ALL THAT GLITTERS

THE WORKING CLASS IN AMERICAN HISTORY

Editorial Advisors

David Brody

Alice Kessler-Harris

David Montgomery

Sean Wilentz

*A list of books in the series appears
at the end of this book.*

ALL THAT GLITTERS

CLASS, CONFLICT, AND COMMUNITY IN CRIPPLE CREEK

Elizabeth Jameson

University of Illinois Press   ◉   Urbana and Chicago

♾ This book is printed on acid-free paper.

Library of Congress Cataloging-in-Publication Data

Jameson, Elizabeth.
All that glitters: class, conflict, and community in Cripple Creek / Elizabeth Jameson.
        p.   cm. — (The working class in American History)
        Includes bibliographical references and index.
        ISBN 0-252-02391-9 (cloth: alk. paper).
        ISBN 0-252-06690-1 (pbk.: alk. paper).
    1. Gold miners—Colorado—Cripple Creek—History.
    2. Trade-unions—Gold miners—Colorado—Cripple Creek—History.
    3. Gold mines and mining—Colorado—Cripple Creek—History.
                I. Title.   II. Series.
            HD8039.M62U637   1998
        305.5'62'0978858—DC21   97-45357
                        CIP

    1   2   3   4   5   C   P   5   4   3   2

In memory of May Wing and John A. Brennan

For Mary Connor Wing and Ralph O. Wing

And for Daniel, with love

CONTENTS

TABLES

ACKNOWLEDGMENTS

I have lived with this book for a very long time. I began it, in some senses, in 1969, when, as an undergraduate at Antioch College, I worked as an intern at the University of Colorado Western History Collections, organizing the archives of the Western Federation of Miners/International Union of Mine, Mill, and Smelter Workers. That was my introduction to working-class history and to the West. It led to a B.A. thesis on the Western Federation of Miners (WFM) and the radical labor movement and raised questions that led to my dissertation, a community study of the Cripple Creek District. I wanted to explore further how the Western Federation of Miners, known for its commitments to industrial unionism and its endorsements of socialism, really affected the daily lives of working miners and their families.

Inevitably, the questions and the frameworks with which I started changed over time as I got deeper into the place and the people and as new social historians pushed the limits of our tools for understanding the complexities of social relationships and identities. By the time I finished the dissertation, gender, households, ethnic identities, and internal tensions within classes seemed as important to me as the militant class-conscious unionism that first grabbed my attention. I still saw class, race, and gender as separate identities and struggled to explain contradictions among them.

Many intrusions delayed this book, some personal, some professional and intellectual. I chose to complete a public history media project based on oral history interviews before I finished my dissertation because I wanted to return their histories to the elderly people who recorded them, while they were still alive and could share their stories with their families. Later, other projects interrupted. Partly, too, I was working to find a framework that could hold the overlapping diversity of thousands of historical actors. I began to see identities as the inseparable products of class, race, gender, age, religion, family, and other social relationships. Recognizing the complex realities that shaped people's options and guided their choices, it became a greater challenge to write the relationships that linked them and their histories. It is hard to build these frameworks, to find forms for stories that are not always linear, that are about thousands of individual lives and also about the social relationships among them.

I described my dissertation as the product of a long gestation with many mid-wives. The danger is becoming an overprotective parent—it's time for this child to leave home. It is important for readers to know a bit of how this work developed over time, if only to understand the mix of perspectives and methods I've used and particularly how many people I need to thank.

I must first thank Robert S. Fogarty, my mentor at Antioch, who found me the internship organizing the WFM records, told me I had to do it even if I didn't know why, and, most of all, taught me that history matters because it is about people, a conviction he demonstrated in the humanity of his teaching.

Next, I must thank the late John A. Brennan, the director of the Western History Collections, who turned a major collection over to an inexperienced undergradu-ate. Years later I asked him why he did it. He smiled quietly and answered, "That's how we all learn." I will always be grateful.

As a graduate student at the University of Michigan, I was fortunate to work with some extraordinary professors and to learn from a community of feminist scholars. For encouragement and help in the early stages I am especially grateful to Robert Sklar, Marilyn Blatt Young, Kathryn Kish Sklar, and the late Marvin Felheim. Robin Jacoby and Linda Eggert provided continuity and enabled me to see a dis-sertation through to completion.

In Boulder, where I did dissertation research, I had extraordinary support and challenging conversation from friends in women's studies and in a study group or-ganized by the local Union of Radical Political Economists. I particularly want to thank Carol Pearson, Susan Armitage, Kathi George, Suzanne Juhasz, Ann Marku-son, Martha Gimenez, and Sheryll Patterson-Black for pushing the ways I thought about gender and class and for modeling a community that could be both support-ive and, at times, oppositional. John Graham offered extraordinary conversation and energy. His infuriatingly precise editorial eye contributed greatly to my early publi-cations on class and gender and put some of the first cracks in the simple models with which I started. From our first talks through the last footnotes, his empathic connection with long-dead miners' passions has mattered a lot.

A number of people helped with the tiresome details of data processing. I want to thank Douglas Orr for help with programming, Charles Feigenoff for coding, and Julie Heath, Lynne Domash, Kathy Kanda, Edward Agran, Charlotte Fairlie, and Julia Lenfest for helping to check the keypunching. Mike Furulli performed tech-nical wonders to make Lillian Powers's taped interview intelligible. Kathi George at various times checked computer printouts, offered her excellent editorial com-ments, proofread my dissertation, and provided encouragement when I needed it most. More recently, a number of people checked details and tracked down last-minute sources. For their professionalism, efficiency, and energy I thank Evelyn Schlatter, Andrew Rieser, and Judy Morley.

I am indebted to the staffs of the Colorado State Historical Society, the Denver Public Library, the Amon Carter Museum, the Wisconsin State Historical Society, and the United States Federal Records Center in Denver. Colorado Springs Local Union No. 515 of the United Brotherhood of Carpenters and Joiners of America graciously trusted me with the minutes of Cripple Creek Carpenters' Local No. 547. Dayton Lummis of the Cripple Creek District Museum provided help, interest, and a much-needed sense of humor. I owe my greatest debt as a researcher to the staff of the University of Colorado Western Historical Collections: Albin Wagner, Augie Maestrogiuseppe, Kay Evatz, and particularly to Cassandra M. Volpe and John A. Brennan, who always provided outstanding professional support and assistance.

Portions of my research were sponsored by the University of Michigan Horace H. Rackham School of Graduate Studies through a dissertation fellowship. A summer stipend from the National Endowment for the Humanities allowed me to do further research for chapter 7. I owe particular thanks to the American Association of University Women for two years of support through the Sara McAnulty Nevins–Myra Bigelow Wilson and Martha Hoag Clifford Endowed Fellowships. The AAUW demonstrated its commitment to women by treating me like an adult; graduate students will understand. They just sent money and told me they were sure I was doing a good job.

John Graham, Carol Pearson, and Milton Cantor all gave valuable comments on earlier versions of chapter 5. I especially thank Milton Cantor, as well, for long-term encouragement. Ronald Brown and Melvyn Dubofsky commented helpfully on portions of other chapters as conference papers. Duane Smith has for years encouraged my work with characteristic generosity and humor. I am grateful, too, to Robert F. Berkhofer, Jr., Alan M. Wald, and Nora H. Faires for their comments.

I owe an enormous debt to Terrence J. McDonald, who chaired my dissertation. His generosity, insight, and cheerful devil's advocacy got me through a never-easy process and shook my models repeatedly. Many thanks.

I also thank the graduate students at the University of New Mexico for their questions, challenges, and conversation—and particularly Thomas Gentry-Funk for thoughtful papers and talk that came at just the right time. Richard White provided encouragement at a crucial moment. At the University of Illinois Press, Alice Kessler-Harris, Liz Dulany, Richard Wentworth, and Mary Giles have been extraordinarily helpful. Thanks, too, to Bill Nelson, heroic mapmaker extraordinaire.

In the largest sense, I am indebted to a generation of social historians who have collectively shifted our focus to the agency of all people and the significance of daily acts in making history. I am grateful to practitioners of the new working-class, women's, ethnic, and western histories whose work makes it fun to do my own. In the process of revising for publication, I have benefited from the support and careful reading of a number of these colleagues. I want especially to thank Vicki Ruiz, Joan Jensen, David Myers, and Jeremy Mouat for generous criticism and David Brundage for sharing from his own research. Most of all, I thank Mary Murphy for her careful and passionate criticism and for years of good talk.

Besides these colleagues, a number of people gave support as I revised. I want to thank my neighbors on Westerfeld, particularly Butch and Esther Evans, Mike Miles, and Theresa Bauer, for humor, perspective, and an occasional beer; and Marcia Landau, Barbara V. Johnson, Robert E. Bienstock, Linda S. Fuller, Aaron B. Ezekiel, Linda Biesele Hall, and Philip Jameson for all the reasons they know. My family has, I am sure, heard more than they ever wanted to about Cripple Creek. I hope they know how much their support has mattered, even the occasional nudge.

I owe more than I can possibly say to many people in Cripple Creek and Victor for their hospitality over the years. I owe an enduring debt to the people who shared their stories with me: S. C. Gatheridge, Anna McGoldrick, Clara Stiverson, Leslie Wilkinson, Ruby Wilkinson, Beulah Pryor, Kathleen Chapman, Ileen Pryor, Ralph Wing, Mary Wing, and May Wing. Many of these people have died; I am grateful for their trust. I am grateful, too, to their families, who participated in the sometimes unsettling process of seeing personal lives as collective histories. Most of all, I can never adequately thank all the members of the Wing family for all they have given to this project, and to me. I am especially grateful to Mary Connor Wing for bringing me into her family and to the late May Wing for trusting me with her history and insisting that it be told.

Finally, I thank my son Daniel, who lights my world and reminds me daily that history is about memory from one generation to the next.

THE SUMMIT OF PISGAH

> Moses went up from the steppes of Moab to Mount Nebo, to the summit of Pisgah, opposite Jericho, and the Lord showed him the whole land: Gilead as far as Dan; all Naphtali; the Land of Ephraim and Manasseh; the whole land of Judah as far as the Western Sea; the Negeb; and the Plain—the Valley of Jericho, the city of palm trees—as far as Zoar. And the Lord said to him, "This is the land of which I swore to Abraham, Isaac, and Jacob, 'I will assign it to your offspring.'"
>
> Deuteronomy 34:1–4

A small, cone-shaped mountain called Mt. Pisgah overlooks Cripple Creek, Colorado. Named for the slope east of Jordan from which Moses viewed the Promised Land, from its deceptively low and accessible summit a 360-degree panorama unfolds. We can only guess what promises its namer dreamed might lie below in a land that lured thousands to the gold and silver of its streams and slopes. The view from this peak can seem breathtakingly unreal—the old western mining town, patches of golden aspen and dark pines, the craggy blue-green and purple peaks, the hazy reaches of South Park in the distance. But that is only the surface. This landscape hid its rich ores for millennia. It does not easily reveal the stories of the people who tried to mine them, of what they sought or what they found.

Pikes Peak lies to the east. A massive beacon—"Pikes Peak or Bust"—it fueled the dreams of gold-seekers in the Pikes Peak rush of 1859. The gold, however, lay not on its slopes but to the north around Cherry Creek and in many small mining camps, mostly short-lived and long-dead, around South Park, stretching in vast pastel hazes to the northwest. Its remote loveliness tells little of the dreams that drew those early argonauts or of the daily grubbing their hope demanded (map 1).

But south and east of Mt. Pisgah, the next generation of miners left their footprints. When I first saw it in 1973, the town of Cripple Creek had shrunk considerably from its heyday as the commercial center of "the World's Greatest Gold Camp." The mines had closed, its sprawling residential neighborhoods were gone, and the houses were torn down. Vacant lots gaped like missing teeth in its once-bustling downtown. On Myers Avenue, the legendary red light district that once housed an astonishing variety of gambling parlors, saloons, dance halls, and all classes of prostitution, only one building still stood: the fanciest of the parlor houses,

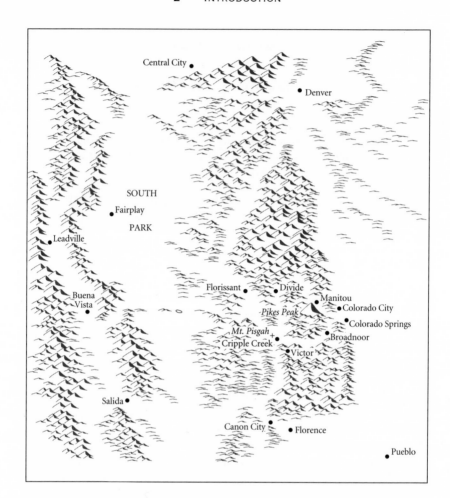

1. Cripple Creek, the Eastern Slope, and the Pikes Peak Region

the Old Homestead, restored and refurbished as a museum. Beyond the Old Homestead, Myers Avenue meandered eastward into Poverty Gulch. There, in 1890, a sometimes cowhand named Robert Womack hit gold in the El Paso lode that had eluded him through twelve years of stubborn prospecting.

Womack's discovery turned a sleepy cow pasture into one of the world's leading industrial mining centers. Cripple Creek captured the imagination of the nation and the interest of most of the financial world during the economically troubled 1890s. It saved Colorado's crashing economy when Congress repealed the Sherman Silver Purchase Act in 1893 and silver mines closed throughout the Rockies. To a

country rocked by a massive depression and to a state shakily based in a silver mining economy, the gold discovery was one of the few bright spots in an otherwise
dismal economic picture. Cripple Creek produced more than $65 million in gold
during its first decade. Deservedly called the World's Greatest Gold Camp, its riches
stabilized the national monetary system. Within a decade, the District, only six
miles square, held ten towns, some thirty thousand residents, and more than seven
hundred producing mines.[1] Their shafts and rock dumps still dot the slopes.

A century after Womack hit pay dirt, a new breed of gold-seekers trekked to this
town born of chance. In 1990 Colorado voters approved limited gaming in Cripple
Creek, beginning October 1, 1991. Since then, motels and casinos have sprouted,
testimony to another sort of gamblers' dreams. The last time I visited, the new Jubi-
lee Casino dwarfed the Old Homestead next door. Myers Avenue had been paved.
Mt. Pisgah was for sale.

Gambles are nothing new in Cripple Creek. But in the 1890s the biggest games
of chance were waged daily underground. Crumbling gravestones and deserted
townsites throughout the old mining district testify to the earlier risks of long-gone
miners. Most of their cabins and the small settlements near the mines burned or
crumbled or were torn down long ago, leaving as little sign of their passing as the
earlier camps of the Fifty-niners.

Poverty Gulch—where Womack's lucky strike began it all—overlooked the town
of Cripple Creek from the east. After Womack struck gold, others followed the
contours of long-extinct volcanoes to explore Squaw Gulch and Beacon Hill to the
south and west; and Squaw Mountain, Battle Mountain, and Bull Hill to the southeast (map 2). People settled wherever there was gold. Mound City sprouted in 1892
with the discovery of ore in Squaw Gulch, as did Arequa, in the gulch between
Beacon Hill and Squaw Mountain. Neither the federal census nor the post office
recognized Arequa, but it remained a miners' community, a string of cabins along
a dirt road leading to the mines along the gulch. Mound City was short-lived. In
1894 Anaconda was settled nearby at the head of Squaw Gulch, and it grew rapidly after 1894 when the Florence and Cripple Creek Railroad (F&CC) came
through.[2] A few foundations mark the former Anaconda townsite. Elaborate timbering barely contains the waste rock above the road that follows the old F&CC
roadbed.

The road leads to Victor, the District's second-largest town. Called the "City of
Mines," it was mostly a city of miners, where the commerce and entertainment
served a largely working-class population. Victor lay at the heart of mining activity,
at the southern edge of the District below Squaw and Battle mountains. There, and
on Bull Hill to the northeast, lay the richest mines and the towns that housed their
miners: Elkton, at the Squaw Mountain end of Arequa Gulch near the Elkton
Mine; Altman, on Bull Hill, once the highest incorporated town in the United

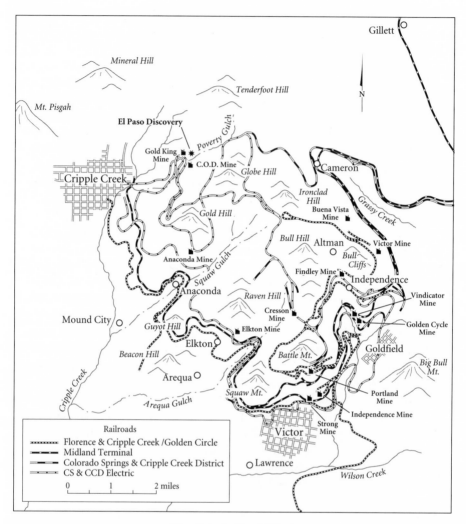

2. The Cripple Creek District

States; Independence, south of Altman, in the center of mining activity on Battle Mountain and Bull Hill; and Goldfield, just below Independence, at the southeast edge of the mining belt. Lawrence, a milling and working-class residential area, stood just south of Victor. Cameron, at the northeast edge of the District, was settled late, in 1900, and grew to a population of five hundred as mines and railroads developed on the north slope of Bull Hill. Gillett, a railroad and milling center, lay outside the mineral region at the northeast entrance to the District (map 2).[3]

These smaller settlements, almost totally working class, held rooming and boarding houses, miners' cabins, and single-family dwellings. The few churches and schools, the union halls, and the bars served as local social centers. In Victor, there were more schools, churches, and union halls, more lodge halls and fraternal societies, more saloons and gambling houses, an opera house that offered everything from Shakespeare to vaudeville, and a sizable red light district. Both Victor and Cripple Creek boasted bustling business centers; Cripple Creek's theaters, saloons, and vice catered to the wealthy as well as to the majority working population.

Most of this is long gone. By the 1990s the fluctuating gold market and heap leach mining revived some mining activity as technology and cyanide made mining profitable again, for a while at least. The new mining, however, generates relatively few jobs compared to the boom days of underground digging. The local work force is more tied to tourism and gambling. Victor survives, a fraction of its former size, still home to retired miners and a few of their descendants. A few houses stand at the old Goldfield and Independence townsites. The weathered wooden remains of Altman lie beyond a "no trespassing" sign that announces "this is privately owned mining property." Even less visible than the physical remains of their settlements are the people who built them, whose lives and labor wrote a chapter in the making of industrial America.

❀   ❀   ❀

I came to the Cripple Creek District drawn not by gold or the beauty of the natural landscape but by a historical panorama I found even more compelling. Those mental landscapes were bounded by two events that might more easily be seen from the top of Bull Hill than from the distanced vantage of Mt. Pisgah. Each sketched in sharp relief the outcome of a miners' strike. Separated in time by a decade, they framed the temporal boundaries of a labor community.

On the afternoon of May 26, 1894, a group of striking miners, representatives of the Western Federation of Miners (WFM) gathered on a mesa below Altman. They brought with them three men, managerial employees of the Strong Mine, who had been trapped underground when the Strong's shaft house was blown up during a confrontation between miners and deputy sheriffs. The miners rescued the trio, held them in the labor stronghold of Altman, and then traded their hostages for six union men imprisoned by the El Paso County sheriff following a gun battle between sheriff's deputies and strikers. The two sides exchanged their prisoners that May afternoon with all the military formality of war. It was one of the final episodes in a pivotal strike.[4]

Labor conflicts punctuated the history of western mining as they did most of industrializing America. Formed after a strike in Idaho's Coeur d'Alenes in 1892, the Western Federation of Miners waged strikes that have aptly been called "labor wars" in Leadville, Colorado in 1896, in the Coeur d'Alenes again in 1899, in Telluride, Colorado, in 1901, throughout Colorado (including Telluride and Cripple Creek) in 1903 and 1904, in Goldfield, Nevada, in 1906 and 1907, in Lead, South Dakota, in 1909, in Calumet, Michigan, in 1913 and 1914, and in Bisbee, Arizona, in 1917.

The 1894 Cripple Creek strike was atypical as mining conflicts went. Typical enough in the defensive nature of its goals—to resist wage cuts and a longer work-day—it was remarkable because the miners won, and in seemingly inauspicious circumstances. As silver mines closed in 1893, throwing thousands of skilled miners out of work, members of the newly founded WFM won an eight-hour day, $3 minimum daily wage, and the right to union membership. Equally remarkable, they won their victory with the help of the state. Gov. Davis Waite intervened against sheriff's deputies from Colorado Springs, the county seat and the mine owners' political stronghold. It was the only mining strike of the period in which the power of the state protected civil peace rather than mine owners' property.

Capital controlled the county government, but the miners elected Waite, a pro-labor Populist, their sole union arbitrator. The governor negotiated the agreement that became the keystone of union strength in the District. The ink on the agreement was barely dry when 1,200 deputies advanced on Bull Hill, refused to disperse until the state militia prepared to shoot, and defied Governor Waite's order to disband until he threatened marital law.[5] Military rule came ten years later during the second Cripple Creek strike, a protracted struggle in 1903 and 1904 called to support striking mill workers in nearby Colorado City.

The first strike established the organizational base from which the miners extended their gains to other crafts. Their numbers gave them considerable leverage in the local economy, and by 1902 members of nine WFM locals had helped organize a majority of all workers in all trades in the District. At least fifty-four local unions included everyone from waitresses and laundry workers to bartenders and newsboys (Appendix B). Their influence extended far beyond the workplaces and union halls to the social life and politics of the towns.

From the vantage point atop Bull Hill, an observer could watch the frenzied action of the second pivotal event, in June of 1904, as a decade of working-class power shattered (chapter 8). In the early morning of June 6, non-union miners came off shift at the Findley Mine and waited at the Independence depot for the 2:15 F&CC train. An explosion ripped through the platform where they stood, killing thirteen strikebreakers and wounding six others. Within hours the wreckage and mutilation spread throughout the District, as employers' mobs deposed elected officials, shot union miners and wrecked their halls, rounded up hundreds of the strikers, and held them in a military "bullpen" in Goldfield. Union sympathizers waved from the slopes of Bull Hill as the militia loaded several hundred union men onto freight cars and deported them to Kansas and New Mexico.[6]

❀   ❀   ❀

These scenes pose questions. How could a decade of union power come to so tragic and cataclysmic an end? What so dramatically altered the outcomes of the two strikes? One obvious answer to those questions lay in the role of the state. The militia, called out by a pro-labor Populist governor to protect the strikers in 1894 was used by an adamantly anti-labor Republican, James Hamilton Peabody, to support capital in 1903 and 1904.[7] But state intervention, decisive as it was, is an insufficient answer. We need to know why the balance of power shifted. The two strikes frame the history of a working-class community; they provide a beginning and an end, but they are not the heart of the story. The role of the state must be placed in the contexts of internal struggles among capital and workers and of daily negotiations that forged a decade of social relationships.

The strikes have been chronicled and their meaning debated in an extensive literature. Historians have been drawn by the violence of WFM strikes; by the union's endorsements of the Socialist Party; by WFM leaders like William D. "Big Bill" Haywood and Vincent St. John, legendary in radical labor circles; and by the union's role in founding two organizations, the Western Labor Union in 1898 (later the American Labor Union) and the Industrial Workers of the World, in 1905 as alternatives to the more conservative American Federation of Labor. These acts stimulated considerable scholarship on the roots, the extent, and the consequences of the union's radical policies.[8] Focusing on Socialist endorsements, strikes, and violence, historians asked why western workers deviated from "mainstream" American labor, an imagined norm defined by eastern craft unions. The brutal conclusions of dramatic labor confrontations drove the historical narrative, so that it became a seemingly inevitable history of losers and their defeats.

Despite a wealth of working-class community studies produced in a quarter-century of new labor and social history, few histories engage the connection between hard-rock miners' lives and their unions. Some important scholarship focused either on daily life or on organized labor. Some historians concluded that western miners and their unions were neither radicals nor reformers, but working-class conservatives primarily concerned with bread-and-butter goals.[9]

❀   ❀   ❀

This book reframes the story. The questions that drew me to Cripple Creek concerned what connected the unions, the union leadership, and the daily lives of rank-and-file workers. Did the Socialist endorsements passed at annual labor conventions represent the rank and file? Did the strikes, however dramatic, and the unions, however successful, make much difference in the mundane textures of individual lives? Those questions expanded the focus from the strikes to the working-class community of the intervening decade and from the unions to working-class identity and association. The questions, therefore, became not whether labor or capital was most violent or whether the unions were radical or conservative, but how workers interpreted their experience and sought to shape it and how working-class sentiment was mobilized in a variety of arenas—private, social, industrial, and political. The story is not just about conflicts between labor and capital but about sources of unity and division within and across classes and the identities and experiences that motivated people to act.

Cripple Creek offered a historical laboratory in which to explore unions and labor politics in the contexts of the workers who created them. Because organized labor was so successful, the period between the two strikes provided an arena to explore the extent and the limits of that success, to locate working-class organization in the web of social relationships that knit a specific community. Cripple Creek allowed me to ask, in effect, not only why the unions were destroyed but also how the outcome might have been different.

These questions led to some unexpected answers. Beginning with miners and their unions, I discovered women, families, and social constructions of gender that affected, in sometimes surprising ways, working-class identities and programs. Beginning with a largely native-born Euro-American population, I discovered that racial politics revolved around people of color who were never allowed in the District, that people who were never there sparked a politics of racist exclusion that redefined class alliances.

Working-class men's identities were rooted in race and gender as well as work. Although union membership in Cripple Creek was impressively high, and although unions were central institutions in working-class life, labor organization nonetheless provided only one important source of identity and association. Workers' choices could not be explained without unraveling the intertwined social relationships that shaped white working-class manhood. The experiences, identities, and institutions at the center of this story include class and labor unions, but they include other sources of identity and community as well—gender, families, households, and fraternal orders; race, ethnicity, and ethnic politics; and an array of political parties and partisan alliances. In all the richness of this social web, class remained a primary focus in Cripple Creek because class relations, in their full complexity, remained central to daily lives and collective histories.

The focus is on relationships—relationships among workers and employers, women and men, single and married men, people of different religions and racial ethnic heritages, and unions and other social and political institutions. These relationships connected personal and group identities; they connected work and class to other sources of social identity and social identities to behavior and action. Ultimately, it's about relationships among people, whose lives, like most lives, were shaped by a variety of human connections and needs. Families and households were as important as unions, and ethnic and religious differences existed within the working class. There were contradictions and strains between home and work, between the union hall and the lodge hall, among workers of different racial and ethnic backgrounds, and between union politics and electoral politics. And just as surely there were shared experiences of work and family, lodge and union, and class and ethnicity that reinforced people's bonds and brought them together.

What nourished working-class community and what undermined it? The answers are significant beyond the boundaries of the old mining district. The Cripple Creek District provides a window on the formation of working-class organization and identities in industrial America. The District was, virtually from the beginning, an industrial enterprise that required considerable capital. In the 1890s corporate control proceeded unevenly. It was perceived in ways that were both contradictory and reasonable, given the slow transformation of older beliefs and social relationships in mining communities. The formation of this working-class community illuminates a period of significant historical change, and hence the formation of industrial society and culture.

The polarized debate about whether the WFM was radical or reformist, visionary or job-protective, is not a particularly useful entry to this history. It was both. The union desired both job security and fundamental social change. For the miners of Cripple Creek, the world of industrial mining held not a promised land of wealth and ease but the possibility that they could shape the new order to reflect their values and address their needs. The promised land lay in the future.

⸙   ⸙   ⸙

Before making the large leap from Mt. Pisgah to industrial society and culture, I should clarify some key terms and assumptions—beginning with "industrial society" and "culture." By industrial society, I mean a society in which social relationships are influenced by an industrial mode of production. Economic power is enacted primarily in relationships governed by factory production, capitalist ownership, wage work, and market exchange. Other forms of production may coexist with industrial production—women may still, for instance, tend gardens and make clothing for their families—but the fundamental economic relationships on which people depend for survival are linked to industry. Cripple Creek was an industrial mining center, and working-class people relied primarily on wages to live.

When I began this book, I assumed that the social relationships that developed in an industrial workplace would generate a working-class culture, a relatively coherent and shared set of beliefs grounded in workers' shared social experiences. I began with a distinction between society and culture that the late Herbert Gutman delineated, borrowing in his own work from anthropologists Eric Wolf and Sidney

Mintz, and from sociologist Zygemunt Bauman. Mintz called culture "a kind of resource" and society "a kind of arena." The word *culture* referred to cognitive systems, whereas *social structures* defined the material contingencies in which people acted.[10] The old model of culture as a relatively unified system of values and beliefs came from cultural anthropology, particularly from the work of Clifford Geertz. That model, which informed much of the new social history, generated work characterized by thick descriptions of particular communities. Its weakness, as Peggy Pascoe has noted, was that it tended to downplay power relations between and within cultures.[11] That occurred in part because historians focused on single sources of cultural identity—on cultures based on class ("working-class culture"), gender ("women's culture"), or racial ethnic identity ("Italian culture").

More recently, cultural criticism—rooted in critical theory, poststructuralist literary criticism, and postmodern anthropology—generated a new approach to culture that focused more directly on power and conflict, particularly within cultures. In this paradigm, culture is not a coherent set of symbols and beliefs that unify a community but a site in which competing groups struggle to control symbols and meanings. Culture, in the words of James Clifford, becomes a "predicament." Cultural critics do not see identity as unified and often downplay social historians' emphasis on historical agency, stressing that consciousness is "always already" shaped by phenomena outside people's control.[12]

Both of these perspectives influence my analysis. Neither, however, adequately describes what I mean by culture and its connection to social relationships, identity, or people's historical agency. I begin with the assumption that people make their own history through daily acts that either preserve or transform existing social relationships and cultural meanings. When women leave abusive marriages or men change diapers, they change gender relationships and alter the symbols connected with what it means to be a man, a woman, or a parent. I assume, too, that how *much* people can change their lives depends on material circumstances, social relationships, and their understandings of their own power and possibility.

Finally, I assume that everyone possesses multiple and often inseparable sources of identity based simultaneously in all the social relationships that link them to other people and shape their possibilities—relationships, among others, of class, race, gender, sexuality, religion, and age. The historical actors in Cripple Creek brought with them a host of beliefs and experiences about what work was and could be; about what men and women could and should be; about what it meant to be white, Irish, Catholic. All of these sources of identity influenced their choices and contributed to the dense web of daily interactions through which they shaped social relationships.

To understand these interlocked relationships I had to connect the elastic and historically changing categories of class, gender, and ethnicity to more concrete and limited historical sources. For the key category of class, I had to connect class, as the participants enacted and interpreted it, with the more concrete fact of occupation, and class relationships to consciousness and ideology. Class and consciousness illustrate the key link between social relationships and individual and group identities. People choose their behaviors in particular social circumstances. The consequences of those choices in turn affect how they envision alternatives and how they behave in the future. As they act and interpret what happens, they selectively emphasize the symbols and cognitive resources from which they draw. If workers are injured by defective machinery, for instance, and the state denies their disability claims, they may conclude that they are powerless, that they must organize to change the law, or that their only power lies in secretly wrecking the owner's machinery. They get the message that they are less powerful than owners in arenas of state power, but they may reach different conclusions about whether they can change power relationships and make different choices from an array of possible responses. The task becomes to distinguish and connect perception and action — to understand how people "see" their worlds and act to shape them.

These conceptual distinctions were reflected in my sources. From newspapers, union publications, convention proceedings, state and federal records, and some few letters and working-class reminiscences and biographies I gleaned important values, preoccupations, activities, associations, and beliefs. The *Victor and Cripple Creek Daily Press* was a particularly valuable source. Owned and operated collectively by most of the District's unions, it published from 1899 to 1903. The largest daily in Teller County, its masthead read "The Only Daily Newspaper Owned by Organized Workingmen." Besides union news, the *Press* proved a rich source for daily life and gossip, and its columns reflected public community values and preoccupations. Oral histories with persons who lived in the Cripple Creek District between 1890 and 1910, and with their descendants, enriched this qualitative sense of working-class life. Through interviews I learned about private understandings and activities, such as household labor and family planning, which were not recorded in more public sources.

I also processed the 1900 manuscript census for the District, which provided data on households, marriage, ethnicity, age, sex, occupation, and home ownership. From newspaper, state, and union sources I collected the names of virtually all local labor leaders, a sample of rank-and-file members, names of persons who engaged in significant strike activity in 1903 and 1904, the names and party affiliations of political activists, and the names of persons active in various lodges and fraternal associations. These samples, combined with the census, described the population and connected social structure to unions, politics, and social organizations (Appendix A).

The census provided a descriptive entry into the local social structure. It did not explain that world, how it was formed, the relationships among social groups, what it meant to the people who lived there, or how they influenced it. I assumed that words and actions *both* matter, that what people said, the words they used to define their own social realities, and the contexts in which they used them should all be taken seriously.

In the Cripple Creek District, one of the words they used frequently and habitually was *class*—in union publications, in daily newspapers, in interviews years later. Class emerged conceptually even on the census, where some people identified their occupation as "capitalist," and in the local jail records, where witty drunks signed in as "J. P. Morgan" and "A. Wage Slave." The language through which people described themselves reflected in rich, concise, and complex ways their systems of perception. To construct meaningful categories for social analysis meant entering a conceptual arena defined as much as possible by the participants.[13]

I defined class as did the miners of Cripple Creek, in terms of relationships to the means of production. Western miners subscribed to the labor theory of value. The WFM contended that the value of commodities was created by the human energy it took to produce them and that people's social positions depended on whether they lived by selling their labor power for wages or from profits derived from the labor of others. The union's slogan summarized succinctly that "labor produces all wealth—wealth belongs to the producer thereof." This was not a foreign ideology but a concept shaped by miners' experience literally creating wealth as they mined gold and silver. It was an assumption that the secretary of the Cripple Creek District Trades Assembly articulated, for instance, when he chided American Federation of Labor president Samuel Gompers for using the "misleading term of 'wage earners,' when speaking of the laboring men who are wealth creators."[14]

But beyond that fundamental economic definition, class was also a social category, with elastic boundaries that involved ties of experience and association. To understand how class relations affected daily behavior and identity required a dialogue between occupational structures and how people interpreted them. For dealing with the 1900 census and other quantifiable material, I assigned occupations to broad categories: wage labor, salaried worker, proprietor, professional, or capitalist.[15] But neither class perceptions nor participation in the labor community was solely determined by occupation. Some miners worked for wages for a time, then leased mine properties or operated bars, and frequently returned to wage labor. Mine leasers were small proprietors; they might employ a small work force. But many leasers were union leaders. James W. Gaughan of Altman illustrates this pattern. A leader of the 1894 strike and the first permanent president of the Altman Miners' local, Gaughan served a term in the Colorado legislature and then was appointed the first Teller County clerk. In 1899 he operated a lease on the Araphaoe Mine. In 1900 he and his brother bought a saloon in Altman, where Gaughan's position as a former WFM leader guaranteed that his bar would function as a meeting place for union labor. Similarly, miners' widows who kept boarding houses were "objectively" proprietors but retained working-class identification and close ties with organized labor.

Finally, it was possible, if not simple, to classify persons who worked outside their homes by their relationship to the means of production but more difficult to classify women, children, and others who did not work for wages. For them, the household defined class relationships. When using the census I assigned non-wage-working family members the class of the head of the household because in Cripple Creek, where the paid work force was overwhelmingly male, a husband's class defined the class of his household and because membership in a working-class household provided access to the labor community.[16] I then explored the connections of households and unpaid labor to economic and social relationships of class and gender.

This difficulty illustrates an important point. Occupation is at best a shorthand reflection of class. The figures in this book help describe social categories. They do not quantify class, which, as E. P. Thompson said, is "a relationship, not a thing."[17]

The census reveals only some of what can be counted about a local population. It provides a scaffolding that requires further elaboration to explain human relationships and their historical meaning. Among every ten adults in the Cripple Creek District in 1900, eight were working-class, six were men, and eight were native-born. Most immigrants were Canadians or northern or western Europeans: Irish, English, Swedes, Germans, and Scots. Most had been in the country for some time; most were naturalized. Nevertheless, more than half of all adults were first- or second-generation immigrants.[18]

What did these numbers mean, in daily experience, for social identity? The numbers help distinguish forms of social relationships—the connections, for instance, among ethnicity and occupation and politics. They are particularly important because of one source I did not have—most local union records were destroyed in the brutal aftermath of the second strike. This history is in part an effort to reconstruct from other sources the stories those lost records held. Statistics provide at least a limited way to examine differences between the rank and file and union leaders because it is easier to find narrative sources for the leadership than for now-anonymous workers. In concert with other sources, the numbers suggest how social relationships might translate into social identities and beliefs.

"Beliefs" cover a broad territory, ranging, for instance, from class sentiments to political ideologies. Class sentiments, as Richard Oestreicher has noted, include relatively unfocused senses of grievance, and, I would add, relatively unfocused senses of pride or achievement as well. But sentiment does not necessarily translate into strategy, action, or collective explanations of shared circumstances. For class sentiments to move people to act, they must be linked to symbols and programs and mobilized by individuals or organizations.[19] Thus, for instance, miners resisted industrial capitalism in a variety of ways, from quitting their jobs, to stealing ore, to organizing unions, to advocating free silver, to socialism—tactics that expressed a spectrum of consciousness ranging from sentiment to ideology fully mobilized through political action.

The same observations apply as well to other sources of social identity, to understandings shaped, for instance, by ethnicity, race, or gender. Gender sentiments can range from griping about personal relationships and workplace discrimination, to scorching the dinner, to leaving abusive relationships, to working for suffrage, to separatism.

By looking beyond organized labor to social relationships and overlapping cultures a more complete picture of workers' values and institutions becomes possible. We begin by locating them historically. Part 1 of this book introduces the people of the Cripple Creek District and the ways that both capital and labor staked their claims in the new gold camp. Chapter 1 describes the people and explores the backgrounds and assumptions that labor and management brought with them. Chapters 2 and 3 address how capital and labor negotiated their relationships as they each established their claims to power and to the local communities. Chapter 2 chronicles the first strike, which established the ground rules—or the underground rules—for the coming decade. Class relations developed as both capital and labor negotiated internal sources of unity and division and as both sought to consolidate power. Chapter 3 follows the period between the two strikes to trace the emergence of distinct ownership groups with competing interests and managerial philosophies and the development of organized labor and its relationship to the working class.

Part 2 examines social relationships within the working class and across classes and how these affected labor policy. Chapters 4–6 in particular address intersecting identities of class, gender, and race during the height of union power. Chapter 4 considers the overlapping social functions of unions and of multi-class fraternal organizations and what these meant for relationships among men. Chapter 5 explores what concepts of working-class womanhood meant for women and for union policies. Chapter 6 describes how labor interpreted race and ethnicity and how racism influenced relationships within the working class and across classes. Chapter 7 focuses on labor politics during the ten-year period of union strength to probe how working-class ideologies and cross-class alliances came together in partisan politics. In Part 3, chapters 8 and 9 explain how the bonds and tensions within and across classes were mobilized to influence the strike of 1903–4 and its outcome.

❀   ❀   ❀

This history supports two assumptions that frame it—that the material conditions through which people support themselves underlie all social relationships and that, at the same time, people have multiple social experiences and multiple sources of social identity, and these are important whether they empower or disempower. Too frequently, race, class, and gender are seen as significant only for the people who experience discrimination on these bases. But men are affected by gender, capitalists by class, whites by race, and native-born Americans by ethnicity. In Cripple Creek, unstated assumptions about commonalties of race and gender, shared by white men of all classes, were as powerful in shaping local social arrangements as were more explicit declarations about class, gender, and racial differences.

Identity, like culture, is not a single simple thing. In Cripple Creek, people who had complex identities operated simultaneously and differently in a number of social arenas. I distinguish social identities of race, class, gender, and religion not because they operated separately for individual people who were, for instance, simultaneously male, Irish, working-class, and Catholic. Class, race, ethnicity, and gender are conceptual lenses that allow us to explore how sources of identity were mobilized along different axes at home and work, in union halls and lodge halls, in churches and bars, in partisan politics and racial politics, when labor was secure and when it was attacked.

As I immersed myself in the social worlds of Cripple Creek the mining metaphors became irresistible. The gold and silver that early prospectors discovered had eroded from more complex ores beneath the surface. In the industrial age, mine shafts followed those "leads" underground to the complex ores that must be milled and refined to yield their riches. So, too, with working-class social history. The simpler formulations of union and strike history led beneath the "surface diggings" to more complex and interlocking formations of identity and experience.

The Cripple Creek District sat atop rounded hills, the eroded remnants of ancient volcanoes. Beneath their surfaces ran a network of narrow fissures. Salt solutions filled these cracks with the District's dull gray calaverite and sylvanite ores, which must be crushed, heated, and treated with chemicals to release the gold.[20] The intricate fissures, the rock they traversed, and the ore that stabilized their shifting fault lines became for me a visual metaphor. If the local social structure was the rock, the fissures were the interlocking axes of class, gender, and ethnicity, sometimes stabilized by the complex ores of group identity and association, sometimes shifting along their fault lines as events blasted their shared terrains, exposing contradictions and disjunctions. The ore itself could be a metaphor for individual identities, sometimes a complex amalgam of personal and social experience, sometimes, under heat or pressure, separating into constituent parts. Sometimes the gray rock yielded gold; sometimes all that remained was cyanide-laced tailings. What was waste, what was precious, what was fool's gold, and what was real treasure could be gauged only against scales of personal and social value.

❀   ❀   ❀

The unusual mineral formation and its deceptively dull ores raise, at least by analogy, one more question. Is Cripple Creek typical of anything, or is it so exceptional that it has only particular and antiquarian value for historians? Some historians have said just that, asserting that its strikes have been overemphasized and that interpretations of western labor radicalism are based in the false assumption that, as Mark Wyman put it, "The WFM's defeat in Cripple Creek was merely the experience of Tincup, Silver City, Lump Gulch, and Tonopah writ large."[21] Perhaps not. But Cripple Creek was, both materially and symbolically, more significant than Tincup in shaping class relations and working-class agendas and in the lived experience of tens of thousands of miners and their families. Confrontations with capital did not have to occur in every mining town to influence workers' understandings. They had only to happen at critical times and places, given miners' mobility and access to news, to touch people who were not actual participants. Capital understood this and devoted extensive resources to break union labor where it was strongest.[22]

Was Cripple Creek typical? What if it weren't? And what would the answer tell us? Whether or not Cripple Creek was typical, it was pivotal. A decade of working-class success in Cripple Creek nourished labor's visions. The 1904 strike defeat killed the dream of local working-class control and, by demonstrating that change could not happen without a broader base of power, provided one impetus to found the Industrial Workers of the World in 1905. The District provides a case study of a western working-class community that can be compared with others, in the West and elsewhere. It provides more, too—a way to explore the limits and the strengths of a working class mobilized in a number of arenas to shape industrial society and culture. The Cripple Creek District allows us to explore the limits of working-class belief and organization because they reached a degree of potency and coherence there that has seldom been equaled in the United States. At the time, the social terrain seemed as vast and uncharted as the Colorado Rockies must have appeared to the first gold-seekers. Labor's place in the industrial mining landscape remained to be forged, with any number of potential and uncertain outcomes. Only through the eyes of workers who lived the history can we understand their choices.

For the people of the Cripple Creek District, industrial America was a process of daily creation. They built working-class organization for ten years and then waged the strike in which they lost what they had built. But most of the histories of the District have been written from the perspectives of the mine owners who won control in 1904.[23] To restore the actors to the historical landscape we must leave Mt. Pisgah for the dusty streets, the saloons and boarding houses, and the homes, mines, lodges, and union halls that lay below.

Most miners who came to the Cripple Creek District sought not the Promised Land but a living wage. Some also dreamed of a more equitable social order. That promise could seem as far in the future as the hazy horizon beyond Mt. Pisgah and at times as tangible as the deputies charging Bull Hill. However immediate or remote their dreams, working people, through countless daily acts, built their own community in Cripple Creek. They did not know at the time how long they would wander in the wilderness or whether they might someday cross into a future of their own making.

PART 1

CLAIMING THE GROUND

1

NOT A POOR MAN'S CAMP

Miners must have tramped through the Cripple Creek District beginning with the 1859 rush to the South Park gold camps. But for more than thirty years they gave it no more than a casual glance. Whatever promised land seemed to stretch beyond Mt. Pisgah, it was not the gold-rich rock that lay unnoticed and untapped virtually underfoot. A traveler passing through, however, might have encountered a local character no one took very seriously—an unkempt and frequently hard-drinking ranchhand named Robert Womack who was sure that there was "gold in them thar hills." While others flocked to more promising camps—to the San Juans, Aspen, Leadville, Georgetown, Central City, Creede, and countless other bonanzas—Womack stuck to prospecting the odd volcanic formations. He stuck to it for twelve stubborn years despite a general consensus that he was on a life-long fool's errand. But in October 1890 he proved them wrong, at least to a point, when he finally found gold in Poverty Gulch.

Some people, of course, regretted how casually they had dismissed Womack, but his was an unlikely bonanza. The District bore little resemblance to other mining areas, and there was nothing to suggest the hidden treasure beneath its slopes.[1] It had, for instance, no primary ore deposit, or "Mother Lode" common to other U.S. mining regions. In the Tertiary Period a series of volcanic eruptions broke through the rock crust and created a cone and several minor craters. These eroded to form rounded hills broken by a network of especially narrow fissures, into which salt solutions later carried minerals. Prospectors expected to find pure metals and then follow them to the veins from which they had eroded. But in the Cripple Creek District there were few outcroppings of the dull ores and virtually no free gold.[2]

Womack was the only person who believed the area held anything of value except some moderate pasture, and he could have told those who failed to prospect there that they had probably not lost much. Too poor to develop his gold claim, Womack sold it. For twelve years' labor he earned $500 and brief fame as the discoverer of the new goldfield.[3]

Womack was not part of the industrial mining culture. He represented the fate of older prospectors in the industrial era, who were replaced by miners who worked underground for wages. Cripple Creek's mines were always deep-shaft, industrial enterprises worked by wage laborers. Its wealth went to those who had the money or the family contacts to invest in mines, railroads, and smelters. The day of the individual prospector was gone.

⊗   ⊗   ⊗

Many of the West's gold and silver deposits were small, and the camps that surrounded them were transient and temporary. But when there was sufficient ore for profitable exploitation, mining camps quickly became industrial cities, and grub-staked prospectors faded into the background, eclipsed by large corporations and miners who worked for a daily wage. Large-scale lode mining called for substantial capital investment because profitable development required railroads, advanced technology, large mills and refineries, and a skilled work force. Between 1893 and 1897, 3,057 new mining companies incorporated—many for the District's mines— each capitalized at more than $1 million.[4]

As the scale of mining increased, the industry became more lucrative. New tools and new technologies helped shift mining to greater economies of scale and made it profitable to mine low-grade and complex ores. Dynamite and machine drills reduced labor costs below ground, while on the surface the mills that treated Cripple Creek ore began to employ a new cyanide process, discovered in 1890, as well as chlorination. While these innovations increased profits for mine owners, dynamite, cyanide, and power drills that spewed rock dust increased the health hazards for labor in mines and mills.[5]

Labor-management relations became increasingly strained in the mining West as management cut production costs by substituting capital and technology for labor. The changed character of ownership created new economic and social relationships in mining communities. Class was obvious as the social gulf widened between owners and labor. The *Miners' Magazine*, official publication of the WFM, created a remembered "golden age" of mining in the 1870s "when the mines of the West were owned largely by individuals who were not too proud or arrogant to live in the same community with their employees." Many miners idealized the earlier mining camps. Cripple Creek pioneer J. B. Douglas wrote nostalgically of a time when "every man had equal privilege with his fellow men in the race for bread—had free access to the natural resources of the country. The artificial man called a corporation was not heard of."[6]

The "artificial man" and those he represented challenged assumptions developed in the old mining camps, where work and occupation granted title to a claim. A system of common law and custom developed to regulate mineral and water rights, establish a cooperative system for working claims, and govern social custom. Various states and territories gradually recognized the customs that regulated mining. First Colorado in 1861, then Nevada, Idaho, Arizona, Montana, and Oregon, ruled that valid locations and mining claims must be made in accordance with the local laws of each mining district. Senators Thomas Hart Benton and William Seward achieved tacit acceptance of free mining on government land, and miners accepted this as recognition of their possessory rights. As people moved from camp to camp, the customs were diffused and achieved general acceptance and consistency. Sen. William Stewart of Nevada, who had mined briefly in Grass Valley, California, in 1849, proclaimed that the miners' regulations were "thoroughly democratic in their character, guarding against every form of monopoly, and requiring work and occupation in good faith to constitute a valid possession."[7]

The mining frontier was short-lived. It is difficult to know how thoroughly the people who drafted its regulations internalized their challenge to private property rights. But the concept of the work process underlying definitions of ownership achieved heightened significance in the industrial era. Placer mining (sifting or panning gold and silver from streams and gravel beds) involved hard work but relatively little money. One person could locate a placer deposit, but several people were usually required to exploit it. Mining was a small-scale enterprise that required cooperation in camp governance and work alike. The earliest quartz mines were small cooperatives where miners shared the labor and the costs of sinking shafts and blasting tunnels, hoping to be among the lucky few who hit pay dirt.[8]

Independent small-scale mining became idealized out of all proportion to its duration or to how many people it profited. Its cooperative work relationships resonated for miners whose heritage of class relations was considerably more conflictual. Cooperation and trust became essential in industrial mining, where the increased hazards underground meant that miners literally put their lives into one another's hands.

Industrialization, with its changed work process and ownership, cost miners in ways they could easily calculate. The old placer camp cooperation had produced precious metals. When the grubbing was done, miners not only kept the product of their labor but also a very special product—gold—which had direct exchange value. That fact influenced a developing class analysis based in the labor theory of value. When miners became wageworkers they lost a product that clearly demonstrated the costs of corporate control. It was simple to calculate the value of the metals they had mined, compare it with total wages, and calculate what had been lost in profits to absentee owners who did not share the physical risks and who neither worked nor lived in mining towns. Inheriting the principle of work and occupation as the criteria for ownership, it is not surprising that the miners founded the WFM with the motto "labor produces all wealth—wealth belongs to the producer thereof."

Nor is it surprising that capitalists did not agree.

❀   ❀   ❀

The history of the Cripple Creek District is thus a history of contested claims to industrial America. In the rugged terrain of the Colorado gold camp, labor and capital negotiated power, identity, and control of the new industrial social order. It was, in effect, a tale of two classes and, symbolically at least, a tale of two cities. Cripple Creek's mining depended on outside capital. But because major investment came from nearby—from Denver and particularly from Colorado Springs, only eighteen miles northeast of the District—the economic and social distances between capital and labor were enacted vividly in the life-styles of Cripple Creek miners and Colorado Springs mine owners.

In the 1880s Colorado Springs had been a haven for tourists and health-seekers. A sleepy spa in the shadow of Pikes Peak, it grew from the ambitions, both entrepreneurial and personal, of Gen. William Jackson Palmer, who came to the area in 1869 to build a railroad south from Denver to the Rio Grande. Palmer originally wanted to build a supply town for Colorado mining camps along his Denver and Rio Grande Railroad. That plan changed as he determined to create a fit residence for his bride Queen, William Proctor Mellon's daughter, whom Palmer had met in 1869 as he traveled east to find investors. The usual rough railroad stop was instead replaced in 1870 with a town founded on the model of Newport and Saratoga Springs, intended as a pleasant place for the well-to-do. In October 1870 Palmer founded the Denver and Rio Grande Railroad, and on November 7 he married Queen Mellon.[9]

Queen Palmer arrived in Colorado Springs in October 1871 and stayed four months, her longest continuous residence in the town her husband built for her.[10] But others appreciated its refined atmosphere, ban on alcoholic beverages, magnificent scenery, and the mineral baths at nearby Manitou Springs. Except that his wife never lived there, the town became all that Palmer had envisioned—a comfortable retreat for retired capitalists, wealthy consumptives, adventurous Europeans, and young easterners drawn by the romance and promise of the West. For twenty years, until Cripple Creek changed it, Colorado Springs was a genteel retreat "untainted" by the crass speculation and roughness of Colorado's boomtowns.

From the start, Colorado Springs charted the District's development. When Womack found the vein for which he had searched so long, the ore samples he triumphantly took to Colorado Springs assayed as high as $250 per ton. But given Womack's reputation, no one paid much attention. A handful came to prospect; on April 5, 1891, they formed the Cripple Creek Mining District. After some initial hesitation, those who could afford to buy into the new bonanza organized mining corporations, three stock exchanges, and land companies.[11]

The few working-class men who struck it rich in the District quickly left to live in Colorado Springs or Denver. The geographic distance between owners and miners marked class differences much more profound than space could measure. Labor resented most absentee owners and scorned the affectations of polite society in "Little London," as Colorado Springs was not-so-lovingly called. The different communities of capital and labor became a shorthand for fundamentally different understandings of what it meant to own the mines and to work in them. The Colorado Springs *Weekly Gazette* succinctly separated residence and ownership when it declared in 1891 that it would "take time and money, a good deal of them," to explore the District. "Cripple Creek," it announced, "is not a poor man's camp."[12]

By 1893, when more than $2 million in gold was taken from some 150 mines, Colorado Springs eagerly claimed the District and funneled its capital. In its first edition of 1894, the *Weekly Gazette* insisted that Colorado Springs "must continue to be the center of Cripple Creek business" and estimated that "three-fourths of the producing mines . . . and a large part of its best prospects" belonged to Colorado Springs investors. By 1900, 90 percent of the mines were owned by Colorado Springs and Denver capitalists, or eastern or foreign corporations.[13]

❀   ❀   ❀

The idealized past of small-scale mining informed labor's critique of industrial class relations, but Cripple Creek owners and miners alike had, by 1890, directly experienced mining for wages and profits. District miners shared a heritage that included the shafts, pits, and union halls of western silver, gold, and copper towns; of eastern coal and lead mines; and of Cornish tin, Welsh coal, and Irish copper. Nourished by this international mining heritage, a mining subculture developed in the West, beginning with the California gold rush. Thousands who came to Cripple Creek shared that history, but it is easier to document its personal meanings for employers than for labor. More owners' stories were recorded; workers' backgrounds must be gleaned from tantalizing scraps of personal detail pieced together on a framework of statistics.

Cripple Creek's people were the descendants, both actual and spiritual, of older miners. Their backgrounds mapped the migrations that produced the work forces of earlier mines and the successive waves of greenhorns who joined their ranks. The first U.S. census of the District was not taken until 1900, when the area was virtually at its peak of development. But it confirms that many people brought with them a heritage of older working-class understandings and associations.[14] The stories of a few individuals tell more widely shared experiences.

Consider John Welch, the son of a Vermont coal miner, born in Montpelier in 1864. Welch entered the coal mines after his father died in a mining accident on

July 4, 1875—hardly an Independence Day for the eleven-year-old who quit school to take his father's place underground. Sometime in the 1880s, he moved to Leadville, like many who sought the higher wages and lesser dangers of western hard-rock mines. In Leadville, Welch met the Doran family, whose history traced another strand of miners' migrations.[15]

Edward and Catharine Doran, born in Ireland in the early 1830s, married young, probably during the disastrous famine years from 1845 to 1849. They left Ireland, to settle for a time in Wales; perhaps Edward worked the coal mines there. Catharine began long years of childbearing with the birth of their first son, James, in 1852. Sometime between 1854, when Thomas was born, and 1858, when Mary arrived, the Dorans immigrated to Shullsburg, Wisconsin, in the lead mining region that spanned the southwestern corner of Wisconsin, northwestern Illinois, and eastern Iowa. Edward worked as a lead miner, and Catharine cared for their ever-increasing family. Margaret was born in 1862, Anastasia (Hannah) in 1864, Catharine (Kate) two years later, then Eliza, George E. (Ed), and Alice, who was born in 1873. Altogether, Catharine Doran bore twelve children in nineteen years, nine of whom survived.[16]

Shullsburg developed with its lead mining. Indians had shown local lead deposits to early French settlers, and the French and Indians mined sporadically through the 1700s. James Shull mined the area beginning in 1818, and by 1825 small American settlements developed around the mineral deposits. The first Cornish miner arrived in 1827; between 1830 and 1850 a fairly steady stream of Cornish immigrants joined him. Most of the Cornish settled in other Wisconsin lead mining communities, however, which ranged from half to three-fourths Cornish compared to an estimated one-fourth in Shullsburg in 1850. Many of Shullsburg's first citizens, like the Dorans, were Irish. Settlements called Dublin and Irish Diggings grew north and northeast of the town. Pioneer members of St. Matthew's Catholic Church included the O'Neill, Ryan, McLear, Higgins, and McNulty families.[17]

Edward and Catharine Doran joined this community, and perhaps other kin as well—William Doran lived next door to Edward in 1860. By most standards, the Dorans did fairly well. All of the Doran children attended school well into adolescence—no small achievement, particularly, we might guess, for their mother, who could neither read nor write. In 1860 Edward listed assets of $50; ten years later he claimed $765.[18]

By the 1880s, however, lead and zinc mining had declined. Many Shullsburg miners went west, following new mining discoveries. In June 1884, the local *Pick and Gad* lamented, "We have many times been made to feel sorry by seeing so many of our young men leaving every spring to hunt work and wages far away from home and friends, among the mines of Colorado." The new silver mines around Leadville drew many Shullsburg miners, including the extended Doran family, who settled there sometime before 1888. We can establish the year because that was when Hannah Doran and John Welch married.[19]

All the Doran children followed paths common to second-generation Irish in western mining camps. Most of the boys mined; the other girls, like Hannah, married miners. Young Catharine (Kate) married James McConaghy, an Irish immigrant who worked as a hoist engineer. Their daughter May was born in November 1890. Three months later Kate died, and in 1893 James took three-year-old May to Victor, in the Cripple Creek District. James's brother John McConaghy moved there, too, as did his brother-in-law, Ed Doran, with his wife, Mary.

In 1893 John and Hannah Doran Welch followed them all to the new gold camp. Their son Thomas was born there the following year, in his parents' tent in Altman during the first miners' strike. After the strike, the Welches moved to a new home they built in Goldfield. Kathleen was born there in 1895, then Edward, Annie, and young John. John Welch was, according to Kathleen, "a great union man." He and Hannah passed on to the next generation of Welches, Dorans, and McConaghys their stories of the strikes and of the labor community.

The families' intertwined migrations illustrate common family settlement patterns. In the transient world of western mining, people moved to the next big ore find, and, if it seemed large enough to provide long-term work, then friends and families followed. Friends and families also helped men locate jobs. James and John McConaghy, Ed Doran, and John Welch all eventually worked at the Gold Coin Mine in Victor. Sometimes unmarried miners who did not share such rich family ties tried to create kinlike bonds. Single miners sometimes formed "partnerships," working and living together and sometimes moving together from camp to camp. Many were, like John Welch and Ed Doran, miners' sons who had worked underground elsewhere before they came to Cripple Creek.

W. F. Davis was such a single miner when, in his mid-twenties, he came to the District in 1899. Perhaps Davis, like other Missouri-born westerners, traced his family to the lead mines around Joplin. He had been mining since he was sixteen, in Idaho's Coeur d'Alenes from 1891 to 1898 and then in Alaska for a year. He returned to Wallace, in the Coeur d'Alenes, transferred his union membership from the Western Labor Union, and joined the WFM on April 29, 1899. Imprisoned during the 1899 Coeur d'Alenes miners' strike, Davis left Wallace, mined briefly in Butte, and then moved to the Cripple Creek District. In 1900 he was twenty-six, divorced, and living in the Goldfield boardinghouse of a widow, Louisa Geary. Two years later he was elected president of the Altman Miners' Union, and, on Christmas 1902, he married Mattie Bowman.[20]

Davis's close friend, Sherman "Kid" Parker, also lived at Louisa Geary's in 1900. Parker's and Davis's partnership extended beyond bachelor living quarters to union activities as well. Already active in the Altman local in 1900, Parker served as its secretary while Davis was president. He left the District briefly to work in the Leadville silver mines. When he returned in June 1901, he bought the Topic Saloon in partnership with Andy Short but sold out to Short a year later and went back to mining in July 1902. The next month he married Bessie Delphi, a Colorado native, whose mother, Isabella Ramsey, kept boarders to augment her husband's wages from the mines. Like many miners' daughters, Bessie Delphi Parker married young—she was nineteen, her husband thirty-four. Their age difference was not atypical in an area with more male workers than marriageable women.[21]

John and Hannah Welch, W. F. and Mattie Davis, and Sherman and Bessie Parker could, in many respects, represent their neighbors. Like them, Henry and Mary King and Jeremiah and Celia Kelly came from eastern states, the Kings from Pennsylvania and the Kellys from New York. King moved to Colorado in 1881, when he was twenty-five, and mined in Eagle County. He married Mary in Denver in 1884 and moved to the District in 1893, where he became a charter member of Victor Miners' Union No. 32. By 1900 he had held numerous union and lodge offices, including president of his local, and had served a term as mayor of Goldfield.

The Kellys, like the Dorans, were second-generation immigrants. Jerry Kelly's father was born in Ireland, and Celia Kelly's mother in Scotland. When the census-taker found them in 1900, Jerry was forty-six and Celia thirty-two. They had been married fourteen years, had three children, two of whom were living, and owned their home in Victor. Kelly joined Victor Miners' Union No. 32 in February 1895 and was quickly elected its financial secretary.[22]

Finally, consider a few people who might represent other trades and other classes. Hans Hansen, like a minority of the District's workers, was neither native-born nor a miner. A Dane, Hansen migrated to the United States in 1866, leaving behind his wife Karen, who was pregnant with their son Christopher. It was five years before they joined him. We can glean only traces of what happened next. Karen Hansen bore ten other children, only two of whom survived. Edna and Nels were both born in Missouri, in 1883 and 1885. By 1900 all the Hansens were U.S. citizens, and they owned a home in Elkton. Both Hans and Nels worked as blacksmiths. Perhaps, like many District blacksmiths, they worked for the mines, repairing machinery and straightening drill bits. But they both belonged to Cripple Creek Federal Labor Union No. 64 rather than to a WFM local, so perhaps their work was not mining-related. Christopher worked as a laborer but had been out of work six of the twelve months before the census-taker's 1900 visit. The fact that three of the Hansens were wage-earners may have buffered periodic unemployment.[23]

If few workers found wealth in the District, some achieved modest success. Frank P. Mannix, born in Malone, New York, in 1862, became a printer, moved to Minneapolis in 1879, and two years later to Denver, where he set type for newspapers and sold real estate. In early 1896 he settled in the District, where he helped found the Victor *Record* and then published the *Victor Evening Times*. He joined the Typographical Union in 1881 and remained active in both the Victor local and the Cripple Creek District Press Club. Reportedly he once owned part of Womack's Poverty Gulch claim but lost it. Instead, he found modest security in his newspapers and in his elected position as Teller County clerk.[24]

All of these men had ties to organized labor and to the various political parties it supported in the District. But how typical were they of the rank and file and of those who remained outside the union fold? If the questions census-takers ask reflect common roots and experiences, then in all respects except, perhaps, the relative numbers who were married and owned homes, they might represent many of their neighbors.

Their ethnic backgrounds resemble those of most District residents. The first western hard-rock miners ran the Chinese out of California's underground mines and Nevada's legendary Comstock Lode. Their descendants in Cripple Creek never let them in, and so, unlike earlier mining towns, almost no Chinese lived in the District.[25] Otherwise, its residents reflected the ethnic origins of earlier hard-rock camps. They were, like the people of previous gold rushes, predominantly born in the East or Midwest if they were native-born and in Canada or northern or western Europe if they were immigrants. The foreign-born were particularly likely to trace their roots to Ireland, England, Wales, Scotland, Germany, and Scandinavia (table 1). A much lower proportion of the adult population was foreign-born (23 percent) than had been the case in earlier mining camps.[26] But 28 percent were second-generation immigrants—some of them, like Welch, second-generation miners who had grown up in hard-rock or coal towns and followed their fathers underground.[27]

The differences between their communities and their parents' reflected changes in the underground fraternity. There were proportionately more Irish and fewer English than in some earlier mining areas and more Canadians, many of whom were children of Irish, Cornish, and Welsh immigrants who had mined in the Canadian West. The Cornish were the most skilled miners in the American West in the 1850s. Some early Irish miners came from West Cork and had worked in the copper mines near Berehaven. The County Cork surnames of Sullivan, Harrington, Murphy, Shea, O'Neill, Lynch, and McCarthy were all common in Cripple Creek. Other parts of Ireland were amply represented, and the immigrant population shared common international journeys from one mining camp to another.[28] Some of the Irish mined in California, Nevada, or other western hard-rock camps before they or their sons brought their skills to the new gold camp. Some mined copper in Michigan's Upper Peninsula, lead in Wisconsin or Iowa, or coal in the Pennsylvania anthracite mines. Whether they learned mining in West Cork or on the Comstock, by the 1890s the Irish were recognized as highly skilled miners.

TABLE 1
Predominant Birthplaces of Adults, Cripple Creek District, 1900

Place of Birth	Second-Generation Immigrants		First- and Second-Generation Immigrants		
	N	% Adult Population	N	% Adult Population	% Adult Population
Colorado	1,269	6.3	. . .	. . .	. . .
Illinois	1,737	8.6			
Indiana	744	3.7			
Iowa	1,283	6.4			
Kansas	769	3.8			
Kentucky	431	2.1			
Michigan	571	2.8			
Missouri	1,359	6.8			
Nebraska	316	1.6			
New York	1,275	6.3			
Ohio	1,188	5.9			
Pennsylvania	1,281	6.4			
Texas	214	1.0			
Wisconsin	666	3.3			
Canada	804	4.0	495	2.5	6.5
England	756	3.8	994	4.9	8.7
France	44	0.2	157	0.8	1.0
Germany	534	2.7	1,093	5.4	8.1
Ireland	846	4.2	1,788	8.9	13.1
Scotland	318	1.6	563	2.8	4.4
Sweden	635	3.2	122	0.6	3.8
Wales	153	0.8	182	0.9	1.7
	17,193	85.5a	5,394	26.8a	47.3a

Source: Manuscript census, Teller County, Colo., 1900.
a. Totals represent only predominant birthplaces, not the total adult population, some 23 percent of whom were foreign-born and 28 percent of whom were children of immigrants.

Native-born residents of the District were likely to be from states with significant coal or metal mining, such as Ohio, Pennsylvania, Illinois, Michigan, Missouri, Wisconsin, Iowa, Kentucky, or Colorado, or from nearby agricultural states such as Nebraska or Kansas (table 1). The census cannot reveal people's class backgrounds or everywhere they lived or worked. But many individuals, as the census suggested, had experience in western hard-rock mining, in coal or base metals further east, or in both. At least some of those born in farm states had mined before they came to the District, drawn to Colorado by earlier mining excitements in Leadville, Aspen, Central City, Idaho Springs, or the San Juans. One survey of 218 Colorado metalliferrous miners in 1899 and 1900 revealed an average of 16.7 years spent in mining. The first miners' local in the District, Altman Local No. 19, was formed by men who had been silver miners in Aspen and Leadville. When the silver mines closed they took their skills to the new gold camp and named their WFM local "Free Coinage." Transfer cards and records of the Victor Miners' Union, the largest local of any craft in Colorado, showed people who mined copper for a time in Butte, silver in Leadville, then gold in the Cripple Creek District. And a number of individuals, such as John Welch, came from coal mining backgrounds. John Calderwood, the primary WFM leader in the early days of Cripple Creek unionism, entered the coal mines at age nine. John J. Mangan, a charter member of Anaconda Miners' Union No. 21, came from School County, Pennsylvania, to Leadville in 1879 and then moved to Anaconda in 1892.[29]

Some eastern coal miners were clearly union veterans. Independence miner Con Coll came originally from Coaldale in Schuylkill County, Pennsylvania, as did his friend, a man named Davis, who came to the District after he "left the [Pennsylvania] mines to declare against corporate greed and for manly principles." A Schuylkill County miner brought a heritage of union organizing that dated at least from the 1840s, when miners in Schuylkill, Luzerne, and Carbon counties struck for higher wages and better working conditions. His class experience, like Con Coll's, was rooted in the histories of many Irish men who, fleeing the British and the potato famine, became American miners. During the 1840s and 1850s some twenty thousand came to Schuylkill County, where in 1842 they waged the first regional strike in the industry. In the 1860s they helped organize Workingmen's Benevolent Associations (WBAs) there and in Carbon County. The Schuylkill WBA struck for an eight-hour day in 1868. Its membership soared, particularly after an 1869 mining disaster killed 179 Luzerne and Schuylkill County miners. By 1870 the WBA had thirty thousand members, or 85 percent of Pennsylvania anthracite miners, and a written agreement. Pinkerton detective James McParland infiltrated the union and labeled the leadership a gang of foreign terrorists called the Mollie Maguires; fourteen union leaders were hanged in 1877. Descendants of the Pennsylvania coalfields met McParland again and again after the famous labor spy moved to Colorado to manage the Rocky Mountain Pinkerton agency.[30]

By the 1890s most western miners migrated frequently because the industry was unstable or because they were blacklisted for union activity. They sold their skill for wages, sometimes working on base metals, and less frequently on coal, as well as the gold and silver of older prospectors' dreams. Of 434 members initiated into Victor WFM Local No. 32 between February 1894 and December 1895, thirty-four (8 percent) transferred in from another WFM local and 110 (25 percent) transferred out to another local. These figures are especially impressive because the Western Federation was not founded until 1893 and did not achieve stable leadership or growth until 1896. A few transferred from other locals in the District, but most came from other silver or gold camps such as Aspen, Leadville, Ouray, and Silverton. Miners left to go to other silver and gold camps and also to copper mining areas like Butte. Such working-class migrations charted the journey of Charles T. Dillon, who came to Colorado from Chicago to work on the survey of the Denver and Rio Grande Railroad. Dillon moved to Bingham, Utah, in 1881, and mined copper there for four years and in Butte for two. In 1887 he moved to Idaho, where he mined silver until he went to Altman to mine gold. Similarly, Charles E. Phillips, born in Halifax, Nova Scotia, mined in Clear Creek County and the San Juans for thirteen years before coming to the Cripple Creek District.[31]

Miners migrated internationally, sometimes lured by hopes of opportunity and sometimes forced to move by mining economies or politics. They shared a widely dispersed lore of labor struggle. In December of 1900 a small group of Boer miners came to the District while the Boer War interrupted South African mining. Five of them visited Altman, "principally to see the remains of the fort which was erected during the [1894 Cripple Creek] strike on Bull Hill, having read of the affair in the Transvaal papers at that time." Then at least one, John Boyle, went to Butte. In 1902 James Tobin left the District to return to South Africa and, according to the Victor and Cripple Creek Daily Press, to retrieve the tools he had buried in the Transvaal when the war forced him to leave.[32] The fact that Transvaal miners were drawn to the District by tales of the 1894 strike victory is one testimonial to an international mining working class that identified with labor struggles from Schuylkill to the Cripple Creek District to the Transvaal.

We cannot know the significance of that shared history to each of the thousands of miners who lived and worked in Cripple Creek. But literally hundreds of local press references establish the mining backgrounds of District residents. Gossip columns in the Press between 1899 and 1903 recorded at least 152 persons who moved to other western mining areas, including several who intended to mine coal in northern Colorado, 131 who came to the District from other mining areas, and only forty-three who moved to non-mining locations. News of other camps spread quickly. In 1900 a number of local miners went to the new goldfields in Nome, while District residents who had moved to Tonopah, Nevada, warned their old neighbors to stay away because there were no jobs.[33]

Miners' frequent moves from camp to camp applied to other crafts as well. Construction workers, for instance, moved in and out of mining camps depending on the work available. Many came to the District in 1896, when two fires destroyed much of Cripple Creek, and again in 1899, when another blaze consumed downtown Victor. But after rebuilding, construction work slackened, and between 1900 and 1902 sixty-five members of the Cripple Creek, Victor, and Independence carpenters' locals left to transfer into Denver Carpenters' Local No. 55.[34]

Carpenters' options were broader than miners'. Carpenters could move from Victor to Denver; miners could only go to the next mining town. That meant, however, that the people, the institutions, and the customs were all likely to be familiar. Although there are not sources available to measure mobility in and out of the District, it is clear that Cripple Creek miners shared the high geographic mobility of other camps. That did not mean, however, that miners were rootless or anomic, but rather that wherever they went they were likely to meet people they knew from other mining towns. Former Aspen residents, for instance, formed an Aspen Association in Cripple Creek "for purely social objects."[35]

Marriage and families encouraged residential stability, but the more-settled core of the labor community had ties to other mining towns. For more women than men, western mining camps had always been home. Forty percent of the adult population was female. Because there were roughly three men for each two women of marriageable age, most women married (table 2). Often significantly younger than their husbands, many women also became young widows.[36] Many were miners' daughters, a fact reflected in the greater proportions of women than men who were born in the West. Hard-rock miners' daughters brought lifetimes of mining town experience to the new gold camp.[37]

Many married miners tried to establish some home base, even though they might have to commute to see their families as they moved in search of work. Other families, however, moved together from camp to camp. May McConaghy, who moved with her father and stepmother to Victor in 1893, lived in Victor and Goldfield until 1897 or 1898 and then moved to another gold camp in Rossland, British Columbia. The McConaghys returned to the District, lived in Victor and Cameron, then moved back to Leadville, to a new mining camp on the Cochitopa, and back to

TABLE 2
Marital Status by Sex, 1900

	Men		Women		District	
Marital Status	N	%	N	%	N	%
Single	571	45	148	18	719	34
Married/spouse present	536	42	568	69	1,104	53
Married/spouse absent	79	6	33	4	112	5
Widowed	41	3	69	8	110	5
Divorced	7	1	4	—	11	1
Unknown	32	3	1	—	33	2
	1,266	100	823	99	2,089	100

Source: Manuscript census, Teller County, Colo., 1900, random sample of 2,089 adults.
Note: Column 4 does not total 100 percent due to rounding.

Leadville again. May McConaghy married O. E. Wing in Leadville in 1907. A few years later, the Wings moved to Goldfield. May Wing lived most of the rest of her ninety years in the District.[38]

Mobility rates miss the complexity of such in-and-out migration patterns and also their importance in diffusing social customs and understandings. Wherever they moved, many miners and their families had relatives or friends from other camps; May Wing, for example, had Doran aunts and uncles in Leadville and in the District. They also had access to familiar associations through lodges and unions. Mobility in hard-rock mining did not bring isolation and anomie so much as rapid diffusion of shared histories, values, and social institutions.

⊛   ⊛   ⊛

Part of that shared history was a tradition of union organizing that included earlier coal and metal mines. In the hard-rock West, unions dated from the 1860s and Nevada's Comstock Lode. Miners began to organize as the Comstock industrialized, when the miners of Virginia City formed a Miners' Protective Association on May 30, 1863. Within six years miners organized local unions in most of the major lode mining centers—in Grass Valley, California; Central City, Colorado; Silver City, Idaho; and Pioche, Nevada. Most were formed by old Comstock miners and patterned their constitutions on those of the Virginia City and Gold Hill unions. Other isolated locals were organized, including the Working Men's Association of Butte, formed in 1878, which became the "Gibralter of unionism" as Local No. 1 of the WFM. In 1889 the first formal association of miners in different localities was established, when four Idaho locals formed the Coeur d'Alenes Executive Miners' Union.[39]

Leadville was the major Colorado mining town from 1877 until the Cripple Creek boom. It drew a number of Comstock miners and others from the East and Midwest. In January 1879 Leadville miners founded a Miners' Cooperative Union as a Knights of Labor Assembly and then reorganized it along the more militant policies of the Comstock unions. But the National Guard helped break the Leadville union in a bitter strike only a year later, leaving Leadville the only major non-union camp in the mining West.[40]

In the San Juan Mountains of southwestern Colorado, Telluride and Silverton miners organized unions in the early 1880s. Southwestern Colorado mine owners formed the San Juan Miners' Association in 1883 and mounted a successful assault on the $4 dollar day in Telluride and Silverton. Miners reorganized in Leadville in 1885 and founded unions in Aspen and Breckenridge in 1886, at Red Cliff in 1887, at Central City in 1888, again at Leadville and Aspen in 1890, at Red Mountain in 1891, and at Creede, Ouray, Rico, and Telluride in 1892 (map 3). Many of these were Knights of Labor Assemblies that offered mutual aid and sometimes more militant resistance as mine owners repeatedly tried to cut wages.[41]

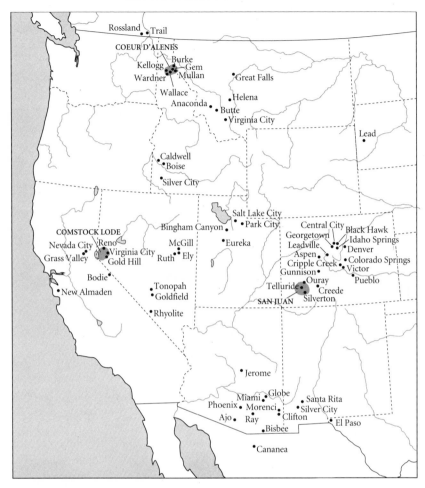

3. Major Western Hard-Rock Mining Areas

The early miners' unions claimed labor's right to the wealth it created and provided mutual aid to buffer the costs of industrial mining. Because all mining labor shared the considerable dangers underground, hard-rock miners insisted on industrial organization—the organization of all workers in an industry in the same union, regardless of craft or skill—and on a uniform minimum wage for all mine workers. They based their cooperation in the understanding that everyone's safety was interdependent. New technologies like heavier drills, which were difficult for older miners to handle, reinforced that awareness. As owners tried to demote older, experienced workers and cut their wages, younger miners organized to help and to avoid being discarded as they, too, aged.[42]

Working-class cooperation was often defensive as miners protected jobs and re-sisted wage cuts. The first locals on the Comstock established a $4 minimum daily wage for all mining labor. By 1892 Coeur d'Alenes miners struck to resist a wage reduction from $3.50 a day for all underground workers to $3 a day for miners and $2.50 for surface workers. The Executive Miners' Union corresponded with unions in Montana, Colorado, and Idaho, proposing to form a central organization, and the 1892 strike provided further impetus. Representatives of fifteen local unions met in Butte on May 15, 1893, to form the Western Federation of Miners. The Cripple Creek District was not represented, but Colorado was—Aspen, Creede, Ouray, and Rico sent delegates.[43]

The spirit of the old mining camps continued in the industrial era not in the state law, which defined ownership and property rights for the new industrial corpora-tions, but in the miners' unions. In every mining town older miners brought tradi-tions and history with them. Experienced miners taught newcomers their skills. New workers generally started as trammers, either physically moving the ore cars to the hoist or driving animals that drew the tram cars. They might also start as muckers and shovel ore into the cars, which required sufficient knowledge to rec-ognize ore-bearing rock. Finally, they went to work with experienced miners to learn how to drill and set dynamite charges to break out the most ore and the least waste rock. Muckers and trammers began to learn the trade as they helped set up machine drills for the more skilled "machine men."[44] Younger men also learned mining lore and history from older miners as they talked underground. The talk continued after work as they gathered in the union halls and lodges, boarding-houses, saloons, gambling parlors, and dance halls that were as much a part of the mining landscape as the mine shafts themselves.

By the 1890s established miners with long experience in western mining identified as wageworkers with special skills rather than as individuals seeking par-ticular metals. That identity was forged by immigrant miners recruited for their expertise, by second-generation immigrants from eastern mines, and by the experi-ence of the western mines. Cripple Creek offered the steady wages and stable min-ing that supported a community they could help shape.

❀   ❀   ❀

Among the people of Cripple Creek there were differences of background and experience that affected perceptions and behavior. Like those in the earlier hard-rock camps, the people of the Cripple Creek District were predominantly young, male, and working class, and most work was mining-related. In 1900, 61 percent of all workers and 51 percent of all adults were employed in occupations directly re-lated to mining. Four adults out of five depended on blue-collar labor for their sup-port (table 3). The vast wealth of the area promised extensive long-term mining and

TABLE 3
Adult Population of Cripple Creek District by Class, 1900

Class	N	%
Working class (blue collar)		
Mining unskilled	19	0.1
Mining semiskilled	117	0.6
Mining skilled	2,025	10.2
Miner	7,437	37.3
Unskilled	1,863	9.3
Semiskilled	1,982	9.9
Skilled	2,267	11.4
	15,710	78.8
Salaried/clerical		
Salaried workers	634	3.2
Salaried mining	236	1.2
	870	4.4
Business		
Proprietors	2,037	10.2
Mining proprietors	15	0.1
	2,052	10.3
Professionals		
Professionals	632	3.2
Mining professionals	99	0.5
	731	3.7
Capitalists		
Capitalists	209	1.0
Mining capitalists	150	0.8
	359	1.8
Other		
Other	190	1.0
Mining other (prospectors)	27	0.1
	217	1.1
District totals	19,939	100.1

Source: Manuscript census, Teller County, Colo., 1900.
Note: Persons without listed occupations were assigned the class of the head of household; persons in households in which no one listed an occupation were omitted. Column 2 does not total 100 percent due to rounding.

brought more women and more stability than did smaller, short-lived camps. The Cripple Creek District, where three of five adults married, housed a higher proportion of families than earlier mining towns (table 2).[45]

All mining camps had higher sex ratios (the number of men per hundred women) than the nation as a whole. The United States varied between 102 and 105 men per hundred women from 1850 to 1900. In 1900 the Colorado sex ratio was 121, roughly that of Teller County, with 55 percent men age twenty-one or older and 45 percent women. The District itself had roughly three men for each two women, a sharp contrast to Grass Valley, California, in 1850, for instance, where men outnumbered women seventeen to one. Cripple Creek more closely resembled Butte, Montana, also a mature industrial mining center, which was, like Cripple Creek, 60 percent male in 1900.[46]

The higher proportion of women in Cripple Creek came with the promise of steady employment. The local communities became known as good "family towns," where married miners could expect to find wages, schools, and communities that supported stable family settlement. Roughly a fourth of the District's population in 1900 consisted of children under age sixteen.[47] Family settlement was one recognition that hard-rock mining was a wage-earning occupation, not a temporary route to quick wealth. It was less common than earlier for miners to leave families elsewhere, expecting to return after they "struck it rich."[48] Men who thought of mining as a life-long occupation were more likely to marry and settle where they worked, which became more possible with the age and skill that enabled them to support households.

Class and skill affected domestic life—how people lived, where, and with whom. Younger unskilled workers were less likely to live with families, and more likely to live alone or in boardinghouses. Skilled workers were more likely to have wives and children, and those in skilled mining occupations were significantly more likely to live with families than were District adults in general.[49] Capitalists and people in white-collar mining occupations were the most likely to live in nuclear family households and less likely to have boarders or unrelated adults in their homes or to be boarders themselves (table 4).

These differences were most apparent for employed persons, who were more likely than the population as a whole to live alone or board and less likely to live in a family household. That is, they were more likely to be male and unmarried than the "average" adult because that average included women, most of whom married and few of whom worked for wages. Miners, the largest group of unmarried men, were the most likely to live in households with unrelated adults and in boardinghouses such as Louisa Geary's and Isabella Ramsey's (table 4). Some of these men lived together and listed themselves as "partners" on the 1900 census. It is possible that, as in other predominantly male environments, some of these household partnerships involved emotional and erotic intimacy. In focusing on heterosexual relationships I do not mean to ignore this possibility. There are, however, few sources through which to explore sexuality. The only direct hints of homosexuality I found were occasional references in the *Press* to a miner called Countess McPherson, a member of Altman Miners' Union No. 19, who was, apparently, a cross-dresser. The

TABLE 4

Household Status by Class, 1900

Occupation	Single Person N	%	Nuclear Family N	%	Extended Family N	%	Family and Boarders N	%	Unrelated Adults N	%	Boarding-house N	%
Working class												
Employed[a]	80	8	411	39	117	11	204	19	67	6	208	20
All adults[b]	80	5	732	47	191	12	262	17	67	4	214	14
Salaried/clerical												
Employed	1	2	21	44	7	15	7	15	1	2	11	23
All adults	1	1	35	49	12	17	11	15	1	1	12	17
Business												
Employed	4	3	50	40	16	13	23	19	9	7	22	18
All adults	4	2	89	46	25	13	37	19	9	5	28	15
Professionals												
Employed	3	5	28	47	8	13	12	20	1	2	8	13
All adults	3	3	46	50	16	17	18	19	1	1	9	10
Capitalists												
Employed	1	4	13	57	5	22	2	9			2	9
All adults	1	3	24	65	5	14	5	14			2	5
Other												
Employed	2	12	3	18	2	12	5	29			5	29
All adults	6	5	67	54	16	13	21	17			14	11
District totals												
Employed	91	7	526	39	155	11	253	19	78	6	256	19
All adults	95	5	993	48	265	13	354	17	78	4	279	14

Source: Manuscript census, Teller County, Colo., 1900, random sample of 2,089 adults, less twenty-five missing observations.

Note: Some figures do not total 100 percent due to rounding.

a. 1,359 adults in the random sample who listed occupations.

b. All adults, less twenty-five missing cases. Persons without occupations were assigned the class of the head of household. This category includes adult women, most of whom had no listed occupation.

Press occasionally noted what Countess wore to the theater and on one occasion reported: "Countess McPherson fell dead in love with the female impersonator in the German village [at a carnival] Thursday night and wanted to stay until the show was over and escort her home. The boys finally dragged him away by force."[50] Such occasional glimpses aside, I can only guess at the emotional contexts of most households.

Men with families were older, more skilled, and made more money than single men. They were skilled miners, skilled workers in other trades, salaried mine workers, professionals, and capitalists. Most workers, like Davis and Parker, achieved some measure of security before marrying. Many women, like Bessie Delphi, married older men whose skills and incomes helped them support families. Those most likely to have children were those with the highest skill levels and incomes: professionals, capitalists, proprietors, and skilled workers.[51]

Placers and boomtowns attracted young, single, rootless individuals who could afford the time for speculative work. Deep-shaft mining attracted older men with considerable experience underground. Certainly the District drew its share of drifters and dreamers, and its adult population was relatively young, but the core of the working-class community was slightly older men in their late twenties, thirties, and forties and women of working-class origins.[52] They bought homes, built schools, and founded unions, staking their collective claim to the communities they built.

Some of the District's early settlers shared memories of bitter confrontations with owners over wage cuts, dangerous new technology, and late paydays. Others hoped that they might this time be among the lucky few who struck it rich. Still others, including the owners who reaped the greatest rewards, came from very different backgrounds and held different assumptions. Both workers and owners included people with experience of labor relations in industrial mining and newcomers to the arena.

The Cripple Creek working class inherited the strands of a collective history of the placer camps, where work and occupation defined ownership; of the early deep-shaft operations, where outsiders who did not share the physical risks came to own the mines; and of mines and union halls from Schuylkill County to the Comstock. Experienced miners came to Cripple Creek understanding the interdependence of mining labor and committed to industrial unionism and working-class cooperation. They shared that history with younger greenhorns and working-class hopefuls. Together they wrote the next chapter.

Few mine owners shared miners' experiences or their values; many had already clashed with labor over the rights and responsibilities of private property. Almost no owners lived in Cripple Creek, and the daily class negotiations tested the extent to which miners' local social and political power could balance outside economic control. The changed nature of ownership showed in the fact that only 1.2 percent of District adults were mine managers and superintendents and fewer than 1 percent owned mines. The profits for which miners risked their lives underground enriched absentee owners and benefited *their* communities. The costs of class were particularly apparent because much of the gold traveled only as far as Colorado Springs.

Still, several circumstances during the District's first decade mediated the impact of concentrated outside control on relations between labor and capital. Despite vast differences between owners' and workers' life-styles, the owners' proximity sometimes obscured their growing social distance from workers. They were accessible; miners could go to Colorado Springs to negotiate face to face.[53] Further, ownership was by no means unified during the first decade, and no owner or group of owners controlled a large enough block of property to dictate policy. Therefore, although workers resented outside ownership they also had some leverage because employers often accommodated labor if that gave them an advantage over business rivals.

Owners' differing managerial assumptions were partially rooted in their own class backgrounds. The working-class origins of a few influenced them to negotiate with organized labor, and their accommodations undermined the anti-union policies of more conservative owners. Too, labor organized to make conflicts costly. And miners dealt most often not with owners but with mine managers, superintendents, and foremen whose backgrounds were similar to their own and who could sometimes buffer relationships between labor and capital.

Biographical information for twenty-five mine superintendents reveals backgrounds that resembled those of miners in the older mining camps, where many of them had begun their careers. Eight, or 35 percent, were immigrants, and the English and Irish backgrounds of the old mining frontier predominated. Twelve of the native-born came from states where there was significant mining. All but two had mined underground, and all had worked in the industry. Their collective experience spanned the mine shafts of England, the Michigan copper range, Pennsylvania and Scottish coal, and all the major hard-rock camps of Colorado, South Dakota, Montana, Utah, Idaho, Arizona, Alaska, California, New Mexico, British Columbia, Washington, and Nevada. Before coming to the Cripple Creek District, the superintendents had mined in some 106 previous localities, an average of 4.24 prior mining camps apiece.[54] Not surprisingly, they came more commonly from working-class backgrounds than did the owners. Of the twenty-five, seventeen had spent their working lives as miners. Five had been mine superintendents; most of them had entered the mines as youngsters. The sole professional was a mining engineer; the one proprietor had leased a mine (table 5).

Similar biographical information for thirty-five major mine owners, including virtually all who significantly influenced District labor relations and politics, reveals backgrounds that differed significantly from those of miners, mine managers, and District residents as a whole. All of them were native-born and came from the East or Midwest.[55] Fourteen (40 percent) had owned mines elsewhere, mostly in other Colorado mining districts but also in California, Arizona, South Dakota, and the lead mining region around Joplin, Missouri. Only five (14 percent) had ever worked as miners or prospectors, and few had ever worked for wages (table 5).[56] The owners were much more likely than their miners or managers to be native-born, to have non-working-class backgrounds, and to have avoided the physical labor and practical experience of mining. They were much less likely to actually live in the Cripple Creek District. Only two of the thirty-five owners lived near their mines in 1900, whereas all the miners, and all but one of the superintendents lived in the District.[57] If working a claim and occupying it had remained the criteria for ownership, most would have lost their mines.

TABLE 5
Predominant Adult Class of Cripple Creek District Mine Owners
and Superintendents prior to Involvement in the District

Class	Owners[a]		Superintendents[b]	
	N	%	N	%
Working class	5	14	17	68
Salaried worker	1	3	5	20
Merchant	9	26	1	4
Professional	5	14	1	4
Capitalist	13	37		
Unknown	2	6	1	4
	35	100	25	100

Sources: Mine owners: Sargent and Rohrbacher, *The Fortunes of a Decade*, pp. 16–50; Sprague, *Money Mountain*, pp. 91–108, 170–89, 193–205, 233–41; Sprague, *Newport in the Rockies*, pp. 166–95; Waters, *Midas of the Rockies*, p. 23; superintendents: Sargent and Rohrbacher, *The Fortunes of a Decade*, pp. 116–32.

a. The mine owners represented in this sample were: David H. Moffat, Warren Woods, Harry E. Woods, Frank M. Woods, J. R. McKinnie, Edward M. De La Vergne, Irving Howbert, George Bernard, Edward R. Stark, David N. Heizer, William A. Otis, Harlan P. Lillibridge, Verner Z. Reed, John E. Hundley, W. S. Montgomery, Frank G. Peck, E. S. Johnson, J. K. Miller, W. F. Anderson, John E. Phillips, Charles N. Miller, J. Maurice Finn, Edwin Arkell, J. A. Sill, W. R. Foley, J. P. Fitting, James Burns, James Doyle, John Harnan, Winfield Scott Stratton, Charles MacNeill, Spencer Penrose, Charles Tutt, Albert E. Carlton, and Sam Strong.

b. The superintendents represented in this sample were: F. M. Symes, John W. O'Brien, Martin C. Gleason, J. H. Emerson, John Stark, R. A. Trevarthen, Herbert Starkweather, J. M. Wright, W. M. Bainbridge, Milo Hoskins, A. J. Campbell, Charles Walden, Fred S. Johnson, Jerry P. Horgan, F. O. Ganson, Sol Camp, Oliver B. Finn, Richard H. Burrows, A. D. De Masters, Newton S. Wilson, Nathaniel Wilson, Joseph Luxon, William H. Shell, H. L. McCarn, and George L. Keenor.

Among the owners, there were nonetheless important differences that influenced how they treated workers and how labor regarded them. Numerous ownership groups interlocked in the directorships of the various mining, milling, railroad, and power companies. But among these complex webs of capital existed three broadly distinguishable backgrounds—older, and generally more conservative, mining magnates; new owners of middle-class or affluent origins; and a few from working-class backgrounds. A cultural gulf of varying depth divided labor from the first two groups, whereas owners from working-class backgrounds generally had more amicable relationships with their employees.

This group, the least typical of District owners, significantly affected labor relations during the first decade, particularly Winfield Scott Stratton, whose Independence Mine made him the first Cripple Creek millionaire, and James Burns, James Doyle, and John Harnan, who discovered the Portland Mine, one of the District's richest producers. It was relatively rare and difficult for men of their backgrounds to own major mines; they tended to be more accommodating to labor than were owners whose previous experience was further removed from their employees'.

Stratton was born in Jeffersonville, Indiana, in 1848, the son of a Mississippi River ship's carpenter. He left Indiana when he was twenty and worked two years as a carpenter in Lincoln, Nebraska, before moving to Colorado Springs to do carpentry and contracting. For seventeen years Stratton alternated carpentry with mining studies and sporadic prospecting. He worked in a gold reduction mill in Summit County, Colorado, studied metallurgy at the Colorado School of Mines, and mineralogy at Colorado College in 1884. In the spring of 1891 he persuaded a plasterer, Leslie Popejoy, to grubstake him to locate and develop claims in the new Cripple Creek District for half the profits. On July 4, 1891, Stratton staked two claims on the south slope of Battle Mountain, which he called the Independence and the Washington in honor of the day. When some assays from the Independence showed $380 in gold per ton, Stratton sold a lot in Denver and his house and lot in Colorado Springs and hurried to buy out Popejoy.[58]

In February 1892 Stratton hit a streak of gold in the Washington. He sold the claim twice, once to a Washington syndicate that paid him $10,000 before forfeiting its bond and once to some California promoters who defaulted. The first ore shipments netted him $25,000, and with his new wealth Stratton turned to the Independence. After months of digging he broke open one of the huge boulders on the claim and found ore running more than $12 a ton in gold. The crushed boulders yielded $60,000, which enabled him to sink a chute, fortuitously enough, directly into an ever-widening vein. With that unlikely string of luck, Stratton became the District's first millionaire.[59]

To cook for his first small group of miners, Stratton hired John Harnan, a former Pennsylvania coal miner, who, in his spare time, began prospecting the slope behind the Independence. At the top of Battle Mountain, Harnan came upon James Doyle, a carpenter, and James Burns, a plumber, who were working a small prospect hole they called the Portland after their hometown in Maine. Their claim was only a sixth of an acre; a full lode claim was ten acres. Doyle had staked it, but, failing to find anything and needing help, he went into partnership with Burns. Burns had located five claims, none of them worth much, but he traded Doyle a half interest in one of them for half of the Portland. When Harnan told the two men that they were digging in the wrong spot, they offered him a third interest to find the right place. Doyle and Burns had sunk a twenty-foot hole along a vein. Harnan put in a cross-cut at six feet and hit gold assaying fifty-two ounces a ton.

Colorado law permitted owners to follow veins from their property onto other claims, and, given the Portland's small size, lawsuits were inevitable. So the three men erected a shack over their shaft and smuggled out sacks of ore at night to buy groceries and accumulate cash for their looming legal battles. They applied for a full lode claim, on the grounds that they were the first to discover gold on top of the mountain. The owners of surrounding claims filed twenty-seven lawsuits to stop them. At that point Stratton stepped in and offered them $75,000 in exchange for stock. With $71,000 and some stock, the four men bought the conflicting claims to settle all twenty-seven suits by purchase. The tiny Portland grew to 240 acres that produced more than $62 million. Stratton incorporated the Portland Gold Mining Company and was its largest stockholder and first president. Burns succeeded him and shaped company policy for years.[60]

There was no typical mining success story, but the circumstances that enabled four working men to acquire the richest mines on Battle Mountain, in the richest part of the mineral belt, were as atypical as they come. They got in early. Only the wealthy could acquire claims after they had been located and developed, and initial skepticism about Womack's discovery created a brief possibility for poorer prospectors to locate property before others began to buy in. As skilled craftsmen without families, they had some savings and could spend months prospecting and developing their own claims. Few married miners could do that. They found high-grade ore very near the surface, another unusual stroke of luck, so their profits offset the high costs of sinking and timbering shafts, paying wages, and buying machinery. They developed their mines with profits from the surface gold and with the proceeds from Stratton's defaulted downpayments.

Burns and Stratton in particular had considerable influence on labor relations during the District's first decade and temporarily mediated the policies of other owners. Older mining magnates were much less inclined to negotiate with labor. Rich and powerful, they either expanded their already substantial holdings to the new gold camp or liquidated their silver interests to invest in the District. Two leading representatives of this group, David H. Moffat and Eben Smith, together controlled many of the District's major producers. Moffat, born in Orange County, New York, in 1839, came to Denver in 1860. In 1867 he became cashier of the First National Bank of Denver—of which Smith was a major stockholder—and in 1880 was the bank's president. Moffat moved into mining in 1879 as vice president of Leadville silver king Horace Tabor's Little Pittsburgh Consolidated Mining Company. He continued to invest heavily in Colorado mines and railroads.[61]

Moffat was Colorado's major mine owner when Womack hit pay dirt. Many Cripple Creek miners knew him—their conflicts dated from the 1880 Leadville strike. In 1893 Moffat called the managers of his silver mines to Denver and announced that to compensate for the reduced price of silver he must cut his miners' $3 daily wage to $2 or close his mines.[62] Instead, many silver miners moved to Cripple Creek. Moving only postponed their confrontation with Moffat, as he and Smith invested in the District. The Smith-Moffat holdings eventually included the

Bi-Metallic Bank of Cripple Creek, the Metallic Extraction Company, the Florence and Cripple Creek Railroad, and a multitude of mines. Their Victor Mine alone paid 20 percent monthly dividends by the mid-1890s. Smith's personal budget ran from $20,000 to $30,000 a month.[63]

Smith and Moffat lived in Denver and seldom visited the District. They remained in close touch with their mine managers, however, and although they made major policy decisions they did not deal directly with labor. They were particularly distant from their miners because many Smith-Moffat managers came from non-working-class origins and shared more, culturally and politically, with their employers than was generally the case. One, a young man named Sherman Bell, came to the District in 1893. Bell served as a deputy sheriff during the 1894 miners' strike and later went to Cuba as a Rough Rider in the Spanish-American War before becoming assistant manager of the Independence-Wilson Creek Consolidated Company in 1900 and then the manager of all the Moffat mining properties in the District. Bell would be a leading player in the 1903–4 strike.

Moffat allowed little to compromise his primary goal of personal gain. But some owners, less successful in the silver camps, accommodated friendly—if often paternalistic—relationships with their employees. These owners occupied a middle ground between Burns and Stratton and Smith and Moffat. The principal representatives of this group were Warren Woods and his sons Frank and Harry. Warren Woods was born in Ohio in 1834 and farmed and later operated a grocery in Illinois, where Frank and Harry were born. Harry Woods went to Colorado in 1878 and developed holdings for the family in the Leadville and Creede mining areas, while Frank and Warren maintained a small business in Ohio. In 1893 they joined Harry in Colorado to organize the Woods Investment Company, which began selling town lots for the new city of Victor, below the rich Battle Mountain gold deposits. While digging the basement for a hotel in 1894 they struck pay dirt, an accidental bonanza they dubbed the "Gold Coin." Their holdings eventually included the Economic Gold Extraction Company, the Pike's Peak Power Company, the Golden Crescent Water and Light Company, the Teller County Mining Supply Company, the United Mines Transportation Company, twenty-four mining companies, and the Colorado Springs and Cripple Creek District Railroad (the "Short Line").[64]

Although the Woods family built mansions in Colorado Springs, labor generally liked the family better than other Springs millionaires because they were the only ones who gave much back to the District. Devout Baptists committed to the stewardship of wealth, the Woods believed that investing in their employees' social welfare would promote smoother industrial relations. In that spirit they built a $40,000 club house for their workers and a vast amusement facility, Pinnacle Park, in Cameron.[65]

The final major ownership group was neither friendly to labor nor patronizing of its welfare. Their labor philosophy was closest to the older mining magnates', although they were generally younger than other owners and had never owned mines before. They came from respectable-to-wealthy eastern families and were able to buy into District ventures largely on the strength of family ties. Four representatives of this group were Albert E. Carlton, Charles MacNeill, Charles Tutt, and Spencer Penrose, who ultimately exerted greater collective influence on District class relations than all the other owners.[66]

Carlton, born in Warren, Illinois, in 1866, moved to Colorado Springs in 1889. His father, H. M. Carlton, underwrote his sons' first business venture by giving Bert and his younger brother Leslie each $10,000. With that capital they started the Colorado Trading and Transfer Company to haul coal and ore. Albert won a monopoly contract in 1894 to haul the Midland Terminal Railway's freight and built his empire from there, finally becoming the major mine owner in Teller County.[67]

MacNeill, the son of a physician, came to Denver from Chicago with his father in 1885 at age fourteen. He studied milling processes throughout the state and became the manager of an experimental chlorination plant at Lawrence in the Cripple Creek District. Chlorination was a new process imported from the Transvaal, and MacNeill made it work until the mill burned in December 1895. He befriended Tutt and Penrose, and together they set out to dominate low-grade ore refining. They formed the Colorado-Philadelphia Reduction Company and built a large chlorination plant in Colorado City, next to Colorado Springs. Buying and building other mills in Florence and Canon City, they came to be called "the mill trust."[68]

The "Philadelphia" in Colorado-Philadelphia came from Tutt and Penrose's hometown, where they had been boyhood friends. Their fathers, both physicians, had studied together at the University of Pennsylvania, but Dr. Tutt had died when his son was an infant, and Charles Tutt went to work after finishing high school. He came to Pikes Peak in 1884, when he was twenty, and sold real estate and insurance in Colorado Springs.[69]

On December 10, 1892, Spencer Penrose joined Tutt. Penrose's father was professor of obstetrics at the University of Pennsylvania, and his mother, Sarah Hannah Boies, was a descendent of seventeenth-century New Englanders whose first American ancestor had graduated from Harvard in 1642. After he, in turn, earned his Harvard degree, Spencer Penrose moved to Las Cruces, New Mexico, in 1888 to run a fruit and produce company. Tired of selling hay and vegetables, he was drawn to Colorado Springs by his brother Richard's accounts of its cricket, polo, and sparkling social life. Charles Tutt met the train when Penrose arrived. Penrose, according to local lore, told Tutt that he was out of money, needed a job, and wanted a drink. Tutt drove him to the Cheyenne Mountain Country Club in Broadmoor, which had a bar, and offered him a half interest in his real estate business and his Cripple Creek mine, the C.O.D., for $500 if Penrose would run the Cripple Creek branch of the business. Penrose didn't have the funds, but Tutt wanted a partner more than immediate capital. The two men eventually built an empire that led to the United States Reduction and Refining Company and a fortune in Utah copper. Penrose, according to the same lore, never paid Tutt the $500.[70]

Of all the young easterners, only Tutt was married in the early days, and the crowd gained a reputation in the District's gambling halls and parlor houses. That, as well as their privileged backgrounds, led labor to perceive them as wealthy opportunists and dub them the "socialites." But by 1896 they were absorbed with business, and all but Carlton moved to the Springs.[71] Although not all came from wealthy families, they had sufficient family influence and credit to buy mines and mills, and their social backgrounds and experiences differed vastly from their workers'.

There were, then, four discernible types of owners: those from working-class origins, linked through their joint ownership of the Portland, who were generally accommodating in their dealings with labor; the benevolent paternalists, represented by the Woods family; the older, largely anti-union, magnates; and the young opportunists, or "socialites," who were also resistant in their relations with employees. The groups were not always distinct. Their interests sometimes overlapped, but they also competed in ways that significantly affected labor relations in the District. The consequences of the conflicting interests of capital and labor were not fully apparent until 1904, in part because capital was not united.

Stratton in particular refused to enter the club of Colorado Springs millionaires. Living modestly in a house he built during his days as a carpenter, his somewhat eccentric generosity became legendary. He donated lots to El Paso County and the U.S. government to build a new county courthouse and post office. He gave Colorado Springs a new streetcar system and Cheyenne Park. His housekeeper, Anna Hellmark, received rental property and a lifetime pass on the streetcars. He gave a five-story building for the Colorado Springs Mining Exchange, annual Christmas gifts of coal to every poor family in Victor, bicycles for all the laundry girls of Colorado Springs, and $5,000 to Robert Womack. Stratton left the bulk of his estate for the Myron Stratton Home, where El Paso County orphans and elderly citizens were to be treated not "as paupers usually are at public expense" but "decently and comfortably clothed and amply provided with good and wholesome food and with the necessary medical attendance, care and nursing to protect their health and insure their comfort." When Stratton died, ironically, Teller County had been created, so no one from the Cripple Creek District qualified for the home. Colorado Springs, with the affectations Stratton scorned, gained the most from his wealth.[72]

Stratton confounded his fellow mine owners with his labor policies and politics. "I am spending fifty thousand dollars a month . . . and every cent of that money goes to union labor," he once announced. He paid daily wages of $3 to $5, saying that it was not "right for a former workingman to take advantage of the necessities of his fellow men." To underscore the point, long after he became a multimillionaire Stratton joined Colorado Springs Carpenters' Local No. 515, to become the wealthiest union carpenter in the country. He endorsed William Jennings Bryan for president in 1896, saying that "the maintenance of the gold standard would be best for me individually, but I believe that free silver is the best thing for the working masses of the country." He offered to bet $100,000 against $300,000 on a Bryan victory because he had "a great respect for the intelligence and patriotism of the working people" and believed that they would "see their duty and interest at the polls is for free silver." He delivered his final insult to the elite of Colorado Springs when the Mining Stock Association hosted an elaborate dinner in his honor on January 16, 1902, in thanks for the new Mining Exchange building. It would have been a huge success, except that Stratton didn't show.[73]

Stratton was more sympathetic to his employees than were most mine owners. But even he and Burns shared little of the mining heritage with the thousands of miners who worked for them. Only two major owners had any mining experience: Stratton, from his idiosyncratic prospecting and studying, and Harnan, from the Pennsylvania coal mines. MacNeill had professional experience in ore refining, but he was not working class in either background or values. Stratton died in 1902. Not until he was gone did the young easterners act on their hostility to organized labor.

❧   ❧   ❧

Although class differences were sometimes muted, nonetheless significant differences in experience separated labor from most owners. The road from Colorado Springs to the District crossed a social chasm. Except for a lucky few, prior wealth and class connections enabled people to buy and develop Cripple Creek mines. To see the significance of class, we need only consider the very different fates of Robert Womack and Spencer Penrose. Both came to Cripple Creek penniless. Both reportedly liked a good drink. Womack, who spent twelve years working to discover Cripple Creek's gold, could not afford to develop his mine, sold it for $500, and died poor. Penrose, because of his family connections, got his start as a mine owner for $500 he did not have and reportedly never paid but died a multimillionaire. By the time Cripple Creek was developed, ownership no longer had anything to do with work or with occupation. Cripple Creek might have been home for working people, but the *Weekly Gazette* was right. Cripple Creek was not a poor man's camp.

Cripple Creek, Colorado, in its heyday at the turn of the century, with Mt.Pisgah in the background, facing northwest from Gold Hill. (Courtesy Colorado Historical Society)

Cripple Creek and Mt. Pisgah from Gold Hill, 1997. (Author photo)

Anaconda, Colorado, mine tailings and surrounding mines, including the Mary McKinney and the Morning Glory. (Photo by L. C. McClure, courtesy Denver Public Library)

Former Anaconda townsite, 1997. (Author photo)

Portland (upper right) and Independence mines (center left) on Battle Mountain, with mine dumps, tailings, and processing plants. The Colorado Midland freight cars are on standard-gauge tracks; the Florence and Cripple Creek Railroad narrow gauge track is passing under its trestle. (Photo by L. C. McClure, courtesy Denver Public Library)

Stratton's Independence Mine, 1997. (Author photo)

Cripple Creek restaurant, early 1890s. (Photo by W. E. Hook, courtesy Colorado Historical Society)

Altman, Colorado, with Pikes Peak in the distance. Caption on the photograph reads "Highest incorporated town in the world—Elevation 11200 feet." (Photo by R. J. Harlan, courtesy Colorado Historical Society)

Deputies Battery A, 1894 strike, under El Paso County Sheriff M. F. Bowers and County Commissioner Wier Boynton. (Courtesy Colorado Historical Society)

The miners' "fort" on Bull Hill during the 1894 strike. (Courtesy Colorado Historical Society)

The Strong Mine after it was blown up on May 25, 1894. (Courtesy Colorado Historical Society)

Colorado National Guard near Altman, with Bull Hill at right, 1894 strike. (Courtesy Colorado Historical Society)

"Examining the Ore Vein," unidentified mine. (Photo by L. C. McClure, courtesy Denver Public Library)

(Below) Victor Miners' Union Hall, 118–122 North Fourth Street. From *Miners' Magazine*, September 1902. (Courtesy Denver Public Library)

(Above) Philip Schuch's Assay Office, Cripple Creek. Left to right, Philip Schuch, Jr., Earl Aikin, unknown, and Dean Aikin. (Courtesy Colorado Historical Society)

Philip Schuch's Assay Office after it was blown up on February 24, 1902. (Courtesy Colorado Historical Society)

2

STAKING THE CLAIMS

On August 17, 1893, Isabella Mine superintendent H. E. Locke informed his work force that he was extending their workday from eight hours to ten, with an hour for lunch. With that announcement, Locke fired the opening shot in the contest for class power in the Cripple Creek District.

The miners refused to work under the new schedule. Their dispute about work hours involved much more than the working conditions in a single mine. The Isabella became the test case to determine who would control working conditions in all the mines. All sides contested their claims in a nearly year-long strike.

The length of the workday was only a surface issue in complex negotiations to determine the relative power of labor and competing capitalists. In the summer of 1893 Locke challenged labor confidently, knowing that it was no particular loss to close the Isabella for a while. Its principal owner, J. J. Hagerman, was also the president of the Colorado Midland Railroad. Until either its Midland Terminal Railroad (MT) or Smith and Moffat's rival Florence and Cripple Creek line (F&CC) reached the District, transportation costs would cut profits considerably. As the railroads laid their tracks, silver mines closed throughout Colorado. Miners, idled by a strike, would have few options. It would not hurt to leave the ore underground while capital established control.

There were a few wild cards—some mine owners worked shorter shifts and a notoriously pro-labor Populist occupied the governor's mansion. But from the perspectives of investors who hastily moved from silver to Cripple Creek gold, it seemed that Locke had picked a fine time to assert the rights of management.

❀   ❀   ❀

Patterns of capital consolidation, labor organizing, the changing allegiances of the state, and the economic strategies of competing owners all shaped local class relations. These factors combined to delineate roughly four periods of class relations from Womack's first lucky strike through 1904 and the end of union power. Different ownership groups predominated in each period, but until the second WFM strike they held one another in check and never united in their policy toward labor.

Economic activity during the first period, from 1890 to 1894, revolved around the ore discoveries and the investments in mines and railroads that assured the District's growth. As development began, miners rushed to the area, founded unions, and organized to regulate working conditions. In 1894 the Western Federation of Miners won its strike to establish a $3 minimum wage, an eight-hour day, and the right to union membership. By the end of 1894 labor-management relations stabilized around that agreement.

During the second period, from 1895 to 1899, owners developed their mines and constructed mills to treat low-grade ore. Labor built on the strike victory to organize more miners, unionize other crafts, and develop regional labor networks. By 1899 the Colorado State Federation of Labor (CSFL), the Western Labor Union (WLU), and the Victor and Cripple Creek Trades Assemblies coordinated and supported the efforts of individual locals.

Gold production peaked by 1900, when miners dug $20 million in gold from 475 mines. Settlement followed the gold, to reach an estimated thirty-two thousand District residents the same year.[1] From 1899 to 1903 the most powerful owners consolidated their holdings and integrated mining, refining, and transportation facilities. Organized labor also reached its peak membership and influence. Representing a majority of all workers, District unions performed pivotal social and political functions, particularly after Teller County was created in 1899.

The final period, the Cripple Creek strike of 1903–4, involved not only the obvious conflict between capital and labor but also competition among owners who fought for economic supremacy.

❀   ❀   ❀

The first period proved pivotal for all that followed. Between 1890 and 1894, both capital and labor staked their initial claims. It was not immediately clear that there was enough gold to warrant large-scale investment. Until the District established its value, the first miners found a rough, impermanent encampment typical of short-lived mining booms. The population was overwhelmingly male and the housing scarce, crude, and inadequate. But by 1894, when some 175 mines produced almost $3 million in gold, around ten thousand people had settled in the District, and the towns of Altman, Anaconda, Cripple Creek, Elkton, Gillett, and Victor all thrived.[2]

The towns developed as the mines did. The early hopefuls found a motley settlement of tents and cabins called Fremont, which soon combined with a second small settlement, Hayden Placer, to become the town of Cripple Creek. When Womack discovered gold, the Cripple Creek townsite belonged to two Denver real estate developers, Horace Bennett and Julius Myers, who had acquired the land as payment for a bad debt. Bennett and Myers platted a town on their land in November 1891 and named the two main streets for themselves. Bennett Avenue became the main business thoroughfare. Myers Avenue, one block south, immortalized the name of retiring Julius Myers as the site of one of the West's legendary vice districts. In 1891, however, the streets were only lines on paper. Capital was scarce, and the few settlers predominantly poor. Investors waited for the camp to prove itself. By late in the year Colorado Springs was sufficiently convinced of the District's value to begin raising capital. Business representatives took an exhibit of Cripple Creek ores and assays to the Denver Mining Congress, and the county commissioners decided to build roads to the District. Private investors formed a pipeline and reservoir company to bring water to the towns.[3]

Newcomers found a thriving camp. Electric lights illuminated parts of Cripple Creek by 1892, and a local telephone exchange began operating in December 1893, followed by telephone service to Colorado Springs. The town of Cripple Creek at last had a water supply. There was still not enough housing, however. What little was available was often rude and primitive. A miner might take refuge at the local saloon, which the local press aptly called "a miner's club."[4]

Saloons provided shelter of a sort, but not for "good" women and their children. Family settlement increased with mining development, and with it the demand for schools and housing. The first school bonds were approved in June 1893; within a year six school buildings dotted the various camps. A decade later nearly four thousand pupils attended nineteen schools. Family settlement brought churches as well. A gospel tent opened for services in 1892. By 1894 Baptist, Methodist, Methodist Episcopal, and Catholic congregations worshipped each Sunday. More than thirty churches held services in 1900. By one measure, however, Cripple Creek remained a typical mining camp—saloons outnumbered churches five to one.[5]

It was typical, as well, in the rush to establish control of the mines that were the only reason for the frenzied settlement. The struggle for economic control began as soon as it was apparent that Womack had found enough gold to warrant investment. By August 1891 more than six hundred people were prospecting, and the first major investors had risked their capital. Edward M. De La Vergne, the first Colorado Springs capitalist to visit the District, purchased the Gold King Mine in Poverty Gulch and shipped the first stock of tools to Cripple Creek in March 1891. David. H. Moffat bought the Victor Mine on Bull Hill for $65,000. Count James Pourtales of Colorado Springs and Judge W. J. Kerr of Pueblo paid $50,000 for a half interest in the Sunshine Placer, and Pourtales began developing the Buena Vista Mine.[6]

Most of the District had been staked off and claimed by early 1892. Several stamp mills processed the ore. Owners, informed of rich deposits discovered at ten to thirty feet, quickly incorporated and expanded their holdings. Pourtales and other Buena Vista investors formed the Bull Mountain Mining Company, bought twenty adjoining claims, and offered a million shares at a dollar each. William Lennox, E. A. Colburn, J. F. Maybury, and associates of Colorado Springs incorporated the Gold King Mining Company. Charles Tutt and his associates incorporated the C.O.D. James J. Hagerman, president of the Colorado Midland Railroad, bought his first claims for $50,000. Moffat and C. L. Roudebush of New York bought the Legal Tender, the New York, and eighty acres on Wilson Creek for $100,000. Moffat opened the Bi-Metallic Bank in Cripple Creek and then merged some fifty claims to incorporate the Anaconda Gold Mining Company, capitalized at $5 million, with Eben Smith as general manager. Roudebush called it "the biggest mining deal in the history of the state," predicting that where "people formerly worked with teaspoons, we will work with steam shovels. We will be shipping a hundred tons of ore per day inside of thirty days, from Gold Hill." The F&CC route through Anaconda did nothing to tarnish the company's prospects. Another merger followed in early 1894, when Smith, Moffat, Lennox, Giddings, and William E. Jackson, president of the Florence and Cripple Creek, incorporated the Battle Mountain Gold Mining Company, with a closed capital stock of $5 million.[7]

Stratton and the Portland group largely controlled the rich southern rim of the mineral belt. Then the Woods family struck pay dirt at their Victor hotel site. Warren and H. E. Woods and some associates incorporated the Columbine Victor Deep Mining and Tunnel Company, capitalized at $2 million. Three eight-hour shifts worked their new Gold Coin Mine by April 1893. Output increased threefold from 1892 to 1893, when the District yielded, by some estimates, more than $2.4 million in gold. Still, with some two hundred mining companies, only thirty-two mines produced ore in 1893, and none had sunk shafts deeper than 250 feet.[8]

In the early years, mine owners had to solve a number of technical problems before they could profitably mine the complex ores, which had high treatment costs. They had to build railroads and treatment facilities and deal with the vexations of water—too much in the mines, too little in the towns. Smith and Moffat raised development capital for a $5 million drainage tunnel and for railroads to transport the ore.[9]

The 1893 financial depression interrupted expansion. Ultimately, however, the District boomed as silver crashed. Colorado smelters substituted silicous gold ores for silicous silver ores, and skilled silver miners flocked to the new gold camp. The Cripple Creek postmaster reported that his money order business flourished on paydays because miners sent money "to their families in Leadville, Aspen and other silver camps in Colorado."[10]

Partly, too, development awaited the railroads. The Buena Vista, with more than $150,000 in ore in sight, waited to ship "until the railroad gets in the camp."[11] Before railroads reached the District, transportation and treatment costs totaled about $25 a ton, a prohibitive sum with low-grade ores. Moffat's Florence and Cripple

Creek Railroad reached the District on May 26, 1894, connecting the mines to the Denver and Rio Grande in Florence. In 1892 the Colorado Midland, a subsidiary of the Santa Fe Railroad, which operated between Colorado Springs and Aspen, began constructing the Midland Terminal Railroad to connect with its tracks at Divide. Delayed by finances in 1893, it reached Cripple Creek in December 1895. Its route followed the richest mineral deposits on the east slope of Bull Hill (near Hagerman's Isabella) and on Battle Mountain (map 2).

Mine owners who owned stock in the two railroads also competed to control refining. The Colorado Springs owners, some of whom also had interests in the Midland, wanted the mills in Colorado Springs. Moffat and his associates built reduction facilities in Florence along their own tracks.[12]

With the principal mines located and rails connecting the mines with mills and markets, major mining development got underway in 1895. The Golden Circle Railroad began operating in 1896, connecting the various towns and unincorporated settlements with the larger mines. A final railroad, the Colorado Springs and Cripple Creek District Railroad (the "Short Line"), financed by the combined Stratton, Portland, and Woods interests, completed its forty-five mile, standard-gauge route from Colorado Springs in March 1901 (map 2). The F&CC initially controlled the Golden Circle, but in 1899 the Short Line bought it. At the same time, Moffat relinquished control of the F&CC to the Midland Terminal — it had lost money after the MT reached the District.[13]

The rail lines completed, owners turned their attention to establishing control of the mills along the tracks outside the District itself. Labor focused on building its local base. In 1899 the District won a long campaign to separate politically from Colorado Springs. Teller County was formed from portions of El Paso and Fremont counties. Before 1899, Colorado Springs tipped the balance of political power to the employers, but Teller County brought potential working-class control of county government and sparked a lively debate within the unions over political philosophies and tactics. For capital, freight and reduction costs remained key issues, and competing ownership groups jockeyed to control mills and railroads. The competition intensified as shifting economic alliances resolved into several distinct groups with integrated holdings in mining, transportation, and refining. As the economy contracted after 1900 they battled to control the profits from low-grade ore.

⊛   ⊛   ⊛

For labor, everything rested on the organizational base in the mines secured during the first stages of development. As the first deals were made, the first shafts sunk, and the first houses built, miners and carpenters founded the first unions. Fremont Carpenters No. 506 existed briefly during 1892, Cripple Creek Carpenters No. 298 functioned during 1893 and 1894, and a Miners' and Prospectors' Protective Association, reportedly the only "form of government at Cripple Creek camp," was formed in January 1892. The Protective Association conducted funerals, decided claim disputes, and was reputedly "a terror to claim jumpers." In 1893 the miners of Barry (later Anaconda) formed a union. The carpenters' and barbers' unions and the miners' band marched in the 1893 Memorial Day parade.[14]

The District was not represented in Butte at the 1893 founding convention of the Western Federation of Miners. But shortly after the new federation was formed, Altman miners asked the Colorado WFM organizer, Alexander McIntosh of Aspen, to come help them. Free Coinage Miners' Local No. 19 was chartered in Altman on August 20, 1893, three days after Locke announced the ten-hour day at the nearby Isabella. The new union soon enrolled three hundred members. John Calderwood, who had represented Aspen at the WFM convention, moved to the District and took over as McIntosh's deputy. Within two months Calderwood organized three more WFM locals in Cripple Creek, Victor, and Anaconda and was elected president of the Altman union.[15]

The first priority was uniform wages and hours. Most miners earned $3 a day, although some received $2.50, and the workday varied from eight hours to ten.[16] The "working-class" owners—Burns, Doyle, Harnan, and Stratton—operated nine-hour shifts at their mines. The Tutt and Smith-Moffat properties worked ten hours and were among the most intransigent. The Isabella, owned by Colorado Midland Railroad president J. J. Hagerman, became the focus of the controversy following Locke's August 17 proclamation.

The Isabella miners responded unequivocally—they did not show up for work the following Monday. Locke telephoned Colorado Springs for instructions, withdrew the order, resumed operations on eight-hour shifts, and asked El Paso County sheriff M. F. Bowers to send him two deputies for protection. The mine owners met to try to establish uniform shifts. The WFM, in turn, geared its strategy to a uniform eight-hour day. The union targeted the Burns Mine, which worked nine hours, and in December 1893 asked manager Frank T. Sanders to adopt an eight-hour schedule. Sanders refused, and on December 26 two hundred miners met at the Burns shaft house and called out the work force.[17]

A number of mines, allied either with Hagerman's MT Railroad or the Smith-Moffat F&CC, counterattacked in early January 1894, announcing that on February 1 they would enforce a ten-hour day. The Pharmacist, formerly an eight-hour mine, offered a ten-hour day, or $2.50 for eight hours. Similar notices went up at Hagerman's Isabella and at Smith and Moffat's Victor and Anaconda mines. On January 20, as tension mounted, union miners ran H. E. Locke and one of his deputies, a man named Rabideau, out of camp. Eight miners were arrested, pleaded not guilty, and posted $200 bonds.[18]

Two days before the ten-hour rule was to be implemented, the miners offered to compromise if the eight-hour mines agreed not to lengthen their shifts. When the owners did not respond, the miners, on February 2, gave management ten days to adopt the union rule of $3 for an eight-hour day before they called out everyone working more than eight hours. The owners instead announced that they would close their mines on February 7. That day the union struck all mines working more than eight hours, making it a moot point whether a strike or a lockout was in effect.[19]

Fewer than half of the producing mines were involved, under a fourth of the working miners locked out. Calderwood estimated that 1,200 to 1,300 miners worked in the District, approximately 800 of whom had joined the WFM. About half were working eight hours for $3 when the strike was called. Working miners paid a $15 monthly strike assessment to support the strikers. Outside labor and local businesses provided further help: a grocery gave $400 credit, Cripple Creek businessmen loaned the union $1,000, the San Juan miners sent $700, and the Butte unions donated $800.[20]

The mine owners were divided. Some held firm for ten hours, others quickly settled with the union. The Kismet and Santa Rita Mines immediately accepted eight hours. More critically, James Burns, to his colleagues' dismay, praised his employees for joining the WFM and announced that every worker had "a right to improve his status by bargaining collectively." Calderwood negotiated a special agreement with Stratton and Burns for $3.25 for a nine-hour day shift and $3 for an eight-hour night shift, an agreement that held for two years until they switched to the standard eight hours. The Independence started on the new schedule on March 19, and the Portland adopted it within weeks. But a number of mines stuck with nine hours, and some threatened to cut wages to $2.50. The *Gazette* reported that with "the prospect of railway construction soon to be completed," many mine owners preferred to "save their money and strength" until they could work "much more economically than at present."[21]

Mine owners who held substantial railroad investments were the least interested in negotiating. The nine-hour properties represented a coalition of the Smith-Moffat mines and Colorado Springs owners, many of whom owned Midland Terminal stock. The principal holdouts included William Lennox, E. W. Giddings, Judge Ernest A. Colburn, Edward De La Vergne, Sam Strong, James J. Hagerman, and the Smith-Moffat properties. The nine-hour mines filed for an injunction, and on March 14 a district judge ordered miners not to interfere in any way with mining operations. De La Vergne's Summit and Raven and Smith and Moffat's Anaconda and Victor mines tried to open, but no more than five men appeared to work at each. The superintendent of the Victor asked the sheriff to send deputies for protection. Bowers hastily deputized six men, but a group of miners intercepted them near

Altman and disarmed them. The Altman mayor, city marshal, and police magistrate, all of whom belonged to the WFM, arrested the deputies for disturbing the peace and carrying concealed weapons. After they produced their deputy sheriffs' credentials, the Altman officials released the prisoners but kept their guns.[22]

That night Sheriff Bowers asked Gov. Davis H. Waite to send troops. Waite dispatched three companies, and Bowers swore in fifty deputies. The troops, under the command of Brig. Gen. E. J. Brooks, arrived at Cripple Creek on the morning of March 18. Brooks and Adj. Gen. T. J. Tarsney met with the sheriff, county officials, and Cripple Creek business representatives, all of whom insisted that civil authorities could not maintain the peace. That evening, union representatives met with Brooks and Tarsney and told them that the miners had not resisted county officials and that "no disturbance of any kind had occurred beyond the ordinary small offenses that are constantly occurring in mining camps." They insisted that the union was not involved in holding the deputies because the union was in session at the time. The generals telephoned these findings to the governor, and the trustees of Altman sent a telegram: "Military arriving in Cripple Creek. Did you send them, and what for? Everything quiet here." Waite, a Populist from Aspen who had long-standing ties with the miners, recalled the troops on March 20. The anti-union *Gazette* reported that the "miners gave them a hearty cheer when they left the camp while the *citizens* deplored their departure."[23]

Before the state troops left, Bowers made a hasty trip to Colorado Springs for warrants and on March 19 demanded military aid in serving them. Tarsney refused, saying that Bowers had no reason to fear interference. All eighteen men for whom Bowers held warrants surrendered voluntarily. Sixteen were dismissed without trial, and an El Paso County jury acquitted the remaining two.[24]

Before the troops ever arrived, Bowers went to Altman, arrested the mayor, city marshal, and Calderwood, and took them to Colorado Springs, where they were released on bail. Returning on March 22, Calderwood complained that he had been arrested without a warrant and jailed for four days without a hearing. He was finally charged with using boisterous language and with threatening two unspecified men.[25]

Representatives of both sides got together on April 1 to try to negotiate. The mine owners, led by J. J. Hagerman, offered $2.75 for eight hours, with a twenty-minute lunch break. The strikers unanimously rejected the offer. A week later, while most union members were attending the funeral of a union miner, handbills appeared throughout the District announcing that there would be a miners' meeting in Anaconda at 11 o'clock—the same time as the funeral. Union men rushed to Anaconda, where they found former deputy Rabideau holding a bogus meeting to feign labor support for the ten-hour day. They beat Rabideau and ran him out of camp once again.[26]

The miners could afford to hold out for their demands. By April, twenty-eight mines were working on the eight-hour schedule in addition to the Portland and Independence. Only seven were idled by the strike. Local business and the Cripple Creek *Crusher* began encouraging Moffat and Hagerman, the primary holdouts, to settle. A local stockbroker noted that since most miners were working, it could "hardly be supposed that this majority" would "consent to a reduction of wages or a lengthening of hours to enable the minority to find employment."[27]

In early May some mine owners offered to provide arms to El Paso County and pay for deputies to open the remaining mines, but the District stayed relatively quiet. Then, in mid-May, Bowers deputized some 1,200 men, and on May 20 sent nearly two hundred to occupy the mines near Victor. Calderwood called them "the scum from nearly all the cities in Colorado."[28]

Anticipating attacks, the strikers entrenched themselves on Bull Hill. They built a fort, or a mock fort, and were thought to be well armed. This may have been clever subterfuge. Stories passed down through the Welch family suggest that the miners tried to appear more formidable than they were. Kathleen Welch Chapman repeated her mother's story of one confrontation:

> There wasn't too many people up there, you know—and the men went out and they had their wives come along with them. And Mama said she wrapped Tom in a blanket and went along. And the men took their coats off, and their hats, and put them up in a tree and put the guns up in there. And then, of course they were milling around, you know, and oh, they just thought that the *world* was up there, this militia did, when they seen them. They come up through Gillett. And when they could look up there and see all them guns shining through with the sun on them, boy, they stopped and they turned around and went back to Colorado Springs *on the run!*[29]

It is not clear how much retelling and memory altered this account. If it occurred, the incident involved sheriff's deputies rather than the militia. The story does demonstrate a working-class oral tradition that challenged official accounts. In any event, considerable apprehension existed about the fort and about what would happen when the mine owners tried to resume operations with non-union labor.[30]

On May 24 between 150 and 200 deputies proceeded to Victor. The miners marched down Bull Hill to meet them and massed near the mines on Battle Mountain. They captured the non-union Strong Mine, which was guarded by armed deputies, and ordered the superintendent, foreman, and engineer to come out. The three men went down the shaft instead and were trapped there for twenty-six hours after the shaft house blew up. Which side was responsible for the explosion remained a subject of perennial local debate.[31]

After the confrontation on Battle Mountain, the deputies withdrew down the F&CC tracks, where they camped for the night. On May 25 some three hundred strikers set out to attack them. An advance party ran into a deputies' outpost, and both sides fired. Rabideau and a striker named Herman Crawley were killed, and two others were wounded. Six strikers were taken prisoner and jailed in Colorado Springs. Union miners rescued the three men trapped in the Strong Mine and held them as hostages to exchange for the imprisoned union men.[32]

Pressure mounted for a settlement. On May 26 Governor Waite asked the strikers to lay down their arms. He also declared that Bowers's deputy sheriffs were illegal because many came from other counties and Colorado law specified that sheriffs could deputize only citizens of their own counties. Swearing in hundreds of deputies and giving them new arms, said Waite, constituted forming an army, which usurped the powers of the governor. He charged that the mine owners were paying for the deputies and demanded that they disperse. The same day a committee from Colorado Springs—Colorado College president William S. Slocum, union sympathizer the Rev. Evans Carrington, and Trades Assembly president Charles Collais—went, at Hagerman's request, to Bull Hill to explore arbitration and to arrange an exchange of prisoners. That afternoon on the mesa below Altman the two sides traded the three Strong mine employees for the union prisoners.[33]

The strike ended, as many had predicted, as the railroads entered the camp. The F&CC reached Victor (and the mines the deputies had occupied) on May 26 as both sides moved to settle. The tracks reached Cripple Creek on July 2.[34]

The miners met with Waite at Altman on May 30 and appointed him their sole arbitrator. Waite and Calderwood left for Colorado Springs but did not arrive until June 2 because of railroad difficulties. Hagerman met the governor at Colorado College and negotiated an agreement conceding the miners' demands. He reneged, however, when other mine owners persuaded him not to sign it. Word got out that Calderwood was at the college. As a mob surrounded the building, Calderwood and Waite slipped out a back door and escaped to Denver on the governor's train. Two days later Hagerman and Moffat met with Waite, conceded the $3 daily wage and eight-hour day, promised not to discriminate against union members, and urged "other mine owners and employers of mining labor, in said Cripple Creek District" to accept their agreement.[35] Although they did not represent other owners, they were the only significant holdouts, so their agreement settled the strike. Their mines opened as the railroad cut their shipping costs.

The settlement, however, did not end the conflict. As the District started celebrating, Bowers and his 1,200 deputies advanced from Divide on a forced march to Bull Hill. Waite immediately called out the state militia on June 4, but because of heavy rains and washouts it did not reach the District until the afternoon of June 7. On the night of June 6 the deputies broke camp, cut all telegraph and telephone lines, and jailed all newspaper reporters in the area. Then they advanced on Bull Hill and exchanged shots with the strikers' pickets. Another small skirmish occurred the next morning. Finally, the militia arrived and camped between the miners and the deputies. The following day the deputies headed up Bull Hill in order, Bowers said, to secure the roads and help him make arrests. They returned to camp only after General Brooks threatened to fire on them.[36]

The militia then moved to Altman. The deputies, defying the governor's orders, refused to disband and proceeded to arrest citizens in Cripple Creek and to occupy the Independence Mine. Because the deputies refused to disperse, Generals Brooks and Tarsney recommended that the governor declare martial law. Waite threatened to call out "the unorganized militia"—potentially every able-bodied man in Colorado from eighteen through forty-five—to "suppress their insurrection." Finally, on June 10, Tarsney arranged a meeting among county officials, prominent mine owners, and the militia officers. They agreed to withdraw the deputies, return the mines to the owners, and provide military protection to both mines and miners. The miners agreed to relinquish their arms and return any property taken from the mines. Persons for whom the sheriff had warrants would surrender to arrest, and troops would remain at least thirty days at Anaconda, Cripple Creek, and Victor.[37]

The next day the deputies returned to Colorado Springs and were disbanded. In the Altman town hall, Bowers read the names of several hundred men for whom he had arrest warrants. Thirty-seven strikers were indicted, and Bowers filled the county jail for more than a year. Four were convicted of assorted charges. In March 1895 D. M. McNamara was convicted of assault with intent to commit robbery and sentenced to two and a half years, but the Colorado Supreme Court reversed the decision on appeal. Jackson Rhines was sentenced to six months in county jail for two counts of assault. Robert Lyons and Nicholas Tully were sentenced to six and eight years, respectively, for blowing up the Strong Mine, but both were pardoned by A. W. McIntire, a Republican who succeeded Waite as governor.[38]

Among those who refused to testify against Lyons and Tully was one of the sheriff's deputies, Sherman Bell. Many believed that Sam Strong, who owned the mine, was responsible for blowing it up. Lennox and Giddings, who were leasing the mine, later sued Strong, alleging that he had arranged the explosion to break the lease, but Strong was acquitted of the charge. The miners insisted that no union man could receive a fair trial in Colorado Springs and considered Tully, Lyons, and Rhines union heroes.[39] On June 23, when General Tarsney, a lawyer by profession, was defending some of the miners in Colorado Springs, he was kidnapped from the Alamo Hotel, driven out of town, stripped, and tarred and feathered. No one was tried for the crime.[40]

Waite's intervention demonstrated the pivotal power of the state, just as the Altman officials demonstrated the potentially critical role of local government. Bowers's allegiance to his wealthy constituents was equally apparent. A precarious political tension existed between Colorado Springs, largely Republican and allied with capital, and the District, largely working class and Democratic or Populist. Some charged that Waite hoped to swing El Paso County to the Populists, others that the deputies were delegated to drive Populists out of the county. There is some evidence that county officers used Bowers's indictments to Republican advantage, offering to drop charges against miners who supported the Republican ticket and threatening to prosecute those who refused. Given anti-labor sentiment in Colorado Springs, convictions were probable.[41]

The strike negotiated the terms of class relations for the coming decade. It also delineated emerging consolidations and differences among owners. The Independence and Portland owners provided a critical check on Hagerman, Moffat, and their nine-hour cohort. James Doyle signed Calderwood's bond and testified for Lyons at his trial. The conservative owners had asserted the rights of private property and of each laborer to "contract" individually for wages and working conditions. The uneasy balance of state, county, and local control held their power in precarious check. The combination of divisions among the mine owners, the miners' successful union organization, and state power together undermined the conservative mine owners, who nonetheless chose an economically propitious moment to settle.[42]

The 1894 strike highlighted fissures of class, ethnicity, and culture. Politics and religion as well as class divided conservative mine owners from their employees. Contemporary rhetoric framed the strike as a conflict between Irish Catholic miners and predominantly Episcopalian mine owners. One Colorado Springs minister, a supporter of the nativist American Protective Association (APA), charged that labor would end the strike if the owners hired Catholic mine superintendents. "If this is true," he proclaimed, "then the A.P.A. was not organized a day too soon." The Colorado Springs press, which portrayed the miners as lawless brutes, claimed that Denver and District newspapers were more sympathetic to labor because their reporters were "bigoted Catholics" in sympathy with "the O'Connells of the union" and that Catholic newspaper "spies" reported the deputies' movements to the union.[43]

We cannot know what proportion of the miners were Irish Catholics. Certainly, many were. After the strike it became a source of working-class pride to be called a "Bull Hill Redneck," local slang that connoted not only Irish Catholicism but also staunch union loyalties.[44] The phrase held more negative connotations in Colorado Springs, where the *Gazette* alleged that the Mollie Maguires and the Rednecks led a reign of terror and anarchy. "The 'Mollies' and the 'red-necks' exercised a complete terrorism over the peaceable," it reported. John Calderwood, a Scottish Catholic fond of quoting Pope Leo XIII and allegedly blacklisted from the Pennsylvania mines for joining the Mollies, personified the Catholic union menace to Colorado Springs.[45] The militance of the Rednecks, like the resistance of conservative capitalists, was rooted in class relationships and reinforced by shared reli-

gious, ethnic, and social experience. Immigrant Irish Catholics shared class understandings forged in Irish nationalism, and in wage work from County Cork to
Schuylkill County to the Comstock. The Protestant mine owners of Colorado
Springs traced their roots and class ties to New England Protestants and Philadelphia's Main Line.

The strike left both capital and labor organized to consolidate their gains. Moffat
and his associates controlled the Florence and Cripple Creek; a number of mines on
Bull Hill and around Anaconda, including the Victor Mine and the Anaconda Gold
Mining Company; and the Bi-Metallic Bank. Stratton, Burns, Harnan, and Doyle
controlled virtually all the mines on Battle Mountain. Other Colorado Springs owners integrated and expanded their holdings, including Howbert, Pourtales, De La
Vergne, Tutt, Colburn, Lennox, and Hagerman, some of whom also held stock in
the Midland Terminal. These groups continued to compete as they consolidated their
mines and integrated them with railroads and refining facilities.

The strike victory held the key for organized labor. By July 1894 some 1,200 miners worked in the District.[46] Union control of the basic industry provided the basis
to organize the rest of the District's work force. As mining resumed, all sides regrouped for their next steps.

3

IN UNION THERE IS STRENGTH

In late October 1896, H. R. Newhouse walked from one Cripple Creek construction site to another. Finding four non-union carpenters at work, he gave them until 9 o'clock the next morning to join the union and pay their dues. When Newhouse returned to check the following day, the four men saw him coming, picked up their tools, and left the jobsite. Proceeding up Bennett Avenue, Newhouse talked to workers at the new National Hotel, who complained that they were being paid regular wages for overtime. They could not prove it, however, so Newhouse merely recorded the problem. Next he talked to a local contractor, Jack Stewart, about the non-union men who laid floors for him. Stewart explained that the men were working to pay a debt and asked Newhouse not to say anything. At another site Newhouse found a carpenter who owed the Pueblo carpenters' local four years of delinquent union dues. He confronted two non-union carpenters at the new Mining Exchange Building. On the outskirts of town, he found more men who had not yet joined the union and some whose dues were five months in arrears.[1]

Newhouse's log recorded the tedious and mundane details of union organizing. Like other "walking delegates," he literally walked from job to job, making routine checks to ensure that all carpenters carried union cards and paid their dues. Sometimes local unions paid organizers, sometimes the Trades Assemblies picked up the tab, sometimes organizers volunteered their time, and sometimes they worked for part of the initiation fees they collected.[2] Their daily rounds built union labor.

Newhouse was busy in 1896. Two fires, on April 25 and 29, had destroyed most of downtown Cripple Creek, including much of the Myers Avenue vice district, and five thousand were homeless. The city rebuilt, erecting more stable structures to replace the ramshackle frame buildings of the boom days. Construction workers flocked to the District, and local unions rushed to organize them, offering, in addition to periodic visits from Newhouse and his cohorts, union wages and the fellowship of the local labor community.

The carpenters, like all non-mining labor, owed their leverage not only to the diligence of H. R. Newhouse and other walking delegates but also to the Western

Federation of Miners. The 1894 strike victory anchored District labor. It established the right to organize and ensured the support of the crucial mining work force for other crafts. From the end of the first WFM strike until 1899 District labor focused on building labor organizations at the District, state, and regional levels. As soon as the strike was settled, Cripple Creek locals formed a District Trades Assembly to organize other crafts and coordinate labor activity. The District Assembly operated from 1894 to 1896. Then the locals from the southern end of the District withdrew to form the Victor Trades Assembly. For five years two trades assemblies were headquartered in Victor and Cripple Creek. They merged in 1901 to form the Cripple Creek District Trades and Labor Assembly.[3]

The 1894 strike victory laid the foundation for the local union movement and established District labor's influence in regional union networks and in the WFM itself. Cripple Creek was the first big win for the Western Federation. Calderwood left during the strike to attend the second annual convention. The convention delegates condemned the El Paso County officials and accused Sheriff Bowers of colluding in "a conspiracy with the so-called Mine Owners' Protective Association of Cripple Creek District" to imprison innocent citizens "for no crime other than that they were members of a labor organization."[4]

The 1894 strike provided one impetus to establish the Colorado State Federation of Labor (CSFL) "for the better organization of all the producing classes." Eight District locals sent delegates to the founding convention in 1896.[5] The CSFL expanded rapidly, and the District, already one of the most organized areas in the West, wielded enormous influence. The annual CSFL convention met in Victor in 1897 and in Cripple Creek three years later. The number of CSFL affiliates doubled, and membership tripled by 1898, when thirteen District unions and both Trades Assemblies sent delegates and Joy Pollard of the Altman WFM local was elected state president.[6]

Cripple Creek unions exercised leadership, too, in the Western Labor Union (WLU), which the WFM helped found in 1898 to establish a class-conscious western rival to the American Federation of Labor (AFL). WFM leaders challenged the AFL for dividing the skilled crafts from other workers and for proclaiming the identity of interests of capital and labor. As machinery collapsed skill levels, they argued, it also increased labor productivity, and the benefits of increased productivity rightfully belonged to labor, not capital. The WFM charged that AFL craft organization created a "labor aristocracy" that divided workers and subverted class unity. Instead, the miners advocated industrial unionism—the organization of all workers in each industry into a single union, regardless of job or skill—in order to match the power of industrial corporations. As alternatives to the AFL, the Western Federation helped found the Western Labor Union (1898–1902), the American Labor Union (1902–5), and the Industrial Workers of the World (1905–   ).[7]

District labor—industrial and craft unions alike—echoed WFM challenges to the AFL. Both Trades Assemblies affiliated with the WLU, and P. N. McPhee of Cripple Creek Carpenters No. 547 and Federal Labor Union No. 19 was elected second vice president. M. J. O'Donnell, a Victor miner, was the first secretary-treasurer, and M. A. Andrews of the Cripple Creek Typographical union succeeded him. The Cripple Creek WFM locals accepted transfer cards when WLU members worked underground.[8]

District labor exercised leadership in numerous WLU affiliates. The United Association of Hotel and Restaurant Employees was formed in 1900 as a WLU union, and the Cripple Creek Cooks and Waiters locals joined immediately. R. E. Croskey of Cripple Creek, a thirty-five-year-old English immigrant, served as the first president of the new union, and J. B. Cummings and Ben Skelton of Victor were elected to the first executive committee.[9]

By the turn of the century Cripple Creek influenced the entire western labor movement through the WFM, CSFL, and WLU. Local union leaders were regularly elected to office in all three organizations.[10] John M. O'Neill, a member of Victor Miners No. 32, became the voice of hard-rock miners in 1901 when he was appointed editor of the WFM's *Miners' Magazine*.

❀   ❀   ❀

In the decade after the 1894 strike, capitalists also worked to expand their power. Owners bought more mines and developed them, consolidated their holdings, and integrated mines, railroads, mills, and smelters. Labor and capital negotiated differences as they arose, with the strike agreement providing a minimal common ground. The potential for further friction between the Moffat interests and the Bull Hill Rednecks remained checked by labor's friendly relationships with Burns and Stratton on Battle Mountain and by the more moderate, if sometimes condescending, management of the Woods family's interests.

Competition among District mines spawned industrial conglomerates to control gold production from underground diggings to the rails and refineries. Larger companies absorbed smaller ones, until by late 1897 only seventy-six companies operated District mines. Organized labor weighed each purchase with apprehension, fearful that consolidation would upset the balance of power between capital and labor.[11]

By 1903 the big investors had vastly increased their mining property and integrated extensive mining investments with transportation systems, refining facilities, and power plants to serve their mines. Soon after the strike, Smith and Moffat expanded significantly in the rich southern part of the District, absorbing the Portland Town and Mineral Company, a number of mines on Bull Hill, and two hundred acres with mineral rights.[12] Then, in 1899, they quite literally consolidated their power in the southern part of the District, constructing the La Bella Mill,

Water, and Power Company in Goldfield, which operated the F&CC and Golden Circle railroads and supplied power, water, and light to mines, mills, and samplers. Its pipe lines carried water to the Smith-Moffat mines, and its compressors powered drills to produce more than a thousand tons a day. Surplus power ran hoists, pumps, compressors, crushers, and other mining machinery throughout the District. Moffat then organized a massive consolidation of transportation and power companies. In late 1899, despite state efforts to block the transaction, the Moffat-controlled Denver and Southwestern Railroad Company merged the Florence and Cripple Creek Railway, the Midland Terminal, the Metallic Reduction Works, the La Bella Electric Power Company, and Carlton's Colorado Trading and Transfer Company. The power of the new conglomerate alarmed competitors, who countered by constructing the Short Line from Colorado Springs (chapter 2).[13]

With tracks completed to Bull Hill, a number of companies expanded there and on the adjacent slopes of Ironclad Hill. The Woods syndicate was the major player, buying part of the Gillett townsite, the old Grassy townsite, substantial acreage on Bull Hill, and the Cameron Mines, Land, and Tunnel Company. The company then built the town of Cameron to house workers for its extensive new holdings.[14] The Woods ultimately combined their vast properties into two conglomerates, the Gold Coin, and the $5 million United Gold Mines. The Woods syndicate, like Smith and Moffat, organized its own power company, Pike's Peak Power Company, which began operating in late 1900 and provided power for the Short Line, the Woods Economic Mill, the electric light systems of Cameron, Gillett, and Anaconda and for the Woods mines.[15]

The Woods family's purchases helped revitalize Victor after the 1899 fire, a boost to labor in symbolic terms as well as for the jobs they provided. The family built a new Gold Coin shaft house, the only one in the country with stained glass windows. "It would be a good thing for the Cripple Creek District," the *Press* editorialized in August 1901, "did it possess a few more such progressive business men as the Woods People." It also praised the family because "unlike many of the fortunate ones who . . . struck it rich" they did not "carry their money out of the district."[16]

The Woods purchases were part of a realignment that began in 1899 as both Stratton and the Smith-Moffat syndicate began selling properties. Smith and Moffat sold substantial holdings on Bull Hill to the Woods family, Burns, and Stratton, among others. But the most significant sales went to Carlton, Tutt, Penrose, and MacNeill. Tutt, Penrose, and MacNeill bought Smith and Moffat's Granite, Pinos Altos, and Commonwealth mines. Tutt and Penrose helped incorporate the Palmyra Leasing Company to operate a number of mines on Bull Hill. As the "socialites" bought Smith-Moffat holdings in the southeastern part of the District they forged increasingly strong links between the two groups.[17] Carlton began expanding from transportation to mining, and Smith and Moffat targeted him as a likely buyer. W. P. Dunham, general manager of the Smith-Moffat Independence Consolidated, reported in April 1902 that he could sell the mine "within twelve months at a very handsome profit" and was "absolutely sure that A. E. Carlton would pay an advance at any time for this control." Dunham wrote in December 1902 that he "went after Carlton the other day up in Cripple Creek. . . . I think if I keep after him I will finally get him landed with the Victor."[18]

The Smith-Moffat cutbacks shuffled local ownership, a process that accelerated as Stratton, too, began to sell. In 1899 he sold his enormously profitable Independence Mine to the London-based Venture Corporation for $11 million. Stratton remained a major Portland stockholder and used much of his profit from the Independence to buy, between 1899 and 1901, virtually all of Womack Hill, around Poverty Gulch, and enormous tracts on Gold, Globe, Ironclad, and Bull hills. He finally controlled roughly a fifth of the producing property in the District. Stratton intended to try to prove his theory that the Cripple Creek veins converged at great depth—rather in the shape of a goblet. He failed in that purpose but remained an enormously powerful employer.[19]

The wave of consolidations reorganized the most powerful ownership groups: Stratton held more than six hundred acres in two major properties on Bull Hill and in Poverty Gulch; the Woods Investment Company emerged as a major economic power in the District and merged the Woods holdings into two major companies; and Carlton extended his operations from fuel and freight to begin his rise as a mine owner. The sales of the Independence and of various Smith-Moffat properties shifted ownership alliances and marked the rising power of Tutt, Penrose, MacNeill, and Carlton.

But it was in ore refining that the young socialites began to flex their financial muscle. The struggle among competing capitalists accelerated as they fought to control the profits from mills and smelters. Moffat built a cyanide mill at Florence. Tutt, Penrose, and MacNeill established a chlorination facility at Lawrence and then, in December 1896, opened the largest chlorination plant in the country, the Colorado-Philadelphia Reduction Company in Colorado City, adjacent to Colorado Springs.[20]

Many owners feared dependency on the Tutt-Penrose mills and on the smelters of the American Smelting and Refining Company (ASARCO), commonly called the "smelter trust," both of which, they thought, charged high reduction fees. Formed in 1899 and capitalized at $65 million, ASARCO controlled roughly two-thirds of all U.S. smelting and refining. Its Colorado holdings included the Globe, Grant, and Pueblo smelters and Smith and Moffat's Bi-Metallic in Leadville. Moffat served briefly on the first board of directors. To counter ASARCO and the Tutt-Penrose mills, James Burns approached more than twenty major mines about building new reduction facilities. Also in 1899, the Woods family opened their Economic Gold Extraction plant in Arequa Gulch.[21]

The power of refining conglomerates created a management headache. In early 1900 a combine of all mills and smelters refused to treat ore running less than two ounces, or $40 a ton, infuriating owners and leasers of low-grade mines and the miners who lost their jobs. The power of the competing ASARCO and Tutt-Penrose mills increasingly concerned District owners. In December 1900 ASARCO bought the Guggenheim smelting properties, including the Philadelphia Smelting and Refining Company in Pueblo. Four months later, in April 1901, ASARCO hiked its smelting charges and sent contracts to the major mine owners that required them to ship to its plants for five years. At the same time, it reserved the right to refuse more than two hundred tons a month per company, to decide disputed ore values, and to pay mines $19 an ounce, which was less than the fixed market price of $20.67.[22]

The ASARCO ultimatum came two months after Tutt and Penrose opened yet another chlorination mill, the Standard, capitalized at $1.25 million. MacNeill managed the Standard, as he did "all the milling interests controlled by Messrs. Tutt and Penrose." The Colorado-Philadelphia had already bought the National Gold Extraction Company smelter at Florence; the three Tutt and Penrose reductions works—the Standard, the Colorado-Philadelphia, and the National—could treat at least nine hundred tons of Cripple Creek ore daily. More than half the District's output went to the Tutt-Penrose mills, which claimed to be taking a loss to meet ASARCO's prices. To compete, the socialites established their own refining conglomerate, the United States Reduction and Refining Company (USR&R). Incorporated in New Jersey and capitalized at $10 million, USR&R owned five mills: the Colorado-Philadelphia and the Standard in Colorado City and the National, Union, and Smith and Moffat's Metallic in Florence. The new corporation treated more than $7.5 million in ore before the end of the 1901.[23] ASARCO immediately raised its rates.

USR&R and ASARCO controlled most ore refining. The only competition came from the Woods family's Economic Mill and two Florence mills—the Union Gold Extraction Company and the Dorcas Mill. With Moffat's interests in both ASARCO and USR&R, his increasing control of the railroads, and with Tutt and Penrose buying mines to match their mills, Burns first tried to unite other owners to resist their power and then countered by integrating his own operation. Burns called for a community of interests among the owners in the "fight between the mines and the smelter trust" and urged the Mine Owners' Association (MOA) to withhold ore from "the smelter and mill trusts" to force them to lower their "exorbitant treatment charges." Most of his cohorts refused, fearing that a boycott would "ruin the stock market." Burns resigned as MOA president, left the association in disgust, closed the Portland, and made the fight alone. The smelters quickly lowered their charges. Burns announced that he would build the largest chlorination facility in the state near Colorado Springs on the new Short Line Railroad he had helped organize. He never returned to the Mine Owners' Association.[24]

Burns completed his Portland Mill in 1902. It and a new bromide mill, the Telluride, both located in Colorado City, joined the accelerating competition. When the Portland Mine's contracts with trust smelters expired at the end of January 1902, Burns curtailed operations and laid off four hundred workers until his mill opened in April rather than pay ASARCO's high treatment charges.[25]

Yet bigger changes lay ahead. On September 14, 1902, Winfield Scott Stratton died.[26] With Stratton gone, jockeying accelerated among the remaining owners. In little more than a decade a few distinct ownership groups had emerged that had integrated holdings and competing philosophies about the rights of management and of labor. The Smith-Moffat business interests were increasingly interlocked with Tutt, Penrose, MacNeill, and Carlton, who acquired a number of Smith-Moffat mines and their Metallic mill. The socialites patronized the older magnates' railroads, which in turn supported Carlton's freight and coal monopolies in the District. Burns had integrated the Portland Mine, the Portland Mill, and the Golden Circle and Short Line railroads to carry his ore. The Woods Investment Company had consolidated vast mine holdings, its interest in the Short Line and Golden Circle, and its own mill. Burns, the Woods family, and some allies consolidated to challenge the linked power of Smith and Moffat and the young socialites. Besides the Short Line, built to challenge the Midland Terminal, Burns backed a new trading and transfer company to compete with Carlton's Trading and Transfer Company. The Short Line purchased the Golden Circle and switched its power source from the Smith-Moffat La Bella facility to the Woods electric plant, uniting the Woods interests and Burns against the Smith-Moffat alliance with the socialites.[27] The business rivalries that preoccupied the owners until 1903 resolved into competing camps. Until 1903, however, owners' efforts to integrate the industry absorbed most of their energies and left labor free to consolidate its own power.

⚜   ⚜   ⚜

The four years from 1899 to 1903 marked the height of working-class power. Unions organized a majority of all workers in all trades, extended their influence throughout the mining industry and the regional labor movement, and increased their political power as well. The WFM, like the mine owners, turned from its base in the District mines to the new mills and smelters. In 1899 the WFM wrote industrial unionism into its constitution, and the language on jurisdiction was changed to include "all persons working in and around mines, mills, and smelters" rather than mines alone. As ore refining became a major management concern, the WFM moved to organize local mill and sampler employees, chartering a new millmen's union in Gillett, Banner Mill and Smeltermen No. 106 in Victor, and three locals of hoist engineers. Altman Engineers No. 75 was chartered in 1898; (Victor) Excelsior Engineers No. 80 and Cripple Creek Engineers No. 82 were chartered in 1899.[28]

District labor membership climbed after 1899 as new locals organized and as membership drives swelled the ranks of established unions. The *Pueblo Courier,* voice of the CSFL, reported that there was "much activity in union circles in the Cripple Creek and Victor mining district just now, and besides new members to nearly all the old unions, new organizations are being formed almost nightly." These included the Cripple Creek and Victor Federal Labor Unions, which covered crafts too small to support their own locals. One of the first acts of the newly merged Cripple Creek District Trades and Labor Assembly in 1901 was to elect organizers for Cripple Creek and Victor.[29]

Secure in their membership base, the local unions bought the Gold Nugget Publishing Company and, on June 27, 1899, began publishing a daily newspaper. Their Victor and Cripple Creek *Daily Press* proclaimed that it was "the first and only daily paper in the world owned, operated and controlled by men who toil in mine and shop and store, the men whose activities keep the wheels of this globe in motion and make civilization possible." The *Press* promised to serve labor as "an advocate and defender" by challenging publications that represented the "all powerful combination of capital." Editor J. J. Callahan believed that the *Press* had a critical educational mission in the campaign for working-class power because "being in the majority, there is no valid reason why we, the common masses of the people, should not control the destinies of this nation if we but rise to an intelligent conception of our power." In 1901 the *Daily Press* was chosen the official newspaper of Teller County, a symbolic recognition of labor's influence that also netted the revenues for printing county notices.[30]

The *Press* began publishing the year Teller County was created, a legislative victory that labor claimed liberated the District from the political domination of Colorado Springs. To underscore labor's political power, Gov. Charles Thomas appointed James Gaughan to serve as the first county clerk and recorder. The first permanent president of the Altman WFM local, Gaughan was one of the strikers Sheriff Bowers arrested during the 1894 strike. As a member of the Colorado House of Representatives, he led the campaign to create Teller County.[31]

Labor used its political clout to get the city of Cripple Creek to pay union scale and Teller County to enforce an eight-hour day for clerks. The all-union Goldfield city council legislated a $3 minimum wage and eight-hour day within city limits.

Graders on the Short Line immediately called a strike because they were being paid only $2.50, and the city marshal announced that the labor ordinance would be "strictly enforced."[32]

Effective organizing involved a variety of tactics, including social pressure, boycotts, and, when necessary, strikes. Labor disputes were not uncommon, but they were usually quickly resolved. Preoccupied with consolidating their own industrial control, employers generally accommodated labor. During March and April 1899, for instance, the CSFL reported three strikes or lockouts in the District. The new Gillett Mill and Smeltermen's local settled a ten-day lockout when union representatives and County Clerk Gaughan negotiated an eight-hour day. F&CC switchmen struck for new switch engines, wage increases, and reduced hours. Their tactic was simple—they stopped the ore-bearing freight trains while three union representatives went to Denver to negotiate their demands. Midland Terminal employees won a one-day strike for sixteen demands, including wages, hours, order of promotion, trials of discharged employees, and grievance rights.[33]

Workers felt sufficiently powerful to push their demands, and each success increased their faith in collective action. If conditions were unsatisfactory, generally a brief work stoppage won a union victory or at least an acceptable compromise. Between 1899 and 1903 the *Press* reported at least thirty-four minor strikes, primarily over wages and working conditions, most of them quickly negotiated.[34] Repeated success encouraged labor to expect that employers would accommodate union demands.

Strikes, nonetheless, remained a last resort. Generally, unions simply announced their wages and hours and boycotted businesses that resisted. To establish this tactic, seventeen members of the Cripple Creek Trades Assembly deliberately courted arrest under the Colorado boycott law by supporting a boycott called by the Painters' and Decorators' and Barbers' unions. Their acquittal established the right to boycott, winning, the *Press* boasted, "a distinct victory for unionism."[35] During 1901 alone, the *Press* advertised boycotts of more than twenty products or firms.[36] Using the *Press* to publicize banned goods and establishments, organized labor established six o'clock closing for retail clerks, prevented laundries from shipping clothes out of the District to non-union shops, made boardinghouses and restaurants hire union help, established the six-day week for cooks and waiters, and eliminated non-union products from saloons, groceries, and other retail houses—in short, enforced demands for union recognition, wages, and hours for most District workers.[37] Few male workers earned less than the miners' $3 minimum daily wage. Bricklayers and masons earned $6 for eight hours in 1899; stonecutters, $5; plumbers, steamfitters, hod-carriers, mortar mixers, and plasterers, $4; and tinners, brick-carriers, and stonemasons' helpers, $3.50. The Barbers' Union set a $5 scale to shave a corpse.[38]

Boycotts worked for workers who produced consumer goods or sold services to local residents. For miners, however, a gold boycott would have been a quixotic tactic at best. Occasionally, though, miners could use the boycott when mine owners' diverse interests offered workers something besides gold to target. That happened in 1900 when the Vindicator Mine refused to allow WFM posters in the shaft house. The Altman Miners' and Engineers' locals asked the CSFL to meet with Denver brewer A. J. Zang, a director of the Vindicator, to protest the "attitude of the management of the company" because "they do not want to have union men working on their property, but Mr. Zang wants union men to buy his beer." District WFM unions persuaded the State Federation to boycott Zang's beer until the Vindicator and Anaconda mines established union shops.[39]

For all District workers, the WFM remained pivotal; if the miners' unions were weak, everyone would be jeopardized. The 1894 strike won the right to join a union but not a closed shop. All miners, whether or not they joined the union, received union wages and hours. Labor organizations provided more than wages and hours, however. Although all workers enjoyed these basic benefits, only union members received social services. Local unions assisted their members when they were ill and unemployed, buried the dead, and provided insurance (chapter 4). To encourage miners to join, the WFM relied on union benefits and services, on its ability to control working conditions, on class loyalty, and on social pressure.[40]

The WFM's power to regulate work rules provided an important inducement to join. One periodic point of contention concerned management attempts to stop "high-grading," or thefts of rich ore from the mines. In 1897 some mine owners solicited $100 monthly contributions from each company to hire Pinkerton detectives to ferret out high-graders.[41] In 1900 eight large mines announced a stripping order requiring all underground workers to undress in one room of the change house and pass nude to another room, observed by a guard, when they changed clothes coming on and off shift. The Independence (called Stratton's Independence, Ltd. by its new British owners) became the test case for the new stripping order.[42]

On Sunday, September 23, the Independence closed at the end of the day shift and announced that it would accept job applications the next day under the new rules. Five hundred miners massed that night in Victor's Armory Hall. They announced that they would help stop ore thieves but would not work under the new rules. They also appointed a committee to persuade Independence manager H. A. Shipman to reconsider. The negotiators finally achieved a compromise that required miners to strip to underclothes and shoes to pass from one room to another. The miners accepted this compromise the night of the September 24.[43]

It was a tenuous truce. A detective searched all miners on the Independence as they came off shift on October 25 but discovered no ore thieves. When the searches were repeated the next day, all three hundred miners walked out. A mass meeting in Victor, including 90 percent of the Independence work force, resolved that thereafter miners would "leave the mine in their digging clothes." Reportedly, four men from the ore house and two underground miners either quit or were fired as a result of the searches and were blacklisted from working in the District. The miners elected another committee to meet with Shipman and report back to a miners' meeting the following day. Shipman suggested that underground workers strip to their underwear and that a few from each shift be searched. The miners countered that suspected ore thieves could be searched according to law but that there should be no mass searches and that the mine should reinstate the workers it had discharged. Shipman met with the WFM District Executive Board on the night of October 28. He agreed to abolish the Pinkerton detective system, to appoint a guard for the change rooms from candidates the union proposed, and to accept a closed shop. Finally, Shipman and the District Executive Board agreed that the men would strip at shift change to undershirt, drawers, low shoes, and stockings and pass from one room to the next observed by the guard. Any miner suspected of high-grading could be searched by a fellow union member in the presence of the watchman. The mine resumed operation under the new agreement on November 1. The union agreed to help catch highgraders and expel members convicted of theft at any closed-shop mine. Shipman announced that "a man is benefited by joining the union," and that he would use his "personal influence to have him join the union." Although the stripping controversy was not entirely resolved, the WFM won an important concession. In return for promising to fight high-grading, it negotiated a closed shop.[44]

High-grading could be seen as a form of low-level resistance to the wage system. It occurred throughout gold and silver mining, and the WFM went to great pains to separate its public image from the ubiquitous thefts. When five men were arrested for high-grading on the Elkton, Victor Miners No. 32 vehemently denied that "the members of the miners unions of the Cripple Creek District are engaged in the practice of ore stealing." The local insisted that most union miners were "honest and honorable men" and that there was more high-grading on non-union mines than on union properties. It promised to uphold "the letter and the spirit of the 7th Commandment."[45]

Safety and health care, from labor's perspective, were more pressing issues than the ore thefts that preoccupied management. Mining was extremely dangerous work. Miners worked through their WFM locals to prevent occupational hazards and to provide medical care for themselves and their families. Union health care programs were based in miners' ideological commitments to fraternal solidarity, mutual aid, and democratic control. In the Cripple Creek District, their insistence on working-class control was expressed in opposition to company-controlled com-

pulsory insurance funded by withholding wages. Miners opposed compusory insurance because it was mandatory, the service was often inadequate, company doctors often testified against injured workers in liability suits, and the insurance covered only workers, not their families, and then only while they were on shift. Many
unions and lodges, in contrast, offered full family coverage. In 1895 the Smith-
Moffat properties began deducting $1.50 a month for accident insurance and raised
the amount withheld to $2 in February 1896 to cover a contract physician. In Sep-
tember the miners on their Victor Mine protested, and management discontinued
the deduction. In December 1900 Daniel P. McGinley, secretary of the Altman
local, pulled the work force from the Wild Horse Mine because improper timbering had caused a number of accidents and the miners received poor medical service for their compulsory medical insurance. Labor fought compulsory insurance
in the legislature as well as the workplace. In 1899 State Representative James
Gaughan introduced a bill to prohibit wage withholding, but it stalled in the state
senate while Gaughan devoted his energy to the Teller County bill. The WFM
District Executive Board then resorted to direct action and announced that after
January 1, 1901, everyone working under its jurisdiction must "be paid their wages
in full with no deductions whatever for insurance, doctor or hospital fees or for any
other purpose whatsoever." The WFM convention delegates that year called for a
law to ban compulsory insurance.[46]

Labor's ability to affect such issues as stripping orders and deductions for company doctors tangibly demonstrated the rewards of strong unions. But benefits alone
did not account for high WFM membership figures. In such a highly organized
area there was considerable social pressure for union loyalty, and that pressure was
probably the most effective organizing tool. The *Press* editorialized that the "non-
unionist should be treated as a social leper, avoided as the plague. No unionist
should talk to him, no unionist should go where he goes; the women of the unionist household should avoid him." One effective organizing tactic was for secretaries of WFM locals to check miners' union cards as they went on shift and let peer
pressure do the rest. When Jerry Kelly, financial secretary of Victor Miners No. 32,
checked cards at the Gold Coin in May of 1900, only one miner refused to com-
ply, reportedly asserting that he "cared nothing for the Miners' union or its representative." The rest of the miners refused to ride down in the cage with him, creating a stalemate that the superintendent solved by paying the man's dues.[47]

The next day, Kelly and E. J. Campbell, secretary of Cripple Creek Miners No.
40, visited the Independence, where approximately a hundred WFM members
worked alongside six to eight holdouts. Kelly addressed the assembled work force.
"Those boys refuse to join our union," he began. "If our organization is not good
enough for them, do you want to ride with them?"

"No!" was the unanimous answer from the hundred union men, and they rode down the shaft in the cage to their work.

Mr. Kelly then talked with the non-union men, saying that he and Mr. Campbell were not there to distress or coerce anyone, but that he would like to have them join the union.

The men then took counsel with Superintendent Summers who had an informal talk with them. He told them frankly that he had no power and no desire to compel them to do anything against their wishes, but he would like to see them members of the union and all working harmoniously. He advised them to go to work, and expressed the hope that when they were visited by the union men that all would be satisfactorily settled.[48]

With encouragement from management, the entire Independence work force paid up and joined.[49]

The WFM increased the pressure, trying to achieve a de facto closed shop throughout the District. In 1901, amid rumors that some mines planned to cut wages and go to ten-hour shifts, the WFM mounted a closed-shop campaign. The WFM District Executive Board declared that effective September 15, 1901, "anyone working in or around the mines, mills or power plants of the Cripple Creek district" who was not a member in good standing of a WFM local would "be considered a scab, an enemy to himself to us and the community at large" and would be "treated as such."[50] The *Press* emphasized the critical importance of the WFM for all the other District unions, many of which had won closed shops, and for local merchants whose prosperity relied on union wages. WFM District Executive Board president John Curry of Victor said that seven-eighths of all miners were organized. The others were "either for us or against us"; there was "no middle ground." It was unfair for them to enjoy union benefits if they did not help maintain them.[51]

Membership rose dramatically as the September 15 deadline approached (Appendix B). The District Executive Board announced on September 14 that it had accomplished its objective because virtually all workers in the WFM's jurisdiction had joined. An estimated five to six thousand miners carried union cards, representing approximately 90 percent of the mining workforce. The union announced that it would, in the future, publish the names of persons who refused to join, and in July 1902 the WFM established a universal scab list.[52] The miners virtually achieved a closed shop in practice if not formally.

Some owners charged that organizing exceeded the bounds of social persuasion. Employers charged that the unions maintained their power through violence, but miners denied the accusations. The Altman miners' local denied that it had kidnapped and beaten a Bull Hill miner or that it "encouraged violence as a means to attain the grand aims of our organization." Whether the unions sanctioned it or not, some violence did occur. In 1900 seven masked men "escorted" two stationary engineers out of the District because they undermined the union scale of $4 for eight hours by working twelve hours a day for $3 at the Gillett pipeline pumping station. Two years later, Altman miners' president William F. Davis investigated whether a man named Jack Burke was paying union scale on a mining contract. According to the *Press*, an "altercation" ensued in which "Burke was shot in the fleshy part of the back." Davis claimed self-defense, charging that Burke had threatened to kill him. He was acquitted after a trial that lasted only five hours and took only fifteen minutes of jury deliberation.[53]

Organizing varied from mine to mine and changed with the competitive climate among owners. After Burns left the Mine Owners' Association, friction increased between labor and the more anti-union owners, especially around the Bull Hill mines. Without the moderating influences of Burns and Stratton within the MOA, the mine owners most opposed to organized labor became increasingly hostile and began to contest the terms of the 1894 agreement, particularly the right to belong to a union and what that meant in practice. Charging that the unions fostered violence, the owners prepared a counteroffensive to the 1902 organizing drive. In the fall of 1901, while the WFM drive was underway, some mines spread rumors that a strike was imminent. Ignoring union denials, they erected stockades as if they anticipated conflict. The MOA then charged that the union beat and robbed two non-union mill workers. Forty-three mining companies posted handbills saying that they would hire whom they pleased. If their employees were assaulted, kidnapped, threatened, or maltreated they would consider it "conclusive evidence that the Miners union is hostile to the interests of the entire camp" and would "protect to the full extent of the law all employees against any attempt on the part of any union or organization of whatsoever nature to force or coerce our employees to join." The Altman and Cripple Creek locals denied the accusations. Victor Miners No. 32 branded the charges "false as hell" and offered to help apprehend the perpetrators. The *Press* insisted that union miners had a far greater stake in maintaining local order than did the nonresident owners. It charged that the mine owners' handbills in fact provoked violence because criminals could rob with impunity, secure that the unions would be blamed for their crimes.[54]

The handbills were only an opening salvo. The employers organized a State Federation of Mine Owners in April 1902 to fight all their enemies—smelters, railroads, and unions alike. George Bernard of the Elkton and Judge A. E. Colbran represented Colorado Springs owners at the founding meeting. As they organized, anti-union owners repeatedly charged that the power of organized labor rested on coercion and violence. The unions answered that corporate callousness and greed were responsible for much more mundane workplace violence such as the mine accidents that were a daily fact of labor in the District. When the new state MOA labeled the WFM a violent organization, the *Press* replied that a grand jury should investigate "the many fatal accidents that have occurred in this district through the criminal carelessness of greedy mine owners."[55]

A more unusual crime of violence against property underscored labor's claim that employers, more than workers, used force to protect their interests. Because the unions consistently resisted stripping orders, the owners shifted their campaign to stop high-grading from the mines to the high-grade market in the communities. Stolen ore was commonly fenced through assayers. At 3 in the morning of February 24, 1902, explosions rocked the District as a number of assay offices were dynamited. Miraculously, because many assayers and their families lived on the premises, no one was killed. After the bombings, property owners who rented to assayers received anonymous typewritten letters warning them not to rent to persons who bought stolen ore. The *Colorado Chronicle* voiced the common but unproved assumption that "thugs" hired by the MOA set the explosives.[56]

❀   ❀   ❀

Despite renewed resistance from some owners, Cripple Creek claimed, by 1901, to be the most organized area in the country. Although it is impossible to determine the exact membership of all District unions, it appears that a majority of all workers in all crafts were organized between 1901 and 1903 (Appendix B). In 1901 the *Press* claimed that some five thousand union members worked in the District. In 1902, at the height of labor power, at least fifty-four union locals operated there. The *Press* claimed that nearly ten thousand members belonged to thirty-eight of those locals, a figure which, if accurate, represented one District resident in three, almost half the adult population. In January 1903 thirty-nine local unions belonged to the Trades Assembly and another eight operated independently. Many owned their own halls, including Victor Cooks and Waiters No. 9 and all four miners' locals. By 1902 Victor Miners No. 32 held its $30,000 building debt free. The *Press* gloated that there was "no city on the face of the globe superior to and very few equal to Cripple Creek in the exemplification of the axiom 'In union there is strength.'"[57]

The organizations with which District labor affiliated, the WFM, CSFL, and the WLU, all advocated fundamental social and economic change. The WFM affirmed the principle that "the land, including all the natural sources of wealth, is the heritage of the people," and therefore "occupancy and use should be the only title" to it. Before the Socialist Party was founded in 1901 the Western Federation advocated a variety of political strategies. It supported union members for public office and endorsed the initiative and referendum, the eight-hour day, free coinage of silver at sixteen to one, and government ownership of public utilities. It urged political discussion to determine remedies for "wage slaves of the corporations and trusts that flourish on wealth produced by labor." The WFM later advocated both cooperative mining and socialism. The WLU favored government ownership of all

"natural monopolies," and the CSFL advocated independent working-class political action because "the power of the capitalist class rests upon institutions essentially political." The State Federation advocated numerous reforms, including the
initiative and referendum, state ownership of coal mines, and an eight-hour law for
mines, mills, and smelters. It demanded "that the means of production and distribution be owned by the whole people" and recommended the "study and discussion of socialist principles."[58]

District labor leaders likewise endorsed a wide range of political reforms and radical programs. Portrayed as revolutionaries and thugs in the Colorado Springs press
in 1894, they were relative moderates in the WFM in the early days. District delegates voted with the minority in 1895 to affiliate with the American Federation of
Labor.[59] But Cripple Creek unions increasingly criticized the AFL for dividing the
working class and sharpened their challenge to industrial capitalism. In the aftermath of a bitter labor struggle at Telluride in 1902, the *Press* argued that "the cap-
ture of the government by the laboring people is the solution of the question by
which capitalists can be shorn of their power to oppress and exploit." Labor struggles
like those at Leadville, Telluride, and Bull Hill taught that workers must control the
state. "If the powers of wealth and of the state" were "used to disrupt labor unions,"
then they should be "met with the united opposition of organized labor. . . . Arouse
ye," the *Press* invoked, "to the Class Struggle!"[60]

The WLU announced in 1902 that it would challenge the AFL and changed its
name to the American Labor Union (ALU). Initially, the name *Western* Labor
Union connoted a geographic jurisdiction, reflecting western unionists' belief that
the AFL ignored them. The name change to *American* Labor Union challenged
the AFL to a national contest about ideological and tactical differences. The WLU
had recognized class struggle, advocated industrial unionism, and called for fundamental economic and social change, convictions that animated the ALU and
later the IWW, of which it was a founding member. The Western Federation provided the major support for founding the WLU, was its largest affiliate, and was
instrumental in the decision to take on the AFL. District labor endorsed the move.
The *Press* proclaimed that the ALU had "done more for the laboring men of the
west during its four years of existence than the American Federation has in twenty
years."[61] From the vantage of labor's zenith in Cripple Creek in 1902, a class-conscious labor movement must have held enormous promise.

As the struggle between the AFL and ALU embroiled organized labor throughout
Colorado, the District Trades and Labor Assembly became increasingly hostile to the
AFL. But unlike the Denver and Colorado Springs Trades Assemblies, both divided
by opposing AFL and ALU factions, the District organization allowed local unions
allied with either the AFL or the ALU to affiliate. The District Trades Assembly was
itself an ALU affiliate, but it still supported the union label drives of AFL unions.[62]

Greater philosophical unity existed among District labor than between craft and industrial unionists elsewhere. The principles that animated the Cripple Creek labor community went far beyond bread-and-butter concerns. Mining dominated both the economy and the work force, and miners' philosophies influenced all District labor. Even the construction trades, traditionally considered among the more conservative crafts, were influenced by close associations with miners and by class relationships in mining. Many carpenters worked as mine timbermen or on mine construction. The Victor and Cripple Creek carpenters' locals opposed Samuel Gompers' reelection as AFL president in 1896 and later advocated that the United Brotherhood of Carpenters and Joiners of America affiliate with the WLU instead of the AFL. The recording secretary of Cripple Creek Carpenters No. 547 meticulously reported the speeches of Eugene Debs and WFM president Edward Boyce to the Cripple Creek Trades Assembly. Both Debs and Boyce attacked the concept of skill lines upon which craft unions were based.[63] Carpenters regularly refused to march in parades with the state militia, a common position of the miners because the militia so often broke strikes.[64]

❀   ❀   ❀

Shared labor philosophies did not mean that union leaders necessarily agreed on partisan politics or on how to achieve a more egalitarian society. The union leadership charted various routes to a cooperative commonwealth while advocating shared hopes and visions. Had their beliefs diverged widely from their members', they presumably would not have been elected and reelected to union office. It is impossible to determine the beliefs of all of the thousands of workers they represented. But it is possible to compare the leaders' social statuses with those of all District workers as an index of how their experience might shape union policy.

The leaders differed from their constituents in several important respects. Although fairly representative ethnically, they were slightly older than the rank and file, proportionately more married, more often heads of households, and more settled in homes of their own. They were, overall, more stable residents of the District than the frequently transient, younger, and single working population.

In other respects they were quite representative. Approximately the same proportions as all District adults were native-born and first- and second-generation immigrants. Although Irish were not particularly over-represented in the leadership as a whole, at the highest levels—those elected to state and national offices—there were disproportionate numbers of second-generation Irish (about 17 percent). This was more than double the proportion among all workers, evidence of the impressive influence of the Bull Hill Rednecks (table 6). Their representation in the leadership reflected their long experience in mining and the fact that, not surprisingly, the leaders were slightly older than the rank and file. Given similarities in Irish

TABLE 6
Predominant Countries of Birth and of Parents' Birth, Immigrant and Second-Generation Union Leaders

Country	District		Workers		Local Leaders		District Leaders		State/National Leaders		All Leaders	
	N	%	N	%	N	%	N	%	N	%	N	%
Immigrants												
Canada	804	4	25	2	7	3	2	3	3	3	12	3
England	756	3	35	3	7	3	2	3	3	3	12	3
Germany	534	3	34	3	6	2	4	6	1	1	11	3
Ireland	846	4	62	6	20	8	3	5	6	6	29	7
Scotland	318	2	25	2	7	3	1	2	4	4	12	3
Sweden	635	3	44	4	8	3	0		0		8	2
Wales	153	1	7	1	3	1	0		0		3	1
	4,046	20	232	21	58	23	12	19	17	17	87	22
Second Generation												
Canada	495	3	15	1	6	2	0	0	2	2	8	2
England	994	5	34	3	8	3	0	0	3	3	11	3
Germany	1,093	5	41	4	11	4	4	6	6	5	21	5
Ireland	1,788	9	79	7	21	8	5	8	19	17	45	10
Scotland	563	3	15	1	5	2	0		2	2	7	2
Sweden	122	1	8	1	1	—	0		0		1	—
Wales	182	1	39	4	8	3	3	5	3	3	14	3
	5,237	27	231	21	60	22	12	19	35	32	107	25

Source: Manuscript census, Teller County, Colo., 1900, and union sample. Figures for workers based on 1,087 people with working-class occupations in a random sample of 2,089 adults, 463 of whom were first- or second-generation immigrants. Union leadership figures from a sample of 443 union leaders.

names, it was harder to match the names of Irish union members with the census than for any other group. It was not always apparent, for instance, which John Sullivan was the union leader. Thus, estimates of Irish leadership may be somewhat low.[65]

Long experience underground and long involvement with organized labor were likely to generate the popularity and respect that would elect them to office.[66] The higher the level of union office, the older the leaders. Roughly a third of those elected to positions of state or national leadership were forty-one or older; almost two-thirds were over thirty (table 7).

Even more significant than their ages, union leaders were considerably more likely than the rank and file to be married (59 percent of the leadership compared with 44 percent of workers) (table 8). The older and more skilled a man was, the more likely he was to have a family. Only one man in three was married by age thirty; four in ten had not married by forty.[67] Union leaders, overwhelmingly male, married in higher proportions than all workers. Moreover, some younger men in the union leaders sample, like Sherman Parker and W. F. Davis, had not yet been elected to union office in 1900, when the census recorded them as single. Both had married by the time they became union officers but were counted as single in the leadership sample that depended on 1900 information. The 1900 census provides only a rough index to marriage among the leadership; the figures may well be low.

Married workers were older and less transient than their single counterparts. They stayed around long enough to become well known and to be elected to union office. Perhaps, too, family responsibility encouraged men to become active in unions to safeguard their families' welfare. And perhaps it was easier for men who had domestic services provided at home to afford the time for union activism.

Consistent with their age and family status, union leaders were also more likely than all workers to own homes. Home ownership on the census was listed for the head of household only. Whether we consider all workers, or household heads alone, union leaders were much more likely to own homes than were the workers they represented or than other adults (tables 9 and 10). The working class owned homes in roughly the same proportion as the District population—18 percent of all workers and of all District adults were homeowners. Twice as many union leaders owned homes—36 percent. In 1900 almost half (48–49 percent) of working-class heads of households and all District household heads were homeowners. Of the 212 union leaders who actually held offices in 1900, when home ownership was reported, 44 percent owned homes. Of these, 146, or 69 percent, were heads of households, of whom 64 percent were homeowners.[68] Thus, the union leaders of 1900, the group most directly comparable to the census population, were over two-and-a-half times more propertied than the working class as a whole and over 16 percent more than all household heads. The 1900 census did not list property val-

TABLE 7
Age of Union Leaders in 1900

Age	District		Workers		Local Leaders		District Leaders		State/National Leaders		All Leaders	
	N	%	N	%	N	%	N	%	N	%	N	%
<16	11	1	9	1	3	1	0	0	0		3	1
16–20	188	9	79	7	14	5	3	5	1	1	18	4
21–30	711	35	364	34	82	31	19	29	37	34	138	32
31–40	627	30	348	32	103	40	20	31	37	34	160	37
41–50	333	16	182	17	47	18	20	31	29	26	96	22
51–60	143	7	68	6	10	4	3	5	6	6	19	4
61–70	40	2	18	2	2	1	0		0		2	1
>71	10	1	5	1	0		0		0		0	
	2,063	101	1,073	100	261	100	65	101	110	101	436	101

Source: Manuscript census, Teller County, Colo., 1900, and union sample. District figures are from a random sample of 2,089 adults, less 26 whose ages were unknown. Working-class figures from the same random sample for 1,087 individuals who listed working-class occupations, less 14 whose ages were unknown. Union leadership figures from a sample of 443 union leaders, less 7 of unknown age.

Note: Some columns do not total 100 percent due to rounding.

TABLE 8

Marital Status of Union Leaders in 1900

Marital Status	District		Workers		Local Leaders		District Leaders		State/National Leaders		All Leaders	
	N	%	N	%	N	%	N	%	N	%	N	%
Single	719	34	526	48	100	38	25	37	36	32	161	37
Married	1,216	58	479	44	150	57	38	57	72	65	260	59
Widowed	110	5	56	5	10	4	2	3	2	2	14	3
Divorced	11	1	9	1	1	—	0		1	1	2	—
Unknown	33	2	17	2	2	1	2	3	0		4	1
	2,089	100	1,087	100	263	100	67	100	111	100	441	100

Sources: Manuscript census, Teller County, Colo., 1900, and union sample. District figures are from a random sample of 2,089 adults; figures for workers are from the same sample for 1,087 with working-class occupations. Union leadership figures from a sample of 443 union leaders, less 2 of unknown marital status.

TABLE 9

Union Leaders and Home Ownership, 1900

	Rent		Own		Unknown		Not Head of Household	
	N	%	N	%	N	%	N	%
Local leaders	65	25	90	34	10	4	98	37
District leaders	19	28	25	37	2	3	22	32
State/national leaders	30	27	42	38	4	4	36	32
All leaders	114	26	157	35	16	4	156	35
Working class	258	17	272	18	31	2	985	64
District	355	17	370	18	46	2	1,318	63

Sources: Manuscript census, Teller County, Colo., 1900 and union sample. District figures are from a random sample of 2,089 adults; figures for the working class are from the same sample for 1,546 persons who listed working-class occupations and other members of their households.

Note: Some figures do not total 100 percent due to rounding.

TABLE 10

Union Leaders and Home Ownership, Heads of Households Only, 1900

	Rent		Own		Unknown	
	N	%	N	%	N	%
Local leaders	65	39	90	55	10	6
District leaders	19	41	25	54	2	4
State/national leaders	30	40	42	55	4	5
All leaders	114	40	157	55	16	6
Working class	258	46	272	49	31	6
District	355	46	370	48	46	6

Sources: Manuscript census, Teller County, Colo., 1900, and union sample. District figures are from a random sample of 2,089 adults, 771 of whom were listed as heads of households. Working-class figures are from 561 working-class heads of households in the same sample.

Note: Some figures do not total 100 percent due to rounding.

ues, and the size and value of houses certainly varied, but this single available index of economic worth suggests significant differences between the rank and file and their leaders.

The leadership, then, was composed of older and more experienced workers who could marry and establish homes and families. Even the unmarried leadership was older and more settled than the rank and file. Their experience of work and of class relationships reinforced their union allegiance and equipped them for public authority. Age, marriage, home ownership, and skill together were likely to generate fully mobilized union activism and class analyses, the combined results of experience and limited alternatives. Most leaders could not, like younger, rootless workers, quit and move on if they were unhappy with working conditions. A 1901 lockout on the Portland Mine, for instance, prompted some miners to leave, "especially," the *Press* reported, "the single men."[69] Married men had fewer options. They could choose various recreational escapes such as drink, gambling, or other entertainment—or they could organize for change.

The same stability that supported class leadership also nourished social and political associations among union leaders and the managers with whom they negotiated. They shared positions of community leadership outside the workplace. Union leaders became visible symbols of the security and influence that union labor could achieve—and of what the rank and file might hope to attain. Highly effective organizers, they established the organizational base for working-class power in the workplace and for social authority in the broader communities as well.

PART 2

HIGH-GRADE AND FISSURES

4

Sirs and Brothers

Labor Day, at the height of Cripple Creek's union era, was an elaborate three-day extravaganza. For little Kathleen Welch, the Labor Days of her childhood evoked a wonderland of merry-go-rounds, ball games, and horseshoes at Pinnacle Park, of picnics shared with other union families, and speeches by the governor of Colorado and other "people like that, you know, that was really worthwhile." Labor Day began with a parade. An estimated three thousand union members marched in 1899, five thousand in 1901 and 1903. Kathleen's father, John Welch, always marched, as befitted a proud veteran of the Bull Hill strike. Welch was, according to his daughter, "a great union man" who taught his children "his ideals of that union—'for people and among people.'" He marched, however, not with his WFM local but with his religious fraternal association. "He was a Knights of St. John," Kathleen remembered, "and he always wore his uniform, and, oh, them were great!"[1]

John Welch, like many union men, sought fellowship in the lodge hall as well as the union hall. He belonged to the Ancient Order of United Workmen in addition to the Knights of St. John and the WFM. More than a hundred local chapters of some forty lodges and fraternal associations operated in the District.[2] On Labor Day and the Fourth of July, politicians, bands, and the lodges marched beside the union locals in rituals of community that crossed class lines. Labor Day itself bridged class boundaries in Cripple Creek to demonstrate labor's community influence. The *Daily Press* reported in 1899 that an estimated ten to twelve thousand had attended the festivities, including "the miner, the merchant, the clerk, the artisan, the professional man."[3]

For workers like John Welch, unions were pivotal institutions in a larger network of social relationships that stretched from workplaces to union halls and from boardinghouses to local saloons, dance halls, and lodge halls. Unions operated both as social centers and as the primary sites to define working-class concerns and mobilize to address them. Workers negotiated allegiances of class, gender, ethnicity, and religion in their unions and in other social arenas as well. The parades in which

John Welch marched linked people who might otherwise seem separate—union labor with managers and professionals and the Catholic members of the Knights of St. John and Knights of Columbus with Protestant Masons, Odd Fellows, and Knights of Pythias.

Men of different classes associated with one another in local lodge halls and taverns and in the workplace itself. Their relationships defined more than class. They charted the meanings of democratic possibility, manhood, and ethnic and religious loyalties. To understand the significance of working-class organization, unions must be set in their social, political, and community contexts, and union members must be located in their wider social networks.

Labor unions served multiple functions that connected them with other social institutions in the Cripple Creek District. Beyond the workplace, they organized holidays and social events; provided social services, health care, education, and recreation; and exerted considerable influence in politics and daily life. The unions, like the mixed-class lodges and fraternal societies, addressed social needs common to industrial hard-rock mining. In an unstable economy that produced frequent moves from mine to mine and town to town, both unions and lodges offered places to rekindle friendships and rituals to establish bonds of class and brotherhood that might substitute for local kin. In an industry characterized by risk and danger, unions and lodges provided relief and assistance in times of sickness, injury, hardship, and death. Both organized mutual responsibility to buffer individual vulnerability in a capitalist marketplace.

Lodges differed from unions, however, in the ways they interpreted capitalist social relations. Many lodges sought to recreate in their rituals the fellowship and relationships of preindustrial artisans.[4] In an industrial work culture characterized by class hierarchy and competition, they provided a ritual order in which all members could rise through the ranks to become Master Masons, Patriarchs, Chiefs, Knights, or Ladies. Unions, on the other hand, supported social kinship based in class, more critical interpretations of class hierarchy, and more oppositional responses to capitalism. An overlapping range of responses and accommodations to industrial realities could be found in the informal fellowship of the local saloon or pool hall, the cross-class fraternity of local lodge halls, and the multiethnic, working-class loyalties of union halls.

Patterns of daily recreation and entertainment established the boundaries of acceptable contact across class, ethnic, and gender lines. Theaters provided some of the limited public entertainment acceptable for mixed-sex audiences. Both Victor and Cripple Creek boasted large opera houses where touring companies presented such productions as *The Mikado, The Tempest,* and *The Three Musketeers.* "Respectable" women were barred from saloons, gambling houses, dance halls, and bawdier events, as well as from all-male union smokers. Neither could they attend the frequent prizefights, a major attraction for men. Jim Corbett, John L. Sullivan, and Jack Dempsey all trained in the District; Jack Johnson worked as a porter at the Gold Coin Club; and a number of lesser pugilists drew capacity crowds.[5] Excluded from saloons, gambling halls, and prizefights where men of all classes mingled, and from many all-male union functions, women formed their own clubs or gathered in private homes. Some set aside an afternoon or a day a week to do "fancy work" and visit with women friends.[6]

Beyond their private social networks, women, to a lesser extent than men, participated in all-women's or mixed-sex lodges, in the unions as members or supporters, and in family-centered labor recreation. Restricted from much public recreation, respectable women participated in unions most often in auxiliary roles as relatives of male members. They were barred from many lodge rooms as well, but by the late nineteenth century some lodges allowed women to participate. Some created women's affiliates such as the Daughters of Rebekah (Odd Fellows), Ladies of the Maccabees (Knights of the Maccabees), Rathbone Sisters (Knights of Pythias), Women of Woodcraft (Woodmen of the World), and the women's auxiliaries of the Knights of St. John and the Ancient Order of Hibernians. Some sponsored mixed-sex degrees or orders for women and men, including the Masonic Order of the Eastern Star, the Degree of Honor (Ancient Order of United Workmen), Daughters of Pocahantas (Improved Order of Red Men), and Royal Neighbors (Modern Woodmen of America).[7]

Women more commonly belonged to lodges than to unions. So did men of other classes—managers, professionals, proprietors, and owners. Some lodges, like the unions, bridged ethnic and religious differences. Others were more closely defined by religion or ethnicity. The Sarsfield and Sheridan clubs and Ancient Order of Hibernians were restricted to persons of Irish descent. Religion defined the membership of the Catholic Knights of Columbus, the Knights of St. John, and largely Protestant lodges like the Masonic Orders, from which Catholics were banned on pain of excommunication. Membership in the Odd Fellows and Knights of Pythias brought lesser penalties for Catholic members. The Holy Office in 1894 denied the sacraments to Roman Catholics who joined either lodge. Two years later it relaxed the ban to allow nominal membership for those who would suffer a "grave temporal loss" (e.g., insurance protection). Between the poles of the Masons and the Knights of Columbus lay a variety of more ethnically inclusive and nonsectarian lodges such as the Elks, Maccabees, and Woodmen of the World.[8]

The multiple social arenas in which workers operated affected class relations on several levels. Unions and lodges reinforced the social bonds of men who belonged to both. Cross-class fraternal ties with owners and managers helped mediate potential labor conflicts and blunted the oppositional edge of class relations. These associations affirmed labor's active participation in class relations; they did not abolish class. In virtually every social arena, union strength wove workers into the local community and emphasized labor's social respectability. The strength of the local unions guaranteed working men a place of dignity and respect and something they called "manhood" in community affairs. Working-class manhood functioned as a coherent identity during the union era. Still, internal tensions existed within the cross-class fraternity that linked workers with men of other classes whose own manhood did not depend on labor unions to secure social power.

In the largely masculine and working-class contexts of public discourse, the dignity of labor was linked to the dignity of men. Most people spent most of their time working. The conditions of work were their daily realities, and work relationships were their fundamental social contacts. Shared work conditions and workplace dangers forged social ties and social identities. This was especially true in mining because it was so hazardous and family welfare depended on the health of the wage-earners. Injury, sickness, and death lurked as constant dangers.[9] The WFM *Miners' Magazine* and the *Daily Press* carried frequent notices from District unions of members' deaths and funerals.[10] The Colorado Bureau of Mines reported ninety-eight serious accidents in the District from 1893 to 1896. But myriad lesser injuries created more common instabilities for working-class households. Although seemingly trivial, bruises and cuts from falling rocks or from machinery could cost several days' work. Including these daily hazards — and certainly only a fragment of them — the *Press* reported nearly a thousand accidents in under four years.[11]

Common accidents included drilling into missed (unexploded) shots, falling down shafts, being hit by falling rock, and falling from cages or scraping against the sides of shafts because hoisting platforms lacked sides or adequate guard rails. A host of "freak" accidents, too varied to classify, also occurred. Powder exploded prematurely or blew up because it was negligently thawed over hot stoves. Men breathed noxious gases, got bits of rock or drill steel in their eyes, or were run over by tram cars. One miner died when an iron rod fell the full length of a mine shaft before piercing his head.[12]

Workplace dangers underscored the significance of skill and the interdependence of labor. The safety of each worker depended on the skills of all; an incompetent timberman or fuse-setter endangered everyone. Some owners briefly shared the hazards of mining in the smaller, preindustrial mines. In the era of industrial capitalism, however, accidents often resulted from the economies of absentee owners. Corporations took scant responsibility for their workers' welfare, and hiring was in the hands of people who did not share the risks.[13] C. F. Dillon, financial secretary of Free Coinage Miners No. 19, charged that "the employment of tenderfeet or unskilled miners" caused a "frightful" number of accidents between 1895 and 1900.[14] Other accidents resulted from faulty machinery, inadequate materials and labor, and ignorance. When electric hoists were introduced in the District, for instance, some were not properly grounded, and a number of miners were electrocuted. The Victor Trades Assembly charged criminal negligence and asked the state mine inspector to investigate. Inadequate timbering of mine shafts led to cave-ins and reflected the priorities of those who had little to lose. J. C. Sullivan of Victor Miners No. 32 voiced a common attitude among miners when he charged that "so many corporations think men are cheaper than timber that they don't put in the timber."[15]

Disease, too, presented constant dangers, including occupational illnesses such as the silicosis known as "miners' consumption." Some of the larger drills spewed so much rock dust that they were called "widow makers." Respiratory illnesses were especially dangerous for men who had inflamed lungs, but infections threatened everyone, regardless of occupation. Diphtheria, measles, smallpox, and other communicable diseases posed perennial threats.[16]

One of the first tasks of local unions, therefore, was to provide for sickness and death. The financial secretary of Free Coinage No. 19 wrote that part of the object of the WFM was "to assist one another in every way. When one of our brothers dies we give him a decent burial, and when sick and disabled we are bound by the constitution to look after him and see that he is not thrown on the cold charity of the world." Unions paid sick benefits, cared for widows and orphans, organized funerals, and shipped bodies out of the District for burial.[17] Victor Miners No. 32 offered a $10 weekly sick benefit and spent $4,000 during 1902 to care for the ill and for funerals. The Altman local paid $2,235 in sick benefits in 1898 and 1899; in the first six months of 1900 it dispensed $980 in sick benefits and buried three members. In 1903 the District WFM locals assisted victims of at least 193 accidents and conducted the funerals of thirty-five members. Some locals employed physicians for a monthly fee to care for sick and disabled members; others hired nurses for them.[18] Kathleen Welch Chapman fondly recalled union benefits as part of what her father meant when he said that unions were "for people." "Now, if there was a family that was very hard up or very tight for money, why [the unions would] help them out. . . . I can remember people in Victor coming to Goldfield when Papa'd maybe have a cold or be sick or couldn't go to work or something. There'd be maybe a half a dozen men come at night to see if he was getting along and if he needed anything."[19]

Communal support accompanied material assistance. When Henry King died in a mining accident, it was his wife's "express desire that a union man make whatever remarks are deemed necessary or appropriate." The service was held in the Victor union hall, and union miners were among the pallbearers. D. F. O'Shea, vice president of the ALU, delivered the eulogy on behalf of all the District unions. When Mary King buried her husband in Denver, lodge brothers and sisters accompanied her, along with a *Daily Press* reporter and a friend from the WFM Women's Auxiliary.[20]

King's funeral illustrates the overlapping social functions of unions and lodges, both of which cared for the sick and buried the dead. In 1896, for instance, W. W. Ferguson of the Grand Army of the Republic (GAR) visited a sick comrade named Vance. The GAR appropriated its entire small treasury for Vance's care and then buried him when he died. When H. F. Johnson was hurt on the Vindicator Mine, Little Bull Tribe of the Independent Order of Red Men (IORM, or Red Men) arranged for his care. The Elks held an annual memorial service to commemorate members who had died. Although hardly complete lists, the *Press* reported lodge sponsorship of twenty-three funerals in 1899, nineteen in 1900, and sixteen in 1901. Both unions and lodges provided sick and death benefits and hired contract physicians to care for their members. Many offered further security through group life insurance.[21]

Like the unions, fraternal associations grew dramatically in the latter half of the nineteenth century, in part because they responded to the dislocations of industrial workplaces. Roughly half of the District's fraternal organizations offered some form of life insurance. The *Press*'s reports of insurance payments suggest the prevailing anxiety about accidents, disease, and death. In 1900, for example, after Andrew J. Ray was killed in the Ajax Mine, the Woodmen of the World paid his wife $3,000 from Ray's insurance. Mrs. Mitchell Roscoe expressed her appreciation that the Woodmen of the World so promptly paid her late husband's $3,000 insurance benefit. The *Press* reported that Mr. Hicks, who had belonged to the Ancient Order of United Workmen (AOUW), had left his family $2,000 in lodge insurance benefits. "Would to God that every man would emulate the example of Mr. Hicks and thus provide for his loved ones," the report intoned.[22]

The insurance, benefits, and charitable aid of lodges and unions all provided safety nets against adversity. An outpouring of aid, for instance, buffered Jerry Farrell's family when Farrell died the night his wife delivered their sixth child. Farrell carried $1,000 in insurance, the Knights of St. John supported the family for some time, and the Knights of St. John Auxiliary held a benefit ball to help them. Similarly, Beulah Pryor reported that the Victor Elks lodge regularly provided free firewood to her mother, who struggled to support her children by taking in laundry and keeping boarders.[23]

Regular dues and assessments funded some benefits. Others required special fund-raising events. Benefit dances and entertainments served recreational purposes as well as altruistic ones. Fun and fund-raising reinforced the common social ground on which mutual responsibility rested. A small sample of union functions included benefit balls for a former secretary of Victor Miners No. 32, Arthur Beaver, to help him travel to some hot springs to relieve his paralysis; for G. W. Baugh, who lost a leg in the Elkton Mine; for George Newcombe, a former miner on the Mary McKinney, who had "struck some rough places in the road" and needed financial aid; and for William H. Eller, who was blinded by a premature explosion on the Last Dollar Mine. In addition to the union aid, Eller's co-workers collected $206 to help him. When a man died, his co-workers often contributed a day's pay to help his family.[24]

Although lodge assistance certainly helped many needy people, the underlying message of fraternal social welfare was different from the unions'. If a miner were injured at work, union benefits emphasized class solidarity and the unfair risks that workers bore for owners' profits. Lodge assistance focused on immediate needs but rarely on underlying causes. Fraternal aid mediated the consequences of risks that did not equally threaten all brothers. Unions, however, responded to the shared risks of hazardous employment, assigned responsibility to owners, and sought alternatives to the privatization of both risk and welfare.

Only unions provided strike relief and unemployment benefits and raised money for striking workers elsewhere. Five different locals hosted balls in 1902 to aid striking Pennsylvania coal miners. An extensive campaign in 1899 raised at least $1,500 for the striking miners of the Coeur d'Alenes and their families. The fund-raisers held mine owners responsible and pushed the local middle class to choose sides. By printing the names of those who contributed to the Coeur d'Alenes fund, the *Press* pressured merchants to prove their loyalty to the local miners who were their customers. The Raymond-Whittenberger Mercantile Company of Independence defensively denied that it had refused to donate. The McGill Trading Company uncomfortably explained that it could not, as a business firm, sign union resolutions about the Coeur d'Alenes strike. But when union canvassers reported its policy to the Trades Assembly, McGill management hastily donated money "for the sufferers in Idaho."[25]

Working-class mutual aid served several ends. At the most basic level, labor helped because help was needed and to affirm a simple sense of decency and human dignity. But on a larger scale, working-class assistance testified to shared risks and responsibility. The frequent accounts of mining accidents were constant reminders of what corporate profits cost labor. Shared feelings of loss, anger, and exploitation lent coherence to working-class experience and gave collective meanings to frustration, tragedy, and pain.

The local lodge halls and union halls overlapped as community meeting places and recreation centers. Frequently, the same space operated as headquarters for unions and lodges alike. The larger fraternal orders and the larger unions owned their own buildings, which they rented to other organizations. Thus, in 1897, before it built its own hall, Victor Miners' Union No. 32 met in the Odd Fellows' Hall, perhaps because Henry King, who at various times held offices in the WFM, the Independent Order of Odd Fellows, and the Ancient Order of United Workmen, was president of the Victor Odd Fellows at the time. The Retail Clerks met at the GAR Hall. In 1902, when more unions owned their own buildings, the Cripple Creek Carpenters' Union hall housed the Red Men, Knights of St. John, Knights of Columbus, and the Degree of Honor; the Fraternal Brotherhood met at Electrical Workers' Hall; and the Cripple Creek IOOF Temple provided quarters for seven other fraternal orders. In Victor, the Miners' Union Hall rented meeting space to the Elks, AOUW, Knights of Pythias, Knights of Columbus, and Woodmen of the World. The Rathbone Sisters, Yeomen, Knights of the Maccabees, and Degree of Honor met at the WFM Engineers' Hall. Other lodges met at the Masonic Hall.[26]

The unions and lodges shared social terrain as well as meeting space. They hosted myriad smokers, socials, dances, and other entertainments in their meeting halls, some for members only, some as communitywide events. The Knights of Pythias (KP) held monthly balls; nearly a thousand attended a smoker hosted by the Cripple Creek AOUW in January 1900. In a single week in 1902, the *Press* reported a Rathbone Sisters entertainment that netted $50 for a needy member, a joint installation of the GAR and Women's Relief Corps, joint installations of the Knights and Ladies of the Maccabees in Cameron and in Victor, a reception sponsored by the Ladies of the GAR, a basket picnic given by the Brotherhood of American Yeoman, an oyster supper of the Degree of Honor, and a Rathbone Sisters social. In parallel fashion, many union dances, banquets, smokers, and other entertainments were open to everyone. The *Daily Press* advertised at least twenty-eight union picnics, smokers, dances, ball games, and socials during 1900 that were open to the public. The Victor Typographical Union gave a smoker for some two hundred people, the Cripple Creek Journeymen Barbers held a masquerade ball, Cripple Creek Carpenters No. 547 gave a smoker, and so on. Anaconda Miners No. 21 showed warographs, or early motion pictures. The Anaconda, Victor, and Altman miners' locals held annual anniversary balls to celebrate the dates they were chartered, and Cripple Creek Miners No. 40 hosted a ball each Thanksgiving.[27]

Frequently, the strictly social qualities of union entertainment served other ends as well. Private social hours commonly followed union meetings. Altman Engineers No. 75 reported:

> We meet every Tuesday evening, and one meeting night in each month we give an entertainment of some kind, an evening of music, a smoker or a social, our next being a grand ball. The object of this social part is to strengthen our treasury and to break the monotony of business routine, which takes place night after night until everybody wearies and many neglect attendance at the union and a quorum becomes hard to attain. An evening of social pleasure not only strengthens the fraternal feeling among the members, but entices the engineer on the outside to come and see what is going on, and eventually he comes in and makes a good union man.[28]

The programs of labor socials emphasized working-class education as well as recreation. One union smoker, for instance, progressed from a speech about industrial conditions in the southern Colorado coal fields, through singing and dancing, to a talk by the state labor commissioner, to a boxing match, a flute and piano duet, a comic recitation, and talks by local union leaders on economic conditions in the District, all while the audience consumed considerable union labor tobacco. A single Cooks' and Waiters' social offered speeches by representatives of the American Labor Union, the Socialist Party, the Building Trades Council, and by hoist engineer W. H. Leonard on "Our Political Emancipation," as well as a three-round boxing match, monologues, and music. The District Trades and Labor Assembly held monthly open meetings "for the discussion of any public question that is before the people of our district." The meetings opened with music, songs, and essays followed by one or two speakers and then general discussion.[29]

Working-class entertainment bridged boundaries of age, class, and gender. Women and children attended some union socials, which introduced the next generation to organized labor. As a small child, Lowell Thomas, whose father was a local physician, performed at union gatherings in Victor, and children commonly entertained at some of the less rowdy events.[30] Women, children, proprietors, and professionals supported organized labor by attending union functions. Most women and children were there because of family ties to male union members; class remained the basis from which they bridged differences of age and gender. Similarly, brotherhood provided the foundation of social kinship that linked men in lodges and unions and across classes.

But brotherhood carried many meanings. Depending on the lodge, "fraternal feeling" could evoke ties of the artisans' workplace (Masons), of the Civil War battlefield (Grand Army of the Republic), or of the struggle for Irish liberation (Ancient Order of Hibernians). In contrast, when the Altman engineers said that "social pleasure" strengthened "fraternal feeling among the members," their object was working-class solidarity.

The emphasis on working-class education so evident in much union hall "social pleasure" was meant ultimately to create a movement culture in which shared understandings would support working-class action. Those efforts built from the tradition of earlier mining camps where miners shared books and discussed literature and working-class politics. Bill Haywood wrote of his days as a young miner in Nevada, "I did not have many books of my own, but the miners all had some. One had a volume of Darwin; others had Voltaire, Shakespeare, Byron, Burns, and Milton. . . . We all exchanged books, and quite a valuable library could have been collected among these few men. Some received magazines, and there were four or five daily papers that came to the camp."[31]

Organized labor formalized libraries for working people to help support working-class self-help. The Denver Knights of Labor established a reading room in 1885, in part as an alternative to saloon culture and in part to introduce workers to Laurence Gronlund, Karl Marx, and Henry George. In the Cripple Creek District, as in Denver and in many mining towns, the unions established the libraries. The Trades Assembly operated free public libraries in Cripple Creek and Victor to foster working-class consciousness. The libraries stemmed from a Trades Assembly resolution that advocated "the establishment of reading rooms wherever possible, reading matter supplied on all social and economical questions to the end that the working classes may become familiar with the land question, the money question, the transportation question, temperance question, the labor exchange question and all other political and social questions, that all laboring people should know, in order to lift themselves out of the social and economic conditions of oppression that ignorance has placed them in."[32] Asserting that "knowledge is power," the Trades Assembly proposed to the State Federation of Labor and the WLU that all union locals should have libraries and establish public reading rooms whenever possible.[33]

In 1902, as the Trades Assembly prepared to implement its policy, the Victor Women's Club, composed largely of the wives of merchants and professionals, planned to petition Andrew Carnegie for funds for a town library. The unions objected. Labor preferred to build its own reading rooms, the Trades Assembly responded. It regarded Carnegie's money "as 'blood money,' coined from the sweat and blood of our fellow workmen," and considered the proposal "an insult to organized labor."[34]

Long before the Women's Club proposed the Carnegie Library, the Trades Assembly appointed a committee composed of a delegate from each District union to "devise means of establishing a library and free reading room for working people," levied a one-cent monthly assessment to establish libraries throughout the District, and sponsored a fund-raising ball for the project. The first library opened at the Victor Miners' Union headquarters for the use of "any man of good morals, whether affiliated with a union or not." In 1902 a second library opened in Cripple Creek, which, according to Haywood, held eight thousand volumes. When Cripple Creek Miners No. 40 built a new hall, both the Trades Assembly and the Cripple Creek branch of the Union Library moved there as well. The Victor city council agreed to pay the rent for the Victor library, and the unions asked the Cripple Creek Council to follow suit, so all library funds could go for books.[35] The union libraries, founded in opposition to capitalist philanthropy, became quasi-municipal institutions.

The unions' free public libraries extended the educational efforts of individual locals. Victor Federal Labor Union No. 64, for instance, maintained a reading room and club room for its members that provided magazines and literature as well as card tables, chess, and checkers. Like the Denver Knights of Labor, it hoped to "induce the members to spend their evenings there instead of at saloons." Electrical Workers No. 74 kept a reading room with newspapers, magazines, and scientific journals. The (Victor) Excelsior Engineers No. 80 organized a debating club and a school to maintain craft skills. A board of examiners tested hoistmen and issued cards certifying "first class engineer[s]." Weekly classes covered such topics as "The Slide Valve Engine," "The Corliss Engine," "Mechanical Force of Electricity and Three Phase Wiring," and "The Rise and Advantage of the Engine Indicator." The local's club room held books and models "for the benefit of all who wish to study." Altman Engineers No. 75 likewise discussed "some very practical questions on engines and pumps."[36]

❋   ❋   ❋

The union library, it is worth emphasizing, announced that it was open to any *man* "of good morals, whether affiliated with a union or not." Whether the word choice in this case was literal or generic, it underscores the connection of manhood with labor's community influence. Working-class manhood connoted skill, strength, dependability, dignity; the ability to command a fair wage and respect; and to behave responsibly at work, at home, and in the community. It also connoted organized power. Working-class manhood was affirmed in the unions' prominence as social institutions for the whole community. This was especially evident on Labor Day and July Fourth. Christmas and Thanksgiving lasted a day apiece and received passing mention in the *Daily Press*, but July Fourth and Labor Day were two- or three-day extravaganzas. Some mines closed for Christmas, and some gave their employees a half day off. Most businesses and all of the mines closed for the Fourth and for Labor Day and usually paid their employees early so they would have cash to celebrate.[37]

Themes of independence, equality, and working-class dignity connected the two holidays. On March 15, 1887, Colorado became the second state to declare Labor Day a legal holiday, and the District celebrated with a vengeance. The *Press* editorialized that "with the exception of this narrow ridge constituting the Rocky Mountain region, American producers of human necessaries are down in the scale of wagegetting where all effort must be directed in a neverending struggle for base animal existence."[38] Labor Day represented what became possible after unions guaranteed the basics.

Generally, one of the WFM locals organized a picnic, and the rest of organized labor arranged the remaining events.[39] After the Labor Day parade, thousands moved on to Pinnacle Park in Cameron for the picnic, speeches, contests, and games. The 1899 program that drew "the miner, the merchant, the clerk, the artisan, the professional man" included dancing, baseball games, and other sports: climbing a greasy pole, a slow burro race, sack races, a fat man's race, a potato race,

a three-legged race, horse racing, and, above all, drilling contests, which were perennial mining-town staples. Small prizes rewarded the winners in other events, but
drilling contests offered at least $100—and generally considerably more. All con-
testants had to show their union cards. The contests drew the next generation of
workers—a drilling contest for boys under sixteen carried a $10 prize.[40]

Labor Day was more than a social event. It was also an opportunity to demonstrate
working-class skill, display union strength, teach labor history, and build a more educated, organized, and class-conscious union movement. The *Press* editorialized that
Labor Day would lead workers to "think along certain grand and essential political
lines" and "become fully alive to the necessity of unity amongst the laboring class."
The educational function of the holiday was to teach workers that "if it is of benefit
to the wealthy to get closely together in order to further their individual interests by
collective effort through trusts and combines, then it is to our interests as sellers of
our muscle to follow the example." Labor Day would promote "the evolution of the
race from wage slavery" to a future when cooperation would replace the "present
morality destroying and crime breeding competitive dog-eat-dog system."[41]

Labor Day orators proclaimed the imperative of collective action in politics and
at the work place. Lt. Gov. D. C. Coates spoke in 1902. The former president of
the State Federation of Labor, Coates was nominated to the 1900 statewide fusion
ticket through labor's influence (chapter 7). A long-time socialist who joined the
Socialist Party soon after it was founded in 1901, Coates offered the Labor Day crowd
a class analysis of industrial conditions. In 1903, during the second Cripple Creek
strike, WFM president Charles Moyer lambasted Gov. James H. Peabody for sending the militia to break strikes throughout Colorado.[42]

It is not particularly surprising, in one of the most organized areas in the country, that workers celebrated Labor Day with eloquent enthusiasm. But labor
influence was equally inescapable on the Fourth of July. Although the lodges,
merchants, and professional men were more prominent, the events themselves
were similar, and the message often became even more pointed in the critical connection of working-class power with democracy. The 1899 Victor program reflected
both class and masculinity with a twenty-round prizefight, an "artificial earthquake"
caused by exploding five tons of giant powder, an ore-shoveling contest, and four
drilling contests—double-handed down hole, double-handed upper hole, double-
handed down hole for amateurs, and double-handed down hole for boys age fourteen and under. Adult contestants, as usual, had to produce WFM cards. Further
festivities included the parade of lodges, unions, and fraternal organizations, bal-
loon ascensions, a "Grand Mask Carnival," and more contests—hose races, a bucking bronco contest, greased pole climbing, a greased pig chase, and more races.
Gov. Charles S. Thomas addressed the crowd.[43]

The Cripple Creek celebration that year boasted three parades. The Trades Assembly led off on July 3, there was a general parade on the Fourth, and the fraternal organizations paraded July 5. The July 3 program emphasized mining skills with the ubiquitous drilling contests, capped that night with a masked carnival. The Fourth itself began with a thirteen-gun salute, followed by races and games, lightweight wrestling, the parade, a speech, horse races, and ore shoveling followed by fireworks and illuminations of Mt. Pisgah and Pikes Peak. July 5 featured rodeo skills, with a roping contest, horse races, and bucking bronco contests as well as baseball and masked balls.[44]

Independence Day allowed workers to claim democratic principles and older visions of republican equality and to redefine them in terms of industrial class relations. The underlying ideology of public celebrations articulated, in effect, a labor theory of civic value in which democracy depended on working-class power to resist capitalist control. Labor Day orators were, if anything, understated compared with Fourth of July speakers who reiterated that capitalism threatened democracy and only organized labor could save it. In 1899 the *Press* editorialized that the country had "fallen on evil days" with "money making our laws, Standard Oil sending the federal army to destroy our labor organizations, — the only barrier between the people and absolute serfdom, courts declaring laws favoring the people unconstitutional, Croesus Hanna pulling the strings that work an automaton called a president, a Rockefeller defying the power of our courts to investigate his robbery of the people, press and pulpit joined in an unholy alliance to prevent any change in the existing order of plutocracy and capitalist anarchy."[45]

Governor Thomas elaborated the message in Victor, delivering a "Scathing Arraignment of Organized Capital." Thomas charged that "the absorption of common wealth by commerce" threatened the integrity of American institutions and that America was "dominated by the thralldom of what has been called an economic oligarchy." Justice and equality, the governor concluded, were threatened by "powerful interests favored by the government." A second speaker, James B. Belford, focused more directly on the 1899 Coeur d'Alenes miners' strike. Belford put an upbeat spin on capitalist concentration, concluding that trusts were unconscious pioneers of "state socialism which promises equal opportunities to all" and that combinations of capital and of labor were "but schools" to teach "the principles of state socialism" so that "through their agency an industrial democracy" might emerge.[46]

We cannot know how local proprietors and mine managers responded to the insistent theme that democracy depended on working-class power, if not ultimately on state socialism. Yet men of all classes heard and even invited these messages. In 1900 the Business Men's Committee organized the Fourth of July. Its fund-raising committee was a model of cross-class cooperation, consisting of Edward Bell, a

Democratic politician, grocer, and director of the Cripple Creek stock exchange; Oscar Lampman, an undertaker; and Charles Outcalt, president of Cripple Creek Miners No. 40. The Business Men invited WFM president Edward Boyce to deliver the major address.[47]

Boyce equated the McKinley tariff with the Stamp Acts, challenged the sanctity of private ownership, and advocated by analogy the legitimacy of popular revolt against established governments that protected the rich. "History records no such destruction of property in this country," Boyce proclaimed, "as was witnessed during the ten years just preceding the declaration of Independence." He compared the Revolution to strikes in "Chicago, Hazelton, Cleveland, Leadville" and "the Coeur d'Alenes" and charged that President McKinley kept troops "for the same purpose that animated George III, to deprive the people of their rights." Capitalist politicians and U.S. imperialism endangered the principles of the American Revolution, Boyce proclaimed, charging that conditions in Cuba and the Philippines were "worse under a Republican president than . . . under a king." The WFM leader stressed that capitalism was destroying democracy. "We labor under the hallucination . . . that we live in a land where all men are equal; we rave about equal rights for all and special privileges for none; at the same time we pass laws that create millionaires and make paupers and divide the people into two classes: Masters and Slaves." Presidents Cleveland and McKinley, he said, were "as completely under the control of the plutocratic element of this Republic as King George was under the influence of the aristocracy of England." Thus, Boyce concluded, government had "become destructive of the ends for which it was created" so labor needed a new "government for the people, not for the benefit of trusts and combinations. . . . We need a new Declaration of Independence to teach workingmen that they should not lay in a filthy bull pen for seven months without a trial. That it is their duty as free men to resist such persecution to the end, and like Adams and Hancock organize the 'Sons of Liberty' and prove to their persecutors and monopolists that there is enough of the spirit of the men of 1776 left in their veins to assert their rights."[48]

Boyce staked labor's claim to core American values through several interrelated themes. The most obvious was that unequal economic power undermined democracy, as he equated labor with the revolutionaries of 1776 and capital with the British king and aristocracy. The analogy was particularly potent from the Irish-born Boyce. A native of County Donnegal and a member of the Clan na Gael, Boyce's rhetoric must have resonated particularly for the Bull Hill Rednecks.[49] He not only insisted that labor must check capitalist influence to safeguard democracy but also that resistance must be collective and even sometimes revolutionary.

Whether or not workers embraced Boyce's revolutionary rhetoric, they heard it because unions had secured the territory for public discourse. Labor's strength guaranteed that anyone who chose to celebrate Independence Day would hear Boyce's message, including the businessmen who invited him to speak. Boyce might well have engendered considerable apprehension about the potential of labor's public power. But for the moment that power was part of the holiday display and part of what democracy promised for Cripple Creek workers.

❀   ❀   ❀

That sense of possibility rested not just on flamboyant rhetoric but on daily interactions and informal recreation that demonstrated the centrality of labor in local communities. Popular union leaders were also visibly active and respected in other social arenas. Sherman Parker, secretary of Free Coinage Miners No. 19, for instance, helped arrange a prizefight in Independence. He, like Daniel McGinley, James Gaughan, and several other Altman union leaders, left mining briefly to run his saloon, where his prominence ensured the patronage of union miners. D. C. Copley of Altman Engineers No. 75 and a WFM Executive Board member, played in the Independence town orchestra.[50]

How did cross-class community ties affect working-class consciousness and organization? Did friendly relationships with local merchants, managers, and owners undermine class as a source of identity and action and support more accommodationist responses to capitalism? To approach that complex question it is necessary to understand that workers considered themselves active partners in cross-class exchanges and acted, they thought, from collective strength. They anchored their strength in working-class organization and linked it to the prominent and respected roles of labor in local communities.

Given the importance of work and of relationships among men in the mines, working-class dignity was codified in terms of gender. The drilling contests were one clear display of working-class manhood. Local celebrations charted the social terrains that white men shared. The separate union and lodge parades on July 3 and 5 in 1899 did not divide labor from the fraternal orders; they enabled men to march with both their unions and their lodge brothers. The same rituals revealed social divisions of race and gender. White men of different classes shared public prominence as they marched and celebrated together. Women joined men to provide food at picnics and partners for the balls. More often, women and African Americans participated in community holidays from separate and subordinate positions. In 1899, July 5 was ladies' day. The contests included a girls' foot race, a talking contest, a fat women's race, a pie-eating contest, a lean women's race, a baby show, and dancing. The honored guest of the day was Harriet Wright, a Colorado legislator notable for her pro-labor record as well as for breaking new political ground for women. The July Fourth program offered racially segregated and racist events for blacks only—watermelon and pie eating, buttermilk drinking, and buck and wing dancing.[51] The celebrations mirrored the extent to which concepts of manhood bridged class differences among white men and the social boundaries of race and gender that segmented the working class.

Given the prominence of white working-class men, it is important to recognize how class and masculinity were fused conceptually in working-class manhood. Public displays of manhood involved men of all classes, but manhood in a union community carried working-class meanings: physical skill, interdependence, the dignity of labor, a breadwinner's responsibility, and civic leadership. In workplace relationships, working-class men defined their dignity at least in part through their ability to negotiate from strength and to be treated with respect as "sellers of muscle."

Manhood in cross-class relationships depended on forms of familiarity, fairness, and respect. Thus, cross-class relationships did not seem so much accommodations to capitalism as demonstrations of collective working-class dignity and strength. Workers chose which owners and managers they liked, changed their minds when circumstances warranted, and altered their tactics as well. Unions' approval of owners and managers who respected organized labor, and workers' expressions of praise and affection, all implied that labor's regard was important. The Portland, and especially James Burns, enjoyed general popularity. The *Press* reported with approval the Portland's annual Christmas gift of a $5 gold piece to all its employees. When Burns married in 1900, his workers bought him a five-piece monogrammed silver service for a wedding gift. The El Paso Mine employees gave superintendent Frank May a diamond stud "in appreciation of what had been done for the welfare of the miners employed by him." In 1902 the miners on Stratton's Independence, where H. A. Shipman negotiated the closed shop, gave diamond rings to Shipman, who was by then the former general manager, to Superintendent Sam Lobb, and to Assistant Manager R. J. Grant. A "little smoking session" followed the presentations at Shipman's home.[52]

Some cross-class associations occurred on common social ground; others were friendly but paternalistic. Labor appreciated generous owners and egalitarian displays of fellowship. Workers rejected with equal vehemence managerial decisions that challenged their dignity or required subordination. This pattern was especially apparent in relations with the Woods family, widely perceived as fair to its employees and generous for its contributions to working-class social life.[53] The family built Pinnacle Park at Cameron—a vast picnic ground, zoo, and amusement park that it regularly donated for Labor Day. Soon after the park opened the Woods family gave a "grand picnic" there for the District. They also hosted an annual New Year's reception for the employees of all their mines. The *Press* said, "The Woods people are famed for entertaining the notion that there is nothing too good for the men who make their wealth for them and the families of those men. They pay the best wages going without grumbling and treat their employees as human beings and the

equals of their employers." Their Cameron employees, offering thanks for hospitality on New Year's, emphasized "the clean, manly methods employed in all dealings with your employes" and expressed the "esteem in which the working people
hold those multi-millionaires who can so nobly assist in the uplifting of their brother
men."[54]

In 1898 the Woods Investment Company organized the Gold Coin Club for its
employees and erected a clubhouse for them opposite the Gold Coin Mine in
Victor. The original Gold Coin Club House was completed only to be burned in
the Victor fire of 1899. Reconstructed, it was dedicated at an elaborate party in February 1900 that featured dancing and a banquet. John Welch worked on the Gold
Coin, and he and Hannah attended the party.[55] Their daughter recalled:

> Papa worked on the Gold Coin there in Victor. And that was a wonderful place. And
> that great big place, . . . that nice building right across from where the Gold Coin is,
> that was the club house for the men. . . . I can remember that night so well. I wasn't
> very big. Yes, Mama and Papa went. I can remember how nice they looked. They got a
> baby-sitter to come in and set with us. . . . We lived in Goldfield, and they went up to
> Victor to the opening. And . . . they said they had such a good time. Well, they danced
> and they had a big banquet.[56]

The two-story Club House held a library with "six hundred volumes of well-cho-
sen books," a large athletic room, a bath room where men could bathe when they
came off shift, a billiard hall and chess tables (games cost half the rate charged in
saloons), and a few bedrooms for office employees. Anyone who worked six continuous months for the company could belong. The WFM *Miners' Magazine* "regretted that other mining companies and wealthy corporations [were] not so gen-
erously disposed as the Woods Investment Company."[57]

Nonetheless, labor's approval lasted only as long as employers treated workers
with respect. In 1901 the town of Cripple Creek denied the Woods Investment
Company a franchise for electric lights, and in retaliation the company refused to
employ Cripple Creek residents. The Trades Assembly protested the policy as "ty-
rannical, iniquitous, and totally unjustifiable." The *Press* reported "much ill feeling and indignation" because "the Woods people had acquired all they own in this
district right here, by a stroke of good fortune; . . . they found it in the ground where
God (not the Woods) deposited it; and . . . now they propose to use the power of
this wealth to oppress the people—to crush and trample underfoot the liberties of
the citizens."[58] Hans Hansen, a Socialist and a leader of Victor Federal Labor Union
No. 64, sarcastically suggested that ownership of the earth implied "the ownership
of the people that live on that part of the surface of the earth." Hansen argued that
"labor alone gives value," so that labor created the Woodses' wealth, providing, he
figured, $9.13 in profit for each $1.42 paid in wages.[59]

As the rage over the company's order illustrated, labor's approval required that owners and managers recognize union power and workers' dignity. Cross-class cooperation rested delicately on a form of egalitarian exchange labor codified as "manly methods." When employers exerted power workers considered unfair, or interfered with union organizing, then labor responded from a class analysis and emphasized that working-class men created the wealth and therefore the power of those who owned the gold and exploited their labor. The shared terrain of brotherhood lay atop fault lines of class divisions that could shift the social exchange when employers abandoned "manly" respect to assert control. Capitalist paternalism could fracture cross-class fraternity.

❀   ❀   ❀

For the most part, however, between 1894 and 1903 cross-class contact supported generally amicable labor-management negotiations that depended on mutual recognitions of dignity and power. Cross-class ties, knit in daily exchanges at work, in recreation, and in the lodges to which both employers and workers belonged, drew the middle class to local union halls and Labor Day celebrations. When Cripple Creek Miners No. 40 dedicated its new hall, for instance, a thousand people attended the gala, and the "number of business and professional men present caused favorable comment." Prominent union leaders and businessmen commonly belonged to at least one fraternal organization, frequently to the same ones. Martin Gleason, superintendent of the Consolidated Mines Company's properties, who "had the reputation of not discriminating in the employment of men," was a former member of Free Coinage Miners No. 19 and belonged to the AOUW. Henry King, who held numerous offices in Victor Miners No. 32, was also an officer of the Victor Odd Fellows and the AOUW. Both Henry and Mary King were active in the AOUW's Degree of Honor, and Mary King belonged to the Odd Fellows' Daughters of Rebekah and the WFM Women's Auxiliary as well. J. W. Higens, a president of Cripple Creek Carpenters No. 547, belonged to the Modern Woodmen of America (MWA). John Calderwood, the 1894 strike leader, was an officer in the Knights of Pythias and the Victor Elks; W. S. Stratton, a millionaire mine owner, belonged to the Elks and the Masons.[60]

Especially in the smaller mining towns, mine managers socialized with their employees, who were also the majority of their neighbors. Sherman Bell, who was in 1901 the assistant general manager of the Independence Consolidated Gold Mining Company and in 1903 the manager of all Smith-Moffat mining properties in the District, lived near the properties he managed, in Independence, an overwhelmingly working-class community of miners and their families. Bell was a Republican, an Elk, and a member of the Knights of Pythias and the Goldfield Masons. Active in community affairs, in 1901 he served as the marshal of the day for the Fourth of July celebration. He won immense popularity for buying Christmas dolls for all the little girls of Independence. One local couple named their son for him.[61]

Bell was particularly active in local lodges, and in 1902 was appointed the acting major of the Third Battalion, Second Regiment, Colorado Brigade, in the uniform rank of the Knights of Pythias, which competed in regional and national drill contests. His appointment included the Victor, Leadville, Colorado Springs, and Central City jurisdictions. In August 1902 he led a local contingent to participate in military drills at the national Knights of Pythias convention. The members of Victor's KP Company 8 won the national championship and returned home to a heroes' welcome.[62]

Bell had close associations with the District's working-class leaders through lodges and through his involvements in mutual aid. In 1900, for instance, he helped organize a benefit ball that raised $500 for a Mrs. Tompkins and her children. The two leading ticket-sellers were Bell and Steve Ryan, a man who was in many ways Bell's opposite—a Democrat, probably of Irish descent, and an active member of Altman Stationary Engineers No. 75. Ryan served as a trustee of his local in 1900, on a committee to host a joint visit of the WFM and WLU to the District the same year, and on the WFM District Executive Board in 1901. His wife Ella belonged to the Rathbone Sisters, the Knights of Pythias Auxiliary.[63] Bell, a Republican mine manager, and John Calderwood, a former WFM organizer, were prominent in the same lodge.

This anecdotal evidence of cross-class association is confirmed by an analysis of some 616 lodge members and officers. Stable and prominent citizens, they included many business people and professionals, as well as many union leaders (table 11).[64] Lodges brought together salaried workers, capitalists, professionals, and workers, especially miners. Widowed, single, or divorced women also found community in some lodge halls. Although class proportions varied from lodge to lodge, all had cross-class memberships.[65]

To distinguish among the various groups, it is useful to separate the organizations by function as well as by ethnic and religious restrictions. The most notable difference existed between fraternal benefit societies and lodges. Fraternal benefit societies flourished particularly during the late nineteenth century, when many were founded to provide insurance for ordinary people. The AOUW, for instance, which boasted some five to six hundred District members in 1902, was described as "a gigantic co-operative fraternal insurance scheme" organized to provide insurance at cost. Fraternal benefit societies levied regular assessments for sick and death benefits and for life insurance. The lodges' primary purpose was more social. Lodges depended on short-term assessments and other voluntary fund-raising to support short-term assistance in times of sickness, accident, disability, and death. The fundamental distinctions among organizations were whether or not they offered life insurance

TABLE 11

Class of Lodge Members, 1900

Class	District		Lodge Members	
	N	%	N	%
Working class	15,710	79	419	69
Salaried/clerical	870	4	38	6
Business	2,052	10	65	11
Professionals	731	4	45	7
Capitalists	359	2	14	2
Other	217	1	25	4
	19,939	100	606	99

Sources: Manuscript census, Teller County, Colo., 1900, and lodge sample (Appendix A).

Note: Those in households in which no one listed an occupation were excluded. Column 4 does not total 100 percent due to rounding.

and the limitations placed on membership. Hibernians must be between sixteen and forty-five and in good health. Miners could belong to the Maccabees if they did not engage in blasting, but they paid more for insurance. The Modern Woodmen of America enrolled only persons eighteen to forty-five, excluded all hazardous occupations, including all miners who worked underground, and purported to operate only in the "healthful" states of Illinois, Minnesota, Iowa, Nebraska, Wisconsin, Michigan, Kansas, North Dakota, South Dakota, Missouri, Indiana, and Ohio.[66] Four branches, however, operated in Altman, Cripple Creek, Gillett, and Victor.

Unlike lodges, which existed primarily for social purposes, the primary appeal of benefit societies was insurance as well as sick and funeral benefits. Lodges, in contrast, provided benefits on a more irregular and voluntary basis. The Benevolent and Fraternal Order of Elks, for instance, traced its origins to a social association of actors who organized for drink and fellowship when an 1866 New York law closed both taverns and theaters on Sundays. The Elks ultimately expanded membership to all white men over twenty-one who believed in a Supreme Being, and the group offered "charity which is inoffensive, untraced, and unsuspected."[67]

The various lodges and benefit societies served overlapping functions. Most benefit societies offered sociability and ritual as well as insurance; most lodges offered charitable assistance. The Knights of Pythias created an Endowment Rank that operated like a benefit society to provide insurance. The benefit societies prominent in the Cripple Creek District included the AOUW and its Degree of Honor, the Knights of the Maccabees and Ladies of the Maccabees, the MWA and the Royal Neighbors, and the Woodmen of the World and the Women of Woodcraft. The Yeomen, Eagles, Hibernians, and Knights of Columbus all offered insurance as well.[68] In addition to the Elks, District lodges included the Masonic Orders (Masons, Knights Templars, and Order of the Eastern Star); the Pythian Orders (Knights of Pythias, Knights of Khorassan, and Rathbone Sisters); the Independent Order of Red Men and its Daughters of Pocahantas; and the Odd Fellows and Daughters of Rebekah.

Religion, ethnicity, and occupation all restricted membership in particular organizations. The Sheridan and Sarsfield clubs and the Ancient Order of Hibernians were restricted to persons of Irish descent, the B'nai Brith was restricted to Jews, and the Knights of Columbus and Knights of St. John were restricted to Catholic men. Catholics could not belong to the Masonic Orders without risking excommunication and were sanctioned from participating in the Pythian Orders or Odd Fellows. The Maccabees and Modern Woodmen restricted membership on the basis of work hazards, and many orders restricted membership or insurance on the basis of age. It appears, however, that these restrictions were not always followed in practice. Despite restrictions on hazardous occupations, 34 percent of the members of the District's male fraternal benefit societies were miners in 1900. The highly restrictive MWA had a thriving branch in Altman, where virtually everyone was engaged in mining.[69]

Nor did religious restrictions always dictate the choices of individual Catholics. The Land League and working-class allegiance both supported Irish resistance to church authority in Colorado. In the 1870s Bishop Joseph Machebeuf drew opposition from Denver Catholics for his pro-British politics and alleged discrimination against Irish priests. In 1904 most of Colorado's Irish workers ignored Denver Bishop Nicholas Matz when he urged them to vote for Governor Peabody, an anti-labor Republican. From all reports, relationships between Catholics and their priests were friendly in the Cripple Creek District. Father Edward Downey was himself a member of the Victor Elks Lodge.[70] But we cannot assume that all Catholics followed church rulings on lodge membership—or on anything else. John Calderwood, reportedly a devout Catholic, was president of the Knights of Pythias, and Steve Ryan's Irish heritage did not stop Ella Ryan from joining the Rathbone Sisters. The Ryans may not have been Catholic, of course. If they were, they ignored the Church's position on lodges.

In the Cripple Creek District, the more restrictive benefit societies and the Masonic Orders generally had lower-working-class memberships than did the other lodges, ranging from roughly 50 to 60 percent working class in the lodge sample. The Catholic organizations were the most heavily working class (85 percent), presenting a contrast to the model of cross-class association David Emmons found in Irish organizations in Butte. There were proportionately fewer miners in the benefit societies than in the lodges (34 percent compared to 41 percent). But these observations bear considerable qualification. First, the lodge sample itself is not a complete or scientific sample of lodge members and is only a rough, suggestive index of participation. Second, a number of benefit societies had high working-class memberships. The AOUW and Woodmen of the World samples were both 79 percent working class, for instance.[71]

The most notable general pattern is cross-class association, together with levels of working-class membership higher than those found for lodges in other communities. Seven lodge members in ten (69 percent) were working class, a figure that exceeds that of late-nineteenth-century or early-twentieth-century Providence, Boston, Oakland, Buffalo, and Belleville, Illinois. District figures exceeded even the extremely high working-class participation in the Lynn, Massachusetts, Odd Fellows that John Cumbler documented. The 58 percent working-class participation in District Masonic Orders is high compared with other localities, although still 21 percent lower than workers' representation in the District population.[72]

Overall, the lodges reflected the working-class character of the communities. Ethnically, too, lodge members reflected the District. The Masonic Orders, the Protestant and nonreligious lodges, and the fraternal benefit societies were all 76 to 78 percent native-born. Ethnic background, however, was more skewed for particular groups, most notably in Irish and Catholic organizations, four in ten members of which were foreign-born and at least as many of Irish heritage. There were no Irish Masons in the sample.[73] Between these poles lay all the secular or nondenominational fraternal beneficiary societies and all the non-Masonic and non-Catholic lodges, which were more working-class, foreign-born, and Irish than the Masons and less so than the Catholic organizations.[74]

Just as lodges bridged class and ethnic differences, they spanned politics and ideology as well. The sixty-three members of the AOUW in the lodge sample, for instance, included at least seven Democrats, four Republicans, a Silver Republican, a Populist, two members of the local Co-operative Party, and a Social Democrat. There were eight Democrats, five Republicans, a Silver Republican, and four Populists among twenty-eight Elks. Twelve Eagles included three Democrats, two Republicans, a Populist, and two Socialists. In a few lodges, however, particular politics may have predominated. Almost half the Masons whose political affiliations could be determined were Republicans, and virtually all the political activists in the Sarsfield Club were Democrats, differences that reflected religious, cultural, and class distinctions between the organizations.[75]

Whatever their ideologies, lodge members often shared a common bond of family responsibility. Three out of four (74 percent) were married, compared with 58 percent of all adults and 48.5 percent of all men. Eight in ten (78 percent) were either heads of households or wives.[76] Because the lodge sample was heavily male, and it was harder for men to marry, the difference is especially significant. Again, however, there were some distinctions. The Catholic lodge members were the least married (60 percent), in part because they included fewer women than the other groups. The fraternal benefit societies had the most married members (79 percent), who apparently heeded the *Press's* admonition to provide insurance for their families (table 12).

Like the union leaders, lodge members were also more likely to own homes than were other adults—34 percent compared with 18 percent of District adults and 61 percent of household heads compared with 48 percent District-wide.[77] They were among the most stable residents of the District, married, heads of households, and homeowners. Home ownership, though, did not entirely correspond to differences in class and marital status. The Masonic Orders, with the fewest working-class members, had the highest levels of home ownership (78 percent of all household heads). But the next most propertied group were the Catholics (67.5 percent of household heads), both less married and more working-class than the others.[78] Lodge membership, like union leadership, expressed stability that was established by some combination of social ties, marriage, home ownership, and financial responsibility.

Many of the most prominent labor leaders were also active in lodges. Of the 443 union leaders discussed in chapter 3, at least seventy-eight, or 18 percent, were active in lodges and fraternal organizations as well. This group, which composed 13 percent of the lodge sample, included only those union members whose lodge

TABLE 12

Marital Status of Lodge Members by Type of Lodge

Lodge Type	Single		Married		Widowed		Unknown[a]	
	N	%	N	%	N	%	N	%
Masonic orders[b]	15	28	37	70	1	2		
Men only	12	32	24	65	1	3		
Fraternal beneficiary[c]	44	17	211	79	9	3	2	1
Men only	35	20	132	76	6	3		
Charitable and beneficiary[d]	58	27	150	71	4	2		
Men only	50	32	106	68	1	1		
Catholic[e]	22	37	36	60	1	2	1	2
Men only	20	35	35	61	1	2	1	2

Source: Lodge sample.

Note: Some figures do not total 100 percent due to rounding.

a. No one in this sample was divorced.

b. Masons, Knights Templars, and Order of the Eastern Star.

c. Ancient Order of United Workmen, Degree of Honor, Knights of the Maccabees, Ladies of the Maccabees, Modern Woodmen of America, Royal Neighbors, Woodmen of the World, Women of Woodcraft, Fraternal Order of Eagles, and Yeomen.

d. Benevolent and Protective Order of Elks, Independent Order of Red Men, Daughters of Pocahontas, Knights of Pythias, Rathbone Sisters, Independent Order of Odd Fellows, and Daughters of Rebekah.

e. Women's Auxiliary of Ancient Order of Hibernians, Sheridan Club, Sarsfield Club, Knights of Columbus, and Knights of St. John.

membership was reported in the *Press* and who could be linked to the 1900 census; there was considerably more overlap between unions and fraternal associations. The fact that working-class leaders were prominent in the mixed-class lodges demonstrated labor's prestige and extended working-class influence. Leadership in one arena reinforced prominence in another.

But the brotherhood of the lodge halls differed subtly from working-class fraternity, and the differences could strain working-class solidarity. The lodges included more women, whose membership reflected the family responsibilities of so many lodge members. Even more than for the union leadership, family status and stability divided fraternal associations from the younger, less married, and more mobile segment of the working class, the men who were more likely to seek recreation in bars and dance halls than at lodge hall dances. Fraternal recreation, in turn, directly threatened at least one craft. Non-union musicians frequently played for lodge socials. In many instances the scab musicians belonged to unions of other crafts and played occasionally at lodge functions without joining the Musicians' Protective Association. Union musicians protested that this practice was unfair because they depended on music for a livelihood. They could not "exist on the work derived from larger public dances alone" and so "should be given a chance at all the work there is to be had in this line." The musicians blamed lodge entertainment committees and the members of organized labor who went to "these dances and encourage[d] such tactics by dancing after scab music."[79]

In lodge hall recreation as in other social arenas, different sources of identity exerted competing loyalties. Lodges did not, in Cripple Creek, undermine working-class identity or autonomous working-class organization, as they did in less unionized areas. Although many union members came into close contact with management through their lodge and community activities, the *Press* drew an important distinction between unions and fraternal organizations. Pointing out that Cripple Creek unions guaranteed some of the best wages and hours in the state and aided the "sick and helpless members," it editorialized that District workers should join unions to "assist your fellow workmen in carrying the burden of holding the district to its present high standard, besides creating a safe guarantee against sickness and adversity." By contrast, although the majority of fraternal organizations did "much and great good," the *Press* said, they were limited "by reason of their fundamental principles which confined their mission to the channel of individualism."[80]

Lodge members collectively procured fraternal benefits, but insurance remained an individual responsibility of a man for his family. Family ties and responsibilities linked the men and women of the mixed-sex lodges and the husbands and fathers of different classes who shared lodge-hall fellowship. The lodges, however, envisioned family welfare as a breadwinner's concern, whereas unions emphasized social causes and collective responsibility. That difference distinguished fraternal brotherhood from working-class manhood and the oppositional critique of capitalism that underlay union aid. Like the unions, lodges provided diversion and buffered members against some of the personal risks inherent in corporate mining. But unions saw such services as temporary balms until the economic and political systems could be transformed and workers would no longer be forced to bear the costs of corporate profits. Lodges treated industrial dislocation and adversity as exceptional occurrences in an otherwise satisfactory system and tried to "patch" the lives of unfortunate lodge members until they were back on their feet. The significant overlaps in lodge and union memberships, however, qualify any interpretation of fraternalism as simple accommodation to capitalist social relations. As long as workers exercised collective strength through the unions, cross-class fraternity provided an additional strategy for working-class welfare and demonstrated the dignity of working-class men. But an unstated assumption went unexamined—the notion that the needs of workers, owners, and managers were equally served by the organizations to which they all belonged. That belief appeared particularly credible when lodges and unions cooperated in joint responses to death and need.

On January 24, 1901, Daniel P. McGinley died of pneumonia at age thirty-seven. The daily news reports as his illness dragged on expressed widespread concern, affection, and esteem. McGinley had served three terms as the financial secretary of Altman's Free Coinage Miners No. 19 and was elected to the WFM and CSFL executive boards. A prominent member of the Elks, the Red Men, a former commander of the Independence American Order of Protection (AOOP), he belonged to the Sheridan Club and was an active Democrat as well. He was, in short, active in virtually every sphere of community association—working-class, fraternal, ethnic, and political. He had also owned a bar. Members of every District WFM local and of all of McGinley's lodges and political clubs attended his funeral.[81] The Gillett Mill and Smeltermen No. 92, Cripple Creek Jeffersonian Club, Independence Harbor No. 36 of the AOOP, Victor Miners No. 32, Anaconda Miners No. 21, and the Cripple Creek District WFM Executive Board all published resolutions of grief. The resolution from McGinley's own local, Free Coinage No. 19, concluded that he lived

> For the cause that lacked assistance,
> For the wrongs that need resistance,
> For the future in the distance,
> And the good that he could do.[82]

McGinley was the sole support of his parents, who lived in Emporia, Kansas. Their mortgage was due, and their son's death left them in severe need. McGinley's organizational network therefore cooperated to host a benefit ball at Miners' Union Hall in Altman to raise money for the elder McGinleys. The Musicians' Union played for free. The arrangements committee was composed of representatives from Free Coinage Miners' Union No. 19, the Cripple Creek Order of Red Men, the Independence American Order of Protection, and the Sheridan Club of Cripple Creek. As with the benefit for Mrs. Tompkins, Steve Ryan represented the Altman Engineers' union and Sherman Bell represented the Victor Elks lodge.[83]

McGinley had not shared Bell's Republican politics, his religion, his Masonic membership, or his class interests. As long as labor and management successfully negotiated their minor differences and labor posed no immediate threat to private ownership, Sherman Bell and Daniel McGinley could meet at the local bars, the Elks Hall, and holiday celebrations. Such cross-class friendships partially stabilized relationships between capital and labor. But the language of fraternity skirted workplace relations that were more hierarchical and paternal than egalitarian and brotherly. Lodges worked to resolve this tension through rituals that formalized hierarchy and converted it to entertainment. As lodges became profit-making institutions that marketed costumes and rituals in addition to benefits, they moved increasingly from the model of mutual responsibility to the restrictions of the Maccabees and the MWA that excluded many working miners.[84]

Fraternal inequalities were symbolically represented in the Uniform Rank of the Knights of Pythias, which won public recognition under Bell's leadership as major. Like the Masonic Knights Templar and the Odd Fellows' Patriarchs Militant, the Uniform Rank, characterized as "the military department" of the order, was devoted to elaborate costumes and spectacle. One critic of the Patriarchs Militant complained that the military branches responded to the "overwhelming desire among the younger members of the Order to strut before the world, — clad in the habiliments of war when no danger threatened, to dress themselves in showy uniforms." This particular construction of manhood in Cripple Creek connected working-class Pythians in a military hierarchy with a mine manager commandant. The Uniform Rank appealed to militarism and authority rather than to brotherhood and craft.[85]

The Uniform Rank was created during the massive labor conflicts of 1876 and 1877.[86] The dominant theme in Cripple Creek, however, during the union era was brotherhood, not paternalism. Until the second Cripple Creek strike, working-class men remained confident that they controlled the terms of fraternal friendships in Cripple Creek. Their rhetoric and displays of brotherhood stressed egalitarian values based on mutual respect and dignity. The appeals to brotherhood and manly methods glossed over differences between working-class manhood and other concepts of masculinity based on paternal authority, hierarchy, militarism, violence, and control. "Dear Sir and Brother," a common salutation that began most labor correspondence, implied egalitarian respect and kinship. The words carried similar connotations for the Sir Knights and Brothers of the local lodge halls. Whether all sirs could, in the same senses, be brothers in the workplace was more dubious. Still, during the union era, class distinctions could be submerged and mediated through the social conventions of fraternity.

5

IMPERFECT UNIONS

In August 1901 Colorado labor commissioner James T. Smith journeyed to Cripple Creek to attend a union smoker hosted by WFM Miners' Local No. 40. Sandwiched on a program that included three boxing matches, music, a buck-and-wing dance, recitations, and numerous other speakers, Smith stood before an overflow crowd fortified by "an abundance of smoking material and liquid refreshment" and discussed "the advantages possessed by communities in which organized labor was strong." Later that evening State Federation of Labor president H. E. Garman underscored Smith's message, hammering home the point that union wages protected working-class families. "Good wages," Garman concluded bluntly, "means a good, decent home."[1]

A crowd estimated at more than a thousand cheered Garman and Smith.[2] It is a safe bet, however, that no women were there. According to the union ideal, women and children remained sheltered in their "good, decent homes." No decent woman would set foot in masculine spaces like smokers and saloons, where men forged the bonds of working-class manhood in rooms that reeked of sweat, union-label tobacco, and union-label beer.

Working women, however, found their own particular space in the labor movement and working-class discourse. Labor Commissioner Smith invited working women as well as men to write to him, and he published their opinions in his biennial reports. In 1902 a Cripple Creek housemaid penned an analysis that would have played well at any union smoker. The time had come, she declared, when "a clear, well-defined class interest" separated "the laboring class from their employers." Therefore, the "working class must become class conscious and enter politics through the Socialist movement." Class-conscious politics would achieve a more just society. There would be no wage system and no profits. Instead, workers would establish an industrial government:

> not to manipulate politics and parcel out patronage, but to take charge of and direct and control production and distribution. The actual workers in each industry will con-

trol that industry, waste will be eliminated, earnings will be vastly increased, and the hours of labor will be shortened to less than half what they are at present. Almost all the work now is performed by people who are working for wages. They would surely work better if they were getting all that they earned, instead of a very small part of it. . . . Reform measures may help a little, but not until we get the co-operative commonwealth will the question be settled so that it will stay settled.[3]

The housemaid's dream of a "cooperative commonwealth" was familiar in labor circles. The image came from Laurence Gronlund's *The Cooperative Commonwealth*, published in 1884, which introduced Marxist ideas to many American readers. The housemaid repeated Gronlund's central argument that the wage system must be abolished and that the state should take over the means of production. The revolution that would bring state socialism was inevitable, but violence was not. Class conflict could be resolved at the ballot box, and an orderly revolution won through democratic politics. Socialists, Gronlund emphasized, were "respectable." He invited professionals and "thoughtful" small-scale middlemen to join in creating a new era of cooperation.[4] In the Cripple Creek District, Gronlund's "respectable" architects of the cooperative commonwealth could be found at the lodge halls and Fourth of July celebrations where union leaders gathered with local merchants and professionals.

Like any visionary ideology, the cooperative commonwealth resonated in different ways for its many adherents. Dreams of a better world carried unstated assumptions about ideal social relationships, including what women's and men's roles would be in an ideal cooperative order. In the Cripple Creek District, assumptions about what was good and natural for each sex stood as unexamined and as significant as the distances that barred working-class wives from union meetings and prostitutes from "respectable" women's parlors. The geography of gender was charted from "truths" so widely accepted that they required no elaboration.

Two key assumptions about work and intimacy framed working-class gender relations: mining was men's work, and "good, decent homes" sheltered patriarchal families. Men who succeeded in both arenas represented working-class aspirations. Labor spoke most often through local union leaders, whose identities were defined simultaneously by their positions as wageworkers, as white men, and often as husbands, fathers, and heads of households. Their experiences of work and intimacy differed in particular ways from those of women wageworkers, working-class wives and daughters, and the unmarried majority of working-class men (tables 8 and 13).[5] Although the leaders' status defined an ideal to which other working men could aspire, policies based on their experience generated particular conflicts within the working class for people who did not share the productive or the domestic realities of the union leadership.

TABLE 13
Occupation by Sex, 1900

Occupation	Men N	Men %	Women N	Women %
Working class (blue collar)				
Mining semiskilled	7	1	0	0
Mining skilled	80	7		
Miner	514	43		
Unskilled	127	11	44	29
Semiskilled	127	11	25	17
Skilled	131	11	31	21
	986	82	100	67
Salaried/clerical				
Salaried workers	32	3	2	1
Salaried mining	14	1		
	46	4	2	1
Business				
Proprietors	100	8	23	15
Mining proprietors	1			
	101	8	23	15
Professionals				
Professionals	35	3	17	11
Mining professionals	9	1		
	44	4	17	11
Capitalists				
Capitalists	11	1	1	1
Mining capitalists	11	1		
	22	2	1	1
Other				
Other	7	1	7	5
Other mining	3			
	10	1	7	5
District totals	1,209	103	150	100

Source: Manuscript census, Teller County, Colo., 1900, 1,359 persons who listed occupations in a random sample of 2,089 adults.

Note: Some columns do not total 100 percent due to rounding. Totals for each class were calculated separately to minimize the distortions of rounding, particularly for working-class categories.

Work roles and family roles were neither natural nor inevitable. They were so-cial constructs, as were the circumstances that assigned different significance and values to men's and women's activities. The housemaid's analysis contained a definition of work that was appropriate for the male work force but for only a small minority of District women. "*Almost all the work now,*" she wrote, "*is performed by people who are working for wages.*"[6] The housemaid, presumably, earned wages for domestic service. But her definition of work excluded most working-class women in the District, who received no wages for their domestic labor. Their exclusion from the paid work force rested on the unexamined assumption that women should not work in the mines, a social belief that seemed entirely natural, although women did, in fact, perform mining labor in other times and places.[7]

Gender was as inextricably bound to class relationships and class identities as it was to the division of labor in mining towns. The industrial structure of gold min-ing supported both intense class allegiances and gendered definitions of work. Manhood was defined by wage work and breadwinning, womanhood by domes-ticity and relationships to working-class men. Effective labor control meant that a secure home life was at least partially accessible for working-class families. With a male-dominated work force and an excess of men of marriageable age, paid work for women was limited, and most adult women were economically dependent on male breadwinners. Women's jobs provided domestic support for unmarried men—they were cooks, waitresses, seamstresses, retail clerks, dance hall workers, and prostitutes. Many were small proprietors of boarding and rooming houses, res-taurants, and groceries (table 13). Schoolteaching was the largest female profession. An unusual number of professional women practiced in the District—at least four physicians, one osteopath, one dentist, and twenty-five nurses in 1902.[8] Married women, however, rarely worked outside the home. They might take in laundry, cook, clean, or manage boardinghouses, but not teach or engage in public busi-ness. According to one woman who grew up in the District, "Women just didn't get jobs, women belonged in the home."[9]

More than 95 percent of District men listed occupations on the 1900 census; 19 percent of the women did. Paid occupations do not fully represent women's work, however. Because there were roughly three men of marriageable age for each two women, most women married and were significantly younger than their spouses. Among women over age sixteen, seven out of ten lived with their husbands (table 2). Their work was largely unpaid domestic labor.

❊   ❊   ❊

The language organized labor used to discuss gender was sufficiently common and sufficiently elastic that we must understand it in context. "True manhood" and "true womanhood" were common phrases in nineteenth-century America, so common that Barbara Welter used the "Cult of True Womanhood" to label an ideology that prescribed white middle-class women's roles from 1820 to 1860. Welter's true woman was pious, pure (that is, asexual), domestic, and submissive to male authority. These expectations were rooted in changes that occurred as production moved from households to factories and eroded Euro-American women's work manufacturing commodities in their homes. The popular version of true womanhood reflected women's loss of central productive roles and restricted them to a special social function. Women, through their influence within the household, were to provide a stabilizing moral center; men were to be aggressive, acquisitive, and competitive.[10] Both roles were defined as natural and biologically ordained. Men were expected to work to provide for themselves and their families. Women were to be private and decorative and support men by establishing comforting domestic retreats from a competitive marketplace. These concepts of appropriate gender behavior were formulated in an age of laissez-faire individualism that judged deviation from accepted sexual spheres as an indication of individual failure. The gender ideals marked the social status of the few who succeeded in a capitalist marketplace.

Welter's formulation of true womanhood could be achieved at best by only a small Euro-American minority of middle-class and wealthy urbanites. Her choice of the word *cult* implied both the negative judgment she applied to a role she found subservient and constraining and the inflexible list of gender attributes a woman must achieve in order to be "true." In practice, however, true womanhood was a flexible idea that could express the domestic realities and aspirations of women and men of different classes and races. The patterns, language, and cultural signs of domesticity helped women in widely different circumstances make sense of their lives. Domesticity, true manhood, and true womanhood were flexible ideologies, not cults or templates for all gender roles and relationships. Domestic ideologies are best understood through the actual behaviors and perceptions of people in particular circumstances.[11]

For the Colorado labor movement, true manhood and womanhood owed more to an industrial workers' culture than to the domestic prescriptions of an antebellum elite. During the 1880s, "labor's true women" in the Knights of Labor forged what Susan Levine called a labor feminism, which included women's rights to representation and authority in labor organizations, equal pay, and equal respect for their productive work at home or in the factory. That vision, like the Cripple Creek housemaid's, did not challenge a domestic sphere for women. Women could preserve moral values from their homes and "at the same time infuse the public world with a more moral, humane, and cooperative character." Labor's version of true womanhood fused the concerns of the industrial workplace with the issues of the nineteenth-century women's movement, particularly temperance and suffrage. The Knights' version of domesticity supported cooperation and collectivity in opposition to the competition and individuality embedded in capitalist social relations. "Home and work," Levine asserted, "combined to shape the very core of the Knights' vision. Work, or productive toil, provided pride and meaning in life and home provided strength. The two were linked together in the ideal of the cooperative commonwealth."[12]

There were problems with the Knights' vision of the ideal commonwealth. Women's equality depended on a workers' movement that would support domestic harmony, independent producers, and egalitarian social relations. In that ideal world, women would return home from the paid work force. The industrial system, however, separated home and work.[13] And in Cripple Creek it removed women from decision-making authority in the labor movement.

Cripple Creek unions considered the achievement of stable and respectable families an important measure of collective success and also realized that labor organization was necessary to gain secure homes. District labor's versions of true manhood and true womanhood, like the Knights', carried both particular class meanings and romantic and moral assumptions about women's and men's innate qualities. There was considerable distance between labor's public discourse and workers' daily realities and behaviors. Labor's versions of true working-class womanhood idealized the productive and domestic relationships of union leaders whose skill, experience, and dedication to organized labor provided the security that allowed them to marry, settle, and raise families. Their work and their intimate relationships differed in important ways from the public ideal, from the experiences of most rank-and-file workers, and from the lives of most working-class women.

The public language of class and gender emphasized the particular contexts of work and intimacy in the mining economy. Wage work was largely the province of white men. Most women were married and performed domestic labor. Single, working-class men often found companionship with other men and erotic intimacy with dance hall workers and prostitutes. The working-class domestic ideal ignored the daily labor of working-class housewives and the intimate relationships of unmarried men. The contradictions multiplied for the women who earned their livings in the District's brothels and dance halls. Arguably the largest group of women wage earners, they were excluded from the working-class community and the protection of organized labor. The failure to integrate comprehensions of class and of gender weakened working-class policy and subordinated and privatized women.

Forty percent of the District's adult population was female. Taking into account their relationships to both production and intimacy, or reproduction, three groups of women in the District could reasonably be considered working class. Women wageworkers, most of whom were unmarried, performed "respectable" wage work. Prostitutes and dance hall workers did "unrespectable" wage work. Whether married or single, the fact that they accepted pay for physical intimacy violated the moral boundaries labor defined for good women. The women of working-class families, most of whom were married, performed unpaid domestic labor and were by far the largest group. Most women were considered working class by virtue of ascribed status, because their husbands, fathers, or brothers worked for wages. Their security depended on the men's incomes, health, and generosity and on the regularity of work in the mines.

Women shared the class understandings and social support of the labor community, but organized labor rarely addressed the private world of the family or the specific needs of working-class women. Women discussed female concerns among themselves, but these private understandings did not affect the public role prescriptions of the labor press. Even women wage laborers who "earned" their class status remained subordinate to male union members, and all District workers relied on the economic control of the men's WFM locals.

Women wageworkers shared the class philosophies of male unionists and espoused them with eloquence. In 1902 a Cripple Creek stenographer told the Colorado Bureau of Labor Statistics that there was no essential difference between chattel and wage slavery: "Chattel slaves labor for their masters, are poor, dependent upon the whims of owners for food, clothing, and shelter and are kept in mental darkness. Free laborers (God save the world) toil for their employers, are poor, dependent upon the caprice of monopolists for wages with which to procure food, clothing, shelter. . . . One system of exploitation is simple and direct in its execution, the other is complex and roundabout."[14]

The stenographer used a common racial metaphor to describe class when she distinguished chattel slavery and wage slavery. Like the housemaid, however, she omitted the indirect exploitation of working-class wives. However powerful their responses to capitalism, neither directly addressed the experience of most women, whose relationships to capitalism and to their husbands were not common subjects of working-class analysis. But Mabel Barbee, the daughter of a Cripple Creek prospector, recognized the harshness of her mother's life, "the bare, ugly camp, so alien to her nature; the wide gap between her dream of a home and the drab reality of the house on Golden Avenue; her never-ending loneliness."[15] The distance between that daily reality and the class outlook and faith in political action of stenographers and housemaids reflected an important tension for working-class women. They were expected to accept a class analysis of industrial conditions, and definitions of natural and moral gender qualities that transcended class lines. If the male world was divided into workers and employers, the world of women was divided into good women and bad. Men defined themselves by their relationships to production, to other men, and to families; they defined women by their relationships to men and to morality. Defining work as wage labor only, the unions ignored women's arduous domestic and reproductive toil.

The *Press* reflected the masculine domination of the mining camp. The frequent prizefights were front-page news, and union and lodge smokers received full coverage. The *Press* did reflect, at least indirectly, some of the relational concerns of unmarried men. Lydia Pinkham never advertised in its columns, but a wide variety of "male complaint" remedies promised to protect men from the dangers of the sexual marketplace and cure everything from impotence to an astonishing list of venereal diseases. Cupidene, Nervita Pills, and Vitaline vied with local doctors who specialized in sexual problems. Dr. Schultz's cure included a "very new system of inhalation of compound vapors," and the Doctors Sims and Sims, "expert medical electricians," delicately claimed to work wonders with "first class electrical equipment." Mormon Bishops' Pills, "in use over fifty years by the leaders of the Mormon Church and their followers," promised to cure "lost manhood, impotency, lost power, night losses, spermatorrhoea, insomnia, pain in back, evil desires, seminal emissions, lame back, nervous debility, headache, unfitness to marry, loss of semen, varicocele, or constipation . . . quickness of discharge, and nervous twitching of the eyelids."

Manhood was understood in terms of sexuality, strength, and breadwinning. It was also defined in relation to class membership and union fealty, which in turn enabled a man to be a good provider. "True men" were concerned with strength, skill, sexuality, and their "fitness to marry." Once married, they also worked hard to support their families. Union wages made that support possible, and manhood was less tied to rugged individualism than to militant unionism. The *Press* said that a "man who is not alive to his interests enough to join a union of his craft is unworthy to be the husband of a good woman or the father of innocent children." Scabs were derided for their "lack of manhood"; to be a loyal union member was to be a "man—not a makeshift."[16] Womanhood, in contrast, was defined in domestic terms. Most women's class status derived from their husbands' or fathers' relationships to the means of production; their class participation was indirect and depended on male organization. Concepts of sexual sphere remained publicly unchallenged in Cripple Creek because unions were strong enough to guarantee wages that could support families. Labor redefined manhood and womanhood in class terms. True men were union men, and true women were loyal union wives.

Whatever their class analysis, the men and women of Cripple Creek did not question their domestic relationships with one another. Men attached male pride to breadwinning. Hoistman James McConaghy considered it a "disgrace" for a woman to work outside the home because it meant he "wasn't a good worker; he was lazy, he wasn't able to take care of his family." One woman wrote that a working-class wife should be able to "earn a dollar or two without advertising it to the neighborhood."[17] Women's class allegiance derived from responsibilities to husbands and households; they were encouraged to be class-conscious housewives and mothers. The strongest demonstration of class loyalty was to "find a man who's a union man." In a WFM song, "Scab, Scab, Scab," a woman rejects her suitor for being a strikebreaker:

> And when I popped the question she said, "You make me sad,
> Do you know I can marry a union man? Do you think I'd look at a scab?
> My father is a W.F.M., my brother is the same,
> My mother joined the Auxiliary—I guess I'll not take your name."[18]

❀   ❀   ❀

Western labor assumed, with some accuracy, that it treated women in a progressive manner. It met, in large measure, the standards of "labor's true women" and of the nineteenth-century women's movement. Although there were few mixed-sex occupations in the District, labor endorsed equal pay for equal work and opposed politicians who disagreed. Women could vote in Colorado and were considerably more active in District politics than in the unions.[19] It was not unusual for women to vote in the old mining districts. They fought for the full franchise and won the vote in school elections when Colorado achieved statehood in 1876. Seventeen years later, Colorado became the first state to enfranchise women by a vote of the male electorate. In the intervening suffrage campaigns, pro-suffrage votes correlated with the Greenback vote from 1878 to 1884 and with the Union-Labor vote in 1888. In 1893, during the Populist insurgency, women won the full franchise with the support of Governor Waite, who declared that with the limited franchise "the heavens have not fallen and the efficiency of the public schools has been greatly improved."[20]

A coalition of middle-class women's clubs, the Women's Christian Temperance Union, suffrage clubs, organized labor, and working-class women cooperated to win the suffrage victory. The National American Women's Suffrage Association sent Carrie Chapman Catt to Colorado, and the Knights of Labor sent Leonora Barry to work in the 1893 campaign. The major support at the polls came from Populist hard-rock metal miners. The Cripple Creek District ratified woman suffrage in 1893 by a vote of 548 to 254. Altman, then the labor stronghold, favored votes for women 92 to 27. The year after the suffrage victory the District followed through on the promise of civic authority when two women were appointed to a police court jury, the first women in Colorado to serve in that capacity.[21]

District labor prided itself on these achievements, defined them as valuable working-class tools, and considered them sufficient to women's needs. It achieved many precepts of the Knights' labor feminism. But there was one critical exception—women exercised little authority in the labor movement itself. Labor assumed that women's needs had been met with the franchise and that only class issues remained. Organized labor saw the ballots and the purchasing power of working-class women as tactical weapons to support unions.

Labor incorporated domesticity into its critique of industrial capitalism. When artisans' homes were their workshops, wives might contribute to craft production. Their productive work in the home was apparent, as was their domestic and reproductive labor. The Knights' true women represented an industrial transition. Some women did wage work, and local labor assemblies recognized wives' home labor with a voice and vote. But in Cripple Creek the wage system itself obscured women's productive labor. Cripple Creek was not the producers' commonwealth the Knights of Labor had envisioned. The capital required for industrial mining ruled out working-class ownership.

In Cripple Creek, labor's understandable emphasis on men's wage work shifted class analyses away from the domestic labor that supported the paid labor force. Miners could not work unless they were clothed and fed. But organized labor's public discourse ignored women's domestic labor to emphasize the union's protective role toward working-class families. Thus, labor attacked capitalism because it forced women to do wage work and destroyed the home. The *Press* insisted that a man should receive wages "sufficient to keep his wife and children out of competition with himself, and give them the same opportunities for improvement and intellectual and moral training and comfortable living as are enjoyed by those who do not labor. No other condition of society is just."[22] Labor did not examine how capitalism exploited the unpaid labor of working-class women to supply the domestic needs of the industrial work force.

The domestic realities of working-class families did not challenge a domestic ideology based in separate spheres for women and men. After marriage, the worlds of husbands and wives were often quite separate. Women were home-centered; men's lives revolved around work and work associations. Men spent more waking hours at work than at home. After work, many relaxed downtown at the saloons, union halls, and lodges.[23] Their homes were retreats as well as emblems of union achievement. Tying respectable family life to unions, the *Press* contrasted District miners' homes with those in unorganized areas:

A comparison of the home of the average industrious miner of the Cripple Creek district and . . . its contents with that of a coal miner in the eastern states . . . would be a revelation to that class of people who look upon a man who delves in the earth and who gets black and dirty when on shift as an inferior sort of animal, ignorant and brutal, drinking up his wages and beating his wife and living in dirt and squalor. Instead of those conditions the opposite are the rule. Their homes are neatly furnished, carpets on the floors, kitchen furnished with all the conveniences a good housewife is so proud to own. . . . The father, when off shift, is neatly dressed, and with his papers and books becomes intelligent and well posted. The mother, though often hard worked, finds time to put on a neat, clean dress in the evening. The children attend school, and are comfortably clothed and well fed.[24]

The language of family in this passage introduces a father, mother, and children—not a miner, domestic worker, and future wageworkers and domestic workers. At home, in the domestic arena, kinship defined human relationships, not people's relationships to the productive process. The fact that workers, when off shift, could come home and be family men was a union achievement. So was their ability to keep children in school and out of the paid work force. District unions celebrated their power to keep workingmen's wives and children out of the work force and safe from dance halls and brothels, victories won only because "organized labor was strong."

For working-class women, union control made the Cripple Creek District more pleasant than many mining camps. It stood in stark contrast to non-union coal towns, where workers lived in company houses, traded at company stores, sent their children to company schools, and were paid in company scrip. District workers owned or rented their own homes, were paid in cash, traded with private merchants, and elected school officials and most other office-holders. For women, such benefits meant greater material and social security, emotional support, and a clearer class analysis of daily difficulties than was available to most working people. Union aid in times of sickness and death was of enormous benefit to women, as was the emotional support offered when trouble occurred. Although nothing could totally ameliorate human loss or economic uncertainty, unions did much to relieve suffering, provide friendship and support, and give class meaning to life—and death—in the District.

The unions addressed the stresses of economic and emotional ties to working-class men by providing social explanations for the difficulties of working-class families. Union social gatherings helped ease the isolation of private households. For ten years women benefited from union control. With their security and home life dependent on male organization, they placed class loyalty above their particular needs.

Working-class women had few ties with middle-class women. They were isolated from the local women's clubs, whose members were mostly wives of merchants and professionals. More preoccupied with civic projects and culture than with class, women's clubs sometimes came into conflict with organized labor (as in the controversy about a Carnegie Library discussed in chapter 4). More to the point, their domestic realities were not the same as working-class women's. Cripple Creek housemaids probably worked for middle-class women whose homes were more likely to have running water and "modern conveniences" than would be the case for the homes of miners' wives.[25]

Class and gender were not separate categories of experience in Cripple Creek. They combined to construct daily social relationships among different classes of women and men. Daily work and intimate relationships differed for working-class men, working-class women, middle-class women, and middle-class men. Work was divided by both class and gender. The social structures of an industrial mining economy maintained considerable separation between women and men, home and workplace. Gender roles appeared natural and biologically determined, whereas class relationships appeared historically constructed and changing—and therefore changeable. Because gold mining could support male breadwinning and female domesticity, women owed much to a labor movement in which they had little authority or voice and which defined their roles as supportive and subordinate.

An analysis that fused class and gender was unlikely in these circumstances, but its absence created critical rifts in working-class programs. Believing that union wages and woman suffrage met women's essential needs, Cripple Creek unions projected class goals that assumed separate spheres rather than interdependent relationships. The result was an incomplete analysis of industrial capitalism that left out the relationship of the household to the economy and omitted the social and economic value of housework. The *Press* occasionally recognized that miners' wives "were often hard worked" but did not publicly acknowledge women as economic partners. Visions of an equal and humane society did not project equality between women and men. Unresolved tensions in the workplace increased tension and hierarchy at home, exacerbated by women's dependence on men's wages.

The uneasy coexistence of strong loyalties to working-class organization and definitions of work that devalued women's labor created separations among women and within a working class segmented by sex and marital status. Working-class women were divided by whether or not they worked for money, and women wageworkers by whether they worked in a reputable or disreputable market. The incomplete class analysis that presumed women's dependence created stresses for all working-class women, whether respectable wageworkers, prostitutes and dance hall workers, or workingmen's wives. It also generated tensions between union leaders and the unmarried rank-and-file majority.

Women wageworkers received an inconsistent blend of support as workers and chivalrous patronage as women. It was assumed that women held jobs only in the absence of a male breadwinner. The common fear prevailed that women took men's jobs and depressed wages. For every woman who worked, a man would "be out of a job through the ingenuity of capitalism to economize on the profit reaping system."[26] District unions organized women to diminish that threat, but male workers commonly believed that women worked only temporarily and only to support themselves, not families. Those women whom labor did organize generally worked in industries that employed white men. Union organizers ignored women who worked in dance halls, brothels, and private households.

Union men believed that their treatment of women was progressive, and for the time it was. The Typographical Union was proud that it was "the first organization of men to recognize the rights of women to equal work." Not all District workers agreed, however, and many either patronized women or considered them incompetent to work outside the home. R. E. Croskey proclaimed that no woman could "cook in a restaurant or hotel," because when "you put a woman at a range with three half springs to keep broiling with a long fork and a bowl of consomme coming up at the other end, she gets flustered." Croskey was a Socialist, the secretary of the District Trades Assembly, and national president of the ALU's Hotel and Restaurant Employees Union. But perhaps more important in this instance, he was married to a woman fifteen years his junior.[27] She probably *was* a less experienced cook than he, and the marital norms of the union leadership significantly shaped gender ideology.

Deviation from accepted work spheres was sexually as well as economically threatening. Deeper masculine fears surfaced when the Denver Women's Club lobbied to hire a female police officer. The *Press* was against it, claiming that hiring a woman for the job would "result in the effeminacy of the human race." Worse yet, wives would "confer with the young lady next door who is working the night shift on the force, and those aged and sacred excuses for coming home at 2 in the morning will not hold as much water as a sieve."[28]

Several hundred District women belonged to unions, especially to the Retail Clerks, Laundry Workers, Cooks and Waiters, Hotel and Restaurant Employees, and the Typographical locals. Clerks and typographers, who most often had equal work and wages, benefited particularly from union membership. But women's and men's jobs were generally different, and women's union wages were often lower than men's. The 1900 census of manufactures listed fifty women working in the District in non-mining manufacturing for an average $368.09 annually and 735 men whose average annual wage was $838.68. The wage scale enforced by the Cripple Creek Laundry Workers was generally lower than the $3 minimum daily wage for miners, and the lowest wages were for "women's work." The scale for a sixty-hour week ranged from a minimum of $15 for male drivers to $8.50 for towel supply girls and $7.50 for mangle girls. Laundry wages were slightly better in Victor, where the weekly scale ranged from $9 for mangle girls to "men working inside, not less than $18" for fifty-four hours.[29]

Women's wages in Cripple Creek were somewhat higher than national scales. So was the cost of living, and work was often part-time and temporary. Ten waitresses hired to serve a convention overflow crowd staged a walkout in 1902 because they received the regular scale of $14 a week and board instead of the $3 a day and board usually paid temporary help. When the grievance committee of the Hotel and Restaurant Employees could not resolve the issue, the union struck. As one woman explained, "We wait a week or a month for two days' employment, and get four dollars for it. Extra work is during a rush. It is hard and wearying work because there are so many people to wait upon, and a waitress earns every cent she gets. My brother earns four dollars a day at the mines, and comes home fresh and ready for a frolic, but I am so tired and weary that I must go to bed if I would be in any shape to work the next day."[30] It is likely, too, that this waitress worked a "double day," doing housework when she got home, and that her brother did not. Thus, her need to go to bed might also cut short her second shift of work.

Even in "women's occupations," women were seldom a majority of the work force, and all the unions were male strongholds. With the possible exceptions of a short-lived Dressmakers' Union in 1896 and Female Clerks No. 238, which existed briefly and claimed some sixty members in 1899, there were no all-female locals. Women were also a decided minority in mixed-sex unions. Clerks organized the largest group of women, numbering at least sixty members of Federal Labor Union No. 19 in 1900, when that local had more than two hundred members. The WLU listed sixty-five women members in the District in 1901, a year when District unions claimed more than four thousand members.[31]

Few women achieved union leadership. Several served as secretaries of the clerks' locals, but more were found on arrangements committees for socials and in other more "feminine" roles. Nellie Kedzie, one of the few women prominent in the District labor movement, represented the Cripple Creek Federal Labor Union at the State Federation of Labor convention in 1900. The *Press* reported that she "spoke well for early closing" and "seemed at home, too." But her influence in the masculine world of organized labor was sufficiently novel (or sufficiently threatening) that one facetious reporter could only ascribe her forcefulness to the fact she had once survived being "run over by a street car in Denver."[32]

If District labor patronized working women, at least their class and moral status was unambiguous—they were wageworkers and they were good women. Class and morality interacted with greater complication for workingmen's wives and for "bad" women. Prostitutes performed wage labor, but perceptions of prostitutes' class status depended on their race and the class of their clientele. Cripple Creek's red light district reflected the race and class system in its geography. Myers Avenue between Third and Fifth streets held the dance halls and "resorts," as well as the fancier parlor houses—the Old Homestead, Royal Inn, Mikado, Laura Bell's, and Nell McClusky's, and a few one-woman cribs. Conventionally attractive and younger white women staffed the big houses that served wealthier customers. The Old Homestead, renowned as the playground of mining kings, kept a separate building on the back of its lot, where a few African American women worked apart from the white women in the "big house." Further down Myers came the smaller houses. When Myers Avenue ran into Poverty Gulch the crib area began, holding, in order, the dwellings of French, Japanese, Chinese, Mexican, Indian, and African American prostitutes, as well as two African American houses.[33]

Organized labor's reverence for good women stood in stark contrast to the "row" and to living and working conditions there. In 1901 and 1902 the *Press* covered at least fifteen suicide attempts by prostitutes and dance hall women. Male reporters attributed most suicides to desertion by pimps or lovers; even in this final choice they defined women through their relationships with men. The "soiled doves" could not be approved but could be seen as victims of exploitation, forced into their vocations by a capitalist economy. "Under our present social and industrial system," the *Press* intoned, "the breeding and propagation of the female prostitute class is as inevitable and unavoidable as the appearance of the maggot in the putrid carcass that lays in the July sun."[34] Prostitution was inevitable, too, given mining-town demography. Single men found companionship in cribs and dance halls, where they bought dances, alcohol, and conversation as well as sex.

Dance halls compromised women and men, but it was hard to condemn the women who worked there. The *Press* portrayed women sex workers as victims but carefully avoided clients' roles in sexual commerce and reserved its greatest venom for pimps. "The inmates of such places . . . deserve pity rather than censure. They are victims of conditions which should not exist in any country. But for the men who live from the product of these women's shame, we have no words adequate to express our contempt."[35] Although labor partially recognized that women became prostitutes to support themselves and because they had few economic options, the distanced stance of union publications denied working men's intimate knowledge of the tenderloin. At best, the *Press* portrayed the women as victims of capitalists and pimps; it never realistically described their options and choices.

Prostitutes could earn more than most women wageworkers. One young woman worked in a Cripple Creek dance hall to help support her family after her father developed silicosis. She had previously earned only $2.50 a week in a Denver department store. Lillian Powers, who worked as a prostitute in Victor and Cripple Creek, entered "the life" because it was her best option as an uneducated woman. She first worked as a domestic, but "there was no money in it. My God, you worked for two dollars a week!" Then she worked in a laundry. "Well, most of those laundry girls was out doing business. . . . They said, 'Well, you're foolish to work around, work so hard. Go on, get you a friend to pay your way'. . . . So I did." Powers worked briefly in a dance hall but did not like it. "That's too much booze." She preferred working out of her own crib. Instead of the $2 a week she made as a domestic servant, she charged a dollar a "date" and sold beer for a dollar a bottle.[36]

The *Press* occasionally recognized that low wages elsewhere pushed women to become prostitutes, yet public allegiance to genteel morality was sufficiently strong that labor never considered organizing dance hall workers, much less prostitutes. True to the union spirit of the community, however, dance hall women went on strike in 1902 to oppose a 10 percent cut in their share of liquor sales and established a Dance Hall Girls' Protective Association. Although the strike succeeded, the union was apparently short-lived, and the women never applied for membership in the Trades Assembly.[37]

If they had, they would have been disappointed. In late 1902 and early 1903 the Trades Assembly mounted a campaign to close the dance halls and resolved that "no person employed in dance halls in the Cripple Creek District" would be "recognized as members of organized labor by this assembly, nor in any way receive its support." Union musicians protested that the policy would "work hardship on many members of our union who are working in those places, as will be seen by the fact that more than 50 per cent of the wages paid to musicians in the District is paid by dance halls." Musicians' Protective Association No. 49 was likely correct in asserting that "we do not think the action of the assembly in this matter represents the majority of the union people of the district." But the values of the married union leaders prevailed. The musicians requested a referendum vote of union members, but the Trades Assembly refused because the large miners' locals had already voted almost unanimously to endorse closing the dance halls.[38]

It is not clear from the *Press*'s reports whether few WFM members dissented from the policy or whether majority votes in most WFM locals endorsed it. In either case the domestic circumstances and life-cycles of married men clarify the extent and limits of labor's moral crusade. Moral and sentimental definitions of domesticity distinguished the domestic work of working-class wives and daughters from the domestic and sex work of other women. Organized labor could demand dignity for the "sellers of muscle" but not for the "sellers of sex and companionship." Whatever their private feelings or behavior, most miners maintained a public stance against vice.

Male recreation, particularly married men's amusements, defined the boundaries of labor's policies on public morality. Organized labor publicly disavowed dance halls and prostitution, but it never directly attacked saloons Many union leaders still drank downtown, and some owned bars. District unions did attempt to provide an alternative to saloon culture, a goal they shared with the Woods family's Gold Coin Club, which boasted that its billiards and chess cost half as much as at local saloons. Likewise, the club room of Victor Federal Labor Union No. 64 offered card tables, chess, and checkers to "induce the members to spend their evenings there instead of at saloons."[39]

Labor was much more aggressive in numerous campaigns to regulate gambling and prostitution. A man might patronize dance hall workers and prostitutes in his youth, but he did not want his daughter to grow up to be one. Although men's life-cycles took them from the companionship of the "half world" to the home world, it was hard for a woman to walk the same path. That double standard underlay working men's proud boast that union wages saved "families from the soup house and the brothel."[40]

Men could drink in lodges and union halls as well as saloons. They could even dance and find female companionship at union balls and lodge hall socials. But they could not purchase casual sex outside the tenderloin. The labor movement organized bartenders but not prostitutes, dance hall workers, or barmaids. These solutions to the moral conflict between home and the tenderloin disregarded the realities of most people who worked in the vice districts and of any unmarried men who desired more erotic companionship than chess and boxing could supply.

❀   ❀   ❀

The definition of union wives as good women failed to distinguish them from women of other classes, including the few women mine owners or the Victor Women's Club that wanted a Carnegie library. The boardinghouse keepers and restaurant owners whom organized labor boycotted for anti-union hiring practices were good women, too. Virtue and domesticity were inadequate analytic tools to define working-class womanhood. Labor's class analysis said that capitalism forced women into prostitution. The cooperative commonwealth would end prostitution by guaranteeing men wages that could support dependent women and patriarchal households.

Women accepted, in public discourse at least, that they should provide a refuge from the workplace. If a working man provided a comfortable home, he expected wifely support. One woman wrote that a working man should be able to come home to a "rosy wife" who could "sing at the wash tub" and find "nothing under the sun that makes her as merry as housecleaning." She should save money and be agreeable, because "the working man has all the vicissitudes he wants when he goes to his work." But she recognized that women's supportive roles were rooted in economic dependence and suggested that a happy marriage required that a woman take "to the altar a sum of money to give her some share of independence for life."[41] That, of course, was not likely.

Women were assumed to be preoccupied with home, morality, children, and femininity. One page of the Sunday *Press* was devoted to news of the various unions and to columns on labor philosophy. The page also featured fashion items. Next to a story about a waitresses' strike or an article "For the Abolishment of the Wage System" appeared fashion photos of "A Moire Blouse Jacket," "The 'Zenana' Coat," and "Smart Paris Costumes." Working-class women were encouraged to be pretty and popular and strive for male approval. They were advised to "dress as well as your means will allow, dress becomingly, and dress modestly; give every attention to your underclothing." While the *Press* lauded men for their civic and work activities, it ran popularity contests for women—for the most popular teacher, the most popular married woman, or the most popular clerk in the District. Jennie Wolf, "the popular and attractive saleslady at Pierce Cigar Store," won a theater box. The *Press* had no doubt that she would "be a charming hostess and sustain her position with grace and dignity."[42]

Labor demanded respect for feminine gentility. Even union politics could not absolve the man who swore in the presence of a lady. Ed Boyce could criticize President McKinley on the Fourth of July, but there were limits to what a man could say when women were present. Shortly after McKinley was shot in 1901, the *Press* reported that

> Residents of Victor Avenue in the vicinity of Sixth Street are incensed over the speech of one Jim Olvie in that locality yesterday noon. . . . Yesterday Mrs. Ed. Vinton, wife of a letter carrier, remarked that the president was growing better. Olvie is alleged to have expressed his regret with much profanity and some obscenity in the presence of ladies and particularly to Mrs. Walenberg. The latter is the wife of P. Walenberg, a member of the executive board of the miners' union, and a lady of respectability and refinement. Olvie, she states, referred to the president as a s— of a b— and hoped he would die.[43]

Women might expect chivalrous amenities, but the public veneer often hid more mundane realities. For all the genteel language condemning Jim Olvie, the simple fact was that Olvie called McKinley a son-of-a-bitch, and Mrs. Walenberg apparently rushed to quote him to the *Press*. Although it may have been conventional to avoid profanity in front of women, most had probably heard some. Behind the restrained prose of the labor press lay occasional glimpses of less-than-idyllic marriages. One item, for example, reported that a man named Joe Chenowyth had slashed his wife with a razor because dinner was not ready. Most women I interviewed remembered men who spent their paychecks for drink or knew of women who had been battered; some had personally witnessed domestic violence.[44] Beneath the protestations of domestic respectability were some unhappy women who elected the only ways out they knew. Some sixty divorces were reported in the *Press* between 1899 and 1901. Women were the plaintiffs in most of these actions and were much more likely to claim cruelty and desertion than were men.[45]

Some couples lived apart, and wives left the District for months at a time. Separations were generally explained in acceptably genteel terms. Vacations were to benefit the wife's health, and couples lived in separate cities for the health of the family or the children's educations. Although some families lived apart through necessity rather than choice or because they felt it important to establish some home base rather than move with each fluctuation of an unstable industry, for others, separations may have been solutions for domestic discord.[46]

The distanced language of the labor press obscured most women's realities of work and family concerns related to childbearing and child rearing. The idealized picture of working-class domesticity contained a kernel of truth. Women *were* "often hard worked." The language of idealized domesticity likely reflected labor's desire to claim respectability, one ingredient of the public authority that union leaders shared with professionals and merchants, and of their common identities as married breadwinners. Elizabeth Hampsten, analyzing class differences in the language of rural women, observed that nineteenth-century language instruction "strongly advocated rising class expectations" so that more public documents used more formal and genteel language. "I have found," she wrote, "that this language of composition differs markedly from the conversational talk encountered in the letters and diaries of working women," whose "highly oral" written language was similar to that used in oral history interviews.[47] Although the public language of the labor press supported notions of female submissiveness, purity, and leisured domesticity, other sources suggest that the District's working-class women understood their lives quite differently. Domestic ideology was sufficiently pliable to function differently in the public discourse through which labor presented itself and the private discourse in which working-class women and men expressed their relationships.

Married women rarely engaged in wage work outside their homes, but they frequently tended vegetable gardens and small livestock, made clothing, did housework, and provided income by keeping boarders, cooking, or doing laundry at home. Mine shutdowns, strikes, and accidents made women periodically responsible for supporting families. A man's death meant that a woman must work for wages, take in boarders, or otherwise support herself and her family. When, for instance, Anne Ellis's husband was killed when he drilled into a missed shot in the Vindicator Mine, the Knights of Pythias arranged the funeral. After Ellis released the mine from liability it gave her $600, and each man who worked on the Vindicator donated a day's wages. Beyond that, Ellis was on her own with two children to support. At first she lived by selling baked goods — her landlady promised to "see that all the girls" of the nearby sporting district bought Ellis's wares. Later she kept boarders.[48]

Family needs shaped women's work. Women were much more likely than men to live with families — 92 percent as opposed to 69 percent of the male population. Only 2.4 percent of all women lived alone or with unrelated adults, obligated to care only for themselves. Women cared for both the elderly and the young. As people aged, they were more likely to live with extended families, board, or live with unrelated adults. More than 65 percent of the adult female population lived in households with children, but only 47 percent of the men did.[49] Children meant increased financial responsibility for a father. For women, both children and the elderly meant more work.

When the census takers visited in 1900, more than a third of all women cared for adults outside their immediate families. Twenty-one percent kept boarders, and another 15.5 percent cared for extended family or other adults. Sometime in their lives, most working-class women probably cared for extended kin or boarders. Women served the domestic needs of the surplus male population, keeping lodgers or boarders in their homes, running boarding and rooming houses, doing laundry at home or in commercial establishments, and selling sex and companionship. About four men in ten (37 percent) lived in boardinghouses or in family households that kept boarders (table 14). Nearly an equal proportion of women lived with boarders or extended families, but most of these women were domestic caretakers rather than boarders themselves. Boarders meant more work for a woman but more income for her family.

The life of a working-class woman in Cripple Creek, then, was generally quite different from the sheltered domesticity the labor press suggested. A young woman might work for wages for a short time before marriage, generally in poorly paid service occupations that did not provide her the financial independence to live alone. Her choices became sex work or marriage. She was likely to marry before her mid-twenties and to combine housecleaning and childcare with some household production. She might supplement the family income by keeping boarders or doing cooking or laundry at home, but her world was largely domestic. That did not mean it was leisured. Quite the opposite. Most working-class women spent most of their lives doing domestic work for others. And they frequently had little to show for their lives of labor. Two-and-a-half times more women than men were widowed (table 2), but only one widowed person in five owned a home.[50] Home ownership was

TABLE 14
Household Type by Sex, 1900

Household Type	Men		Women		District	
	N	%	N	%	N	%
Single person	77	6	18	2	95	5
Nuclear family	500	40	502	61	1,002	48
Extended family	138	11	127	15	265	13
Family and boarders	233	18	130	16	363	17
Unrelated adults	78	6	2	—	80	4
Boardinghouse	239	19	43	5	282	14
	1,265	100	822	99	2,087	101

Source: Manuscript census, Teller County, Colo., 1900, random sample of 2,089 adults, less incomplete data on 2 persons.

Note: Extended families included eight households that housed a nuclear family and unrelated adults not identified as lodgers or boarders. Of the families that housed boarders, four also included unrelated adults not identified as lodgers. Columns 4 and 6 do not total 100 percent due to rounding.

particularly significant for widows because they frequently had dependent children and because their homes, as boardinghouses, provided one of their best avenues to self-support. Kathleen Welch Chapman remembered that keeping a rooming house gave her widowed Grandmother Doran a measure of independence. Catharine Doran lost that autonomy and all her possessions in the Victor fire of 1899, however. "I don't remember ever, Grandma ever having anything for herself after that," Chapman said. "She just stayed around [with her daughters]."[51]

As this picture of dependent old age suggests, women's daily domestic experiences contradicted the rosy picture the *Press* painted. Far from leading easy and sheltered lives, women expected marriage to be a working partnership and appear to have understood the value of their family labor. Despite the image of comfortable homes with "modern conveniences" the *Press* offered, no woman I interviewed had a washing machine before 1915, and few had running water. They cooked on coal or wood stoves; hauled water for cooking, cleaning, and washing; sometimes carried and heated water for baths for men on different shifts at the mines; did the family baking; sewed and mended; raised and processed vegetables at high altitudes; and cared for children, spouses, extended family, and boarders. All of this was more than a full-time occupation. One woman I interviewed baked fifteen loaves of bread twice a week. Leslie Wilkinson remembered clearly how hard his mother worked: "Bake day, mending day. A certain day for a certain thing. That's what I remember, those special days that my Ma had. Ironing, cooking, and washing, every day. Then her day, Friday, was mending day. She always sat down and mended everything that had to be mended. . . . Oh, it went on to maybe eleven o'clock at night, my mother'd be ironing, the door wide open." Kathleen Welch Chapman described how much housework had changed from her childhood, when she scrubbed clothes on a washboard and hauled fuel in and ashes out. Hannah Welch, she said, was "never was idle. I never knew Mama to be idle."[52]

Cripple Creek women expected and found lives of hard work. As one woman said when asked what she expected of marriage, "Just what I got. A lot of hard work. And if you were lucky you didn't have too many children." Women's work multiplied as their families did, and they shared information about the female life-cycle, including how to avoid pregnancy. The strains of childbearing and the work involved in caring for small children distinguished women's lives from men's. As one woman told me, "One thing that was nice, after you went through menopause, you didn't have to worry. You don't have to figure on a calendar and figure up so many days, you know."[53] It is not surprising, then, that women discussed the consequences of sexuality if not sex itself.

Although information about a number of birth control techniques was available in print before 1873, the passage of the Comstock laws, which made it illegal to mail contraceptive information, pushed the subject even further underground. Still, women discussed sexuality and related topics. One woman told me that she did not know how her mother "kept from having more than she did." As a child, she was locked out of the living room while her mother's friends visited and the "woman talk was going on."[54] Like Leslie Wilkinson's mother, many women maintained a day or a part of a day when they did sewing or fancy work and their friends visited. Others frequently spent a day with close friends or female relatives and shared work and "woman talk."

Whether or not a woman's mother explained the facts of life to her, some older woman usually offered advice. One woman I interviewed told me that her mother-in-law told her to douche to avoid pregnancy.[55] May Wing, who grew up in the Cripple Creek District and other Colorado mining towns and who was married in Leadville in 1907, described how older women told younger women about sexuality: "Well, usually when a girl was going to be married, these old ladies would tell them. I imagine if my mother had been alive, she would. But my second step-mother, she used to talk to us girls a lot. And then they was a lady that lived next door. When she heard I was going to be married, she asked me over to tea one day. She asked me if I knew anything, and then she told me a lot of things."[56] The variety of contraceptives reported indicates a lot of woman talk:

Now, I know, when I was married, the older women, they used Vaseline a lot. They said a greased egg wouldn't hatch. And then a lot of them used salt. They would use this, you know, that they put in ice cream, this rock salt. . . . I never did use the rock salt. Because we were told that it wasn't a good thing to use—it affected the mind. . . . And then, of course, we were more or less a little bit careful. I suppose the Catholics called it the rhythm, you know, and we were taught on that. Well, of course, we were always told as long as you nursed a baby, you wouldn't conceive. You see, you wouldn't menstruate. So I didn't, I nursed [my son] until he was eighteen months old. . . . They was a lady come through one time, and she asked if we used birth control, and she had a recipe, or a receipt, whichever you'd call it. She took cocoa butter, and you took a shoebox, with the top on it, and then you put holes in it. Then you put this melted cocoa butter in it. Then there was something else she used to put in it—what was it? They used to use it to wash . . . the babies' eyes out. Boric acid. So much boric acid with so much cocoa butter. And you made these—they'd be a little cone, like, and you'd use those. We made them together, this [friend] and I; we met the lady. . . . Yes, it worked. And in later years, in the magazine, you saw where there was a rubber kind of a thing, that you would insert in your vagina. Like a diaphragm.[57]

Women's identities revolved around their labor, both productive and reproductive. Working-class women were not preoccupied so much with true womanhood as with distinguishing good women from bad. Productive work was good if performed for one's family. Wage work might be good unless it implied that a man was not an adequate provider. Paid sex work was bad. A good woman worked hard for her family and may have enjoyed sex or initiated it.[58] She was defined largely by what she was not—a woman of the half world or, in some people's view, a woman who worked outside the home for wages at all. "A single woman—a good woman didn't usually work. There was enough at home to help mother with," one woman said. A good woman "wasn't a woman on the Row, or she didn't have men chasing her. Or she didn't chase men. That was a good woman."[59]

Though the women I interviewed distinguished good women from bad, they were by no means as innocent of the red-light districts or as disapproving of the women who worked there as public discourse suggested. Most girls were at least aware of prostitution, because in both Cripple Creek and Victor they had to walk through the red-light districts to go to school. In Cripple Creek the interurban trains ran down Myers Avenue, and in both Cripple Creek and Victor the opera houses stood in the heart of the tenderloin.[60] In the smaller towns, prostitutes were not segregated, but they were still stigmatized. Leslie Spell recalled that when he was a child in Barry (later Anaconda), some dance hall women rented the house next door. "One of those girls had a small son who always played alone in his backyard. When my small brother Cline climbed to the top of our fence and asked him to come over to play the little boy said: 'No, my mother is a whore and says I am to stay home.' Cline came running to mother and asked, 'Mama, what's a whore? Boy says his mother's one and he can't play with me.'"[61]

Some women expressed sympathy for prostitutes and understood that their choices were rooted in limited options. One felt that the red light district was a good thing because it protected the virtue of good women's daughters. And one was, as an adult, friends with a retired prostitute who married a local man. Good women and bad women were a little like the children, separated by fences that hid how similar their lives might have been.[62]

❀   ❀   ❀

Although there was a women's community that revolved around work and the female life-cycle, and although the women themselves seem to have been more realistic about their lives and about "bad" women's options than the labor press suggested, private relationships among women did not affect labor's public prescriptions of appropriate gender roles, nor did good women shape working-class policy. Union policies reflected the life-cycles of working-class men, who, when they were younger and learning their trades, found companionship with other men, dance hall workers, and prostitutes. When they gained years and skill, they earned higher wages, married younger women, and rigorously separated their families from the world of sexual commerce. Their public discourse labeled labor's women as "good," and therefore preoccupied with home, family, and civic morality, an assumption that shaped understandings of women's social power and labor politics.

Some union tactics, particularly consumer boycotts, required women's support. Working-class women controlled daily consumer purchases. But because they did not earn the family paychecks, their purchasing power did not buy female authority. Instead, the labor press projected images of dependent helpmates who must be kept from betraying organized labor by buying non-union goods. Because purchasing power was a vital union weapon, labor courted women for their control of household budgets and told them that they belonged to unions through their husbands. As one woman wrote, "My husband is a member of a labor union. Am I not his better half? The good husband brings his union wages to his wife. That is as it should be. But if the wife spends the union wages for nonunion goods, she is undoing the work of the labor unions."[63] The District Trades Assembly formed a Women's Auxiliary to organize support for union label drives, saying: "The results of researches made by the home industry committee have convinced the assembly that so long as the wives and home keepers of union men remained in a measure indifferent to the sources from which the necessities of life were supplied, just so long would their efforts in behalf of the blue label be but partially successful."[64]

Suffrage bought women some recognition, but it was often offered in genteel domestic and moral terms. Labor assumed that women were less partisan than men and that special appeals were necessary to win their votes. Those appeals were based on neither feminist nor class goals, but on the presumed moral and domestic concerns of working-class women. Women were asked to support Democrats in 1900 because Republicans squandered education funds and because women were "more intimate with the home and school life of the children than the husband." The WFM decided to organize women's auxiliaries in 1902, in part because it was adopting a policy of political action and it "estimated that by organizing the women just about two hundred thousand votes will be added to the political strength of the organization." The *Press* acknowledged women's political importance, agreeing with Elizabeth Cady Stanton that "the question of trusts, imperialism, free silver, and other political issues are of no consequence or importance whatever compared to the emancipation of women."[65] There was, however, more opportunism than conviction in this pronouncement, which was intended to encourage women to vote against an anti-union politician who had opposed suffrage.

Allegiance to womanly virtue and working-class domesticity generated political hostility toward prostitutes, probably the largest group of women wage-earners in the District. This stance undermined possibilities for the political success of organized labor in the important 1899 election. After Teller County was created in 1899, making possible working-class control of county government, the unions formed the Co-operative Party and joined with Populists to run a labor slate for county offices. Assuming that union strength guaranteed male support and that only the women's vote must be won, organized labor made the only real campaign issue the suppression of gambling and prostitution.[66]

Labor adopted the "good civic housekeeping" argument of many suffragists and asked women to prove their right to vote by opposing local vice. "The ladies have an opportunity to show that the right of suffrage has not been thrown away upon them—the opportunity to throw their influence for purity in politics," the *Press* announced. The labor candidates would enforce laws "for the protection of the homes against those who debauch the husbands and fathers." Women should support the labor slate because when women demanded "justice by enfranchisement they did not have to ask how organized labor stood upon that." The *Press* reminded voters that "every gambler, every keeper of a bawdy house, every man in the Cripple Creek District who makes a living by violating the law, is working and fighting for either the democratic or republican candidates for county offices." Some women organized the Women's Co-operative-People's Club to support the ticket. But purity was no vote grabber. The Co-operatives came in an abysmal third to the Democrats and the Republican-Silver Republican coalition.[67]

Neither union power, the class understandings developed by organized labor, nor the daily concerns of working-class women sufficiently explain the tactics adopted in the 1899 election campaign. A highly organized and class-conscious labor community projected political goals and tactics, not from class understandings but from moral concepts of home, family, and sex. Mining town demography doomed labor's crusade against vice. It was foolish to rely on men to oppose prostitution when more than 45 percent of all men and half of all workers were not married. Other political issues were certainly more riveting. Moreover, eliminating vice would have reduced municipal revenues. Saloons and gamblers paid license fees, and prostitutes and dance hall women paid monthly taxes to work legally: $16 for madames, $6 for parlor house prostitutes, and $4 for crib women and dance hall workers. In addition, all prostitutes had to pay for periodic physical examinations.[68]

Labor never targeted the saloons. A married man could drink moderately without losing his manhood—in some circles he had to drink to demonstrate it. But the definition of working-class domesticity permitted, and perhaps required, attacks on dance halls and prostitution. The 1899 election strategy could not bridge the gap between daily experience and the idealized gender roles union leaders espoused. Women were neither as sheltered nor as powerful as the union rhetoric suggested. Labor's moral politics targeted many women's jobs and unmarried men's heterosexual options and denied the economic importance of women's household labor and wage work. The most notable failure of the 1899 election was that labor did not encourage working-class women to write their own political platform. Their real daily concerns might, for instance, have generated demands to extend sewer lines and running water to working-class neighborhoods.

Industrial change not only produced the conditions that encouraged miners to organize but also masked the role of domestic work in the productive process and made wage work the province of men. It is not surprising that women and households were not integral parts of class understanding; that analysis began to be formulated only as the economic role of the household became more narrowly restricted to consumption and as married women moved in greater numbers into the paid work force. So long as domestic and productive roles appeared separate, men could be seen primarily as workers and women primarily as homemakers. These goals were accessible in Cripple Creek for a married working-class minority. Until they changed nationally for the white middle class, their inherent interdependence received little serious analysis.

The failure to include women in policymaking expressed masculine definitions of respectability and success and the prevailing male perception of women as subordinate. By idealizing women's economic dependence on their husbands and men's economic responsibility for their families, labor reinforced an economic hierarchy. If women were dependent on male wages, men were equally dependent on unpleasant jobs and could not easily risk unemployment by individually challenging working conditions.[69]

Organized labor combated individualism by providing social explanations and responses for the economic position of working-class men. But successful unions and an overwhelmingly male work force paradoxically reinforced the domestic ideals of an individualist age. The ability to provide for a family was such an important measure of working-class manhood that labor idealized the domestic achievements of the married leadership. These definitions of masculine respectability and working-class success rendered women's work socially invisible, generated political programs that alienated many working-class men, and excluded the unorganized women who served laboring men in the demimonde and at home. Ultimately, the unions' moral political crusades failed because they did not speak to significant issues for working-class constituents. They were not the most compelling daily concerns of miners or of working-class wives. And they threatened dance hall musicians, bartenders, and women sex workers whose jobs they targeted.

6

A WHITE MAN'S CAMP

An odd assortment of citizens, united in a common cause, gathered at the Victor Miners' Union Hall in February 1902. Mine manager Sherman Bell presided. A succession of politicians, businessmen, and labor leaders addressed the crowd. Representatives of all three Victor WFM locals spoke: William Fechyew and T. D. Foster from the Victor Miners' local, F. W. Frewen, secretary of Excelsior Engineers No. 80, and C. M. Green of the Banner Mill and Smeltermen. Trades Assembly president A. R. Bernier, WFM District Executive Board member Joy Pollard of Altman, *Daily Press* lodge editor Mrs. D. H. Elder, and WFM *Miners' Magazine* editor John M. O'Neill spoke as well. The union leaders shared the platform with Bell; with two local merchants, Samuel G. Porter of the Cripple Creek Coal and Transportation Company and clothier R. E. Ellsberry; and with three politicians—former Victor mayor W. J. Donnelley, Victor city engineer F. V. Bodfish, and former Colorado attorney general Eugene Engley.[1]

Although their cause was political, the speakers parted company each election day. Sherman Bell, Frank Frewen, and Fred Bodfish were Republicans. Bernier was a former Populist turned Democrat. Donnelley, elected mayor on the Co-operative ticket in 1899, supported William Jennings Bryan for president in 1900. Porter and Foster were Democrats, Engley and O'Neill had moved from radical populism to the Socialist Party. Fechyew, a former Social Democrat served, in 1902, on the Colorado Socialist Party executive committee.[2]

Mrs. Elder apparently devoted herself to lodge work. The wife of a union hoistman, both Elders belonged to the Yeomen. Mrs. Elder also belonged to the AOUW's Degree of Honor and the King's Daughters. She wrote for the Yeomen *Shield* in addition to editing lodge news for the *Press*.

The issue that united this unlikely crew spanned differences of politics, class, and, to varying degrees, ethnicity and gender. Regardless of occupation or ethnic heritage, they all claimed a common racial identity as whites.[3] They gathered to lobby Congress to renew the Chinese Exclusion Act of 1882 and to extend it to ban Japanese. The president of the Victor Miners' Union presented resolutions to the meeting. Everyone agreed that given "the higher standard of living of the Caucasian race than that of the Mongolian race" it was "an utter impossibility for the white race to compete with the Mongolian race in the labor market."[4] They supported Asian exclusion to maintain Cripple Creek, and by extension the United States, as a "white man's camp."

Although Euro-American miners rallied to preserve "white men's camps" throughout the mining West, the racial and gender assumptions of that concept went largely unexamined. The phrase "a white man's camp" was common, but its precise meanings varied. "Whiteness" meant different things in different places. The Victor meeting was one of countless acts that defined the racial boundaries and racial-ethnic hierarchies of particular communities.[5]

Anti-Chinese campaigns punctuated western mining from the early days of the California gold rush and the Comstock Lode. But anti-Chinese racism by no means exhausted the racial and ethnic prejudices of the western working class. Local racial boundaries depended in part on regional racial ethnic populations, on when each group arrived, on regional economies, and on local occupational structures. All of these factors contributed to the complex historical constructions of racial-ethnic identities and relationships throughout the mining West. In Rossland, British Columbia, most gold miners came from Britain, the United States, or Canada and traced their ethnic origins to England, Scotland, Ireland, or Wales. But significant minorities of Swedes, Italians, and Germans also labored there. More Italians and Chinese lived in Rossland than in Cripple Creek, but they faced heavy discrimination. In Utah, native-born miners and immigrants from northern and western Europe tried to exclude Greeks, Japanese, and Mexican Americans from their WFM local. Cripple Creek miners never let them in the District. The coal camps along the Union Pacific railroad in Wyoming first drew workers from England, Ireland, Wales, China, and Japan, but after 1900 the UP recruited southern and eastern European rather than British or Asian labor. By 1910 the coal towns of Sweetwater County, Wyoming, housed almost two-thirds immigrants, predominantly eastern Europeans barred from Cripple Creek—Hungarians, Austrians, Italians, and Slavs (Croatians, Czechs, Poles, Serbs, Slovaks, and Slovenes). In Butte, but not in Cripple Creek, Italians and Finns worked the mines by 1910, as well as the Irish and Cornish. This did not mean that ethnic relationships were amicable. In 1912, for example, five hundred Finnish miners fired by the Amalgamated Mining Company complained to the WFM leadership that the Butte Miners' Union overwhelmingly refused to support its Finnish members. In Arizona and New Mexico a dual labor system separated "white" workers from Mexicans and Mexican Americans. In Colorado, Mexicans and Mexican Americans might work in the coal mines or sugar beet fields but not in the hard-rock gold and silver mines. A "white man's camp" in Cripple Creek meant excluding Asians, southern and eastern Europeans, and Mexican Americans—but not African Americans.[6]

People defined race and ethnicity in particular historical circumstances within a larger social web of shared identities and concepts of difference. "Whiteness" subsumed differences among disparate Europeans, just as American slavery had reduced a variety of Africans to the single category "black." "Whiteness" in Cripple Creek defined who was barred from the District. For the ethnic people who lived there, whiteness connected many ethnic heritages that remained important sources of individual and social identity. Race and ethnicity were both exclusive and inclusive concepts. They defined who was kept out and what linked and separated the diverse people who could stay.

Ethnicity did not rigidly determine behavior. Like all social identities, race and ethnicity were malleable concepts. In Cripple Creek, as elsewhere, people continually redefined the meanings of their ethnic identities. Ethnic cultures provided reservoirs of symbols, observances, values, and behaviors among which people could choose and which they could change through daily practice. Those cultural reservoirs, most of all, held memories—shared histories through which people located their own experience and understood social relationships.[7]

Ethnic identities coexisted with identities of race and religion. Whiteness could link many people who might also, through necessity or choice, maintain distinct ethnic and religious identities. Like other social identities, race and ethnicity had material roots. Organized labor's racial policies expressed a conflicted mixture of coexistence, respect, and racist stereotyping, depending on which racial ethnic group was involved and its relationship to the union work force. Workers created racial barriers and social boundaries through daily relationships that constructed the local work force and tied it to regional economies.

The District's holiday parades reflected local social boundaries fairly precisely. Working-class white men marched together with other white men—merchants and professionals—and separate from white women and African Americans. These divisions reflected shared identities of race and gender. They also reflected what linked the local work force with community power. With a few exceptions, the workers, merchants, and professionals who met at local lodge halls and celebrated holidays together belonged, collectively, to what the Knights of Labor had called "the producing classes." The white male public community and public power structure crossed the line between the working and middle classes. Merchants, professionals, and skilled workers, particularly settled residents and married homeowners, located themselves at the center of local civic authority.

White women and African American women and men also worked, to be sure, but they did not share public authority, nor did they threaten the white male occupational structure. The local work force was segmented by race and gender. Women performed domestic labor and service work, either at home or in the paid work force. African American men worked mostly as saloon porters, janitors, and cooks; African American women as domestic servants. Women of all races and African American men did not impinge to any great extent on white men's work or public status.

To ensure that no one else did, fierce local barriers excluded Asians and southern and eastern Europeans. The shared bonds of white manhood became most explicit through racist anti-Asian politics that crossed class lines. The regional mining economy provided other alternatives for Mexican Americans and "new" immigrants from southern and eastern Europe. These "outsiders" could work elsewhere in Colorado, and District workers clearly preferred that they do so. They might work in the mills and smelters of Colorado City or Denver, in the steel mills in Pueblo, or in the coal mines of northern and southern Colorado, but not in the gold camp.[8] Rather than organize Chinese, Greeks, Slavs, Italians, or Mexican Americans, the "white" miners of Cripple Creek banned them and joined with merchants and managers to campaign for Asian exclusion.[9]

While they policed their racial barricades, District miners minimized the interethnic discord that divided European immigrants in earlier mining camps, where animosities between the Irish and the Cornish splintered the working class. From the 1860s, there was strong Irish-Cornish rivalry throughout the West, fueled by the bitter history of Ireland and by tensions between skilled Cornish miners and anyone less experienced. In contrast with the early hard-rock camps, Cornish-Irish hatred did not publicly divide District labor.[10] Some anti-Irish and anti-Catholic prejudice clearly persisted in Cripple Creek, but shared class interests among workers also blunted ethnic differences among older northwestern European immigrants.

It would be foolish to assume that the prejudices that were so evident among the previous generation of miners and that endured in other localities magically disappeared in Cripple Creek. But they were not prominent in public discourse and had little evident impact on labor policy. Why should this be so?

First, the overwhelming majority of District residents and of the working class were native-born Americans. There were fewer immigrants than in other mining communities. There was also greater residential integration among the native-born and immigrants than in some other mining towns. Greater residential concentrations of immigrants existed in the southeastern corner of the District, in the communities of Goldfield, Independence, and Altman around the Bull Hill and Battle Mountain mines, a fact that reflected that more immigrants were miners. But there were few real ethnic residential enclaves. Scattered clusters of households had common ethnic roots, and there was a small settlement called "Swede Gulch" near Anaconda, but for the most part Irish, Germans, Scots, English, Canadians, Swedes, and Welsh lived close to one another, to their second-generation descendants, and the native-born majority. In one Independence rooming house, one could meet the Clancys from Ireland, a Sweeney from Michigan, Enoch from Ohio, Mathews from England, Johnson and Peterson from Sweden, and a Stewart from Canada. At Sarah Carlisle's boardinghouse, the English-born proprietor and a Scottish chambermaid filled lunchboxes daily for eleven miners: Sarah's husband Samuel, also an English immigrant; two Irish immigrants; a German; a Canadian; two second-generation Irish; a second-generation Englishman; a Louisianan born to an English father and German mother; and two native-born men with native-born parents. The Anaconda hotel run by D. F. and Josephine O'Shea, both second-generation Irish, housed the O'Sheas, their two children, three Canadian-born miners, three Swedes, one German, one man born in Scotland to Irish parents, two second-generation Irish, a second-generation German, eight native-born miners whose parents were native-born (including two named O'Bryan and Flynn), and a miner's wife whose father was German and mother was Irish. The homes around the O'Shea hotel housed Welsh, Canadians, Irish, Scots-Irish, English, native-born citizens, and one second-generation German whose wife was Hungarian. These examples, pulled at random from the 1900 manuscript census, illustrate ethnic immigrants' proximity to other groups, even in some of the more heavily immigrant neighborhoods around the mines.[11]

In part, no immigrant group was large enough or separate enough to form a distinct ethnic enclave. In part, too, skill divisions among Cornish, Welsh, and Irish miners were largely a thing of the past. Although some Irish immigrants on the older hard-rock frontiers had mining experience, many began as unskilled mine workers, while the Cornish brought their mining experience with them. By the 1890s, however, the Irish were among the most skilled miners in industrial hard-rock towns, a product of their experience in the older hard-rock camps and in eastern lead and coal.

Many of the older, skilled miners were immigrants with long experience in western mining. More miners, therefore, were foreign-born than any other group of workers in the District. One worker in four (25 percent) was an immigrant, as were 29 percent of miners and 25 percent of proprietors. In contrast, 13 percent of salaried workers, 15 percent of professionals, and 5 percent of capitalists were foreign-born. Put another way, an immigrant in Cripple Creek was more likely to be a miner or other wageworker and less likely to be white-collar than was a native-born citizen.[12]

But in contrast to the earlier mining towns, immigrants constituted a minority of both miners and the working class. In 1860 more than half of Grass Valley's male workers and almost half of Nevada City's were immigrants. Roughly one Grass

Valley workingman in five was born in Ireland, another in England, mostly from Cornwall. In the Comstock mines, the Cornish and Irish each comprised a third of all miners; only one miner in five was native-born. A majority of Idaho miners in 1870 were Chinese, and almost half the remaining miners in five Idaho camps were immigrants.[13] Butte's population in 1900 was 26 percent first- or second-generation Irish alone, excluding other ethnic immigrants. But in Cripple Creek in 1900, only about three miners in ten were immigrants. The Irish population, although the largest Euro-ethnic group, was proportionately half the size of Butte's. First- and second-generation Irish combined comprised only 13 percent of the District's population, compared with 26 percent in Butte; fewer than 4 percent were born in England (table 1).[14]

The corollary to the District's distinct demography was that it was less advantageous there than elsewhere to maintain ethnic identities in order to get jobs in the mines. Maintaining ethnic identity for some groups was at least in part a matter of choice. Ronald James has argued that for the Cornish, who were white, English-speaking, and Protestant, and might have expected more ready acceptance than other immigrants, Cornish identity retained positive value because it marked Cornishmen as skilled and experienced miners. It helped them get hired by Cornish shift bosses and superintendents. Irishness functioned in much the same way in some Butte mines. Ethnicity thus held a positive economic value for Cornishmen seeking work in Grass Valley or on the Comstock or for the Irish in Butte.[15] In Cripple Creek, some Irish and Cornish men controlled hiring, but both shift bosses and miners were more native-born, and bosses were more ethnically diverse than elsewhere. There was less need to compete, too, because there was enough work to go around, particularly for highly skilled, experienced immigrant miners. Ethnicity could, in such circumstances, be a source of identity and pride without the need to mobilize ethnic rivalries in the marketplace.

If immigrants were more likely than the native-born to be working class and to be miners, that was no social handicap during the union era. Certainly, miners were at greater physical risk than anyone else in the District, but they were also the largest and key occupational group. They belonged to the most influential unions in a union camp and earned the relatively high wages of mining labor. In Grass Valley in 1860 and 1870, the foreign-born, especially the Irish, were at the bottom of the property hierarchy.[16] Home ownership is the only available index for wealth in the Cripple Creek District, and although the size and value of homes varied, by this single index it was no economic handicap to be an immigrant or a miner. Proportionately more immigrants owned homes in 1900 than did native-born Americans, and miners were among the most propertied. Nearly 48 percent of all household heads owned their homes. Only four occupational groups exceeded that average. They were, in order, miner, professional, mining capitalist, and skilled mining worker (table 15). Second-generation immigrants were the most likely to own their own homes (53 percent of households), followed by immigrants (51 percent) and then the native-born (47 percent). Native-born children of native parents were the least propertied (45 percent).[17]

There were, however, significant differences in home ownership, depending on nationality. A majority of all immigrants were propertied, except the Canadians and the Welsh, but proportionately more Irish owned homes (62 percent) than other immigrants.[18] The historical significance of property as a source of stability for the Irish may explain some of the differences in home ownership. But home owner-ship and the stability it signified was most strongly connected to age and skill and the occupational status that accompanied them. Immigrants were generally older than their neighbors (table 16). Age translated to more mining experience, which in turn generated the means to buy property. It was reflected in marital status as well; immigrants were more likely than others to be widowed.[19] Specific immi-grants, particularly the Irish and English, were most likely to buy homes, to be miners, and to have the years and experience that bought stability, property, and respect. All of these factors—age, marital status, skill, occupation, and home own-ership—reflected the long experience in mining that made skilled immigrants and their children the elite of the local working class. Home ownership reflected the fact that a union town with extensive long-term mining offered miners the chance to settle and establish a home and family. For merchants, professionals, and work-ers with more portable skills it was a place to make money and, perhaps, to leave.

Diverse ethnic heritages made Cripple Creek a cosmopolitan cultural meeting ground. The traditions and celebrations of many ethnic cultures enriched local social life. A number of ethnic organizations flourished. Irish residents could join the Sheridan and Sarsfield clubs or the Ancient Order of Hibernians. The small Jewish community built Temple B'rith Abraham in 1900 and formed a B'nai B'rith chapter with some seventy members. The Swedish citizens of Anaconda and Cripple Creek organized a social group called the Belmont Club, and the Scandi-navians of Victor hosted socials. Scandinavian Democrats formed a Scandinavian Bryan and Stevenson Club in 1900 and an organization of Swedish American Democrats the following year. Scots established the Lodge of Royal Highlanders and the Caledonian Club of the Cripple Creek District and regularly celebrated Robert Burns's birthday. They established a Burns memorial fund and sponsored a concert to raise funds for it; Gov. J. R. Orman presided, and *Miners' Magazine* editor John M. O'Neill spoke on "Burns as a Hero and Educator to Mankind." The Welsh celebrated the birthday of their patron saint, St. David. The Irish and much of the rest of the District celebrated St. Patrick's Day. The *Press* was printed in green ink on March 17, 1900, the Swedes gave a St. Patrick's Day ball, and the Sheridan Club hosted celebrations for the District's Irish.[20]

TABLE 15
Home Ownership by Occupation, Heads of Households Only, 1900

Occupation	Rent		Own		Unknown	
	N	%	N	%	N	%
Working class						
Mining semiskilled	3	60	1	20	1	20
Mining skilled	24	44	27	50	3	6
Miner	106	37	159	56	20	7
Unskilled	31	66	13	28	3	6
Semiskilled	43	60	26	36	3	4
Skilled	51	52	46	47	1	1
Salaried/clerical						
Salaried workers	6	46	5	39	2	15
Salaried mining	6	55	5	45		
Business						
Proprietors	39	43	42	47	9	10
Mining proprietors	1	100				
Professionals						
Professionals	13	45	16	55		
Mining professionals	3	60	2	40		
Capitalists						
Capitalists	6	55	5	45		
Mining capitalists	4	50	4	50		

Source: Manuscript census, Teller County, Colo., 1900, 771 heads of households in a random sample of 2,089 adults, less 9 household heads whose occupations were unknown and 32 who fell into the "other" category and whose home-ownership status as a group would mean little.

TABLE 16
Proportion of Adult Population under
Thirty-one and Forty-one by Nativity, 1900

Birthplace	Under Thirty-one	Under Forty-one
Canada	25%	60%
England	39	64
Germany	26	67
Ireland	25	60
Scotland	37	69
Sweden	36	83
Wales	21	79
District	45	75

Source: Manuscript census, Teller County, Colo., 1900, random sample of 2,089 adults.

O'Neill's tribute to Burns and the Swedes' St. Patrick's Day ball suggest that ethnicity could serve as a bridge among groups as well as a protective social boundary. Differences among northern and western Europeans, or between them and native-born Americans, surfaced only rarely in public documents. The one exception was the frequent reference to "Rednecks," which, in public discourse at least, was not a slur but a term of working-class pride and respect. Many Rednecks were older, highly skilled, property owners. Far outnumbered by the native-born, even in mining, the Irish commanded considerable status for their skill and prominence as union leaders.

Still, the extent of interethnic harmony is difficult to gauge without access to records that might reflect greater discord, like local union minutes. Interviews and other sources suggested that Catholics and Protestants expressed some animosity that was mobilized particularly around class conflicts during strikes.[21] The Colorado Springs press equated Irish Catholics with lawlessness and union militancy in the 1894 strike, associations that also surfaced in memories of the second strike.

Anti-Catholic prejudice in the District appears to have centered more on class issues than on religion itself. Two people recalled in interviews that "APA" and "Redneck" were schoolyard taunts. (APAs, members of the American Protective Association, were nativists who opposed all immigration, not just for Catholics. The Victor APA chapter was headquartered at the Masonic Temple.) Because those two individuals were an Irish Protestant and a German Catholic, the terms clearly carried significance beyond the simple designation of Irish Catholicism. The German Catholic woman had, as a child, associated "Redneck" only with a color and retorted by calling her tormentor a greenhorn. She remembered the insult specifically in the context of the 1903–4 strike and learned that Rednecks were presumed to be pro-union. The Irish Protestant recalled bad feeling between the religious groups when she was a child. "The Catholics were Rednecks. And they had another organization—the APAs. Well, the worst thing that could be said to a child, if they were a Protestant, then it was a Redneck, or vice versa."[22]

The religious and ethnic divisions expressed in the terms *APA* and *Redneck* reflected class as well. Given the higher proportions of immigrants within the working class and the native-born, Protestant backgrounds of most owners, the terms could on occasion serve as shorthand for "owner" and "worker." But the same divisions could threaten working-class unity. When Eugene Debs addressed the Cripple Creek Trades Assembly in 1896, he counseled that there was "no use quarreling about A. P. Aism or any other ism. . . . If you hate somebody you begin to poison yourself."[23]

It is not clear just how prominently organized religion figured in the lives of many District adults. When Father Edward Downey arrived in Victor in 1894, among two thousand residents he could locate only some twenty-five families that claimed any religious affiliation at all, twelve of them Catholic. The first Catholic church in Victor, dedicated on St. Patrick's Day 1895, served a congregation of twenty Catholic families. By 1900 there were Catholic churches in Altman, Anaconda, Cripple Creek, Gillett, Goldfield, and Victor. When St. Victor's Church was dedicated during the second strike, Victor's Catholic congregation had grown to 350 families.[24]

The impact of religious differences within the working class was, in public discourse, minimal. The *Press* only rarely mentioned anti-Catholic prejudice. There were religious distinctions among some lodges, but many drew members from diverse ethnic backgrounds and religious affiliations. Occasionally, though, religion became an overt issue in local politics. In 1895 an El Paso County fusion Democratic-Republican-Populist ticket united diverse constituencies and prompted a Republican newspaper to quip that "A. P. and 'red-neck' did not go yesterday in that feast of union and brotherly love." The APA was active in Anaconda politics in 1896 (both local tickets had APA sponsorship), which may have provided the context for Eugene Debs's anti-APA comments when he spoke to the Trades Assembly that year. And during the 1900 school board election contest between W. E. Pruett and P. J. Lynch, the *Press* reported that religion was "being interjected into the school campaign" in a political debate.[25] "Religion and politics were dragged in when the appointment of teachers was under discussion and President Hills and Mr. Wells indulged in criminations and recriminations, and Mr. Pruett intimated positively that there was one thing which he was unwilling to do to secure his election, but did not specify whether this was the recommendation of a Catholic teacher or the acquiescence in ballot box stuffing in his own interest."[26] Despite these reports of anti-Catholic prejudice, there is no evidence that it divided the District's unions. The *Press* used Pruett's presumed anti-Catholic politics to encourage working-class support for an Irish Catholic candidate. There is considerably more evidence of respect for Catholic union leaders than of religious divisions.

❁   ❁   ❁

Cripple Creek was, nonetheless, hardly a perfect melting pot. Race clearly mattered. African Americans were not welcomed as equal members of the labor community, although there were probably friendlier relations with the small African American population than existed in many parts of the country. Prejudice against Asians and the new immigrants from southern and eastern Europe eclipsed older ethnic rivalries among Caucasian immigrants. Although these prejudices had less apparent impact on the local union movement than had the ethnic divisions of the earlier mining frontier, they established racial hierarchies. Shared racism supported cross-class political alliances that separated the unions from other workers. District miners bridged ethnic differences among white men but fostered deep prejudices toward working-class men of other races.

Four groups were not welcome in the ethnically diverse labor community: African Americans, Asians, Mexicans, and southern and eastern Europeans. Of these, only African Americans lived in the District in significant numbers, and relationships with them, although certainly conflicted, were probably easier than with the excluded groups. At least they were allowed to stay. Teller County was home for 310 African Americans in 1900 but only five Asians. Most of the African Americans (188) lived in Cripple Creek, forty-three in Victor, and the remaining seventy-nine in the smaller towns or outside the District itself. Most lived and worked in Cripple Creek's Third and Fourth Wards near the vice and entertainment districts. The largest single occupation for African American men was saloon porter; others worked as janitors, cooks, laborers, and in a variety of unskilled and semiskilled occupations. African American women who worked for wages were likely to be washerwomen, cooks, and servants.[27]

Labor's attitude toward African Americans was at best conflicted racism. The *Press* printed racial slurs and equated whiteness with fairness and blackness with vice and violence. It referred to "nigger minstrels," "coons," "Negro Brutes," and "Negro Ravishers." A loud shirt was a "nigger shirt." The *Press* claimed that bloodhounds would follow the smell of an African American "in preference to any other." When the Pinto Mine granted its workers a half day off on New Year's Eve, the *Press* hailed it as "the whitest mine in the state."[28]

Most *Press* coverage of African Americans concerned crime and violence in the red light districts and behavior that violated separatist norms. Annie Carter, a white woman and an alleged prostitute, was ordered to leave town on charges of vagrancy, of frequenting Mahogany Hall (the African American dance hall at the entrance to Poverty Gulch, where there were reputedly "no restrictions, even the real can-can allowed"), and of having "an undue regard for a carbon colored coon of that resort." When Clara Tucker, an African American, slashed white miner George Garrett with a razor, some of Garrett's co-workers promised to "assist him in attending to the colored portion of the row." Many news stories accused African American prostitutes of robbing their customers or other residents of the demimode.[29]

But when the *Press* shifted its focus from vice and violence it covered news of the African American community without epithet. The paper printed notices of deaths and funerals of African American residents and covered social events. For the most part, African Americans organized their own social life apart from the rest of the District. They established churches and political organizations; for example, a Colored Republican Club and, more surprisingly, an organization of African American Democrats. The "Just a Few" Club sponsored dances and socials.[30]

Although segregation remained the norm, relationships between African Americans and whites could be friendly and sometimes respectful. The Republican Party made a point of including African American delegates to party conventions, and white delegates resigned their positions to guarantee African American representa-tion. Professor Hepner, a local musician, donated the use of his hall to the "Just a Few," and Cripple Creek miners let African Americans use their union hall for a private dance. The Cripple Creek city council declared Emancipation Day an official holiday, and the *Press* covered the festivities and referred to the women who organized the celebration as "Mrs." and "Miss." Victor city officials accepted invi-tations to attend.[31]

Although organized labor and the small African American community coexisted relatively amicably in social circumstances that did not directly touch most white workers, racism surfaced when race impinged on work and job control. The unions' harshest racial language involved African American strikebreakers. The charges had some basis in fact—western employers did import African Americans to break strikes, mobilizing the racist divisions inherent in a racially segmented work force. In Cripple Creek the most powerful symbol of this practice occurred during the Coeur d'Alenes miners' strike of 1899, when President McKinley dispatched fed-eral troops, including an African American company from Brownsville, Texas, and placed the strike area under martial law. The African American soldiers became powerful symbols who fused images of government force and strikebreaking with racism. When the *Press* attacked a local mine manager named Weaver for hiring an incompetent engineer, for instance, it connected Weaver with the divisive rac-ism of the Coeur d'Alenes strike. "To show the kind of man this Weaver is a few days ago one of the employees was reading an edition of the Miners' Magazine and made some comments relative to negro soldiers in the Coeur d'Alenes insulting the miners' wives when Weaver remarked that the negroes were as good as the women, he guessed."[32] Bill Haywood charged that employers and the state used race to inflame the already tense strike situation in Idaho. The tactic worked in Cripple Creek, where labor equated race with threats to working-class control and directed its anger against the African American soldiers.[33]

Closer to home, contractors hired African American scabs during an 1899 Victor hod carriers' strike. Two firms refused to let the strikers return to work and instead hired African American laborers from Cripple Creek to replace them. The *Press* blamed local Republican newspapers for suggesting that organized labor did not sup-port the strikers, thus leading the contractors to believe that "they would be upheld in this manner of taking revenge on the strikers" and outside laborers to think that "they were justified in coming to get work."[34] It was possible to manipulate race, how-ever, because organized labor marginalized local African Americans as outsiders.

Racial divisions surfaced again in 1901 during a barbers' organizing drive. On March 3, 1901, the Barbers' Union demanded that barbershops close at 7 o'clock instead of 8. The Trades Assembly endorsed the demand, which was implemented uneventfully, except at one shop owned by an African American barber. In June

1901 the *Press* reported that the "colored barber . . . on the east side of Third street between Myers and Warren avenues had been declared unfair for refusing to join the union." He also refused to close at 7 o'clock like the union shops, so the Trades Assembly sent a committee to determine whether union men patronized him. Three months later, in September 1901, someone dynamited a barbershop owned by an African American, John Tyler, and Tyler was killed.[35] It is not certain that Tyler was the barber who was declared unfair. His shop was on South Third Street, but so was that of another African American barber, Mack MacLeod, and it is not clear whether labor boycotted Tyler, MacLeod, or someone else. It is clear that race was injected into a disagreement that involved only union allegiance. The African American barber apparently could have joined the Barbers' Union had he had wanted and had he been willing to follow local craft rules.

These local racial conflicts occurred in circumstances that affected few African Americans. The unions admitted an occasional African American who worked in a predominantly white trade. In other situations, unions policed the racial boundaries of their crafts. African Americans likely did not support the hod carriers and barbers because organized labor did not support African Americans or include them as equals. Some unions, such as White Cooks No. 92, which existed briefly in 1900 and 1901, openly banned them. But such racism did not go uncontested. Cripple Creek Carpenters No. 547 instructed its delegates to the Cripple Creek Trades Assembly "to vote against admitting the Cooks to Trades Assembly until said Cooks make some provisions to protect the Colored Members." The carpenters, like the miners, rented their hall to African American clubs.[36] The Cripple Creek Hod Carriers' Union buried John White, an African American member who died in 1899.[37] For the most part, however, organized labor ignored African American workers and the segregated occupations in which they worked. There was, for example, no Saloon Porters' Union.

Few African Americans were miners. When the Wild Horse Mine hired an African American, the other miners protested to Superintendent Martin Gleason, who "gave a good sermon on brotherly love and cited the fact that they had embraced the black race thirty-five years ago." Gleason's "Christian talk" did not work, however, and "the men refused to go down with the negro." The man apparently left, and some of the Wild Horse employees came to the *Press* to complain about Gleason "for attempting to make them play the black to win."[38] Although Gleason had belonged to Free Coinage Miners No. 19, many of his union brothers did not share his version of brotherly love.

❁   ❁   ❁

The unions' conflicted attitudes toward African Americans had little immediate impact, if only because there were so few African Americans in the Cripple Creek

District. A few belonged to unions, but most worked in unorganized occupations. Labor was more prejudiced against groups more prominent in western work forces: Asians, Mexicans, and southern and eastern Europeans, who were not allowed in the District at all. Cripple Creek was known as a white man's camp not because African Americans were excluded but because Chinese, Japanese, Slavs, Italians, Greeks, and Mexicans were not welcome.[39]

Organized labor justified its biases as necessary self-protection, presuming that the people it excluded would work for less than union scale. One miner wrote that his co-workers should join unions to avoid a situation in which "the Dagoes, Japs or Chinese will walk in and take a chance with those cheap guys who today are willing to work for $2.50 or $2.00 a day." A former District resident recalled, "And with the working element, if there was any, any threat to anyone coming into the camp and working for cheaper wages, like if your Spanish people would come in, they were driven out of town, the town guns would stone 'em out. They wouldn't let them come in at all. That was always. They never let anyone come in who would work for cheaper money. Make life so uncomfortable they'd leave. They didn't have a chance to live up there."[40]

Mexicans, Greeks, Italians, and Slavs, all of whom worked in Colorado and Wyoming coal mines, were portrayed and treated as inferiors in the District. The *Press*'s repertoire of ethnic slurs included the word *dago*. When labor-backed gubernatorial candidate J. R. Orman was accused of employing Greeks, the *Press* hastily denied the charge. In an effort to enlist middle-class support for organized labor, the unions appealed to nativist fears. The *Press* urged merchants to support the unions or else "the camp would be overrun by Italians, Austrians and Slavs, as in Leadville, where the merchants complain of no business because the foreigners live on nothing and send their money abroad!"[41]

Racism and nativism were not, however, universal. Some workers argued that ethnic prejudices undermined class unity. A Victor subscriber to the *Colorado Chronicle*, an independent socialist labor newspaper, connected the interests of "older" northwest European immigrants and the "new" immigrants whom labor barred from the District. The reader objected to implications that "Greeks, Italians, Germans, Swedes, Danes, French, and Irish" scabbed, insisting that many staunch union members were immigrants, and many scabs and union detractors were native-born. District unions, however, largely distinguished between the "good" and "pro-labor" older immigrant groups from northern and western Europe and the "bad" newer immigrants from southern and eastern Europe. Like African Americans, few people from those countries lived in the District; there were only eighteen Italians in Teller County in 1900 and no Greeks.[42] That fact was probably the most significant evidence of how working-class racism operated in Cripple Creek. Few African Americans or Chinese worked in the regional mining economy to threaten the hegemony of miners of northern and western European origins. Italians, Greeks, Mexicans, Mexican Americans, and Slavs all moved into Colorado and Wyoming coal mines after 1900 but were barred from the gold camp.

There were few Asians in the District or elsewhere in Colorado. Census-takers recorded only five persons of Asian birth in 1900, all of them in the Cripple Creek vice district. Because red light districts were underenumerated, five may be a low figure. But unlike earlier boomtowns there were no Chinese miners; the majority of prostitutes were Anglos or African Americans.[43] Organized labor worked hard to keep it that way, reserving its greatest venom for the Chinese and Japanese, who posed little apparent threat.

Hard-rock miners carried a long history of prejudice against Asian immigrants. Miners barred the Chinese from working in the larger camps of the hard-rock frontier, and opposition to Chinese miners remained a hallmark of the mining labor movement. From the early 1850s labor and the state had persecuted Chinese placer miners. California charged a special foreign miners' tax, and miners' courts and the laws of various mining districts legislated the Chinese out of one camp after another. If legislation did not work, mobs either drove them out or killed them. Chinese were generally prevented from working underground by superintendents who would not hire them and miners who would not work with them. In California they worked underground without opposition only in the deadly quicksilver mines. When they were employed in the more isolated mines they received less than a third of the wages paid to white miners.[44]

Instead of organizing the Chinese or fighting to raise their wages, white miners organized to exclude them. When some hundred Chinese were hired to work in the stamp mills at Unionville, nearly a hundred miles northeast of the Comstock, miners there promptly organized the Workingmen's Protective Union "to protect the interests of the white workingman against the encroachments of capital and Coolie labor; and to use all *legal* means of ridding the country of Chinamen." Comstock miners helped organize the Grand Council of the State of Nevada, which promised to use "all the resources of petition and argument to check the tide of coolie importation." But, the delegates added, *"if we are pushed to the wall, then the end must qualify the means."*[45]

Following the lead from the Comstock, the Grass Valley Anti-Coolie Association organized in September 1869 "to prevent the employment of Chinese," and the Amador County Laborers' Association listed among its aims "to discourage competition of inferior races." The anti-Chinese campaigns achieved the Chinese Exclusion Act of 1882 and fueled a number of anti-Chinese riots throughout the West in 1885 and 1886. The most violent occurred in the coal mines of Rock Springs, Wyoming, in 1885, when the Knights of Labor led a mob to slaughter twenty-eight Chinese and drive hundreds from their homes.[46]

Older miners brought this legacy to Cripple Creek. In 1892 there were reportedly no "Chinamen to be seen" because from "the foundation of the camp the thoughtful celestial ha[d] been rigorously excluded from its limits by the unanimous resolution of the miners."[47] Their determination to exclude Asians gathered momentum as the 1902 expiration of the Chinese Exclusion Act approached. Organized labor distinguished between old and new European immigrants but extended anti-Chinese sentiment to all Asians as Japanese immigration increased at the turn of the century.

The only *Press* references to local Chinese or Japanese were to prostitutes, with somewhat more justification than in the case of African Americans because the only persons of Asian birth in the District were prostitutes.[48] Labor equated vice with Asian heritage but did not analyze how the exclusion laws had led to a virtual slave trade by restricting the immigration of Chinese women.[49] In 1902 Cripple Creek Federal Labor Union No. 19 asked the police chief "to run the Japanese harlots and their lovers out of town." When he complied, the Trades Assembly unanimously praised the union and the chief for "expelling from the city the Japanese women and their consorts."[50]

On earlier mining frontiers owners had imported Chinese workers to depress wages or to work the placers. But there were no placers in the Cripple Creek District, and Caucasians of all classes united to exclude Chinese and Japanese. Anti-Asian politics also spanned the divide between the WFM and the American Federation of Labor (AFL), which the *Miners' Magazine* dubbed "the American Separation of Labor." The Western Federation of Miners, the Western Labor Union, and the AFL united to oppose the immigration of Asian workers. All the officers of the WFM and WLU endorsed Japanese exclusion in 1900, and WLU president Daniel McDonald warned the 1900 convention delegates about "the alarming number of Japanese laborers being brought to this country." Although he considered Japanese "more intelligent and better educated" than the Chinese, he claimed that they would "work for wages that even a Chinaman" would refuse. McDonald considered Japanese more dangerous than Chinese because they wanted to learn skilled trades, would "work for a mere pittance," and were "keen to imitate" American customs and dress in American clothing. Although "somewhat preferable to the Chinese by reason of . . . neatness of style and cleanness of dress," Japanese threatened women workers in "household, laundry work and the like." McDonald therefore urged that the Chinese Exclusion Act be renewed and extended to all Asians.[51]

District labor agreed. The *Press* argued that "the re-enactment of the act against Chinese should carry with it a remedy for the unsatisfactory immigration laws in general." The District Trades Assembly urged the Colorado congressional delegation to extend the Exclusion Act and broaden it to "include all Asian races." The

State Federation of Labor followed suit. Its president, H. E. Garman, said he believed the moneyed classes favored admitting cheap Asian labor.[52]

In late 1901 a new Chinese exclusion bill was introduced in Congress. Organized labor asked the Cripple Creek Chamber of Commerce to sponsor a mass meeting to tell Congress "that we don't want Chinese in Cripple Creek." Two representatives of the WFM District Executive Committee addressed the Chamber's board of directors, who passed a resolution asking Colorado congressional representatives to support the act. The Chamber agreed to cooperate with the Trades Assembly and Cripple Creek's mayor, F. J. Crane, in sponsoring a mass meeting to express public sentiment.[53]

The *Press* encouraged workers to attend, saying, "Labor saving machinery and consolidations of capital have brought a condition before the laborers of the United States which threatens a radical change in every affair of life. It requires no prophet to see that the struggle between labor and capital is rapidly assuming a place the seriousness of which must call for earnest thought and careful action. Just now the admission of China's cheap workmen into competition with American labor would mean a disturbing factor, the result of whose presence is beyond human calculation."[54]

The combination of union power and the racial prejudices of the business community erected a united front on Asian exclusion that crossed class lines. The Trades Assembly endorsed a Law and Order League "to exclude all aliens who do not wish to become American citizens and adopt American customs," a cruelly ironic policy for Chinese and Japanese, who were not allowed to file for citizenship. According to the *Press*, the League proved that "the business man is as much interested in the exclusion of these Asiatics as is all branches of labor." Mine manager Sherman Bell presided at the mass meeting in Cripple Creek, where, as in Victor, labor, business, and government representatives united for Asian exclusion. The speakers included Joy Pollard of Free Coinage No. 19; a local judge; county attorney Frank J. Hangs, who later served as a WFM attorney; and other labor representatives. Pollard introduced a resolution to extend the exclusion law. The meeting unanimously endorsed it in the name of "the Chamber of Commerce and the people of the Cripple Creek district."[55]

Several months later the Victor Miners' Union hosted the exclusion rally described at the beginning of this chapter. "Several expulsions from the gold camp in past years may have given John Chinaman some idea of our social preferences, but he won't know how really exclusive we are until after the meeting in Miners' Union hall," the *Press* declared. The Victor meeting again united capital and labor and cut across partisan political lines. The *Press* reported that some people "believed that the presence of Mongolians would be inimical to socialistic success" as "evidenced by the numerous references to socialism that broke out in the addresses of several of the speakers." Socialism was a dubious attraction for Republicans Sherman Bell, Frank Frewen, and Fred Bodfish, but they and other local Republicans broke with Colorado GOP leaders who supported legal protection for Japanese laborers to keep their homes and jobs. The socialist *Colorado Chronicle* attacked the Republican position, charging that the "republican party is pre-eminently the corporation party and would applaud the acts of corporations and public officers in importing foreign labor, giving them protection and making conditions worse for American labor."[56]

Just as District Republicans were less tolerant than the state GOP leadership, some District socialists broke with the *Chronicle* to oppose Asian exclusion. J. J. Callahan, in 1899 the first editor of the *Daily Press*, had years before connected the principals of socialism and racial equality. The red flag of socialism, he said, "represents peace, not war; love, not hate; unity, not discord. It symbolizes the common red blood of the race, and says that the whole human family, springing from a common origin, should be as a brotherhood not divided by the prejudices of race, color, creed or nationality. If we must have flags then let us have one which represents universal brotherhood; one which says to the Mongolian, 'You are the equal of the purest Caucasian,' and to the African, 'your black skin is no brand of inferiority.'"[57]

In the same tradition, Hans Hansen, a Socialist, spoke to the exclusion debate, arguing that if all men were created equal and entitled to life, liberty, and the pursuit of happiness, then "the Japs have the same right as anybody else."

> But let us suppose the Japs are driven out; who is to take their place? Some tell us that would give white women and children a chance. Well, I don't want my wife or children to take their place. Others say there are Irish enough to take their place, but if it be right to drive the Japs out, is it not right to drive the Irish out also, and if right to drive the Irish out is it not equally right to drive all the Europeans out. Suppose that the whole population was driven out until there were but two persons left in the whole country. And if one of those two owned all the land and tools, would not the landless one be the slave of the land and tool owner just as much and just as truly as the landless masses are the slaves of the land owners at present . . . ?
>
> The landless is always at the mercy of the land owner; hence, I would suggest that it would be better to drive out the landlords and leave the Japs, for the Japs support themselves and more too, but the landlord is simply a drone in the hive for labor to feed, he is a dead load for labor to carry.[58]

Hansen urged labor to ignore Asian exclusion and "steer straight for Socialism and the co-operative Common Wealth."

Few of Hansen's fellow workers agreed. The American Labor Union offered a partial explanation for the plight of Chinese workers but argued that Asian exclusion and industrial unionism would together pave the road to socialism:

> As long as men have left the power and the will to strike against wrong and oppression there is hope left for the final emancipation of the working class. In the opposite case

hope has departed. In China there are no labor strikes. The workers there have been ground down through centuries of ceaseless toil an[d] oppression until they have lost all the moral and intellectual attributes of decency and are mere animals of toil. This condition of the Chinese working class make of them "good servants," which is highly satisfactory to the capitalistic class—but at what cost to the qualities of true manhood and womanhood! The "pure and simple" trades unions could not have saved the working people of China from this fate; nor can it save the workers of this nation from a like fate—it can only defer the time. But by adopting the tactics of the "new trades union" movement it cannot only prevent this curse, but it can do more—it can wrest the powers of government from the control of capitalism, take every parasite from the burdened backs of toil, build the Socialist commonwealth and give to labor all the good things of life—material, mental, moral and physical.[59]

District labor dreamed of a cooperative commonwealth that denied entry to most African Americans, Mexican Americans, Slavs, Greeks, Italians, Chinese, and Japanese. In the wake of Colorado labor's vehement exclusionist stand, union miners called a mass meeting in Ouray in 1902 to drive the remaining Chinese from the San Juans. They drove the Chinese out of Silverton.[60]

Although it argued that the "pure and simple" trades unionism of the AFL could not halt the oppression of industrial workers in China or anywhere else, the ALU nonetheless joined ranks with the AFL to support a "pure and simple" race policy. In 1902 the WFM, ALU, and AFL all supported Asian exclusion. The next year they parted company. In 1903—after Chinese exclusion was again secured—Big Bill Haywood announced that thereafter the WFM would try to organize Japanese and Chinese workers in and around mines. The ALU, despite deep internal dissent, followed suit. The ALU's *American Labor Union Journal* advocated admitting "Mongolians" into the organization in order to stop splitting the ranks of labor and proposed that labor withdraw its support for Asian exclusion. The 1903 ALU convention amended its constitution to declare that "no working man or woman shall be excluded from membership in local unions because of creed or color."[61]

It was easier to endorse inclusion than to practice it. By 1903 District labor was focused on the second strike, and there is no evidence that the new WFM and ALU policies changed local racial politics. The general ethnic character of the District did not change much with time. By 1910 the second strike and the decline of mining caused Teller County population to drop to 14,351, a dramatic 50 percent decline. The remaining residents guarded their jobs. There was little in Cripple Creek to attract new immigrants. Although the overall proportions of native-born and foreign-born residents remained the same, the proportions of English and Irish dropped as older, skilled miners aged or left. In 1910 there were still only three Italians, twenty-five Finns, and thirty-two Greeks in Teller County and thirteen "Indians, Chinese, Japanese, and all others." By 1930 the Teller County population had dropped to 4,141, of whom only 10 percent (428) were immigrants, among them thirty-four Irish, ninety-seven English, and a hundred Swedes but only five Finns. No Greeks, Italians, or Mexicans lived there.[62]

Confronted with technology that reduced skill levels, and with increasingly powerful capitalist consolidations, some western miners understood that they must bridge divisions of skill and ethnicity among white men. They advocated industrial unionism and patched older antagonisms among the native-born and various northern and western Europeans. But there they stopped. Union miners at the turn of the century faced no threat from older immigrants, who were highly skilled and commanded union wages. Instead, they feared competition from Asians, Mexicans, and immigrants from southern and eastern European. Fears of competition and depressed wages were easily manipulated to divide workers and to make union labor, from the perspectives of those it excluded, a hostile camp ringed with racial barricades. Labor's attitude toward those groups was at least as hostile as the earlier animosity between Cornish and Irish miners and the movements for Chinese exclusion in California and on the Comstock. Unions only partially analyzed how capital used ethnic prejudices to divide and weaken working-class organization, and they applied that analysis inconsistently. Nor did District unions attempt to organize newer immigrants and help them acquire skills, as the Irish had managed to do a generation earlier.

As workers erected barriers to bar "non-whites" from organized labor, they constructed shared identities as white men. The language of racist exclusion carried gendered assumptions as well. During the Coeur d'Alenes strike, the African American soldiers became enemies not only for strikebreaking but also for insulting miners' wives. The *Press* attacked Mine Manager Weaver not simply because he approved of the soldiers but because he said they "were as good as the women, he guessed." Daniel McDonald, the WLU president, warned members about Japanese immigrants who threatened women workers in "household, laundry work and the like," and Hans Hansen responded that he did not want his "wife or children to take their place." Given the severe barriers to Japanese and Chinese women entering the United States, Japanese and Chinese men did "women's work" for one another as well as for whites. Because they washed laundry, cooked in noodle shops, and performed domestic work, their racial status was in part constructed by identifying them with devalued and subordinated women. At the same time, the image of white working-class womanhood, protected and sheltered from non-white men, was mobilized to construct and defend a racist hierarchy. The ALU journal feared competition from Chinese workers who had been so oppressed that they had become "mere animals of toil." It responded to their oppression, however, not through a class analysis that demanded solidarity but as a threat from people who had been so "ground down" that they endangered "the qualities of true manhood and womanhood!"⁶³ This language reflected how deeply race and gender anchored the identities of white working-class men. Gender and race were so inextricably bound to working-class identities that threats to labor became emasculating threats to white manhood. Whiteness and masculinity in turn created common social ground with men of other classes and linked them in cross-class alliances.

In its attitude toward Chinese and Japanese in particular, District labor echoed the policies of the AFL. When the AFL excluded unskilled workers the Western Federation and ALU responded that its policies divided the working class. But they favored Asian exclusion. Their members in Cripple Creek routinely barred Chinese, Japanese, Mexicans, Mexican Americans, Italians, Slavs, and Greeks. District labor encouraged racial divisions between African Americans and Euro-Americans that divided the working class, caused an African American barber to be attacked and perhaps murdered, drove Mexican Americans from the District, and joined with employers to support Asian exclusion.

From the standpoint of organized labor, none of these acts appeared momentous because none of the people labor excluded joined the white male work force to divide local unions. The corrosive significance of working-class racism underlay the impressive solidarity white workers achieved. Race had little apparent impact on white workers allowed to live in the District, but the shared racism of business and labor grounded identities of white manhood that split workers along racial fault lines. Cross-class racist alliances with employers supported an ideology of racial hierarchy. Reflected in a racially separated work force and in a regional economy that channeled southeastern Europeans and Mexicans to the coal mines, that hierarchy undercut working-class unity and the inclusive vision of industrial unionism that the WFM and ALU articulated. District labor tacitly affirmed common identities as white men with the employers who joined them to fight for Asian exclusion. White manhood bridged class divisions to create common social ground—more common ground than local unions offered the African American, Chinese, Japanese, Italian, Slav, Greek, and Mexican American working men whom unions barred from their "white man's camp."

Benevolent and Protective Order of Elks, Lodge No. 367, Victor, posed in front of Donnelley Building. Father Edward Downey is standing in the first row, second from right. (Courtesy Denver Public Library)

Hose race, Cripple Creek, 1896. (Courtesy Colorado Historical Society)

The Gold Coin Club, 413 West Diamond, Victor, opened on March 5, 1900. This photograph was originally published as part of a brochure to accompany the Colorado Exhibit that the Woods Investment Company contributed for the Pan-American Exhibition. (Courtesy Denver Public Library)

Crapper Jack's Saloon and Dance Hall, Myers Avenue, Cripple Creek. Dance hall workers and customers line up at the bar. (Courtesy Denver Public Library)

Camp Goldfield, October 1903, the National Guard headquarters during the 1903–4 strike, near Goldfield, Colorado. (Photo by R. G. Leonard, courtesy Colorado Historical Society)

Soldier on duty (upper right) during the 1903–4 strike. (Courtesy Colorado Historical Society)

Militia taking the *Victor Record* work force to the bull pen. (Courtesy Colorado Historical Society)

The Independence Depot of the Florence and Cripple Creek Railroad, June 6, 1904, following the explosion that killed thirteen nonunion miners and climaxed the strike of 1903–4. (Courtesy Colorado Historical Society)

This unidentified photograph, labeled "Goldfield Strike 1904—Lynching, Military Strikes—Cripple Creek 1903–04" fits written accounts of Sheriff Henry Robertson's meeting with mine owners on June 6, 1904, in all respects except that the rope is actually around the victim's neck. (Courtesy Colorado Historical Society)

Victor Avenue and Fourth Street, between 2 and 3 in the afternoon of June 6, 1904. Special police (many of them WFM members), deputized by City Marshall Michael O'Connell, shortly before he and they were dismissed. (Courtesy Colorado Historical Society)

The Victor City Council being force-marched up Fourth Street by military after being arrested; Victor riot scene, June 6, 1904. (Courtesy Colorado Historical Society)

Arrival of soldiers and deputies with prisoners after the Battle of Dunnville, June 8, 1904. (Courtesy Colorado Historical Society)

Victor Miners' Union Hall, 1997. (Author photo)

Abandoned home on road to Altman townsite. (Author photo)

Goldfield, 1997. (Author photo)

Mt. Pisgah, 1997. (Author photo)

7

CLASS-CONSCIOUS LINES

Three union leaders opposed one another in the 1903 election for Cripple Creek city clerk. The Republican candidate, E. M. Turner, was the former president of the Cripple Creek (city) Trades Assembly; the Democrat, D. F. O'Shea, was the former president of the District Trades Assembly; and the Socialist, R. E. Croskey, was the incumbent secretary. The District Trades Assembly sponsored a debate "to find out why these three men being . . . united on the industrial field, cannot agree on the political field."[1]

It was a good question. We still work to understand why the class-conscious militancy evident in working-class community studies was not expressed in electoral politics.[2] Western labor historians still debate what the Socialist endorsements of the Western Federation of Miners (WFM), the Western Labor Union (WLU), and the American Labor Union (ALU) meant for the rank and file.

The labor organizations with which District labor affiliated—the Western Federation of Miners, Western Labor Union, American Labor Union, and Colorado State Federation of Labor—all endorsed the Socialist Party before 1903, and the rank and file elected Socialists to prominent leadership in the Cripple Creek labor movement. But Socialists lost at the polls. Neither the Trades Assembly nor the *Daily Press* endorsed the Socialist Party. As we seek to understand these choices, Cripple Creek redirects our questions from socialism to the shifting political allegiances of Colorado labor during a period of intense partisan realignment.

GETTING PAST THE DEBATE ABOUT SOCIALISM

A debate about whether western labor was radical or accommodationist dominated western labor history through the 1980s. Some scholars equated radicalism with strike violence or the Socialist Party and tried to determine whether there was a radical tradition in western hard-rock communities by counting strikes or Socialist votes.[3] The problem with these interpretations was that they discounted any working-class commitment to economic transformation or fundamental social change which was not expressed by voting Socialist, acting violently, or striking. Often, however, labor made tactical choices to seek security and immediate reforms while advocating more visionary agendas. Workers in Cripple Creek, as elsewhere, took different routes from the union hall to the voting booth. Labor's aspirations and electoral choices need to be located in the shifting political configurations of the 1890s and early 1900s. The choices become clearer against the backdrop of Colorado politics.

To understand labor's politics it is useful to identify what, from a union perspective, politics—or the state—might provide. In broad terms, the state was a potential avenue to union survival, to a variety of reforms, and, some workers thought, to fundamental changes in economic ownership and control. Survival translated to electing officials who supported unions, or who at least would not try to smash them. The 1894 Cripple Creek strike showed how important public officials were for the survival of a local union movement as pro-union local officials and Governor Waite countered Sheriff Bowers and his deputies. After the strike, control of local politics and patronage ensured that unions could organize and that union rules and wages were enforced.

Beyond survival, organized labor at every level advocated a variety of Populist and progressive reforms. These ranged from free silver, to the initiative and referendum, the secret Australian ballot, the direct election of U.S. senators, and graduated inheritance and income taxes. State power offered the most to labor, however, when it regulated the workplace. The reform that District labor wanted above all others was an eight-hour law for miners.[4]

Every party that won labor endorsement—Populist, Democrat, Social Democrat, and Socialist—advocated some political reform. The dividing line between populist/progressive reforms and radicalism was articulated around two issues, one ideological and one tactical. The ideological debate concerned private property and collective ownership. The State Federation advocated nationalization of telephones, telegraphs, railroads, and mines; municipal ownership of utilities; and land ownership based solely on occupation and use. A majority of the District's delegates to labor conventions voted for the WFM, WLU, and the State Federation's Socialist resolutions. But even more advocated producers' and consumers' cooperatives that could be achieved without political action or state support. That was not the case for socialism, at least if it were to be won at the polls, as many workers, however naively, envisioned.

More immediately, however, the political debate centered on tactics. Workers' partisan choices only partially expressed the changes they ideally desired. They also grappled with the practical realities of a winner-take-all electoral system, which created considerable pressure for political alliances.[5] Workers often voted not their ultimate desires but their practical judgments about independent working-class politics and the wisdom of risking the protection and reform labor could gain through broad-based political coalitions.

PARTY POLITICS

Labor developed its political strategies amid volatile realignments in Colorado politics, which in the 1890s involved numerous fusion coalitions among political parties and frequent shifts in individual partisan allegiances. Extremely unstable alliances and political organizations made it difficult to infer social beliefs from partisan activity alone. People who articulated similar goals chose different political paths to reach them. From 1894 to 1904 more than ten political parties operated in the Cripple Creek District, not counting numerous short-lived municipal parties. I have identified sixty voting patterns among politically active persons, and there were certainly many more. Co-operative Party supporters became Social Democrats and then joined the Socialist Party, for example. Populists became Democrats and then Socialists; other Populists became Silver Republicans or Republicans. Silver Republicans became Republicans. Democrats and Republicans became Socialists.[6]

Working-class progressives of the 1890s identified not with the Socialist Party, which was not founded until 1901, but with the People's Party. Colorado populism initially went far beyond free silver. The Cripple Creek District, like Colorado, strongly supported Populist candidates. Colorado gave Populist presidential candidate James B. Weaver 57 percent of the vote in 1892; elected a Populist governor, Davis Waite, the same year; and voted overwhelmingly for William Jennings Bryan for president in 1896 and 1900. Republican senator Henry M. Teller, for whom Teller County was named, formed the Silver Republican Party rather than support McKinley and the gold standard. As populism first narrowed to free silver and then was absorbed into the major parties, labor developed a variety of radical and reform allegiances and sought new allies.[7]

Colorado populism built from a decade of popular unrest in the 1880s, expressed politically through the Greenback, Greenback-Labor, and Union-Labor parties. Their constituents—Farmers' Alliances, independents, the Knights of Labor, Nationalist Clubs, and the United Order of Anti-Monopolists—came together to form an Independent Party in 1890. Independents advocated the Australian ballot, free silver, government ownership of railroads and telegraphs, and state ownership of all ditches and reservoirs; they opposed national banks and alien land ownership. For workers, the party endorsed an employers' liability act, a labor arbitration board, and an eight-hour day. In 1890 the Independent vote came from areas characterized by native-born Protestants, farming, and debt; it carried only two counties. The Democrats won in mining areas that had large numbers of men, Irish, English, and

Roman Catholics.[8] The Democratic constituency connected with the Independent reform platform through the Colorado Populist Party.

Formed in Denver on September 8, 1891, the People's Party of Colorado built from the foundations of the independent movement of 1890. Strongly working class in orientation and membership, its platform went far beyond free silver, an issue that united most Coloradans. As Davis Waite put it, "Except for a few damned fools, the people of Colorado without distinction of party, are . . . in favor of free coinage of silver at 16 to 1." The damned fools included prominent mine owners, who remained, for the most part, with the goldbug Republicans. Few silverites went as far as Waite, who wanted a silver standard and proposed sending Colorado silver to Mexico to be minted for use within the state, a plan even most Populists rejected. Cripple Creek miners, however, supported the idea and sent T. C. McCoy to represent them at a special convention Waite called to discuss his proposal.[9]

Although most Coloradoans, including Cripple Creek gold miners, supported free silver, the reasons they did so distinguished their politics. Agrarian Populists wanted currency inflation; miners wanted jobs. In the mountains and cities, most voters favored any policy that would save Colorado silver mining, jobs for miners, profits for owners, and a healthy economy supported by their wages and dividends. Colorado Democrats and Republicans supported silver or some form of bimetallism. But for radical Populists, free coinage was only one reform among many, and some favored a more inflationary greenback policy.[10] Submerging these differences, the Populists forged a coalition that attracted Democratic support in some areas and Republican support in others. Political fusions generated complicated alliances throughout the decade, which brought pressures to moderate the radical Populist agenda.

To the radical Waite wing of the Populist Party, the silver crisis was only a symptom of government by the rich and powerful. Under Waite's leadership the party issued "a declaration of war by the producing classes against all forms of legislation which enable any man to exploit the labor of another." Governor Waite's behavior in the 1894 strike became a symbolic rallying point for Populist labor. Colorado Populists in turn endorsed reforms that characterized labor politics in the 1890s. Waite wanted to regulate railroads, restrict convict labor, prohibit child labor, and legislate employers' liability, compulsory arbitration of labor disputes, and the eight-hour day. He opposed Pinkerton detectives or any other "private armed force" that broke strikes or infiltrated unions. Like organized labor, Waite favored the free coinage of silver, state ownership of coal mines, the popular election of U.S. senators, and the Australian ballot. He also opposed imperialism and capital punishment.[11]

The Populist coalition drew on a tradition that included socialists, greenbackers, silverites, bimetallists, single-taxers, agrarians, and workers, all of whom, except the greenbackers and agrarians, were represented in the Cripple Creek labor movement. That the District's brand of populism was rooted in working-class experience was vividly demonstrated in early 1894, when John Sherman Saunders, an electrician and miner, organized a local branch of Coxey's Army. Jacob S. Coxey, an Ohio businessman and farmer, and Carl Browne, a California labor organizer, had called for a march on Washington to support their plan for a public works program. Coxeyites wanted the government to finance jobs on extensive road improvements with $500 million in new paper currency. Saunders gathered his troops in the midst of the 1894 miners' strike, when working-class feeling was riding high. Victor residents hanged an effigy of goldbug Republican senator Edward Wolcott, draped with a banner emblazoned "Down with Plutocracy." In late April and early May, some two hundred District men formed legions of Coxey's Industrial Army and got as far as Pueblo on donated rail cars. There they built their forces to 450 and commandeered a train for the journey east. The railroads kept trying to stop them by leaving engines on the tracks, but the skilled craftsmen built bypasses around the obstructions. Their mission ended in Scott City, Kansas, where they surrendered, confronted by a U.S. marshal, the general superintendent of the Missouri Pacific, fifty-five armed deputies, and a corps of reporters.[12]

Some of the Coxeyite enthusiasm endured, however, to nourish Populist organizing. In 1899 Carl Browne visited the District as part of a western tour to establish a new labor organization, the Sovereign Citizens, and organize Populist Cottage Home Clubs and another march on Washington—this time to demand stock regulation and a capitalization tax. The Altman Sovereign Citizens boasted ninety-eight members, among them many District labor leaders and radical Populists who later joined the Social Democratic or Socialist parties.[13]

Radical Populists resisted fusion alliances, fearing that they would compromise the Populist agenda. Cripple Creek Populists split over whether to run combined slates with other parties. Fusionists often out-voted the radicals. The silver coalition broke and regrouped through 1900, with consequently volatile partisan shifts. In the Cripple Creek District there were fusion alliances in at least ten local or county races between 1895 and 1901. These united, in various permutations, Democrats, Populists, Silver Republicans, Republicans, the National Silver Party, and the unions' independent Co-operative Party. Democrats, Populists, and Silver Republicans joined forces in 1895, 1898, and 1900; Democrats, Republicans, Silver Republicans, Populists, and the National Silver Party united in the Cripple Creek municipal elections of 1897; the local Co-operative Party and the Populist Party ran a joint slate in 1899; the Silver Republicans, Republicans, Co-operatives, and Populists ran jointly in the Victor and Cripple Creek city elections in 1900, as did the Co-operatives and Republicans in the Victor municipal elections in 1901, the Democrats, Co-operatives, and Republicans in Gillett in 1901, and the Democrats and Populists in Altman the same year. The silver consensus that united various parties undercut the original broad platform of Colorado Populists, and in 1898 and 1900 they joined victorious fusion slates with Democrats and Silver Republicans. As the Colorado Populist Party compromised to achieve silver coalitions, labor in the District and statewide debated whether to join the fusion bandwagon or pursue independent working-class politics.

In Cripple Creek as in other hard-rock areas, organized labor mobilized support for populism. Variables related to hard-rock mining accounted for 69 percent of the Waite vote in 1892, and the Populist vote correlated strongly with gold and silver mining throughout the decade, with men engaged in mining, and with foreign-born populations, particularly the Irish.[14]

In El Paso County elections the politics of class pitted the District's miners opposite staunchly Republican Colorado Springs. The county voted Republican almost two to one in 1888; four years later the new gold camp swung it into the Populist column. The District voted Populist by roughly three to one, while the Springs went Republican by almost two to one. The Republican *Colorado Springs Weekly Gazette* announced that "El Paso welcomes the addition to her voting strength in spite of their majority being on the wrong side." In the 1893 off-year election the Republicans took the county but not the District, where the local Labor Party won handily.[15]

The 1894 governor's race exposed class tensions within the Populist coalition and sparked the debate over fusion that recurred for the next decade. Waite alienated many moderate Populists, including *Rocky Mountain News* owner Thomas Patterson, who disapproved of the governor's behavior in the 1894 Cripple Creek strike. Patterson's delegation of moderate, pro-fusion Populists, primarily concerned with free silver, was not seated at the 1894 state Populist convention, which re-nominated Waite by acclamation. The Silver Democrats nominated Charles Thomas. But the real contest was between Waite and A. W. McIntire, a Republican who branded the Populists "socialistic and anarchistic" and charged that Waite frightened eastern investors. McIntire, who had strong ties to the nativist American Protective Association (APA), conflated workers, immigrants, and Populists. As an economic depression and the 1894 strike victory threatened Republican owners, McIntire fanned their fears with inflammatory campaign rhetoric against labor, immigrants, and Catholics. The *Colorado Springs Weekly Gazette* joined the red-baiting, accusing Populists of defending the red flag "of the Paris commune, the Chicago massacre, and the Bull Hill insurrection."[16]

Waite won only 41 percent of the vote, and Thomas a minute 4.6 percent. McIntire won handily. Altman and the other mining towns in the southern part of the District voted overwhelmingly Populist. Waite carried the Cripple Creek District but lost the town of Cripple Creek, which went narrowly Republican by twenty-five votes. John Calderwood wrote to Waite that the mine owners had brought in new men just before the election to vote for McIntire, and Populists charged that Sheriff Bowers's deputies intimidated some voters to swell the Republican vote.[17] (It is important to remember, in this context, that votes were cast by separate party ballots, a practice that made intimidation easy and underlay Populist and labor demands for an Australian secret ballot.) Cripple Creek housed more professionals, merchants, and would-be capitalists, a fact that may have distinguished its vote as well.

The 1894 election divided along well-articulated philosophical lines, but those issues became less clear with subsequent fusion campaigns. Fusion itself became an issue, with radical separatists opposing political mergers and moderates advocating compromise. Fusion triumphed in 1895, when El Paso County Republicans faced a coalition slate the *Weekly Gazette* called "Demopopublican," a combination of Independent Silver Republicans, Populists, and Democrats. That year the District again split along economic, and possibly nativist, lines. Cripple Creek, Anaconda, and Lawrence went narrowly Republican, while Victor, Altman, Goldfield, and Gillett carried the fusion ticket.[18] Labor charged that the Republicans tampered with votes and pressured miners, threatening to prosecute them for their 1894 strike activities if they did not vote Republican.

As the 1896 presidential election approached, Waite feared that fusion with the Teller wing of the Republican Party and the Bryan-Bland wing of the Democrats would subordinate fundamental change to silver. He therefore called for an early Populist national convention so the party could nominate William Jennings Bryan first and attract disaffected Democrats and Republicans. But Waite's broadly defined radical populism suffered a major defeat when Thomas Patterson won control of the Colorado delegation to the national Populist convention and Waite's rival delegation was not seated. Colorado's Senator Henry M. Teller refused to support McKinley or the GOP's equivocal stand on silver and led like-minded dissidents out of the party. The junior senator, Edward O. Wolcott, stuck with the goldbugs. In the state gubernatorial race, Silver Republicans and Democrats united behind former governor Alva Adams, while the Populists and National Silverites backed Morton Bailey. Radical Populists, outflanked by Patterson's fusionists, nominated Waite. But most of Waite's support evaporated amid fears of a hopelessly splintered Populist vote. A group of Victor miners joined in asking Waite to withdraw from the race. Bryan carried Colorado handily, with 158,000 votes to McKinley's 26,279. He even won El Paso County, taking Cripple Creek by more than five to one. Adams defeated Bailey; Waite's vote was negligible, even in the District.[19] In 1897 a disillusioned Davis Waite saw fusion leading inevitably to Populist failure and charged that the same party organization and bosses who corrupted the old parties had subverted Populist principles and rank-and-file authority.[20]

Free silver provided the basis for coalition politics that effectively undermined the original working-class platform of the Colorado Populist Party. In 1898 and 1900 the Populists joined victorious fusion slates with the Democrats and the Teller Silver Republicans. The Democrats named the gubernatorial candidates and allocated the other offices to the other two parties. The silver consensus created tensions among working-class Populists, who divided about political coalitions and their implications for organized labor. In 1898 those tensions focused on the victorious gubernatorial candidate, Democrat Charles Thomas, who had bitterly opposed Waite and supported mine owners during the 1894 strike. His opponent, however, was the despised Edward Wolcott. Thomas acknowledged his working-class supporters by at least nominally supporting an eight-hour law and carried the District handily. Republicans took Colorado Springs, but the fusion forces won El Paso County.[21]

It was the last county election that would pit the District against Colorado Springs. In further recognition of District labor's support Thomas endorsed the creation of Teller County in 1899, and with it the possibility of a working-class county government. The governor won further union allies when he appointed James Gaughan the first county clerk.[22] Gaughan, a leading architect of the local silver coalition, had been arrested for his role in the 1894 strike and was the first permanent president of Altman's Free Coinage Miners' Union. Subsequently elected to the state legislature, he wrote the Teller County bill and shepherded its passage.

When the fusion forces won control of the Colorado Populist Party in 1898 they opened a debate within organized labor about the reforms that coalition politics promised versus broader working-class agendas and the risks of independent political action. Colorado organized labor joined the fusion politics of the 1890s but not without internal dissent. The delegates to the 1897 CSFL convention hotly debated whether to work within established parties or to form a labor party. Delegates to a special convention of the State Federation held in Victor to discuss political options decided not to form an independent labor party that year. But there was enough sentiment for a separate workers' party that the Republican *Weekly Gazette* warned against "all attempts at class government."[23]

In the District itself the pivotal 1899 elections sparked an intense debate about labor politics. For the first time, working-class votes could swing the county elections. In the 1899 spring election, thirty-four of the District's unions founded the Co-operative Party and won the mayor's race in Victor. The Coeur d'Alenes miners' strike of 1899 pulled some workers toward independent politics. The Co-operatives charged that Republican president William McKinley and Idaho's Democratic governor, Frank Steunenberg, were "equally culpable . . . in the crime against labor and liberty."[24] But Co-operatives abandoned their independent class focus in the ill-fated fall county elections when they fused with the Populists and stressed morality over class issues.

The 1899 fusion debate generated a heated struggle between James Gaughan, a key player in District fusion politics, and J. J. Callahan, the editor of the union-owned *Daily Press*, which began publishing in 1899. Callahan, a long-time social-ist and labor activist, had previously edited the Denver *Labor Enquirer* and the Idaho *State Tribune*. In 1887 he served on the executive committee of the Denver United Labor Club, which played a leading role in the Colorado Union Labor Party. He later moved to Aspen and supported the Populist Party.[25]

Callahan was committed to a labor press that could challenge capitalist power. Socialism, he said, would "when better understood, kill power, privilege and mo-nopoly in the gifts of nature to man. This being thoroughly understood by the capi-talist press, it follows very naturally that they will try to keep the people from get-ting at the true meaning of Socialism." No simple ideologue, Callahan had long struggled to find effective organizational vehicles for his convictions. In 1887 he helped lead Denver unions out of the Knights of Labor in a pragmatic decision to opt for a strong trade union movement. He argued that there was no choice but to leave the "rotten" Knights and join the American Federation of Labor, which had a "bright future" and recognized "the interdependence of all who work for wages."[26]

As *Press* editor, Callahan fiercely advocated independent politics, arguing that cross-class political coalitions would splinter the working class and compromise its agenda. Criticizing a speech that Governor Thomas had delivered in Victor, Calla-han announced, "We care little for Mr. Thomas or any other politician and will discuss them only from the standpoint of a workingman." He opposed a fusion of Silver Republicans and the Co-operatives, warning the Co-operatives that coalition politics had already killed the Colorado Populist Party and advising workers to avoid "the same old plan as the lion adopted in his fusion with the lamb."[27]

Callahan represented a tradition of independent labor politics expressed serially through the Union Labor, Populist, Social Democratic, and Socialist parties. His editorials endorsed the initiative and referendum, the single tax, and socialism. But he did not speak for long. On September 17, 1899, Callahan triumphantly reported that Gaughan had abandoned fusion and would "let the co-operatives manage their own affairs." Callahan, however, no longer managed the *Press*'s editorial policy. The board of directors, on which Gaughan served, instructed the business manager to stop further political editorials. "For the benefit of our enemies (we have made some and are glad of it)," wrote Callahan, "we will say that they need not lay to their souls the flattering unction that they got us fired—we quit."[28]

Callahan spoke for a portion of District labor that continued to advocate inde-pendent labor politics. Gaughan represented many working-class Populists who moved, through fusion alliances, back into the major parties. Gaughan's fusion forces prevailed in 1899, as the Co-operative Party joined with the Populists. In 1900 the Co-operatives fused with the Republicans, Teller Silver Republicans, and Popu-lists to elect three aldermen in Cripple Creek; Co-operatives and Populists won municipal offices in Goldfield, Altman, Victor, and Gillett.[29]

Labor was torn between trying to win elections through political coalitions with local merchants and managers and organizing around class issues that encouraged political separatism. Individuals came to different decisions about political tactics, in part because they drew different conclusions from common experiences. The history of WFM strikes encouraged some to subordinate long-term social change to immediate survival strategies. Winning elections became more important than ideology when the allegiance of a sheriff or a governor could determine strike outcomes.[30] The 1894 strike encouraged working-class support for Populists in particular, but the hostility of Democratic and Republican officials during the Leadville strike of 1896 and the Coeur d'Alenes strike of 1899 led other workers to distrust both major parties.

Most union leaders supported fusion in 1899 and 1900 rather than independent labor politics, either because they thought coalition politics were the only way to win elections and ensure union survival, or because they considered them effective vehicles for reform politics, or because they chose to subordinate radical agendas to survival and reform. Some considered the Populists working-class allies but opposed fusion with either Democrats or Republicans. P. J. Devault, secretary of the Cripple Creek Trades Assembly, said of the major parties that "it would be difficult to choose between them when they are judged by their actions towards the laboring people," but he endorsed the Co-operative–Populist ticket of "candidates who are from our own ranks and on whom we can rely to do us justice."[31]

The tensions surrounding political coalitions peaked at the turn of the century as Colorado labor briefly attempted independent political action but abandoned it to support a statewide fusion slate of Democrats, Populists, and Silver Republicans. As labor debated political options, it became apparent that workers drew different lessons from labor's political and strike experience. Some concluded that labor and capital had opposing interests and that the only solution was a socialist state. Others cited labor successes as evidence that meaningful reforms, and even socialism, might be achieved through electoral politics. The Cripple Creek Socialist Party platform in 1903 developed a standard Socialist analysis of labor's exploitation and the need to overthrow capitalism. Votes rather than workplace organizing or armed struggle would achieve that goal. There was "only one weapon with which the working class can successfully oppose the capitalist class—and that is the ballot." WFM president Charles Moyer told the 1903 WFM convention delegates that "through organization, education and a united effort at the ballot box" organized labor would "abolish the system of wage slavery and bring about a condition under which the producer may reap the benefits of that which he produces."[32]

Whether Colorado labor emphasized survival, reform, or socialism, before 1903 it focused on electoral strategies to achieve these goals. The *Daily Press* celebrated the elections of union members and their patronage appointments, regardless of their political parties. The paper hailed with equal enthusiasm the Democratic City Council in Cripple Creek and the Co-operative–Republican Council in Victor, both of which awarded patronage jobs to union members.[33]

The Co-operative failure of 1899 led some District labor leaders to abandon independent political action and seek instead to influence the major parties. The 1899 Co-operative–Populist election defeat led the *Press* to endorse the Democrats. John Curry, president of Victor Miners No. 32, announced that workers "must, if they ever desire success, ally themselves with either the democratic or republican parties." He took this position he said, following the 1899 Co-operative defeat and after fifteen years in "the third party field." Curry opposed a state labor ticket because "Teller county is probably the best organized county in the state, and in the light of recent events is not to be relied upon." The Democrats offered "more of the practically attainable reforms," whereas third-party politics were "rainbow chasing." A self-styled Elkton "Radical" agreed, arguing that "some of us seem to be more anxious to build a party than to effect a reform."[34]

Many union activists, however, in the District and throughout Colorado, advocated independent working-class politics. In early 1900 the CSFL polled its affiliates about whether to nominate an independent labor ticket. Five of the six District locals that responded favored the proposal. Eleven locals, however, did not bother to vote. Of 18,400 votes cast statewide, 14,500 favored independent politics. The State Federation therefore called a special convention for March 1900 to nominate candidates for an independent labor ticket. Eight District locals and the Victor and Cripple Creek Trades Assemblies sent delegates. The convention endorsed the independent labor ticket and nominated three candidates for each office, from which the membership at large, in a statewide referendum, selected the candidates. Between March and the annual CSFL convention in June, political separatism drew fire as local union members hotly debated whether to support the independent labor slate. The Altman Miners' local instructed its delegates to the June CSFL convention to oppose the Labor Party. The Cripple Creek Trades Assembly finally left its delegates uninstructed.[35]

District residents had a front-row seat for the debate because the State Federation met in Cripple Creek. CSFL president D. C. Coates favored independent political action to transform "the present competitive method of production and distribution to one of co-operation and public ownership," but not, he said, until the rank and file was ready. The delegates apparently were not. They rejected a resolution to "ignore the old parties, and investigate Socialism and kindred schools of thought." They then narrowly, by a vote of seventy-three to sixty-nine, withdrew their labor ticket.[36]

A group of the losing delegates responded by founding a State Labor Party and nominating an independent slate anyway. The *Press*, fearful that a third party would split the vote, attacked it as "the masked batteries of McKinleyism." M. J. Galligan, a Labor Party nominee, agreed and withdrew from the ticket. Rumor had it that the gubernatorial nominee, D. C. Copley of Independence, a hoist engineer who belonged to Altman Engineers' Local No. 75 and served on the WFM Executive Board, would also desert. The new party was stillborn because its nominees declined to run.[37]

They did not all jump on the fusion bandwagon, however. In July the Social Democracy Club of the Cripple Creek District called a state convention. Some former Labor Party nominees accepted slots on the Social Democratic Party ticket, including D. C. Copley. The Cripple Creek District dominated the Social Democratic Party (SDP) leadership. In addition to Copley, three other nominees lived in the District, as did four members of the state executive committee. Most, like Copley, were union leaders as well. They represented at least six District unions, including the Victor, Cripple Creek, and Altman WFM locals.[38]

The Social Democrats viewed the trade union movement as the "inevitable manifestation of the struggle between capital and labor" and supported both immediate reforms and long-term radical goals. They advocated the initiative, referendum, mandate, and the eight-hour day. But they went further to demand the abolition of capitalism, the establishment of socialism, and the public ownership and control of the means of production and distribution. In the meantime, it was "the duty of all socialists to participate in all struggles of organized labor to improve its conditions under the present system."[39]

The Social Democrats won few votes, either in the District or statewide. The Altman miners, who instructed their delegates to oppose the labor slate, provided the four-vote margin at the CSFL convention that led most of organized labor to support the Democrat/Populist/Silver Republican fusion ticket. The office of lieutenant governor on that slate went to the Populists, who first nominated John Calderwood. Governor Thomas objected vehemently to nominating the 1894 strike leader, so the Populists substituted D. C. Coates, who joined Democrat James Orman on the winning ticket. Thomas and other moderate Democrats did not like Coates, either, but finally accepted him in preference to Calderwood and to keep the Populists in the fusion fold.[40]

Born in Yorkshire in 1868, Coates reportedly dated his class-consciousness from his childhood in the Durham coal fields. He emigrated with his family in 1881 to Pueblo, Colorado, where he worked in the steel mills until he was fifteen. Coates then became a typographer. After completing his apprenticeship in 1888, he worked in Denver and then for a brief time at the *Coming Nation* in Greensburg, Indiana. Returning to Pueblo, he bought a labor paper in partnership with Otto F. Thum. Their *Pueblo Courier*, an official paper of the WFM and WLU, bore the masthead "Socialism the Fundamental Solution." Coates had spearheaded the drive in the Pueblo Trades Assembly to call the founding convention of the CSFL. He served as secretary of the State Federation from 1897 to 1899, and as president during 1899 and 1900. He supported the Populist ticket in 1892, Bryan and Sewell in 1896.[41]

Although District union activists organized the state Social Democratic Party, and Copley led its slate, the *Press* endorsed the fusion ticket because the Democratic Party was "nearer to the people" than the Republican Party and because the second highest office on the fusion slate went to a "representative of the laboring classes, a zealous union man." The labor daily never addressed the local split over socialism and fusion. It pushed the fusion slate and attacked Orman's Republican opponent, Frank Goudy, the county attorney of El Paso County, who had prosecuted union miners after the 1894 strike. Perhaps District labor discussed the political split at a mass meeting the Trades Assembly called "to consider the political situation." The *Press* did not cover the meeting.[42]

Labor's Democratic support in 1900 was a vote for reform. Few union members, apparently, wished to risk union survival by supporting the SDP. The *Press* emphasized that a split working-class vote would elect Goudy, a dedicated union enemy. It published the sworn statements of three WFM members, Robert J. Lyons, D. M. McNamara, and Jackson Rhines, all convicted of various charges related to the 1894 strike. The *Press* made front-page news of the three men's testimony. Goudy, they reminded readers, had said that they should be convicted simply because they were union members. The fusion Democrats, in contrast, included Coates on the ticket as a labor representative. Coupling the threat of Goudy's anti-union politics with the fusionists' promise of political patronage for union labor, fusion Democrats persuaded the CSFL to abandon an independent labor ticket and District labor to ignore the alternate Social Democratic slate. After the election Orman recognized his labor support by appointing miner and former state legislator Patrick J. Lynch to fill a vacancy as Teller County commissioner.[43]

While the majority of organized labor supported the fusion slate, Social Democrats continued the radical tradition and paved the way to organized labor's Socialist endorsements. Coates, the labor candidate on the fusion slate, became a more tangible bridge between the pragmatic politics of fusion and the independent politics of socialist labor. He joined the Socialist Party while in office. Because he served as governor when Orman was out of the state, radicals claimed him as the nation's first Socialist governor.[44]

The *Press* and *Miners' Magazine* expressed the political tensions within organized labor. They united in their enthusiasm for Coates but split over the presidential candidates. The *Press* admitted that the Democrats might not offer "all a workingman could desire" but counseled, "If we can't get what we want, let us take the best we can until a future day." The *Miners' Magazine* preferred Bryan to McKinley but charged that Democrats were using Bryan's popularity rather than embracing the Populist platform. Instead, the WFM urged labor to support the Social Democratic ticket of Eugene Debs and Job Harriman.[45] District labor voted for Bryan.[46]

Two years earlier, Bryan had met a tumultuous welcome when he visited the District. The trustees of Altman's Free Coinage local and five hundred citizens hailed his "triumphal entry into the white house," and the *Press* announced that Bryan was "the only honest man, of great prominence, in American politics today." District residents presented Bryan with a silver and gold loving cup, made with a ratio of sixteen parts silver to one part gold, and he ruefully told a Victor crowd that he hoped to rescue from error the nineteen local voters who voted against him in 1896. Ten thousand cheered him in Cripple Creek, and when he spoke in Anaconda Bryan reportedly drew the largest crowd in that town's short history. Bryan's warm reception contrasted starkly with vice-presidential candidate Theodore Roosevelt's campaign visit the following year. There were conflicting partisan versions of the so-called Victor incident. The Republican version charged that a Victor mob ran Roosevelt out of town. Labor, however, said that Roosevelt's escort, Senator Wolcott, became flustered over some boys "hurrahing for Bryan," that Wolcott lost his temper, and Roosevelt fled the confrontation with the pro-Bryan labor crowd. The Republicans tried to capitalize on the image of lawless working-class fusion mobs. District labor treated it as a joke.[47]

The fusion slate swept the District. Bryan won 9,275 votes to McKinley's 4,452, Orman beat Goudy 8,070 to 4,648, and Coates bested his Republican opponent 8,411 to 4,337. Fusion candidates for state senator and state representative won easily. The legislature—fifty-six Democrats, fifteen Silver Republicans, twenty-two Populists, and seven Republicans—retired Wolcott and replaced him with fusion Populist Thomas Patterson. The *Press* gloomily hailed McKinley's victory as "Four More Years of Full Stomachs for the Trusts."[48]

The Democratic Party quickly swallowed the rest of the 1900 fusion alliance and absorbed the Populist and Silver Republican parties. In early 1901 eight Populist senators joined the Democratic Party and urged other Populists to follow suit. In 1902 Colorado's entire congressional delegation—Silver Republican senator Henry Teller and Populists Patterson and Representative John Shafroth—abandoned their respective parties for the Democratic fold. In Cripple Creek the *Daily Press* joined the bandwagon and endorsed the Democratic slates that won the 1901 local elections in Cripple Creek and Victor.[49]

The 1901 Victor elections further elaborated the political tensions within organized labor. The municipal contests pitted union members against one another. Labor's Co-operative Party fused with local Republicans, who included four members of the Victor Miners' local on the ticket: John Horgan, John Harper, George Emery, and Jerry Kelly. Victory, however, went to a cross-class slate of Democrats.

Union members Gustaf Nelson and Henry Robertson joined a Democratic ticket headed by mill manager Nelson Franklin. The fusion nominees, despite their alliance with the Republicans, were anything but conservative. Horgan supported Bryan and Stevenson in 1900. Kelly, the financial secretary of Victor Miners No. 32, ran for justice of the peace as a Populist in 1902 and then joined the Socialist Party and ran for mayor of Victor as a Socialist in 1903. His wife, Celia Kelly, was the Socialist nominee for city treasurer the same year. The *Press* admitted that the four Co-operative–Republican nominees were good union men but said that they were being used to ensure control of the local election machinery for the Republican "Wolcott machine." The WFM mill workers' local, Banner Mill and Smeltermen No. 106 of Victor, endorsed mill manager Franklin and his mixed-class ticket rather than the fusion slate.[50]

The victorious Henry Robertson, a member of Victor Miners No. 32, used the Victor city council as a political stepping stone. In November 1901 he was elected sheriff as the Democrats swept Teller County.

The 1901 county elections also marked the local electoral debut of the new Socialist Party. Socialists won only some four hundred votes, with the highest totals going to three local union members—coroner candidate Fred Hinnen; R. H. Meany, who ran for surveyor; and J. C. Provost, the Socialist candidate for assessor. But most of their fellow workers deserted them. The *Press* claimed that 80 percent of organized labor voted Democratic. A year later Socialist support rose slightly to some five to six hundred votes. Ida Crouch-Hazlett of Victor won 595 votes for Congress, J. C. Provost drew 560 votes for governor, and Hans Hansen received 551 votes for regent of the State University. But the old silver coalition held as the Democrats again swept the county offices.[51]

Coalition politics, however, paved the way for anti-fusion Democrats to take control of the party. The Orman-Coates team was too radical for many moderates. In 1902 anti-fusionists won control of the state convention, repudiated Orman, and nominated Edward Stimson for governor. The excluded Populists nominated Judge Frank Owers of Leadville, who had been a Waite Populist, and turned the contest into a three-way race.[52]

The year 1902 marked the last significant effort of the Colorado People's Party, as Owers evidently knew. Calling himself an Independent Democrat, he told District voters, "You may call yourselves Populists, but you are Democrats. The Populistic planks of today are eventually the planks of other parties." Teller County gave Owers 1,129; James H. Peabody, the Republican candidate, 3,643; and the Democrat Stimson, 4,547. Peabody won, in large measure because of Owers's effect on the three-way race. Stimson lost fourteen counties the Orman fusion slate had carried in 1900, most of which had been Waite counties in 1892 and 1894. Democrats lost the election because they lost the Populists.[53]

COLORADO LABOR POLITICS

The debate over fusion captures the crux of Colorado labor politics. Labor's socialist endorsements, which long dominated the discourse among labor historians,
must be located in the broader context of choices between political coalitions and
independent working-class politics. In the Cripple Creek District and throughout
Colorado, fusion politics diluted radical populism and ultimately swallowed the
Populist Party. Fearful of anti-labor conservatives and attracted by promises of immediate reforms and political patronage, state labor endorsed fusion rather than
more radical alternatives, a decision that expressed the practical difficulty of trans-
lating long-term union goals into mainstream politics. Cripple Creek workers voted
for Socialist resolutions at labor conventions and fusion slates at election time.

However divided labor might be on election day, the Colorado labor movement
united to support a variety of economic and democratic reforms. The 1902 ballot
included reform proposals that organized labor had achieved through fusion politics. Chief among these was an eight-hour law for miners and smelter workers,
which had been endorsed by the Colorado Populist Party and was first enacted in
1899. The 1899 law was modeled on a Utah law that the U.S. Supreme Court had
declared constitutional in 1898. The Colorado State Supreme Court, however,
declared the 1899 eight-hour law unconstitutional virtually before the ink was dry.
Infuriated, District workers demanded that "the constitution be changed to fit the
law." They achieved precisely that through a constitutional amendment on the 1902
ballot to permit an eight-hour law in mines, smelters, and other dangerous industries. Two other amendments, the Bucklin and "Australasian" tax measures, would
permit counties to tax land alone, following the single tax theories of Henry George.
Teller County voted virtually unanimously for the eight-hour amendment (4,712
to 332) and passed the Australasian tax 2,348 to 1,547.[54]

Rank-and-file workers supported labor's ballot initiatives, but not the Socialist
Party. Both the responsiveness of the Orman administration and labor's local political influence buttressed arguments that working-class interests were best served
through reform coalitions. For the *Daily Press*, coalition politics meant revenue in
the form of advertising from the county and from local merchants. The *Press* frequently opposed the radical politics of the CSFL and the WFM. Many miners
believed that local political patronage held the key to union survival. The union
leadership split over whether to court local politicians and business leaders or organize independently around working-class issues. District workers did not necessarily dispute the analyses that led union leaders to socialism, but they divided about
the best political tactics to achieve an array of working-class goals.

The Socialist Party was founded only two years before the second Cripple Creek
strike, and thus Socialist votes are a limited index of radical sentiments in the Dis-

trict. Labor's Socialist resolutions, too, do not adequately convey the range of working-class political agendas, which from 1890 through 1904 consistently combined reforms with more radical analyses of class relationships and labor exploitation. Colorado labor supported reforms to increase popular control of government and state control of the economy. The founding convention of the WFM in 1893 advocated the free coinage of silver and the eight-hour day, repealing all anti-boycott laws, disbanding the state militias, establishing mine inspectors, and licensing stationary engineers. The delegates demanded that the federal government return to the people all mineral and other lands "unlawfully held by railroads and other corporations," establish government ownership of all railroads and telegraph lines, create postal savings banks, and enact the direct election of U.S. senators. In 1894 the WFM called for "laws beneficial to the masses of the people" and the repeal of "all laws which place capital above labor." Seeking electoral reforms to achieve radical ends, miners pledged to "work unceasingly to establish the initiative and referendum and thus make the people the actual rulers instead of plutocrats and politicians." Six years later the *Press* called the initiative and referendum the "Father of Reforms" through which voters could enact government ownership of utilities and railroads.[55]

Workers founded the Colorado State Federation of Labor in 1896 to organize "all the producing classes of this State and in order to better their condition, socially, politically and morally." The delegates to the founding convention supported the initiative and referendum, eight-hour laws, and the free coinage of silver. By a narrow five-vote margin they rejected a resolution urging the Populist Party to nominate Eugene Debs for president, because Debs would "lead the toiling masses to victory, and do all in his power to save this country and its people from the worst system of wage slavery in the history of the human race." The State Federation, like the WFM, demanded nationalization of telephones, telegraphs, railroads, and mines, advocated municipal ownership of utilities, and favored the initiative and referendum. In 1897 it proposed that land ownership depend solely on occupation and use and that the single tax on land be adopted to help achieve that aim. Two years later it called for "the rallying cry of freedom from the thralldom of the greed of organized capital." It paid lobbyists to take labor's programs to the state legislature.[56]

The Western Labor Union, founded in 1898, voted the following year for government ownership of all natural monopolies. The same year the WFM proclaimed that occupancy and use should determine land ownership and called for graduated income and inheritance taxes, government ownership of public utilities, the free coinage of silver, and a national monetary system to issue money "direct to the people without the intervention of the banks."[57]

In Cripple Creek and throughout Colorado, labor repeatedly wrestled with political priorities. That debate, always spirited, reflected how deeply workers believed in their own political power. The labor press cheerfully predicted that because seventeen state legislators held union cards in 1899 Colorado would be "the first state in the Union to be controlled by those who produce wealth." The Orman-Coates victory encouraged workers to believe they could achieve reforms through legislation. To draft laws, the State Federation hired John H. Murphy, a WFM attorney who had written the Utah eight-hour law that the Supreme Court upheld. Then the CSFL instructed its president, H. E. Garman, and secretary, J. K. Robinson, to lobby the legislature for labor proposals, including a land tax proposal consistent with single-tax theories. Garman got an employers' liability bill introduced to the Senate and helped get the land tax and eight-hour amendments before the voters in 1902.[58]

The State Federation's allegiance to the Orman-Coates ticket and the reform legislation it supported overrode more radical goals from 1900 to 1902 during the fusion administration. The CSFL did not, like the WFM and ALU, endorse the Socialist Party in 1902 because the delegates to the annual convention felt "some obligation to the Fusion forces for the constitutional amendments and other acts" and believed "that we can do a great deal in the future in the way of legislation." The CSFL did, in 1902, demand the initiative and referendum and the public ownership of the means of production and distribution, and it recommended the study and discussion of socialist principles by union labor.[59]

The District Trades Assembly, like the State Federation, supported the Australasian tax and eight-hour amendments, but it also expected to win more fundamental economic change through legislation. The assembly responded to a series of coal strikes by advocating state ownership, urging the legislature "to enact laws necessary to enable the state to operate its coal mines for the benefit of the commonwealth of Colorado." The *Press* alternately asserted labor's political strength and backed off in ambivalent fear of exerting too much pressure. It warned, for example, that failure to enact a promised employers' liability law would alienate working-class voters and "seriously jeopardize the success of the Democratic Party at the next general election" but then retreated and announced that labor's "natural home" was "the Democratic party." It dismissed third-party alternatives because Democrats were "so much more in sympathy with organized labor than the Republican party that there is no difficulty in a union man making a choice."[60]

Many union members disagreed. Radical Populists who had long opposed fusion turned instead to socialism. All the major Colorado labor organizations endorsed the Socialist Party. Prominent labor leaders—Edward Boyce, Charles Moyer, Bill Haywood, and John O'Neill of the WFM; J. C. Sullivan and David C. Coates of the CSFL; and Daniel McDonald of the WLU/ALU—all worked to win labor support for socialism. During the 1900 debate about independent political action WFM convention delegates, "believing that beneficial reforms in industrial conditions can be accomplished only through radical changes in present governmental institutions," declared that "the wage system should be abolished and the production of labor distributed under the cooperative plan." They further declared representative government "a failure" and advocated direct legislation as "the first step necessary to enforce legislative reforms." That same year the CSFL resolved to "ignore the old parties, and investigate Socialism and kindred schools of thought with a view of finding the true solution of the labor problem."[61]

If there was a time when Colorado labor believed that it could peacefully create a new society "within the shell of the old," that time was 1901. Lieutenant Governor Coates, welcoming delegates to the WFM convention, announced that labor must have "absolute abolition of the wage system." The miners agreed that a "complete revolution of social and economic conditions" was "the only salvation of the working classes." The Western Labor Union and the WFM both declared that the "capitalist class is in complete possession of the means of production, and thereby control the Republican, Democratic and Populist parties." Because the working class had "nothing in common with the capitalist class either politically or industrially," workers could not "expect to derive any benefits from affiliating with and supporting the capitalist parties" and so should take steps to "separate . . . as a political body from all parties controlled by the capitalist class." The State Federation, like the *Press*, was not yet convinced that capitalists controlled the fusion coalition. But the next year the CSFL overwhelmingly recommended "the study and discussion of Socialist principles by the members of local unions." The WLU endorsed the Socialist Party and "earnestly" appealed to all workers to follow its lead. The WFM adopted independent political action and recommended "the adoption of the Socialist party of America by the locals of the Federation in conjunction with a vigorous policy of education along the lines of political economy."[62] Looking far beyond political reform and patronage, the WFM organization committee explained, "A working man in political power in a capitalistic system is of no more value to us than to the capitalist. Labor must own its own tools of production and distribution. Co-operation must take the place of competition. Labor must employ itself and secure for itself the full product of its toil. It is to this end and this alone that we demand political power."[63]

The WFM reaffirmed its Socialist commitment in 1903, declaring that the Socialist Party was the only party "that demands that the land and the machinery of production shall become the property of all, and that labor shall receive the full product of its toil." The following year it advised "the toiling masses of humanity" that the party offered the only way to "complete emancipation from the present system of wage slavery." The CSFL, the WLU, and the ALU all agreed.[64]

DISTRICT UNIONS AND PARTISAN POLITICS

Convention delegates from the District unions supported the Socialist Party endorsements at least as strongly and enthusiastically as WFM delegates as a whole. Delegates who voted for Socialist resolutions were subsequently reelected to represent their lo-cals and to other union offices. The same Socialists, however, who were elected and reelected to union office lost when they ran for public office as Socialists.[65]

Labor continued, even with Socialist Party endorsements, to juggle immediate reforms and long-term Socialist goals. Letters from Cripple Creek workers to the state labor commissioner reflected the breadth of labor's reform sentiment. Like the reso-lutions adopted at labor conventions, they advocated working-class organization and education, compulsory arbitration, the initiative and referendum, the single tax, and the eight-hour day. Working-class correspondents spoke of a widening gulf between the classes, of trusts as the forerunners of socialized production, and of reform mea-sures to provide partial relief until workers achieved the ultimate remedy of the cooperative commonwealth.[66] But workers who voiced the same analyses of class ex-ploitation offered different solutions. People who agreed about union policy fre-quently disagreed about electoral politics. During the 1900 campaign, for example, WFM attorney John Murphy came to Cripple Creek to work for the fusion ticket. A staunch Democrat, Murphy's politics placed him, like many union members, in opposition to friends and labor associates. Murphy's long-time friend J. E. Seeley of Goldfield was running for presidential elector as a Social Democrat. During Murphy's visit the men publicly debated their political differences.[67]

The Murphy-Seeley debate portrayed in microcosm the pervasive political fer-ment of the mining West, iterated and reiterated in local union halls, labor con-ventions, union publications, and in the bars, workplaces, and street corners of western mining communities. In 1902 Cripple Creek Engineers No. 82 asserted that it was "necessary that we go into politics for our self preservation, and to offset the encroachments of organized capital." Because the Socialist Party was "the only party organized for the benefit of the toilers," the engineers wanted the WFM to endorse it, and they encouraged all unions to work to elect the Socialist ticket. At the same time, Altman Miners No. 19 wanted to reduce the hours of labor "in pro-portion to the progress of production" and to hire a Socialist and labor speaker to educate workers. They favored both an assessment to purchase cooperative min-ing property for the federation and government ownership of all means of produc-tion and distribution. Cripple Creek Miners No. 40 supported cooperative mining even more strongly, recommending that the WFM Executive Board incorporate a Western Federation of Miners Mining and Milling Company and that 25 percent of per capita tax be used to grubstake miners to locate property for it.[68]

Cooperative mining was one thing, the cooperative commonwealth yet another. Despite general agreement on the need for more cooperative social relationships, District labor delegations split their votes on the Socialist resolutions. At the 1902 WFM convention, District delegates favored socialism by more than two to one. The dissenters came from the Cripple Creek and Victor Miners' locals and the

Victor Engineers; delegates from the old labor strongholds on Bull Hill favored socialism. Tom Hurley of Altman said that "it was time labor was asking for all it produces. . . . We have it in our power to wipe capitalism out, and we are cowards if we don't do it." The solution, he said, was "to own mines of our own." W. H. Leonard of Altman said that the Socialist Party was "the only one standing true for labor." Delegate Bond of Victor disagreed. He did not "oppose the propagation of Socialism" but believed that "to force men into one political party or another would not be wise." The time had come, he said, "for independent political action, but not to declare for any party. The way to do was to get a little reform at a time."[69]

District delegates again voiced their differences at the 1903 WFM convention. *Miners' Magazine* editor John O'Neill, of Victor Miners' Local No. 32, consistently advocated "the ownership of the means of production and distribution by the workers of the world." But John Harper, president of the Victor local, disagreed. The federation, he said, should eliminate politics entirely because political action had led to the 1903 strikes and was thus "responsible for the present serious condition of the Federation." Two delegates from Cripple Creek Miners No. 40 also divided on politics. E. J. Campbell, a Democrat, said that it was "impossible to make progress by advocating radical political policy and radical union policy at the same time." George Seitz, a Socialist, said that membership had grown after the WFM endorsed socialism. He favored "a political program in the interests of the working people." Joy Pollard of Altman wanted to organize and educate but "leave partisan politics alone." W. A. Morgan of the Victor Engineers favored organization, education, and independent political action, and F. B. Krallman of the Altman Engineers wanted to "inculcate in the minds of the members the correct use of the ballot." Executive Board member D. C. Copley believed that "the political policy is the only one we can look to with hope of emancipation from industrial slavery."[70]

The divided delegations accurately represented disagreements at home. While the WFM, WLU, and CSFL supported the Socialist Party, the *Press* endorsed the Democrats. In 1901 its board of directors and management "decided that the Daily Press could be of much more aid to organized labor by the support of Democratic principles than by any other course."[71] The *Press* did not speak for all of organized labor, however; its Democratic endorsements provoked periodic opposition from local unions and the Trades Assembly. Business often swayed the *Press*. In 1902, when the it endorsed Democrat Clint Tillery for school director, the *Press* reported that Cripple Creek and Victor businessmen had supported Tillery because he was a "good business manager." But the District Trades Assembly dismissed Tillery because two of his opponents were union members: J. C. Provost of the Plasterers, a Socialist, and C. T. Smith of the Retail Clerks, a Republican.[72]

The *Press* was frequently more moderate than the unions. The Trades Assembly pursued challenges to private enterprise, including a proposed cooperative coal yard. In 1902 it appointed a committee "to secure a coal mine to be operated by organized labor," because it was "impossible to obtain industrial freedom until labor owns the means of production and distribution." Although the Socialist delegates considered cooperatives "another half-way measure," the Trades Assembly appointed a committee to look into establishing cooperative stores. The assembly instructed its WLU convention delegate to propose that all locals appoint cooperative agents to establish "co-operative enterprises, such as stores, butcher shops, boarding houses, coal mines, factories" and "inculcate the co-operative principle into the minds of the membership."[73]

In early 1902 the Trades Assembly began devoting an hour at the first two meetings each month to discuss "such political questions as pertain to the welfare and happiness of humanity in general and union people in particular." J. W. Martin, state organizer for the Socialist Party, addressed the body in January. In September a Mr. Osborne, former organizer for the International Brotherhood of Painters and Decorators, spoke on the class struggle. The topic for February 1902 was the Bucklin tax amendment. The *Press* reported that "while it is not looked upon as a panacea for all ills, the sentiment was strongly in its favor, the members seeming to think that half a loaf was better than no bread, especially as it was shown that the best governed country in the world — New Zealand — started its reform movement with a measure almost identical with the Bucklin bill." The assembly gathered some five thousand signatures to support the bill and worked actively for the Australasian tax and eight-hour amendments in the 1902 election. It pledged to vote only for candidates who supported the initiative and referendum. The *Press* reported protests from "advanced Socialist members [who] contended that it was only a palliative measure" that sidetracked the main issues, whereas "the opportunist wing of that party seemed to favor the measure as did the balance of the delegates."[74]

The political topic at the April Trades Assembly meeting was "Resolved, That the Socialist Party is the only political party that offers a solution of the wage problem to the wage slave." The *Press* reported that the subject "brought out so many interesting facts that one hour was found to be not nearly long enough and the resolution was laid over for debate at the next meeting." The Socialists who disdained "half-way measures" gained influence with the elections of J. C. Provost and Hans Hansen to represent the Trades Assembly at the CSFL convention.[75]

There was ample opportunity for District residents to learn about socialism. Despite its Democratic allegiance, the *Press*, during 1901, ran columns on socialism by local miner George Seitz as well as by nationally prominent Socialists. The "State Federation Notes" discussed the "Slavery of Private Ownership," and Populist carpenter P. N. McPhee called "For the Abolition of the Wage System." During 1902 Socialist education appeared weekly in the *Press*'s "Labor Notes" column, largely because R. E. Croskey, a Socialist and the secretary of the Trades Assembly, wrote the feature. The Teller County Socialist Club organized in June 1901 "for educational propaganda to give the public a better understanding of socialism." It also fielded candidates, announcing that "No Fusion Will Be Countenanced." One of its first nominees was J. J. Callahan who so vehemently opposed fusion politics in 1899. Socialists would accept "No Fusion; No Compromise," the state party announced in 1902.[76]

Socialist clubs soon organized throughout the District and sponsored public educational forums. The Socialist Club of Independence sponsored an address on economic questions and on Chinese exclusion. The Cripple Creek Socialist local met every Sunday at Miners' Union Hall, the Victor local met every first and third Sunday, the Arequa Gulch local gathered several times a week in the school house for meetings and lectures. In March 1902, Socialists nominated an all-union ticket for the Altman elections. George Hooten of Anaconda Miners No. 21, endorsed by both local parties for mayor of Anaconda, wanted it "distinctly understood" that he was "not a Democrat, but a straight Socialist." Anaconda and Goldfield, too, soon hosted active Socialist Clubs.[77]

District labor dominated the state Socialist Party, as it had the Social Democratic Party before. In 1902 four of the five members of the Executive Board lived in the Cripple Creek District, Charles LaKamp of Goldfield served as state secretary-treasurer, and District labor activists claimed a number of slots on the Socialist ballot.[78] Organized labor and Socialists cooperated to bring Socialist speakers to the District. The Trades Assembly invited Eugene Debs. No stranger to District labor, he had addressed the Cripple Creek Trades Assembly in 1896. Local Socialists invited Father Hagerty, the Socialist priest, who spoke in Cameron, Goldfield, and Victor in June 1902. Debs came in August and spoke at Pinnacle Park and the Victor Opera House. The *Press* ignored both speeches.[79]

The paper's coverage of all Socialist orators was sparse at best; its coverage of Socialist labor leaders was somewhat better. In April 1902 WFM President Boyce and Lieutenant Governor Coates addressed the District miners. Boyce attacked pure-and-simple trades unionism of the Gompers variety and called for socialism and working-class political unity. Socialism might be advanced, he thought, if miners owned and operated mines and smelters. Coates called on workers to be as strongly united politically as they were industrially.[80]

District workers remained divided about socialism but appeared, through 1902, to unite in support of cooperatives. The *Press* proclaimed that "co-operation in organization is the source of strength of unionism, and co-operation in the matter of ownership will some day be the basis of all prosperity." At the 1902 WFM convention, delegates from Cripple Creek Miners No. 40, who opposed the Socialist Party

endorsements, joined with Socialist miners from Altman to advocate a WFM mining cooperative. The *Press* said that the "most radical opponents of Socialism" could
"find no fault with this plain business plan for the benefit of organized miners."[81]

The surface unity masked ideological differences that soon erupted in the Trades
Assembly. Socialists considered cooperatives half-way measures that might help
pave the way to a Socialist state. Moderates' cooperative vision, however, was closer
to the Knights of Labor's dream of producers' and consumers' cooperatives. They
considered local merchants and professionals potential allies as members of "the
producing classes." For these reformers, cooperatives were business enterprises to
help workers compete more effectively within the capitalist system. Socialists dominated the Trades Assembly by early 1903 and blocked a union cooperative store.
"Our socialist delegates do not want any half-way measures," the *Press* reported,
"and will be satisfied with nothing short of the Co-operative Commonwealth."[82]

The *Press* insisted that the Socialist resolutions of the WFM, ALU, and CSFL did
not represent the rank and file. They should, therefore, have been submitted to a
referendum vote, not adopted by "a few self appointed class-conscious dictators." The
Press restated its political position in July 1902: "The Press will support the Democratic Party because it is the party of the laboring man. It will oppose the Republican Party because it is the party of the capitalists. It will oppose the Socialist ticket
because if it ever does gain strength enough to become a factor in politics, it will but
serve as a boost to the Republican party."[83] E. P. Steen, secretary of the Electrical
Workers' local, suggested in response that the *Press* hold a referendum of readers to
determine whether they wanted to learn more about socialism and whether they
thought that their delegates misrepresented them. Steen, a Democrat in 1902, ran
for office as a Socialist in 1903. He believed that because "these representatives were
the leaders of thought in their respective organizations," that "if the rank and file are
not now Socialists, they soon will be." The *Press* countered, "We are satisfied, the
Democratic party is satisfied and the Socialists can grin and bear it."[84]

The *Press*'s politics became increasingly problematic in the District and beyond.
John O'Neill charged in the *Miners' Magazine* that the *Press* had "sold itself for a
'mess of pottage,' namely, a slice of the county printing." O'Neill claimed that some
people associated with the *Press* were dishonest, and that the paper was repudiated
by the "honest miners" of the District. It was, consequently, "gasping for existence."
He charged that the "same Press that now shouts for the Democratic party offered
to support the principles of socialism provided the Western Federation of Miners
would rescue the demoralized sheet from financial difficulties which now threaten
to bury it in a dishonored grave." The *Press* retaliated by calling O'Neill an "ingrate
and degenerate" whose attack stemmed from "the excrescence of a disordered liver"
and who had not "drawn a sober breath" during his term in the state legislature.
The paper tacitly admitted, however, that some of its constituents repudiated its

politics. "Because of the objection of some of the members of the miners unions to the Press's political policy," it wrote in reply to O'Neill's allegations, "a committee went to Denver and made a proposition to the Western Federation of Miners to turn the paper over to them and let them run it as they saw fit."[85]

The *Press's* politics caused increasing discord beginning in 1902, as Stimson took control of the Democratic Party and as Socialist influence increased rapidly within local unions. Given the political divisions within organized labor, the Trades Assembly declined to endorse anyone in the 1902 state elections. Its former president, A. Bernier, was running for the legislature on the Democratic ticket, the Victor Miners' local unanimously endorsed Populist Frank Owers for governor, and Socialist gubernatorial candidate J. C. Provost was a Trades Assembly delegate. The *Press* supported the Democrats. The paper's policy was particularly divisive because it endorsed H. E. Insley, the Democratic nominee for state auditor who had served as an El Paso County deputy in the 1894 strike. The *Press* claimed that Insley had not served voluntarily. The WFM, the District Trades Assembly, and the Altman WFM local denounced him as an enemy to organized labor and called on all workers to vote against him.[86]

At least partly as a consequence of the Insley controversy, the paper's management and board of directors referred its political policy to the stockholders at their annual meeting on December 3, 1902. The stockholders voted for a non-partisan policy. The *Press* announced a "New Year's resolution" on January 4, 1903, that it would be "nonpartisan and independent politically." It would support candidates as individuals. Union members would "receive our unqualified endorsement and if there should be two or more union men nominated for the same office we can cheerfully recommend all of them and let the voters decide." The *Press* had certainly cheerfully recommended any number of candidates who were neither union members nor working class. The new policy meant that "whenever a candidate for public office is condemned by the labor organizations the Press [would] be free to oppose his election without breaking faith with any political party." The paper editorialized that it had "freed itself from political bondage and [could] devote itself to the cause of unionism." It had also freed itself from the county's printing business. The *Press* remained the official organ of Cripple Creek but not of Teller County.[87]

The union era in Cripple Creek coincided with an era of intense political realignment, and it is not particularly remarkable that organized labor's political allegiance remained in flux. Short of socialism, however, its political agenda remained fairly consistent through 1903. The CSFL Executive Board met from January 12 to 15, 1903, and drafted bills for an eight-hour law, the initiative and referendum, the licensing of barbers, and to prohibit storing explosives in or around mines. The District Trades Assembly also demanded an eight-hour bill and a law to establish unrestricted liability for work-related injuries. Corporate opposition blocked the constitutional amendment to enact the initiative and referendum that labor had long supported. The eight-hour amendment, which won overwhelming popular support in 1902, mandated the legislature to pass an eight-hour bill. The legislature, however, passed neither an eight-hour law nor the initiative and referendum. Governor Peabody refused labor's requests to include either measure in his call for a special legislative session in 1903.[88] For some labor leaders these failures proved that the major parties subverted working-class programs. For others they suggested that all politics was a waste of labor's energy.

Socialists gained influence in the Trades Assembly from 1901 to 1904. The body passed a resolution in late 1902 calling on President Roosevelt to nationalize coal lands and railroads. The secretary of the assembly was to send the resolution to the president and to the Colorado congressional delegation, and District labor representatives were to give the document "all possible publicity." Some delegates who were not Socialists countered by proposing a policy that would prohibit any partisan matter from coming before the assembly until it was adopted by an affiliated union. No political resolutions could be published or sent outside the District until all affiliates held a referendum vote, with the expense of the referendum to be borne by the sponsoring union. The resolution went to the Trades Assembly Executive Board to be redrafted because it was considered too stringent. It was, finally, "the sense of the assembly that a full discussion of any and all political and economic subjects should be permitted but not endorsed and broadcast as the opinion of the body without full deliberation and all members having a chance to vote upon them."[89]

The political controversy in the Trades Assembly reflected a gap between the growing numbers of union leaders who embraced socialism and the more accommodationist politics of the rank and file. Most of organized labor, like the *Press*, endorsed candidates for office on the basis of their union membership rather than their political affiliation. But the distance between the leaders and union members was neither stark nor complete. Cooks and Waiters No. 24, for example, endorsed the platform of the Socialist Party and donated $10 to the 1903 Socialist campaign.[90]

On the eve of the 1903–4 strike, all of the larger labor bodies with which local unions affiliated had endorsed the Socialist Party or its platform, the *Press* and the Trades Assembly were officially nonpartisan, and the Democrats won most District elections. The State Federation of Labor put its resources into lobbying for progressive legislation, and District labor supported its efforts. There was a broad working-class consensus for a number of reforms, including the eight-hour day and the initiative and referendum. Many thought democratic reforms were intermediate steps toward working-class control of the economic and political systems. In 1903 the State Federation of Labor adopted a resolution that linked the initiative and referendum with socialism:

Whereas the power of the capitalist class rests upon institutions essentially political and

Whereas, We recognize the inadequacy of pure and simple trades unionism to grapple with the same; therefore be it

Resolved, by the Colorado State Federation of Labor in its eighth annual convention assembled, that we demand the initiative and referendum and the imperative mandate as a part of the organic laws of the state and nation.

We further demand that the means of production and distribution shall be owned by the whole people, and we recommend to our affiliated unions the study and discussion of the principles of Socialism.[91]

We cannot know how many Cripple Creek workers, like the CSFL, linked progressive reforms to a socialist state. They had not, by 1903, united behind the Socialist Party. A scant two years after the Socialist Party was founded, however, the *Press* and the Trades Assembly had backed away from major party politics, and Socialists exercised considerable influence in the District unions. Socialist Party members J. C. Provost and R. E. Croskey were elected president and secretary of the Trades Assembly. Croskey also served as first vice president of the Colorado State Federation of Labor, and J. C. Sullivan of Victor, also a Socialist, was elected president. Croskey carried all but one District local in the CSFL election, receiving 2,013 votes to 122 for his opponent. Sullivan won 1,552 votes to fellow Socialist D. C. Coates's 565.[92]

Most District workers occupied a political spectrum to the left of center and advocated objectives that ranged from social reform through the major parties, to establishing, through electoral politics, the socialist cooperative commonwealth. What united these positions was faith in labor's political power. Workers believed that, given education and organization, they could achieve fundamental change through democratic processes.

CHOICES

Through 1904 Colorado unions remained torn between independent working-class politics and more broad-based reform coalitions. The dominant sentiment within organized labor moved from the radical populism of the early 1890s through shifting fusion alliances, until in 1903 workers debated whether to support the Democrats, who inherited the silver coalition, the Socialists, who represented independent working-class politics, or all candidates who belonged to organized labor, regardless of their party.

Given these political realignments, what affected the ballots of individual voters? What separated Democrats and fusionists from radical Populists, working-class separatists, and the influential Socialist minority? Some answers may be gleaned by link-ing the 1900 census with political activists—those who ran for public office, campaigned for candidates, or were delegates to party conventions (Appendix A).

The census must be used with care. The 1900 election is the only one for which some census information could be directly connected with political party affiliations, because the census was taken that year. Some census data—birthplace, sex, and birth date—do not change, but others—occupation, marital status, and household composition—do. So did partisan choices. Thus, for example, an activist listed as married in 1900 was not necessarily married when he or she supported the Populist Party. I used the census to explore the 1900 election (about which it reveals the most) and, more cautiously, for what it could say about other people who had been politically active between 1894 and 1904. Republicans appeared on the ballot throughout this period. Populists were most active from 1892 to 1898, and the last major Populist campaign occurred in 1902. Democrats appeared on the ballot every year, gaining power from 1898 to 1902. Silver Republicans were active between 1896 and 1900; Social Democrats and the largely female Bryan and Stevenson Clubs in 1900. The Socialist Party began organizing in 1901. Thus, Socialists were older, and more had married, since 1900 when the census was recorded. Populists were generally younger, and more were likely single. But even accounting for such factors, data for the ten-year period did not differ markedly from data for 1900.

Family, property, and a stake in the community encouraged political activism of all kinds. Most political activists, regardless of party, were older than their constituents and more likely to be married, have families, and be propertied homeowners than the adult population as a whole. Most were over thirty. Republicans and Silver Republicans, however, were older than activists in other parties. More than a third of the Republican activists in the 1900 election were in their fifties. A fifth of all the Republicans in the sample and 40 percent of the Silver Republicans were born between 1840 and 1850.[93] They could remember the Civil War. Perhaps they identified the party with Lincolnian democracy rather than with the goldbug McKinley. Lincoln was a powerful figure for labor and in Colorado politics generally. Silver Republicans traced their roots to the original Republican Party, "born in answer to the cry for a champion of liberty," and compared Bryan favorably to Lincoln. So did Democrats. The GOP ridiculed an El Paso County Democrat who claimed to be "a Democrat after the idea of Jefferson and Lincoln and Bryan." Goldfield Republicans organized the Goldfield Lincoln Republican Club, and the Silver Republican Party changed its name in 1900 to the Lincoln Republican Party.[94]

Organized labor frequently compared chattel and wage slavery and saw Lincoln as a champion of free labor. Age might explain how some labor leaders translated working-class loyalties into voting Republican. Consider, for example, W. W. Ferguson, president of Victor Federal Labor Union No. 64 and the Victor Trades

Assembly, member of the WLU Executive Board, and delegate to CSFL conventions. A Populist during 1899 and 1900 and an officer of the Cottage Home Club, Ferguson then became a Republican for two years before running for office as a Democrat in 1903. He was also a Civil War veteran and a member of the Victor GAR.

Commensurate with their age, more political activists were married and lived in family households than the adult population as a whole. Silver Republicans, Populists, Socialists, and Social Democrats lived with families in higher than average proportions.[95] More activists from all parties were married than District adults as a whole—from 68 percent of the Co-operatives and Socialists to 92 percent of the Silver Republicans. To some extent, as with the Republicans (88 percent of whom were married), marital status was related to age, but even the younger Socialist Party leaders were disproportionately married in 1900.[96]

Men dominated the political leadership, but Bryan and Stevenson Clubs provided a political outlet for women in 1900. Women also constituted a sizable minority of Democratic and Populist activists, a legacy of Populist support for woman suffrage in 1893.[97] Although some have speculated that women were a conservative electorate, there is no evidence that this was true in Cripple Creek, where most women political leaders worked in left-of-center parties.

Like the lodge and union leaders, political activists were more likely than all adults to be propertied homeowners. Although only 18 percent of all District adults and 48 percent of all household heads owned homes in 1900, 46 percent of those active in the 1900 elections owned their homes and 69 percent of household heads. Among those politically active any time between 1894 and 1904, 39 percent owned homes in 1900—64 percent of household heads. Younger Socialist Party and Social Democratic leaders were only slightly more likely than average to be homeowners; nearly half the Socialist household heads owned homes. The older Co-operative and Populist leadership exceeded property ownership among Democrats and Republicans. Fully 82 percent of all Populist leaders and 70 percent of the Co-operatives owned homes in 1900, and several younger Socialists married and bought houses shortly after the census was taken.[98] Family, property, and a stake in the community encouraged political activism of all kinds; they did not promote conservatism.

The most notable ethnic influence in local politics was the high level of Irish activism in support of Democrats and Populists and the representation of second-generation Irish among Socialist Party leaders. Most activists, like most adults, were native-born Americans; the only significant exception was a slightly higher proportion of immigrants among the leaders of labor's Co-operative Party, reflecting the higher proportions of immigrants among skilled workers.[99] Immigrant and Irish activism expressed the political choices of organized labor and reflected the influence of Rednecks in both arenas.

Workers' representation in the leadership of most parties was seldom proportionate to their numbers in the local population (79 percent all of adults). Silver Republicans and Republicans included proportionately few workers in the party leadership (54 percent and 31 percent, respectively). Working-class leaders predominated only in the independent working-class Co-operative Party and in the Socialist parties. Only the Socialist Party, with 86.5 percent of its activists from working-class households, and the Social Democrats, entirely working-class, exceeded the proportions of workers in the District.[100]

Organized labor nonetheless exerted considerable influence in District politics. Almost a third of all the political activists identified belonged to unions. In 1900, 21 percent of all Democratic activists, 34 percent of the Populist leadership, 70 percent of the Social Democrats, and only one Republican (3 percent) belonged to unions.[101] The more radical their politics, the more these political leaders clustered in the upper levels of union leadership. The *Miners' Magazine* and the WFM leadership endorsed the Social Democratic presidential ticket in 1900. Union members who were Democratic activists were most likely to belong to the rank and file or be local union leaders; Populists were most likely to be elected to District, state, or national union offices; and Social Democrats clustered in the highest levels of union leadership. There were as many Social Democrats as Democrats among the District's state and national union leaders in 1900, and more Populists (table 17).[102]

Union members supported the parties that advocated labor's political agenda. Most prominent Socialists were also prominent in the labor movement. Some 70 percent of all identified Socialist Party and Social Democratic Party members also belonged to unions, as did a known majority of the Co-operative activists (54 percent). Free silver was reflected in the fact that four in ten Silver Republican activists (38.5 percent) and half of the Populists (47 percent) were also prominent in organized labor. Proportionately fewer major party leaders held union cards — 29 percent of Democrats and 22 percent of Republicans.[103]

The extent of labor influence in District politics also reflected the deep investment of many workers in their local communities, particularly mining labor. Other people might seek economic opportunities in the gold camp, but their skills and interests allowed them to move. The political left reflected the interests of union miners who sought to settle, establish homes and families, and shape social relationships in the District.

Socialists, Co-operatives, and Populists were more likely than members of the major parties to live in smaller towns that were residential centers for miners and their families and where a militant union tradition nourished their political radicalism. Silver Republicans clustered in the commercial center of Cripple Creek, and Democratic and GOP activists lived predominantly in Cripple Creek and Victor. Populists, Co-operatives, Social Democrats, and Socialists (members of all

TABLE 17
Political Activists' Level of Union Participation by Affiliation

	Rank and File		Local Leader		District Leader		State and National Leader		Unknown	
	N	%	N	%	N	%	N	%	N	%
Democrat	18	25	31	42	9	12	15	21	0	0
Republican	4	21	7	37	2	11	5	26	1	5
Silver Republican			3	75			1	25		
Populist	5	19	6	23	3	12	12	46		
Co-operative	4	27	3	20	2	13	6	40		
Socialist	1	4	5	19	6	22	14	52	1	4
Social Democrat	1	14	1	14	5	71				
Co-operative–Populist	1	6	5	28	3	17	8	44	1	6
Bryan and Stevenson Club	1	14	4	57	1	14	1	14		

Sources: Political sample and union sample.
Note: Some figures do not total 100 percent due to rounding.

the more radical and independent labor parties) all lived in disproportionate numbers in smaller, working-class towns around the mines, especially in Altman, the center of union activity in the 1894 strike, in nearby Independence and Goldfield, and, for the Co-operatives, in the mill and railroad town of Gillett. Altman, Goldfield, and Independence together housed only 13 percent of all District adults, but 42 percent of the Populist leaders lived in one of those towns, 43 percent of the Co-operatives, 32 percent of the Socialists, and 30 percent of Social Democrats.[104]

These smaller towns were overwhelmingly working-class. In contrast to Cripple Creek and Victor, which offered many meeting places and diversions, the union halls of the smaller communities functioned as primary centers of social and political life. The unions offered opportunities to discuss union history and class politics. Altman held a special identity as the early bastion of District unionism. The *Press* urged workers to stand together and vote for the Co-operatives in 1899 because they were united by the "illustrious example of three dollars for eight hours' work wrung from the millionaire mine owner by the fearless sons of labor on Bull Hill." The "fearless sons of labor" created an environment that supported class-conscious politics. During the Co-operative campaign of 1899 the Democratic rally at Altman reputedly witnessed the "severest frost of the season." "Attendance was slim and enthusiasm was nil" because of local support for the Co-operative–Populist ticket. The 1899 contest for Co-operative votes was close in Goldfield and Anaconda; only the Bull Hill bastions of Altman and Independence gave the Co-operative Party an electoral majority. In 1900 the Altman *Press* correspondent reported, "Politics are warm and McKinleyites are scarce on the hill."[105] The popular vote followed the residential patterns of the party leaders. Older, married, perhaps of Irish descent, they developed political identities in the workplace and in communities where class relations were matters of daily discussion.

By 1902 Altman, Goldfield, Anaconda, Cameron, and Elkton all had active Socialist Party locals. The smaller mining communities welcomed leaders of organized labor and the political left. Cheering miners and shaft house whistles greeted WFM and WLU delegates who visited Altman in 1900.[106] Such enthusiasm drew orators to Bull Hill and stimulated more sophisticated political discussion than might be heard in much larger communities.

Not surprisingly, most of the Altman town officers were union members. Their power was important symbolically as well as for their concrete political influence. Altman demonstrated "that workingmen [could] own and operate a town successfully." The *Press* used Altman to exemplify the ideal business practices demonstrated by the wise government of organized labor, calling it a "model municipality" for its good streets, water works, city building, fire department, municipal services, and lack of debt. Known as a good family town, Altman had few disturbances and only one police officer. These accomplishments, the *Press* declared, showed that "men who create the wealth know something of the true value of wealth, and if given representation in accordance with taxation, they see to it that an adequate return is realized for public funds expended."[107]

Altman's all-labor city government was, for most of the union period, officially Populist. Populism also drew strong support in other small towns. The Goldfield Populists' 1900 platform closely paralleled organized labor's, opposing private ownership of public utilities, endorsing the initiative and referendum, and supporting the Filipinos and Boers in their fights for liberty and the striking Idaho miners "persecuted and driven from their homes by a democratic governor and a republican president." It was no accident that local Populists, and later Socialists, articulated the political positions of Colorado labor. The labor leadership came disproportionately from the political left of the mining camps, and Populists and Socialists were committed union leaders. In his analysis of Colorado Populism, James Wright identified labor, particularly the WFM leadership, as "persisting dissenters" who continued the radical Populist tradition in the Socialist Party.[108] Cripple Creek confirms his conclusion.

The rank and file apparently had not, by 1904, followed the leadership to vote for the Socialist Party. But neither did radical politics alienate them; they elected and reelected radicals to the highest union offices. In some locals, partisan politics seem to have had little influence on union elections. Cripple Creek Carpenters No. 547, for example, elected as president at various times C. S. Buck, a Democrat; J. W. Higens, a Republican; P. N. McPhee, a Populist; and John W. Dinwiddie, a Socialist. All four espoused the labor theory of value, the need for working-class organization, and the need to check capitalist power through political action.[109]

The political paths that union leaders chose demonstrated the different avenues through which individuals pursued political efficacy. William R. Phelps, president of Victor Miners No. 32, a member of the *Press*'s board of directors, and delegate to CSFL and WFM conventions, chaired labor's Co-operative Party. In 1900 he served as a delegate to the Teller County Silver Republican convention. Phelps fit the pattern of a pro-labor Lincolnian Republican; born in 1852, he had been a drummer boy in the Civil War.[110]

D. C. Copley, also a Republican in 1898, chose differently. He served as secretary of Altman Stationary Engineers No. 75, as a delegate to WFM and CSFL conventions, as president of the Cripple Creek District Executive Board of the WFM, and as a member of the WFM Executive Board from 1902 to 1904. In 1900 he supported the Co-operative Party and ran for governor as a Social Democrat. By 1902 he was an active Socialist Party leader.

John Calderwood, the 1894 strike leader, took an opposite course. President of Altman's Free Coinage Miners No. 19 in 1894 and a member of the WFM Executive Board from 1894 to 1896, throughout the 1890s and as late as 1900 Calderwood remained an active Populist. He served as an officer of Carl Browne's Cottage Home Club in 1899 and was the preferred Populist nominee for lieutenant governor in 1900. Ironically, because he was rejected as too radical and replaced by D. C. Coates, by 1903 Calderwood was a Republican, although still a union supporter.

Jerry Kelly, financial secretary of Victor Miners No. 32, was more representative of the union leadership and ran for public office sequentially as a Co-operative, a Populist, and a Socialist. Daniel P. McGinley, secretary of the Altman Miners' local, was just as typical. McGinley, who died in 1901 before the WFM endorsed socialism, belonged to the Populist Sovereign Citizens Club, supported the Co-operative–Populist fusion ticket in 1899, and then worked as an ardent Democrat from 1900 until his death.

Different partisan choices expressed in part how people interpreted the functions of political parties and labor unions. Most parties were cross-class coalitions; unions were wholly working class. Political choices expressed what individuals thought they could win through the state rather than at the workplace. It was possible for a union member to vote for working-class imperatives in union elections and opt for patronage and protection on election day. Many who desired fundamental social and economic change did not join the more radical political parties because they felt that immediate reforms and union survival were necessary to achieve long-term social change. Others, who held similar goals for reform and social transformation, believed that independent working-class organization in politics and at the workplace promised the only meaningful change.

The greater involvement of the union leadership in more independent and radical political alternatives, including the Socialist parties, reflected Socialist commitments to organizing politics and production. It also demonstrated how commitments to independent labor politics were mobilized through discussions and personal contacts at union meetings and conventions.

WFM POLITICS REVISITED

The WFM's Socialist endorsements generated a series of questions for U.S. labor history. The first concerned why western labor was so much more radical than an assumed moderate (eastern) "mainstream" of American labor. By the 1970s some historians argued that the WFM was not radical, regardless of the Socialist resolutions, because unions spent most of their time on bread-and-butter issues or because union members did not vote Socialist, or because locals were rarely involved in violent strikes. David Emmons concluded that the Irish miners of Butte were working-class conservatives, concerned primarily with jobs and working conditions.[111]

The complex commitments of individuals to workplace organizing and a variety of political parties renders any simple labels inadequate to describe labor politics. To argue whether western labor was reformist or radical is to engage a false dichotomy; it was both. The Butte Irish composed only a portion of the Butte working class, and some Butte Irish voted for the WFM Socialist resolutions. Even those who did not were not necessarily political conservatives. Joseph Calloway of the Butte Miners' Union, who voted against the WFM Socialist resolution in 1902, said that "he was glad to hear the principles as represented by Mr. Debs, and wondered how such a man could have been incarcerated in prison for standing for such principles." He voted against the resolution because he opposed "any action which would create any division of the ranks." Delegate B. M. Lindsay of Butte Stationary Engineers No. 83, who also voted against the resolution, "said he was a Socialist and voted that ticket, but at the same time he acknowledged every man had a right to cast his vote according to his own conscience." Lindsay favored "keeping trades union and political parties separate."[112]

Thus, even negative votes on Socialist Party resolutions did not fully reflect political sentiment within the unions. It distorts the complexity of labor's goals to weigh unions' commitments to bread-and-butter gains and job security against long-term aspirations for fundamental change, as if these were necessarily opposed desires. Such oppositions confuse distinctions between what workers sought to gain in the workplace and what they sought from local, state, or federal governments.

If a radical is one who advocates fundamental social and economic change, then to varying degrees the Cripple Creek working class was radical. If a reformer works to achieve change in existing institutions, then even the radicals pursued some reform agendas, notably the eight-hour law. More important, however, the full range of workers' social and economic analyses was not reflected in electoral politics. The fusion coalitions undermined the radical Populism of the early 1890s. Portions of organized labor, understandably enough, accepted reforms as a strategy for union survival and supported Democratic, fusion, and even Republican slates. These alliances expressed their faith in cooperation among "the producing classes," a sentiment articulated earlier through the Knights of Labor.[113] That tradition influenced the *Daily Press* as it asserted that it was conservative and businesslike, endorsed managers and merchants for public office, and hailed the working-class officials of Altman for being good businessmen.

An evolving radical tradition found expression through Waite Populism, the CSFL's attempts to form an independent labor party, the District unions' Co-operative Party, and later in the Social Democratic and Socialist parties. By 1903 anti-fusion Democrats had swallowed the Populist and Silver Republican parties. The *Press* and the Trades Assembly had declared that they were nonpartisan. District labor had backed away from major party politics and decided to support union members for public office, regardless of party. To that extent, District labor had moved toward independent labor politics.

Cripple Creek does not offer simple definitions of working-class politics, but it does challenge some assumptions about American radicalism, particularly that radicals were likely to be foreign-born, unmarried, and rootless. If radical Populism in the 1890s and then membership in the Social Democratic or Socialist parties were radical political choices, then Cripple Creek radicals were more likely to be native-born, married, and settled than most District residents and leaders of other political parties. They were the home guard, not the bindlestiffs; their radicalism was rooted in the communities they built and the homes they guarded.[114] They shared a heritage of union activism and labor conflict. Their constituents, few of whom voted Socialist, respected them and consistently reelected them to high union offices.

Given their stability and commitment, Socialists might have won other workers to their views. Certainly, many conservatives were afraid that they might. By 1903 labor's Socialist endorsements alarmed Colorado employers who considered organized labor a threat to capitalist enterprise. Organizing through Mine Owners' Associations and Citizens' Alliances, they used the specter of Socialist labor to justify their attacks on unions as they had used fears of Waite Populism a decade earlier.

Labor policies continued, even with the Socialist Party endorsements, to express a mixture of desires for survival, immediate reforms, and long-term radical goals. Local political power convinced some workers to vote for union supporters regardless of party and others that socialism could be won at the ballot box. But neither independent third parties nor fusion coalitions triumphed to win state support for reform, socialism, or even survival. Labor's eight-hour amendment won overwhelming popular support in 1902, but the legislature failed to enact it and Governor Peabody refused to support it. For some labor leaders these failures suggested that the major parties subverted working-class programs. The leaders supported the Socialist Party because, in the words of one miner, labor was "impotent to better conditions, unless it took political action along class-conscious lines."[115]

Fears that the Socialist Party endorsements would threaten organized labor led to political disagreements among union leaders. Some, particularly those who lived in Cripple Creek and Victor, where most merchants and professionals lived, supported cross-class reform coalitions. Others favored independent working-class politics, reinforced in their radicalism by their neighbors in smaller working-class towns. Some union leaders proudly marched with the merchants and employers who were their lodge brothers, campaigned with them for public morality and Asian exclusion, and voted for Populists or Socialists like the union brothers with whom they shared the fellowship of labor conventions and union halls. Others endorsed fusion politics, trusting that the fraternity of the local bars, lodge halls, and party conventions cemented working-class influence in electoral politics.

The most widely shared legacy of the decade of union power was a belief, among working-class fusionists and radicals alike, that a more equitable society could be won through working-class organization and peaceful political processes. Labor pursued survival at the local level, where party did not matter as much as patronage and union allegiance. Fusion candidates supported reforms to make the workplace safer and the political process more democratic and to use taxes to equalize wealth. The collapse of the fusion alliance and the three-way governor's race in 1902 sent James Peabody to the governor's mansion. Socialism could not be won locally, and the absence of a strong independent party left labor politically weak. Until 1904, however, labor's local power sparked a vital debate about political strategy. Radical Populists, Democrats, Silver Republicans, fusionists, and Socialists all worked to construct politics "along class-conscious lines."

Part 3

All That Glitters

"As If We Lived in Free America"

Delegates from mines and mills throughout the West opened the annual Western Federation of Miners convention in Denver on May 23, 1904. They soberly surveyed the state of their union, battered by more than a year of protracted strikes in the Cripple Creek District and elsewhere throughout Colorado. A week later, while they were still meeting, the Colorado state militia, the Cripple Creek District Mine Owners' Association (MOA), and the anti-union Citizens' Alliance (CA) staged a Decoration Day parade in Victor. About a hundred soldiers and strikebreakers marched, followed by twenty-seven Elks, eighty school children, forty adults, eleven members of the GAR, and a few mine owners in carriages. Victor Miners' Union representatives reported that "all the law abiding citizens" refused to march in a parade with "scab herders." Spectators were scarce.

The union immediately printed circulars inviting liberty-loving citizens to assemble that afternoon for their own parade. On that short notice some 1,500 people turned out. More than seven hundred marched behind the banner of Victor Miners' Local No. 32. The WFM women's auxiliaries mustered 247, and the Newsboys' local about forty. About a hundred school children paraded, along with Victor city officials, the Goldfield fire department, members of other unions, the Red Men, the Daughters of Pocahantas, and many individuals. More union miners would have marched, but James Burns's union work force was on shift at the Portland Mine. The procession was more like the Fourth of July than Decoration Day.[1]

The people who gathered on such short notice paraded their pride and support for embattled union labor. Later, they could tell their children that they marched in the last union parade in the Cripple Creek District.

        ◈   ◈   ◈

The end began quietly enough. During August 1902 WFM Executive Board member D. C. Copley organized Colorado City mill workers whose new Colorado City Mill and Smeltermen's Union No. 125, like the District WFM locals, belonged to WFM District Union No. 1. The millmen's union included workers from Tutt,

Penrose, and MacNeill's Standard Mill (USR&R), James Burns's Portland Gold Mining Company mill, and the Telluride Reduction and Refining Company. USR&R hired Pinkerton detective A. H. Crane to infiltrate the millmen's local, then used Crane's information to fire forty-two union men. On February 14, 1903, a committee protested the dismissals with vice-president and general manager Charles MacNeill. At the same time, union representatives requested that the minimum wage be increased from $1.80 to $2.25 a day and that the millmen have the right to belong to a union. MacNeill refused to negotiate, ostensibly because no member of the committee worked for Standard (it included one Portland employee, one Telluride employee, and one of the workers MacNeill had fired). Because MacNeill refused to bargain, the millmen struck at the USR&R's mills. El Paso County deputy sheriffs provided security at USR&R expense until the county assumed the costs; MacNeill and several strikebreakers were appointed deputies for the duration of the strike.[2]

The same day that the union committee visited MacNeill, it met with Frank G. Peck, secretary-treasurer of the Portland Gold Mining Company, and Hugh W. Fullerton, general manager of the Telluride Reduction Company. Two weeks later they both refused to recognize the union, and the strike spread to their mills on February 28. The companies hired strikebreakers and demanded more protection, which El Paso County sheriff W. R. Gilbert asked James H. Peabody, the newly elected governor, to provide. On March 3, MacNeill presented Gilbert's request to Peabody. Gilbert later testified that there was no disorder; the mayor, police chief, and city attorney of Colorado City all opposed his request for troops. Peabody nonetheless ordered his new adjutant general to activate some three hundred National Guard troops, who guarded company property and escorted non-union workers for the next seventeen days.[3]

Cripple Creek miners considered the Colorado City mills part of local industry. They refined Cripple Creek ore, and their workers belonged to Cripple Creek District Miners' Union No. 1. "If the millmen's union is to be so easily crushed," the *Press* warned, "it is but a step to Cripple Creek where more crushing will be done." Industrial unionism required the miners, if necessary, to "do their duty to their organization and GO OUT TO A MAN." The District Trades Assembly pledged its moral and financial support to the District Union "in any trouble it may be forced into."[4]

The WFM's industrial unionism, like its political goals, pushed it to organize beyond the mining towns. To maintain economic power as capital consolidated mines, railroads, and smelters, the union had to organize mill and smelter workers as well as miners. To achieve change through the electoral process required an activist state and political allies outside the mining communities. Both workplace control and politics forced labor to move beyond the relatively secure boundaries of the District. There it must face employers and a new governor who shared neither labor's assumptions nor the cross-class social relationships of the local labor community. What that meant was not yet apparent in 1902, as Copley moved to organize the mill workers who refined Cripple Creek gold.

Between August 1902, when Copley organized Local No. 125, and February 1903, when MacNeill refused to bargain, a pivotal event occurred. When the Colorado fusion coalition collapsed in 1902 the unresolved political tension between moderates and radicals left an opening for conservatives to attack organized labor. In the resulting three-way gubernatorial race the Democrats and Populists won a combined majority of the votes, but Republican James Hamilton Peabody took the office by a plurality. That began a nightmare for Colorado unions. Employers knew that Peabody, a Canon City banker, was no friend of organized labor, and they gave him every opportunity to prove it.[5]

During Peabody's two-year term, major strikes rocked the northern and southern Colorado coal fields, the mills and smelters of Denver and Colorado City, and the hard-rock communities of Clear Creek County, Telluride, and the Cripple Creek District. The strikes have been interpreted either as the inevitable consequence of labor's Socialist endorsements—which threatened Colorado employers as much as the earlier Populist insurgency and the aborted Independent Labor Party—or as labor's attempts to achieve by direct action the eight-hour day that the state supreme court and legislative inaction had denied. The various strikes, however, originated with diverse local issues and escalated because anti-union owners could mobilize state support.

Conservative employers organized nationally through the National Association of Manufacturers and the Citizens' Industrial Association and in Colorado through Citizens' Alliances and Mine Owners' Associations, all of which considered most unions, including the WFM, dangerously radical. Peabody helped found the Canon City Citizens' Alliance. His allegiance was as clear as Davis Waite's had been ten years before. Over the protests of local authorities, he dispatched the National Guard to Telluride, the southern coal fields, Colorado City, and the Cripple Creek District. The troops arrested WFM president Charles Moyer and held him in Telluride from March 29 to July 5, 1904, on charges of "military necessity as well as military discretion." Peabody, however, sent no troops to Idaho Springs, where businessmen deported fourteen striking union miners from Clear Creek County. He appointed mine manager Sherman Bell to be adjutant general of the National Guard and named USR&R owners Charles MacNeill and Spencer Penrose as aides-de-camp on his personal staff, appointing his two "Colorado Springs Colonels" while the National Guard was "protecting" their mill from striking WFM millworkers.[6]

The 1903–4 Cripple Creek strike jeopardized everything that labor had built in the previous ten years. Ideological consistency and ultimate social goals became abstract luxuries. Union survival was the only real issue. Colorado labor reacted defensively to recurrent waves of crises for a year and a half, as issues that had been quickly negotiated for a decade suddenly became non-negotiable and former friends became enemies.

Published accounts of the Cripple Creek strike and the Colorado "labor wars" of 1903–4 have emphasized the violence of these conflicts between capital and labor, but they have missed divisions among employers and within the middle class that also drove the struggle.[7] Only part of the interpretation concerns who was violent, although that was the contemporary focus of ideological discourse. A more important question concerns who controlled the ideological interpretation of violence. Anti-union employers used the state to threaten both their business rivals and organized labor and justified their acts in terms of democratic values. Both the enormity of actual events and their subsequent portrayal require some retelling. The strike story in this chapter precedes an analysis in chapter 9 of the strike and its significance.

❀   ❀   ❀

The unions believed that they dealt from strength, because they represented a majority of all workers in the District. Despite political divisions, labor had elected a number of union members to public office in the towns and county, including Sheriff Henry Robertson and law enforcement officials in Victor and many of the smaller towns.[8] And if workers disagreed about socialism, mine owners were divided as well. Politically they were more united than the miners; some owners were Democrats, but most were Republicans. Some, such as the Woods family and James Burns, supported amicable if paternalistic relations with organized labor. But the conservatives—including Smith and Moffat, MOA president Ernest Colburn, MOA secretary Clarence Hamlin, Albert Carlton, Charles Tutt, Charles MacNeill, and Spencer Penrose—wanted to stop the WFM from extending its organizational power to the mills, and if possible to destroy the union. Tutt, Penrose, and MacNeill also wanted a business victory over their rival James Burns, who built the Portland Mill rather than use their USR&R plants and who quit the Cripple Creek Mine Owners' Association to protest their high refining charges.

At the heart of the strike lay the industrial integration of mining and smelting interests. The industrial unionism that motivated the organizing drive among the millworkers was meant to match an industrywide union work force against integrated mining, transportation, and refining conglomerates. Conservative mill owners sought to keep the union from extending its influence to refining. At the same time, business rivalries and differences in management philosophies also drove the strategies of conservative owners and the governor who proved a powerful ally.

Peabody's vision of industrial relations became apparent when he appointed Sherman Bell as his adjutant general, giving him command of the National Guard and the armed power to tip the scales in strike after strike. Bell, the manager of the Smith-Moffat interests in the Cripple Creek District, took a pay cut from his manager's salary of $5,000 a year to $1,800. Labor charged that the mine owners had covered the salary difference and that Bell's appointment was part of a plot to provoke strikes, instigate violence, blame the WFM, and crush the union. The *Press*'s coverage of Bell's appointment, however, initially reflected his close ties to District labor through the local lodges and the Asian exclusion campaigns. District workers assumed that the fellowship of the lodge halls would extend to the bargaining table and that coalition politics would protect their unions and right to organize. Bell's appointment was reportedly "received with great pleasure by his large circle of friends." But after the militia seized strikers' tents and forbade picketing in El Paso County, the *Press* charged Bell with "attempting to force trouble with the strikers for the purpose of establishing a bull pen" and called him the "Mine Owners' appointee" and a "blatherskite."[9]

❀   ❀   ❀

True to pattern, the unions treated Bell as a friend until he violated the code of "manly methods." And, following the methods that had worked for a decade, the WFM threw the organized strength of District miners behind the millworkers' organizing drive. The miners acted from ten years of success with short, effective strikes, believing that a brief show of solidarity would win for millworkers the right to organize. Accordingly, the WFM threatened to strike mines that shipped to the unfair mills, intending to dry up the ore supplies. When the management of the Standard, Portland, and Telluride refused to recognize the Smeltermen's local, the Executive Board of District Union No. 1 asked all mines to stop shipping ore to those mills. On March 5—two days after MacNeill asked Peabody to send troops to Colorado City—the MOA refused. Two days later, Peabody conferred with MacNeill and Peck and asked WFM secretary-treasurer William D. ("Big Bill") Haywood for the union's terms to end the strike. Haywood responded immediately: an eight-hour day, reinstatement of the fired union workers to their jobs, no discrimination against union members, and the guaranteed right to organize and belong to a union. Although Peabody asked Charles Moyer and company officials to meet with him in Denver on March 14, he apparently was not hopeful about the meeting's outcome. At Bell's urging, he asked Secretary of War Elihu Root whether an "allotment of Krag guns" was available, because a "serious strike was imminent."[10]

Portland and Telluride officials accepted the union's terms nonetheless, and by March 23 their mills were completely unionized. Once the Portland and Telluride mills settled, the mine owners' battle over reduction charges became a submerged issue in the strike. James Burns reportedly said, "It will be a cold day when MacNeill closes down the Portland mine or mill."[11]

MacNeill refused to fire his strikebreakers in order to reinstate the union workers or to discuss wages and union recognition. The WFM sued Sheriff Gilbert and the National Guard officers for violating civil liberties, illegally seizing property, and using the state to break the strike. Peabody offered to withdraw the troops if the WFM dropped the suit, and on those terms he deactivated the militia.[12]

Again, on March 16, the District Union threatened to strike unless ore shipments to USR&R ceased. Many of the District's largest mines supplied USR&R's ore bins, including, of course, properties that Tutt, Penrose, and MacNeill themselves owned and the Smith-Moffat mines that Bell had managed. To further complicate strike relationships, the socialites were intermittently negotiating to buy some of the Smith-Moffat mines. USR&R's major suppliers were the Strong and the Gold King, owned by MOA president Ernest A. Colburn and his partners E. W. Giddings, Charles Dudley, William Lennox, and Senator Scott; the Granite, owned by Tutt, MacNeill, Penrose, and Clarence C. Hamlin; Smith and Moffat's Vindicator and Independence Consolidated; and Carlton's Findley. Collectively, they employed some 1,750 men, 80 percent of whom belonged to the WFM.[13] Many of these mines were in the southeastern section of the District and thus pitted the most intransigent mine owners against the militant Bull Hill locals.

On March 17 MacNeill offered to reinstate the strikers when possible and meet with an arbitration board selected by Peabody or the chief justice of the Colorado supreme court. He refused Moyer's proposal of a board composed of one member chosen by MacNeill or Peabody, one by the WFM, and the third selected by those two. That afternoon the union struck all mines and samplers that supplied ore to the United States Reduction and Refining Company.[14] It was not a happy St. Patrick's Day for the Bull Hill Rednecks.

The miners assumed that by drying up the Standard's ore supply they would force MacNeill to negotiate. Three mines—the Vindicator, Strong, and Mary McKinney—agreed to stop shipping, and approximately 750 miners were called out of the other mines. "All is quiet in Victor tonight," the Press reported. "There will be no reason to call for state troops and Sherman Bell will not be given the opportunity to show the residents how important he is." Two days later, the Independence Consolidated, which Smith and Moffat owned and Bell managed, remained the only major mine affected. The miners' locals reported that they were flooded with membership applications.[15]

Peabody appointed an advisory board that asked District employers to help settle the conflict. MacNeill, under considerable pressure from District businesses, refused to reinstate the strikers but said that he would take them back as vacancies occurred, except for fourteen—presumably those he considered the primary "agitators." The executive committee of District Union No. 1 recommended, by a split vote, to accept MacNeill's terms. Many District WFM leaders felt that it was important to find some strategy to reinstate the fired union members so they could continue organizing. Moyer, who sided with the minority, accepted the decision, and the Colorado City and Cripple Creek strikes were settled on March 31 on MacNeill's terms.[16]

USR&R offered jobs to sixty of the strikers, but forty-seven turned them down because they were not offered their old jobs or because they were offered the positions of other union members. Another forty-two persons were denied employment because, they claimed, they belonged to the WFM. Only one union member was offered his previous job; MacNeill hired non-union workers to replace the strikers.[17]

In June the committee on strikes and lockouts recommended to the 1903 WFM convention delegates "that the miners in all mines furnishing ore to said Standard mill be called out, if necessary" to secure the same conditions that the Portland and Telluride had accepted. District delegates reported that their members were divided, and only the delegates from Altman were certain that their members would strike if asked. Some felt that the millworkers should have, as an organizing strategy, taken any job MacNeill offered. Many apparently felt that the millmen had not done much to help themselves and had handled the strike badly, and that someone from the District should have been in charge. Moyer continued to insist that MacNeill honor his agreement to reinstate his workers by giving them their old jobs. The convention unanimously endorsed the committee's recommendations, and District miners authorized the District Union Executive Board to call a strike if necessary.[18]

Just when labor needed its own newspaper to print the union's side of the story and win public support, the *Press* folded. In May 1903 the paper stated that "in trying to stay by the principles of the Federation it had lost business and was in debt." Unless the WFM assumed its debts, the newspaper would stop publishing. The WFM Executive Board deferred action, the *Press* soon closed, and the Victor *Record* became the only pro-union paper in the District.[19]

In Colorado City the Portland and Telluride worked an eight-hour day and paid the new union scale, with a $2.25 minimum daily wage; the Standard paid $1.80 for eight hours. Then the Telluride threatened to cut wages. Union millworkers voted to strike at USR&R on July 3 to achieve the union scale and reinstate union workers, but almost no union members were left at USR&R. Most Standard employees stayed on the job, and the discrepancies between the two union mills and the Standard remained unresolved. On August 8, after failing once again to negotiate with MacNeill, District Union No. 1 called a strike on all mines that shipped ore to Colorado City; 3,552 miners were on strike in the Cripple Creek District by August 11.[20]

By drying up the ore to all Colorado City mills instead of USR&R alone, the union apparently hoped to enlist the pressure of other mine owners to settle the strike. The Mine Owners' Association announced, however, that it could not influence the outcome because no local issues were involved. The WFM replied that all branches of the mining industry were represented in the MOA and that owners of mines, mills, samplers, and smelters influenced one another, just as miners supported workers throughout the industry. Moreover, some mine owners also owned mills and smelters, and competing District mine owners controlled the Colorado City refineries. On August 15 thousands attended a union picnic at Pinnacle Park to hear Moyer, Haywood, CSFL president John C. Sullivan, and other union leaders discuss the strike. "If the mine owners of the Cripple Creek district desire that peace should prevail in this district," Moyer declared, "all they have to do is to say to the United States Reduction and Refining Company, or Mr. MacNeill, 'If you desire to further reduce our ores, you must pay the men in your employ reasonable wages.' "[21]

Owners remained divided. The El Paso Mine resumed operations on August 18 behind a ten-foot fence with seventeen armed guards, some deputized by Sheriff Robertson and paid by the company. Cripple Creek businesses organized a Citizens' Alliance and cut off credit to striking miners. The WFM countered by opening cooperative stores at Cripple Creek, Victor, and Anaconda in late August and later a fourth store at Goldfield. James Burns's Portland Mine settled with the WFM and reopened on August 26, still a union property. Sympathizers sent strike support. The Federated Trades Assembly of Duluth paraded outside employment agencies and circulated ten thousand handbills in Minnesota mining towns to discourage strikebreakers.[22] The strikers' strategy worked quickly; the Standard Mill closed for lack of ore on September 2. The same day, Cripple Creek mine owners asked Peabody for troops.

A number of minor incidents had occurred in the District, some of them strike-related and some probably not. The shaft house of the Sunset-Eclipse mine and the home of a union member both burned. A union picket, Ed Minster, stopped a scab who was going to work at the Golden Cycle Mine. Minster apparently had a gun but put it away. John Hawkins, an Anaconda justice of the peace, was knocked down in Altman. Someone beat Thomas Stewart, a non-union worker who was building a fence around the Golden Cycle Mine, presumably to protect scab miners. The MOA offered rewards for information about the Sunset-Eclipse fire and the assaults on Hawkins and Stewart and asked Sheriff Robertson to appoint deputies to guard the mines and mills involved in the strike. Robertson complied, and the companies paid the costs. Robertson, however, refused to ask Peabody for troops. So the mine owners made the request, saying that they feared "a reign of terror," and Mayor French of Victor concurred. Robertson insisted that he could control the situation. He had arrested Minster and was seeking Hawkins's and Stewart's assailants. The District Union said it would not tolerate lawlessness and denied involvement in the assaults. Moyer argued that it was illegal to send troops because there had been no invasion or insurrection and no problem enforcing the laws of the state. On September 3, Peabody sent a commission to investigate that consisted of Brig. Gen. John Chase and Lt. Thomas E. McClelland of the National Guard and Attorney General N. C. Miller. That night Peabody and Bell met with E. A. Colburn and W. H. Bainbridge, the president and treasurer of the Cripple Creek Mine Owners' Association, who agreed that the mine owners would pay the costs if Peabody sent the militia to the District. Bell would issue certificates of indebtedness against the state, due in four years at 4 percent interest, which the soldiers and merchants could cash with the MOA.[23]

As the mine owners sealed their agreement, Chase, McClelland, and Miller arrived in Victor to meet with Mayor French, Postmaster F. M. Reardon, and other "leading citizens." In Cripple Creek the trio consulted Mayor W. L. Shockey, who refused to ask for troops; Sheriff Robertson, who said that he had the situation in hand; and members of the MOA and CA. The commissioners left the District at 4:10 A.M. without consulting any union representative. They telegraphed the governor from Colorado Springs that the lives of people in the District were in imminent danger, that property and personal rights were in jeopardy, and that a "reign of terror" existed. On September 4, 1903, the governor called out the National Guard. The next day, more than a thousand troops occupied the District.[24]

The WFM, the Victor city council, and Sheriff Robertson all protested. County commissioners charged that the troops had been called out to suppress "a riot that does not now and that never did exist, and to protect property and individual residents of the county that are not in danger." Mass meetings in Victor and Cripple Creek supported local officials and collected more than two thousand signatures protesting the governor's action.[25]

The MOA announced that it planned to reopen the mines and continue the fight until the WFM was "swept from the district," and the Citizens' Alliance applauded Peabody for sending the troops. Bell was direct about his purpose: "I came to do up this damned anarchistic federation." His junior officer, Thomas McClelland, declared, "To hell with the constitution, we aren't going by the constitution." Bell justified the ensuing reign of terror as a "military necessity, which recognizes no laws, either civil or social."[26]

❈ ❈ ❈

By September 10, soldiers were stationed at all the large mines that had been struck and patrolled the major roads. A Pinkerton detective reported that there was "no radical talk or threats of any kind that I can hear, on the part of the miners," that the soldiers and miners were becoming friendly, and that some soldiers sympathized with the strikers. He reported rifts among the mine owners. The Golden Cycle owners in particular charged that MacNeill gave them "too little returns for their ore."[27]

Despite reports that the strikers were peaceful, the troops began arresting union leaders. Charles G. Kennison, president of Cripple Creek Miners No. 40 and a member of the District Union executive committee, was riding an F&CC train on September 10 when he and J. E. Sturdevant began to argue about strikebreakers. Sturdevant hit Kennison, who drew a gun that caught in the bell rope. Sturdevant hit him again. Deputy Sheriff James W. Gaughan, still a WFM member, arrested Kennison for assault with intent to kill—in all likelihood to maintain civil authority rather than surrender Kennison to the militia. Sherman Bell dispatched forty-three soldiers to arrest Kennison, who was already in the county jail. He posted bond and was released the following day. The troops did arrest Charles Campbell, H. H. McKinney, and three other men and held them in the old Goldfield jail, known as the "bullpen," on the grounds of "military necessity." The men had allegedly threatened the militia, but Bell filed no charges against them. The troops next arrested union leader James Lafferty. And, at 1 A.M., September 12, seven soldiers seized Sherman Parker, secretary of Free Coinage Miners No. 19 and president of District Union No. 1, and took him from his home to the bullpen. District court judge W. P. Seeds issued writs of habeas corpus for Campbell, McKinney, Lafferty, and Parker and ordered Generals Bell and Chase to produce them. The habeas corpus cases were called September 18, with former Attorney General Eugene Engley representing the miners and Lieutenant McClelland appearing for the militia. When Seeds insisted that the four men be produced in court, some ninety soldiers surrounded the courthouse, an infantry company escorted the prisoners, and fourteen armed troops entered the courtroom, bayonets fixed. The next day the military did not bring the prisoners to court, and Seeds refused to proceed without them. The troops, however, did go to seize Kennison and take him to the bullpen. On September 23 the soldiers again surrounded the courthouse and trained a Gatling gun on the building. A detail of sharpshooters was stationed on the roof of an adjacent hotel, and thirty-four armed soldiers escorted the prisoners to court. Engley and WFM attorney John Murphy refused to proceed with the troops present. Military counsel Samuel D. Crump claimed that the soldiers could arrest people and hold them without charges because a *qualified* state of martial law existed. Peabody said that he had not declared martial law, but had dispatched the troops to aid civil authorities.[28]

The militia repeated its performance the next day. Thirty soldiers were present when Seeds ruled for the union. Asserting that "fundamental principles of American liberty" were at stake and "the military should never be permitted to rise superior to the civil power," he ordered the prisoners released. General Chase "de-

clined" to obey. He released the union leaders later, however, on Peabody's telegraphed instructions. The union immediately filed writs of habeas corpus to release
Kennison and three others in military custody.[29]

As all this transpired the soldiers invaded the Victor Miners' Union Hall, searched
it, arrested a number of union members, held most of them prisoner for short periods, and then released them. Among those they imprisoned were Joe Lynch, the
city marshal of Independence; William Dodsworth, the president-elect of the Victor Miners' Union; and County Commissioner P. J. Lynch, who expressed shock
and betrayal. Of Sherman Bell he said, "Here is a man who has known me for ten
years, and he knows that there is not a more law-abiding citizen of the community
than I am."[30]

The district court ruled that Bell was violating the law and ordered him and
Chase arrested for the unlawful imprisonment of Sherman Parker and others. But
Attorney General N. C. Miller held that military officers on duty were immune
from arrest, and Bell announced that no civil officer would be allowed to serve civil
processes to any National Guard officer on duty.[31]

Having defied the civil courts and elected officials, the military next turned its
attention to the press. The night of September 29, soldiers arrested the work force
of the Victor *Record*, taking editor George Kyner and four printers to the bullpen
because the paper had criticized the militia and printed official WFM statements.
Emma F. Langdon, a linotype operator whose husband was one of the imprisoned
workers, sneaked into the *Record* office, barricaded herself inside, and printed the
next edition, headlined "Slightly Disfigured but Still in the Ring," which she delivered to the bullpen. At Peabody's instructions the militia released the *Record*'s
staff to Sheriff Robertson, charged them with criminal libel for reporting that a
militia member was a former convict, and allowed their release after they posted
bond.[32]

In concert with the military harassment, the MOA began pushing companies to
fire union miners. The Woods Investment Company caved to the pressure, and
Frank M. Woods announced on September 30 that all employees must quit the
WFM at the end of the day shift. They walked out instead, including the superintendent, shift bosses, and all workers at the Woodses' Economic Mill. Only an estimated 2,900 miners worked in the District by October 10, including 500 union
men at the Portland and some 700 at other union mines. Despite MOA claims that
900 non-union miners were working in late September, a Pinkerton detective estimated that the real figure was closer to 225. In mid-October, 817 soldiers were stationed at mines throughout the District—at Camp Goldfield, which was the main
encampment on Battle Mountain, and at Camp Vindicator, Camp El Paso, Camp
Golden Cycle, Camp Elkton, and Camp Cripple Creek. But Peabody withdrew
all but two hundred by October 20.[33]

The financial fallout of the strike hit the entire District. In November the First National Bank of Victor and the Bi-Metallic Bank of Cripple Creek went bankrupt and closed, at least in part because miners left the District and withdrew their savings. The union charged that Peabody deactivated the troops because the MOA was not paying the bills. Almost $160,000 was outstanding on the certificates of indebtedness, the soldiers were owed $38,000, and the Citizens' Alliance merchants who supplied the military had unpaid accounts that ranged from $8,000 to $21,000. The two bank failures exacerbated a dismal local economy. Merchants could not get credit, and working people lost their savings. Community divisions widened as moderates and the small middle class took sides in the struggle. The WFM increased strike relief, and Bell informed Peabody that he would have to disband the troops because he could not procure coal, hay, oats, food, or other supplies. The federal government sent a thousand Krag-Jorgensen rifles and sixty thousand rounds of ammunition to the District, but they were of dubious value because Peabody threatened to recall the remaining soldiers if MOA funds did not come through.[34]

Labor concentrated on the local political race for county assessor and united behind P. J. Devault, secretary of the Trades Assembly, who ran on an Independent Citizens ticket. Claiming that the MOA and CA controlled both the Democrat and Republican candidates, the unions promised that Devault would make the mines pay their fair share of taxes. He was elected by three hundred votes on November 3, despite the united efforts of the employers for the Republican. Independent labor politics finally succeeded in mid-strike.[35]

Labor's peaceful victory at the ballot box, however, did not dominate press accounts. Instead, the news media painted a picture of union lawlessness based on incidents the WFM charged were staged to justify the troops. On September 14, E. E. Hartman of the Short Line Railroad told the military that some spikes had been removed from the tracks near the Economic Mill. On the night of November 14, the track walker on the F&CC Railroad discovered more spikes missing on a curve near Anaconda and warned the engineer, who was transporting businesspeople to Cripple Creek from a military ball in Victor. Two nights later a track walker again discovered that spikes and bolts had been removed from the rails near Anaconda, and the engineer was warned in time. H. H. McKinney, a lapsed member of the WFM, was arrested and confessed to two detectives—D. C. Scott, employed by the F&CC, and K. C. Sterling of the Mine Owners' Association—that he had yanked the spikes. McKinney charged as accessories Sherman Parker, president of District Union No. 1; W. F. Davis, president of the Altman local; and Thomas Foster, an Altman WFM activist. McKinney soon repudiated his confession and told WFM attorney Frank J. Hangs that he had been promised immunity and $1,000 to lie. He wrote to his wife that he did not know who had removed the spikes.[36]

Parker, Davis, and Foster were tried in February 1904 for attempted murder before a jury selected from a special panel of ranchers and timbermen from outside the District. Much of the testimony corroborated the strikers' charge that employers had staged the incidents. Changing his story yet again, McKinney admitted all three derailing attempts. He testified that Foster helped twice and that Scott and Sterling had promised him $500 for the job. Charles Beckman, a detective who had worked undercover as a member of Victor Miners No. 32 since April 1903 and whose wife was an undercover member of the Ladies' Auxiliary, said that he reported to Sterling as they plotted the derailing. Sterling admitted that he was employed on secret work by the MOA and that he, Beckman, and Scott had tried to induce WFM members to derail a train. Scott testified that only Beckman and McKinney tampered with the rails and spikes and that he and Sterling had witnessed the November 16 attempt. He said, however, that Davis and Parker loaned him money and tools. W. W. Rush, an F&CC engineer, said that Scott had asked him to identify a good place to derail a train and warned him that the rails had been tampered with. The night of the second attempt, Detective Sterling told Rush "that they had removed the entire rail—to move his engine slowly and when he heard torpedoes to stop the train." When he heard the torpedoes, Rush said, he discovered that only a few spikes had been removed, and his train proceeded safely. When the prosecution rested, R. E. Lewis, the Republican judge, dropped the charge against Foster and released Davis for lack of evidence.[37]

The defense claimed that the derailings were planned and performed by MOA detectives in order to persuade President Theodore Roosevelt to send federal troops. V. W. Mather, a butcher, swore that on the night of November 16 he saw Scott and another man at work on the train tracks. Many people testified that Beckman had tried to involve them or that they were with the union defendants during the nights in question. A. A. Rollestone, the cashier of the Bank of Victor and a member of the Citizens' Alliance, testified that on the night of the November 14 attempt he was with Parker from 10 P.M. until 2 A.M., along with Thomas Cornish, manager of Stratton's Independence. All union defendants were unanimously acquitted. McKinney was ordered held for trial, but A. E. Carlton and two other mine owners paid his bond. District Attorney Henry Trowbridge dropped the case in May 1904. McKinney was then seized at the MOA's offices, arrested for perjury in the train-wrecking case, and released on $300 bond, which the MOA covered.[38]

If the train-wrecking attempts created only the illusion of violence, that illusion became tragically real on November 21, when superintendent of the Vindicator Mine Charles H. McCormick and shift boss Melvin Beck died in an explosion on the six-hundred-foot level. A shattered pistol and some copper wire were found at the scene, but the coroner's jury could not determine what had caused the explosion. The mine was under military guard, only non-union men worked there, and no union members could enter by the shaft. Sheriff Robertson, Deputy District Attorney J. C. Cole, and Vindicator employees at the mine when the explosion occurred all concluded that the explosives were taken to the six-hundred-foot level through the working shaft. Nonetheless, the MOA charged an "inner circle" of the WFM with murder, and the military arrested fifteen strike leaders for the crime. Their cases were never prosecuted because no evidence was produced to link them to the explosion.[39]

The local confrontation of labor, employers, and the state mirrored conflicts throughout Colorado, which had become an industrial battlefield. By late November some twenty thousand coal and metal miners were on strike.[40] Some struck for the eight-hour day, responding directly to the legislature's failure to enact the public mandate. But other conflicts, like those in Colorado City and Cripple Creek, began with local issues. No single cause united the strikes unless the promise of potential state support prompted employers to refuse to settle issues they had previously negotiated.

Despite that support and some five hundred troops, employers claimed that they could not control the District, and the governor and attorney general agreed that the civil courts had undermined the state by releasing military prisoners. On December 4, 1903, Peabody declared martial law, citing the attempted train-wrecking cases and the Vindicator explosion to prove that Teller County was in a state of insurrection and rebellion. "The military will have sole charge of everything, and those whom the military think ought to be arrested will be landed in the 'bull pen,'" Sherman Bell announced. "If an order is issued to arrest all Socialists, they will be landed in the 'pen.'" Peabody tried to soften Bell's statement, explaining that he had declared "qualified martial law" so the military could hold prisoners who had been "released on flimsy or whatever pretexts." Only in such cases would "the writ of habeas corpus . . . be suspended."[41]

The military harassment that followed was often a confrontation between District labor and anti-union District employers. Within days of declaring martial law, Peabody ordered Frank Reardon, the postmaster of Victor and a brigadier general in the National Guard, to muster a new company, Company L, Second Regiment, Colorado National Guard, which was composed of eighty members of the Victor Citizens' Alliance. Harry T. Moore, president of the Alliance, was captain; A. A. Rollestone, cashier at the Bank of Victor, was first lieutenant; and Citizens' Alliance secretary A. C. Cole was second lieutenant.[42]

The state immediately demonstrated what the qualified suspension of habeas corpus meant in practice. On December 3, the day before Peabody declared martial law, the District court ordered the militia to produce prisoners. Sam Crump admitted that there were no charges against three of the men whom Judge Seeds ordered released. Three others were turned over to the sheriff, who set bonds. But as soon as one man, Victor Poole, was released, the militia seized him and took him from the courthouse back to the bullpen. On December 7, Judge Seeds ordered Poole produced, and two days later Peabody suspended Poole's habeas corpus rights, in order, he said, to ensure public safety. Declaring the military subservient to civil authorities, Seeds again ordered Poole's release. The military appealed to the Colorado supreme court, charged Poole with assault with intent to kill in a Goldfield saloon on March 15, 1902, and turned him over to the sheriff. He was tried on January 9 and released because no witnesses testified against him. The supreme court case was dropped because he had been surrendered to civil authorities.[43]

The attack on habeas corpus rights was only the opening shot. Within weeks the military suspended most of the Bill of Rights, turning next to freedom of the press. The night that Peabody declared martial law, Maj. H. A. Naylor informed George Kyner that the Victor *Record* was under military censorship and that he could no longer publish official WFM statements. Neither could he print his editorial for the December 5 morning edition, which charged that Peabody had declared martial law because the troops had not broken the strike in "a manner satisfactory to the mine owners of the district." Kyner did publish his editorial, which concluded, "The Record does not know at this time how far it will be allowed to express its opinion under the reign of military law, but we propose to proceed just as if we lived in Free America."[44]

The military immediately declared a ban on publications that criticized the government of the United States or Colorado and on news items or editorials that commented on the military forces of Colorado. It simultaneously suspended the right to bear arms, ordering all private individuals to surrender their arms and ammunition to the District commander by noon on December 8. And it abolished the right to freedom of assembly, prohibiting assemblages in the streets.[45]

Cripple Creek attorney John Glover, formerly a Populist member of Congress from Missouri, challenged the weapons ban, informing the press that he had two unregistered guns in his office and that Col. Edward Verdeckberg could collect them "when the supreme court ratifies his criminal usurpation against the liberties of the people of this country, and before that whenever he is bold enough to do murder under his illegal orders." Verdeckberg sent troops to arrest Glover, who locked himself in his office. The soldiers decided to rope the door shut and starve him out. Glover, however, thought they were trying to break in and fired but did not hit anyone. He was shot in the arm and surrendered before being released to two Golden Cycle Mining Company officials, who assured the authorities that Glover would make no more inflammatory statements. Allowed to seek treatment in a Colorado Springs hospital, Glover was subsequently arrested again and held in the bullpen until martial law was lifted in February. Reportedly, Glover's release and reimprisonment were connected to an ownership battle in which Albert Carlton was challenging John T. Milliken and L. E. Hill for control of the Golden Cycle. Glover represented the Milliken faction, which filed six suits against Carlton for defamation of character.[46]

As military harassment escalated, a number of union leaders joined Glover in the bullpen. A. G. Paul, secretary of Cripple Creek Miners No. 40, was imprisoned from December 10 to 23. On December 11 a squad of soldiers surrounded the Victor Miners' Hall and refused to let anyone enter or leave. Two days later, troops seized WFM Executive Board member D. C. Copley but released him the next day on Peabody's orders. The following week, a detail of soldiers invaded a Victor WFM meeting to arrest James Baker of the WFM Executive Board, who was in the District to open the cooperative store at Goldfield. Told to leave the District or face the bullpen, Baker left immediately. M. E. White of the ALU Executive Board was arrested when he arrived in Cripple Creek on December 28. The militia held White for two days, put him on a train, and told him never to return. On January 16, Norman Morrison, a defense witness in the train derailing cases, was arrested for quarreling with a merchant. The next day, soldiers searched his mother's house in Independence, arrested her for harboring criminals, and took her to Victor, where Colonel Verdeckberg ordered her released. Mrs. Morrison, a member of the WFM Women's Auxiliary and of the District Trades Assembly, ran a boardinghouse popular with union miners.[47]

The military declared that after January 7 troops would arrest anyone "found loitering or strolling about, frequenting public places where liquor is sold, begging or leading an idle, immoral, or profligate course of life, or not having any visible means of support." The WFM posted placards instructing members that they were not vagrants because they were supported from their own strike fund and thus had visible means of support. They were also advised not to leave their homes and to return if forced to leave. The militia tore down the union's placards and arrested and briefly held a child who was distributing them. Soldiers then arrested five men for having no visible means of support and for being agitators. They escorted them to the county line—despite a civil injunction against deporting any WFM members from the District.[48]

Sherman Parker, who had been held for attempted train-wrecking, was released when he posted bond on January 4, 1904, but arrested yet again as he left jail and held until January 20. Finally freed, Parker managed a brief visit with his wife Bessie—who was pregnant—before fleeing to Denver. Saying that he left so that he might spend a few days with his wife without being persecuted by the military (who had invaded a Victor Women's Auxiliary meeting to search for him), Parker turned himself in to the Denver chief of police. Peabody charged that Parker had proved "that as soon as those fellows secured a release they would skip out." The Denver police chief refused to release Parker to Sherman Bell without a request from the proper civil authorities. The military then charged Parker with assaulting Thomas Stewart the previous September, and Sheriff Robertson came to Denver to arrest him on the new charge. Robertson took him back, accompanied by Detective Scott, whom General Bell sent to supervise. Parker refused to pay his $1,000 bond so that he could not be released from civil custody and returned to the bullpen. The military then dropped the assault charge for lack of evidence. No longer subject to the civil authorities, Parker was released on January 25, rearrested, and taken back to the bullpen.[49]

The next day, the most violent event to that point rocked the District. As non-union miners came off shift at Stratton's Independence Mine on the night of January 26, the cage was drawn into the sheave wheel at the top of the shaft. The cable was cut, the cage dropped, and fifteen men fell to their deaths. The coroner's jury found that the engineer had lost control of the engine because of management's negligence in installing a safety device to prevent overwinding and because the disk brakes of the hoisting engine had been detached. The WFM accused the mine management of violating safety statutes. Management countercharged that the union had tampered with the machinery, despite the fact that the mine was within the main militia encampment at Camp Goldfield. After the accident 168 men reportedly quit at Stratton's Independence. The union claimed that fewer than seven hundred strikebreakers remained in the District.[50]

Two days later, Peabody announced that peace and good order were being restored and suspended martial law, effective February 2. He withdrew all but fifty soldiers and suggested to Clarence Hamlin that "the olive branch, the hand of friendship, should be extended to the striking miners, and that harmony between the employer and employee should be brought about." With martial law suspended, Sherman Parker and John Glover were turned over to the civil authorities and released on bond. By February 4 all WFM prisoners were out on bail, and on March 2 charges were dropped against Parker, W. F. Davis, Stephen Adams, and Charles G. Kennison for the Vindicator Mine disaster.[51]

But the remaining soldiers withheld "the hand of friendship." On March 12 troops occupied the Victor Union Hall, searched it for Charles Moyer, who was not there, and arrested Peter Calderwood, manager of the Anaconda Union Store, for displaying union posters. Three days later they arrested E. J. Spencer, also for displaying the posters. Peabody finally withdrew the remaining troops on April 12.[52]

The standoff solved neither the strike nor the battle among competing capitalists. While martial law was in force, the MOA pressured the remaining union mills outside the District, including the Dorcas Mill in Florence, which handled ore from a number of union mines and whose workers belonged to WFM Local No. 184. On December 9, 1903, the MOA ordered the Dorcas to fire all its union employees and employ no WFM members in the future. Dorcas manager J. M. Hower, Jr., initially refused but capitulated when the MOA threatened to divert his ore supply. Hower offered his workers union scale and eight hours if they would quit the union. They walked out instead. Next the employees of the Horse Shoe Mining Company, a union coal mine that supplied the Dorcas's coal, announced that they would quit if the Horse Shoe furnished coal to non-union operations. Their manager then told Hower to rehire his union workers or lose his coal. United Mine Workers organizer John Gehr went from house to house in Florence, gathering individual coal orders so the Horse Shoe would not suffer for its pro-union stand. The WFM asked the Portland (which remained a union mine) to furnish ore to Hower, who resisted further MOA pressure and refused in February to fire seventeen union miners from a Dorcas lease in the District.[53]

Hower was caught between organized labor and powerful mine owners as both sides tried to control ore supplies to mills and smelters. That was the WFM's tactic; the MOA countered by cutting shipments to all mills that employed WFM members. The Portland then diverted ore from its own mill to buttress the union Dorcas Mill.

The battle for industrial control escalated with the end of martial law. On March 10, 1904, the MOA instituted a working card system and required all miners to obtain an MOA permit to work in the District, effectively blacklisting all WFM members from MOA mines. The organization extended the pressure to leasers, announcing that they must all submit monthly lists of their employees for MOA approval. The Home Gold Mining Company resisted and announced that it would employ only union miners. The importance of the leasing work force became apparent in mid-March, when the WFM called out some 350 union miners on leases that shipped to non-union mills.[54]

Mine owners declared that with the new card system the District was a non-union camp, and the strike was over. Strikers stayed out, however, and received steady support from workers throughout the country. The WFM spent more than $93,000 in strike relief in the Cripple Creek District from August 1903 through March 1904, not including legal fees, organizers' salaries, or incidental expenses such as a $1,600 mortgage payment for the Cripple Creek WFM hall.[55]

The strike cost the owners as well. The MOA assessed District mines and mills to build a war chest to fight organized labor, combat ore theft, and help elect anti-union candidates. In December 1903 the WFM happily reported that USR&R had passed its dividend because of the strike but that the Portland, with its union work force, had paid 6 percent.[56] Certainly, the strikes cost the people of Colorado. The WFM charged that Peabody had "rented the armed power of the state" to the Mine Owners' Association and the Citizens' Alliance and that the citizens of Colorado were paying the rent. The Cripple Creek campaign ultimately cost almost $400,000; military expenses for all the 1903–4 Colorado strikes exceeded $700,000.[57]

Although many miners left the District to seek work elsewhere, morale and union membership remained generally high. In December 1903, after almost a year of strikes and work disruptions, the Trades Assembly claimed to represent 5,300 workers. Its affiliates included the District Ministerial Alliance, which joined to demonstrate that "the church of Jesus Christ" supported "the common people who heard Him gladly" and because "a gross injustice [had] been perpetrated upon an innocent and law-abiding people." The union claimed that the mines were producing less than half their normal output.[58]

Miners thought they were winning the strike. Some worked in union mines. The union had adequate relief funds to support strikers, but the strike was clearly hurting the non-union companies. The costs of keeping soldiers in the strike area had become prohibitive. The MOA was not paying the bills as promised, and the union felt that without military interference it could force owners to negotiate. Employers, trying to attract competent workers, offered $3.50 a day for ordinary miners and $5 a day for machinemen. The WFM claimed that incompetent miners had drastically increased operating costs by breaking out huge quantities of waste rock with the ore; that the USR&R mill in Florence was running less than half the time; that the Golden Cycle, Last Dollar, and Vindicator mines had all closed for lack of competent miners; that the pumps had been pulled at the Independence Consolidated and the mine allowed to fill with water to the nine-hundred-foot level; and that high-grading was rampant among the non-union miners at the El Paso. The executive committee of District Union No. 1 reported that most mines were operating at a loss and claimed that the MOA was barely holding on, hoping that WFM members would repudiate the union's leadership at the annual convention in May. Ira Jarvis, president of Victor Miners No. 32, claimed on May 17 that conditions in the District were brighter than they had been since the beginning of the strike.[59]

There conditions stood when the WFM opened its annual convention in Denver on May 23, 1904. A week later, as the marchers demonstrated their loyalty in the hastily arranged Decoration Day parade, District WFM delegates reported on the strike situation. Sherman Parker and W. F. Davis of Free Coinage No. 19, F. M. Ney of Victor Miners No. 32, E. L. Whitney of Cripple Creek Engineers No. 82, and W. A. Morgan of Victor Engineers No. 80 all confidently predicted that the union would win the strike. Parker reported that there were originally between 3,000 and 3,500 strikers, that 900 to 1,000 families were receiving strike relief, that 800 union miners were working on fair properties, and that 300 strikers had returned to work as scabs. The convention appointed three delegates, R. E. Allen, Malcolm Gillis, and H. B. Seaman, to go to the District, investigate conditions, and report back to the convention on June 6. The committee confirmed the District delegates' reports. The three committee members met with Clarence Hamlin, who, they said, behaved as though the strike were over and the WFM broken. They also met with WFM members, who demonstrated "an anxiety and a desire" to settle the strike but remained determined "to wage the fight to the end, if some honorable arrangement cannot be attained for a settlement."[60] The WFM membership was not repudiating the leadership as the MOA had hoped.

By the time the committee reported, however, an honorable settlement was out of the question. At 2:15 A.M. on June 6, 1904, an explosion ripped through the platform at the Independence depot of the Florence and Cripple Creek Railroad. Twenty-five non-union miners from A. E. Carlton's Findley Mine and two others from the Deadwood were waiting for the 2:15 train. Thirteen were killed—many of them mutilated—and six were wounded.[61]

Sheriff Robertson rushed to the scene with all the deputies he could find. So did Carlton and Findley manager James S. Murphy. Sherman Bell activated local units of the National Guard, putting Maj. H. A. Naylor in temporary command, and Company L assembled at the armory. Coroner M. J. Doran took charge of the bodies, but at 9 A.M. Naylor and Murphy demanded that Doran, a member of organized labor, surrender the bodies to J. H. Hunt, a local undertaker.[62]

When he arrived at the depot, Robertson roped off and searched the area, questioned witnesses and nearby residents, telegraphed other counties for bloodhounds, and swore in some one hundred deputies. His investigation uncovered nearly seventy-five yards of wire, one end of which was wound around a chair leg and part of a revolver, presumedly parts of a device that exploded between 150 and 200 pounds of dynamite.[63]

News and rumors spread quickly. All the mines closed except the Portland, freeing scores of non-union miners to gather in Victor. The District split into opposing camps—those who assumed that the WFM was responsible and those who presumed it was innocent. Armed and angry men assembled on the streets of Victor, and Robertson closed all saloons.[64]

The Mine Owners' Association and Citizens' Alliance gathered at Victor's Military Club in the armory, determined to depose elected officials whom they considered pro-labor. They began with Sheriff Henry Robertson. When Robertson met with them voluntarily, the employers demanded his resignation. When he refused, they produced a coiled rope, fired several shots, and offered him the choice of resigning or being hanged. Robertson resigned. The owners then persuaded the county commissioners to replace him with Edward Bell, a member of the MOA and CA, whose $10,000 bond they had already arranged. Sheriff Bell immediately fired Robertson's undersheriff, James Gaughan, and replaced him with Citizens' Alliance secretary L. F. Parsons. Within days the MOA and CA forced more than thirty officials to resign, imprisoned many of them, and replaced them with opponents of organized labor.[65]

Next, the employers provoked what can only be called mob violence. Over the objections of the county commissioners they called a public meeting for the afternoon of June 6, to be held in a vacant lot across the street from the Victor Miners' Union Hall. Michael O'Connell, the city marshal of Victor, swore in some hundred deputies to try to stop the meeting. Mayor French then fired O'Connell, revoked his deputies' commissions, and replaced him with Major Naylor. A crowd of several thousand gathered. Clarence Hamlin arrived to speak, accompanied by Sheriff Bell and MOA attorney Sam Crump. Hamlin demanded that the WFM be destroyed. "The badge of the Western Federation of Miners is a badge of murder," he declared, "and everyone who is responsible for the outrage at Independence should be driven from the district." Alfred Miller, a union miner, objected. He was carrying a rifle, which his brother, Chris, fearing trouble, tried to take. Chris Miller's action was misinterpreted, and it sparked a riot. Seven men were shot, two fatally, and some fifty union miners fled to their union hall.[66]

Sheriff Bell called out Company L, commanded by Lt. W. Travell, manager of the Stratton's Independence, who surrounded the union hall and opened fire. Four miners were shot in the ensuing battle before the union men surrendered and were taken to the armory. The Citizens' Alliance seized union records, wrecked the union hall, and deployed mobs to wreck all the WFM halls in the District, loot the four WFM cooperative stores, and destroy the merchandise. By midnight they had ravaged every union store and union hall in Teller County. George Kyner and the *Record* work force were arrested yet again, held briefly, and released. Squads of soldiers, sheriff's deputies, and armed citizens roamed the District, seizing union members. The militia imprisoned approximately 175 people in dirty, bug-infested bullpens at Victor, Independence, and Goldfield and held them without sufficient food until the Women's Auxiliary was finally allowed to feed them.[67]

Among those arrested were many deposed public officials, including Robertson, O'Connell, Doran, and five members of the Goldfield city council. On June 7 a committee of mine owners demanded that District Attorney Henry Trowbridge fire his deputy, J. C. Cole, and replace him with Sam Crump. Although Trowbridge complied, Crump resigned, to be appointed special prosecutor for the union cases at a $10,000 salary. The WFM convention delegates, still meeting in Denver, offered a $5,000 reward for the arrest and conviction of those responsible for the explosion. But the employers controlled the state government and most public media, which mobilized behind the presumption of labor's collective guilt. On June 6 Edward Bell deputized all the mine owners, managers, and superintendents. In place of Governor Peabody, who was attending the St. Louis World's Fair, Lt. Gov. Warren Haggott declared Teller County in a state of insurrection and rebellion and called out the National Guard. Sherman Bell arrived in Victor at midnight on June 7, ordered Company L of Victor and Company H of Cripple Creek to report to him for duty, and activated additional troops.[68]

Gen. Sherman Bell led the charge on organized labor, starting with some sixty-five union miners who were prospecting at Dunnville, a new mining camp eight miles south of Victor. On June 8, Bell, thirty soldiers, and a hundred deputies went to seize the prospectors. In the ensuing gun battle, John Carley, a union miner, was killed, and fourteen others were arrested. The miners collectively possessed two rifles, three shotguns, and five revolvers. The troops and deputies were fully armed.[69]

The MOA and CA had insisted since March that there would be no peace until WFM members were driven from the District, and on the morning of June 7 Clarence Hamlin announced their plan to deport union miners. The two employers' organizations appointed a seven-man commission to decide who must leave. People who wanted to stay had to renounce union membership and accept MOA cards. At 5 P.M., deputy sheriffs took twenty-eight men, none charged with any crime, put them on a train, and deported them to Denver.[70]

When he arrived in the District, Sherman Bell approved the deportation procedures and converted the examining committee into a "military commission" to decide who among Sheriff Edward Bell's growing numbers of prisoners would be driven from their homes. By the end of July the commission had questioned 1,569 men and recommended that 238 be deported, that charges be filed against forty-two, and that 1,289 be released. The militia loaded the deportees onto trains, took some to Denver and others to the Kansas and New Mexico state lines, unloaded them, and ordered them to stay away from the District. Chris Hansen, Hans Hansen's son and one of the deported miners, said that "the main cause for deportation was the fact that I was guilty of being a Socialist and union man, and would not give up my union card and help them make this a non-union camp." Among the others expelled were WFM attorney Frank J. Hangs and John Harper, the former president of the Victor WFM local and manager of the Victor union store. In addition to the "official" deportees, civilian mobs also drove many others from the District. On the night of July 6, five union members, including the president and secretary of the Retail Clerks' local, were beaten, robbed, taken out of Victor, and told they would be hanged if they returned.[71]

In the chaotic aftermath of the Independence explosion, union sympathizers were converted, by force or by conviction, to the anti-union cause. On June 8 the *Record* ran an editorial urging the WFM to call off the strike, not because it believed the union had anything to do with the explosion but because it believed that there would have been no violence had there been no strike and because it thought the strike was lost. That night eight armed men destroyed the office and machinery, an act for which the union was blamed despite the fact that the printers said that they recognized two Citizens' Alliance members in the wrecking party. No one was arrested, but the *Record* resumed publication as an anti-union paper, leaving unions without a public voice in the District. Peabody approved Kyner's claim for $4,206, and the state covered his losses.[72]

The WFM had been the keystone of organized labor in the Cripple Creek District, and its defeat crushed the District's unions. The Citizens' Alliance asked local businesses to refuse to employ anyone affiliated with the Trades Assembly, ALU, or WFM. More than a hundred merchants and mine owners vowed on June 14 that "neither walking delegates, agitators nor labor unions [would] be allowed to say who [could] labor in Teller County, or . . . do business here." The WFM and the Trades Assembly would "no longer be tolerated."[73]

The National Guard attacked the remaining pro-union holdouts at the point of production by stopping all work at the remaining union mines. On June 9 Sherman Bell accused the Portland Mine of "employing and harboring large numbers of dangerous, lawless men," charged that it hindered "the restoration of peace and good order," and directed that the mine be closed and all dangerous men found there be arrested. Earlier in the strike Peabody had written, "I anticipate Mr. Burns will be permanently deposed, and I hope obliterated from that vicinity." Bell, aiming at just that goal, enforced his order at the 4:30 shift change and hastily deported many of the Portland's union miners. Two days later he issued identical orders to close the Pride of Cripple Creek and the Winchester and Morgan leases at Anaconda.[74]

James Burns sued to restrain the governor and the National Guard from interfering with the Portland's operations, filing a $100,000 damage claim against Peabody, Sherman Bell, Edward Bell, the sheriff's deputies who helped close the mine, and Clarence Hamlin and other MOA members. But Burns was fighting a battle on two fronts. Besides Bell, the USR&R, and the Mine Owners' Association, Burns fought to keep control of the Portland. Frank G. Peck—the secretary-treasurer of the Portland Gold Mining Company who had originally refused to negotiate with the union millmen—represented a group of Portland stockholders who disapproved of Burns's pro-labor policies. At a special June 19 meeting, the directors of the Portland Gold Mining Company repudiated Burns's actions, ordered the suits withdrawn, and directed that the mine be reopened with non-union men. Two days later the Portland resumed operations as a non-union mine and required all job applicants to present MOA cards. Portland Mill employees had to certify that they were not affiliated with the WFM. In February 1905 Burns lost his battle for control of the Portland, and a new board of directors endorsed the MOA's policies.[75]

The military harassed strikers' families who had drawn supplies from the four union stores. After mobs wrecked the stores on June 6, the WFM arranged with two grocers, John Ganley of Cripple Creek and John Kettelson of Victor, to furnish supplies to deportees' families under the direction of the women's auxiliaries. The

WFM Executive Board instructed the women to stop taking supplies to men imprisoned in the bullpen and to save them for their children and themselves. On June 14, Col. Edward Verdeckberg ordered that all aid must be channeled through the military and ordered Ganley and Kettelson not to sell any more goods on WFM orders. After that, the women's auxiliaries distributed most of the strike relief in secret. As union men were arrested and deported, women led the local resistance, supervising all relief and raising bonds for those who had been imprisoned. The militia did not physically attack the women, but it did harass their leaders. McClelland ordered two auxiliary members, Mrs. James Printy and Mrs. Blixer, brought to the bullpen on June 8 and then told them to cease their "insolent criticism and denunciation of the military." That night he hauled in eight more auxiliary members and then released them. Later, soldiers took auxiliary members Estella Nichols of Cripple Creek and Margaret Hooten of Anaconda to the bullpen and ordered them to stop their work.[76]

Finally, on July 26, 1904, Peabody ended martial law and deactivated the National Guard. But the situation remained grim. Major Naylor, who remained as acting marshal of Victor, refused to let deportees return. Sheriff Bell advised them to stay away because he did not think he could protect them if they came back. In a wave of whitecapping (violent intimidation by masked mobs) still more union members and sympathizers were beaten and driven from the District. The managers of the Victor and Cripple Creek union stores, John Harper and T. H. Parfet, returned on July 16 to inventory their remaining goods and conclude union business. Despite Sheriff Bell's promises of protection, seven or eight masked men took Harper from his home on the night of August 9, beat him, and drove him out of the District. T. S. Leland, pastor of the Victor Methodist Church, preached a sermon in late July in which he voiced sympathy for the strikers and criticized the militia, the Citizens' Alliance, and the MOA. Leland had also served on the coroner's jury that found management responsible for the fatal accident at Stratton's Independence, and he was one of the Ministerial Alliance members who established ties with the Trades Assembly. On August 10 three men threatened to hurt him if he did not leave town that evening. Leland instead began keeping armed men in his house for protection. Two union miners, Arthur Parker and L. R. Jenks, were there the night of August 28, when Sheriff Bell and four deputies arrived and exchanged shots with them. Bell said the miners had tried to shoot him; Jenks and Parker said they thought the intruders were whitecappers and that they opened the door as soon as they realized it was Bell. The sheriff arrested them and Leland and charged all three with assault to murder, conspiracy to murder, and assault with deadly weapons. The same day that Leland was ordered to leave, five masked men shot into the home of George Seitz in Cripple Creek. The widowed Seitz, a Socialist and former president of Cripple Creek Miners No. 40, shared the home with his children. He returned their fire and was taken to the Cripple Creek jail for protection. His assailants were never caught.[77]

The threats and violence escalated throughout August. The WFM sold the remaining goods from its stores to the Interstate Mercantile Company, a corporation chartered in Montana. It was suspected, correctly, that the Interstate acted for the WFM. Opened on August 16, the Cripple Creek store was back in business only four days before a mob wrecked and looted it, driving the managers, clerks, and other union sympathizers from the District. No help arrived from the sheriff's office across the street. Among those deported were T. H. Parfet; Eugene Engley, Colorado attorney general during the Waite administration; Deputy Clerk and Recorder Michael J. O'Neill; WFM attorney Frank J. Hangs; Frank Aikins of Excelsior Engineers No. 80 and local manager of the store; clerks Charles H. Wasson and Stephen Leahy; H. M. Heimerdinger of Butte, an attorney, clerk of the District court of Silver Bow County, Montana, and manager of the Interstate Mercantile store; Albert L. Pierce, August Girodot, James Redd, and Patrick Maloney; and J. W. Higens, a contractor and former president of Cripple Creek Carpenters No. 547, who had helped organize the Colorado Industrial League, an association of pro-labor business owners. They were driven from town in two groups, one to Florissant and one to Canon City, and told not to return. Two miles out of Cripple Creek on the Canon City road, the whitecappers beat and flogged Parfet, told the deportees to keep walking, and fired shots over their heads.[78] Higens later described his deportation to the press:

> My little girl came in and said there was trouble in town, and I went down to see what it was. When I walked up to the crowd, A. E. Carlton, the banker, pointed at me and said "There is one you want," and the next instant they had me fast. . . .
>
> About a week ago Carlton came up to me and asked me to withdraw from the bond of William Graham, one of the imprisoned miners, and I refused to do so. This is the offense for which I was deported. J. K. King, a well known man there, shoved a gun in my face and told me not to make any resistance. . . . It was a little after 5 o'clock when the mob got me and about 6 o'clock when the leaders started up over the mountains. They rode along with guns, talking in insulting language, saying: "Have you the ropes[?]" "how many ropes do we need?" "Oh, one is enough[.]" "Will it be hanging or shooting or dropping them into a pit?"
>
> We walked along silently, and had gone most of the distance, when two of the guards saw my gun. I had not tried to use it when they jumped on me, although it was reported that I tried to do so. One of them grabbed at me, and the other grabbed the gun. He did not quite get hold of it, and I reached for it, too, and had I secured it would have begun shooting. One of them struck me with a sixshooter. I tried to aim, but they got the gun away, struck me on the head a fierce blow, hit me on the shoulders and chest and kicked me. Had I ever begun firing we would all have been killed, for our guards would have begun shooting, too. They did not help me in any way after I was wounded,

and as I walked along I bled profusely from the cut, the blood running down my clothes and into my shoes. When we had gone out three or four miles, they stopped on the crest of a hill, and the leader said: "Gentlemen, this is the last time we will ever give you any show at all. If you ever return it will be a bullet or a rope." They went off yelling: "They can't come back." We walked on toward Box Canyon, down the road and along Spring Creek to the county road and down to Florissant. The railroad surgeon at Florissant dressed my wound and bandaged my head. We got into Florissant at 2:20 A.M. and took the train for Denver at 8 o'clock Sunday morning.[79]

Higens's wife reported that armed men watched their home all night. Unable to return without risking his life, Higens lost his home and property in the District, including two houses, three lots, and a contract on a cyanide mill for the Anaconda Mine.

Higens was but one of hundreds of union advocates persecuted for supporting organized labor. On August 31 a mob whitecapped George Hooten of Anaconda Miners No. 21 and manager of the Anaconda WFM store, robbed him of $65 and a gold watch, whipped him with cartridge belts, and deported him. Attorney Frank Hangs returned to the District on September 1, but left again that afternoon when Sheriff Bell refused protection. Michael O'Connell, the deposed marshal of Victor who had been imprisoned in the bullpen and county jail, was finally released and reached Denver on August 5. He died the next day, allegedly falling from his room on the fourth floor of the Markham Hotel. Deported miners charged that he had been murdered by "paid assassins." The WFM accused the MOA and CA of hiring thugs to terrorize union sympathizers. The full impact of the mob violence cannot be known because, in addition to the documented cases, many people who feared that the militia or the mob was after them left town rather than be deported.[80]

By the end of August, news of deportations, whitecappings, and rumors of intended victims raged throughout the District. Sheriff Edward Bell denied most of the reported deportations, charging that the disturbances were "occasioned by the united efforts of the Western Federation to create an impression of alarm regarding life and property in this locality and bring disrepute and odium on my administration of the sheriff's office." Most of the reports, he said, "emanate directly from an organization known as the Woman's Auxiliary, which is an adjunct of the Western Federation."[81]

After the August 20 riot, Frank Hangs filed criminal charges for assault to kill, malicious mischief, and criminal destruction of property against Nelson Franklin, P. B. Russell, John Sharpe, Cliff Newcombe, Henry Dahl, A. E. Carlton, Harry ("Kid") Waters, Frank Vanneck, H. H. Babcock, A. C. Cole, Harvey Gregory, A. T. Holman, and some fifty others. The Interstate Mercantile Company asked for an injunction to restrain the Citizens' Alliance, the MOA, and a number of individuals from interfering with its business. The District court continued to try to uphold civil authority and issued a temporary order on September 6. Three days later, H. M. Heimerdinger and several of his employees returned to reopen the Cripple Creek store. On November 7 a permanent injunction was issued against the Citizens' Alliance and a number of prominent citizens, including T. E. McClelland, A. E. Carlton, Nelson Franklin, and Edward Bell.[82]

But the injunctions could not undo the damage. Organized labor had taken a crippling blow. The ultimate strike casualty was that working people lost faith in their right and power to help shape the industrial social order. Union workers affirmed in defeat the principles that had failed them. On June 15, 1904, the National Guard marched a trainload of union deportees to the New Mexico state line and left them there.

Standing on the stone that marks the line between the state of Colorado and the territory of New Mexico, Charles Anderson raised a half a loaf of bread aloft and shouted defiance back at General Bell's soldiers: "Give me liberty or give me death." Another deported Cripple Creek miner, who stood near him, started to sing: "Sweet Land of Liberty, of Thee I Sing." Others took up the words—just those two lines—without a tune, and they watched the soldiers and deputies from Cripple Creek who walked back over the alkali plain to their train, which was waiting a mile away.[83]

For the working people of Cripple Creek, hope for a democratic future withered in that arid terrain.

9

LOOK AWAY OVER JORDAN

Go up to the summit of Pisgah and gaze about, to the west, the north, the south, and the east. Look at it well, for you shall not go across yonder Jordan.

Deuteronomy 3:27

On a cold, gray day in February 1979, I drank coffee and talked with May Wing, as I had at intervals for almost three years. We talked, as we often had, about her childhood in the District, about how the strikes touched her family, and about children, friends, work, and men. Over time, as we recorded her oral histories, our relationship changed, and she added new details to familiar stories. I became, I think, some combination of adopted kin and personal scribe. She increasingly controlled our interviews and summoned me when she felt it was time to get on with recording her life. And she became more fiercely insistent about the importance of her work. This day she stated simply, "I lived the history that I can tell." Then she added, "And of course the history today in the books that's written . . . a lot is not really the true thing, as it was lived."[1]

The lived histories I recorded held the bitter legacy of the second strike. People told stories about working-class life before 1904 that their children and grandchildren often had not heard. Labor's history had been largely unrecorded, lost with the union records the mobs destroyed, the leaders they drove from the District, and the fear that silenced many. To stay in Cripple Creek, miners had to renounce their union. Most, in order to keep their jobs, hid any hint of union allegiance. By the time I brought my tape recorder to gather buried stories, most remaining memories of the union era belonged to elderly women whose fathers had been union miners. Still girls during the strike, they had married men who did not begin mining until after the WFM had been driven out. Their husbands could, therefore, swear that they had never belonged to a union and could work and settle in the District. The men could still be blacklisted, though, which made it dangerous to talk about organized labor and the strike. By the time I came to the District, the mines had closed, the men had died or retired, and the survivors did not want their memories to die with them.

Time and experience had shaped those memories. Personal and social perspectives affected how each person remembered the past. The stories I recorded reminded me constantly that all history is partial. But Cripple Creek's history had been told largely from the partial perspectives of the mine owners who won the second strike. To preserve labor's history was partly to dredge for long-buried versions of the past.

WHO BLEW UP THE INDEPENDENCE DEPOT?

The first step in preserving labor's history was to rethink the written versions of labor's defeat. Employers claimed that strike violence, culminating with the June 6, 1904, Independence depot explosion, proved that the unions harbored violent Socialists and dynamiters who threatened civil peace. That "fact" justified how they and the state combined to destroy organized labor.

We can probably never know with certainty who planted the dynamite under the Independence depot platform. Some evidence supports the WFM, which insisted that the mine owners arranged the violence. The tragic massacre at the depot was never fairly investigated; the Mine Owners' Association and Citizens' Alliance immediately deposed elected officials as they tracked the perpetrators and replaced them with men who assumed the strikers' guilt. The speed with which employers assumed control suggests possible foreknowledge. By managing investigations and censoring the local press, employers and the military controlled events as well as how they were recorded.

When employers and government officials accused the WFM of violent and anarchistic behavior, the union threw the charges right back. "For a year now," the *Miners' Magazine* wrote in September 1904, "the capitalist press has been telling us of the lawlessness of the striking miners in Colorado, but notwithstanding that the capitalist class in Colorado is in possession of every branch of the state government—executive, legislative and judicial—not one miner has yet been convicted of crime." The reason, the union insisted, was that the mine operators themselves were to blame. The WFM detailed a history of violent crimes in Colorado for which it held employers responsible. The union pointedly observed that no one was arrested after the 1894 strike, when Adjutant General Tarsney was tarred and feathered by "the hired deputies of the Mine Owners' Association." No owners, it continued, were "bullpenned" when fifteen men, by negligence or design, fell to their deaths on Stratton's Independence. No one was punished for dynamiting eight assay offices in 1902, after the mine owners threatened to close down assayers they accused of fencing ore.[2]

The WFM denied that it was involved in the assault on Stewart, the Vindicator explosion, the attempted train-wreckings, or the Independence depot explosion. It charged that employers overthrew the civil authorities to protect the Mine Owners' Association and alleged that "preconcerted action had been taken to depose the civil authorities; the successors of the regularly elected sheriff of the county and marshal of Victor had been selected, the bonds of the usurpers having been arranged." The mob violence, it claimed, was intended to crush the unions, particularly the cooperative stores that "had been thorns in the side of the citizens' alliance."[3]

More than a year after the strike's chaotic climax, Harry Orchard, a former member of the Altman WFM local, confessed that he had murdered Frank Steunenberg in Caldwell, Idaho, on December 30, 1905. A sheep rancher in 1905, Steunenberg had been the governor of Idaho during the Coeur d'Alenes strike of 1899—the Democrat whom miners blamed equally with a Republican president for persecuting strikers. Orchard implicated an "inner circle" of the WFM in the Steunenberg murder, particularly WFM president Charles Moyer, Secretary-Treasurer W. D. ("Big Bill") Haywood, and George Pettibone, a Denver merchant who had been a WFM activist in the Coeur d'Alenes. The three were abducted to Idaho, imprisoned for more than a year and a half, and finally acquitted. In his confession, Orchard also alleged that the inner circle had hired him to set the explosives at the Vindicator Mine and the Independence depot.[4]

Orchard's is a complicated story which, as historian Melvyn Dubofsky wrote, lies "probably as much within the province of psychopathologists as of historians and amateur detectives." Perhaps Orchard told the truth. Perhaps he acted alone. Perhaps he knew nothing about the Cripple Creek crimes but claimed the credit for his own peculiar reasons. And perhaps he worked for the Mine Owners' Association. Before the Steunenberg murder, Orchard reportedly told a companion, G. L. Brokaw, that he had been a Pinkerton employee for some time.[5] He confessed his crimes to James McParland, manager of the Pinkerton Rocky Mountain office. Steve Adams, a former Altman WFM activist, was arrested and pressured by McParland to corroborate Orchard's story. Adams charged that Orchard and McParland had colluded and that Orchard had to rewrite his confession because "he could not repeat it the second time anything at all like the first one." One witness swore that Orchard had visited detective D. C. Scott at the F&CC depot at least three or four times between January 1 and June 6, 1904, and that he once consulted for six hours with Scott, MOA detective K. C. Sterling, and another individual. One of the soldiers on duty during the strike said that the militia knew to let Orchard come and go unhindered. Having gathered these hints, WFM defense attorney Edmund F. Richardson, in a biting cross-examination, forced Orchard to admit that he had worked as a Pinkerton operative during the Cripple Creek strike.[6]

Orchard implicated the WFM in the Cripple Creek strike violence, and close ties existed among the Idaho authorities who prosecuted the Steunenberg case, the Cripple Creek District mine owners, MOA attorney Samuel Crump, and Sheriff

Edward Bell. The WFM therefore gathered considerable testimony about Cripple Creek as it prepared the defense for the Steunenberg trials, starting with Steve Adams's trial, which preceded Haywood's.[7] The union's evidence, as well as eye-witness statements from 1904, supported WFM charges that the mine owners instigated violence in the Cripple Creek strike.

William B. Easterly, an Altman activist and president of WFM District Union No. 1 in 1903, testified at the Haywood trial that the only person who discussed violence at Altman WFM meetings during the strike was a visiting member who turned out to be a mine owners' detective. Francis J. Ellison, the investigating officer after the Vindicator explosion, said he was certain that Orchard was lying. Ellison reported that while he was on active duty the militia was often ordered to start trouble with the strikers.[8]

As they prepared Adams's defense, WFM attorneys gathered considerable testimony suggesting that the mine owners had anticipated the Independence depot explosion. Denver attorney Edmund F. Richardson gathered much of this information and recorded it in his trial notes and affidavits. Lewis Samsel of Victor, a friend of MOA attorney Sam Crump, told Richardson that Crump said two weeks before the explosion that the union stores were going to be looted. Jesse Throwers and George Sherman, partners in the Cripple Creek Club, said that they had overheard Albert Carlton and Charles MacNeill discuss provoking a riot. Hi Wilson, a Teller County deputy sheriff when the Independence explosion occurred, said that he had arrived at the depot by 4 A.M., with Robertson and Deputy J. Knox Burton, and that they had Chris Miller watch the wire and chair leg until the bloodhounds arrived. Some witnesses said that one of the bloodhounds sniffed the chair leg and wire and headed straight for the Vindicator Mine. An onlooker, Ira Blizzard, then telephoned MOA detective K. C. Sterling and told him that the dog was following the trail. Sterling allegedly said to call off the dogs, that they were on a false scent, and that he knew who the dynamiter was. Others said that the same dog later went past the Findley sampler and took a roundabout path to a point about twelve miles from Independence, where the criminal had presumably been picked up. A number of witnesses said that they saw the dog go from the chair leg to MOA detective Al Bemore's house and to the powder house at the Vindicator Mine.[9] Others said that they saw Bemore carry the powder from the Vindicator the afternoon of June 5. Bemore, according to at least one source, admitted meeting with Findley manager James Murphy, Carlton, two gunmen, and Orchard on the afternoon before the explosion, and that he got the powder to put under the platform.[10]

Frank Aiken, deputy assessor of Teller County, arrived at the depot almost immediately after the explosion and served on the coroner's jury that investigated the crime until Coroner Doran was deposed. A railroad worker who was there told Aiken "that if they had held the shift, as they had been told to, no one would have been hurt." The union attributed the same remark to a mine owner and said that an MOA detective had told the men for two weeks before the explosion not to "stand upon depot platforms, that something was likely to happen."[11]

Some of the most damning testimony came from A. C. Cole, a former Victor High School teacher and a prominent Republican who served as secretary of the Victor Citizens' Alliance from December 1903 to June 1, 1904, and who was second lieutenant of Company L during the strike. Cole reported that Melvin Beck, the shift boss who died in the Vindicator Mine explosion, had said several times—including the day before the explosion—that something must be done to keep the soldiers in the District and "that something was going to be pulled off at the Vindicator that would prevent the soldiers from going away."[12]

Cole charged that prominent members of the MOA had asked him to help with plans that were "similar to, or the same proposition, as the pulling off of the Independence station." When he refused, Cole said, he was "immediately relieved of his position as secretary of the Victor Citizens' Alliance." The impressive show of union strength on Decoration Day, he said, "excited the animosity of the Mine Owners' Association." Afterward, MOA and Citizens' Alliance leaders "declared repeatedly that the Western Federation men must be driven out of the Cripple Creek District, and that something had to be done to give an excuse for driving them out." The Victor militia, according to Cole, had an "unusual number of drillings," considerable ammunition was brought to the armory on June 5, and the militia was ordered to prepare for instant call. "It was freely talked among the members of the militia company, and The Mine Owners' Association, and The Citizens' Alliance that something was going to happen . . . and they looked for it on or before the next morning," Cole said.

Around 10 P.M. on June 5, Capt. Harry Moore came to military headquarters. Apparently nervous and excited, Moore checked that the arms and supplies were ready for immediate use. That night, most of the militia and prominent members of the Citizens' Alliance stayed at the Baltimore Hotel in Victor. Few slept, according to Cole, "in anticipation of some event." Most were awake when news of the explosion came. They reportedly said that Edward Bell would be made sheriff when the trouble happened. The militia was instructed to clean out the WFM members when "the shooting began" during the afternoon of June 6. "It was generally understood and freely discussed that a riot was to be precipitated," Cole charged. He was, he said, present and knew "all about" the destruction of the *Record* plant on June 8, the planned deportations, and the looting of the union cooperative store on August 20. He was also "familiar with the general conspiracy to drive out The Western Federation of Miners which existed practically from the beginning of the strike in 1903." Finally, Cole said that he knew Harry Orchard and knew that Orchard worked for the Mine Owners' Association.

Another member of the Victor militia, J. M. Huff, corroborated Cole's story. He said that "it was general talk among the members of the company, on June 5th, 1904, that something was coming off and to be ready. He had never been summoned that way before, and no disturbances had been recorded since March 10th." Other members of the militia told the same tale. J. M. Orwing, a sergeant in the Cripple Creek militia unit, claimed to have seen two MOA gunmen, Harry ("Kid") Waters and Harry Guyton, murder a man named Jack Bowman to keep him from telling what he knew about the Independence depot explosion.[13]

Much of Cole's account dovetailed with the sworn statement of A. H. Rogers, a union miner who said he quit the WFM during the strike because Albert Carlton had threatened to call in a loan on his property. Rogers acted as a guard at Carlton's Golden Cycle and Findley mines until the militia was activated and after that served as Carlton's guard and general helper. He reported that Carlton asked him to help assault "old man Stewart in order to get the militia into the district." After the militia arrived, Rogers reported to General Bell. He helped target union men for the bullpen and planted evidence to justify their arrests. Rogers claimed that on the day of the fatal Vindicator explosion he was told that something was going to happen at the mine. He also claimed to know that the accident at Stratton's Independence resulted from an MOA plan.[14]

Rogers said that he met Albert Carlton at the Findley on the afternoon of June 5, 1904, and was told to be available for the next several days. After the explosion, Carlton told Rogers to arm himself. MOA gunmen were told to kill as many union men as possible, and Carlton told them to destroy the union store. Rogers reported that in July 1904 Crump asked him to find men who, for $500, would lie under oath that they had seen Haywood and Pettibone in Independence on June 5. In fact, Rogers said, he had seen Orchard and detective K. C. Sterling together several times, the last time at the Findley ore house a few nights before the Independence depot disaster.[15]

Rogers recorded his story in a sworn statement on December 19, 1906. He then apparently gathered statements from other people who implicated Carlton, Crump, and others in events connected with the Cripple Creek strike and with the WFM trials in Idaho. During this period he apparently worked as a double agent and also obtained information from members of the MOA and Citizens' Alliance who thought he worked for them. Attorney Richardson's notes record that Rogers interviewed Frank Wilson, who lived near the Independence depot in June 1904. Wilson reportedly said that around June 1 James Murphy and A. E. Carlton had asked him to move up the hill above the mine. Then Carlton offered to buy Wilson's house if he would move. The morning after the explosion, Wilson saw Murphy and asked, "Jim, was this the reason you wanted me to move?" "Yes," Murphy replied, "but someone has made a terrible mistake, as we never intended something like this should have been done." Carlton asked Wilson not to mention being asked to move. In return he guaranteed Wilson employment, money, and assistance as needed. Paul Gilhorn, the night blacksmith on the Findley, told Rogers that James Murphy had told him and other regular employees not to come to work the night of the explosion, a story his co-workers corroborated. Gilhorn was anti-union, but he believed that agents of the mine owners had dynamited the depot.[16]

Rogers also interviewed Frank Gillese, the engineer at Stratton's Independence who was running the hoist when the cage went into the sheave wheel. Gillese was certain that a mine employee had tampered with the engine. Several times before, a bolt had been removed from the brake, and Gillese had reported the vandalism to the master mechanic, who always laughed. A mine owners' committee asked Gillese to implicate WFM Executive Board member D. C. Copley, but he refused to do so. The mine lay within the guard line at Camp Goldfield, and only people with military passes could get in. Finally, Gillese reported that the wife of MOA gunman Kid Waters had told a friend of Gillese's wife that Waters had said on his deathbed that he and H. F. Guyton went to Denver and murdered Michael O'Connell by hitting him with a sandbag and dropping him out his hotel window. According to this fourthhand hearsay, Waters and Guyton did the job "at the solicitation of the Mine Owners' Association of the Cripple Creek district."[17]

Finally, a man "calling himself Dick Reese" came to the office of WFM attorney Edmund F. Richardson. Reese claimed that he had worked for the Mine Owners' Association during the summer of 1904. He told Richardson that on June 2, 1904, a number of men met at the armory. The group consisted of Kid Waters, Jim Warford, Harry Guyton, Jack Bowman, Harry Orchard, Tom Brown, and Reese, most of whom were MOA gunmen; two Pinkertons; and mill manager Nelson Franklin (the former Democratic mayor of Victor), along with A. E. Carlton, Frank M. Reardon, A. T. Holman, Captain Moore, and Major Naylor. Reese said that Reardon offered $500 to any five men who would explode boxes of powder under the Independence depot after the train had passed. The explosion was not intended to hurt anyone, but rather was to "gain sympathy for their side, and to break up the Western Federation." Waters chose the five men—reportedly Waters himself, Harry Guyton, Jack Bowman or Jim Warford, Harry Orchard, and Tom Brown. Reese said that Waters told him that the explosion would happen early on June 6. Richardson wrote in his notes that he thought Reese was telling the truth, but that "at the same time, he was so nervous that I became convinced that he was either a dope fiend or had been in such constant fear of his life that . . . he was scared of his shadow." Richardson was "satisfied that he could not have made the story up, but . . . equally convinced that he could not tell that or any other story, true or false, if put on the witness stand."[18]

If Reese told the truth, his fears were understandable. When he approached Richardson on April 9, 1907, most of the people he identified as MOA hirelings were either dead or in prison: Kid Waters and Jack Bowman were dead; Waters and Guyton had allegedly murdered both Bowman and Michael O'Connell; Jim Warford and Thomas Brown were serving life sentences for murdering two union men, one of whom, Chris Miller, had guarded evidence at the Independence depot for Sheriff Robertson; and Harry Orchard awaited trial in an Idaho jail.

THE QUESTION OF VIOLENCE

Historians and partisans have long debated who was responsible for the violent events in Cripple Creek. Whether or not individual members of the Western Federation of Miners committed violent acts during the strike, violence was not union policy. It was, however, the policy of the Mine Owners' Association, the Citizens' Alliance, and the militia. Whether or not they staged the fatal accidents at the Vindicator, Stratton's Independence, and the Independence depot, they fomented the Victor riot that caused two deaths, killed another miner in the "Battle of Dunnville," and destroyed union property. They also had people charged with no crimes arrested and deported, deposed elected officials, and at least tacitly approved assaults and whitecappings. They took deportees hundreds of miles from their homes under military guard and abandoned them without food or shelter.

The violence of mine owners and the state magnified a prevalent culture of masculine violence. Violence provided daily amusement in the form of the prizefights that punctuated the front pages of labor's *Daily Press*. It was also a daily possibility for miners and their families, who lived with the constant threat of violent death underground. Both sides likely committed violent acts at some time. Management blew up assay offices; labor beat scabs and ran non-white workers out of camp. The strike record testifies that men on all sides habitually prepared for violence and either carried guns or hired them. Violence as a shared assumption and mode of behavior deserves further analysis. For this history, however violence itself becomes less the issue than how it was deployed, by whom, and to what ends.

The parallels between the 1903–4 strikes and the 1894 Cripple Creek strike are inescapable. Battles among competing capitalists were submerged issues in both strikes. The state, in both instances, held the balance of power between labor and capital. In 1903, however, the unions were taken off guard. Cripple Creek unions used tactics that had worked for ten years. They assumed that a brief work stoppage would bring the owners to a negotiated settlement. But strikes with different immediate causes escalated to full-scale confrontations throughout Colorado. Employers and the state responded similarly in all strike areas. Owners allowed negotiable conflicts to escalate because they knew they had a friend in the governor's mansion.[19]

In terms of the historical outcome, the question of who actually planted the dynamite at the Independence depot is less important than whose explanation was accepted—and how that justified the consequences. Each side blamed the other, but the employers controlled the official version of events. As long as unions posed no threat to private ownership, some mine managers, merchants, and professionals met amicably with workers at local lodge halls and saloons. But conservative employers never embraced organized labor. When Socialist sentiment became sufficiently strong that the *Press* declared itself nonpartisan, many local merchants withdrew their advertising. When the militia closed the *Record*, the only remaining local voice of District labor was gone. Thus the owners could attribute violence—real or manufactured—to the "socialist dynamiters" of the WFM and justify using state force to destroy union labor.

Both sides lay ideological claim to shared American values. Both capital and labor affirmed democratic principles and proclaimed them on Labor Day, the Fourth of July, and through cross-class political alliances. They framed their fight less about the respective rights of capital and labor or the relative merits of capitalism and socialism than over who had broken the rules of civilized democracy—over who had been most violent. That debate did not generate the most interesting lessons of the strike, which concerned working-class identity and local social relationships.

CHOOSING SIDES

The strength of shared class interests drew the overwhelming majority of miners to strike in support of the mill workers and affirm the ideology of working-class interdependence that grounded the WFM's industrial unionism. Their strike experience demonstrated that cross-class politics could not protect organized labor.

The strike also demonstrated the limits of white manhood as an identity to unite working-class resistance or bridge class differences. When industrial conflict shattered the mutual respect and "manly methods" that working-class dignity demanded, then relationships based in white manhood shifted along social fault lines of class and gender. Local merchants and professionals chose whether to support working-class lodge brothers and political allies with whom they shared civic authority as members of the "producing classes" or whether to support local mine managers and mine owners who held the keys to state power. The grocers who agreed to distribute strike relief, the businessmen who joined the pro-labor Colorado Industrial League, and the ministers who affiliated with the Trades Assembly all represented that portion of the local middle class who continued to stand with organized labor. Other merchants, leasers, and professionals were pressured to side with anti-union owners who also controlled freight rates and access to credit, particularly Carlton, who controlled the local freight business. Many were clearly conflicted about doing so. Citizens' Alliance members and militia officers A. C.

Cole and A. A. Rollestone both demonstrated the ethical limits of their opposition to union labor. Yet the middle class elicited no sympathy from Charles Moyer, who told WFM convention delegates in 1904 that

> The lesson taught by the business element of the Cripple Creek district, the almost immediate withdrawing of all credit, the organizing of Citizens' Alliances, should be convincing evidence that the friendship of this class reaches no farther than the pocketbook. It took the business man of the Cripple Creek district but a very short time to betray his true colors; always in favor of union wages, because they brought more money to his till, like the non-union man in times of peace and the scab in times of trouble, ever willing to share the benefits secured by organized labor, yet at the first alarm that his profits might be affected or some union man whom he has robbed for years might ask for a dollar's credit, he cries, "The Cash System," but the same old profits.[20]

Class overshadowed all other sources of social identity during the strike. Numbers are most comforting and most absurd when they prove the obvious, and that is the case with statistics about strike participation. The clearest and least surprising generalization is that union supporters were likely to be working class and union opponents were likely not to be. The exceptions were strikebreakers, whose names the union published in scab lists and who could therefore be located on the 1900 census.[21] Not surprisingly, anti-union leadership came predominantly from salaried workers and capitalists, especially salaried mine workers and mining capitalists. Equally predictably, all who were arrested or deported, who were union strike organizers, or who were forced to resign public office after the Independence depot explosion were working class. Virtually none of their opponents were (table 18).[22]

Class also manifested itself in ethnic differences among the participants. Approximately three strike activists in ten were immigrants, somewhat higher than the 23

TABLE 18
Strike Sympathies by Class, 1900

Class	Pro-Union		Anti-Union		District Adults	
	N	%	N	%	N	%
Working class	213	88	108	67	15,710	79
Salaried	2	1	22	14	870	4
Business	19	8	14	9	2,052	10
Professional	3	1	4	2	721	4
Capitalist	0	0	12	7	359	2
Other	4	2	1	1	217	1
Total	241	101	161	100	19,929	100

Sources: Manuscript census, Teller County, Colo., 1900, and strike sample, less four missing observations. District figures omit nineteen persons in the unskilled mining class (0.1 percent of the population).

Note: Column 2 does not total 100 percent due to rounding.

percent figure for all District adults but about equal to the proportion of foreign-born miners.[23] Disproportionate numbers of immigrants were arrested and deported, perhaps because so much of the conflict centered in the southeastern corner of the District. The military seized or deported many men from the Goldfield area near the mines that Sherman Bell managed, and that area was slightly more foreign-born than the District as a whole. The Rednecks continued to bear the brunt of owners' hostility.[24]

Mine owners tried to manipulate ethnic divisions by hiring immigrant strikebreakers. At the beginning of the Colorado City mill strike, twenty-five Bohemians, recruited to scab, reportedly quit work instead. Next, the *Press* reported that the mill managers were "importing dago scabs" and warned, "This is a move which the citizens of Colorado do not take kindly to." Cripple Creek mine owners tried to hire immigrants who did not speak English and did not know about the strike. On September 18, 1903, they imported fifty-one scabs, most of whom were Finns and Norwegians. When District newsboys followed them, yelling "scab" the few who spoke English explained that the mine owners had assured them that there was no strike. Eighteen came to union headquarters that night and promised not to scab. The rest, taken to the Independence Mine under heavy guard, refused to go underground. The militia marched twenty-three through Cripple Creek under heavy guard. Emil Peterson, a Dane who had learned about the strike, yelled "Don't go to work" in Danish and ran, escaping under fire. The rest of the strikebreakers—who were working at bayonet point—managed to escape by September 22 and left the District at the union's expense. Later, four "subjects of Germany" recruited as strikebreakers in Duluth, Minnesota, refused to work when they learned about the strike, and they spent four days in the bullpen. The WFM, attempting to dissuade potential strikebreakers at the source, sent organizers to other metal mining regions. Joy Pollard, a member of Free Coinage Miners No. 19, went to the copper mines in Michigan's Upper Peninsula. Realizing that the owners manipulated language barriers, Pollard printed circulars in Italian, "Austrian" (Serbian), Finnish, Polish, and Swedish.[25] Thus, in a limited way the miners developed strategies to bridge ethnic divisions. Certainly they responded more effectively to immigrant strikebreakers than they had when the same ethnic workers tried to join the District work force.

The effect was the same, however—to keep new immigrants out. Union miners did not overcome their prejudice against southern Europeans, Mexicans, or Asians and warned during the 1904 election that a vote for Peabody was a vote for low wages and "Japanese labor."[26] Those prejudices survived the strike, in part because mine owners shared them too deeply to exploit them and did not recruit Chinese, Japanese, or Mexican strikebreakers. To that extent labor's bonds with Sherman Bell remained intact.

As with ethnicity, the geography of strike participation reflected the class struc-ture of the District and the residential base of the union and Socialist leadership. Union supporters were more likely to live in smaller communities close to the mines, particularly in Victor, Goldfield, and Independence, where the conflict centered around the Smith-Moffat and Carlton mines, and also in Anaconda and Elkton, where the Elkton and Mary McKinney mines were strongly anti-union. Labor's opponents came particularly from Cripple Creek and also from Anaconda, Victor, Independence, and Goldfield, where most of the Smith-Moffat companies and some of Carlton's properties were located, as well as some of MOA president Ernest Colburn's and MOA secretary Clarence Hamlin's mines. The opponents were largely scabs and militia members recruited from anti-union companies, par-ticularly from management. To simplify accurately, Sherman Bell's union miners were prominent strike leaders, and Bell and his managers also recruited scabs from their own work forces (table 19). These residential patterns became even more pro-nounced among strike leaders. Anti-union activists lived predominantly in the busi-ness center of Cripple Creek, and some lived in Victor. Union support came dis-proportionately from Victor, Anaconda, Elkton, Independence, Goldfield, and Altman; no significant anti-union leadership came from the old union stronghold on Bull Hill.[27]

More strike activists on both sides were married than District men as a whole: 58 percent of pro-union activists and 63 percent of the anti-union forces, compared

TABLE 19
Strike Sympathies by Residence, 1900

Class	Pro-Union		Anti-Union		District Adults	
	N	%	N	%	N	%
Cripple Creek	44	18	51	32	7,541	38
Anaconda	9	4	19	12	755	4
Elkton	16	7	8	5	765	4
Altman	8	3	6	4	460	2
Independence	23	9	16	10	921	5
Goldfield	22	9	10	6	1,232	6
Victor	96	39	33	21	4,770	24
Lawrence			1	1	173	1
Gillett	2	1	1	1	284	1
Rural	25	10	14	9	3,007	15
Total	245	100	159	101	19,908	100

Sources: Manuscript census, Teller County, Colo., 1900 and strike sample.
Note: Column 4 does not total 100 percent due to rounding.

with 49 percent of all men. Those arrested and deported reflected the marital norms of the District more than the men who deported them. Only four identified members of the MOA, Citizens' Alliance, or deportation committees were single, whereas thirty-four (39 percent) of those arrested and sixty (46 percent) of the deported were single in 1900, close to the 45 percent figure for all men.[28]

Strike activists, even in 1900, were disproportionately likely to own homes, and union sympathizers were slightly more likely to be homeowners than were their opponents. Four in ten activists on both sides of the conflict owned homes, compared with 18 percent of all workers and all adults. Among heads of households, 63 percent of union supporters and 59 percent of their opponents owned homes, compared with 48 percent for the District. Those most affected on the union side of the struggle—people who were arrested or deported or who were organizers or strike-relief distributors, or those forced to resign public offices—were much more likely to be homeowners (38 percent overall, and 62.5 percent of household heads) than were the leaders on the other side of the conflict (30 percent overall, 41 percent of household heads).[29]

Marital status and home ownership, again, were determined for 1900 not 1904, and many of these men had subsequently married. W. F. Davis and Sherman Parker, for instance, both of whom were arrested numerous times and both of whom served on the District strike committee, were both single boarders in 1900 but had married and established homes before the strike began. Figures for marital status, therefore, can only be suggestive.

Marriage data suggest that men's marital status affected their choices among available modes of resistance. It was easier for single men to leave the District than it was for married men, who stayed to wage the fight. Their choices refute stereotypical portraits of labor activists and strikers as rootless, single, and anomic individuals who could afford the risk of a labor conflict. Contrary to the belief of Stephan Thernstrom and others that home ownership and residential stability led to working-class conservatism, strike activists were those with the greatest stakes in the outcome—stable married men who owned homes.[30] Their unmarried and unpropertied co-workers could more easily leave, but workers with families, homes, and roots fought to protect them.

The higher proportions of single men among those who were arrested and deported for their union allegiance demonstrates in part that the rank and file endorsed the strike and did not repudiate union leadership. The lower proportions of married men among the deportees compared with all pro-union strike activists testifies to how ties to families, homes, and communities affected options and influenced choices. Commitments to home and family motivated men to stay and fight for working-class control. But when labor lost in the chaotic summer of 1904, union men had to choose whether to drop their WFM membership or be deported. Married homeowners felt considerable pressure to cave in to the MOA policy rather than risk their jobs and property and leave their families or uproot their wives and children. The most committed union leaders and Socialists had no choice—they were deported. The other deportees were some of the most committed leaders, who chose to sacrifice jobs, homes, and community for their principles. They included the most dedicated unmarried leaders and rank-and-file union members, who chose to stay and fight although they could more easily have left during the strike. The choice to be deported or renounce the union silenced or dispersed the Socialist and union leadership.

As the strike polarized class relationships, labor modified its ideology of sheltered womanhood. Just as women have been allowed to perform jobs traditionally held by men and receive at least brief public recognition for their contributions during wartime, organized labor lauded the women who provided essential strike support. The *Miners' Magazine* proclaimed that the women had demonstrated that "every fibre of their nature was permeated with the spirit of unionism." Women continued to provide domestic support during the strike and to maintain working-class social life. Their activities achieved new, more public significance in the strike context. The Victor WFM Auxiliary, for example, gave a leap year ball, card party, and supper, with tickets "furnished free of charge to sisters whose husbands were out on strike." They hosted entertainments to raise relief funds, cared for the sick and needy, and worked "to improve the condition of [their] class morally, financially, intellectually and socially."[31]

In addition to traditional "feminine" tasks, women took on more public roles usually reserved for men. After the deportations, they raised bail bonds, fed imprisoned miners, and distributed strike relief despite the military ban. Emma Langdon, hailed as a "Colorado Heroine" for publishing the *Record* when its work force was jailed, became the first woman elected an honorary member of the WFM.[32]

Before the strike, images of sheltered wives and families had symbolized union achievement. During the strike, labor used domestic imagery to emphasize the excessive and invasive force deployed against the working class. Thus, when soldiers invaded the Women's Auxiliary meeting, when mine owners' gunmen intimidated women and children, and when the militia separated husbands from their families, the union attacked employers and the state for violating womanhood and destroying the home. But reverence for white womanhood became a double-edged sword. Union wives and daughters could do things the men could not because the militia hesitated to use physical violence on women and children. Soldiers harassed women who crossed military lines to distribute strike relief, but they did not imprison or shoot them. Women and children taunted scabs and soldiers and waved at trainloads of deportees.[33] Particularly after the deportations, women formed the backbone of the local resistance, and the WFM Executive Board praised them for their "noble and heroic stand."[34]

The strike provided a context to legitimize and recognize activist working-class women. When class action became imperative, women left their homes and the fiction of sheltered domesticity. Emma Langdon, who wrote that "women's natural sphere should be in the home and not in public life," nonetheless acted on her class allegiance during the strike. In addition to defying the military to print the *Record*, she served as secretary of the Victor Women's Auxiliary, vice president of the Trades Assembly, and chair of the executive board of the Typographical Union.[35]

Understanding that class antagonisms threatened their homes, women abandoned the public pretense that separated domestic and public spheres. They accurately connected men's work with family welfare. During the strike crisis, women, too, could act with public bravery to defend their families. The connection between resistance and family was apparent as May Wing fondly recalled the strike heroism of her grandmother, Catharine Doran, and her aunts, Mary Doran and Hannah Welch.

> I did have an uncle that lived in Goldfield. His name was Ed Doran. And Grandma was there, Aunt Mary was expecting. So Uncle Ed, of course, got out. Well, he got word that they were going to raid the house. Of course, the militia had the way of doing, in the middle of the night they'd come after the men and take 'em to the bullpen and then they'd send 'em out. But Uncle Ed got word that they were going to come that night, so he left. Grandma never said just exactly where he went or where he hid. But she was there when they came, and they tore that house to pieces! They even looked in the breadbox. Well, that got Grandma's goat. And she said, "Shure'n he's not little enough to put in the breadbox! Now every God blesset one of you get out of this house and leave this woman alone!" She said, "You can see what condition she's in. Now," she said, "git!"
>
> Then I had another aunt that lived there. Her name was Hannah Welch. . . . And she had two great big butcher knives, and she kept those knives razor sharp. And she always said if one of those militia men ever come in her house in the middle of the night, they'd leave with less than they brought in![36]

Organized labor reconfigured class and gender during the strike to redefine working-class comrades and enemies. Just as working-class manhood connected class and gender in a proud identity, masculine inadequacy marked labor's foes. Charles Moyer depicted the men who forsook the union to scab as failed brothers, husbands, and fathers. "For those who, at the first volley, surrendered their honor, violated their obligation and deserted their brothers in time of need, we can have nothing but contempt. To these traitors can be charged the long-drawn-out struggle in the Cripple Creek District, and they will surely receive their reward. A man who will violate his sacred oath will not defend the honor of his family and should be banished from all honorable society." Working-class women could be strong and heroic during the crisis. But labor derided the soldiers as "pimply faced, chalky complexioned kidlets" who needed the "attention of specialist physicians in order to be cured of certain secret habits." The CSFL's *Pueblo Courier* taunted that there was "mighty little manhood left in Colorado's capital, and not enough in Colorado's militia to fertilize a protoplasm."[37]

As labor embraced working-class women as allies, it rejected former lodge brothers who acted as enemies. "If the members of the Western Federation of Miners are criminals," the *Miners' Magazine* asked rhetorically, "is it not strange and singular that the mine operators harbored those criminals for ten long years?" And, more difficult yet, "Is it not true that the mine operators met these men as brothers in the various fraternal societies?"[38]

The fraternity of the lodge hall shattered under the force of class conflict and the small middle class was forced to choose sides. Members of the same lodges took opposing sides as lodge brothers arrested and deported one another. Among the 616 persons in the lodge sample, thirty-five could be identified as pro-union during the strike and eight as anti-union. Among twenty-eight Elks, one was a member of the deportation committee, one belonged to the Citizens' Alliance or Mine Owners' Association, and one was a union strike relief distributor. One member of the Odd Fellows was arrested by the militia, one was deported, and one belonged to the Citizens' Alliance. One of the thirty-four Masons was arrested, and one belonged to the CA or MOA. A few lodges, however, seemed less divided. The sixty-three members of the Ancient Order of United Workmen (AOUW) in the sample included five who were arrested, four who were deported, and a union organizer. Indeed, the list of officers of the Victor AOUW in 1903 read like a directory of leaders of the Victor Miners' Union. They included Henry King, who had been mayor and treasurer of Goldfield, president of the Victor local, a delegate to CSFL conventions, and who was, in 1903, president of the *Press*'s board of directors; Michael McCarthy, who had served as conductor of the Victor local and on union committees; John Harper, president of the Victor local in 1902 and 1903, a member of the *Press*'s board of directors, and manager of the union's cooperative store during the strike, who was jailed and deported; and Arthur Evans, deported in 1904 and a union trustee in 1903. The Chamber of Commerce, however, included at least five men identified as anti-union activists, four of whom belonged to the CA or MOA, and no union supporters.[39]

Brotherhood could not be constructed in lodge halls if it did not exist outside them. No rituals could dissolve real social hierarchies or erase distinctions of class and power. The military hierarchy of the Knights of Pythias drill team represented class relationships during the strike. Nowhere was that more evident than in the Knights of Pythias itself, where Sherman Bell had practiced his martial prowess by training the drill team for its championship. Other Pythians served in the National Guard during the Cripple Creek strike, including Col. Edward Verdeckberg, and Maj. H. A. Naylor, who had been Bell's drill captain in the Knights of Pythias. Bell and Naylor arrested and deported men who were both union members and lodge brothers. When Naylor married May Stevens at her parents' home in Victor in 1900, the only people other than family at the ceremony were E. W. Stone, who was both a fellow KP officer in 1903 and an active member of Victor Miners No. 32, and J. L. Brinson, a member of the Cripple Creek KP, an Elk, an active Democrat, and a union supporter during the strike. Bell's troops deported Frederick Warburton, the newly elected chancellor commander of the Victor Knights of Pythias lodge. Reverend Leland, harassed for supporting labor, was, like Bell, a Mason and a Knight of Pythias.[40]

If mixed-class lodges did not blunt class antagonisms during the strike, neither did cross-class political coalitions. Although Democrats were much more likely to favor the union and Republicans much more likely to support employers, members of both major parties participated on both sides of the conflict. The more radical and working-class parties—Populists, Co-operatives, Social Democrats, and Socialists—all overwhelmingly sided with labor. Not surprisingly, Socialists and Social Democrats were prominent among the organizers and among those imprisoned and deported.[41] They were well-known union leaders, obvious threats to employers, and many lived in Independence, Goldfield, and other small towns, where the mine managers in the militia knew them. They were prime targets.

That the military hounded Socialists such as Sherman Parker and W. F. Davis was not surprising. The strike's political lessons proved more unsettling for fusion advocates because political coalitions did not, after all, deliver protection. Union men elected to public office and appointed to patronage posts through cross-class political alliances were simply deposed, imprisoned, and/or deported after the Independence depot explosion. Democrat Nelson Franklin helped depose fellow Democrat Henry Robertson, and Republican A. E. Carlton deported fellow Republican J. W. Higens. As chair of the Democratic executive committee in 1902, Franklin had supported Robertson's candidacy for sheriff. But when the lines were drawn, it was more important that Robertson was a miner and Franklin a mill manager and promoter of the Eagle Sampler than that they were both Democrats. Robertson's former membership in the WFM and Franklin's affiliations with the Citizens' Alliance and the Mine Owners' Association guided their behaviors during the strike more than their shared party allegiance possibly could. Edward Bell, who replaced Robertson as sheriff, was a director of the Cripple Creek Mining Exchange. He shared more materially and ideologically with Albert Carlton, the Republican mine owner and banker with whom he cooperated, than he did with Henry Robertson, a former miner and fellow Democrat whose office he seized.[42] The political support to crush Cripple Creek unions came from the Republican state administration, but it came equally from Edward Bell, a Democrat.

No Politics as Usual

The problem, of course, was not just coalition politics. It was the failure of electoral politics and democratic process. A mob with no constitutional authority deposed officials elected with labor support and forcibly replaced them with persons hostile to organized labor. Regardless of political party, Cripple Creek workers shared a belief in democracy, a faith that reform and revolutionary change alike could be won at the ballot box. But some public officials supported the lawless takeover of local government. Victor postmaster F. M. Reardon, as a general in the National Guard, served as a member of the deportation committee. The WFM charged that Reardon allowed strike sympathizers' mail to be opened and read, and the union telegraphed Theodore Roosevelt, "Can you not prevent federal officers from committing such crimes?"[43] Roosevelt either could not or chose not to. One of the bitter lessons of the strike was that the Fourth of July orators were right—democracy did not work when capital controlled the state. That lesson did not end with the forced resignations in the summer of 1904.

Reeling from the brutal Peabody years, organized labor made what was for some a difficult decision to support Alva Adams, the Democratic candidate for governor, rather than the Socialist, acting on the certainty that organized labor would be doomed if Peabody were reelected. The State Federation of Labor declared that the only issue that mattered was "Peabody and his policy toward labor" and supported the Democratic Party to secure "relief from Peabody and his policy."[44]

District mine owners flexed their muscles with bipartisan vigor, pressuring employees to attend both the Democratic and Republican primaries and to support Peabody for governor and Edward Bell for sheriff. They openly threatened that the deportation committees would "rush" both primaries. Albert Carlton reportedly said that he would name the next county officers.[45]

Labor feared that Peabody's supporters would prevent miners from voting at all. The *Rocky Mountain News* quoted Major McClelland as saying that Peabody would carry Teller County because those in control would not permit "those ____ miners to vote, except the way we want them, in Teller." Clarence Fitch, assistant secretary of the MOA, reportedly threatened that miners who voted against Peabody would never work in the District again, and voters refused to ride to the polls in Democratic carriages for fear of being blacklisted.[46]

Their fear was more than justified. On election day, November 9, two union miners, Chris Miller and Isaac T. Liebo, were serving as poll watchers in Goldfield. Jim Warford, a mine owners' gunman who had been appointed a Teller County deputy sheriff, told them to leave. When Miller and Liebo refused, Warford shot them—one in the back, both fatally. Miller—who had guarded the evidence at the Independence depot—died instantly, and Liebo died later. A detail of deputy sheriffs was dispatched to Goldfield. Shortly thereafter, at 10 A.M., three men tried to deport County Clerk and Recorder Frank Mannix as part of a plan to allege vote tampering, if need be, to ensure a Republican victory. Sheriff Bell caught and arrested the would-be deporters, among them a Republican campaign worker, William Carruthers.[47]

The news about Miller, Liebo, and Mannix spread quickly and frightened citizens stayed away from the polls. Teller County went Republican for the first time, and members of the MOA, the CA, and officers of the local militia companies won most county and municipal offices. Edward Bell was elected sheriff, and Clarence Hamlin was elected district attorney. The State Federation of Labor's *Clarion Advocate* reported that "Teller county went for Peabody, but it took 1,000 deportations, hundreds of beatings, scores of murders and God only knows how much fraud to accomplish this result."[48]

Democrats protested the Teller County election, filing charges of wholesale bribery and fraud and claiming that voters were intimidated by the deportations, violence, and premeditated murders of Miller and Liebo. They charged that miners had been threatened with the loss of their MOA cards and jobs if they did not vote for Peabody, and that ballots were opened to determine how individuals voted. By late November some 250 miners' cards had been canceled. The first act of the new county commissioners was to increase the county attorney's annual salary from $600 to $1,800 and appoint T. E. ("to hell with the constitution") McClelland to the job.[49]

Even with the Teller County ballots, Peabody lost the election to Adams by some ten thousand votes. Both sides charged election fraud, both with probable cause. Democratic repeat voters in Denver went from poll to poll, while Republican fraud was equally rampant elsewhere throughout the state. Adams was sworn in and took office, but Peabody contested the election, and a tense legislature investigated. Peabody's allies appointed MOA detective K. C. Sterling custodian of the Colorado Senate, with former MOA gunmen, including Kid Waters, as his deputies. By January 4 the state capitol building was barricaded, and lawmakers had to pass the scrutiny of former MOA hirelings to enter. Sherman Bell guarded the basement, and Sterling's civilian guards worked as doorkeepers for both houses.[50]

On January 11, 1905, representatives of Colorado Fuel and Iron, Victor Fuel, ASARCO, various public utility companies, two railways, and the Colorado Mine Owners' Association met to plan how to seat Peabody. Rumors of bribery ran rampant, including reports that the Denver Tramway Company and ASARCO were offering $2,500 to $5,000 per legislative vote. The special commission the legislature appointed to investigate the contested returns was chaired by W. H. Griffiths, a Cripple Creek newspaper publisher and, the unions charged, an MOA apologist. Sam Crump served on Peabody's legal team. After hearing hundreds of witnesses, the committee announced that it could not determine a winner, and the legislature thereupon devised a "compromise." Peabody replaced Adams as governor, on the condition that he resign within twenty-four hours and allow his lieutenant governor, Jesse McDonald, to take the office.[51] Thus, Colorado had three governors in a day that ended with the appointment of a man who had never run for the office.

After the 1904 election, charges were dropped against most of the people indicted for instigating the Victor riot. The seventeen remaining defendants included the WFM officers and Executive Board and Sherman Parker and W. F. Davis. Charges were eventually dropped in some of the cases, and all the others were acquitted. Charges were also dropped against Arthur Parker, L. R. Jenks, and the Rev. T. S. Leland for conspiracy to murder Sheriff Bell. A jury in Castle Rock, on the plains south of Denver, acquitted Parker and Jenks of the remaining charges related to the raid on Leland's home.[52]

Jim Warford and Thomas Brown were arrested for the election day murders of Miller and Liebo, convicted of murder, and sentenced to life imprisonment. A. H. Rogers visited Warford in prison and Warford reportedly said that Ed Bell told him to go to Goldfield to kill Miller and Liebo on election day 1904. Warford, according to Rogers, said that he was "supposed to be taken care of" and that "Bell, Holman, Gleason, Carlton, and Bainbridge all said that if I killed one or both of them that they would see that I got out all right, but you know how they all went back on me when I had that racket with Bell." Chris Miller, whom Henry Robertson had appointed to guard evidence at the Independence depot, was silenced like so many others who held the key to that tragedy. Two of the MOA gunmen whom attorney Richardson's informants linked to the explosion were also dead, and three more were in prison. A Republican governor pardoned Warford and Brown after they served less than four years. Harry Orchard died in 1954 in an Idaho prison.[53]

LABOR UNORGANIZED

The WFM refused to concede defeat in the Cripple Creek District and continued to care for the families of strikers and deportees. On December 28, 1904, it organized Cripple Creek District Miners' Union No. 234 to replace the nine WFM locals. Finally, on December 7, 1907, the members of Local No. 234 asked the WFM Executive Board to declare the strike over, arguing that there was still a lockout of union miners but that the strike had ended June 6, 1904. Colorado City Mill and Smeltermen No. 125 had been defunct for two years. The Executive Board finally declared the Cripple Creek strike officially over, and in 1909 the Colorado legislature appropriated $60,000 to reimburse the WFM for the state troops' destruction of the cooperative stores and the Victor union hall.[54]

The small WFM local held on for years. The WFM proudly staged its 1912 convention in Victor. Nonetheless, as the few remaining WFM stalwarts knew, for all practical purposes organized labor in the Cripple Creek District had died with the victims at the Independence depot. By 1905 only one District local, the long-beleaguered Musicians' Union, still belonged to the Colorado State Federation of Labor. Strike failures split Colorado labor. The WFM, deciding that one reason it lost was its lack of broad national support and that neither industrial unionism nor socialism could be won on a local level, founded the Industrial Workers of the World. The State Federation joined the American Federation of Labor.[55]

Cripple Creek demonstrated the limits of even the most impressive local union movement to achieve working-class goals. Workers could not win industrial union-ism, legislative reforms, or socialism in isolated localities. It became clear, too, that cross-class civic authority was no match for armed state power. However clear these lessons were, and whatever other lessons the strike might have taught, they came too late to matter. The Cripple Creek working class had lost its leadership and the institutional base to act through unions at the workplace or through independent class politics at the polls.

Ideological differences among workers no longer mattered in the Cripple Creek District. Employers could effectively blacklist miners by returning their cards to the Mine Owners' Association.[56] Fear and accommodation governed labor relations. The real victors were the most conservative mine owners, particularly Tutt and Penrose, who broke the millmen's local at their Colorado City mill, and their friend Albert Carlton. The strike provided the opportunity not only to banish organized labor but also to consolidate the power of anti-union owners over companies that had accommodated unions. The message became clear as first the Woods family and then Burns were forced to swallow MOA policy.

The conservatives prospered. MacNeill, Tutt, and Penrose converted their Cripple Creek riches into the Utah Copper Company. Tutt sold out, did well, and died wealthy; Bingham Canyon made MacNeill and Penrose multimillionaires. In 1907 they bought out Peabody's interests in his Canon City bank. The *Miners' Magazine* intimated that they forced him to sell, saying that they "crushed him to the wall with as little mercy as Peabody manifested toward the miners who were torn from their homes and deported by an armed mob." Albert Carlton won con-trol of the Golden Cycle Company, which gradually took over most major mines in the District and built its own mill. Carlton's mill controlled assays and returns to independent mines, and his bank controlled credit to local merchants and miners.

By the 1920s and 1930s the District was in many respects a company town. Golden Cycle controlled wages, hiring policy, and leasing conditions and wielded consid-erable power in local politics. District residents reported that there was always a Golden Cycle man on the school board and city council. Whenever a bond issue for new schools was proposed, they charged, the company would threaten to shut the mines if it passed. Discrimination based on religion and ethnicity became a shorthand, too, for class; residents charged that to be promoted within Golden Cycle one had to be "a Republican and a Mason."[57]

The Cripple Creek District never really recovered from the strike. Many mines never reopened, and many union miners never returned. Their hard-won homes deteriorated until they were torn down and sold for building materials during World War I. The towns and businesses never returned to the bustling pre-strike prosperity. The losses of the Cripple Creek strike of 1903–4 were borne daily by thousands of people who for ten years built a working-class community and then risked it to establish the right to organize for other workers. The strike exacted an incalculable human price when union miners were forced to leave. Their fates represented organized labor's writ small.

Like countless miners left homeless by blacklists and mine closures, many simply went to other mines in other places. Just as miners from Leadville, Aspen, and the Coeur d'Alenes had come to the promising new mines of Cripple Creek, many of the District's dispossessed miners took their skills to new gold camps in Nevada and elsewhere. W. F. Davis, who came to Cripple Creek after he was jailed in the 1899 Coeur d'Alenes strike, first fled to Cheyenne and then moved to Goldfield, Nevada, in January 1905, where he transferred into WFM Local No. 220. Davis lost considerably more than his home. Mattie Bowman Davis and their infant both died during the strike.[58]

Davis's old partner Sherman Parker also joined the trek to Goldfield. He died there in the fall of 1906, leaving Bessie Delphi Parker a widowed mother at age twenty-three. Davis served on the committee that wrote resolutions of condolence for the family and the press. Their resolution praised Parker's "efficiency in serving the interests of his class against the attacks of its hyena-hearted enemies," for which he was "repeatedly jailed, bull-penned, abused and threatened," but who remained "a man they could neither intimidate nor corrupt." W. F. Davis, affirming the values of working-class manhood, described Parker as "a man, a true man and a loving man."[59]

Frank Mannix, the pro-labor Teller County clerk and recorder, was forced to leave when he refused to resign his office. Mannix also went to Nevada, where he continued his careers in politics and publishing. In Rhyolite he published *The Bullfrog Miner*, the columns of which defended the WFM and attacked the conservative *Cripple Creek Times* and the Citizens' Alliance for anti-labor pronouncements. From Rhyolite, Mannix went to Tonopah and was elected the treasurer of Nye County. He died there in 1914.[60]

Jerry Kelly, who served six terms as financial secretary of Victor Miners No. 32, was deported for his commitments to socialism and the WFM. Forced to leave

Victor, he, too, went to Nevada, to mine in Tonopah and Goldfield. He remained but a brief time because of ill health. The 1906 WFM convention paid Celia Kelly for six and half months' "rent" for the use of her home after the Victor Miners' Hall burned in the 1899 Victor fire, using the payment as thinly disguised relief for her husband's disability. Jerry Kelly died of miners' consumption in November 1906. He was fifty-two.[61]

Workers whose skills were not tied directly to mining could continue as labor and political activists in other communities. Three former District union leaders served as delegates to the 1907 convention of the Colorado State Federation of Labor. R. E. Croskey represented Journeymen Cooks No. 18 of Denver, P. N. McPhee represented Denver Carpenters No. 55, and J. C. Provost served as a delegate from the Denver Building Trades Council. Hans Hansen, the Danish immigrant who was deported along with his son Christopher, moved to Colorado City and continued to work and write for socialism. In 1904 he ran for presidential elector as a Socialist, listing himself on the ballot as "Hans Hansen, Deportee." In 1906 he thoughtfully analyzed the internal divisions in the Industrial Workers of the World, and the following year he organized rallies to protest the arrests of Moyer, Pettibone, and Haywood for Frank Steunenberg's murder. He encouraged workers to "teach our children never to take up arms against their own class," because "a soldier is simply a tool in the hands of his oppressors." In Hansen's case, the troops drove the Socialist out of Cripple Creek but reinforced his political commitment.[62] Many deportees continued as Socialist Party leaders in Colorado and other western states.[63]

If one person in these pages could tell what the labor community of Cripple Creek meant for working miners, and what its defeat cost, that person was John Welch. Informed that the militia was coming to deport him "the next trainload they took out," Welch left in the middle of the night and went back to Leadville to mine. Hannah Welch took the children and joined him there for a time after the militia harassed her son Tom and her nephew Eddie Bulger as the boys were going fishing. Kathleen Welch Chapman remembered:

The militia drove up there and stopped them. And they wanted to know where they were going. They told them, and they said, "Oh, no, you're not. You're hauling out food for the union men someplace." "Oh, no," Eddie said, "we're not. We don't have anything, only our lunch." Anyway, they pulled the two kids down off of the horse. Eddie was about six years older than Tom. And pulled them down, took their lunch, throwed it down on the grass. Took the saddle off the horse, and every little nook and corner of that saddle they went through to see if they were taking something. Well, they just put the saddle back on the horse and come back down home, and you know that made a wreck out of Tom. He was about, I'd say, ten, eleven years old, something like that. And he was just a wreck. He couldn't sleep at night. He'd just wake up—or he wouldn't wake up, but he'd scream in his sleep, you know. So Mama said, "Well I can't stand that." So she packed us up and took us to Leadville, where Papa was, until the darned thing would quiet down or get over. And we were up there for over a year and a half. Then we came back to the District.[64]

Hannah and the children stayed in their home in Goldfield, while John Welch worked in various mining communities and visited his family when he could, because "a union man couldn't get a job and he wouldn't work on them scab cards for anything." After he was buried in a cave-in at a Minturn mine, which crushed his chest and injured his legs, Welch finally came home. Unable to mine, he worked as a watchman at the Trilby, a small mine that resisted the MOA. When he became too ill to climb the hill to the mine or to do much work, young Tom Welch left school after the eighth grade to take his father's place. Just as John Welch entered the work force when his father died in a Vermont coal mine, Tom Welch, born in a tent during the Bull Hill strike, became the family's breadwinner. In time, Kathleen also contributed her wages as a housekeeper and laundry worker. John Welch died of his injuries at age forty-eight. His children remembered the union benefits, the social support, the vibrance, and the power of the union community their father had built and cherished. They knew in bitter detail what they had lost.

The individual fates of W. F. and Mattie Davis, Jerry and Celia Kelly, Frank Mannix, Hans, Karen, and Chris Hansen, Sherman and Bessie Parker, and John and Hannah Welch represent in microcosm the fates of thousands of people who worked and lived a while in Cripple Creek. Some remained active in organized labor and politics, working to win again the social power they had experienced, however briefly, in the District. Others simply lived their private lives as best they could and left control of public affairs to the strike victors. Their lives continued to revolve around daily labor and their families. Most worked until they died.

The WFM continued to try to buffer the losses for strike victims and their families. In December 1905 it paid funeral benefits of $75 each to the widows of Chris Miller, Isaac Liebo, Michael O'Connell, and John Carley. It also donated $100 to Celia Kelly immediately after Jerry Kelly died. Mrs. Carley, whose husband was killed in the "Battle of Dunnville," requested and received periodic aid for years.[65]

That assistance, of course, was no substitute for incalculable personal losses. Miners died and lost their homes because they could control neither the technical nor the social hazards of their industry. The casualties went far beyond individual lives. They lost, too, their shared social visions and collective history. Fear of company retaliation was so profound that some people never shared childhood memories of the strike with their children, so many memories died. Because employers had controlled contemporary press reports and seized union records after the Independence explosion, they controlled not only events but also the history of those events. After the mines closed in the early 1960s, the elderly residents finally felt free to tell their stories.

The history they wished to preserve was not a nostalgic past or a tale of tragic loss. It was about complicated people who lived complex and often mundane lives. They sought neither romance nor riches, but a community that they could shape, a place where work would be honored and workers dignified. The survivors remembered a world in which union labor won social standing, industrial control, and political influence.

If this is not simply a history of loss, neither is it a history of one-dimensional heroes or victims or of lives driven solely by class allegiances. The shared social terrain of race, gender, and class created overlapping sources of identity and association. Shared identities of white manhood in particular opened arenas of social and political association for the ten years of union power. The respectability and civic authority that went with being a man, a husband, a homeowner, and a union leader persuaded much of organized labor that the road to wider working-class power lay in workplace organizing, coalition politics, and dignified dealings with employers who recognized "manly methods" in labor relations. The same local authority persuaded a growing minority that they could extend workplace and political power to win a Socialist cooperative commonwealth through democratic processes. But the proud and complex identities of white working-class manhood broke along racial lines during the union era—and along class lines during the strike. Participants defined their manhood as they chose which side they were on.

Class relations, in ways that were not always apparent, were negotiated in every social encounter. Different identities appeared more salient in different contexts— gender in saloons, lodge halls, and family kitchens and class in union halls and workplaces and during the strike. The imperfect links between the political allegiances of organized labor and partisan politics, among ideologies of race, class, and gender, existed at least in part because different sources of identity and different social relationships operated in different arenas and circumstances. Labor's social power masked the underlying tensions inherent in being a working-class community leader—a person active in unions, lodges, recreation, and politics. The measure of union achievement was to be fully human in all these arenas, to be, like Sherman Parker, "a man, a true man and a loving man" whom capital "could neither intimidate nor corrupt."

These were not separate identities. Lodge halls and precinct conventions were also arenas in which people negotiated class recognition. That regard proved to be as short-lived as many a prospector's dream, but the short history of labor's social influence was as significant as the long memory of its loss.

The real and important internal contradictions within Cripple Creek's working-class community were matched by rifts among mine owners, whose disagreements about union labor and refining charges operated as submerged issues in the strike. The conflict between capital and labor partially masked competition among capitalists that generated pressure for mine management to adopt MOA policy and for small merchants and local professionals to choose sides. Like the rock that held Cripple Creek's complex ores, the labor community contained fissures. Divisions of race and sex and partial class analyses were enacted daily in cross-class social and political ties, in divisions among white and non-white workers, and among working-class women and men. Under the pressure of industrial conflict, class loyalties bridged many internal rifts, just as gold ore filled and stabilized cracks in the volcanic rock. The complex social terrain divided along class lines.

When the unions were smashed—and with them the institutional base for working-class power—what remained to anchor daily relationships were identities of family, race, religion, and gender. These were powerful enough to motivate wrenching decisions to renounce the unions and shroud labor's history. Still, they could provide only private and personal motives and explanations as people negotiated unequal social relationships. They did not offer the means, the power, or the hope for change.

Finally, lacking the institutional power to challenge class relationships at work, miners turned to the fellowship of their lodges, and especially to the families for whom they had risked so much and for whom they had stayed. Years later, survivors recalled the strike defeat in terms of domestic loss. Asked what difference the second strike made for working people, Kathleen Chapman replied, "Oh my, it changed it awful! You've been through Goldfield. Well, you should have seen the homes that was up there in Goldfield. They were beautiful, some of them. They were just gorgeous. Well, people just got up and left, you know, and left their homes like it was, and lots of them never come back to them. People would go in and destroy the homes and pick up what they wanted, and the houses went to wrack, and they tore them down, and—oh, it just—it just used to make me sick all over."

ALL THAT GLITTERS

Whatever the Promised Land seemed to offer from the top of Mt. Pisgah, for many miners and their families that promise was home. Neither promise nor loss can be seen from the summit of Pisgah. From there we can view broader patterns but not the lost dignity that meant being able to resist a stripping order, to keep children in school instead of working, to parade proudly on Labor Day, or to go home to a house you owned.

It has been a constant temptation to end this book with a return to the summit of the biblical Pisgah—to point out that Moses, having wandered for forty years in the desert, was, like the union leadership, allowed only a distant glimpse of the Promised Land but was not allowed to cross the Jordan and touch its soil, that the union miners, like the children of Israel, sojourned there only briefly before their long diaspora. It would be a tidy if pretentious ending. That story, though, leaves out the women and children who maintained daily life and memory and the people who contested ownership of the Promised Land. Without them, the biblical story, however inspiring, cannot explain what anchored daily choices or connect the past and present.

The last time I drove to the top of Mt. Pisgah, May Wing went with me. She had lived in the Cripple Creek District most of her then-eighty-eight years, but this was the first time she had gone to the top of the mountain. Occasionally she pointed out a landmark. Mostly we shared the incomparable panorama in silence. Suddenly, a tourist startled the quiet of the bright morning. Holding out a rock that glistened in the sunlight, he asked, "Can you tell me, is this gold?"

"No," May answered shortly.

"You'd know it if you saw it?" he persisted.

"I'd know it if I saw it," she replied brusquely. "And that's not it. But," she added softly, "I've seen some beautiful ore in my time."

Appendix A

Methodology

Much of the quantitative data come from the 1900 manuscript census for Teller County, Colorado, which enumerated 29,002 residents for the entire county, whereas District boosters claimed a population of some 50,000. The most reliable population estimates come from geographer Robert Guilford Taylor's *Cripple Creek*. Taylor based his estimates on some thirty-six sources, including public relations and Chamber of Commerce releases, District directories, advertising, press reports, published historical research, the U.S. census, and U.S. postmasters' stipends based on the volume of mail. He estimated the District's peak population in 1900 as 32,000.[1] Comparing Taylor's population estimates with the manuscript census, the populations of the towns appear to have been underestimated as follows: Cripple Creek, 2,853 (22 percent); Victor, 1,014 (17 percent); Gillett, 26 (5 percent); Anaconda, 41 (4 percent); Goldfield, 309 (12 percent); and Altman, 241 (27 percent).[2] Cameron was not founded until 1900, after the census was taken.

Some of Taylor's estimates may be faulty. For example, the census may have listed a number of Altman residents as living in the unincorporated portions of Precinct 26, which included Altman. Taylor did not specify figures for unincorporated areas, which also may be under-represented. Comparing my knowledge of local geography with the manuscript census, I believe that the under-enumerated areas included at least the red light districts of Cripple Creek and Victor, and, to a lesser degree, working-class neighborhoods in Cripple Creek, Victor, Goldfield, and Altman. These under-enumerations likely resulted from several factors, including census policy regarding counting the population of the red light districts and local politics. Census-takers in 1900 were Republican patronage employees, and they appear to have under-counted the areas where they would have been least welcome, particularly the most militant working-class neighborhoods in Altman, Victor, and Goldfield.

The bias in the census meant that I could not use it to describe prostitutes and their households, and, more important, the under-enumerations meant that some union and political leaders (likely Populists, Co-operatives, and Socialists in particular) could not be located and included in the union, strike, political, or lodge samples. If anything, their inclusion would reinforce my conclusions. The neighborhoods that were under-enumerated included family neighborhoods, so the census bias did not exaggerate the numbers of stable, married homeowners.

For occupation, class, and ethnicity, figures were computed for the entire adult population. For most data I relied on a 10 percent random sample of the adult population (persons sixteen and older and younger people who listed occupations) for reasons of economy and because a random sample of some two thousand is statistically reliable. There were thirty-seven persons under age sixteen, or 1.8 percent of the adult population in the random sample of 2,089. Although they were not included in the rest of the quantitative analysis, I counted all children by class to determine the total population and explore class differences regarding marriage and parenthood. For union affiliation, politics, lodges, and strike activity, figures were computed for the full samples.

Most census variables required only straightforward coding: age, marital status, race, sex, father's country of birth, mother's country of birth, individual's state or country of birth, position in household, and home ownership. I divided occupations into classes and further divided them by skill level and by whether or not they were mining-related. Skill levels were used only for occupations for which they could be determined with reasonable accuracy. Most workers listed themselves as miners and did not specify their work. One hundred and forty-one persons who listed their occupation as engineer were listed with skilled mining labor on the assumption that most of them were hoist engineers. There were few mining engineers in the District, and they and railroad engineers usually specified their occupations.

Two men reviewed my occupational classifications: Ralph O. Wing, who worked as a miner, ore sorter, and assayer from 1933 to 1962 and who had discussed changes in the work process with his father, O. E. Wing, who began as a hoist engineer around 1905; and S. C. Gatheridge, who began mining in Cornwall in 1896 and mined in the District from 1905 to 1921. In the tables, "occupation" refers only to those actually engaged in the occupation. "Class" includes people in their households, unless those persons listed occupations of their own.

As I researched, I maintained file cards on individuals who were active in politics, unions, lodges, or in the 1903–4 strike. When someone is identified in this text as belonging to a particular lodge or political party or as holding a particular union office, that information came from the file cards. After the census was coded, I matched these persons with the census whenever possible. This was obviously impossible for persons who did not live in the District when the census was taken, or who were not enumerated, or whose names were so common that they could not be matched with certainty. This was most difficult with some Irish names. It was not always apparent, for example, which of the six John Sullivans who were miners belonged to Victor Miners No. 32.

THE UNION SAMPLE

The names of union leaders were gathered primarily from the records of the Western Federation of Miners and the Colorado State Federation of Labor, the biennial reports of the state labor commissioner, and from reports of union elections and other union functions in the *Victor and Cripple Creek Daily Press*. A leader was defined as one who held union office or served on union committees. A local leader was one who held office in his or her local union or served on a local union committee. A District union leader held union office at the District level, as a delegate to the Cripple Creek District Trades and Labor Assembly or a Building Trades Council, or as a member of the board of directors of the *Daily Press* or of the WFM District Union No. 1 Executive Board. A state or national leader held office in a state or national labor organization (the CSFL, WFM, WLU/ALU, or his or her international union) or was a convention delegate to a state or national labor organization. Each person was counted at the highest level of leadership attained. The names of virtually all union leaders were gathered for those elected from 1899 to 1903, when the *Press* published. The names of secretaries of many locals were available in the reports of the state labor commissioner; the names of convention delegates and of those who held office in the CSFL or WFM were available in the existing records of those organizations. The sample is thus biased for the period of greatest union activity, when more sources were available. The census was also taken during that period.

The names of the rank and file are less complete. They were gathered from three sources: from the only available membership ledger, that of Victor Miners No. 32 for 1894 to 1903, which provided the names of some four hundred individuals initiated during 1894 and 1895; from occasional letters to newspapers or references to a person's union membership in the local press; and from death and funeral notices. Given the high incidence of early death from mining accidents and infectious diseases, these were not particularly biased by age, and in any event they represented very few cases in the sample. In most instances I compared union leadership to all workers rather than to the rank and file, because workers, given the high level of union membership (Appendix B), were fairly representative of the rank and file.

THE LODGE SAMPLE

The names of lodge members were gathered from local newspaper stories, particularly from the *Press*, which covered lodge elections and social events. It also ran death and funeral notices for lodge-sponsored burials, which appeared to be as representative as those in the union sample. The sample therefore includes more lodge leaders than ordinary members and more persons who belonged between 1899 and 1903 than any other period. It does, however, include names of many ordinary lodge members who were leaders either in the unions or in politics, or who were socially prominent for other reasons. Stories about union leaders or about candidates for public office, for instance, sometimes mentioned their lodge affiliations. Thus, the sample is biased somewhat for community leadership; in light of that fact, the proportion of working-class lodge leaders is impressive.

THE POLITICAL SAMPLE

The names of people active in political parties or in political fusion campaigns were gathered from the local, labor, and Socialist press, including the *Daily Press*, the *Colorado Springs Weekly Gazette*, the *Denver Colorado Chronicle*, the *Denver Rocky Mountain Socialist*, the *Colorado Springs Pink Iconoclast*, the *Pueblo Courier*, the *Pueblo Labor Advocate*, and the *Miners' Magazine*. The *Press* printed lists of delegates to all party conventions from the precinct level up; the *Gazette* sometimes did, particularly for the Republican Party. All the publications covered party conventions and election campaigns and printed the names of candidates and of members of party executive committees.

A politically active person was defined as one who ran for public office, was a delegate to a party convention, was a member of a political club or organization, or who actively supported a particular party or ticket.

The sample is skewed in several ways. It is, again, most complete for 1899 through 1903, when the *Press* published. It also contains the names of more Democrats than any other group, not only because the Democratic Party was the majority party in the District in those years but also because, for most of its history, the *Press* endorsed the Democratic Party and gave it favored coverage. Most important, however, the Democrats elected more delegates to local, county, and state conventions than did other parties. They simply held larger conventions, and delegate lists were a primary source of names. The Democrats and Republicans identified include many convention delegates. The Populist, Co-operative, and Socialist parties, however, held open conventions, at least locally. Anyone who wanted could attend and participate. Although that was democratic, it meant that the more radical and working-class parties did not publish lists of convention delegates. Hence, I had to rely on sporadic news coverage of the conventions or of meetings of Socialist locals, the names of candidates and prominent campaign workers, notices of Socialist Party meetings, and letters to the press. That there are fewer people from these parties in the sample, therefore, is partly related to differences in how party representatives were selected. It is also reflects that from 1899 to 1904 fewer members of these parties were in the District than of the major parties. The fact that the census undercounted radical working-class neighborhoods further diminished their numbers in the sample.

Finally, because the samples of Social Democrats and Socialist Party members are small, some comment about their representativeness is in order. The Social Democratic Party was active in the District only in 1900; that sample includes mostly the names of candidates for office or members of the state executive committee. These represented the small minority who insisted on independent labor politics in 1900 and are likely fairly representative of that group. I included them largely because they were the only radical alternative in 1900. Without them the figures for 1900 would compare only the major parties. Most of the Social Democrats joined the Socialist Party. Only thirty-eight Socialist Party members are in the sample for the reasons given above. They include, however, a fairly representative group of the local party leadership and equal 5 to 10 percent of the Socialist vote from 1901 to 1904.

THE STRIKE SAMPLE

Strike participants on both sides were reported in the *Miners' Magazine*, in the *Press* until it ceased publication, and in government reports. They were coded for level of involvement. Two categories were used for analysis: strike participants and strike sympathizers. Strike participants included, on the union side, those who were arrested, deported, served on the strike committee, worked as organizers in the District or elsewhere soliciting strike relief and discouraging strikebreakers, those who distributed strike relief in the District, and those forced to resign public office for presumed pro-labor loyalties. The anti-union participants were members of the Citizens' Alliance, the Mine Owners' Association, or of the deportation committees. The strike participants were included in the strike sympathizers sample, which was divided simply into pro- and anti-labor groups. To these activists were added, on the pro-union side, names of persons who signed petitions endorsing the strike or protesting sending troops to the District and the names of persons who indicated their sympathies in the press. On the anti-union side, the sympathizers included those the union identified as strikebreakers or as "gun thugs" hired by the Mine Owners' Association. The strikebreakers comprise virtually all the working-class persons in the anti-union category.

THE ORAL HISTORIES

I conducted oral history interviews with a number of residents and former residents of the Cripple Creek District from 1975 to 1979. Some of these were persons born long after 1905. There were, however, seven who were children, teen-agers, or young adults in the District during the period of this study: Kathleen Chapman, S. C. (Charlie) Gatheridge, Anna McGoldrick, Beulah Pryor, Clara Stiverson, Leslie Wilkinson, and May Wing. Four others were born between 1903 and 1930: Ileen Pryor, Ruby Wilkinson, Mary Wing, and Ralph Wing.

Neither group constitutes a "sample" or represents more than a group of personal histories that offer some rare firsthand accounts of working-class social life and private experience. Of the older group, Charlie Gatheridge was the only person I was able to interview who actually mined during the period, although he did not come to the District until 1905, after the strike. He nonetheless heard stories about the strike from his cohorts, and I interviewed him primarily about the work process and work relationships underground, which had not changed a great deal by 1905. Most of the older people I could interview were women, because miners often died before their wives did. Of the women, May Wing was born in 1890 and Kathleen Chapman in 1895, and both remembered the strike in detail. Beulah Pryor, born in 1896, remembered living under military guard as a strikebreaker's child. Clara Stiverson's father owned a saloon next to the Victor Union Hall, and she heard his stories of the Victor riot and recalled a few strike-related events. I interviewed the next generation to find out what version of labor history they had inherited and to gather their experience of living and working in the District after the strike.

I located people to interview in a variety of ways. I went to the Cripple Creek District and asked elderly people how long they had lived there and whether they would talk to me. That is how the Wilkinson interviews occurred. I gave a number of talks about my research, and people in the audience identified themselves as descendants of residents. I met Clara Stiverson's daughter that way. A number of interviews came from my contacts with the Wing family, and one interview often led to the next. Hence, I interviewed Anna McGoldrick because she was a friend of James and Catherine Wing. She introduced me to Charlie Gatheridge, who lived at her nursing home.

A number of these people were related. May Wing and Kathleen Chapman were cousins. Ileen Pryor and Ralph Wing are the children of May and O. E. Wing. Beulah Pryor was Ileen Pryor's husband's stepmother. These relationships did not necessarily mean, however, that people's experiences, particularly their experience of the strike or of working-class culture, were the same. Kathleen Chapman's father was an active union member who supported the union during the strike and who left the District to avoid being deported. May Wing's father was a hoist engineer who had no particular union sympathies; he was not in the District during the strike. Beulah Pryor came to the District during the strike when her stepfather came to work as a strikebreaker.[3]

APPENDIX B

UNION MEMBERSHIP

Membership in District labor organizations cannot be accurately determined because the minutes and records of most local unions were either lost or destroyed by mobs as they wrecked and looted union halls following the explosion at the Independence depot on June 6, 1904.

I could, however, construct at least partial lists of District unions and their memberships. Lists of local unions came from the biennial reports of the Colorado state commissioner of labor and from the records of per capita receipts of the Colorado State Federation of Labor. I augmented these with CSFL convention proceedings, the WFM Official Charter Book, a list prepared by the United Brotherhood of Carpenters and Joiners of America of local unions chartered in Colorado, and by press references from the *Miners' Magazine* (1901–11), the *Colorado Springs Weekly Gazette* (1891–99), and the *Victor and Cripple Creek Daily Press* (1899–1903), which published a directory of local unions.[1]

All of these are partial sources. Not all District locals affiliated with the CSFL, answered the questionnaires of the state labor commissioner, or purchased union directory listings in the *Press*. Each source, however, included some the others excluded.

The only consistent source of membership figures was the membership records of the CSFL. Yet even those figures are, in some cases, misleading. There are some wide discrepancies between the per capita tax reports to the State Federation, those to other bodies, such as the WFM and the WLU/ALU, and press references, all of which sometimes suggest higher membership figures than do the CSFL records. In some cases, locals may have reported inflated memberships to newspapers. It was common practice, however, for local unions to affiliate with larger labor organizations based on fewer members than they actually had.[2] They did this to save money by paying lower per capita tax, or because they were unhappy with the organization's policies, or because they felt they had enough influence without claiming all the convention votes to which their full memberships entitled them. Under-reporting seems clearly to have happened in some cases. In April 1902, for example, Cripple Creek Federal Labor Union No. 19 paid per capita tax to the CSFL for 324 members; in May 1902, it claimed 300, and in June, 280. At the same time, however, the secretary-treasurer of the Western Labor Union reported that FLU No. 19 was the largest WLU affiliate, with some 700 members. In May and June 1901, Victor Miners' Union No. 32 paid CSFL per capita tax on 800 members while claiming 1,100 in the local press. From September 1901 through

June 1902, Anaconda Miners' Union No. 21 paid CSFL per capita on 150 members, but in January 1902 the *Press* reported its membership as 500.[3] Particularly when a local claimed a membership in round figures (for example, 150) for a long period, I suspect that it was not reporting total membership.

Both the *Daily Press* and the labor commissioner reported membership totals for the District that at first seem inflated compared with CSFL figures. Yet given evidence of under-reporting, and local unions that existed but for which no membership figures are available, these higher estimates may be more credible than they first appear. A list of local unions and Trades Assemblies that could be documented from 1892 to 1905 follows. I identified two local unions for 1892, five for 1893, six for 1894, seven for 1895, twelve for 1896 and 1897, twenty-three for 1898, twenty-seven for 1899 (although I know that at least thirty-four locals existed that year because thirty-four were said to have founded the Co-operative Party and thirty-three of thirty-four were said to have bought the *Press*), forty-six for 1900, forty-seven for 1901, fifty-four for 1902, forty-seven for 1903, thirty-seven for 1904, and ten for 1905.

UNIONS

Cripple Creek Bakers and Confectioners No. 171 (1902–3)
Victor Bakers and Confectioners No. 191 (1898–1903)
Barbers' Union (1893)
Cripple Creek Barbers No. 92 (1900–1904)
Victor Barbers' Protective Union (1898)
Cripple Creek Bartenders' Union No. 1 (Bartenders' Protective Association) (1900–1901)
Cripple Creek Bartenders No. 215 (1902–4)
District Bartenders' Protective Association No. 16, WLU (1902)
(Cripple Creek) Bill Posters' Union (1902)
Cripple Creek Bricklayers and Masons No. 6 (1898–1903)
Cripple Creek Building Laborers No. 4 (1901–4)
(Victor) Amalgamated Meat Cutters and Butchers' Workmen of North America (1902)
Cripple Creek Carpenters No. 289 (1893–94)
Cripple Creek Carpenters No. 547 (1895–1917)
Gillett Carpenters No. 91 (1896)
Independence Carpenters No. 178 (1897–1903)
Victor Carpenters No. 584 (1895–1906)
Cripple Creek Cigarmakers No. 397 (1900–1902)
Cripple Creek Branch, Colorado Springs Cigarmakers No. 402 (1903)
Cripple Creek Butcher and Grocery Clerks (1898)
Grocery Clerks' and Butchers' Union (1900)
Cripple Creek Retail Clerks No. 150 (1899–1904)
Cripple Creek Retail Clerks No. 238 (1899–1901)
Victor Retail Clerks No. 124 (1900–1904)
Cripple Creek Cooks and Waiters No. 24 (1897–1904)
Cripple Creek White Cooks No. 92 (1900–1901)
Victor Cooks and Waiters No. 9 (1897–1904)

Dairymen's Association of Victor, Goldfield, and Independence (1902)
Dance Hall Girls' Protective Union (1902)
Cripple Creek Dressmakers' Union (1896)
Cripple Creek Electrical Workers No. 70 (1900–1904)
Cripple Creek Federal Labor Union No. 19 (1899–1904)
Cripple Creek Junior Federal Labor Union No. 139 (1902–3)
Cripple Creek Junior Federal Labor Union No. 3 (1903–4)
Victor Federal Labor Union No. 64 (1900–1904)
Victor Junior Federal Labor Union No. 1 (1902–4)
Victor Hod Carriers and Building Laborers No. 130 (1900)
Cripple Creek Lathers No. 6718 (1898)
Lathers No. 60 (1900–1903)
Cripple Creek District Laundry Workers' Union No. 259 (1902–4)
Miners' and Prospectors' Protective Association (1892)
Barry Miners' Union (1893)
(Altman) Free Coinage Miners No. 19 (1893–1905)
Anaconda Miners No. 21 (1893–1905)
Cripple Creek Miners No. 40 (1894–1905)
Victor Miners No. 32 (1894–1905)
Altman Engineers No. 75 (WFM) (1898–1903)
(Victor) Excelsior Engineers No. 80 (WFM) (1899–1905)
Cripple Creek Engineers No. 82 (WFM) (1899–1905)
Gillett Mill and Smeltermen No. 92 (WFM) (1899–1904)
(Victor) Banner Mill and Smeltermen No. 106 (WFM) (1900–1905)
Cripple Creek District Union No. 234, WFM (1905–   )
Musicians' Union (1894)
Cripple Creek Musicians' Protective Association (1898–99)
Cripple Creek Musicians No. 49 (1900–1904)
Newsboys' Union (1894)
Cripple Creek Newsboys (1900)
Newsboys No. 109 (1901)
Victor Newsboys No. 32 (1902–4)
Cripple Creek Newspaper Writers No. 3 (1901–4)
Cripple Creek Painters and Decorators' Union (1896–99)
Cripple Creek Painters and Decorators No. 94 (1900–1901)
Cripple Creek Painters and Paper Hangers No. 501 (1901–4)
Victor Painters and Decorators No. 127 (1898)
Victor Painters and Paper Hangers No. 127 (1899)
Victor Painters and Paper Hangers No. 40 (1896–97)
Victor Painters and Paper Hangers No. 40 (1899–1904)
Victor Painters and Decorators No. 40 (1898)
Cripple Creek Plasterers No. 52 (1900–1902)

Victor Plasterers No. 73 (1900)
Cripple Creek Plumbers No. 24 (1901)
Victor Plumbers No. 158 (1900–1903)
Victor Postoffice Clerks No. 855 (1902–4)
Cripple Creek Letter Carriers No. 613 (1900–1904)
Victor Letter Carriers No. 687 (1900–1904)
Cripple Creek Electrical Trainmen's Protective Union No. 1 (1901)
Cripple Creek Electrical Trainmen No. 1 (1902–4)
Railway Employees' Union No. 272, ALU (1902)
(Victor) Order of Railway Telegraphers (1898)
(Victor) Gold Coin Order of Railway Conductors No. 375 (1901)
(Victor) Bull Hill Lodge Switchmen No. 64 (1900)
Pike's Peak Union No. 1, Tin, Sheet-Iron and Cornice Workers of the Cripple Creek District (1899)
Cripple Creek Sheet Iron Workers (1901–2)
Victor Sheet Metal, Tin, Iron and Cornice Workers No. 90 (1900–1904)
Cripple Creek Signwriters' Union No. 1 (1898–99)
Local Journeymen Stone Cutters' Branch of Cripple Creek District (1899)
Victor Journeymen Tailors No. 280 (1900–1904)
Cripple Creek Theatrical Stage Employees No. 52 (1900–1904)
Cripple Creek Typographers No. 227 (1896–1903)
Victor Press Employees (1896)
Victor Typographers No. 275 (1898–1904)
Cripple Creek District Printing Pressmen and Assistants No. 83 (1900–1904)
Cripple Creek District Trades Assembly (1894–95)
Cripple Creek Trades Assembly (1896–1900)
Victor Trades Assembly (1896–1900)
Cripple Creek District Trades and Labor Assembly (1901–4)

Although some locals technically existed after 1904 (that is, they still held charters in their international unions), for all intents and purposes unionism ended in the Cripple Creek District in the summer of 1904. The charters of the remaining WFM locals were revoked in 1905, with the exception of District Union No. 234, the membership of which was negligible. Victor Carpenters No. 584 surrendered its charter in 1906. Cripple Creek Carpenters No. 547 maintained its charter until 1917, when it merged into the Colorado Springs local, but its membership was small, and only seven stalwarts attended most meetings.[4]

Membership figures are virtually nonexistent before 1896, when the Colorado State Federation of Labor was founded. Therefore, membership totals, such as they are, were attempted only for 1896 through 1904 (table B-1).

TABLE B-1
Membership in Local Unions, Cripple Creek District, 1896–1904

Local Union	CSFL Figures			Other
	Average	High	Low	
1896				
Miners No. 19				400
Miners No. 21	87	100	60	
Miners No. 40	171	177	165	790
	258	277	225	1190
Highest total figure for year = 1,290				
Number of missing locals = 9 of 12 (75 percent)				
1897				
Carpenters No. 547	217	302	140	
Carpenters No. 584	75	78	73	
Cooks and Waiters No. 9	61	67	60	
Cooks and Waiters No. 24	74	96	50	
	427	543	323	
Highest total figure for year = 543				
Number of missing locals = 8 of 12 (67 percent)				
1898				
Bakers & Confectioners No. 191	8	9	8	
Victor Barbers	31	35	30	
Bricklayers & Masons No. 6	41	53	35	
Carpenters No. 547	43	77	15	
Carpenters No. 584	68	78	59	
Cooks & Waiters No. 9	60	60	60	
Cooks & Waiters No. 24	68	105	42	
Lathers No. 6718	23	23	23	
Miners No. 19	182	200	170	
Miners No. 21	31	36	23	
Miners No. 32	497	550	450	
Miners No. 40	100	100	100	
Musicians' Protective Association	55	100	50	
Cripple Creek Painters & Decorators	28	30	25	
Painters & Decorators No. 127	20	20	20	
Railway Telegraphers				16
Signwriters No. 1	10	10	10	
Typographers No. 227	20	24	17	
Typographers No. 275	12	15	10	
	1,297	1,525	1,147	16
Highest total figure for year = 1,541				
Number of missing locals = 5 of 13 (38 percent)				
1899				
Bakers & Confectioners No. 191	9	10	9	
Bricklayers & Masons No. 6	58	96	50	
Carpenters No. 547	110	172	76	

Local Union	CSFL Figures			Other
	Average	High	Low	
Carpenters No. 584	131	200	74	
Cooks & Waiters No. 9	63	80	50	
Cooks & Waiters No. 24	125	180	92	
Federal Labor Union No. 19	174	234	66	
Federal Labor Union No. 64				250+
Miners No. 19	217	250	170	
Miners No. 21	41	54	36	
Miners No. 32	471	520	352	
Miners No. 40	123	160	100	
Engineers No. 75	42	52	33	
Musicians' Protective Association	59	67	50	
Cripple Creek Painters & Decorators	29	30	25	
Painters & Paper Hangers No. 127	20	20	20	
Retail Clerks No. 238				60
Signwriters No. 1	10	10	10	
Typographers No. 227	24	30	20	
Typographers No. 275	14	21	12	
	1,720	2,186	1,245	310+

Highest total figure for year = 2,496+
Number of missing locals = 7 of 27 (26 percent); at least
   34 unions that year founded the Co-operative Party.

1900

Local Union	Average	High	Low	Other
Bakers & Confectioners No. 191	10	10	10	
Barbers No. 92	73	81	61	
Bartenders' Protective Association	50	64	10	69
Bricklayers & Masons No. 6	93	125	51	
Carpenters No. 547	176	182	159	
Carpenters No. 584	228	245	179	
Carpenters No. 178	30	30	30	
Cigarmakers No. 397	30	42	20	
Cooks & Waiters No. 9	57	60	50	
Cooks & Waiters No. 24	121	180	90	
White Cooks No. 92	39	40	33	
Electrical Workers No. 70	57	66	34	
Federal Labor Union No. 19	222	269	159	
Federal Labor Union No. 64	132	160	125	
Hardware Clerks No. 75				25
Lathers No. 1	10	10	10	
Miners No. 19	239	250	200	
Miners No. 21	75	108	48	
Miners No. 32	610	904	483	
Miners No. 40	227	300	160	
Engineers No. 75	43	58	33	
Engineers No. 82	30	38	25	
Mill & Smeltermen No. 92	50	68	32	
Musicians No. 49	67	67	67	

TABLE B-1 (CONT.)

Local Union	CSFL Figures			Other
	Average	High	Low	
Painters & Decorators No. 94	32	40	26	
Painters & Paper Hangers No. 40	30	37	23	
Printing Pressmen No. 83	17	20	10	
Retail Clerks No. 124	33	50	30	
Retail Clerks No. 150	33	39	30	
Stage Employees No. 52	16	16	16	
Switchmen No. 64	20	20	20	
Typographers No. 227	18	30	15	
Typographers No. 275	12	14	9	
	2,880	3,623	2,248	94

Highest total figure for year = 3,653
Number of missing locals = 13 of 46 (28 percent)

1901
Bakers & Confectioners No. 191	10	10	10	
Barbers No. 92	79	80	76	
Bricklayers & Masons No. 6	42	51	33	
Carpenters No. 547	154	174	133	
Carpenters No. 584	142	179	113	
Carpenters No. 178	23	28	18	
Cigarmakers No. 387	17	20	14	
Cooks & Waiters No. 9	80	80	80	
Cooks & Waiters No. 24	112	130	65	
White Cooks No. 92	40	40	40	
Electrical Workers No. 70	50	63	38	
Electrical Trainmen No. 1	56	67	14	
Federal Labor Union No. 19	288	421	176	
Federal labor Union No. 64	123	150	92	
Miners No. 19	325	514	200	
Miners No. 21	145	170	124	
Miners No. 32	855	916	800	1,100
Miners No. 40	453	635	300	
Engineers No. 75	41	56	20	
Engineers No. 82	51	72	32	
Mill & Smeltermen No. 92	34	59	23	
Musicians No. 49	129	150	100	
Newsboys No. 109				100
Painters & Decorators No. 94	33	33	33	
Painters & Paper Hangers No. 501	24	26	19	
Painters & Paper Hangers No. 40	26	30	20	
Printing Pressmen No. 83	23	32	18	
Retail Clerks No. 124	53	60	50	
Retail Clerks No. 150	27	30	24	
Stage Employees No. 52	12	16	11	

| Local Union | CSFL Figures | | | Other |
	Average	High	Low	
Sheet Metal, Tin, Iron and Cornice				
Workers No. 90	14	16	10	
Typographers No. 227	15	15	15	
Typographers No. 275	10	11	9	
	3,486	4,334	2,710	1,200

Highest total figure for year = 4,618
Number of missing locals = 14 of 47 (30 percent)

1902				
Bakers & Confectioners No. 191	10	10	10	
Barbers No. 92	67	79	64	
Bartenders No. 215	75	95	63	
Bartenders No. 16				40
Bricklayers & Masons No. 6	26	33	17	
Amalgamated Meat Cutters & Butchers				18
Carpenters No. 584	105	113	100	
Cooks & Waiters No. 9	66	80	53	
Cooks & Waiters No. 24	112	130	100	
Electrical Workers No. 70	38	64	27	
Electrical Trainmen No. 1	67	67	66	
Federal Labor Union No. 19	272	421	163	700
Federal Labor Union No. 64	101	150	74	
Laundry Workers No. 259				60
Miners No. 19	369	425	323	
Miners No. 21	141	150	125	500
Miners No. 32	951	1,026	885	1,400
Miners No. 40	535	600	485	
Engineers No. 75	45	52	32	
Engineers No. 82	57	72	50	
Mill & Smeltermen No. 92	24	38	15	
Musicians No. 49	127	150	100	
Victor Newsboys				11
Painters & Paper Hangers No. 501	21	26	18	
Painters & Paper Hangers No. 40	13	20	10	
Printing Pressmen No. 83	33	43	16	
Retail Clerks No. 124	57	50	60	
Retail Clerks No. 150	24	25	23	
Stage Employees No. 52	11	11	11	
Sheet Metal, Tin, Iron, & Cornice				
Workers No. 90	12	17	9	
Typographers No. 227	17	23	14	
Typographers No. 275	10	10	10	
	3,386	3,980	2,923	2,729

Highest total figure for year = 5,154
Number of missing locals = 22 of 54 (41 percent)

TABLE B-1 (CONT.)

| Local Union | CSFL Figures | | | Other |
	Average	High	Low	
1903				
Bakers & Confectioners No. 191	10	17	6	
Barbers No. 92	54	60	50	
Bartenders No. 215	74	95	54	
Bricklayers & Masons No. 6	17	17	17	
Cooks & Waiters No. 9	51	65	32	
Cooks & Waiters No. 24	88	100	50	
Electrical Workers No. 70	30	42	25	
Electrical Trainmen No. 1	67	67	66	
Federal Labor Union No. 19	144	176	100	200
Federal Labor Union No. 64	57	96	24	
Junior Federal Labor Union No. 3	30	30	30	106
Miners No. 19	319	400	166	
Miners No. 21	133	150	121	
Miners No. 32	877	1,002	700	
Miners No. 40	475	530	300	
Engineers No. 75	45	54	37	
Engineers No. 80	145	158	103	
Engineers No. 82	56	72	20	
Mill & Smeltermen No. 92	22	26	22	
Mill & Smeltermen No. 106	66	70	60	80
Musicians No. 49	100	100	100	
Newsboys No. 32	43	50	40	
Painters & Paper Hangers No. 40	10	10	10	
Printing Pressmen No. 83	13	13	13	
Retail Clerks No. 124	73	84	50	
Retail Clerks No. 150	18	23	17	
Stage Employees No. 52	11	11	11	
Sheet Metal, Tin, Iron & Cornice Workers No. 90	9	10	8	
Typographers No. 275	10	10	10	
	3,047	3,538	2,242	386

Highest total figure for year = 3,638
Number of missing locals = 18 of 47 (38 percent)

| Local Union | CSFL Figures | | | Other |
	Average	High	Low	
1904				
Barbers No. 92	54	60	50	
Bartenders No. 215	37	40	35	
Carpenters No. 584	20	25	18	
Cooks & Waiters No. 9	38	45	28	
Cooks & Waiters No. 24	46	65	30	
Electrical Workers No. 70	20	20	20	
Electrical Trainmen No. 1	40	40	40	
Federal Labor Union No. 19	68	70	59	
Federal Labor Union No. 64	37	50	20	

Local Union	CSFL Figures			Other
	Average	High	Low	
Miners No. 19	300	300	300	
Miners No. 21	73	80	56	
Miners No. 32	652	804	450	
Miners No. 40	378	450	235	
Engineers No. 80	103	103	103	
Engineers No. 82	31	50	16	
Mill & Smeltermen No. 92	9	10	9	
Mill & Smeltermen No. 106	69	90	36	
Musicians No. 49	100	100	100	
Newsboys No. 32	40	40	40	
Retail Clerks No. 124	50	50	50	
Stage Employees No. 52	10	10	10	
Sheet Metal, Tin, Iron & Cornice Workers No. 90	50	50	50	
Typographers No. 275	10	10	10	
	2,235	2,562	1,765	

Highest total figure for year = 2,562
Number of missing locals = 14 of 37 (38 percent)

❁   ❁   ❁

Although these data suggest that figures are available for proportionately more locals before 1899, that was probably not the case. After the *Press* began publishing in 1899, its reports indicated the existence of locals not affiliated with the CSFL. It is more difficult to determine the existence of such unions before 1899, and it is likely that there were more than can be documented. It is also important to note that during 1903 and 1904 some locals lost members who left the District during the strike. Others, however, seem to have maintained relatively high memberships, considering the strike, and to have withdrawn from larger labor organizations or reported low memberships in order to conserve funds for strike relief.

At the beginning of 1901 the *Press* claimed that there were five thousand members of organized labor in the Cripple Creek District. In February 1902 the Trades Assembly claimed that its thirty-eight affiliates represented nearly ten thousand. At the end of 1903, when the 1903–4 strike had been going for more than nine months, the Trades Assembly claimed to represent 5,300. The Colorado Bureau of Labor Statistics reported that in early 1901, when only some 25 percent of Colorado wageworkers were members of organized labor, "fully 70 per cent. of those living in the Cripple Creek District were members of labor unions."[5] Initially, using only CSFL membership figures, these claims seem exaggerated. Considering evidence of under-reporting membership to the State Federation of Labor, however, and the numbers of locals for which no membership figures are available, it is possible that the claims of local labor and of the labor commissioner were correct.

The proportion of District workers who belonged to organized labor cannot be determined with certainty given such partial evidence. In 1900 census-takers enumerated some

13,458 persons who listed occupations. Of these, 10,738 (79.8 percent) were working class. Most were engaged in mining: 5,150 listed themselves as miners, and 6,093 worked at the mines, mills, and samplers of the District.[6] Thus, from available membership figures, a minimum of 21 to 34 percent of these workers were organized, with membership figures missing for thirteen of forty-six locals and the likelihood that at least some of the reported memberships were low.

If Robert Guilford Taylor is correct in his population estimates, there were some 32,000 residents in 1900 rather than the 29,002 in Teller County enumerated by the census.[7] If the figures for wage-earners are inflated by 9 percent (the proportion Taylor claimed was missed), then there would have been some 11,700 people engaged in working-class occupations in 1900, approximately 37 percent of the total population (table B-2). The only estimates of organizable workers for other years would be extremely rough and based on the assumption that roughly the same proportion of the population was engaged in working-class occupations.

If these figures are approximately correct—a big assumption—then approximately 17 percent of the working class can be documented as organized in 1896, with no figures available from three-fourths of the local unions and the strong possibility that locals existed that cannot be documented. In 1900 at least 31 percent were organized, with no figures from thirteen of forty-six locals; in 1901 at least 42 percent were organized, with missing data from fourteen of forty-seven locals; and in 1902 a possible 46 percent can be documented, with no figures from twenty-two of fifty-four local unions. If the Trades Assembly represented the five thousand it claimed in 1901, that was roughly 45 percent of the working class before the major WFM organizing drive later in 1901. If the Trades Assembly really represented the nearly ten thousand it claimed in 1902, that figure probably included 80 to 90 percent of all workers. If it represented 5,300 in 1902 and 1903, then it probably represented about half of all organizable workers in the District. It is spurious to pretend that these figures represent anything more than the rough guesses they are. But knowing that available membership

TABLE B-2

District Population and Working-Class Estimates

Year	District Population	Total Workers[a]
1892	2,500	925
1893	8,000	2,960
1894	10,000	3,700
1895	15,000	5,550
1896	21,000	7,770
1897	23,000	8,510
1898	25,000	9,250
1899	27,000	9,990
1900	32,000	11,840
1901	30,000	11,100
1902	30,000	11,100

a. Estimated at 37 percent of the population.

figures are partial, and in many cases low, the level of organization in the Cripple Creek District was impressively high by current standards and certainly for 1900. If the 70 percent figure claimed by the Colorado Bureau of Labor Statistics seems high, an estimate of more than 50 percent seems reasonable.

Mining labor, the critical group, was clearly highly organized by 1901–2. In 1900 roughly 21 percent of the population was engaged in mining labor. If that figure held constant in 1901 and 1902, then there were approximately 6,300 mine workers in those years. In 1901, even with no figures from the Victor Engineers' or Mill and Smeltermen's locals, and even with probable under-reporting to the CSFL, some 41 percent were organized. In 1902, with the same qualifications, a possible 49 percent were. Given the likelihood of under-reporting, it seems reasonable that the labor commissioner was correct in his estimate that 65 percent of all miners were organized in 1901.[8] For mining and non-mining labor alike, the organized were probably the most stable residents of the area, and many of the unorganized may have been transients, increasing the unions' influence on the local economy, social life, and politics.

NOTES

ABBREVIATIONS USED IN THE NOTES

Courier	*Pueblo Courier*
CSFL Collection	Colorado State Federation of Labor Collection, University of Colorado at Boulder Archives
CSHS	Colorado State Historical Society, Denver
DPL	Denver Public Library, Western History Department
GAR Collection	Grand Army of the Republic Collection, Colorado State Historical Society
Gazette	*Colorado Springs Weekly Gazette*
Press	*Victor and Cripple Creek Daily Press*
Smith Collection	Eben Smith (1831–1906) Collection, Denver Public Library, Western History Department
UCB	University of Colorado at Boulder Archives
WFM Collection	Western Federation of Miners/International Union of Mine, Mill and Smelter Workers Collection, University of Colorado at Boulder Archives

INTRODUCTION

1. Production figures vary according to source. The Mining Stock Association, *The Official Summary of Certified Reports of Listed Companies* (Colorado Springs: Mining Stock Association, 1913), claimed figures somewhat higher than the Colorado Bureau of Mines, and figures from the federal government were lower still. *The Official Summary* claimed production of more than $92 million for the first decade, while the $65 million figure is from *Mineral Resources of the United States* (Washington: Department of the Interior, Government Printing Office, annual publication, 1889–1911). The two major sources for production figures were the reports of the mining companies and of the mills and smelters. Particularly in the early years, Denver smelters did not always note the Cripple Creek origin of their ore, and no official figures can account for gold ore stolen from mines.

Population estimates also vary widely. District directories and other publications of local boosters claimed a peak population of 50,000 for the area, whereas the 1900 U.S. Census enumerated 29,002 persons for all of Teller County. The most accurate estimate of District population is found in Robert Guilford Taylor, *Cripple Creek*, Indiana University Publications Geographic Monograph Series, vol. 1 (Bloomington: Indiana University, 1966), pp. 203–5. A geographer, Taylor based his estimates on some thirty-six sources (Appendix A). He estimated the District's peak population in 1900 as thirty-two thousand.

2. Taylor, *Cripple Creek*, pp. 197–98, 201.

3. Ibid., pp. 198–202.

4. U.S., Congress, Senate, Commissioner of Labor, *A Report on Labor Disturbances in the State of Colorado, from 1880 to 1904, Inclusive, with Correspondence Relating Thereto*, S. Doc. 122, 58th Cong., 3d sess. (Washington: Government Printing Office, 1905), p. 79 (hereafter cited as *Labor Disturbances*); *Gazette*, 31 May 1894; John Calderwood, "The Strike of 1894," in Emma F. Langdon, *The Cripple Creek Strike: A History of Industrial Wars in Colorado* (Denver: Great Western Publishing, 1904–5, repr. New York: Arno Press and the New York Times, 1969), pp. 41–42; Benjamin McKie Rastall, *The Labor History of the Cripple Creek District: A Study in Industrial Evolution*, Bulletin of the University of Wisconsin no. 198, Economics and Political Science Series vol. 3, no. 1 (Madison: University of Wisconsin, 1908), pp. 37–40.

5. Rastall, *Labor History*, pp. 45–49; *Labor Disturbances*, pp. 80–84.

6. *Labor Disturbances*, pp. 247–52; George G. Suggs, Jr., *Colorado's War on Militant Unionism: James H. Peabody and the Western Federation of Miners* (Detroit: Wayne State University Press, 1972), pp. 110–11.

7. For Peabody's ties to conservative employers, see Suggs, *Colorado's War*.

8. For the union's Socialist endorsements, see *Official Proceedings of the Ninth Annual Convention, Western Federation of Miners* (Pueblo: Pueblo Courier Press, 1901), p. 10 (hereafter cited as 1901 WFM Convention); *Official Proceedings of the Tenth Annual Convention, Western Federation of Miners* (Denver: Colorado Chronicle, 1902), pp. 94–96 (hereafter cited as 1902 WFM Convention); *Official Proceedings of the Eleventh Annual Convention, Western Federation of Miners* (Denver: Western Newspaper Union, 1903), pp. 209–10 (hereafter cited as 1903 WFM Convention); *Official Proceedings of the Twelfth Annual Convention, Western Federation of Miners* (Denver: Western Newspaper Union, 1904), p. 258 (hereafter cited as 1904 WFM Convention).

For the debate over the roots and consequences of WFM radicalism, see Vernon H. Jenson, *Heritage of Conflict: Labor Relations in the Nonferrous Metals Industry up to 1930* (Ithaca: Cornell University Press, 1950); Selig Perlman and Philip Taft, *History of Labor in the United States, 1896–1932* (New York: MacMillan, 1935), p. 173; Melvyn Dubofsky, "The Origins of Western Working Class Radicalism, 1890–1905," *Labor History* 7 (Spring 1966): 131–54; Melvyn Dubofsky, *We Shall Be All: A History of the Industrial Workers of the World* (New York: Quadrangle/The New York Times Book, 1969), p. 35; Louis Filler, *The Muckrakers: Crusaders for American Liberalism* (New York: Harcourt, Brace, 1939, repr. Yellow Springs, Ohio: Antioch Press, 1950), pp. 217–18; Clark Kerr and Abraham Siegel, "The Interindustry Propensity to Strike," in *Industrial Conflict*, ed. Arthur Kornhauser, Robert Dubin, and Arthur M. Ross (New York: McGraw-Hill, 1954), pp. 189–212; Richard E. Lingenfelter, *The Hardrock Miners: A History of the Mining Labor Movement in the American West, 1863–1893* (Berkeley: University of California Press, 1974); John H. M. Laslett, *Labor and the Left* (New York: Basic Books, 1970), pp. 241–86; David Brundage, *The Mak-*

ing of Western Labor Radicalism: Denver's Organized Workers, 1878–1905 (Urbana: University of Illinois Press, 1994); Sharon Reitman, "The Politics of the Western Federation of Miners and the United Mine Workers of America: Uneven Development, Industry Structure, and Class Struggle," in *Bringing Class Back In: Contemporary and Historical Perspectives*, ed. Scott G. McNall, Rhonda F. Levine, and Rick Fantasia (Boulder: Westview Press, 1991), pp. 203–22; John Ervin Brinley, Jr., "The Western Federation of Miners," Ph.D. diss., University of Utah, 1972; James C. Foster, "Quantification and the Western Federation," *Historical Methods Newsletter* 10 (Fall 1977): 141–48, esp. 143; Ronald C. Brown, *Hard-Rock Miners: The Intermountain West, 1860–1920* (College Station: Texas A&M University Press, 1979); Mark Wyman, *Hard Rock Epic: Western Miners and the Industrial Revolution, 1860–1910* (Berkeley: University of California Press, 1979); David M. Emmons, *The Butte Irish: Class and Ethnicity in an American Mining Town, 1875–1925* (Urbana: University of Illinois Press, 1989); "The I.W.W.: An Exchange of Views," *Labor History* 11 (Summer 1970): 355–72; and William Preston, "Shall This Be All? U.S. Historians versus William D. Haywood *et al.*," *Labor History* 12 (Summer 1971): 437–38, 442.

9. Notable studies of western hard-rock communities include Ralph Emerson Mann, *After the Gold Rush: Society in Grass Valley and Nevada City, California, 1849–1870* (Stanford: Stanford University Press, 1982); and Emmons, *The Butte Irish.* Neither, however, focuses specifically on labor. See also Duane A. Smith, "The San Juaner: A Computerized Portrait," *Colorado Magazine* 52 (Spring 1975): 137–52; and Elliott West, "Five Idaho Mining Towns: A Computer Profile," *Pacific Northwest Quarterly* 73 (July 1982): 108–20, for statistical profiles of mining communities. Important working-class community studies include Alan Dawley, *Class and Community: The Industrial Revolution in Lynn* (Cambridge: Harvard University Press, 1976); Sean Wilentz, *Chants Democratic: New York City and the Rise of the American Working Class, 1788–1950* (New York: Oxford University Press, 1984); Bruce Laurie, *The Working People of Philadelphia* (Philadelphia: Temple University Press, 1980); Susan E. Hirsch, *The Roots of the American Working Class* (Philadelphia: University of Pennsylvania Press, 1978); Brian Greenberg, *Worker and Community: Response to Industrialization in a Nineteenth-Century American City, Albany, New York, 1850–1884* (Albany: SUNY Press, 1985); Daniel J. Walkowitz, *Worker City, Company Town: Iron and Cotton Worker Protest in Troy and Cohoes, New York, 1855–1884* (Urbana: University of Illinois Press, 1978); Richard Oestreicher, *Solidarity and Fragmentation: Working People and Class Consciousness in Detroit, 1873–1900* (Urbana: University of Illinois Press, 1986); Michael Katz, *The People of Hamilton, Canada West: Family and Class in a mid-19th-Century City* (Cambridge: Harvard University Press, 1979); Roy Rosenzweig, *Eight Hours for What We Will: Workers and Leisure in an Industrial City, 1870–1920* (Cambridge: Cambridge University Press, 1983); Stephan Thernstrom, *Poverty and Progress: Social Mobility in a Nineteenth-Century City* (Cambridge: Harvard University Press, 1964).

For critical reviews of the new labor history and the new political history, see Leon Fink, "The New Labor History and the Powers of Historical Pessimism: Consensus, Hegemony, and the Case of the Knights of Labor," *Journal of American History* 75 (June 1988): 115–36; and Richard Oestreicher, "Urban Working-Class Political Behavior and Theories of American Electoral Politics, 1870–1940," *Journal of American History* 74 (March 1988): 1257–86.

10. Herbert G. Gutman, "Work, Culture, and Society in Industrializing America," in *Work, Culture, and Society in Industrializing America: Essays in American Working Class and Social History* (New York: Vintage Books, 1977), pp. 3–78, esp. pp. 15–18.

11. Clifford Geertz, *The Interpretation of Cultures* (New York: Basic Books, 1973); Peggy Pascoe, "Race, Gender, and Intercultural Relations: The Case of Interracial Marriage," *Frontiers* 12 (1991): 5–18, esp. 12–15.

12. See James Clifford, *The Predicament of Culture: Twentieth-Century Ethnography, Literature, and Art* (Cambridge: Harvard University Press, 1988); Thomas Bender, "Wholes and Parts: The Need for Synthesis in American History," *Journal of American History* 73 (June 1986): 127–132; and Gayatri Chakravorty Spivak, "Can the Subaltern Speak?" in *Marxism and the Interpretation of Culture*, ed. Cary Nelson and Lawrence Grossberg (Urbana: University of Illinois Press, 1988), pp. 271–313. For a critique of the deconstructionist concept of "always already," see Diana Fuss, *Essentially Speaking: Feminism, Nature, and Difference* (New York: Routledge, 1989), p. 17

13. When I conducted oral history interviews I initially avoided the word *class*. I later learned that some people thought that was strange. When I asked one woman, for example, if some people were more privileged than her family, she replied, "You know, I wasn't really aware of class until I was about thirteen." Interview with Ileen Pryor, Colorado Springs, Colo., 4 May 1979.

14. R. E. Croskey, ed., "Labor Notes," *Press*, 21 Dec. 1902, p. 3. For the connection of the labor theory of value with artisanal republicanism, and its salience for the Knights of Labor, see Fink, "The New Labor History," p. 119.

15. I am indebted to Ralph O. Wing and S. C. Gatheridge for reviewing my classifications.

16. All persons who listed occupations were categorized by their own occupations. Household members without listed occupations were assigned to the category of the person listed as head of household. In boardinghouses and hotels, boarders' families were classified together, not with the proprietor listed as "head of household."

17. E. P. Thompson, *The Making of the English Working Class* (New York: Vintage Books, 1963), p. 11.

18. U.S. Department of Commerce, Bureau of the Census, manuscript census, Teller County, Colo., 1900 (hereafter cited as manuscript census, Teller County, Colo., 1900); U.S. Department of Commerce, Bureau of the Census, *Twelfth Census of the United States, Taken in the Year 1900, Volume 1* (Washington: United States Census Office, 1901), pp. 740–41, 973 (hereafter cited as *Twelfth Census, Volume 1*). The actual figures were 79 percent working class, 60 percent male, and 83 percent native-born. In 1900, of a total population recorded by the U.S. Census of 29,002, Teller County had 4,822 first-generation immigrants. Of 3,030 foreign-born males age twenty-one and over, most (1,932) were naturalized citizens, 348 had their first papers, 214 were aliens, and there was no citizenship data for 536. Women and children acquired the citizenship of the male head of their household if they, too, were foreign-born.

19. See Oestreicher, "Urban Working-Class Political Behavior," p. 1269.

20. Taylor, *Cripple Creek*, pp. 3–7.

21. Wyman, *Hard Rock Epic*, p. 244.

22. See Michael Neuschatz, *The Golden Sword: The Coming of Capitalism to the Colorado Mining Frontier* (Westport: Greenwood Press, 1986), esp. pp. 133–84.

23. See, for example, Marshall Sprague, *Money Mountain: The Story of Cripple Creek Gold* (Boston: Little, Brown and Company, 1953; reprint ed., New York: Ballantine Books, Inc., 1971), pp. 205–13. The 1979 edition of *Money Mountain* (Lincoln: University of Nebraska Press), unlike the 1953 edition, has some footnotes and lists sources. In this text, it is cited as *Money Mountain* (1979). The original edition is cited as *Money Mountain* (1953). Many labor historians have similarly accepted the mine owners' contentions concerning union violence during the strike and have not examined seriously the union's charges that the mine owners instigated the violence themselves. See, for example, Rastall, *Labor History*.

CHAPTER 1: NOT A POOR MAN'S CAMP

1. See, for example, A. W. Stubbs, "The Miner's Lament," *Gazette*, 30 Jan. 1896, p. 3.

2. Taylor, *Cripple Creek*, pp. 3–7.

3. Sprague, *Money Mountain* (1953), pp. 78–88; Catherine Rinker, "The History of Cripple Creek, Colorado, 1891–1917" (M.A. thesis, University of Colorado, 1934), p. 18.

4. Dubofsky, *We Shall Be All*, p. 22.

5. Dubofsky, "The Origins of Western Working Class Radicalism," pp. 133–34; Robert L. Spude, "Cyanide and the Flood of Gold: Some Colorado Beginnings of the Cyanide Process of Gold Extraction," *Essays and Monographs in Colorado History*, no. 12 (1991): 1–35; *Gazette*, 6 June 1895.

6. Quoted in Joseph R. Conlin, *Big Bill Haywood and the Radical Union Movement* (Syracuse: Syracuse University Press, 1969), p. 15; J. B. Douglas, "Who Owns the Country?" *Miners' Magazine*, Oct. 1901, p. 11.

7. For more on early camp custom and law, see Charles Howard Shinn, *Mining Camps: A Study in American Frontier Government* (New York: Charles Scribner's Sons, 1884, repr. New York: Harper and Row, 1965), esp. pp. 280–88; Duane A. Smith, *Rocky Mountain Mining Camps* (Lincoln: University of Nebraska Press, 1967); and *Congressional Globe*, 19 June 1866, quoted in Shinn, *Mining Camps*, p. 283. Shinn, like Frederick Jackson Turner, emphasized the transformative influence of the environment and the frontier. He, however, saw the mining frontier as fundamentally collectivist rather than individualistic. The mining law he cites supported his claims. The fundamental criteria for ownership were redefined yet again by capitalist ownership. But for industrial miners, the mining frontier's emphasis on occupation and work resonated with the philosophies of the Knights of Labor and the Populist Party that labor created wealth and was entitled to its benefits.

8. Shinn, *Mining Camps*, p. 288.

9. The "Pikes Peak" gold rush left few settlers around the peak itself. Colorado City, established in 1859 as a supply center for the South Park gold camps, dwindled to a virtual ghost town because the large mining booms bypassed the area and Denver captured most of the supply business.

10. Marshall Sprague, *Newport in the Rockies: The Life and Good Times of Colorado Springs* (Denver: Sage Books, 1961), p. 38.

11. Sprague, *Money Mountain* (1953), pp. 39–40, 44–47, 50–56.

12. *Gazette*, 27 June 1891.

13. Production figures from Taylor, *Cripple Creek*, p. 209; *Gazette*, 4 Jan. 1894; Rinker, "History of Cripple Creek," pp. 62–63.

14. For the earlier camps, see Mann, *After the Gold Rush*; Smith, "The San Juaner"; and West, "Five Idaho Mining Towns." West (p. 109) omitted the Chinese from his calculations because he thought they were seriously underenumerated on the census. They were, however, a majority of Idaho miners in 1870. The census was itself a partial source; see Appendix A for issues involved in estimating the District's population.

15. Information about the interconnected Doran, McConaghy, and Welch family histories was provided by John and Hannah Welch's daughter, Kathleen Chapman, and James and Catharine McConaghy's daughter, May Wing. Interview with Kathleen Welch Chapman, Wheat Ridge, Colo., 27 April 1979; interviews with May Wing, Boulder, Colo., 6 March 1976, and Victor, Colo., 21 Oct. 1978.

16. U.S. Department of Commerce, Bureau of the Census, manuscript census, Town of Shullsburg, LaFayette County, Wisc., 1860, 1870, 1880; Town of Leadville, Lake County, Colo., 1900; and City of Denver, County of Denver, Colo., 1920.

The 1860 Shullsburg Census lists Edward Doran as a boarder in the home of J. S. and Esther Earnest, next door to William Doran, twenty-four and also born in Ireland. Although Catharine and the children are not listed, on the 1860 census the Doran household included Edward, Catharine, James (eighteen), Thomas (sixteen), Mary (twelve), Margaret (eight), Anastasia (six), Catharine (four), Eliza (one), and John Williams (twenty-two), a farm laborer. James and Thomas were born in Wales, and the other children in Wisconsin. When the 1880 census was taken the two older boys had left home, and George (nine) and Alice (seven) had been born. By 1900 Edward had apparently died, and Catharine lived in Leadville with her daughter, Alice; Alice's husband, Charles Krizleb, a miner; and their two-year-old son, Freddie.

Edward and Catharine's exact ages are hard to determine from these records. The 1860 census lists his age as twenty-seven, in 1870 both their ages are listed as thirty-six, in 1880 they are both forty-nine, and in 1900 Catharine is listed as sixty-eight. My thanks to Andrew Rieser for tracking all the Shullsburg sources. Several of the children were not called by their given names. Catharine was "Kate," presumably to distinguish her from her mother. Anastasia was always called Hannah by her daughter and niece; she appears as Hannah on the 1900 Teller County Census. I assume that George E. was the "Uncle Ed Doran" to whom both May Wing and Kathleen Chapman referred; he also had a son named Edward.

17. Badger Historical Society of Shullsburg, *The Sesquicentennial History of Shullsburg, 1827–1977* (Shullsburg, Wisc.: Badger Historical Society of Shullsburg, 1977), esp. pp. 11–12, 36–37, 99–101. The first Catholic services were held in 1835, and the first mass was celebrated at St. Matthew's Catholic Church in 1841.

18. 1860, 1870, and 1880 Shullsburg Censuses. In 1870 eighteen-year-old James worked as a laborer but had attended school within the year, as had Thomas, Mary, and Margaret. In 1880 twenty-four-year-old Mary worked as a domestic servant.

19. The Shullsberg *Pick and Gad*, 19 June 1884, and 1 May, 22 May, and 29 May 1884. John and Hannah Welch's marriage date calculated from manuscript census, Teller County, Colo., 1900.

20. Davis's biography, like those of many local union leaders, was compiled from numerous union records, references in the *Press*, and the manuscript census, Teller County, Colo., 1900. These were noted on file cards for each leader as personal details and information about activities and affiliations was discovered. For Davis, see also "Doings in Boise, Idaho," *Miners' Magazine*, 27 June 1907, p. 10.

21. Parker was born in Iowa in 1868. His biography was compiled from union records, *Press* reports, manuscript census, Teller County, Colo., 1900, and from the *Press*, 22 June 1901.

22. Compiled from union records, *Press* reports, and manuscript census, Teller County, Colo., 1900.

23. Ibid.

24. *Press*, passim; *Miners' Magazine*, 25 June 1914, p. 3.

25. District labor's role in Asian exclusion is discussed in chapter 6. For more on anti-Chinese prejudice in earlier hard-rock camps, see Lingenfelter, *The Hardrock Miners*, pp. 5, 107–9, 112–14, 117–19, 127; and Smith, *Rocky Mountain Mining Camps*, pp. 29–34.

26. Figures are based on 20,081 adults (age sixteen or older and the few under sixteen who listed occupations) enumerated in manuscript census, Teller County, Colo., 1900, of whom 247 (1.2 percent) listed no place of birth. Among 15,254 native-born adults, 22 percent were born in the East, 58 percent in the Midwest, 10 percent in the South, and 10 percent in the West. In contrast, Grass Valley was 75 percent foreign-born in 1870, Nevada City, 62 percent, and the five towns West studied in Idaho ranged from a low of 39 percent immigrants in Silver City in 1870 to a high of 63 percent in Placerville the same year. Particularly since West omitted Chinese, it is clear that proportionately more District residents were native-born than in earlier mining camps. When Chinese were added, the adult foreign-born population became 74.2 percent in 1870 and 71 percent in 1880. Mann, *After the Gold Rush*, table 8, p. 229; West, "Five Idaho Mining Towns," table 2, p. 110, and p. 111.

27. This figure includes all persons with parents not born in the United States, including some who were immigrants themselves; for example, those born in Canada to Irish-born parents. It double counts a few persons whose parents were both born abroad but in different countries. It is therefore not an absolute count of second-generation immigrants so much as a measure of those with second-generation access to particular immigrant heritages.

28. Emmons, *The Butte Irish*, pp. 15–16.

29. *Press*, passim; Chapman interview; Wing interviews; James T. Smith, *Seventh Biennial Report of the Bureau of Labor Statistics of the State of Colorado, 1899–1900* (Denver: Smith-Brooks Printing, 1900), p. 83; U.S. Mss. 14a, Victor Miners' Union No. 32, Ledger, 1894–1903, Wisconsin State Historical Society, Madison; Dubofsky, *We Shall Be All*, p. 24; *Press*, 29 Oct. 1899.

30. *Press*, 30 Sept. 1902; Grace Palladino, *Another Civil War: Labor, Capital, and the State in the Anthracite Regions of Pennsylvania, 1840–68* (Urbana: University of Illinois Press, 1990) esp. chs. 3 and 4; Richard O. Boyer and Herbert M. Morais, *Labor's Untold Story*, (New York: Cameron Associates, 1955, repr. New York: United Electrical, Radio & Machine Workers of America, 1974), pp. 44–58.

31. U.S. Mss. 14a, Victor Miners' Union No. 32, Ledger, 1894–1903, Wisconsin State Historical Society, Madison; *Press*, 7 Aug. 1900, 29 Oct. 1899.

32. *Press*, 2 Dec., 30 Dec. 1900, 31 July 1902.

33. For Cripple Creek miners leaving the District to mine coal, see, for example, the *Press*, 15 Dec. 1900. On May 6, 1900, the *Press* reported that some three hundred were planning to go to Nome, and on May 9, 1900, it reported that ninety District residents were on the passenger list of the steamer *Centennial*, leaving Seattle May 20. See also *Press*, 9 Oct. 1901.

34. Local No. 55, United Brotherhood of Carpenters and Joiners of America, Minutes, 1900–1902, UCB. See also Elizabeth Jameson, *Building Colorado: The United Brotherhood of Carpenters and Joiners of America in the Centennial State* (Denver: Colorado State Council of Carpenters, 1984), pp. 9–23.

35. The persistence rate in Grass Valley from 1850 to 1860 was 5 percent, in Nevada City, 7 percent. From 1860 to 1870 there was a persistence rate of 13 percent in Grass Valley and 12 percent in Nevada City. Mann, *After the Gold Rush*, table 46, p. 266. The five Idaho mining towns had an overall persistence rate of 10 percent from 1870 to 1880, with the highest persistence among professionals and merchants. West, "Five Idaho Mining Towns," p. 115, table 8, p. 116; *Press*, 21 Sept. 1899. See also, the *Press*, 9 Nov. 1901, which stated that "Tom Flynn of Butte City, formerly of the Coeur d'Alenes, is here and has secured work on the Vindicator. He is an old time friend of Ed Fleming." Such notes were common.

36. In a random sample of 2,089 adults (with eight missing cases), the the proportions of women and men who were married or widowed within each age cohort were: sixteen to twenty, 4 percent of the men and 27 percent of the women (3 percent widowed); twenty-one to thirty, 35 percent of the men (1 percent widowed) and 81 percent of the women (3 percent widowed); thirty-one to forty, 58 percent of the men (2 percent widowed) and 87 percent of the women (9 percent widowed); forty-one to fifty, 67 percent of the men (6 percent widowed) and 82 percent of the women (12 percent widowed); fifty-one to sixty, 62 percent of the men (11 percent widowed) and 73 percent of the women (27 percent widowed); and sixty-one to seventy, 68 percent of the men (9 percent widowed) and 28 percent of the women (56 percent widowed). Manuscript census, Teller County, Colo., 1900.

37. A random sample of 2,089 adults, with one missing observation, contained 1,265 men, of whom eighty-six (7 percent) were born in the West, and 823 women, of whom ninety-two (11 percent) were western natives. By far the largest group of westerners was born in Colorado—sixty-eight of the men and seventy-three of the women.

38. Chapman and May Wing interviews. This accounts partially for the 5.4 percent of the population who were married but not living with their spouses (table 2). Single miners may have been more mobile than married miners. The higher proportion of married adults in the District may have supported greater geographic stability than in the earlier camps.

39. Lingenfelter, *The Hardrock Miners*, pp. 31–32, 67; "The Western Federation of Miners," *Miners' Magazine*, June 1901, p. 20.

40. Lingenfelter, *The Hardrock Miners*, p. 132.

41. Ibid., pp. 132–33, 194.

42. Ibid., pp. 44–45, 226–27; William D. Haywood, *Bill Haywood's Book: The Autobiography of Big Bill Haywood* (New York: International Publishers, 1929, repr., International Publishers, 1969), pp. 80–81.

43. "The Western Federation of Miners," pp. 20–21; Jenson, *Heritage of Conflict*, pp. 10–18; "Proceedings of the First Annual Convention of the Western Federation of Miners Held at Butte, Montana, May 15–19, 1893, Miners' Union Hall, Butte," microfilm, Graduate Social Science Library, University of California, Berkeley, p. 3 (hereafter cited as 1893 WFM Convention).

44. Interviews with S. C. Gatheridge, Denver, Colo., 21 Feb., 7 March 1979; interview with Ralph O. Wing, Boulder, Colo., 16 Feb. 1979; Brown, *Hard-Rock Miners*, pp. 70–74.

45. In Grass Valley, only 3 percent of the men were married in 1850 and 31 percent in 1870; in Nevada City, 2 percent were married in 1850 and 27 percent in 1870. In five Idaho mining towns an average of 30 percent of the adult population lived in family households in 1870 (not all of whom were married), and 45 percent in 1880. Mann, *After the Gold Rush*, p. 265; calculated from West, "Five Idaho Mining Towns," table 6, p. 114.

46. Mann, *After the Gold Rush*, table 1, p. 224; 1900 sex ratios for the United States, Colorado, and Teller County computed from *Twelfth Census, Volume 1*, pp. 482, 496. The District's population was 59 percent male and 41 percent female; calculated from manuscript census, Teller County, Colo., 1900. Mary Murphy, "Women on the Line: Prostitution in Butte, Montana, 1878–1917" (M.A. thesis, University of North Carolina at Chapel Hill, 1983), p. 6.

47. Calculated from manuscript census, Teller County, Colo., 1900.

48. For how husbands' leaving to seek gold affected families, see Linda Peavy and Ursula Smith, *The Gold Rush Widows of Little Falls: A Story Drawn from the Letters of Pamelia and James Fergus* (St. Paul: Minnesota Historical Society Press, 1990); and Linda Peavy and Ursula Smith, *Women in Waiting in the Westward Journey: Life on the Home Frontier* (Norman: University of Oklahoma Press, 1994).

49. Thirty-nine percent of employed adults and 47 percent of all adults lived in nuclear families; 37 percent of miners, 54 percent of skilled mining workers, 21 percent of unskilled workers, 43 percent of semiskilled workers, and 47 percent of skilled workers. Only 13 percent of skilled mining workers lived in families with boarders, compared with 19 percent of all workers and 17 percent of all adults; 10 percent of skilled mining workers, 20 percent of miners, 35 percent of unskilled workers, 13 percent of semiskilled workers, and 11 percent of skilled workers lived in boardinghouses. The average for all workers was 20 percent; the average for all adults was 14 percent. Manuscript census, Teller County, Colo., 1900, random sample of 2,089 adults—1,359 of whom listed occupations—less 25 missing cases.

50. *Press*, 20 July 1901. The topic of same-sex partnerships in mining awaits further exploration. The topic is important for the history of gender and for constructions of manhood in the real and mythic Wests.

51. The 1900 manuscript census enumerated 3,469 households with children—approximately 26 percent of all households. Persons classified as "other," most of whom were women, were most likely to have children in their homes (86 percent of all "other" headed households), followed by capitalists and proprietors (33 percent of both). Some 24 percent of workers and 25 percent of professionals and salaried and clerical workers had children in their homes. Still, most children came from working-class families (5,441 of 7,171 enumerated, or 76 percent), and the majority of working-class children (2,930, or 41 percent of all

District children) came from miners' families. Within the working class, skilled workers were the most likely to have children (41 percent), followed by miners (26 percent). Manuscript census, Teller County, Colo., 1900, all households except forty-six with incomplete information, including all households in which no one listed an occupation. Children were counted with the head of household, who was usually, but not always, a parent.

52. Manuscript census, Teller County, Colo., 1900. In a random sample of 2,089 adults, less 37 persons younger than 16 or whose age was not listed, 9 percent were sixteen to twenty, 35 percent were twenty-one to thirty, 31 percent were thirty-one to forty, 16 percent were forty-one to fifty, 7 percent were fifty-one to sixty, 2 percent were sixty-one to seventy, and .5 percent were seventy-one or older. Cumulatively, 44 percent of adults were thirty or younger, 74 percent were forty or younger, 91 percent were fifty or younger, and 98 percent were sixty or younger (numbers do not total 100 percent because of rounding). Most male workers in Grass Valley and Nevada City were in their twenties and thirties. The population aged forty and older grew from 9 percent in Grass Valley and 6 percent in Nevada City in 1850 to 36 percent in Grass Valley and 44 percent in Nevada City in 1870. The average San Juan miner in the early 1880s was 32.8 years old. Mann, *After the Gold Rush*, table 2, p. 224; Smith, "The San Juaner," p. 142.

53. This was also true of early Butte. See Emmons, *The Butte Irish*, esp. ch. 5.

54. Their birthplaces were Canada, one; Denmark, one; England, three; Germany, one; Ireland, two; California, one; Colorado, one; Kansas, one; Michigan, one; Missouri, two; Montana, one; New York, one; North Carolina, two; Pennsylvania, two; Washington, D.C., one; and Wisconsin, four. The superintendents were F. M. Symes, John W. O'Brien, Martin C. Gleason, J. H. Emerson, John Stark, R. A. Trevarthen, Herbert Starkweather, J. M. Wright, W. M. Bainbridge, Milo Hoskins, A. J. Campbell, Charles Walden, Fred S. Johnson, Jerry P. Horgan, F. O. Ganson, Sol Camp, Oliver B. Finn, Richard H. Burrows, A. D. De Masters, Newston S. Wilson, Nathaniel Wilson, Joseph Luxon, William H. Shell, H. L. McCarn, and George L. Keenor. Biographical data compiled from Sargent and Rohrbacher for the *Colorado Springs Evening Telegraph*, *The Fortunes of a Decade* (Colorado Springs: Colorado Springs Evening Telegraph, 1900), pp. 116–32.

55. Their birthplaces were Delaware, one; Illinois, seven; Indiana, two; Maine, two; Michigan, one; Missouri, two; New York, three; Ohio, eight; Pennsylvania, four; Wisconsin, one; and birthplaces for four are unknown. The thirty-five were David H. Moffat, Warren Woods, Harry E. Woods, Frank M. Woods, J. R. McKinnie, Edward M. De La Vergne, Irving Howbert, George Bernard, Edward R. Stark, David N. Heizer, William A. Otis, Harlan P. Lillibridge, Verner Z. Reed, John E. Hundley, W. S. Montgomery, Frank G. Peck, E. S. Johnson, J. K. Miller, W. F. Anderson, John E. Phillips, Charles N. Miller, J. Maurice Finn, Edwin Arkell, J. A. Sill, W. R. Foley, J. P. Fitting, James Burns, John Harnan, Winfield Scott Stratton, Charles MacNeill, Spencer Penrose, Charles Tutt, Albert E. Carlton, and Sam Strong. Biographical data compiled from Sargent and Rohrbacher, *The Fortunes of a Decade*, pp. 15–50; Sprague, *Money Mountain* (1953), pp. 91–108, 170–89, 193–205, 233–41; Sprague, *Newport in the Rockies*, pp. 166–95; and Frank Waters, *Midas of the Rockies: The Story of Stratton and Cripple Creek* (Chicago: Swallow Press, 1937).

56. Richard H. Peterson's study of fifty western mining leaders was similar in many regards. Of forty-two whose nativity was known, most had roots in the British Empire or Germany; thirty-five were native-born (20 percent from New England, 34 percent from the Middle Atlantic states, 17 percent from East North Central, 23 percent from the South, and 6 percent from the West). Of forty-one whose fathers' occupations were known, 41 percent were the sons of businessmen, 10 percent were the sons of professionals, 39 percent were the sons of farmers, 5 percent were the sons of public officials, and only 5 percent had working-class origins. Three owners in Peterson's sample were prominent in the Cripple Creek District: Irving Howbert, David H. Moffat, and Winfield S. Stratton. See Richard H. Peterson, *The Bonanza Kings: The Social Origins and Business Behavior of Western Mining Entrepreneurs, 1870–1900* (Lincoln: University of Nebraska Press, 1971), pp. 5–8.

57. Sargent and Rohrbacher, *The Fortunes of a Decade*, pp. 21–50, 116–32; Sprague, *Money Mountain* (1953), pp. 195–96.

58. Waters, *Midas of the Rockies*, pp. 23–24, 33, 51–54, 63–69, 80–89, 107–8, 115–16, 121–27, 157–58; Peterson, *Bonanza Kings*, pp. 28–29.

59. Waters, *Midas of the Rockies*, pp. 128–29, 164, 208–9.

60. Ibid., pp. 138–41. Typically enough, Doyle, who located the claim, profited least. Relations between Doyle and Burns became strained after January 1896, when the Portland's Anna Lee shaft caved in and eight miners were killed. Burns spent more than $100,000 to recover the bodies and compensate the families. As a result, the March dividend was canceled, angering Doyle, who apparently needed the money. The final break came in November 1898, when Doyle sued Burns for $700,000, which he claimed Burns had withheld from his share of Portland profits. Doyle had increasingly little influence over the company. Harnan was a Portland director for years but later moved to Nevada and lost his money. Waters, *Midas of the Rockies*, p. 141; Sprague, *Money Mountain* (1953), pp. 177–79.

61. Moffat was upper class by birth but quit school after completing a common-school education at age twelve, forfeiting the college education his family could have provided. In Denver he operated a book and stationery business and was assistant postmaster and the local agent of the Western Union Telegraph Company before achieving his position at the First National Bank. He had substantial mining investments in Aspen, Leadville, and Creede before he bought into Cripple Creek mines. His railroad holdings included the Denver Pacific, the Denver and South Park, the Kansas Pacific, the Golden, Boulder, and Caribou, and the Denver and Southern. He was president of the Denver and Rio Grande from 1884 to 1891 and built the Florence and Cripple Creek to connect his and Smith's mines to the D&RG lines. His other interests included two water companies, the International Trust Company of Denver, and reduction plants for his mines. He was also active in the Colorado Republican Party. Sargent and Rohrbacher, *The Fortunes of a Decade*, pp. 21–23; Peterson, *Bonanza Kings*, pp. 11, 20, 25, 113, 125, 131.

62. In Moffat's early days as a Leadville mine owner, he and Sen. J. B. Chaffee gutted the Little Pittsburgh mine for dividends. Some believed that Moffat and Chaffee's scheme inspired Chrysolite Mine manager Winfield S. Keyes to provoke the 1880 Leadville miners' strike, which disrupted production long enough for the principal owners to unload their stock

while hiding the Chrysolite's low ore reserves. Lingenfelter, *The Hardrock Miners*, pp. 143–45; Peterson, *Bonanza Kings*, p. 99; Wyman, *Hard-Rock Epic*, p. 167.

63. Their mines included the Granite, Anaconda, Battle Mountain, Victor, Antlers, United, Metallic, Bon Air, Wolftone, Maid, Grey Eagle, Golden Cycle, Gold Knob, and Independence Consolidated Gold Mining Company. The following are all from box 20, Smith Collection: Ledger; Letterpress Book, Victor Gold Mining Co., from April 18, 1893–Sept. 18, 1895; Letterpress Book, Victor Gold Mining Co., Sept. 20, 1895–Sept. 14, 1896; Letterpress Book, Victor Gold Mining Co., from Sept. 15, 1896–May 16th, 1898; Letterpress Book, Gold Knob Mining Co., Nov. 16, 1897–Aug. 29, 1900; Letterpress Book, Inter-Ocean Mining Co., Jan. 11, 1900–May 12, 1900; Letterpress Books and Correspondence, Victor Gold Mining Co.; Cash Account, Nov. 1901, also in Smith Collection.

64. Chapman interview; May Wing interview, 6 March 1976; "The Gold Coin Club House," *Miners' Magazine*, July 1900, pp. 13–14; Sargent and Rohrbacher, *The Fortunes of a Decade*, pp. 24–26; Waters, *Midas of the Rockies*, pp. 161–63; Sprague, *Money Mountain* (1953), p. 134.

65. Sargent and Rohrbacher, *The Fortunes of a Decade*, p. 26; Chapman and May Wing interviews.

66. Other socialites included Harry M. Blackmer, Horace K. Devereux, and Harry Leonard. Sprague, *Money Mountain* (1953), pp. 137–39.

67. Ibid., pp. 137–38.

68. Ibid., pp. 139, 143–44. Stratton and Irving Howbert, a Colorado Springs pioneer, real estate promoter, and the El Paso county clerk, backed the Colorado-Philadelphia venture, a fact that illustrates the interlocking ties among various ownership groups. Howbert, born in Columbus, Indiana, in 1846, moved to Colorado in 1860 with his father, a Methodist minister. In 1861 they settled in Colorado City. A life-long Republican, Irving Howbert was elected county clerk at age twenty-three. In 1879 he became the cashier of the First National Bank of Colorado Springs and eight years later became its vice president. He was elected to the state senate in 1881. Howbert was the president of the Anchoria-Leland Mining Company, a vice president of the Portland, a director of more than a dozen other mining corporations, an organizer of the Colorado Midland Railroad, and president of the Colorado Springs and Cripple Creek District Railway. Extremely bitter about Populist governor Davis Waite's pro-labor intervention in the 1893–94 Cripple Creek strike, Howbert chaired the Republican state committee that defeated Waite's reelection bid. The young socialites held political and managerial views more similar to Howbert's than to Stratton's. Sargent and Rohrbacher, *The Fortunes of a Decade*, pp. 29–30; Richard H. Peterson, "Conflict and Consensus: Labor Relations in Western Mining," *Journal of the West* 12 (Jan. 1973): 7; Irving Howbert, *Memories of a Lifetime in the Pike's Peak Region* (New York: G. P. Putnam's Sons, 1925).

69. Sprague, *Newport in the Rockies*, p. 186.

70. Ibid., pp. 185, 186–87, 189, 194–95, 237–41.

71. Ibid., pp. 191–93; Sprague, *Money Mountain* (1953), pp. 139–44, 195–96.

72. Sprague, *Money Mountain* (1953), p. 134; Sargent and Rohrbacher, *The Fortunes of a Decade*, p. 26; Waters, *Midas of the Rockies*, pp. 191, 237–39, 151–54, 278, 325.

73. Peterson, *Bonanza Kings*, p. 79; Minutes, Colorado Springs UBCJA Local Union No. 515; Waters, *Midas of the Rockies*, pp. 148–49, 167–69, 242–44, 246; *Press*, 16 June 1901.

Chapter 2: Staking the Claims

1. Taylor, *Cripple Creek,* pp. 205, 209. Taylor gives a production figure of slightly over $18 million. Other estimates were closer to $22.5 million. See Mining Stock Association, *Official Summary,* p. 29.

2. Taylor, *Cripple Creek,* pp. 197–202, 205, 209.

3. Ibid., p. 199; Sprague, *Money Mountain* (1953), 73–76; Rinker, "History of Cripple Creek," p. 5; *Gazette,* 3 Oct., 21 Nov., 28 Nov. 1891. F. W. Howbert, brother of County Clerk Irving Howbert, was a leading organizer of the pipeline company.

4. *Gazette,* 4 June 1892; Rinker, "History of Cripple Creek," p. 82; *Gazette,* 4 Jan. 1894, 7 May 1892. For more on saloons, see Jon M. Kingsdale, "The 'Poor Man's Club': Social Functions of the Urban Working-Class Saloon," in *The American Man,* ed. Elizabeth H. Pleck and Joseph H. Pleck (Englewood Cliffs: Prentice-Hall, 1980), pp. 255–84; Elliott West, "Of Lager Beer and Sonorous Songs," *Colorado Magazine* 48 (Spring 1972): 108–28; and Elliott West, *The Saloon on the Rocky Mountain Mining Frontier* (Lincoln: University of Nebraska Press, 1979).

5. *Gazette,* 26 Dec. 1891, 7 May, 14 May, 25 June, 2 July, 30 July 1892, 8 June, 5 Oct., 19 Oct. 1893, 11 Nov. 1894; Omer Vincent Foxhoven, *The City of God in the City of Gold* (n.p., June 1952), n.p.; *Cripple Creek District Directory, 1900* (Colorado Springs: Gazette Publishing, 1900), pp. 90, 112–13, 150–51, 445, 456–57, 527. At least thirty churches were listed; part of the page that listed the Victor churches was torn out. Frank J. Hard, *Cripple Creek-Victor Mining District Directory* (Cripple Creek: Directory Publishing, 1895), pp. 248–50; *A Complete City Directory of Cripple Creek, Victor, and the Towns of the Cripple Creek Mining District* (Colorado Springs: Gazette Publishing, 1897), pp. 588–90; *Cripple Creek District Directory, 1900,* pp. 770–74. Fifty-three saloons were in the District in 1895, 113 by 1897, and 149 in 1900. Most of them were in the two largest towns: Cripple Creek had seventeen in 1895, fifty in 1897, and seventy-three in 1900; Victor had twenty-two in 1895, thirty-three in 1897, and thirty-seven in 1900. For children in western mining camps, see Elliott West, "Beyond Baby Doe: Child Rearing on the Mining Frontier," in *The Women's West,* ed. Susan Armitage and Elizabeth Jameson (Norman: University of Oklahoma Press, 1987), pp. 179–92.

6. *Gazette,* 15 Aug., 26 Sept., 19 Dec. 1891; Foxhoven, *The City of God.* De La Vergne, who came to Colorado during the Leadville excitement of 1878, invested in mines in Gunnison County and managed mines near Silver City, New Mexico. Ultimately, he held large interests in the Virginia M. Gold Mining Company and the Elkton Consolidated. Sargent and Rohrbacher, *The Fortunes of a Decade,* pp. 28–29. For more on Pourtales, see Sprague, *Newport in the Rockies,* pp. 116–27.

7. The Buena Vista, Washington, Blue Bell, Gold King, and Grand View mines found rich ore at ten to thirty feet. *Gazette,* 9 Jan. 1982. For Portales and his associates, see *Gazette,* 20 Feb. 1892; for Lennox et al. and Tutt and associates, see *Gazette,* 20 March 1892. For Hagerman, see *Gazette,* 28 May 1892 and Sprague, *Newport in the Rockies,* pp. 103–8. For more on Hagerman's holdings in the District, which eventually included the Ophir Company, the Mollie Gibson, and controlling shares in the Buena Vista, the Bull Mountain

Mining Company, and the Zenobia, see *Gazette*, 12 Sept., 5 Nov. 1892, 14 Dec. 1893, and *Press*, 31 March 1900. For Moffat and Roudebush, see *Gazette*, 11 June, 18 June, 25 June 1892 (quotation). For the Battle Mountain incorporation, see *Gazette*, 25 June 1894.

8. *Gazette*, 4 Jan., 8 March, 19 April 1894, 28 Jan. 1893.

9. Rinker, "History of Cripple Creek," p. 39.

10. *Gazette*, 6 July, 7 Sept. 1893.

11. *Gazette*, 5 Nov. 1892.

12. W. C. Calhoun, "History of Cripple Creek," *Quarterly Sentinel*, Feb. 1896, p. 13; Rinker, "History of Cripple Creek," pp. 91–92, 94–95; Taylor, *Cripple Creek*, pp. 54–60. Following a route around the east slopes of Bull Hill, the MT went past the Victor, Vindicator, and Buena Vista and on around Battle Mountain near the Independence, Strong, and Portland. The F&CC earned its entire $800,000 construction cost before the MT reached Cripple Creek but never earned more. Moffat turned over control of the F&CC to the MT in 1899. Sprague, *Money Mountain* (1979), p. 168.

13. Rinker, "History of Cripple Creek," pp. 95–96; Taylor, *Cripple Creek*, pp. 60–61. The principal Short Line investors included James Burns, Irving Howbert, E. W. Giddings, Frank M. Woods, and W. S. Stratton.

14. In 1892 carpenters' wages were $3.50 for an eight-hour day, and miners earned from $2.50 to $4.00. *Gazette*, 9 Jan., 5 March, 30 Jan. (first quotation), 28 May (second quotation), 4 June, and 25 June 1892, 20 April and 8 June 1893; "Local Unions Chartered in the State of Colorado," John S. Rogers, general secretary, United Brotherhood of Carpenters and Joiners of America, memo to Edward A. Rylands, executive secretary-treasurer, Colorado State Council of Carpenters, 13 Feb. 1981.

15. Calderwood, "The Strike of 1894," pp. 32–34, 38; Official Charter Book, W.F.M. and I.U.M.M.&S.W., WFM Collection (hereafter cited as WFM Charter Book). Although Calderwood, "The Strike of 1894," p. 37, dates the formation of the Altman local in fall 1893, the charter was issued in August. Anaconda Miners No. 21 was chartered December 29, 1893, Victor Miners No. 32 on January 12, 1895, and Cripple Creek Miners No. 40 on October 1, 1895. WFM Charter Book. Until the other locals were chartered, all four worked under the Altman charter.

16. The major eight-hour mines were the Isabella, Pharmacist, Zenobia, and Pikes Peak; the principal nine-hour companies were the Strong, Granite, Portland, and Independence. Miners on the Victor, Anaconda, Sunset, C.O.D., Gold King, and Ingraham worked ten hours.

17. Calderwood, "The Strike of 1894," p. 37; Rastall, *Labor History*, pp. 19–20, 22 (from the account of E. W. Pfeiffer, a miner on the Isabella in 1893, as told to Rastall in 1903 when Pfeiffer was chair of the Teller County Board of Commissioners); *Gazette*, 28 Dec. 1893. For eight-hour campaigns elsewhere see Rosenzweig, *Eight Hours for What We Will*.

18. Rastall, *Labor History*, p. 21; *Gazette*, 25 Jan., 1 Feb. 1894; Sprague, *Money Mountain* (1953), p. 112. The signatories included James Burns, who soon withdrew, J. J. Hagerman, D. H. Moffat, Sam Altman, Edward De La Vergne, and William Lennox. *Labor Disturbances*, p. 75. The eight union men were Robert Green, James Gaughan, Hugh O'Connell, Hank McCloskey, Frank Luscha, Robert Lyons, Mike Walsh, and George McMillan.

19. *Gazette*, 1 Feb., 8 Feb. 1894; Rastall, *Labor History*, p. 24; *Labor Disturbances*, pp. 75–76.

20. *Gazette*, 8 Feb. 1894; Calderwood, "The Strike of 1894," p. 39; Rastall, *Labor History*, p. 25.

21. *Gazette*, 15 Feb., 5 April 1894; Sprague, *Money Mountain* (1953), p. 113; *Labor Disturbances*, p. 76; Rastall, *Labor History*, p. 29. The nine-hour holdouts included the Summit, Victor, Anna Lee, Pharmacist, Doubtful, Anaconda, Ingraham, and Free Coinage mines.

22. The Gold King, Strong, Isabella, Victor, Summit, Zenobia, Ingraham, and Free Coinage mines requested the injunction. Rastall, *Labor History*, pp. 26–27; *Labor Disturbances*, p. 76.

23. Rastall, *Labor History*, p. 28; *Labor Disturbances*, pp. 76–77; *Gazette*, 22 March 1894, emphasis added. Waite, a former justice of the peace from Aspen, knew Calderwood and some of the other strikers.

24. *Labor Disturbances*, p. 77.

25. *Gazette*, 29 March 1894; Rastall, *Labor History*, p. 28.

26. *Gazette*, 5 April 1894; Rastall, *Labor History*, p. 31.

27. *Gazette*, 12 April, 19 April 1894.

28. *Gazette*, 26 April 1894; Rastall, *Labor History*, p. 32; Message of Gov. Davis H. Waite to Colorado General Assembly, 1895, quoted in *Labor Disturbances*, pp. 77–78; Calderwood, "The Strike of 1894," p. 40. Eben Smith later requested that El Paso County reimburse $536.95 "paid out . . . during the recent strike at Cripple Creek. The parties to whom these bills were paid demanded that the Victor Company guarantee and pay them before they would furnish food and horses to the deputies and as the case was urgent, we did so." Eben Smith to Board of County Commissioners, El Paso County, Colorado Springs, 20 Aug. 1894, Letterpress Book, Victor Gold Mining Co., from April 18, 1893–Sept. 18, 1895, p. 162, box 20, Smith Collection.

29. Chapman interview.

30. Although Kathleen Chapman said "militia," she was referring to the deputies. This slip probably reflected her experience during the 1903–4 strike and feelings among miners and their families about the militia, which, except in 1894, supported the mine owners. *Gazette*, 17 May 1894.

31. There was considerable dispute about who blew up the shaft house; each side blamed the other. *Labor Disturbances*, p. 99; *Gazette*, 31 May 1894.

32. *Labor Disturbances*, pp. 78–79.

33. Ibid., p. 79; *Gazette*, 31 May 1894; Calderwood, "The Strike of 1894," pp. 41–42; Rastall, *Labor History*, pp. 37–40.

34. *Labor Disturbances*, p. 75.

35. Calderwood, "The Strike of 1894," pp. 42–43; Rastall, *Labor History*, pp. 40–44; *Labor Disturbances*, pp. 79–80.

36. This is probably the incident to which Kathleen Chapman referred. Rastall, *Labor History*, pp. 45–47; *Labor Disturbances*, pp. 80–83.

37. Those present at the June 10 conference were Sheriff Bowers, County Commissioner Boynton, W. S. Stratton and Charles Steele of the Independence, Mr. Keith of Victor (prob-

ably Charles A. Keith, representing the Smith-Moffat interests), William Lennox, L. P. Airhart, Generals Brooks and Tarsney, and Colonel Hagel. Rastall, *Labor History*, pp. 47–49; *Labor Disturbances*, pp. 83–84.

38. McIntire apparently questioned both their guilt and the fairness of their trials. Rastall, *Labor History*, pp. 50–51; *Labor Disturbances*, p. 84; *Gazette*, 2 May 1895.

39. Rastall, *Labor History*, p. 33; Calderwood, "The Strike of 1894," p. 41. For the Strong trial, see *Press*, 1 May 1900, 27 March, 20 April, 24 April, 26 April, 27 April, 28 April, 30 April, 1 May, 2 May, 3 May, 4 May, 7 May, 8 May, 9 May, 10 May, 11 May, 14 May, 15 May, 16 May, 18 May 1901. In 1898 Free Coinage Miners No. 19 endorsed Lyons for state mine inspector. *Courier*, 23 Dec. 1898. The *Courier* was the official paper of the Colorado State Federation of Labor.

40. *Labor Disturbances*, p. 85; *Gazette*, 28 June 1894.

41. This account is from Rastall, who was not notably pro-union. Two prominent citizens of Colorado Springs swore affidavits saying that they heard the assistant district attorney outline a scheme to convict every man tried. Petition for Change of Venue, Case *People v. McNamara*, District Court, April 1895, in Rastall, *Labor History*, pp. 57–58.

42. Calderwood was indicted on a number of charges, including blowing up the Strong Mine and attempted murder. *Gazette*, 19 July 1894, 14 March 1895. Harry Blackmer, another of the young socialites, served as prosecutor in the Lyons case and in the trials of the other union miners. Blackmer came to Colorado Springs from Massachusetts in 1885 and was elected county attorney in 1892 and district attorney in 1894. He eventually controlled all the railroads into the District through his holding company, the Cripple Creek Central Railroad. He gave up his Cripple Creek interests in 1912 to invest in Wyoming oil. In 1924 he fled to France to avoid testifying in the Teapot Dome scandal and remained a fugitive for a quarter of a century before making a deal with the Justice Department to drop perjury and evasion charges in return for $20,000 in fines and a guilty plea to tax evasion charges. See Sprague, *Money Mountain* (1979), pp. 248, 317.

43. Two Catholic priests, Fathers Francolon and Bender, responded to the charge of the Rev. H. E. Warner that he had overheard a priest offer to settle the strike if he could appoint certain mine bosses. Sprague, *Money Mountain* (1953), p. 110; *Gazette*, 31 May, 21 June 1894 (quotation).

44. Sprague, *Money Mountain* (1953), p. 110, claimed that a third of the District was composed of Red Necks, but he did not give his source in either the 1953 or 1979 editions of his book. His generally pro-capital account does reflect the fears and prejudices of Colorado Springs conservatives. The prouder, working-class connotations of the term are reflected in the *Press*, passim; Chapman interview; interview with Clara Stiverson, Golden, Colo., 29 July 1975; May Wing interview, 6 March 1976.

45. *Gazette*, 15 Aug. 1894. For further examples of the *Gazette*'s portrayal of all strikers as ignorant, criminal, and/or Molly Maguires (generally presented as synonymous), see *Gazette*, 16 Aug. 1894. Sprague, *Money Mountain* (1953), p. 111, is the source for Calderwood's ties to the Mollie Maguires. Sprague did not cite his sources.

46. *Gazette*, 2 July 1894.

CHAPTER 3: IN UNION THERE IS STRENGTH

1. Minutes, Cripple Creek UBCJA Local No. 547 (hereafter cited as Minutes, Carpenters No. 547), meeting of 27 Oct. 1896, United Brotherhood of Carpenters and Joiners of America Local No. 515, Colorado Springs, Colo.

2. The exact numbers of local unions and their memberships cannot be determined. By 1896 there were at least twelve locals, and by 1898, twenty-two (Appendix B). In the second half of 1898 the Cripple Creek Trades Assembly admitted six new unions. *Courier*, 16 Dec. 1898; *Press*, 5 Feb. 1901, p. 1.

3. *Press*, 23 July 1901; Minutes, Carpenters No. 547, meetings of 13 Feb., 10 April, 29 June, 1 Dec., 8 Dec., 22 May 1897.

4. "Proceedings of the Second Annual Convention of the Western Federation of Miners, Held at Salt Lake City, Utah, May 14, 1894," pp. 1, 10–11, microfilm, Graduate Social Science Library, University of California, Berkeley (hereafter cited as 1894 WFM Convention). In 1895 the WFM executive committee approved a 50 cent assessment to help pay the legal expenses of union members after the strike. Western Federation of Miners, Minutes of Executive Committee, meeting of 3 June 1895, p. 1, Western Federation of Miners Executive Committee Minutes, 1893–95, microfilm, Graduate Social Science Library, University of California, Berkeley (hereafter cited as WFM Executive Committee).

5. "Official Proceedings of the First Annual Convention of the Colorado State Federation of Labor Held in the City of Pueblo, Colo., May 1, 1896," pp. 7, 12, 16, UCB (hereafter cited as 1896 CSFL Convention); John E. Gross, "Official History of the Colorado State Federation of Labor," prepared December 1928, CSFL Collection. The eight locals were Cripple Creek Typographers No. 227, Cripple Creek Painters, Cripple Creek Carpenters No. 547, Victor Carpenters No. 584, Anaconda Miners No. 21, Cripple Creek Miners No. 40, Victor Press Employees, and the Cripple Creek Dress Makers.

6. *Courier*, 2 June 1899; *Proceedings of the Third Annual Convention, Colorado State Federation of Labor, Held at Colorado Springs, Colorado, May 2nd, 3rd, and 4th, 1898* (Pueblo: Courier Printing, 1898), pp. 5–7 (hereafter cited as 1898 CSFL Convention); "Official Proceedings of the Second Annual Convention of the State Federation of Labor, Held in City of Victor, Colorado, April 30, 1897," UCB (hereafter cited as 1897 CSFL Convention). In 1899 the two Trades Assemblies and fourteen District locals were represented. *Press*, 3 June 1900; *Courier*, 9 June 1899.

7. The WFM briefly affiliated with the AFL in 1896, hoping to gain financial support for the Leadville strike. When the support did not come, it withdrew and prepared to found the Western Labor Union as an alternative. For a more complete discussion of the decision to affiliate with the AFL in 1911, see Elizabeth Jameson, "The Creatures of Discontent: The Western Federation of Miners and the Radical Labor Movement, 1893–1916" (B.A. thesis, Antioch College, 1970). The union failed to achieve merger with the United Mine Workers, a primary goal. Crippled by several disastrous strikes, it went into serious decline after 1912, from which it did not recover until the 1930s. It was instrumental in founding the CIO but was expelled in 1950 with other leftist unions for alleged communist domination. Dur-

ing the 1950s union leaders were prosecuted for alleged communist ties, and the union lost members to raids by larger unions. Finally, in 1967, it merged with the United Steelworkers of America, achieving the affiliation with a strong industrial union it had long desired. The merger, unlike the union's intentions in founding the IWW and the CIO, was not inspired by a desire to transform the political economy but rather by concerns for union survival.

8. McPhee was probably representing Cripple Creek Federal Labor Union No. 19, because the carpenters could not affiliate with the WLU. *Courier*, 10 March 1899; *The Coming Nation*, 4 June 1898; *Press*, 30 May 1901; "The Western Labor Union," *Miners' Magazine*, Jan. 1900, pp. 24–26.

9. *Press*, 28 Aug. 1900.

10. Representatives of District unions who held offices in larger labor organizations included John Calderwood, Free Coinage Miners No. 19, WFM Executive Board, 1894–95; James Leonard, Free Coinage Miners No. 19, WFM vice president, 1895, president, 1895–96; Daniel P. McGinley, Free Coinage Miners No. 19, WFM Executive Board, 1899–1900, and CSFL Executive Board, 1899–1900; D. C. Copley, Altman Stationary Engineers No. 75, WFM Executive Board, 1902–4; W. H. Leonard, Altman Stationary Engineers No. 75, WFM delegate to WLU, 1902; G. C. McGimsie, Cripple Creek Carpenters No. 547, CSFL second vice president, 1896–97; Chauncey Miller, Cripple Creek Cooks and Waiters No. 24, CSFL Executive Board, 1897–98; E. J. Baugh, Victor, CSFL Executive Board, 1897–98; Joy Pollard, Free Coinage Miners No. 19, CSFL president, 1898–99, CSFL treasurer, 1899–1900; E. J. Campbell, Cripple Creek Miners No. 40, CSFL first vice president, 1900–1901; P. J. DeVault, secretary, Cripple Creek District Trades and Labor Assembly, CSFL second vice president, 1901, CSFL secretary-treasurer, 1901–2; J. C. Sullivan, Victor Miners No. 32, CSFL president, 1902–4; R. E. Croskey, secretary, District Trades and Labor Assembly, CSFL first vice president, 1903–4; M. J. O'Donnell, Victor Miners No. 32, WLU secretary-treasurer, 1898; M. A. Andrews, Cripple Creek Typographical Union, WLU secretary-treasurer, 1898–99; P. N. McPhee, Cripple Creek Carpenters No. 547, Cripple Creek Federal Labor Union No. 19, WLU second vice president, 1898–99, WLU executive board, 1899–1900; John Troxel, Cripple Creek Cooks and Waiters, WLU vice president, 1899–1900; J. M. Lane, Cripple Creek Butchers and Grocery Clerks, WLU Executive Board, 1899–1900; S. B. Lawrence, Cripple Creek Federal Labor Union No. 19, WLU Executive Board, 1900–1901; D. F. O'Shea, Free Coinage Miners No. 19, ALU vice president, 1902–3.

11. *Gazette*, 28 Dec. 1897; *Press*, 8 May, 16 Oct. 1900.

12. Letterpress Book, Victor Gold Mining Co., Sept. 20, 1895–Sept. 14, 1896, pp. 138, 160, 278, 308, 388, 434, and Letterpress Book, Victor Gold Mining Co., from Sept. 15, 1896–May 16, 1898, pp. 17, 232, 375, 442, box 20, Smith Collection; *Gazette*, 30 Sept. 1897; *Press*, 2 Nov. 1899. For more detail regarding the actual transactions involved in business consolidations, see Elizabeth Ann Jameson, "High-Grade and Fissures: A Working-Class History of the Cripple Creek, Colorado, Gold-Mining District, 1890–1905" (Ph.D. diss., University of Michigan, 1987), pp. 91–131.

13. *Gazette*, 11 Jan. 1898; *Press*, 20 Aug., 1 Dec., 2 Dec., 6 Sept., 14 Dec. 1899, 8 Sept. 1900.

14. Other Colorado Springs capitalists bought into Bull Hill—Clarence C. Hamlin, Verner Z. Reed, Ernest A. Colburn, E. W. Giddings, Charles Dudley, William Lennox, and Senator Scott of West Virginia, Lennox's brother-in-law—bought the Gold King, the Strong, and other mines. *Gazette*, 18 Jan. 1899, 18 Jan. 1898, 16 July, 8 Feb. 1899; *Press*, 13 Sept., 17 Nov., 13 Dec., 21 Dec. 1899, 9 Jan., 10 March, 11 March, 27 March, 3 April, 5 April, 4 Dec., 13 April, 24 May 1900; Sargent and Rohrbacher, *The Fortunes of a Decade*, p. 16.

15. *Press*, 9 April, 22 May, 17 Dec., 2 Feb. 1901, 7 June, 17 June, 27 Nov. 1902. After 1898 smaller mine owners could buy power from the Colorado Electric Plant at Canon City. Victor and Cripple Creek had water facilities that supplied the major mines, if not all the residential areas, and provided steam for the hoists and compressors. In 1902 the Woodses consolidated the power company with the Pueblo Lighting and Traction Company to form the Pueblo and Suburban Traction and Lighting Company. *Gazette*, 3 Jan. 1899, 23 Aug. 1898.

16. *Press*, 3 Oct. 1900, 16 Aug. 1901 (quotation).

17. *Press*, 13 Dec. 1899, 9 Jan. 1901, 10 Feb. 1900, 12 March 1902, 21 March 1900. Smith said he sold the Gold Knob to J. A. Hayes, trustee, "who represents Colorado Springs people." Eben Smith to F. T. Osgood, Goldfield, 3 Jan. 1900, Letterpress Book, Gold Knob Mining Company, Nov. 16, 1897–Aug. 29, 1900, p. 117, Eben Smith to W. P. Dunham and R. H. Reid, 6 Nov. 1901, Eben Smith to R. H. Reid, Denver, 12 March 1902, W. P. Dunham to Eben Smith, 2 April 1902, Eben Smith to C. C. Hamlin, Colorado Springs, 6 Nov. 1901, and Minutes of Meetings of the Granite Gold Mining Co., meeting of 11 July 1902, all in Smith Collection. Clarence C. Hamlin negotiated Smith's sale of the Granite to Tutt, Penrose, and MacNeill. The secretary of the MOA during the 1903–4 strike, he had long-standing ties with the socialites. In 1900 he, Tutt, Verner Z. Reed, and others incorporated the Golden Tery. *Press*, 7 June 1900.

18. Smith and Moffat put the Victor Mine on the market after its upper levels were exhausted and after they had levied stiff assessments on shareholders to sink the shaft deeper. W. P. Dunham to Eben Smith, 2 Dec. 1902, W. P. Dunham to Eben Smith and R. H. Reid, Los Angeles, 8 April 1902, in Correspondence, Smith Collection; R. H. Reid to Octave Cointe, Paris, 7 Jan. 1900, A. O. Clark to Directors, Victor Gold Mining Co., 8 Jan. 1901 (agreeing to pay the assessment on his 200 shares for "the purposes set forth in your circular of October 17, 1900"), circular, 17 Oct. 1900, and Papers, Victor Gold Mining Co., Jan. 1897–Dec., 1901, Smith Collection. Carlton formed a number of temporary business alliances. In addition to his Colorado Trading and Transfer Company, he was, by 1899, a minority stockholder in the Pharmacist, on the board of directors of the Gold Sovereign Mining and Tunnel Company and the principal owner of the Uncle Sam on Bull Hill. He also cooperated with the Woods syndicate to merge a number of mines on Raven Hill into the Doctor-Jack Pot. *Press*, 8 Aug., 27 Aug., 4 Nov. 1899, 7 Dec., 15 Dec. 1900.

19. Verner Z. Reed engineered the Independence sale and received $1 million for his part in the transaction. Waters, *Midas of the Rockies*, pp. 210–28. Stratton's purchases included the Crescent and Monitor mines, the Temomy Mining and Milling Co., the Reno Group, the Shoo Fly, the Fraction, the Lucky Bill, the Lucky Gus, the May Queen, portions of the Jack Rabbit and Jack Rabbit No. 3, the West View, the Hidden Treasure, and part of the Zenobia. See *Press*, 25 May, 2 Feb., 21 Feb., 15 May, 26 Aug., 17 Oct., 20 Sept., 25 Aug., 31

Aug., 28 Aug. 1900, 16 Jan., 26 Jan., 4 May, 5 May 1901; Judge Albert Frost to R. C. Getch, Ashport, Tenn., 14 June 1901, and Judge Albert Frost to Julius Thompson, Nome, Alaska, 25 June 1901, Albert Frost Collection, CSHS.

20. *Gazette*, 1 April 1897; Foxhoven, *The City of God*; Calhoun, "History of Cripple Creek," pp. 22–23. The new cyanide and chlorination processes revolutionized the treatment of low-grade ores. In 1895 some $205 million in gold was recovered worldwide using the cyanide method on tailings. For a technical description of the mill and of the chlorination process, see *Gazette*, 26 Oct. 1898; for more on the cyanide process, see *Gazette*, 6 June 1895, and Spude, "Cyanide and the Flood of Gold." Tutt was president of the of the Colorado-Philadelphia Reduction Co., Penrose, secretary-treasurer, and MacNeill, vice president and general manager. *Gazette*, 3 Sept., 24 Dec. 1896, 28 Dec. 1897.

21. These estimates of ASARCO's power predated its subsequent merger with the Guggenheim smelting interests. James E. Fell, Jr., *Ores to Metals: The Rocky Mountain Smelting Industry* (Lincoln: University of Nebraska Press, 1979), esp. pp. 222–54; *Gazette*, 4 Jan., 11 Jan., 7 Dec. 1898, 18 Jan. 1899; *Press*, 19 July 1899; Carl Ubelhode, Maxine Benson, and Duane A. Smith, *A Colorado History*, 3d ed. (Boulder: Pruett Publishing, 1972), pp. 238–39. Eben Smith owned some two hundred shares of ASARCO stock, valued at about $95,000. Statement from Central Trust of New York, 18 Aug. 1902, Correspondence, Smith Collection.

22. *Press*, 10 Jan. 1900, 1 May 1901; see also *Press*, 3 Aug. 1899.

23. Tutt sold his Alexandria lode to the Standard Mining and Smelting Company for $10,000. The Standard was completed by February 1, 1901, at a cost of $750,000. The USR&R directors included Tutt, MacNeill, Penrose, and W. K. Gillett. Tutt, Penrose, and MacNeill were the executive committee. *Press*, 13 Feb., 6 March, 22 March (quotation), 10 May, 20 Dec., 23 Dec. 1900, 1 Feb., 29 June 1901, 12 March 1902; Ubelhode, Benson, and Smith, *A Colorado History*, p. 239; "Cripple Creek Output Exceeds Two Millions," *Miners' Magazine*, June 1901, p. 33; "Trust Crushes Its Rivals," *Miners' Magazine*, June 1901, p. 37; "Mine Owners Lose Only Safeguard," *Miners' Magazine*, June 1901, pp. 42–43; "Rockefeller Owns the Smelter Trust," *Miners' Magazine*, June 1901, p. 43.

24. *Press*, 23 July 1901, 17 April, 4 July 1900, 24 April 1902 (first quotation); "Open Letter of James F. Burns," *Miners' Magazine*, 27 Oct. 1904, p. 5 (second quotation).

25. *Press*, 26 Sept. 1901, 15 Sept. 1900, 25 May, 6 April, 25 March, 2 April, 4 May 1902.

26. *Press*, 16 Sept. 1902. After Stratton's death, there was considerable anxiety about what would happen to his property until, to labor's relief, it was offered for leases. See *Press*, 13 Jan., 24 Jan., 27 Feb. 1903.

27. The Short Line's challenge started a rate war. The Midland Terminal slashed freight charges and the Short Line cut passenger fares until finally, in April, 1902, both sides called a truce and moved their competition to other arenas. See *Press*, 23 Nov., 24 Nov., 1 Dec. 1901; Sprague, *Money Mountain* (1953), pp. 200–203.

28. *Courier*, 19 May (quotation), 12 May 1899; "In the Cripple Creek District," *Miners' Magazine*, Nov. 1900, pp. 19–21; WFM Charter Book.

29. *Courier*, 28 April (quotation), 14 April 1899; *Gazette*, 16 April 1899; *Press*, 15 Jan., 22 Jan. 1901.

30. *Courier*, 30 Dec. 1898; *Press*, 27 June 1899, 25 Jan. 1901.

31. *Courier*, 31 March 1899. Gaughan was one of the eight miners arrested for running Rabideau out of camp in the first strike and served as a union representative at the failed negotiations of April 1, 1894.

32. *Press*, 24 Oct., 23 Nov., 24 Nov. 1899, 17 Oct., 23 Oct. 1900 (quotation).

33. Carpenters and machinists at the mill received the same wages for eight hours that they had been paid for twelve; mill workers took a pay cut from $3.00 to $2.70 or from $2.75 to $2.50. *Press*, 27 June 1899; *Courier*, 31 March, 28 April 1899.

34. From June to December 1899, the *Press* reported ten strikes that lasted from a day to something over two weeks. Two involved mill workers. The others concerned newsboys, motormen and mason tenders, hod carriers, ironworkers, plasterers, cooks and waiters, teamsters, and machinists at the La Bella plant. Eight were about wages; the two mill strikes were for the eight-hour day. The outcomes of three were not reported; six resulted in at least partial union victories. In 1900 the paper reported sixteen strikes and the conclusions of eleven. The eleven lasted a day to three weeks, except for a more than thirteen-month dispute at the Gillett Mill. Three involved the Gillett mill and smelter workers, four involved miners, two concerned plasterers, and the others involved ore sorters, iron workers, newsboys, graders, switchmen, carpenters, painters and decorators, construction workers, and electrical workers. Six were about wages, two involved the stripping order, five concerned non-union workers at building trades jobsites, and two concerned mine safety. Miners at the Portland were out for three weeks over a combination of the right of union secretaries to organize at the mine, firemen's wages, compulsory insurance, and Burns's decision to close the Portland to protest smelter rates. Ore sorters on the Damon walked out because a new superintendent said that they were more fit for mucking than ore sorting. *Press*, June 1899–Feb. 1903.

35. *Courier*, 28 April, 6 Sept. 1899 (quotation).

36. From June 1899 through February 1903, more than fifty boycotts were advertised. The boycotted products included convict-made building materials, Swift meats, Zang's beer, various non-union cigars and cigarettes, Knoxville woolen mill products, non-union crackers and mattresses, Coors beer, Western Union clocks, and a host of other items. Most boycotts protested non-union labor, child labor, wages, and other issues in workers' strikes elsewhere. Even more commonly, labor boycotted District firms. At least nine boycotts involved boardinghouses or restaurants that refused to hire union workers, and five targeted grocers or saloons that violated early closing or sold non-union products. The unions boycotted Carlton's Colorado Trading and Transfer Company for refusing to hire union labor, the Evans Laundry for shipping laundry out of the District and Colorado Springs laundry wagons for taking it, and the *Denver Post* and its local agent for attacking striking miners at Telluride and for threatening newsboys who honored the labor boycott. The list was enormous, the tactic generally effective. *Press*, June 1899–Feb. 1903.

37. See, for example, the *Press*, 29 Dec. 1899, in which Federal Labor Union No. 19 announced that after January 2, 1900, "the hours of labor for all clerks employed in the retail dry goods stores doing business in the city of Cripple Creek, shall be from 7:45 A.M. until 6 P.M. on all week days except Saturday. The hours on Saturday shall be from 7:45 A.M. until any time agreed upon between the employer and employee." See also *Press*, 12 Dec., 30 Dec.

1899, 13 May, 11 Nov. 1902, 17 Aug., 12 Oct. 1900. Headlines make the point: "Dry Goods Stores Close at 6," "Must Do Work at Home," "Trades Assembly Demands Union Made Cigars," "Waiters Will Rest One Day in Week."

38. *Press*, 22 Sept., 29 Sept., 10 Oct., 31 Dec., 1 Aug. 1899, 8 Feb., 23 Feb. 1900. Hoisting and stationary engineers received $4.00 for eight hours; mine firemen, at least $3.50. *Courier*, 21 April 1899. Not all WFM members received the $3 scale, however. The notable exceptions were some millworkers. In 1900 the Gillett Mill and Smeltermen's local adopted a scale ranging from $4.00 for engineers to $2.50 for roastermen's helpers. *Press*, 28 Feb., 22 May 1900.

39. The Anaconda Mine was sold in February 1900 to a syndicate that included the Woods family, Burns, Stratton, and Howbert. The Vindicator was one of the Gold Knob properties that Smith and Moffat sold in 1899 to a syndicate that included the Woods family and Burns. Zang apparently had interests in both. Colorado State Federation of Labor, Quarterly Report, in Colorado State Federation of Labor, Minutes CSFL Executive Board, June 10, 1899–Nov. 2, 1909, meeting of 8 Sept. 1900, and meetings of 9 Oct. (quotation), 21 Oct. 1900, CSFL Collection (hereafter cited as CSFL Minutes).

40. See for example D. P. McGinley, "A Lecture from Altman," *Miners' Magazine*, April 1900, pp. 30–31.

41. R. H. Reid to N. H. Cone, Goldfield, 21 June 1897, Letterpress Book, Victor Gold Mining Co., from Sept. 15, 1896–May 16, 1898, p. 380, box 20, Smith Collection. The Smith-Moffat interests chose to continue employing their own detective because it was cheaper. They claimed that some of their mines produced no high-grade, and the association refused their offer of $100 a month for all their mines. R. H. Reid to James F. Burns, 21 June 1897, R. H. Reid to J. A. Sill, secretary, Colorado Springs, 25 June 1897, ibid., pp. 381, 384.

42. The name was changed when Stratton sold the Independence to the Venture Corporation in 1899. He was not the owner at this time. Other signatories included the Gold Coin, Portland, Elkton, Mary McKinnie, Last Dollar, and Vindicator. None ever enforced the order. *Press*, 25 Sept. 1900.

43. The miners voted at mass meetings of mine workers not union meetings, but all the Stratton's Independence employees were union members, and a special meeting of Victor Miners No. 32 unanimously endorsed the settlement. *Press*, 25 Sept. 1900; "In the Cripple Creek District," *Miners' Magazine*, Nov. 1900, pp. 19–20.

44. Only the Independence workers voted at the meeting of October 26. *Press*, 26 Oct., 27 Oct. (first quotation), 28 Oct., 30 Oct., 1 Nov. 1900 (second quotation).

45. *Press*, 23 Sept. 1900.

46. Alan Derickson, *Workers' Health, Workers' Democracy: The Western Miners' Struggle, 1891–1925* (Ithaca: Cornell University Press, 1988) is an impressive study of the WFM's efforts to control miners' health care. R. H. Reid to Charles A. Keith, 12 Dec. 1895, and R. H. Reid to Charles A. Keith, 10 Feb. 1896, Letterpress Book, Victor Gold Mining Co., Sept. 20, 1895–Sept. 14, 1896, pp. 93, 194, box 20, Smith Collection; R. H. Reid to T. B. Dean, Goldfield, 28 Sept. 1896, Letterpress Book, Victor Gold Mining Co., from Sept. 15, 1896–May 16, 1898, p. 29, box 20, Smith Collection; *Press*, 2 Dec., 11 Dec., 14 Dec. 1900 (quotation), 8 June 1901.

47. Refusing to ride in the cage with non-members was a common form of social pressure. Union miners on the Last Dollar Mine employed this tactic as well. See *Press*, 10 April (quotation), 9 May, 15 May (quotation), 22 July 1900.

48. *Press*, 16 May 1900.

49. *Press*, 17 May 1900.

50. "Cripple Creek District," *Miners' Magazine*, Oct. 1901, pp. 13–15; *Press*, 6 Aug. 1901; "Cripple Creek Circular," *Miners' Magazine*, Sept. 1901, pp. 19–20.

51. *Press*, 6 Aug., 5 Sept. 1901.

52. *Colorado Springs Gazette*, 15 Sept. 1901 (a daily newspaper, not to be confused with the *Weekly Gazette*); *Press*, 15 Sept., 14 Sept. 1901, 10 July 1902.

53. *Press*, 8 Aug. 1899, 6 Oct., 7 Oct. 1900, 30 May, 3 Oct. 1902. Later, Davis, Ed Minster, the vice president of No. 19, and James Laferty, the conductor, were accused of beating miners to make them join or pay their dues. Davis was at work in the Shurtloff Mine at the time, and witnesses swore that both Minster and Laferty were somewhere else when the assaults occurred. The cases against Davis and Laferty were dropped, and Minster was acquitted. *Press*, 11 Nov., 12 Nov., 15 Nov. 1902, 15 March 1903.

54. The Woods properties and the Portland signed the statement. Among those who did not were all the Stratton properties, Stratton's Independence, and the Vindicator. "Cripple Creek District," *Miners' Magazine*, Oct. 1901, pp. 13–15; *Colorado Springs Gazette*, 15 Sept. 1901; *Press*, 11 Sept., 13 Sept., 14 Sept., 15 Sept. 1901.

55. Frank M. Woods, James Burns, and William Lennox, the elected delegates, did not attend. *Press*, 29 March, 15 April, 28 Dec. 1902.

56. *Press*, 25 Feb., 11 March 1902, *Colorado Chronicle*, 26 February 1902. The *Chronicle*, an independent labor and Socialist newspaper, merged with the *Miners' Magazine* in August 1903.

57. *Press*, 13 Feb., 1 Jan. 1901, 4 Feb. 1902, 27 Jan. 1903, 2 Sept., 3 Dec. 1899, 24 Feb., 22 March, 24 July 1901, 4 Jan. 1903, 26 Nov. 1902, 23 May 1900; *Courier*, 29 July 1898. James Burns purchased $1,000 worth of stock in the Victor Miners' Hall.

58. *Courier*, 19 May (first, second, and third quotations), 16 June 1899 (fourth quotation); *Press*, 1 June 1902; James T. Smith, *Eighth Biennial Report of the Bureau of Labor Statistics of the State of Colorado, 1901–1902* (Denver: Smith-Brooks Printing, State Printers, 1902), pp. 333, 335, 336 (fifth quotation); Smith, *Seventh Biennial Report*, pp. 219–24. The resolution was adopted at the 1902 CSFL Convention.

59. See for example, *Press*, 8 Nov., 28 Nov. 1899, 28 Aug. 1901, 21 May 1902; "Proceedings of the Third Annual Convention of the Western Federation of Miners, Denver, Colorado, May 13, 1895," p. 12, microfilm, Graduate Social Science Library, University of California, Berkeley.

60. *Press*, 28 Dec. 1902.

61. *Press*, 7 June, 8 June, 26 Sept. (quotation), 21 Dec. 1902.

62. *Press*, 18 Nov., 30 Nov. 1902. P. J. DeVault, former secretary of the District Trades Assembly and secretary-treasurer of the CSFL, wrote that a Mr. Pierce, Gompers' representative in Colorado, had shown good judgment in one thing: "keeping clear of the Cripple Creek District. This shows that he understands how to take care of his health." DeVault to *Colorado Chronicle*, 19 Nov. 1902.

63. Minutes, Carpenters No. 547, meetings of 24 Nov. 1896, 3 June 1899. Boyce report-edly challenged "drawing the line of unskilled" at all. Minutes, Carpenters No. 547, meeting of 1 March 1897.

64. See for example, Minutes, Carpenters No. 547, meeting of 5 June 1897. For more on the politics of mining-town carpenters, see Jameson, *Building Colorado*, pp. 9–23.

65. District adults were 77 percent native-born, 23 percent foreign-born, and 29 percent second-generation immigrants. The comparable figures for union leaders were, respectively, 76 percent, 24 percent, and 27 percent. State and national leaders were 82 percent native-born but 32 percent second-generation immigrants. Like the population as a whole, approximately half were first- or second-generation immigrants. Manuscript census, Teller County, Colo., 1900, and union sample.

66. Table 7 reflects only the ages of union leaders in 1900, regardless of when they attained union office. The sample, however, contains more persons active during and after 1899 than from 1892 to 1899. Thus, some of the younger people represented in the table were not yet leaders in 1900. But the ages of 209 persons who held office in 1900 did not differ significantly from the total leadership sample: 26 percent were forty-one or older, compared with 27 percent of the entire leadership sample; 67 percent were thirty-one or older, compared with 64 percent. Computed from union sample, 212 people who held union office in 1900, less three whose ages were unknown.

67. Among men aged twenty-one to thirty, 35 percent were married, 57 percent of those thirty-one to forty were married, and 66 percent of men aged forty-one to fifty. Manuscript census, Teller County, Colo., 1900, random sample of 2,089 adults, with eight missing observations.

68. Among all household heads in the union sample, 55 percent owned homes. Manuscript census, Teller County, Colo., 1900, and union sample.

69. *Press*, 19 May 1901.

CHAPTER 4: SIRS AND BROTHERS

1. Chapman interview. Kathleen Welch was born in 1895, and her childhood memories cover the years when she was approximately three to nine. I cannot be certain that the parades she remembered were all Labor Day Parades, although she vividly recalled Labor Day. Perhaps Welch sometimes marched with his union and sometimes with the Knights of St. John. That detail is less important than the fact that he was active in both.

2. More than forty lodges and fraternal organizations operated in the Cripple Creek District between 1892 and 1904. Many had multiple chapters, so more than a hundred separate chapters existed. These were documented from the local press and from District directories; there may have been more. In the few cases in which acronyms only are listed, the full name of the order is unknown. They were the Altman Athletic Club; American Order of Protection (Altman, Cripple Creek, Elkton, Gillett, Goldfield, and Independence); Ancient, Free, and Accepted Masons (Cripple Creek [two lodges], Goldfield, and Victor); Knights Templars (AF&AM) (Cripple Creek); Order of the Eastern Star (AF&AM) (Cripple Creek, Goldfield, and Victor); RAC [Royal Arch Chapter?] (AF&AM) (Cripple Creek); Ancient Order of Hibernians (Victor); Ancient Order of Hibernians Auxiliary (Victor); Ancient Or-

der of United Workmen (Cripple Creek, Goldfield, and Victor); Degree of Honor, AOUW (Cripple Creek, Goldfield, and Victor); Benevolent and Protective Order of Elks (Cripple Creek and Victor); Women's Auxiliary, Benevolent and Protective Order of Elks (Victor); Brotherhood of American Yeomen (Cripple Creek, Elkton, Goldfield, and Victor); Fraternal Order of Eagles (Cripple Creek, Goldfield, and Victor); Foresters (Cripple Creek); Grand Army of the Republic (Cripple Creek and Victor); Ladies of the GAR (Cripple Creek); Women's Relief Corps, GAR (Cripple Creek and Victor); Home Forum Benefit Order (Altman and Cripple Creek); Independent Order of Buffaloes (Anaconda); Independent Order of Buffalettes (Anaconda); Independent Order of Odd Fellows (Anaconda, Cripple Creek [six lodges], Goldfield [two lodges], and Victor); Daughters of Rebekah, IOOF (Anaconda, Cripple Creek, and Victor); Independent Order of Red Men (Altman, Anaconda, Cripple Creek [two lodges], Gillett, Goldfield, Independence, and Victor); Daughters of Pocahantas, IORM (Altman, Anaconda, Cripple Creek, Goldfield, Independence, and Victor); King's Daughters (Victor); Knights of Columbus (Cripple Creek and Victor); Knights of the Golden Eagle (Goldfield); Knights of the Maccabees (Cameron, Cripple Creek, Goldfield, and Victor); Ladies of the Maccabees (Cameron, Cripple Creek, Goldfield, and Victor); Knights of Pythias (Cripple Creek, Goldfield, and Victor); Rathbone Sisters, KP (Cripple Creek, Goldfield, and Victor); Dramatic Order of Knights of Khorassan, KP (Victor); Knights of St. John (Cripple Creek and Victor); Knights of St. John Auxiliary (Cripple Creek); LOL (Cripple Creek); Lodge of Royal Highlanders (Goldfield); Modern Workmen of America (Altman, Cripple Creek, Gillett, and Victor); Royal Neighbors, MWA (unknown); Order of the Gold Belt (unknown); Sarsfield Club (St. Victor's Church in Victor); Sheridan Club (Cripple Creek); S of MT (Cripple Creek); Woodmen of the World (Cripple Creek, Independence, and Victor); Women of Woodcraft (WOW) (Cripple Creek and Victor).

3. *Press*, 5 Sept. 1899.

4. Mary Ann Clawson, *Constructing Brotherhood: Class, Gender, and Fraternalism* (Princeton: Princeton University Press, 1989), esp. ch. 5.

5. *Gazette*, 21 May 1902, 12 March 1892; *Press*, 10 Dec., 25 Oct. 1902, 10 April, 3 Oct., 9 Oct. 1900, 21 Feb., 19 May, 19 June, 13 Sept. 1901, 16 April, 8 May, 24 May 1902, 25 Feb. 1903; Foxhoven, *The City of God*; Leslie Doyle Spell and Hazel M. Spell, *Forgotten Men of Cripple Creek* (Denver: Big Mountain Press, 1959), p. 76.

6. May Wing interview, 6 March 1976; Stiverson interview; interview with Leslie and Ruby Wilkinson, Cripple Creek, Colo., 7 Sept. 1975; Spell and Spell, *Forgotten Men*, p. 95.

7. On women's auxiliaries and mixed-sex fraternal organizations, see Clawson, *Constructing Brotherhood*, pp. 178–210; Mary Ann Clawson, "Nineteenth-Century Women's Auxiliaries and Fraternal Orders," *Signs* 12 (Autumn 1986): 40–61; and Ida M. Jayne-Weaver and Emma D. Wood, *History of the Order of the Pythian Sisters* (Seattle: Peters Publishing, 1925). For membership requirements for specific orders, see Albert C. Stevens, comp. and ed., *The Cyclopedia of Fraternities* (New York: E. B. Treat, 1907), William J. Whalen, *Handbook of Secret Organizations* (Milwaukee: Bruce Publishing, 1966), and Charles W. Ferguson, *Fifty Million Brothers: A Panorama of American Lodges and Clubs* (New York: Farrar and Rinehart, 1937). The American Order of Protection and the Brotherhood of American Yeo-

men, were also either mixed-sex lodges or provided a degree that admitted women. The King's Daughters admitted women only, as appears to be the case with the Independent Order of Buffalettes, the Ladies of the GAR, and the Women's Relief Corps (GAR).

8. Victor GAR Minutes, Meetings of 31 June, 12 Nov. 1896, 7 Jan. 1897, GAR Collection. Membership requirements for the various organizations are from Stevens, comp. and ed., *Cyclopedia*, and Whalen, *Handbook*, as well as *Press* reports of meetings and elections. The 1896 ruling assumed that Catholics would not attend meetings of the Odd Fellows or Knights of Pythias but would mail their dues and insurance payments. See Whalen, *Handbook*, pp. 63–65, 69–72, 76–82, 84–91, 117–25.

9. Colorado reported 561 nonfatal mining accidents in 1902, 494 in 1903, 539 in 1904, 486 in 1905, 436 in 1906, 300 in 1907, 313 in 1908, 347 in 1909, 274 in 1910, and 247 in 1911. There were 82 fatal accidents in 1902, 67 in 1903, 101 in 1904, 100 in 1905, 82 in 1906, 77 in 1907, 64 in 1908, 51 in 1909, 51 in 1910, and 43 in 1911. The average was between two and three fatal accidents a year per thousand miners employed and around fourteen or fifteen non-fatal accidents per thousand employed. T. R. Henahen, *Twelfth Biennial Report of the Bureau of Mines of the State of Colorado* (Denver: Smith-Brooks Printing, 1912), pp. 124–25. These figures, however, exclude thousands of minor daily accidents.

10. See for example *Miners' Magazine*, Aug. 1900, p. 58, March 1901, pp. 37–40, July 1901, pp. 40–42, and 14 April 1904, p. 15; *Press*, 7 Nov. and 24 Dec. 1899, 13 July and 21 Oct. 1900.

11. After 1896 the Bureau of Mines did not differentiate accidents by location, and from 1893 to 1896 it appears to have reported only the most serious. Figures from 1899 to 1903 gathered from *Press* reports are similarly incomplete. If *Press* reporters happened to know injured workers, they reported their minor injuries in the paper's daily gossip columns, but they could not have reported every minor mishap. These sources report fifty-one fatal and forty-seven nonfatal accidents in the District from 1893 to 1896, and 114 fatal accidents, seventy-four permanent injuries, and 814 injuries from July 1899 to March 1903. See Colorado State Inspector of Metalliferous Mines, *Biennial Report of State Inspector of Metalliferous Mines December, 1894* (Denver: Smith-Brooks Printing, State Printers, 1894), pp. 13–36; Harry A. Lee, *1896 Report of Bureau of Mines Colorado* (Denver: Smith-Brooks Printing, State Printers, 1896), pp. 46–61; *Press*, June 1899–March 1903.

12. The accidents reported by the state for 1893–96, and by the *Press* for 1899 through 1903, included 97 caused by missed shots, 79 cage accidents, 246 from falling rock, and 678 from other causes. Headlines in the *Press* give some sense of the range of accidents as well as how common and concerning they were. See, for examples, "Severely Injured by Explosion" (24 June 1902); "Fell 165 Feet to His Death" (15 Feb. 1903); "Frank Schreiber Entombed in Nellie V Mine" (28 Jan. 1903); "Dynamite Destroys Two Shaft Houses" (17 Aug. 1900); "Another Victim of the Cage—W. B. Squires Killed" (15 Sept. 1901); "Two Miners Suffocated by Bad Air" (18 Jan. 1902); "Death from Carbonic Acid in Mine" (19 Jan. 1902); "Fell Eighty Feet to Death" (23 May 1901); "Blown Up" (27 Jan. 1900); "Thawed Powder" (28 Jan. 1900); "Another Victim of Negligence—Frank Mero Falls 175 in the Luck Gus and Is Killed" (18 July 1899); "His Skull Crushed by Falling Timbers" (20 June 1900); "Had a Finger Pinched Off" (2 Oct. 1901); and "Pierced by an Iron Rod" (22 Sept. 1900). Other workers were also hurt on the job. An F&CC brakeman fractured his skull on an overhead trestle near a mine, for

example. *Press*, 19 March 1903. See also the *Press* reports: "A Brakeman Killed" (16 July 1899); "Killed at the Arequa Mill" (5 June 1900); and "Poisoned by Paint" (23 Nov. 1899). For more on the dangers of new technologies, see Wyman, *Hard Rock Epic*, pp. 84–117; Derickson, *Workers' Health, Workers' Democracy*; and Brian Lee Shovers, "Miners, Managers, and Machines: Industrial Accidents and Occupational Disease in the Butte Underground, 1880–1920" (M.A. thesis, Montana State University, 1987).

13. Sometimes workers or their families sued mining corporations, but negligence was difficult to prove and mining companies seldom compensated accident victims. For suits for corporate negligence, see *Press*, 6 Dec. 1899, 3 Oct., 3 July, 21 Nov. 1900.

14. *Press*, 24 July 1900. See also "Mero's Sad Death," *Press*, 19 July 1899. In this case, the coroner's inquest found the company criminally negligent for not providing reliable machinery and because the hoist engineer "in whose hand the lives of the miners were placed, was inexperienced and incompetent for the position."

15. *Press*, 14 July, 20 July 1899 (quotation), 4 May 1900. The phrase "men are cheaper than timber" was common throughout the mining West. See also "Men are Cheaper: Mine Owner Who Considers Life Worth Less Than Lumber," *Press*, 12 Dec. 1899. Cave-ins were less common in the District than in other areas because many Cripple Creek mines were blasted through solid rock and required little timbering.

16. There were literally hundreds of *Press* references to illness and death from respiratory diseases, measles, and diphtheria. See, for example, "Smallpox in the District," *Press*, 13 Nov. 1900, and "Cases of Chickenpox Developed on Midway," 7 Nov. 1900.

17. In 1896 the Anna Lee shaft of the Portland Mine caved in, killing eight miners. Victor Miners No. 32 buried victim Michael McGuirk and shipped the body of Pat Mee to Denver for burial and the body of Thomas H. Harman, to Madison, Wisconsin. *Press*, 6 April 1900 (quotation); *Gazette* 13 Jan., 30 Jan. 1896; U.S. Mss. 14a, Victor Miners' Union No. 32, Ledger, 1894–1903, Wisconsin State Historical Society, Madison.

18. See *Press*, 5 Oct. 1902.

19. Chapman interview.

20. *Press*, 10 March, 11 March 1903.

21. Grand Army of the Republic, Victor GAR Post No. 100, Meetings of 3 Aug., 17 Aug. 1896; see also meetings of 31 June, 29 Oct., and 5 Nov. 1896, GAR Collection; *Press*, 2 July 1901, 5 Dec. 1899, 4 Dec. 1902. Among District lodges and fraternal organizations, at least the following offered sick benefits: Knights of the Maccabees, Ladies of the Maccabees, Modern Woodmen of America, Ancient Order of Hibernians and its Women's Auxiliary, Knights of Columbus (optional), Independent Order of Buffaloes, Independent Order of Red Men, Knights of Pythias Endowment Rank. Death and/or funeral benefits were provided by the Red Men, Knights of Pythias (endowment rank), Odd Fellows, AOUW, Maccabees, MWA, Royal Neighbors, Woodmen of the World, Women of Woodcraft, Eagles, Hibernians, and Knights of Columbus. See Stevens, comp. and ed., *Cyclopedia*, pp. 118, 121, for benefits summaries for some orders. For unions, see *Press*, 11 Jan. 1903, 13 Dec. 1899, 24 July 1900, 6 Jan. 1903; 1903 WFM Convention, pp. 86–88.

22. *Press*, 16 Oct., 28 Nov., 12 Oct. 1900, 7 Aug. 1901 (quotation). For similar accounts of insurance through the Brotherhood of American Yeomen, see *Press*, 12 June 1901; for the

IORM, see 28 Jan. 1900. Insurance was offered by the AOUW and its Degree of Honor, Knights and Ladies of the Maccabees, MWA and Royal Neighbors, Woodmen of the World and Women of Woodcraft, Fraternal Order of Eagles, Yeomen, Ancient Order of Hibernians, Women's Auxiliary of Ancient Order of Hibernians, Knights of Columbus, Independent Order of Red Men, Daughters of Pocahantas, and the Endowment Rank of the Knights of Pythias. See Stevens, comp. and ed., *Cyclopedia*, and Whalen, *Handbook*, for more on which groups offered insurance. Some workers held insurance in independent companies. That was the case with Charles T. Dillon, the secretary of Free Coinage Miners No. 19, who extolled the benefits of the unions in providing sick and death benefits. When Dillon died, his widow, Josephine Dillon, received $1,000 from his life insurance policy with the New York Life Insurance Company. "I, like a great many other good women, opposed my husband taking out this insurance, but did not realize then, as I do now, what a husband's duty was in that respect," she wrote. *Press*, 5 Nov. 1900.

23. *Press*, 17 Dec. 1901; interview with Beulah Pryor, Colorado Springs, Colo., 6 May 1979.

24. *Pueblo Courier*, 28 April 1899; *Press*, 20 Dec. 1900, 11 Nov., 20 April 1902, 16 Jan. 1903, 23 Aug. 1900.

25. The $1,500 raised was in addition to money that local unions contributed. *Press*, 14 July, 16 July, 23 July, 26 July, 30 July, 1 Aug., 2 Aug., 3 Aug., 4 Aug., 5 Aug., 6 Aug., 8 Aug. (quotation), 9 Aug., 10 Aug., 11 Aug., 15 Aug., 18 Aug., 19 Aug., 24 Aug., 26 Aug., 6 Sept., 17 Sept., 9 Oct., and 13 Dec. 1899, 17 March 1900, 9 Oct., 11 Oct., and 14 Oct. 1902.

26. *A Complete City Directory of Cripple Creek*, p. 433; *Cripple Creek District Directory, 1900*, pp. 155–59, 529; *Cripple Creek District Directory, 1902–3*, pp. 137–40, 420–22.

27. *Press*, 10 June 1900, 22 Aug. 1901, 9 Dec. 1899, 14 Dec. 1902, 7 Feb., 23 March, 11 Nov. 1900, 23 Aug., 1 Dec. 1899.

28. "The Pioneer Engineers," *Miners' Magazine*, April 1900, pp. 21–22.

29. "Smoker at Cripple Creek," *Miners' Magazine*, Sept. 1901, pp. 20–22; *Press*, 12 Feb. 1903.

30. See, for example, *Press*, 27 Oct. 1901. Thomas's uncle was a WFM member. Lowell Thomas, *Good Evening Everybody* (New York: William Morrow, 1976, repr. New York: Avon Books, 1976), p. 24.

31. Haywood, *Bill Haywood's Book*, p. 23.

32. Brundage, *The Making of Western Labor Radicalism*, p. 71; R. E. Croskey, secretary of Cripple Creek District Trades Assembly, quoted in Anna Kirk, "Workingmen's Free Libraries," *Press*, 23 March 1902, p. 11.

33. *Colorado Chronicle*, 4 June 1902.

34. *Press*, 8 April 1902.

35. *Press*, 17 Sept. (first quotation), 9 Feb. 1901, 18 Feb. 1902, 3 Dec., 3 Nov. 1901 (second quotation), 20 Jan., 25 Feb. 1903, 23 March 1902; *Colorado Chronicle*, 30 Oct. 1901; Haywood, *Bill Haywood's Book*, p. 128.

36. *Press*, 9 Jan., 27 Jan., 8 June, 23 Feb., 4 March, 22 Nov. 1900; "No. 80 to the Front," *Miners' Magazine*, April 1900, pp. 19–20; "Excelsior Engineer's Union," *Miners' Magazine*, July 1901, p. 32; "From Victor," *Miners' Magazine*, Aug. 1901, pp. 41–42.

37. *Press*, 26 Dec. 1899, 25 Dec. 1902, 30 Nov. 1900, 31 Aug., 1 Sept., 3 Sept. 1899, 3 Sept. 1901, 2 July 1899, 4 July 1902.

38. Oregon was first. It designated the first Saturday in June as Labor Day on February 21, 1887, and in 1893 changed the date to the first Monday in September. *Press*, 31 Aug. 1902, 3 Sept. 1899 (quotation).

39. Free Coinage Miners No. 19 organized the 1899 picnic, and proceeds went to the Coeur d'Alenes strike fund. Cripple Creek Miners No. 40 organized the 1900 picnic, and Victor Miners No. 32 planned the 1902 picnic. *Press*, 13 Aug. 1899, 4 Aug. 1900, 9 July 1902.

40. *Press*, 5 Sept. 1899 (quotation), 3 Sept. 1901; Haywood, *Bill Haywood's Book*, p. 133. For the 1900 parade, see *Press*, 25 Aug. 1900. For other Labor Day programs and lists of contests, see *Press*, 5 Sept. 1899, 29 Aug. 1901, and 31 Aug. 1902. Miners often challenged workers from other mining towns to drilling contests. Prizes as high as $900 were reported. See *Press*, 27 Sept., 25 Sept., 31 Dec., 30 Sept. 1899, 25 July 1901, 11 May 1902, 3 Aug., 13 July 1901. Although machine drills were used in the mines, these were old-fashioned hand-drilling contests. As Ronald Brown noted, the contests enjoyed their most widespread popularity in the early twentieth century, as industrialization and technology made the skills older miners had perfected increasingly obsolete. See Brown, *Hard-Rock Miners*, pp. 53–56, esp. p. 56.

41. *Press*, 2 Sept., 3 Sept. 1899.

42. *Press*, 2 Sept. 1902; "President Moyer's Address to the Cripple Creek Miners at Pinnacle Park," *Miners' Magazine*, 3 Sept. 1903, p. 6.

43. *Pueblo Courier*, 1 July 1898; *Press*, 30 June, 28 June, 2 July, 4 July, 5 July, 6 July 1899. For the 1900, 1901, and 1902 activities, see *Press*, 22 June, 4 July, 5 July, 6 July 1900, 5 July, 6 July 1901, 15 June, 3 July, 4 July 1902.

44. *Press*, 28 June, 30 June, 2 July, 4 July, 5 July 1899.

45. *Press*, 4 July 1899.

46. *Press*, 5 July, 7 July 1899.

47. *Press*, 7 June, 12 June 1900.

48. *Press*, 6 July 1900. See also "The Fourth in Cripple Creek," *Miners' Magazine*, Aug. 1900, pp. 39–47.

49. David Emmons, "Ethnic Cohesion and Advancement: Irish Worker Conservatism in Butte, 1876–1906," *Journal of the West* 31 (April 1992): 59–65, esp. p. 60.

50. Andy Short, who bought Parker's interest in the Topic Saloon in June 1902, participated on the union side of the 1894 strike; he had returned to the District after a brief period mining in the San Juans. Daniel P. McGinley, an officer of Free Coinage No. 19 and a WFM Executive Board member, also briefly owned a saloon in Altman. So did James W. Gaughan, the first permanent president of Free Coinage Miners' Union No. 19 and an 1894 strike activist, who bought a saloon in Altman in 1900. *Press*, 8 May, 17 June 1902, 15 June 1900, 20 Dec. 1902.

51. *Press*, 6 July, 5 July 1899.

52. *Press*, 25 Dec. 1900, 25 Dec. 1902, 22 Dec. 1900, 26 Dec. 1899, 20 Sept. 1902.

53. Even people who were children at the turn of the century spoke fondly of the Woods family decades later. May Wing reported a rumor that the family had supported strikers and their families during the 1903–4 strike, leading to the Woodses' financial ruin. Although oth-

erwise unsubstantiated, this belief reflects the widespread image of the Woods family as friendly to labor. Chapman and May Wing interviews.

54. *Press*, 9 Aug. 1899, 3 Jan., 9 Jan. 1900.

55. *Press*, 27 June 1899, 23 Feb. 1900; "The Gold Coin Club House," *Miners' Magazine*, July 1900, pp. 13–14.

56. Chapman interview.

57. "The Gold Coin Club House," *Miners' Magazine*, July 1900, pp. 13–14.

58. *Press*, 15 Oct. 1901.

59. *Press*, 18 Oct. 1901; see also *Colorado Chronicle*, 23 Oct. 1901.

60. *Press*, 20 Feb. 1903 (first quotation), 28 Dec. (second quotation), 29 Dec. 1901, 6 Dec. 1900, 11 March, 31 March 1903, 16 Sept. 1902; lodge sample.

61. *Press*, 18 Aug. 1900, 27 April 1901, 10 Jan. 1903, 24 July, 4 Aug., 4 July 1901, 27 Dec. 1900, 15 Dec. 1901.

62. *Press*, 5 March, 2 Aug. 1902.

63. *Press*, 20 Dec. 1900. Ryan and his parents were native-born Americans, so I infer Irish heritage from his name. The Rathbone Sisters was an independent and unofficial auxiliary of the Knights of Pythias that admitted women relatives of Knights of Pythias and the Pythian Orders. If Ryan's wife belonged to the Rathbone Sisters, it is likely that he belonged to the KP. See Stevens, comp. and ed., *Cyclopedia*, pp. 280–81; Jayne-Weaver and Wood, *Pythian Sisters*.

64. The following organizations, for which members could be linked with the manuscript census, Teller County, Colo., 1900, were included in the sample: Sheridan Club, Sarsfield Club, A.F.&A.M. (Masons), Ancient Order of United Workmen, Knights of Columbus, IOOF (Odd Fellows), Daughters of Rebekah, Royal Neighbors, BPOE (Elks), Order of the Eastern Star, Women's Auxiliary of Ancient Order of Hibernians, Altman Athletic Club, Knights of Pythias, Rathbone Sisters, Knights of Khorassan, Woodmen of the World, Women of Woodcraft, Knights of St. John, Knights Templars, Knights of the Maccabees, Ladies of the Maccabees, King's Daughters, IORM (Red Men), Daughters of Pocahontas, Degree of Honor, Modern Woodmen of America, Brotherhood of American Yeomen, American Order of Protection, and Fraternal Order of Eagles.

65. Roughly seven of ten persons in the lodge sample were working class (69 percent, compared with 78 percent of District adults), and four in ten were miners (41 percent, compared with 37 percent of adults). These proportions, however, varied from lodge to lodge. For example, 47 percent of the Elks in the sample, 90 percent of the Odd Fellows, 59 percent of the Masons, and 85 percent of the Knights of Columbus were working class. The Kings Daughters and the Sarsfield Club provide two possible exceptions to my generalization about cross-class memberships; both samples, although small, were 100 percent working class. A few lodges operated in the District but were not represented in the lodge sample. With these few exceptions, cross-class memberships were documented for virtually all District clubs and fraternal associations. Three out of four lodge members (74 percent) were married, and 3 percent were widowed. Manuscript census, Teller County, Colo., 1900, random sample of 2,089 adults and lodge sample of 616 adults.

66. *Press*, 16 Oct. 1900. The Maccabees excluded coal miners entirely, as well as persons who made, sold, or were addicted to alcohol. The MWA voided its contract with a member who worked in a prohibited occupation unless he waived his death benefits. Ferguson, *Fifty Million Brothers*, p. 130; Whalen, *Handbook*, p. 69; Stevens, comp. and ed., *Cyclopedia*, pp. 112–22, 154, 158.

67. Ferguson, *Fifty Million Brothers*, pp. 130, 281–88; Whalen, *Handbook*, pp. 31–38; Stevens, comp. and ed., *Cyclopedia*, pp. 229–230.

68. The Endowment Rank was established in 1877. See Stevens, comp. and ed., *Cyclopedia*, p. 265. For classification of specific orders as lodges or fraternal benefit associations and for the benefits each offered, see Whalen, *Handbook*; Stevens, comp. and ed., *Cyclopedia*; and Ferguson, *Fifty Million Brothers*.

69. Sixty-four of 187 members of the Ancient Order of United Workmen, Knights of the Maccabees, Modern Woodmen of America, Woodmen of the World, Fraternal Order of Eagles, Knights of Columbus, and Yeomen were listed as miners on the 1900 census. Lodge sample.

70. David Brundage, "Respectable Radicals: Denver's Irish Land League in the Early 1880s," *Journal of the West* 31 (April 1992): 55, 57; George G. Suggs, Jr., "Religion and Labor in the Rocky Mountain West: Bishop Nicholas C. Matz and the Western Federation of Miners," *Labor History* 11 (Spring 1970): 190–206; James Edward Wright, *The Politics of Populism: Dissent in Colorado* (New Haven: Yale University Press, 1974), pp. 243–45; Foxhoven, *The City of God*.

71. The significance of cross-class association is a matter of interpretation as much as numbers. Emmons notes that three-fourths of the memberships of the Robert Emmet Literary Association and the Ancient Order of Hibernians in Butte were working class. Emmons, "Ethnic Cohesion," p. 61. See also James R. Orr and Scott G. McNall, "Fraternal Orders and Working-Class Formation in Nineteenth-Century Kansas," in *Bringing Class Back In: Contemporary and Historical Perspectives*, ed. Scott G. McNall, Rhonda F. Levine, and Rick Fantasia (Boulder: Westview Press, 1991), pp. 101–17. In the Cripple Creek lodge sample, the proportionate class membership varied considerably. Among the benefit associations, the more restrictive Knights of the Maccabees was 54.5 percent working class, and the Modern Woodmen of America was 53 percent. The AOUW and the Knights of Columbus, both of which offered insurance, were 79 and 85 percent working class, respectively. Although the lodges were generally more working class than orders that offered insurance, the Elks sample was only 46 percent working class, and the Knights of Pythias, 79 percent. Lodge sample.

72. The Providence IORM in 1872 was 53 percent blue collar, the Knights of Pythias in 1875 was 30 percent, and the Odd Fellows was 46 percent in 1877 and 42 percent in 1896. The Knights of Pythias in Belleville, Illinois, were 52.2 percent blue collar from 1874 to 1881, and in Buffalo, New York, were 49.8 percent blue collar in 1891. Cumbler's figures for the Lynn Odd Fellows were 74 percent blue collar in 1908 and 80 percent in 1914, compared with 90 percent in the Cripple Creek sample. The figures for Masonic lodges in different cities are as follows: Providence, 32 percent blue collar in 1874 and 18 percent in 1898; Oak-

land, 20 percent in 1890 and 22, 30, and 56 percent, respectively, in three different lodges in 1912; Boston, 4 percent in 1899 and 16 and 27 percent in two lodges in 1901. Oakland data from Lynn Dumenil, "Brotherhood and Respectability: Freemasonry and American Culture, 1880–1930" (Ph.D. diss., University of California, Berkeley, 1981), pp. 395, 398. For Providence, see John S. Gilkeson, *Middle-class Providence, 1820–1940* (Princeton: Princeton University Press, 1986), tables 9 and 10, pp. 121–22. For Boston, see Roy Rosenzweig, "Boston Masons, 1900–1935: The Lower Middle Class in a Divided Society," *Journal of Voluntary Action Research* 6 (July-Oct. 1977): 119–26, table 1. For Belleville and Buffalo, see Clawson, *Constructing Brotherhood*, tables 3-3, 3-4, 3-5, pp. 98, 100, 105. For Lynn, see John Cumbler, *Working Class Community in Industrial America: Work, Leisure, and Struggle in Two Industrial Cities—1880–1930* (Westport: Greenwood Press, 1979), table 5, p. 46.

73. Not surprisingly, many in the Irish Sarsfield and Sheridan clubs were foreign-born: three of eight Sheridans and thirteen of fifteen members of the Sarsfield Club. Equally unsurprising, most were Irish. The adult population of the District was 77 percent native-born, compared with 76 percent of the lodge sample. Of twenty-eight Elks in the sample, 36 percent were foreign-born, and most first- and second-generation immigrants were of Irish descent. Thirty-eight percent of twenty-one Odd Fellows were foreign-born; 43 percent of twenty-three Knights of the Maccabees; 37 percent of nineteen Ladies of the Maccabees; and eight of twenty-one Knights of Columbus, whereas only 19 percent of fifty-two Knights of Pythias were immigrants. An average proportion of Masons—23.5 percent of thirty-four in the sample—were foreign-born (Canadian, English, and German). Lodge sample.

74. Excluding the Catholic and Masonic orders, the memberships of fraternal benefit associations in the sample (AOUW, Degree of Honor, Knights and Ladies of the Maccabees, Modern Woodmen of America, Royal Neighbors, Woodmen of the World, Women of Woodcraft, Fraternal Order of Eagles, and Yeomen) were 67 percent working class overall (23 percent immigrant) but only 7.5 percent first- or second-generation Irish. The charitable and beneficiary lodges (BPOE, IORM, Daughters of Pocahantas, Rathbone Sisters, Knights of Khorassan, IOOF, Daughters of Rebekah) were 72 percent working class, 22 percent immigrant, and 13 percent Irish. Lodge sample.

75. Ninety-two Democrats, forty-three Republicans, six Silver Republicans, twenty-nine Populists, eight Co-operatives, thirteen Socialists, and five Social Democrats were included in the lodge sample. The Ancient Order of United Workmen, the Elks, Eagles, Pythians, and Red Men all included a variety of political partisans, while the seven politically active Knights of Columbus were either Democrats or Populists and more than half of the Masons whose affiliation was identified were either Republicans or Silver Republicans. Lodge sample and political sample.

76. Heads of households accounted for 55 percent of all lodge members in the sample, married women for 23 percent; 11.5 percent were boarders. The sample includes members of fraternal organizations from 1899 to 1903. These figures represent only their household relationships in 1900. In 1900, 23 percent were single compared with 34 percent of all District adults; 74 percent were married compared with 58 percent of all District adults; 2 percent were widowed compared to 5 percent of all District adults; none were divorced com-

pared with .5 percent of all District adults; and the status of 4 (.6 percent) was not reported compared with 1.6 percent of all District adults. Manuscript census, Teller County, Colo., 1900, random sample of 2,089 adults and lodge sample of 616 adults (figures do not total 100 percent because of rounding).

77. Among the 616 persons in the lodge sample, 18 percent rented compared with 17 percent of all adults; 44.5 percent were not household heads compared with 63 percent of all adults; and the status of 3 percent was unknown. Among the 342 households heads, 32.5 percent rented compared with 46 percent of all adults; there was no information for 6 percent. Manuscript census, Teller County, Colo., 1900, random sample of 2,089 adults (771 of whom were household heads) and lodge sample of 616 (342 of whom were household heads).

78. Among 342 household heads, 78 percent who belonged to Masonic orders owned their homes and 16 percent rented; 57 percent who belonged to both fraternal beneficiary and charitable and beneficiary orders owned and 40 and 37 percent, respectively, rented; and 67.5 percent who belonged to Catholic organizations owned and 22.5 percent rented. The rest were unknown. Lodge sample of 616, of whom 591 belonged to organizations that could be categorized.

79. *Press*, 25 Jan. 1903.

80. Editorial, *Press*, 22 June 1900. James R. Orr and Scott G. McNall argue, for example, that mixed-class fraternal orders in Kansas muted class conflict and promoted an emerging capitalist order by tying workers to the bourgeoisie and inhibiting the formation of working-class organizations. This analysis emphasizes the need to locate the social functions of fraternal orders in specific class and community contexts. Orr and McNall, "Fraternal Orders."

81. *Press*, 25 Jan., 26 Jan., 27 Jan., 6 Feb., 7 March 1901; "Death of Dan P. McGinley," *Miners' Magazine*, March 1901, pp. 3–4.

82. *Press*, 29 Jan., 6 Feb. 1901; "Communications," *Miners' Magazine*, March 1901, pp. 37–40.

83. *Press*, 15 Feb., 16 Feb., 19 Feb., 23 Feb. 1901.

84. Clawson, *Constructing Brotherhood*, pp. 213–42.

85. Ibid., pp. 233–39.

86. Ibid. pp. 236–37.

CHAPTER 5: IMPERFECT UNIONS

1. "Smoker at Cripple Creek," *Miners' Magazine*, Sept. 1901, pp. 20–22. Some of the material in this chapter has appeared in "Imperfect Unions: Class and Gender in Cripple Creek, 1894–1904," *Frontiers: A Journal of Women Studies* 1 (Spring 1976): 89–117, and in *Class, Sex, and the Woman Worker*, ed. Milton Cantor and Bruce Laurie (Westport: Greenwood Press, 1977), pp. 166–202. Reprinted with permission. Portions have also appeared in "Women as Workers, Women as Civilizers: True Womanhood in the American West," *Frontiers* 7 (1984): 1–8, and in *The Women's West*, ed. Susan Armitage and Elizabeth Jameson (Norman: University of Oklahoma Press, 1987), pp. 145–64.

2. "Smoker at Cripple Creek."

3. Smith, *Eighth Biennial Report*, pp. 55–56.

4. Laurence Gronlund, *The Cooperative Commonwealth* (Boston: Lee and Shepard, 1884, repr. Cambridge: Harvard University Press, 1965), p. 44. The cooperative commonwealth was frequently mentioned in the labor press. For one good contemporary description of the concept, see Eugene V. Debs, "The Co-operative Commonwealth," *Appeal to Reason*, 29 Dec. 1900, reprinted in *"Yours for the Revolution": The Appeal to Reason, 1895–1922*, ed. John Graham (Lincoln: University of Nebraska Press, 1990), pp. 63–64.

5. Of persons with occupations listed on the 1900 census, 44 percent of workers were married, as were 50 percent of salaried and clerical workers, 69 percent of proprietors, 44 percent of professionals, and 78 percent of capitalists. Manuscript census, Teller County, Colo., 1900, 1,359 persons who listed occupations in random sample of 2,089 adults.

6. Emphasis added.

7. The assumption that women should not work underground led to considerable resistance when they sought mining employment in the 1970s. Yet in other times and places, mining was not restricted to men. See, for example, Patricia J. Hulden, "The Rhetoric and Iconography of Reform: Women Coal Miners in Belgium, 1848–1914," *Historical Journal* 34 (June 1991): 411–36; Zoila Hernández, *El Coraje de las Mineras: Marginalidad Andino-Minera en Canaria* (Lima, Peru: La Asociación Aurora Viva, 1986); Angela V. John, *By the Sweat of Their Brow: Women Workers at Victorian Coal Mines* (London: Croom Helm, 1980); Domitila Barrios de Chungara, *Let Me Speak: Testimony of Domitila, a Woman of the Bolivian Mines* (New York: Monthly Review Press, 1978); and Lucy Murphy, "Economy, Race, and Gender along the Fox-Wisconsin and Rock Riverways, 1737–1832" (Ph.D. diss., Northern Illinois University, 1995). For some British coal miners, the exclusion—or protection—of women from the mines was a distinct achievement that they sought to extend to their children.

8. Figures for women's occupations from *Cripple Creek-Victor Mining District Directory* and the *Cripple Creek District Directory*, 1902–3. The 1895 *Directory* listed 353 women, of whom 117 (33 percent) listed no occupation; the 1902 *Directory* listed 1,521, of whom 703 (46 percent) gave no occupation. From those who listed occupations, the following figures were computed: dressmaker or seamstress, 11 percent (1895, 1902); rooming house, boardinghouse, or restaurant proprietor, 29 percent (1895) and 21 percent (1902); other proprietor, 6 percent (1895) and 3 percent (1902); clerk, 8 percent (1895) and 12 percent (1902); stenographer, 3 percent (1895, 1902); cook, 3 percent (1895, 1902); laundress or laundry worker, 12 percent (1895) and 9 percent (1902); waitress, 8 percent (1895) and 7 percent (1902); housekeeper, maid, or domestic, 7 percent (1902); schoolteacher, 6 percent (1902); telegraph or telephone operator, 4 percent (1902); and other, 15 percent (1895) and 12 percent (1902). The 1902 figures do not total 100 percent because of rounding. The actual numbers are certainly underestimates; there were both boardinghouse keepers and professionals who advertised in the local press but were not listed in various District directories. Similarly, it cannot be assumed that women's work was fully recorded on the 1900 census, particularly those who worked in their homes and prostitutes, who were underenumerated. Among the various directories and the *Press*, seven women physicians were documented—Susan Anderson, M. Alice Lake, Josephine Paddock, Katherine Polly, Frances Lane, Harriet Collins, and Estelle Lewis—and at least two women dentists—a Mrs. Dr. Sapero and Mabel Young.

9. Stiverson interview.

10. Barbara Welter, "The Cult of True Womanhood: 1820–1860," *American Quarterly* 18 (Summer 1966): 151–74.

11. For discussions of the racial, ethnic, and class biases of the cult of true womanhood with respect to western women, see Jameson, "Women as Workers"; Rosalinda Méndez González, "Distinctions in Western Women's Experience: Ethnicity, Class, and Social Change," in *The Women's West*, ed. Susan Armitage and Elizabeth Jameson (Norman: University of Oklahoma Press, 1987), pp. 237–51; and Robert L. Griswold, "Anglo Women and Domestic Ideology in the American West in the Nineteenth and Early Twentieth Centuries," in *Western Women: Their Land, Their Lives*, ed. Lillian Schlissel, Vicki L. Ruiz, and Janice Monk (Albuquerque: University of New Mexico Press, 1988), pp. 13–33. See also Linda K. Kerber, "Separate Spheres, Female Worlds, Women's Place: The Rhetoric of Women's History," *Journal of American History* 75 (June 1988): 9–39; Susan Levine, *Labor's True Women: Carpet Weavers, Industrialism, and Labor Reform in the Gilded Age* (Philadelphia: Temple University Press, 1984); Alice Kessler-Harris, "A New Agenda for American Labor History: A Gendered Analysis and the Question of Class," in *Perspectives on American Labor History*, ed. J. Caroll Moody and Alice Kessler-Harris (DeKalb: Northern Illinois University Press, 1989), pp. 217–34; and Alice Kessler-Harris, "Treating the Male as 'Other': Redefining the Parameters of Labor History," *Labor History* 34 (Spring-Summer, 1993): 190–204.

12. Levine, *Labor's True Women*, pp. 121, 144–45.

13. Ibid., pp. 148–49.

14. Smith, *Eighth Biennial Report*, p. 47.

15. Mabel Barbee Lee, *Cripple Creek Days* (Garden City: Doubleday, 1958), p. 169.

16. *Press*, 22 June 1902, 14 Aug. 1901; see also *Colorado Springs Gazette*, 15 Sept. 1901.

17. May Wing interview, 6 March 1976, describing the attitude of her father, James McConaghy; Augusta Prescott, "The Kind of a Woman a Workingman Should Marry," *Press*, 15 Feb. 1903.

18. *Miners' Magazine*, Jan. 1900, p. 15.

19. *Press*, 2 Nov. 1900. Lists of delegates to political party conventions from the municipal to the congressional levels from 1900 to 1903 indicate that roughly 20 percent of all delegates were women. The figures range from no women at one Republican gathering to a third at some Democratic conventions. Women were most often elected city clerks or treasurers or county school superintendents. Delegate lists were printed in the *Press*. In 1899 the Goldfield Republican Club admitted women members, and there were also a number of women's political clubs: the Goldfield Women's County Seat Club, the Women's Democratic Club of Cripple Creek (which successfully fought for women's inclusion on an election campaign committee), the Republican Ladies Club, and the Women's Bryan and Stevenson Club. See *Press*, 9 Aug., 11 Aug. 1899, 2 June, 18 Sept., 5 Oct. 2 Oct., 5 May, 7 May 1901.

20. Wright, *The Politics of Populism*, p. 116; Waite was quoted in Charles Hartzell, *History of Colorado during the Turbulent Reign of "Davis the First"* (Denver: C. J. Kelly, 1894), p. 14. See also Billie Barnes Jensen, "The Woman Suffrage Movement in Colorado" (M.A. thesis, University of Colorado, 1959).

21. Carolyn Stefanco, "Networking on the Frontier: The Colorado Women's Suffrage

Movement, 1876–1893," in *The Women's West*, ed. Susan Armitage and Elizabeth Jameson (Norman: University of Oklahoma Press, 1987), pp. 265–76; Wright, *The Politics of Populism*, p. 203; *Gazette*, 16 Nov. 1893, 29 Nov. 1894. The WFM continued to endorse woman suffrage. 1902 WFM Convention, p. 135.

22. *Press*, 5 Oct. 1902.

23. By 1902 there were 106 saloons in the District. *Cripple Creek-Victor Mining District Directory*, pp. 448–50; *Cripple Creek District Directory*, 1902–3, pp. 607–10.

24. *Press*, 23 April 1901.

25. For class differences, see also West, "Beyond Baby Doe," pp. 179–92, esp. pp. 181–86.

26. *Press*, 21 Dec. 1902.

27. *Press*, 20 April 1902, 31 May 1901. R. E. Croskey was thirty-five in 1900, and Nora Croskey was twenty. They had been married one year.

28. *Press*, 25 Dec. 1901.

29. U.S. Department of Commerce, Bureau of the Census, *Twelfth Census of the United States, Manufactures, Volume 8, Part 2* (Washington: United States Census Office, 1902), p. 67; *Press*, 5 Aug., 19 Aug. 1902.

30. *Press*, 5 Aug. 1902.

31. *Press*, 7 Oct. 1899, 5 July 1900, 4 April 1901. Clerks No. 238 may or may not have been an all-women's local. Usually referred to as "Female Clerks," the *Press* once mentioned the "ladies and gentlemen" of the local.

32. *Press*, 17 June 1900.

33. Leland Feitz, *Myers Avenue: A Quick History of Cripple Creek's Red-Light District* (Denver: Golden Bell Press, 1967), pp. 17–18.

34. *Press*, 24 Aug. 1899.

35. *Press*, 4 Feb. 1903.

36. *Press*, 11 Jan. 1903; interview with Lillian Powers ("German Lil"), 7 Nov. 1952, conducted by Caroline Bancroft and Fred and Jo Mazulla, tape in Mazulla Collection, Amon Carter Museum, Fort Worth. For either an interview with another prostitute with a similar story, or, more likely, a fictionalized account of Powers, see Mabel Barbee Lee, *Back in Cripple Creek* (Garden City: Doubleday, 1968), pp. 50–55. Lee called the woman she interviewed "Two Bit Lil" (a name Powers did not use) and fictionalized much of her writing. For more on dance halls and liquor sales, see Mary Lee Spence, "Waitresses in the Trans-Mississippi West: 'Pretty Waiter Girls,' Harvey Girls, and Union Maids," in *The Women's West*, ed. Susan Armitage and Elizabeth Jameson (Norman: University of Oklahoma Press, 1987), pp. 219–34, esp. pp. 22–25.

37. *Press*, 5 Sept. 1899, 23 April, 27 April 1902.

38. *Press*, 4 Feb. 1903 (first quotation), 10 Feb. (second and third quotations), see also *Press*, 3 Feb., 17 Feb., 18 Feb., 3 March 1903.

39. Brundage, *The Making of Western Labor Radicalism*, p. 71; *Press*, 27 Jan. 1900; "The Gold Coin Club House," *Miners' Magazine*, July 1900, pp. 13–14.

40. For example, after the Victor fire destroyed the local demimonde, the *Press* urged the

city council to restrict the trade to a designated neighborhood. *Press*, 15 Aug., 24 Aug., 26 Aug. 1899; *Miners' Magazine*, 4 Feb. 1904, p. 5 (quotation).

41. Prescott, "The Kind of a Woman."

42. *Press*, 30 Jan., 9 Nov. 1901.

43. *Press*, 12 Sept. 1901.

44. *Press*, 31 Oct. 1899; May Wing interview, 21 Oct. 1978; Chapman interview; Beulah Pryor interview.

45. The grounds claimed were desertion (five men, eleven women, one unknown); cruelty or extreme cruelty (one man, nineteen women); failure to support (eight women); cruelty and failure to support (five women); failure to support and desertion (three women); habitual drunkenness and desertion (one woman); habitual drunkenness, desertion, and failure to support (two women); adultery (one woman); and unknown (one man, two women). Taken from the *Press*, 1899–1901. For more on divorce in the West, see Robert L. Griswold, *Family and Divorce in California, 1850–1890* (Albany: State University of New York Press, 1982); Paula Petrik, "If She Be Content: The Development of Montana Divorce Law, 1865–1907," *Western Historical Quarterly* 18 (July 1987): 261–91; and Glenda Riley, *Divorce: An American Tradition* (New York: Oxford University Press, 1991), esp. pp. 85–107.

46. After the 1903–4 strike, for example, John Welch worked outside the District because he would not renounce the union; the family remained in Goldfield. Chapman interview. The instability of mining as well as previous strikes created similar situations for other families.

47. Elizabeth Hampsten, *Read This Only to Yourself: The Private Writing of Midwestern Women, 1880–1910* (Bloomington: Indiana University Press, 1982), pp. 50–51.

48. Anne Ellis, *The Life of an Ordinary Woman* (Boston: Houghton Mifflin, 1929, repr. Lincoln: University of Nebraska Press, 1980), pp. 204–9.

49. Forty percent of the women but only 26 percent of the men lived in nuclear families consisting of a married couple and children. Manuscript census, Teller County, Colo., 1900, random sample of 2,089 adults, less one missing observation.

50. Of 110 widowed persons in the random sample, 32 percent rented, 19 percent owned their homes, 42 percent were not heads of households, and no data exist for 7 percent. Of the 64 household heads, 33 percent were homeowners, far less than the 48 percent District average, the 51 percent of married heads of households, or even the 41 percent of single household heads. Manuscript census, Teller County, Colo., 1900, random sample of 2,089 adults, with one missing observation.

51. Chapman interview.

52. May Wing interview, 21 Oct. 1978; Leslie Wilkinson interview; Chapman interview.

53. May Wing interview, 21 Oct. 1978.

54. Stiverson interview.

55. Beulah Pryor interview.

56. May Wing interview, 6 March 1976.

57. Ibid. The women who told me about contraception all mentioned various methods that May Wing listed. In addition, Anne Ellis wrote of her own attempt to miscarry. See Ellis,

Life of an Ordinary Woman, pp. 193–94. Beulah Pryor said that she had thought some of the women doctors practiced near the red light districts and helped the prostitutes, the only allusion to abortion I recorded. Pryor interview. For more about sexuality, see Jameson, "Women as Workers," pp. 4–5. Although most of the women interviewed were born in the 1890s, several married before 1910, and I base my speculations on the behavior of the older woman who gave them the information.

58. Several women I interviewed expressed these attitudes. Although I have permission to quote them, and they were present when I played their tapes at public presentations, I have elected not to identify specific women's sexual feelings or experiences.

59. May Wing interview, 6 March 1976.

60. *Press,* 26 Aug. 1899; Lee, *Cripple Creek Days,* p. 39; Feitz, *Myers Avenue,* pp. 20, 30; Stiverson interview; Beulah Pryor interview; May Wing interview, 6 March 1976.

61. Spell and Spell, *Forgotten Men,* pp. 118–19.

62. May Wing interview, 6 March 1976; Beulah Pryor interview.

63. *Press,* 21 Dec. 1902. For different constructions of working-class women's purchasing power, see Dana Frank, *Purchasing Power: Consumer Organizing, Gender, and the Seattle Labor Movement, 1919–1929* (New York: Cambridge University Press, 1994); Susan Levine, "Workers' Wives: Gender, Class, and Consumerism in the 1920s United States," *Gender and History* 3 (Spring 1991): 44–64; Dana Frank, "Housewives, Socialists, and the Politics of Food: The 1917 New York Cost-of-Living Protests," *Feminist Studies* 11 (Summer 1985): 255–85; and Temma Kaplan, "Female Consciousness and Collective Action: The Case of Barcelona, 1910–1918," *Signs* 7 (Spring 1982): 545–66.

64. *Press,* 16 March 1902; see also *Press,* 8 June 1902, 29 March 1903, 29 June 1902.

65. *Press,* 21 March 1900, 3 June 1902, 13 Oct. 1900.

66. The Co-operative Party platform endorsed William Jennings Bryan for president in 1900 and favored an eight-hour law, the initiative and referendum, government ownership of public utilities, more rigid inspection of mines and workshops, the prohibition of sweatshops, and the abolition of convict labor, in addition to condemning local officials for issuing permits to gamblers in violation of the law. Nonetheless, the only issue emphasized in the 1899 campaign was eliminating vice, the only platform issue that could be accomplished locally. *Press,* 19 Sept. 1899.

67. The *Press,* 29 Oct. 1899, lauded Hattie Westover, the Co-operative–Populist candidate for school superintendent, for having the "admirable attributes of a true woman." *Press,* 8 Oct. (first quotation), 10 Oct., 13 Oct. (second and third quotation), 21 Oct. (fourth quotation), 6 Nov. 1899.

68. *Press,* 7 Oct. 1902; Feitz, *Myers Avenue,* p. 22.

69. Frank M. Woods of the Woods Investment Company believed that the fact that many District miners were married promoted friendly labor-management relations. In mining camps where married men were the majority, he said, fewer strikes and labor disturbances occurred. Married homeowners "think of their families and their partially paid for homes and will not rush into a needless labor trouble." Single men, in contrast, were more "hot headed simply because they have no reason to fear the consequences, having none but themselves to look after." *Press,* 7 Dec. 1900.

Chapter 6: A White Man's Camp

1. *Press*, 1 Feb., 4 Feb. 1902.

2. Frewen was elected to the state legislature on the Republican ticket later in 1902. Fechyew belonged to Victor Miners No. 32 from at least 1895. Engley, elected attorney general on Davis Waite's radical Populist ticket in 1892, subsequently joined the Social Democratic Party and the Socialist Party. O'Neill, a former Populist state representative and a member of Victor Miners No. 32, joined the Socialist Party in 1901.

3. The ethnic backgrounds of the speakers that could be determined were: native-born, with native-born parents, Bodfish, Mrs. Elder, and Porter; Donnelley and O'Neill were second-generation Irish. Donnelley belonged to the local Sarsfield Club. His wife, Matilda, was a Polish immigrant. Manuscript census, Teller County, Colo., 1900.

4. *Press*, 4 Feb. 1902.

5. The language of race and ethnicity, if used precisely, becomes enormously complicated. Accurate labels would require the terms used by individuals and by outsiders; thus, "Issei," "Mongolian," and "first-generation Japanese immigrant" could refer to the same person. In this volume I have opted for current terms that identify socially significant groups in turn-of-the-century Cripple Creek and have borrowed Evelyn Nakano Glenn's term *racial ethnic* for the complex system of identity and discrimination that defines race and ethnicity in historical relationships. See Evelyn Nakano Glenn, "Racial Ethnic Women's Labor: The Intersection of Race, Gender and Class Oppression," *Review of Radical Political Economics* 17 (Fall 1985): 86–108.

6. Butte and Rossland most approximated Cripple Creek as mature, industrial, metal-mining towns. Butte's population was more foreign-born and included more Austrians, Italians, and Finns than did the Cripple Creek District. Silver Bow County, Montana, which included Butte, went from 35 to 38 percent foreign-born from 1900 to 1910 and was approximately 40 percent second-generation immigrant (40 percent in 1900 and 38.5 percent in 1910). In contrast, not quite half of District residents were first- or second-generation immigrants in 1900. By 1910 Silver Bow County was 3 percent Austrian, 4 percent Canadian, 7 percent English, 2 percent Finnish, German, and Italian, 8.5 percent Irish, and less than 1 percent Greek, Swedish, and Welsh. U.S. Department of Commerce, Bureau of the Census, *U.S. Census, 1910, Population, Volume 3* (Washington: Government Printing Office, 1913), pp. 226, 1156. As late as 1930, 22.5 percent of the Butte population was foreign-born. Among 8,904 immigrants, 1,473 were born in England, 294 in Northern Ireland, 1,303 in the "Irish Free State," 496 in Sweden, 425 in Germany, 794 in Yugoslavia, 945 in Finland, and 158 in Italy. U.S. Department of Commerce, Bureau of the Census, *U.S. Census, 1930, Population, Volume 3, Part 2* (Washington: Government Printing Office, 1932), pp. 21–32. Complaint of Finnish miners in *Official Proceedings of the Twentieth Annual Convention, Western Federation of Miners, Victor, Colorado, July 15–July 26, 1912* (Denver: Great Western Publishing Company, 1912), p. 21 (hereafter cited as 1912 WFM Convention). The Butte Miners' Union referendum to strike in support of the fired Finns lost by a vote of 1,121 to 4,460. For Rossland, see Jeremy Mouat, *Roaring Days: Rossland's Mines and the History of British Columbia* (Vancouver: University of British Columbia Press, 1995), esp. pp. 121–25.

For Bingham, Utah, see Gunther Peck, "Padrones and Protest: 'Old' Radicals and 'New' Immigrants in Bingham, Utah, 1905–1912," *Western Historical Quarterly* 24 (May 1993): 157–78; Gunther Peck, "Charles Moyer and 'New' Immigrants: The Politics of Race and Ethnicity in the WFM, 1910–1912," paper presented at the Western History Association, Oct. 1991; and Gunther Peck, "Crisis in the Family: Padrones and Radicals in Utah, 1908–1912," in *New Directions in Greek-American Studies*, ed. Dan Georgakas and Charles C. Moskos (New York: Pelia Press, 1991).

For the Wyoming coal camps, see Earl Stinneford, "Mines and Miners: The Eastern Europeans in Wyoming" and David Kathka, "The Italian Experience in Wyoming," both in *Peopling the High Plains: Wyoming's European Heritage*, ed. Gordon Olaf Hendrickson (Cheyenne: Wyoming State Archives and Historical Department, 1977), pp. 24, 68, 88. An ethnicity analysis of the 1910 Sweetwater County census appears in Dee Garceau, "'I Got a Girl Here, Would You Like to Meet Her?': Courtship, Ethnicity, and Community in Sweetwater County, 1900–1925," in *Writing the Range: Race, Class, and Culture in the Women's West*, ed. Elizabeth Jameson and Susan Armitage (Norman: University of Oklahoma Press, 1997), pp. 274–97.

For Arizona copper, see Andrea Yvette Huginnie, "'Strikitos': Race, Class and Work in the Arizona Copper Industry, 1870–1920" (Ph.D. diss., Yale University, 1991); Philip J. Mellinger, *Race and Labor in Western Copper: The Fight for Equality, 1896–1918* (Tucson: University of Arizona Press, 1995).

For Mexican-Americans in the regional economy of northern New Mexico and Colorado, see Sarah Deutsch, *No Separate Refuge: Culture, Class, and Gender on an Anglo-Hispanic frontier in the American Southwest, 1880–1940* (New York: Oxford University Press, 1987).

7. This discussion draws particularly on Micaela di Leonardo, *The Varieties of Ethnic Experience: Kinship, Class, and Gender among California Italian-Americans* (Ithaca: Cornell University Press, 1984), esp. pp. 22–24; and Pascoe, "Race, Gender, and Intercultural Relations," pp. 5–18, esp. 12–15.

8. Immigrants dominated the Denver smelting industry from 1878. The original work force was Welsh and Cornish, whom owners quickly replaced with a succession of Irish, Italians, and, in the 1890s, Austrians, Poles, and Germans from Russia. During the 1903 Denver smelter strike, American Smelting and Refining imported some fifty to sixty Mexican-American strikebreakers from New Mexico, but many left. Brundage,*The Making of Western Labor Radicalism*, pp. 16, 153–54. For Mexicans and Mexican Americans in Colorado coal, see Deutsch, *No Separate Refuge*, esp. chs. 4, 5, and 6.

9. Ethnic labels, in 1900 Cripple Creek as today, were awkward and imprecise. "Slavs," for example, included Slavic people and Serbs and were sometimes called "Austrians." The terms *Mexican American* and *Mexican* used in this text refer to persons of Spanish or Mexican heritage and include persons who might use those terms, *Hispanola*, *Spanish American*, or others to identify themselves. Miners migrated back and forth across the U.S.-Mexican border to work. Most Mexican Americans who came to Colorado were natives of New Mexico or other southwestern states, pushed into the wage economy as Anglos gained economic control. See Deutsch, *No Separate Refuge*.

10. See Mann, *After the Gold Rush*, pp. 50–56; Lingenfelter, *The Hardrock Miners*, pp. 6, 103–5, 186, 190, 195, 225; Wyman, *Hard Rock Epic*, pp. 45, 158.

11. D. F. O'Shea, listed as a hotel-keeper on the 1900 census, served as president of the District Trades Assembly and belonged to the Altman WFM local in 1902–3, when he was vice president of the ALU. I included the O'Shea hotel by accident—I literally pulled three code sheets at random from a pile and chose the first boardinghouse or hotel on each. Historians have documented a variety of ethnic residential settlement in the West, from distinct enclaves of ethnically uniform households to transient ethnically mixed neighborhoods, to forced ethnic heterogeneity in coal camp company housing. There are equally diverse opinions about the significance of ethnic community for immigrants. John Bodnar, *The Transplanted: A History of Immigrants in Urban America* (Bloomington: Indiana University Press, 1985) argued that the family rather than the ethnic community provided individuals' primary support. Skewed gender ratios in western ethnic communities pose the issue of what relationships substituted for family for single immigrants. See also Henry B. Leonard, "American Immigration: An Historiographical Essay," *Ethnic Forum* (1987): 9–23; James Barrett, "Americanization from the Bottom Up: Immigration and the Remaking of the Working Class in the United States, 1880–1930," *Journal of American History* 79 (Dec. 1992): 996–1020. For how ethnicity functioned in different western economic and social contexts, see di Leonardo, *Varieties of Ethnic Experience*; Garceau, "'I Got a Girl Here,'" and Emmons, *The Butte Irish*. In western mining towns, residential patterns varied from the ethnic residential enclaves Emmons found in Butte, to the heterogeneous ethnic neighborhoods in Wyoming company coal towns, to the ethnically mixed residential neighborhoods of the Cripple Creek District, where residence was affected by proximity to the mines but homes were privately owned and rented.

12. Of immigrant workers, 55 percent were miners compared with 45 percent of native-born workers. Some 51 percent of all immigrants and 42 percent of the native-born worked in mining-related jobs. Calculated from manuscript census, Teller County, Colo., 1900, 1,360 people who listed occupations in a random sample of 2,089 adults.

13. Mann, *After the Gold Rush*, p. 86; Lingenfelter, *The Hardrock Miners*, p. 7; West, "Five Idaho Mining Towns," table 1, p. 109.

14. Emmons, *The Butte Irish*, p. 13. In 1900 Butte's predominant immigrants were from Austria, Bohemia and Hungary, 444; from Canada, 2,074; from Denmark, Norway, and Sweden, 896; from England, Scotland, and Wales, 1,982; from Germany, 901; from Ireland, 2,474; and from Italy, 133. U.S. Department of Commerce, Bureau of the Census, *Abstract of the Twelfth Census of the United States, 1900* (Washington: Government Printing Office, 1902), p. 106. Among employed immigrants in the random sample of 2,089 adults, manuscript census, Teller County, Colo., 1900, 39 percent of the Canadians were miners, as were 45 percent of the English, 49 percent of the Germans, 52 percent of the Irish, 64 percent of the Scots, 50 percent of the Swedes, and 62.5 percent of the Welsh. A majority (52 percent) of second-generation Canadians in the random sample were miners. Children of English parents were concentrated in skilled working-class occupations: 15 percent were engaged in skilled mining labor, and semiskilled and skilled labor each claimed 17.5 percent each. Sec-

ond-generation Irish were slightly less likely than their parents to be miners or unskilled workers and more likely to be skilled workers. Of ninety-four second-generation Irish, 46 percent were miners, 12 percent were unskilled workers, and 16 percent were skilled.

15. Ronald M. James, "Defining the Group: Nineteenth-Century Cornish on the North American Mining Frontier," in *Cornish Studies Two*, ed. Philip Payton (Exeter: University of Exeter Press, 1994), pp. 32–47; Emmons, *The Butte Irish.*

16. Of heads of households in 1860, 44 percent of the native-born owned more than $1,000 in real property, as did 36 percent of the British, 17 percent of the Irish, and 40 percent of the Germans and Scandinavians. In 1870, 38 percent of the native-born possessed property worth more than $1,000, as did 18 percent of the British, 13 percent of the Irish, and 34 percent of the Germans and Scandinavians. Calculated from Mann, *After the Gold Rush*, table 40, pp. 258, 260.

17. Figures for household heads only. Among all adults, 17 percent of the native-born, 20 percent of immigrants, and 17 percent of second-generation immigrants owned homes. Computed from manuscript census, Teller County, Colo., 1900, random sample of 2,089 adults, of whom 771 headed households.

18. Among immigrant heads of households, 43 percent of the Canadians owned homes, 55 percent of the English, 52 percent of the Germans, 62 percent of the Irish, 56 percent of the Scots, 55 percent of the Swedes, and 33 percent of the Welsh. Manuscript census, Teller County, Colo., 1900, random sample of 2,089 adults, of whom 165 were immigrant heads of households.

19. About the same proportion of adults (34 to 35 percent) were single, regardless of nativity. Nearly 60 percent of the native-born and second generation were married, as were 53 percent of immigrants. Eight percent of immigrants were widowed, compared with 4.5 percent of the native-born and 4 percent of the second generation. Computed from random sample of 2,089 adults, less one missing observation, manuscript census, Teller County, Colo., 1900.

20. *Press*, 1 Jan. 1903, 26 Oct. 1900, 24 Oct. 1901, 6 Aug. 1899, 20 Jan. 1900, 24 Jan. 1903, 2 May 1902, 2 March, 17 March, 15 March 1900, 17 March 1901, p. 1; see also *Press*, 18 March 1903, 14 March 1902, 24 April 1900.

21. Not all Catholics were Irish, nor were all Irish Catholics.

22. Stiverson interview; May Wing interview, 6 March 1976. May Wing's father, James McConaghy, was a Protestant Irish immigrant. Her mother, Catharine Doran McConaghy, was second-generation Irish Catholic. Catharine McConaghy died when May was an infant, and although she had been baptized Catholic May McConaghy was raised Protestant, surrounded by a mixture of Protestant and Catholic relatives. That she was called a Red Neck suggests that the term was extended to all people of Irish heritage or all union supporters.

23. *Cripple Creek District Directory*, 1900, pp. 529–30; Minutes, Carpenters No. 547, United Brotherhood of Carpenters and Joiners of America, meeting of 24 Jan. 1897.

24. Foxhoven, *The City of God*; *Cripple Creek District Directory*, 1900, pp. 89, 112–13, 150–51, 445, 456, 527.

25. *Gazette*, 10 Oct. 1895, 9 April 1896; *Press*, 6 May 1900.

26. *Press*, 24 May 1900.

27. *Twelfth Census, Volume 1*, pp. 576, 740–41, 648; manuscript census, Teller County, Colo., 1900. Estimates of both groups may be low because of underenumeration of the red light districts.

28. *Press* headlines make the point. See "Constable Arrested the Wrong Coon" (1 March 1902); "Burned the Negro Brute" (17 Nov. 1900); and "Negro Ravisher Lynched" (26 March 1902). See also *Press*, 25 Feb. 1902, 18 May, 29 Dec. 1901, 2 Jan. 1902.

29. *Press*, 22 Dec. 1899 (first quotation), 27 July 1901 (second quotation), 17 April 1902, 12 Sept. 1901; see also *Press*, 27 July, 14 Jan., 8 March 1900, 11 Jan. 1902, 5 Oct. 1900, 22 Jan. 1901. Again, *Press* headlines are instructive: "Negro Murderer Filled with Lead" (29 Nov. 1900); "A Young White Man Stabbed by Old Negro" (12 Oct. 1900); "Negro Brute Attacks Young Girl in Pueblo" (3 Feb. 1902); and "Colored Grafter Put out of Town" (6 Oct. 1900). For a description of Poverty Gulch, see Spell and Spell, *Forgotten Men*, p. 123.

30. *Press*, 5 April, 5 Jan. 1900, 29 Jan. 1903, 19 Dec. 1899, 19 Oct. 1900, 2 Sept. 1899, 27 March, 25 Dec. 1902, 10 June 1900, 26 Oct. 1901.

31. *Gazette*, 13 Sept. 1898; *Press*, 27 March 1902, 19 Oct. 1900, 23 July, 26 July 1902.

32. *Press*, 28 Jan. 1900.

33. Haywood, *Bill Haywood's Book*, p. 87. See also article about African American strikebreakers in Illinois, "Murderous Nigger Scabs," *Press*, 30 June 1899.

34. *Press*, 11 Oct., 17 Oct. 1899.

35. *Press*, 24 July, 20 June (quotation), 25 June, 11 Sept. 1901, 28 Jan. 1903; "Argument of the Federation," *Miners' Magazine*, 1 Sept. 1904, p. 6.

36. Minutes, Carpenters No. 547, meetings of 10 April 1900, 9 May 1903, 4 Aug. 1905, 2 March 1906.

37. *Press*, 19 Dec. 1899. The Cripple Creek Hod Carriers' local was not involved in the Victor hod carriers' strike of the same year. The Victor hod carriers belonged to Victor Federal Labor Union No. 64.

38. *Press*, 22 May 1900. There was also a *Press* reference to an African American mine leaser, Sam Long, who worked part of the Eclipse Mine and was found dead in Eclipse Gulch of unknown causes. *Press*, 25 Jan. 1902.

39. *Press*, 8 May 1900.

40. *Press*, 14 March 1901 (first quotation); Stiverson interview (second quotation).

41. *Press*, 21 July 1901, 4 Nov. 1900, 6 Aug. 1901.

42. *Denver Colorado Chronicle*, 10 Dec. 1902; *Twelfth Census, Volume 1*, pp. 740–41. The *Colorado Chronicle* published as an independent Socialist labor paper from 1901 to 1903 before merging with the *Miners' Magazine* in 1903. For how the AFL distinguished between "old" and "new" immigrants, see Gwendolyn Mink, *Old Labor and New Immigrants in American Political Development: Union, Party, and the State, 1875–1920* (Ithaca: Cornell University Press, 1986).

43. *Twelfth Census, Volume 1*, pp. 740–41. The Chinese were the largest single immigrant group in Nevada City in 1860 and 1870 and a majority of Idaho miners in 1870. Banned underground, they worked the placers. Mann, *After the Gold Rush*, pp. 56, 143, table 8, p. 229; West, "Five Idaho Mining Towns," p. 109. The Comstock housed seventy-five Chinese prostitutes in 1875 and twenty in 1880; in 1880, when Butte's Chinese population was larg-

est, twenty-one of the city's thirty-five prostitutes were Chinese, a majority of all Chinese women in Butte. Marion S. Goldman, *Gold Diggers and Silver Miners: Prostitution and Social Life on the Comstock Lode* (Ann Arbor: The University of Michigan Press, 1981), p. 63; Murphy, "Women on the Line," pp. 55–58.

44. Lingenfelter, *The Hardrock Miners*, pp. 5, 118, 107. For more on anti-Chinese politics, see Sucheng Chan, ed., *Entry Denied* (Philadelphia: Temple University Press, 1991); Alexander Saxton, *The Indispensable Enemy—Labor and the Anti-Chinese Movement in California* (Berkeley: University of California Press, 1971); and Roger Daniels, ed., *Anti-Chinese Violence in North America* (New York: Arno Press, 1978).

45. Lingenfelter, *The Hardrock Miners*, pp. 107–9, 112–14 (quotation, emphasis in the original).

46. Ibid., pp. 117–19, 127; see also Smith, *Rocky Mountain Mining Camps*, pp. 29–34.

47. *Gazette*, 10 Sept. 1892.

48. See, for example, an article about Natawyo Hanoye, a prostitute who was badly burned while using gasoline to clean her clothing: "Was Badly Burned," *Press*, 22 July 1899.

49. During the period of unrestricted Asian immigration from 1850 to 1882, more than a hundred thousand Chinese men but only 8,848 Chinese women came to the United States. The Chinese Exclusion Act of 1882 barred all but the wives of the wealthiest Chinese. The extremely unbalanced sex ratio and the exclusion of Chinese men from Caucasian prostitutes created a demand for Chinese prostitutes. Although Chinese prostitutes were at the bottom of the hierarchy in western tenderloins, there were gradations, including high-status, all-Chinese brothels in San Francisco that served Chinese clients. Stanford M. Lyman, *The Asian in the West* (Reno: University of Nevada Press, 1971), pp. 18–19; Goldman, *Gold Diggers and Silver Miners*, pp. 95–98; Lucie Cheng Hirata, "Chinese Immigrant Women in Nineteenth Century California," in *Women of America: A History*, ed. Carol Ruth Berkin and Mary Beth Norton (Boston: Houghton Mifflin, 1979), pp. 224–44; Sucheng Chan, "The Exclusion of Chinese Women, 1870–1943," in *Entry Denied*, pp. 94–146; Yuji Ichioka, "*Amerika Nadeshiko*: Japanese Immigrant Women in the United States, 1900–1924," *Pacific Historical Review* 2 (1980): 339–57.

50. *Press*, 23 Feb. 1901, 25 Feb. 1902.

51. *Press*, 10 May, 31 May 1900 (McDonald quotations), 30 May, 1 June 1901.

52. *Press*, 18 June, 24 Nov. 1901.

53. *Press*, 1 Dec., 3 Dec., 6 Dec., 7 Dec. 1901.

54. *Press*, 4 Dec. 1901.

55. *Press*, 10 Dec., 15 Dec. 1901. For Pollard's position, see "Imminent Menace of the Yellow Man," *Press*, 26 Jan. 1902.

56. *Press*, 1 Feb., 4 Feb., 2 March 1902 (quotation); see also "Labor Notes," *Press*, 9 Feb. 1902.

57. Denver *Labor Enquirer*, 26 Nov. 1887. I am grateful to David Brundage for bringing this article to my attention.

58. Letter to the Editor, in "Labor News and Notes from the District Unions," *Press*, 23 March 1902.

59. From *A.L.U. Journal*, quoted in R. E. Croskey, ed., "Labor Notes," *Press*, 22 Feb. 1903.

60. *Press*, 6 March, 14 May 1902.

61. Brundage, *The Making of Western Labor Radicalism*, p. 156

62. Huerfano County, Colorado, a coal mining area, was 7 percent Austrian, 5 percent Italian, 2 percent Scottish, 1 percent English and German, under 1 percent Irish and Swedish, and 2 percent Welsh. U.S. Department of Commerce, Bureau of the Census, *U.S. Census, 1910, Population, Volume 3* (Washington: Government Printing Office, 1913), pp. 226, 1156; U.S. Department of Commerce, Bureau of the Census, *U.S. Census, 1930, Population, Volume 3, Part 1* (Washington: United States Government Printing Office, 1932), pp. 304, 317.

63. *Press*, 28 Jan. 1900, 1 June 1901; Letter to the Editor, in "Labor News and Notes from the District Unions," *Press*, 23 March 1902, from *A.L.U. Journal*, quoted in R. E. Croskey, ed., "Labor Notes," *Press*, 22 Feb. 1903.

Chapter 7: Class-Conscious Lines

1. *Press*, 29 March 1903.

2. See Fink, "The New Labor History"; Oestreicher, "Urban Working-Class Political Behavior."

3. See Jensen, *Heritage of Conflict*; Perlman and Taft, *History of Labor in the United States*; Dubofsky, *We Shall Be All*; Kerr and Siegel, "Interindustry Propensity"; Laslett, *Labor and the Left*; Brundage, *The Making of American Labor Radicalism*; Brinley, "The Western Federation of Miners"; Foster, "Quantification and the Western Federation"; and Emmons, *The Butte Irish*.

4. 1893 WFM Convention, pp. 19–20; 1894 WFM Convention, pp. 7–9. On the initiative and referendum see *Press*, 3 Jan. 1900, 5 June 1901; *Denver Colorado Chronicle*, 11 June 1902; Wright, *The Politics of Populism*, p. 227; 1898 CSFL Convention, pp. 27, 30. For the income tax, see *Press*, 5 June 1901, 19 July, 3 Aug. 1899; *Pueblo Courier*, 21 April, 19 May, 26 May, 27 Jan. 1899.

5. For a thoughtful discussion of how the political system, particularly geographic representation and election by plurality, created pressures for fusion, see Peter H. Argersinger, *The Limits of Agrarian Radicalism: Western Populism and American Politics* (Lawrence: University Press of Kansas, 1995), pp. 8–16.

6. The sixty patterns were: (1) Democrat; (2) Republican; (3) Silver Republican; (4) Populist; (5) Co-operative; (6) Socialist; (7) Social Democrat; (8) Socialist Labor; (9) Taxpayers Party; (10) Bryan and Stevenson Club (1900); (11) Co-operative/Co-operative–Populist coalition; (12) Populist/Democrat; (13) Co-operative–Populist coalition/Populist; (14) Democrat and Taxpayers; (15) Co-operative/Social Democrat/Socialist; (16) Independent Citizens Party; (17) Co-operative/Democrat; (18) Co-operative–Populist coalition; (19) Populist/Social Democrat/Socialist; (20) Social Democrat/Socialist; (21) Republican/Co-operative; (22) Co-operative–Populist coalition/Democrat and Populist (same year)/Democrat; (23) Populist/Democrat/Socialist; (24) Populist/Republican; (25) Democrat and Populist/Democrat; (26) Silver Republican/Democrat; (27) Populist/Socialist; (28) Bryan and Stevenson Club/Republican–Co-operative coalition; (29) Populist/Silver Republican/Republican/Democrat; (30) Republican-Silver Republican coalition/Republican; (31) Silver Republican-Republi-

can–Co-operative–Populist coalition/Democrat/Republican; (32) Co-operative–Populist coalition/Democrat; (33) Silver Republican/Republican; (34) Republican–Co-operative coalition; (35) Republican-Silver Republican coalition; (36) Republican and Populist (same year); (37) Silver Republican-Republican–Co-operative–Populist coalition/Co-operative/Republican; (38) Co-operative–Populist coalition/Co-operative–Republican coalition/Socialist; (39) Co-operative–Populist coalition/Populist-Democrat coalition/Democrat; (40) Co-operative–Populist coalition/Socialist; (41) Co-operative–Populist coalition/Co-operative/Democrat; (42) Bryan and Stevenson Club/Democrat; (43) Co-operative/Independent Citizens; (44) Populist/Bryan and Stevenson Club/Democrat; (45) Co-operative–Populist coalition/Republican; (46) Populist/Bryan and Stevenson Club; (47) Republican–Silver Republican–Co-operative–Populist coalition; (48) Independent Citizens/Republican; (49) Democrat/Socialist; (50) Democrat and Taxpayers/Socialist; (51) Populist/Co-operative–Populist coalition/Democrat; (52) Democrat-Populist coalition; (53) Republican–Silver Republican–Co-operative–Populist coalition/Republican; (54) Co-operative–Populist coalition/Bryan and Stevenson Club; (55) Silver Republican/Co-operative/Republican; (56) Co-operative and Socialist; (57) Prohibition Party; (58) Co-operative–Populist Coalition/Populist/Social Democrat; (59) Co-operative–Republican coalition/Populist/Socialist; and (60) Populist/Republican/Democrat.

7. The mining West produced its own brand of populism. The best history of Colorado Populism is Wright, *The Politics of Populism*. For more on Rocky Mountain populism, see Robert W. Larson, *Populism in the Mountain West* (Albuquerque: University of New Mexico Press, 1986); and William Joseph Gaboury, *Dissension in the Rockies: A History of Idaho Populism* (New York: Garland Publishing, 1988). For context and useful agrarian comparisons, see Argersinger, *Limits of Agrarian Radicalism*; Scott G. McNall, *The Road to Rebellion: Class Formation and Kansas Populism, 1865–1900* (Chicago: University of Chicago Press, 1988); and Jeffrey Ostler, *Prairie Populism: The Fate of Agrarian Radicalism in Kansas, Nebraska, and Iowa, 1880–1892* (Lawrence: University Press of Kansas, 1993).

8. Wright, *The Politics of Populism*, pp. 103–4, 107, 109, 117–22.

9. Ibid., pp. 128, 145–46, 172; *Gazette*, 14 Dec., 7 Dec. 1893. Waite quote 29 March 1894, in reply to a query from the *New York Press* about whether the people of Colorado approved Cleveland's veto of the Bland Bill, in Hartzell, *History of Colorado*, frontispiece.

10. See *Gazette*, 9 Aug. 1898, for a resolution from the Colorado Republican Party asserting that "the republican party of Colorado is earnestly devoted to bi-metallism." Obviously seeking to woo the Silver Republicans back into the party, it concluded that "members believe that the place for a Republican bi-metallist is within the ranks of the party, and not out of it."

11. *Gazette*, 4 Jan. 1893.

12. Inez Hunt, "The Poverty Marchers of 1894," *Empire Magazine*, 16 Feb. 1969, pp. 14–18; *Gazette*, 3 May, 10 May 1894; see also Carlos A. Schwantes, *Coxey's Army: An American Odyssey* (Lincoln: University of Nebraska Press, 1985), esp. chs. 12 and 13.

13. *Press*, 18 Aug., 19 Aug., 27 July, 2 Aug., 12 Aug., 15 Aug., 17 Aug. 1899.

14. Wright, *The Politics of Populism*, p. 155.

15. *Gazette*, 12 Nov., 19 Nov. 1892 (quotation), 9 Nov., 16 Nov. 1893.

16. Wright, *The Politics of Populism*, pp. 184–91; "Waite's Flag," *Gazette*, 25 Oct. 1894.

17. Waite received 2,964 votes to McIntire's 2,703 and Thomas's 174. *Gazette*, 5 April, 2 July, 15 Nov. 1894, p. 2; John Calderwood to Davis Waite, 11 Nov. 1894, cited in Wright, *The Politics of Populism*, p. 201.

18. *Gazette*, 10 Oct., 7 Nov. 1895.

19. Wright, *The Politics of Populism*, pp. 205–7, 210–11. Cripple Creek gave Bailey 3,060 votes to Adams's 2,100, Waite's 131, and the Republican Allen's 286. *Gazette*, 5 Nov. 1896.

20. See Argersinger, *Limits of Agrarian Radicalism*, p. 133.

21. Wright, *The Politics of Populism*, p. 216; *Gazette*, 13 Sept. 1898. Thomas received some 2,800 votes in Cripple Creek to Wolcott's 900 and took Altman 328 to 60, Independence 154 to 89, Goldfield 309 to 43, Victor 1,113 to 204, Lawrence 318 to 71, and Elkton 300 to 32. *Gazette*, 9 Nov. 1898.

22. *Pueblo Courier*, 31 March 1899; James W. Gaughan, "Coming Duty of the Toiling Masses," *Pueblo Courier*, 1 July 1898; *Press*, 6 Nov. 1899. Gaughan ran for the office on the Co-operative–Populist ticket in 1899 and lost to his Democratic opponent.

23. 1897 CSFL Convention, pp. 33–37. The minutes do not, unfortunately, record the debate. *Gazette*, 6 May 1897.

24. *Denver Clarion Advocate*, 7 April 1899; *Press*, 4 Nov., 5 Nov., 2 Nov. 1899.

25. Denver *Labor Enquirer*, 17 Jan. 1887, 9 Jan. 1886, 19 Feb., 15 Jan., 24 Sept. 1887. My thanks to David Brundage for bringing the *Enquirer* articles to my attention.

26. *Labor Enquirer*, 26 Nov. 1887. Many radicals were upset when Terence Powderly opposed clemency for the Haymarket anarchists, but Callahan's move to the AFL was primarily tactical. Brundage, *The Making of Western Labor Radicalism*, pp. 90–91.

27. Others charged that the Democrats stole the election through election fraud. *Press*, 16 Nov., 9 Sept. (first quotation), 28 July 1899 (second quotation).

28. *Press*, 29 June, 17 Sept., 19 Sept. 1899.

29. *Press*, 4 April, 5 April 1900.

30. See the editorial endorsing the Co-operative slate, *Press*, 20 Oct. 1899.

31. *Denver Clarion Advocate*, 7 April 1899.

32. *Press*, 24 Feb. 1903; 1903 WFM Convention, p. 21.

33. For patronage appointments of union members by Victor's Republican–Co-operative city council, Cripple Creek's Democratic/fusion council, Democratic/fusion Governor Orman, and others, see *Press*, 14 April, 18 April 1900, 3 March, 20 April 1901, 25 May 1900, 2 April 1901.

34. *Pueblo Courier*, 2 March 1900. The following year, however, Curry introduced a resolution at the WFM convention that the union "endorse the Social Democratic Party." 1901 WFM Convention, p. 106.

35. The six locals that voted were Federal Labor Union No. 19, Bricklayers and Masons No. 6, Free Coinage Miners No. 19, Cripple Creek Miners No. 40, Anaconda Miners No. 21, and Cooks and Waiters No. 24; only Cripple Creek Miners No. 40 voted against the proposal. P. N. McPhee of Cripple Creek Carpenters No. 547 and Federal Labor Union No. 19 served as Teller County chair for the new party. The March convention nominated the following Dis-

trict residents: governor, D. C. Copley, Altman; lieutenant governor, W. W. Ferguson, Victor, and James W. Gaughan, Cripple Creek; secretary of state, Charles E. Outcalt, Cripple Creek; attorney general, Eugene Engley, Cripple Creek; superintendent of public instruction, Mrs. E. Crosse, Cripple Creek; regents of the University of Colorado, John Crosby, Teller County, W. W. Lovett, Cripple Creek, C. Clacle, Cripple Creek, and E. Anderson, Cripple Creek; presidential electors, Joy Pollard, Altman, and W. M. Peters, Cripple Creek; and congressman, Second District, D. P. McGinley, Altman. *Press*, 4 Feb., 13 March, 14 March, 17 June, 29 May 1900; CSFL Minutes, meeting of 3 Feb. 1900, pp. 12, 22–23.

36. The votes of (Altman) Free Coinage Miners No. 19 swung this close vote. *Press*, 5 June, 6 June, 7 June, 10 June 1900; "Chronology of the Month," *Miners' Magazine*, July 1900, p. 57.

37. *Press*, 10 June, 15 June 1900.

38. Other nominees from the District included J. E. Seeley of Goldfield, and G. W. Saunders and George Seitz of Cripple Creek. W. H. Fechyew and Charles LaKamp of Goldfield, T. C. Reid of Independence, and S. B. Lawrence and H. J. Donnelley of Cripple Creek served on the state executive committee. Copley served on the WFM Executive Board; Seitz was a trustee and president of Cripple Creek Miners No. 40 and a delegate to WFM conventions and to the Executive Board of the Trades Assembly; LaKamp belonged to Free Coinage Miners No. 19; Lawrence served as financial secretary and business agent of Federal Labor Union No. 19, as a delegate to CSFL conventions, on the *Press* board of directors, and on the Executive Board of the WLU; and Fechyew, who belonged to Victor Miners No. 32, was a delegate to the Trades Assembly and to the CSFL. W. H. Leonard, president of Altman Stationary Engineers No. 75, chaired the local SDP. *Press*, 31 July, 4 Oct. 1900.

39. *Press*, 31 Aug. 1900.

40. *Press*, 26 June, 19 July, 20 July, 24 July, 13 Sept., 15 Sept., 16 Sept., 14 Oct. 1900.

41. "David C. Coates: Fusion Candidate for Lieutenant Governor," *Miners' Magazine*, Nov. 1900, pp. 9–11; *Press*, 5 June 1900. Most Colorado Populists in 1896, except for the die-hards united behind Waite, voted for Democratic presidential electors in exchange for Democratic support for Populist candidates in state races. See Argersinger, *Limits of Agrarian Radicalism*, pp. 15–16.

42. *Press*, 7 Oct., 1 Sept. 1900.

43. Rhines was sentenced to six months in county jail for two counts of assault. Lyons and Tully were sentenced to six and eight years, respectively, for blowing up the Strong Mine, but both were pardoned by Republican governor A. W. McIntire. *Press*, 26 Oct., 28 Oct., 30 Oct., 31 Oct., 1 Nov., 2 Nov., 3 Nov., 4 Nov., 5 Nov., 6 Nov., 9 Nov. 1900. On Lynch, see *Press*, 17 Jan. 1901. Lynch joined the miners' union in Leadville in 1880, and later mined in Rico, Robinson, Ten Mile country, and the San Juans before moving to Cripple Creek in 1894. He had served one term in the state legislature and helped get the 1893 woman suffrage bill on the ballot. In 1901 he was a shift boss on the Gold Coin Mine and an active Democrat.

44. *Press*, 6 July 1902.

45. The *Press* endorsed the Democratic ticket on July 7, 1900. WFM president Edward Boyce also endorsed the Debs-Harriman ticket. *Press* 6 July, 4 Oct. 1900, 5 Nov. 1902; "The Coming Election," *Miners' Magazine*, Nov. 1900, pp. 6–8; "David C. Coates: Fusion Can-

didate for Lieutenant Governor," *Miners' Magazine*, Nov. 1900, pp. 9–11; "Debs and Harriman," *Miners' Magazine*, Oct. 1900, pp. 7–9.

46. The *Press* endorsed Bryan on May 30, 1900.

47. Roosevelt credited Dan Sullivan with "saving" him from the mob and arranged for him to be appointed Cripple Creek postmaster. The *Press* denied any violence, saying, "We were civil—he could not have asked for enthusiasm." *Press*, 11 July (first quotation), 9 July 1899 (second quotation), 27 Sept., 4 Oct., 7 Oct., 25 Oct. 1900; Spell and Spell, *Forgotten Men*, p. 76 (third quotation). The *Press* heralded Bryan's visit, "Ready We Willing Welcome—Greatest Gold District to Entertain the Greatest Statesman of the Age Today" (11 July 1899). Roosevelt, however, elicited "Citizens Welcome Roosevelt but Will Vote for Bryan" and "Lack of Enthusiasm" (27 Sept. 1900). On December 15, 1900, it ran a front-page photograph of Roosevelt captioned "Vice President-Elect Roosevelt is cleaning up his rifle and moulding his bullets for his big lion-hunting trip in Colorado. Dan Sullivan the Cripple Creek Postmaster will accompany him to carry the game bag and protect Teddy from being kidnapped by bold, bad, free silver men of Victor."

48. *Press*, 7 Nov., 8 Nov., 9 Nov., 10 Nov. 1900; Wright, *The Politics of Populism*, p. 218.

49. Shafroth was a Republican until 1896. *Press*, 2 Jan. 1901, 30 July 1902, 3 April, 4 April 1901; Wright, *The Politics of Populism*, p. 218.

50. *Press*, 3 April, 17 March, 23 March, 24 March, 30 March 1901.

51. Roughly 10,500 votes were cast. *Press*, 6 Nov., 7 Nov., 14 Nov. 1901. Hinnen and Meany belonged to Cooks and Waiters No. 24, Provost to Plasterers No. 53 and Federal Labor Union No. 19. Hinnen took 489 votes, Meany, 485, and Provost, 439. The highest Socialist votes in 1902 went to outsiders. Charles H. Norris received 609 votes for secretary of state, and George R. Arnold received 669 votes for state treasurer. *Denver Colorado Chronicle*, 19 Nov., 17 Dec. 1902.

52. *Press*, 14 Aug. 1902; Wright, *The Politics of Populism*, p. 219.

53. The Socialist Labor Party candidate received 31 votes; Provost, the Socialist Party candidate, 446; and the Prohibitionist, 33. *Press*, 5 Oct., 5 Nov., 6 Nov., 15 Nov. 1902; Wright, *The Politics of Populism*, p. 222.

54. *Pueblo Courier*, 27 Jan. 1899, reprinted from *Railroad Telegrapher*; *Press*, 3 Aug. 1899, 8 Nov. 1902.

55. 1893 WFM Convention, pp. 19–20; much of this platform was reiterated in 1894 WFM Convention, pp. 7–9. *Press*, 5 June 1901, 3 Jan. 1900; *Denver Colorado Chronicle*, 11 June 1902.

56. The 1896 vote was thirty-one to thirty-six. *Pueblo Courier*, 2 May 1896; 1896 CSFL Convention, pp. 18, 22; Wright, *The Politics of Populism*, p. 227; 1898 CSFL Convention, pp. 27, 30; *Press*, 5 June 1901; *Pueblo Courier*, 21 April 1899 (quotation).

57. 1897 CSFL Convention, p. 33; *Pueblo Courier*, 21 April, 19 May, 26 May 1899.

58. *Press*, 19 July 1899, 1 Jan., 5 Jan. 1901, 6 April, 16 March 1902. Murphy, a former railroad foreman, was blacklisted for his actions in the American Railway Union strike of 1894. He subsequently studied law to become a labor lawyer. When the Utah state legislature passed an eight-hour law in 1896, the Mine Owners' Association immediately challenged it. Murphy fought the legal battle through the U.S. Supreme Court, which declared it consti-

tutional. As WFM attorney, Murphy re-fought the same legal issues in a number of states and became known as "Eight-Hour Murphy." Address by John O'Neill, *Official Proceedings of the Twenty-fourth Consecutive and Fourth Biennial Convention of the International Union of Mine, Mill and Smelter Workers, Held at Denver, Colorado, August 2d to 12th, Inclusive 1920* (n.p.), pp. 78–79.

59. *Press*, 12 June, 13 June 1902.

60. *Press*, 29 Jan., 22 Jan., 16 Feb., 6 March, 12 March, 2 Feb. 1901, 4 Feb., 26 Aug. 1902.

61. "Declaration of Principles Adopted by the Western Federation of Miners May 18, 1900," *Miners' Magazine*, Sept. 1900, pp. 13–15, 13; *Press*, 6 June 1900.

62. The WLU vote was fifty-three to thirteen. *Press*, 29 May 1901; 1901 WFM Convention, p. 89; *Denver Colorado Chronicle*, 11 June 1902; *Press*, 13 June 1902; *Miners' Magazine*, Nov. 1901, pp. 10–11.

63. Statement of the Organization Committee, 1902 WFM Conventon, pp. 100–101.

64. 1904 WFM Convention, p. 258. In 1902, for example, the WFM, the ALU, and the Hotel and Restaurant Employees, affiliated with the ALU, all endorsed socialism. *Press*, 4 June, 5 June, 6 June, 7 June, 8 June, 13 June 1902; 1902 WFM Convention, pp. 100–101; 1903 WFM Convention, pp. 209–10.

65. George Hooten, a Socialist, was elected mayor of Anaconda in 1902, however, on the Democratic and Taxpayers tickets. Other Socialists may have been elected as nominees of other parties.

66. Smith, *Seventh Biennial Report*, pp. 106, 111, 116, 118–19, 123; Smith, *Eighth Biennial Report*, p. 56.

67. *Press*, 25 Oct. 1900.

68. 1902 WFM Convention, pp. 74, 163–64.

69. In one vote, District delegates favored the Socialist resolution eight to four; in another, ten to four. J. R. Anderson and E. J. Campbell of Cripple Creek Miners No. 40, Charles M. Lamb of the Victor Engineers, and John Curry of Victor Miners No. 32 opposed the endorsement. Favoring it were D. C. Copley of Altman Stationary Engineers No. 75; E. A. Emery of Cripple Creek Miners No. 40; H. W. Fox, Tom Hurley, and W. B. Easterly of Free Coinage Miners No. 19; and Daniel Griffis and John O'Neill of Victor Miners No. 32 and editor of the *Miners' Magazine*. 1902 WFM Convention, pp. 87–88; *Press*, 5 June 1902. Curry changed his mind frequently; he went from opposing independent action to introducing a resolution in 1901 endorsing the Social Democratic Party. 1901 WFM Convention, p. 106; 1902 WFM Convention, pp. 66–69, 106–7.

70. 1903 WFM Convention, pp. 263–64, 266–67.

71. *Press*, 1 Oct., 2 June 1901. Of thirteen board members in 1901, at least five were Democratic Party activists between 1900 and 1902: C. W. Rorke of Anaconda Miners No. 21, Henry King of Victor Miners No. 32, W. F. Lally and Frank Warlamount of Cripple Creek Miners No. 40, and R. J. Doyle of Free Coinage Miners No. 19. Those who supported other parties between 1899 and 1902 included King (Populist); Charles E. Phillips, Cripple Creek Miners No. 40 (Co-operative–Populist and Co-operatives); Charles E. Outcalt of the same local (Silver Republican–Republican–Co-operative–Populist fusion slate); Joy Pollard, Free Coinage Miners No. 19 (Populist, State Labor Party, pro-Socialist in 1902); P. N. McPhee, Cripple

Creek Carpenters No. 547, Federal Labor Union No. 19 (Populist and Co-operative); and W. B. Easterly, Free Coinage Miners No. 19 (Socialist Party). The politics of three are unknown: G. W. Shepard, Federal Labor Union No. 19; W. D. Seighman, Excelsior Engineers No. 80; and W. H. Klugy, Victor Miners No. 32.

72. *Press*, 12 April, 4 May 1902.

73. *Press*, 26 March, 17 Sept., 30 May 1901, 4 March 1902, 8 April 1901, 17 June (first quotation), 11 March (second quotation), 15 April 1902 (third quotation).

74. *Press*, 7 Jan. (first quotation), 14 Jan., 30 Sept., 9 Feb. (second quotation), 11 Feb., 18 Feb., 29 July, 9 Sept., 7 Oct., 12 Oct. (third quotation), 4 Nov. 1902.

75. Provost was also treasurer of the Trades Assembly. *Press*, 18 May 1902.

76. *Press*, 17 Feb. 1901, 13 April 1902, 18 June, 25 June, 7 July, 13 Aug. 1901, 6 July 1902.

77. *Press*, 2 Nov. 1901, 22 Feb., 30 March 1902, 14 Dec. 1901, 19 March, 16 March, 20 March, 21 May 1902; *Denver Rocky Mountain Socialist*, 4 Jan. 1902.

78. *Press*, 21 May 1902; *Denver Rocky Mountain Socialist*, 4 Jan. 1902. W. H. Fechyew and Hans Hansen of Victor and J. C. Provost and James Gaston of Cripple Creek served on the Executive Board.

79. *Press*, 3 June, 19 June, 24 June, 26 June, 16 Aug., 17 Aug. 1902; *Gazette*, 28 Jan. 1897. George Crosby transcribed Debs's speech in the minutes of Cripple Creek Carpenters No. 547, "Speech of E. V. Debs to Cripple Creek Trades Assembly January 24, 1897," in Minutes, Carpenters No. 547, June 29, 1896–October 9, 1897, pp. 155–62.

80. *Press*, 26 April, 27 April 1902.

81. *Press*, 4 May, 1 June 1902; 1902 WFM Convention, pp. 101, 162–64.

82. *Press*, 27 Jan. 1903.

83. *Press*, 9 July 1902.

84. *Press*, 13 July, 15 July 1902. In 1902 the board included six Democrats and two Socialists; the politics of five members are unknown.

85. *Press*, 7 Sept. 1902; *Denver Colorado Chronicle*, 17 Sept. 1902.

86. *Press*, 14 Oct., 16 Oct., 29 Oct., 14 Nov. 1902.

87. *Press*, 4 Jan., 24 March 1903. The board of directors elected at the same stockholders' meeting included Democrats Henry King and A. B. Bernier of Victor Miners No. 32, George D. Hill and J. R. Anderson of Cripple Creek Miners No. 40, and Chris Keagy of Free Coinage Miners No. 19; and Socialists W. B. Easterly of Free Coinage Miners No. 19, R. E. Croskey of Cripple Creek Cooks and Waiters No. 24, J. J. Mangan of Anaconda Miners No. 21, and J. C. Provost of Plasterers No. 52 and Cripple Creek Federal Labor Union No. 19. P. J. Devault of Musicians No. 49 supported the Co-operative Party in 1899 and the Independent Citizens Party in 1903. The politics of Andrew Boyle of Victor Miners No. 32, W. D. Seighman of Excelsior Engineers No. 80 and Banner Mill and Smeltermen No. 106, and J. F. Murphy of Cripple Creek Miners No. 40 are unknown.

88. *Press*, 29 March 1903. For more on CSFL legislative activity, see *Press*, 10 Feb., 15 Feb., 1 March 1903; 1903 WFM Convention, pp. 13, 98–99.

89. *Press*, 23 Dec., 30 Dec. 1902.

90. *Press*, 19. Oct. 1900, 25 Jan., 3 March, 8 March, 29 March 1903.

91. "Colorado State Federation of Labor," *Miners' Magazine*, Sept. 24, 1903.

92. *Press*, 29 March 1903; CSFL Minutes, p. 73.

93. In the random sample of 2,089 adults—less ten persons over seventy-one and eleven under sixteen—43.5 percent were thirty or younger in 1900, 46 percent were between thirty-one and fifty, and 7 percent were between fifty-one and sixty. In contrast, among the sample of persons politically active in 1900, 76.5 percent of Democrats, 45.5 percent of Republicans, 63 percent of Populists, 90 percent of Social Democrats, and 59 percent of the members of the Bryan and Stevenson Club were between the ages of thirty-one and fifty, and 36 percent of Republicans were between fifty-one and sixty. For parties active in years other than 1900, the full sample confirms the pattern: 80 percent of the Democrats, 65 percent of the Republicans, 61 percent of the Silver Republicans, 69 percent of the Populists, 75 percent of the Co-operatives, and 68 percent of the Socialists were between thirty-one and fifty. Nineteen percent of Republicans and 39 percent of Silver Republicans were between fifty-one and sixty.

94. *Gazette*, 25 Feb. 1897, 20 July 1900, 20 Sept. 1898, 6 Aug. 1899, 18 April 1900.

95. In the random sample of 2,089 adults, less two for whom data are incomplete, 48 percent lived in nuclear family households in 1900, 13 percent in extended families, and 17 percent in augmented families (families and boarders). No political activists were dramatically under-represented in any category; some groups exceeded the 48 percent average for nuclear families by at least 10 percent: 77 percent of Silver Republicans, 64 percent of Populists, 60.5 percent of Socialists, 80 percent of Social Democrats, and 59 percent of the Bryan and Stevenson Club. The proportions living in extended or augmented families all ranged within 5 percent of the average and were generally higher than average.

96. In 1900, compared with 58 percent of all District adults who were married, 74 percent of activist Democrats, 88 percent of Republicans, 92 percent of Silver Republicans, 78 percent of Populists, 68 percent of Co-operatives, 68 percent of Socialists, 80 percent of Social Democrats, and 75 percent of Co-operative–Populists were married. Calculated from political sample and 1900 manuscript census, Teller County, Colo., 1900; District figures from random sample of 2,089 adults, with two missing observations.

97. Among the activists identified, women numbered 18 percent of Democrats, 9 percent of Republicans, 14.5 percent of Populists, 5 percent of Socialists, and 74 percent of the membership of the Bryan and Stevenson Club. Calculated from political sample and manuscript census, Teller County, Colo., 1900.

98. In the full sample, 63 percent of the Democratic and Republican heads of households and 60 percent of the Silver Republicans owned homes. Manuscript census, Teller County, Colo., 1900, and political sample.

99. Among all activists, 23 percent were immigrants and 77 percent were native-born; 48 percent were native-born children of native-born parents. The political sample included 122 immigrants and 149 second-generation immigrants. By far the largest group was Irish: forty-four first-generation and seventy-seven second-generation. Most clustered in the Democratic Party leadership—66 percent of the Irish immigrants and 69 percent of the second-generation. This, however, also reflected the fact that there were many more Democrats in the sample because Democrats published precinct delegate lists. The Irish also represented 45.5 percent of all immigrants (first- and second-generation) affiliated with either the Socialist or Social Democratic parties, and first- and second-generation Irish accounted for almost half

(47 percent) of immigrant Populists. Manuscript census, Teller County, Colo., 1900 and political sample.

100. Among those politically active in the 1900 elections, 54 percent of Democratic activists, 27 percent of Republicans, 53 percent of Populists, 100 percent of Social Democrats, and 59 percent of the Bryan and Stevenson Club was working class, compared with 79 percent of all District adults. Class figures are less reliable for the whole sample because occupations could change over time but in general produced higher working-class totals than for the 1900 sample. The largest discrepancy occurred among Populists (69 percent overall).

101. Of all the political activists, some 29 percent of Democrats belonged to unions, 22 percent of Republicans, 39 percent of Silver Republicans, 47 percent of Populists, 54 percent of Co-operatives, 71 percent of Socialists, and 70 percent of Social Democrats. The comparable figures for those active in the 1900 election were 21 percent of the Democrats, 3 percent of Republicans, 33 percent of Silver Republicans, 34 percent of Populists, 20 percent of Cooperatives, and 70 percent of Social Democrats. Calculated from political sample and manuscript census, Teller County, Colo., 1900. These figures, of course, are only rough indices because other activists may have belonged to unions. For local union affiliations by party, consult Appendix E in Jameson, "High-Grade and Fissures," pp. 534–42.

102. Populists and Socialists almost equaled Democrats numerically among state and national union leaders despite the fact that the sample was skewed to include more Democrats because of the selection process for party convention delegates. The major parties elected precinct delegates and published their names. The Socialists and Populists opened their conventions to anyone who chose to attend and did not, therefore, publish delegates' names. That difference accounts in part for the differences in sample size among the parties (Appendix A).

103. Political sample and union sample. The exact percentages are hardly precise. Other persons were certainly prominent in both politics and the unions, but the high level of union involvement in the various parties remains significant. For the Independent Citizens Party and the Taxpayers Party, both one-election parties in Anaconda, the only identified members were working class. However, the "samples" consist of three persons each, in communities where virtually everyone was working class.

104. In 1900, 38 percent of District adults lived in the town of Cripple Creek: 38 percent of the Democratic activists, 45 percent of the Republicans, 77 percent of the Silver Republicans, 34.5 percent of the Populists, 18 percent of the Co-operatives, 34 percent of the Socialists, 30 percent of the Social Democrats, and 74 percent of the Bryan and Stevenson members. Victor housed 24 percent of District adults: 34 percent of the Democrats, 36.5 percent of the Republicans, and 24 percent of the Socialists but only 15 percent of the Silver Republicans, 16 percent of the Populists, 14 percent of the Co-operatives, 10 percent of the Social Democrats, and 11 percent of the Bryan and Stevenson Club members. Calculated from political sample and manuscript census, Teller County, Colo., 1900.

105. *Press*, 23 Oct., 22 Oct. 8 Nov., 9 Nov. 1899, 28 Oct. 1900.

106. See, for example, *Press*, 13 July 1899; "The Trip to the Cripple Creek District," *Miners' Magazine*, June 1900, pp. 21–22.

107. *Press*, 8 Oct. 1899, 11 Feb. 1900.

108. For Altman, see "Altman Populists," *Press*, 17 March 1900; for Goldfield, see "The Populist Side," *Press*, 19 March 1900; Wright, *The Politics of Populism*, pp. 226–49.

109. Minutes of Local Union 547, United Brotherhood of Carpenters and Joiners of America, 1895–1904.

110. *Press*, 8 Sept. 1900, p. 2.

111. Jenson, *Heritage of Conflict*; Kerr and Siegel, "Interindustry Propensity"; Perlman and Taft, *History of Labor in the United States*, p. 173; Dubofsky, "The Origins of Western Working Class Radicalism"; Dubofsky, *We Shall Be All*, p. 35; Lingenfelter, *The Hardrock Miners*; Laslett, *Labor and the Left*, pp. 241–86. The various explanations include frontier lawlessness, the lack of a stabilizing middle class, social isolation, and responses to rapid and dislocating industrialization. For works that dispute the characterization of the union as radical, see Brinley, "The Western Federation of Miners"; and Brown, *Hard-Rock Miners*; Foster, "Quantification," 141–48, esp. 143, argues that the WFM was not radical because "the mean number of violent, labor-related outbursts was only 0.785 incidents in the lifetime of the average local (about seven years)." Another way to express this statistic is that a local stood a 78.5 percent chance of an "outbreak" and, given the high geographic mobility of mining labor, it was likely that most had experienced a labor confrontation or knew someone who had. Thus, even by this narrow definition of radicalism Foster's data do not support his conclusion. In "Conflict and Consensus," Peterson concludes that labor relations in the industry were generally good. For a more sophisticated approach that also concludes, partially based on Peterson, that the union's radical period was brief and western miners more moderate than they have been portrayed, see Wyman, *Hard Rock Epic*. Emmons, *The Butte Irish*, esp. chs. 6 and 7, argued that Butte's Irish working class was conservative because it emphasized job stability and was engaged in no major strikes. For a heated debate about the existence and causes of class conflict in the mining West, see "The I.W.W.: An Exchange of Views," pp. 355–72; and Preston, "Shall This Be All?" pp. 437–38, 442. For a more complex assessment of labor's changing politics in Denver that reinforces this analysis of Cripple Creek, see Brundage, *The Making of Western Labor Radicalism*.

112. In 1902 the delegates from Butte Miners No. 1 split four to four on the issue, with two not voting. Those in favor included Joseph Shannon, William Haggerty, T. J. Gilmore, and Thomas Brennan; those opposed were James P. Murphy, Frank L. Reber, Joseph Calloway, and Edward Hughes. One delegate from Butte Stationary Engineers No. 83, M. J. Elliott, voted for the motion; Malcolm Gillis, B. M. Lindsay, and Joseph Corby voted against it. Both delegates from Butte Mill and Smeltermen No. 74, Charles Whitely and Henry Rhinehart, voted for the resolution. In 1903 the roll call was a resolution to table the motion. That year the delegates from Butte Miners No. 1 voted unanimously to table, the two delegates from Mill and Smeltermen No. 74 favored socialism, and the two delegates from Stationary Engineers No. 83 split. Delegate John F. Smith from No. 74 said that "education along working class politics should be continued. . . . We should fight the cause of our present condition, and that means the abolition of private ownership of industry." John McMullen of No. 83, who opposed the resolution, said that "all kinds of economic and political questions should be discussed in our unions." 1902 WFM Convention, pp. 96, 66–67; 1903 WFM Convention, pp. 253–54, 266. In 1902 Delegate Ives from the Butte WLU said that "the capi-

talist system would continue so long as the workers divided their votes with the old political parties."

113. On the politics of the Knights of Labor, see Leon Fink, *Workingmen's Democracy: The Knights of Labor and American Politics* (Urbana: University of Illinois Press, 1983); Brundage, *The Making of Western Labor Radicalism*. On the Knights and the movement against contract prison labor in Albany, see Greenberg, *Worker and Community*.

114. See Preston, "Shall This Be All?" Schwantes suggested that the "bindlestiffs," or migratory, more single workers, were the radicals of western labor, whereas the sedentary "home guard" was conservative. "The home guards put down roots, raised families, and, if unionized, after the 1880s accepted to some degree the conservative outlook of the American Federation of Miners and the railway brotherhoods. Yet from their enclaves the mobile, industry-rather-than-craft-oriented bindlestiffs nurtured a tradition of all-inclusive unionism and a spirit of militance that extended from the Knights of Labor in the 1880s to the radical Industrial Workers of the World three decades later." Carlos A. Schwantes, "The Concept of the Wageworkers' Frontier: A Framework for Future Research," *Western Historical Quarterly* 18 (Jan. 1987): 39–55, p. 44. Cripple Creek suggests the opposite.

115. H. W. Fox of Free Coinage No. 19 to 1902 WFM Convention, *Press*, 5 June 1902.

CHAPTER 8: "AS IF WE LIVED IN FREE AMERICA"

1. Reports of the Decoration Day parades from John Harper, former president of Local No. 32 and manager of the Victor WFM cooperative store and Frank Cochrane, secretary of Local No. 32. 1904 WFM Convention, pp. 228, 237–38, 241–43.

2. *Press*, 19 Feb. 1903; *Labor Disturbances*, pp. 112–13; *Press*, 15 Feb. 1903, 11 March 1903; 1903 WFM Convention, pp. 115–19.

3. *Labor Disturbances*, pp. 114–16; *Press*, 26 Feb. 1903, 1 March 1903, 18 Feb. 1903, 19 Feb. 1903, 20 Feb. 1903, 21 Feb. 1903, 22 Feb. 1903, 4 March 1903, 6 March 1903, 7 March 1903; Suggs, *Colorado's War*, pp. 48–50.

4. *Press*, 8 March 1903, 10 March 1903.

5. For Peabody's ties to conservative employers' movements, see Suggs, *Colorado's War*.

6. Ibid., ch. 4, "Link Up: Peabody and the Employers' Movement," pp. 65–83, esp. pp. 76–77, 81–83. For Moyer's arrest, see esp. pp. 167–77.

7. For other accounts, see Suggs, *Colorado's War*, pp. 84–117; Dubofsky, *We Shall Be All*, pp. 49–55; Jenson, *Heritage of Conflict*, pp. 118–50; Rastall, *Labor History*; Langdon, *The Cripple Creek Strike*; Haywood, *Bill Haywood's Book*, pp. 108–73.

8. Union members who held public office in Teller County in 1903 included Sheriff Henry M. Robertson, Under Sheriff James Gaughan, Coroner M. J. Doran, and the county clerk and assessor; in Victor, Day Marshal Michael J. O'Connell, Night Marshal Michael Lamb, Street Commissioner Simon O'Rourke, Fire Chief J. Murphy, Jr., Jailer James Printy, Aldermen J. Murphy, Sr., James J. Tobin, and Hugh Healy, and four police officers; in Goldfield, Police Magistrate H. P. Kean, Day Marshal J. J. Brothers, Night Marshal R. C. McCarthy, and all six aldermen; in Independence, Marshal Harvey Starbuck; in Anaconda, Aldermen A. Peterson, Burt Hutchinson, and Paul Hensen; and Altman Justice of the Peace J. W. Cooper. Officials not identified with organized labor were Cripple Creek mayor W. L.

Shockey; Victor mayor F. D. French; District judges W. P. Seeds, L. W. Cunningham, and R. E. Lewis; District Attorney Henry Trowbridge; Assistant District Attorney J. C. Cole; and County Commissioners W. C. Saunders and E. W. Pfeiffer.

9. Peabody appointed Bell after the Colorado City strike began, on February 20, 1903. *Labor Disturbances*, pp. 147–48; Suggs, *Colorado's War*, p. 81. Labor's changing opinion of Bell was reflected in the *Press's* headlines: "Sherman Bell's Appointment Is Popular," 22 Feb. 1903; "General Bell Returns," 24 Feb. 1903; "'Majah' Bell, Blatherskite," 13 March 1903; "A Chronic Disturber," 21 March 1903. On Bell's salary, see also George Graham Suggs, Jr., "Colorado Conservatives versus Organized Labor: A Study of the James Hamilton Peabody Administration, 1903–1905" (Ph.D. dissertation, University of Colorado, 1964), p. 194.

10. Suggs, *Colorado's War*, pp. 51, 54; *Labor Disturbances*, pp. 117–18; *Press*, 13 March 1903.

11. *Press*, 20 March 1903.

12. *Labor Disturbances*, pp. 118–19, 123; *Press*, 13 March 1903, 14 March 1903, 15 March 1903.

13. Other affected mines were the Stratton's Independence, the Ajax, the Mary McKinney, the Isabella, the Mountain Beauty, the Elkton, the Thompson, and the Blanche. *Labor Disturbances*, p. 120; *Press*, 17 March 1903.

14. *Labor Disturbances*, pp. 120–21.

15. Ibid., p. 121; *Press*, 18 March, 19 March, 20 March, 21 March, 22 March 1903.

16. *Labor Disturbances*, pp. 123–26; *Press*, 25 March, 26 March, 27 March, 28 March, 31 March 1903; 1903 WFM Convention, pp. 26–28, 115–19, 169–70.

17. 1903 WFM Convention, pp. 125–40.

18. Ibid., pp. 169–71; Suggs, *Colorado's War*, p. 85.

19. The paper had a $1,500 mortgage on its property, and $4,340 in debts, balanced by a plant worth $7,300. 1903 WFM Convention, p. 171; Western Federation of Miners Executive Board Minutes, June, 1902–July, 1907, meeting of 23 May 1903, p. 56, WFM Collection, (hereafter cited as WFM Executive Board Minutes).

20. *Labor Disturbances*, pp. 160–61.

21. Ibid., pp. 162–65; "The Situation in the Cripple Creek District," *Miners' Magazine*, 27 Aug. 1903, pp. 7–8; "President Moyer's Address to the Cripple Creek Miners at Pinnacle Park," *Miners' Magazine*, 3 Sept. 1904, p. 6.

22. "The Strike Situation in the Cripple Creek District," *Miners' Magazine*, 3 Sept. 1903, p. 7. Sympathizers sent all sorts of aid. The Socialist Party of Carbondale, Colorado, for example, sent $12 and offered to send a carload of potatoes, because most of its members were farmers. "Western Federation Notes," *Miners' Magazine*, 15 Oct. 1903, pp. 7–8.

23. *Labor Disturbances*, pp. 165–66, 170–75.

24. Ibid., pp. 175–76.

25. Ibid., pp. 176–79; "Governor Peabody Loyal to the Corporations," *Miners' Magazine*, 10 Sept. 1903, pp. 5–6; "Statement of the Western Federation of Miners on the Conflicts in Colorado," *Miners' Magazine*, 10 Sept. 1903, p. 7; "The W. F. of M. Enters a Protest," *Miners' Magazine*, 10 Sept. 1903, p. 8.

26. Dubofsky, *We Shall Be All*, p. 50. McClelland, a lieutenant at the start of the strike, was promoted to major before uttering his famous remark.

27. *Labor Disturbances*, pp. 79–80; "Extermination the Ultimatum," *Miners' Magazine*, 17 Sept. 1903, p. 5; Operative C. H. R. Reports, 9 Sept. 1903, Pinkerton Detective Agency Reports, UCB (hereafter cited as Pinkerton Reports). This detective probably worked for MacNeill. Pinkerton regional manager James McParland reported that MacNeill had been a Pinkerton client periodically from 1892, "and we have at present three operatives detailed on work for him." Ibid. However, other operatives may have worked for different owners. Earlier in the strike, the WFM locals reported that they had discovered seven Pinkertons working under cover as union members. *Press*, 19 March 1903.

28. Gaughan, appointed the first Teller County clerk, lost his first electoral bid for the office. In 1903 he served as deputy sheriff under fellow WFM member Henry Robertson. *Labor Disturbances*, pp. 181–83.

29. Ibid., pp. 184–87; *Miners' Magazine*, 17 Sept. 1903, p. 9; *Pueblo Labor Advocate*, 18 Sept. 1903; "The Governor of Colorado," *Miners' Magazine*, 24 Sept. 1903, pp. 4–5; "The Cripple Creek Situation," *Miners' Magazine*, 1 Oct. 1903, p. 7.

30. Ibid.

31. *Labor Disturbances*, p. 188; "The Cripple Creek Situation," *Miners' Magazine*, 8 Oct. 1903, p. 6.

32. *Labor Disturbances*; "The Cripple Creek Situation," *Miners' Magazine*, 8 Oct. 1903, p. 6.

33. "The Cripple Creek Situation," *Miners' Magazine*, 8 Oct. 1903, p. 6; *Labor Disturbances*, p. 188; Operative C. H. R. Reports, Cripple Creek, 26 Sept. 1903, Pinkerton Reports; "Report of the Operations and Administration of the Troops of the First Brigade National Guard of Colorado on Duty in the Cripple Creek Mining District from September 4, 1903 to April 12, 1904, Edward Verdeckberg, Colonel First Infantry First Brigade, N. G. C. Commanding," p. 29, Edward Verdeckberg Papers, CSHS (hereafter cited as Verdeckberg Papers).

34. *Miners' Magazine*, 29 Oct. 1903, p. 4; "The Cripple Creek Situation," *Miners' Magazine*, 22 Oct. 1903, p. 8; "Situation in the Cripple Creek District," *Miners' Magazine*, 5 Nov. 1903, p. 7; "Situation in the Cripple Creek District," *Miners' Magazine*, 12 Nov. 1903, p. 6; "Situation in the Cripple Creek District," *Miners' Magazine*, 19 Nov. 1903, pp. 8–9; Executive Board Report, WFM Executive Board Minutes, meeting of 12 Dec. 1903, p. 129; WFM Executive Board Minutes, meeting of 1 Dec. 1903, pp. 82, 85, 87–88; *Miners' Magazine*, 3 Dec. 1903, p. 4. The number of soldiers on duty at any given time is unclear. *Labor Disturbances*, for example, reported 200 on October 20; Peabody said there were 317 before October 13. However, National Guard records indicate that 647 soldiers were on duty on October 31 and that a new camp, Camp Economic Mill, was established on November 4, 1903. Verdeckberg Papers, p. 30.

35. "Western Federation Notes," *Miners' Magazine*, 29 Oct. 1903, pp. 7–8; *Miners' Magazine*, 12 Nov. 1903, pp. 4, 6. Devault was an appropriate representative for independent labor politics. The only previous political affiliation I could identify for him was with labor's Cooperative Party in 1899.

36. *Labor Disturbances*, pp. 189–90.

37. Ibid., pp. 190–91; Defense Attorney Richardson's notes, affidavits, and related mate-

rial 1906 to 1909, *State of Idaho vs. Steve Adams*, p. 27, WFM Collection (hereafter cited as Richardson Notes), p. 75.

38. *Labor Disturbances*, pp. 191–92. See also "The Situation in Colorado," *Miners' Magazine*, 25 Feb. 1904, pp. 10–11; "The Situation in Colorado," *Miners' Magazine*, 3 March 1904, pp. 8–10; "The Situation in Colorado," *Miners' Magazine*, 10 March 1904, pp. 7–11; *Miner's Magazine*, 10 March 1904, p. 4; *Miners' Magazine*, 24 March 1903, p. 3; "The Situation in Colorado," *Miners' Magazine*, 24 March 1904, pp. 9–10; "The Situation in Colorado," *Miners' Magazine*, 2 June 1904, p. 11. By the time Rollestone testified, he was serving as first lieutenant of Company L, composed of members of the Victor Citizens' Alliance. Trowbridge justified dropping the charges against McKinney by claiming that since the jury had acquitted the other defendants it was inconsistent to charge McKinney.

39. *Labor Disturbances*, pp. 192–93; "The Situation in Colorado," *Miners' Magazine*, 26 Nov. 1903, p. 7. The *Miners' Magazine* identified those arrested for the crime as C. G. Kennison, W. F. Davis, Sherman Parker, John Schoolcraft, Gus Johnson, J. B. Isbell, Bob Rowland, Victor Poole, Harry Williams, Ed Fleming, H. P. Jones, Frank Crase, and Bob Adams. "Bob" Adams was probably a misprint for Steve Adams. "Western Federation Notes," *Miners' Magazine*, 26 Nov. 1903, p. 8.

40. "The Situation in Colorado," *Miners' Magazine*, 26 Nov. 1903, p. 7.

41. Suggs, *Colorado's War*, p. 103; *Labor Disturbances*, pp. 207, 209, 213; Verdeckberg Papers, 30 Nov. 1903.

42. *Denver Post*, 9 Dec. 1903.

43. *Labor Disturbances*, pp. 215–16; "The Situation in Colorado," *Miners' Magazine*, 17 Dec. 1903, pp. 9, 11–13; "The Situation in Colorado," *Miners' Magazine*, 7 Jan. 1904, p. 10.

44. *Labor Disturbances*, pp. 209–10.

45. Ibid., p. 213.

46. Ibid., pp. 214–15; "The Situation in Colorado," *Miners' Magazine*, 17 Dec. 1903, pp. 9–10; "The Situation in Colorado," *Miners' Magazine*, 7 Jan. 1904, p. 9; Verdeckberg Papers, pp. 12–13.

47. *Labor Disturbances*, pp. 216–17; "The Situation in Colorado," *Miners' Magazine*, 17 Dec. 1903, pp. 8–14; "The Situation in Colorado," *Miners' Magazine*, 14 Jan. 1904, p. 9; "The Situation in Colorado," *Miners' Magazine*, 21 Jan. 1904, pp. 8, 11; "The Situation in Colorado," *Miners' Magazine*, 3 March 1904, p. 10. Despite the intimidation of Baker, a fourth cooperative store opened in Goldfield on December 21.

48. *Labor Disturbances*, pp. 216–18; "The Situation in Colorado," *Miners' Magazine*, 7 Jan. 1904, p. 10; "The Situation in Colorado," *Miners' Magazine*, 14 Jan. 1904, pp. 9–11.

49. *Labor Disturbances*, pp. 218–19, 223; "The Situation in Colorado," *Miners' Magazine*, 28 Jan. 1904, pp. 10–12; "The Situation in Colorado," *Miners' Magazine*, 4 Feb. 1904, p. 6; *Miners' Magazine*, 4 Feb. 1904, p. 4; "The Situation in Colorado," *Miners' Magazine*, 11 Feb. 1904, pp. 8–9.

50. *Labor Disturbances*, pp. 220–23; *Miners' Magazine*, 4 Feb. 1904, pp. 3–4; "Western Federation Notes," *Miners' Magazine*, 4 Feb. 1904, p. 9.

51. *Labor Disturbances*, pp. 218–19; *Miners' Magazine*, 11 Feb. 1904, pp. 8–9.

52. Verdeckberg Papers, pp. 12–13; *Pueblo Labor Advocate*, 18 March 1904; "The Situation in Colorado," *Miners' Magazine*, 18 March 1904, p. 10; *Labor Disturbances*, p. 223.

53. "The Situation in Colorado," *Miners' Magazine*, 11 Feb. 1904, p. 9. The United Mine Workers, which represented the Horse Show miners, organized coal miners; the Western Federation of Miners organized hard-rock metal miners.

54. "The Situation in Colorado," *Miners' Magazine*, 17 Dec. 1903, pp. 11, 14; "Significant Letters," *Miners' Magazine*, 24 Dec. 1903, pp. 6–7; "The Situation in Colorado," *Miners' Magazine*, 24 Dec. 1903, p. 8; "The Situation in Colorado," *Miners' Magazine*, 31 Dec. 1903, p. 10; "The Situation in Colorado," *Miners' Magazine*, 7 Jan. 1904, p. 7; *Miners' Magazine*, 18 March 1904, p. 4; "The Situation in Colorado," *Miners' Magazine*, 18 March 1904, p. 10; "The Situation in Colorado," *Miners' Magazine*, 31 March 1904, p. 9; *Labor Disturbances*, pp. 224–28.

55. McCabe Miners' Union No. 118, for example, gave a Christmas Eve entertainment and dance to raise funds for the strikers and sent more than $500 in donations. The Joplin central labor body sent $164.50, Mother Jones sent $500, and the Galveston longshoremen's local levied a 50 cent assessment to help. "Western Federation Notes," *Miners' Magazine*, 17 Dec. 1903, p. 8; "Joplin Is Loyal," *Miners' Magazine*, 14 Jan. 1904, pp. 6–7; "Western Federation Notes," *Miners' Magazine*, 21 Jan. 1904, p. 7. WFM strike relief calculated from 1904 WFM Convention, pp. 89–106.

56. *Miners' Magazine*, 31 Dec. 1903, p. 4; "The Situation in Colorado," *Miners' Magazine*, 31 Dec. 1903, p. 10.

57. "The Situation in Colorado," *Miners' Magazine*, 31 Dec. 1903, p. 8; *Miners' Magazine*, 25 Feb. 1904, p. 4; *Labor Disturbances*, p. 360.

58. "The Situation in Colorado," *Miners' Magazine*, 24 Dec. 1903, p. 8; Spell and Spell, *Forgotten Men*, p. 130; *Miners' Magazine*, 18 Feb. 1904, p. 4.

59. "Statement of Executive Board on Conditions in Colorado," *Miners' Magazine*, 26 May 1904, pp. 6–7; *Miners' Magazine*, 28 April 1904, p. 5; "Unionism That Cannot Die," *Miners' Magazine*, 28 April 1904, pp. 4–5; "Open Meeting at Victor," *Miners' Magazine*, 28 April 1904, pp. 11–12; *Miners' Magazine*, 5 May 1904, p. 3; "The Situation in Colorado," *Miners' Magazine*, 19 May 1904, p. 11; WFM Executive Board Minutes, meeting of 17 May 1904, p. 140.

60. 1904 WFM Convention, pp. 279–80; Operative No. 42, Reports from WFM Convention, 2 June 1904, Pinkerton Reports.

61. *Labor Disturbances*, pp. 247–48.

62. Ibid.

63. Ibid.

64. Ibid., p. 249.

65. Ibid.; Suggs, *Colorado's War*, pp. 110–11. Published versions of Robertson's "resignation" always mentioned a "coiled rope." A photograph at the Colorado Historical Society, however, shows a man with a noose around his neck and surrounded by an armed mob. The scene matches accounts of the confrontation with Robertson at the armory, although that cannot be confirmed. In any event, Robertson and other officials clearly responded realisti-

cally to threats to their safety when they resigned their offices. For others who resigned offices, see *Labor Disturbances*, pp. 251–52. Edward Bell and Sherman Bell were not related.

66. *Labor Disturbances*, pp. 249–50.

67. Ibid., pp. 250–51; Suggs, *Colorado's War*, p. 111; Operative J. N. L. Reports, Victor, 6 June 1904, Pinkerton Reports; Verdeckberg Papers, p. 97; Spell and Spell, *Forgotten Men*, pp. 137–43; Gay Morgan to W. H. Morgan, quoted in "The Situation in Colorado," *Miners' Magazine*, 14 July 1904, p. 9.

68. *Labor Disturbances*, pp. 252, 259–60; "The Situation in Colorado," *Miners' Magazine*, 16 June 1904, pp. 6–7; "Gradually the Truth Appears," *Miners' Magazine*, 30 June 1904, p. 5; 1904 WFM Convention, p. 293; "Western Federation Notes," *Miners' Magazine*, 16 June 1904, p. 5; Operative J. N. L. Reports, Victor, 6 June 1904, Pinkerton Reports.

69. *Labor Disturbances*, p. 260.

70. Ibid.; "The Situation in Colorado," *Miners' Magazine*, 16 June 1904, pp. 7–8.

71. *Labor Disturbances*, pp. 267–68, 274–78, 295; Suggs, *Colorado's War*, p. 112. The WFM Executive Board claimed on June 14, 1904, that more than four hundred union miners had already been deported. "Statement of the Executive Board of the Western Federation of Miners," WFM Executive Board Minutes, meeting of 14 June 1904, p. 157. See also "The Situation in Colorado," *Miners' Magazine*, 16 June 1904, p. 10; "The Situation in Colorado," *Miners' Magazine*, 23 June 1904, p. 10; "The Situation in Colorado," *Miners' Magazine*, 7 July 1904, p. 8; and "Letter from an Exile," *Miners' Magazine*, 30 June 1904, p. 8.

72. *Labor Disturbances*, pp. 261–64.

73. Ibid., pp. 265–66; "The Situation in Colorado," *Miners' Magazine*, 16 June 1904, p. 10.

74. *Labor Disturbances*, pp. 285–86; Peabody to Maj. Zeph T. Hill, 21 Dec. 1903, quoted in Dubofsky, *We Shall Be All*, pp. 52–53.

75. No non-union men could be found for the mechanical force in the mine, however, so an exception was allowed for those positions. But the militia returned, arrested forty-two skilled union workers, imprisoned them in the bullpen, and closed the mine a second time until July 26. *Labor Disturbances*, p. 286; "The Situation in Colorado," *Miners' Magazine*, 16 June 1904, p. 10; "The Situation in Colorado," *Miners' Magazine*, 23 June 1904, p. 9; *Miners' Magazine*, 21 July 1904, p. 4; "The Situation in Colorado," *Miners' Magazine*, 28 July 1904, pp. 9–10. The new officers were Irving Howbert, Frank G. Peck, Thomas F. Burns, Carl S. Chamberlin, and Dr. D. Rice. The board defeated resolutions forbidding the new management to join the MOA or compel their employees to carry MOA cards and instructing them to sue Peabody for closing the mine. "The Situation in Colorado," *Miners' Magazine*, 16 Feb. 1905, p. 11.

76. *Labor Disturbances*, p. 281; WFM Executive Board Minutes, meeting of 9 June 1904, p. 150; "The Situation in Colorado," *Miners' Magazine*, 16 June 1904, p. 9; "The Situation in Colorado," *Miners' Magazine*, 23 June 1904, pp. 11–12; "The Situation in Colorado," *Miners' Magazine*, 4 Aug. 1904, p. 14. A Pinkerton operative who attended the 1904 WFM convention and apparently worked as a relief distributor reported on June 9, 1904, that he would follow instructions to cut back the relief as much as possible, and say that he was following Haywood's orders. Operative No. 42, Reports, Denver, 9 June 1904, Pinkerton Reports.

77. *Labor Disturbances*, pp. 295, 306–8, 313–14; "The Situation in Colorado," *Miners' Magazine*, 4 Aug. 1904, pp. 11–14; "The Situation in Colorado," *Miners' Magazine*, 1 Sept. 1904, p. 11; "The Situation in Colorado," *Miners' Magazine*, 8 Sept. 1904, pp. 11–12.

78. *Labor Disturbances*, pp. 309–10; "The Situation in Colorado," *Miners' Magazine*, 25 Aug. 1904, pp. 10–13.

79. "The Situation in Colorado," *Miners' Magazine*, 25 Aug. 1904, p. 12.

80. *Labor Disturbances*, pp. 309, 314–15; "The Situation in Colorado," *Miners' Magazine*, 8 Sept. 1904, p. 13; "The Situation in Colorado," *Miners' Magazine*, 11 Aug. 1904, pp. 11–12; Chapman interview; statement of Steve Adams to E. F. Richardson, County Jail, Shoshone County, 2–6 Feb. 1907, Richardson Notes; May Wing interview, 6 March 1976.

81. "The Situation in Colorado," *Miners' Magazine*, 8 Sept. 1904, p. 13.

82. "The Situation in Colorado," *Miners' Magazine*, 1 Sept. 1904, p. 12; *Labor Disturbances*, pp. 315–18; "The Situation in Colorado," *Miners' Magazine*, 8 Sept. 1904, p. 13; "The Situation in Colorado," *Miners' Magazine*, 15 Sept. 1904, pp. 8–9. Most were members of either the Citizens' Alliance or the Mine Owners' Association or they were local mine managers.

83. "The Situation in Colorado," *Miners' Magazine*, 23 June 1904, p. 10.

CHAPTER 9: LOOK AWAY OVER JORDAN

1. Interview with May Wing, Colorado Springs, Colo., 16 Feb. 1979.

2. *Miners Magazine*, 29 Sept. 1904, p. 3; "Argument of the Federation," *Miners' Magazine*, 1 Sept. 1904, pp. 4–6.

3. Ibid.

4. See Dubofsky, *We Shall Be All*, pp. 97–105; Harry Orchard, *The Confessions of Harry Orchard* (New York: McClure, 1907), esp. pp. 68–109, 129–48.

5. Dubofsky, *We Shall Be All*, p. 98; George E. Dickson to Clarence Darrow, 25 April 1906, in Defense Attorney Richardson's notes, affidavits, and related material, 1906–9, *State of Idaho vs. Steve Adams*, Richardson Notes, p. 53. Dickson was a Chicago attorney who did investigation for the defense during the Adams and Haywood trials. He got the story from G. L. Brokaw, who was jailed in Spokane for obtaining money under false pretenses and who said that he was with Orchard for ten days before May 26, 1905. See also George E. Dickson to Edmund F. Richardson, 6 May 1906, Richardson Notes, p. 55.

6. Transcript of *State of Idaho vs. William D. Haywood, et al.*, June 4–July 30, 1907, 8 vols., pp. 337 ff., cited in Dubofsky, *We Shall Be All*, p. 103. McParland's long anti-union history had begun in the early 1870s when he infiltrated the Molly Maguires for Pinkerton. His brother supported the union and was among those deported from Cripple Creek. *Miners' Magazine*, 11 July 1907, p. 3. McParland induced Adams to confess by threatening to have him killed. Adams said that McParland threatened to turn him over to Cripple Creek authorities if he did not cooperate by corroborating Orchard's confession. McParland had also offered money and a commuted sentence for any crime in which Adams incriminated himself if he cooperated. Adams confession, Richardson Notes, pp. 6–7; statement of Steve Adams to E. F. Richardson, County Jail, Shoshone County, 2–6 Feb. 1907, Richardson Notes; Richardson Notes, pp. 64, 69.

7. Edward Bell and Sam Crump went to Idaho, and Haywood said that it was therefore "evident to us that something would have to be done immediately to checkmate Mr. Crump, as all during the Colorado trouble Crump has been an implacable enemy of the organization." William D. Haywood to Mr. R. J. Hanlon, secretary, Silver City Miners' Union No. 66, 20 Jan. 1906, Richardson Notes, p. 96. Haywood also wrote to William B. Easterly, who was in Silver City, Idaho, that "the fact that Attorney Crump and Sheriff Bell are mixed up in the matter is very good evidence to us that there is a conspiracy on foot and an effort to connect the W. F. of M." William D. Haywood to W. B. Easterly, 5 Feb. 1906, Richardson Notes, p. 109.

8. "Doings in Boise, Idaho," *Miners' Magazine*, 4 July 1907, p. 11; news clipping in Verdeckberg Papers, p. 137; John Baer, conversation with A. H. Rogers, 23 Feb. 1907, as reported by Rogers, Richardson Notes, p. 147. Easterly was president of Free Coinage No. 19 in 1900, secretary in 1901 and 1902, a member of its finance committee in 1902, vice president and trustee in 1903, a delegate to the CSFL convention in 1900 and to the WFM convention in 1901, 1902, and 1903, and a member of the *Press*'s board of directors from 1900 to 1903. He was arrested and held in the bullpen during the strike, but all charges against him were dropped.

9. Richardson Notes, pp. 62, 68, 86; *Labor Disturbances*, pp. 253–54; statement of Ira Blizzard, Richardson Notes, p. 63. Lou Miller of the Victor militia; Mrs. Mary Wilson, Mrs. Gibson, L. F. Taylor, and Mrs. Mart Morrison of Independence; and Jane Henry of Colorado Springs all said that they had seen the dog go to Bemore's house. Richardson Notes, pp. 81–84. C. A. Collins, who lived so near the depot that part of his house was blown away, said that he arrived at the scene of the explosion within minutes and that the dogs arrived from Canon City at noon and went straight to Bemore's kitchen door. Collins's brother, F. T. Collins, corroborated his story in the Idaho trials. Richardson Notes, p. 85; "Doings in Boise, Idaho," *Miners' Magazine*, 4 July 1907, p. 12.

10. E. J. Boughton, conversation with A. H. Rogers, 7 March 1907, as reported by Rogers, Richardson Notes, pp. 149–50; Al Bemore, conversations with A. H. Rogers, 24 March 1907 and 2 April 1907, as reported by Rogers, Richardson Notes, pp. 156–57, 159–60.

11. Richardson Notes, p. 89; "A Review of History," *Miners' Magazine*, 6 Oct. 1904, p. 9.

12. Cole's account in Richardson Notes, pp. 72–76. Next to Cole's name someone, presumably Richardson, noted: "Pinkerton Operative No. 28." Cole was among those the union sued after the strike for assault to kill, malicious mischief, and criminal destruction of property. It is not clear whether union officials sued him because of what he did or because they did not realize that he had been removed as Citizens' Alliance secretary before the Independence depot explosion.

13. J. M. Huff, Lou Miller, sergeant in the Victor militia, and J. M. Orwing, Cripple Creek, first sergeant, Company H, Richardson Notes, pp. 76–78. Miller, who corroborated Huff, Cole, and Orwing, added that the order for the August 20 riot came from the MOA and that afterward A. E. Carlton and Nelson Franklin took the looters to the Cripple Creek Club and "set them up to booze."

14. Statement of A. H. Rogers, sworn before Sydney H. Bourne, notary, 19 Dec. 1906, Richardson Notes, pp. 115–26, 115–17.

15. Ibid., pp. 118–23, 131.

16. For Rogers's interviews with potential witnesses, see Richardson Notes, pp. 127–60; Frank Wilson, conversation with A. H. Rogers, 14 Feb. 1907, as reported by Rogers, Richardson Notes, p. 146; Paul Gilhorn, conversation with A. H. Rogers, Collibran, Colo., 27 Feb. 1907, as reported by Rogers, Richardson Notes, pp. 147–49; Charles Crooks, conversation with A. H. Rogers, 10 March 1907, as reported by Rogers, Richardson Notes, pp. 150–51; Cyrus Burns, who ran a compressor on the Findley, 5–6 June 1904, conversation with A. H. Rogers on train to Denver, 4 April 1907, as reported by Rogers, Richardson Notes, p. 160.

17. Frank Gillese, conversation with A. H. Rogers, Eaton, Colo., 18 Jan. 1907, as reported by Rogers, Richardson Notes, pp. 134–40.

18. E. F. Richardson, 9 April 1907, Richardson Notes, pp. 161–62.

19. For Peabody's ties to employers, see Suggs, *Colorado's War*, esp. ch. 4, pp. 65–83.

20. President's Report, 1904 WFM Convention, p. 204.

21. Because the miners could identify many strikebreakers, because their names were published, and because important union opponents operated behind the scenes, the sample is skewed disproportionately toward working-class union opponents. Of 220 miners whose strike sympathies could be determined and linked to the 1900 census, 71 (44 percent) were strikebreakers.

22. Of 84 people in the strike sample arrested during the strike, 55 (64 percent) were miners in 1900; 80 were working class. Four mining proprietors (probably leasers) were the only non-working-class persons arrested. Of 125 deportees, only six were not working class in 1900. Of nine forced to resign public office in 1904, two were proprietors in 1900 and the rest were working class. Strike sample and manuscript census, Teller County, Colo., 1900.

23. Thirty-one percent of pro-union people in the strike sample were foreign-born, as were 29 percent of District miners. Strike sample and manuscript census, Teller County, Colo., 1900, 1,360 persons who listed occupations in a random sample of 2,089.

24. Union sympathizers and activists were disproportionately Irish and Scots, but the strike committee and organizers were still largely native-born. Among 249 persons arrested, deported, forced to resign a public office, or who served as organizers or relief distributors, 168 (67.5 percent) were native-born, compared with 77 percent of District adults. Among 72 Irish immigrants in the sample, 68 were pro-union; 9 of 12 Scots were. Some 21 percent of all adult immigrants were Irish, compared with almost half the foreign-born persons in the sample who were pro-union, 43 percent of immigrants arrested, 45.5 percent of those deported, and only 13 percent of those who expressed anti-union sympathies. Ten Scots were pro-union activists; none actively opposed the union. These figures at least partially reflect the proportionate representation of Scots and Irish in mining. Manuscript census, Teller County, Colo., 1900, and strike sample.

25. *Press*, 18 Feb. 1903, 12 March 1903; Langdon, *The Cripple Creek Strike*, pp. 117–20; "Western Federation Notes," *Miners' Magazine*, 1 Oct. 1903, p. 8; 1904 WFM Convention, p. 234.

26. *Denver Clarion Advocate*, 7 Oct. 1904.

27. Among the large mines most actively involved on the anti-union side of the struggle, the Strong (controlled by Ernest Colburn and his partners Giddings, Lennox, Dudley, and

Scott); the Granite (Tutt, MacNeill, Penrose, and Hamlin); the Stratton's Independence; and the Ajax were all above Victor. The Mary McKinney was near Anaconda, and the Elkton was near Elkton. Much of the conflict centered around the Vindicator and the Independence Consolidated (Smith and Moffat) and the Findley (Carlton) near Independence and Altman, the bastions of the Bull Hill Rednecks. Of the 249 persons arrested, deported, forced to resign public office, or who were organizers or relief distributors on the union side, forty-five (18 percent) were from Cripple Creek, twelve (5 percent) were from Anaconda, eighteen (7 percent) were from Elkton, nine (4 percent) were from Altman, twenty-seven (11 percent) were from Independence, twenty-one (8 percent) were from Goldfield, eighty-nine (36 percent) were from Victor, two (1 percent) were from Gillett, and twenty-six (10 percent) were from rural areas, mostly around the Bull Hill mines.

These figures vary markedly from the residential distribution of District adults for Cripple Creek (38 percent of all adults), Elkton (4 percent), Independence (5 percent), and Victor (24 percent). The differences reflect the class structures of the communities and the particular mining work forces most affected. Of the thirty-nine persons identified as members of the Citizens' Alliance, Mine Owners' Association, or deportation committees, twenty-three (59 percent) lived in Cripple Creek in 1900, three (8 percent) lived in Anaconda, two (5 percent) lived in Independence, one (3 percent) lived in Goldfield, ten (26 percent) lived in Victor, and one (3 percent) lived in a rural area (numbers do not total 100 percent because of rounding). Manuscript census, Teller County, Colo., 1900, and strike sample; District figures from random sample of 2,089 adults.

28. Most strike leaders were men—93.5 percent on the union side and all of labor's opponents in the sample. The skewed gender representation alone accounts for the larger numbers of single adults in the strike sample because proportionately fewer men were married than women. Manuscript census, Teller County, Colo., 1900, and strike sample; District figures from random sample of 2,089 adults.

29. Among 249 persons arrested, deported, forced to resign office, or who served as organizers or relief distributors, 19 percent rented, 38 percent owned, there was no information for 4 percent, and 39 percent were not heads of households. Of the 152 who headed households, 32 percent rented, 62.5 percent owned, and there was no information for 6 percent. Of forty persons who belonged to the MOA, Citizens' Alliance, or a deportation committee, 30 percent owned, 30 percent rented, there was no information for 18.5 percent, and 27.5 percent were not household heads. Of the twenty-nine household heads, 41 percent rented, 41 percent owned, and there was no information for 17 percent (numbers do not total 100 percent because of rounding). Computed from strike sample and manuscript census, Teller County, Colo., 1900.

30. Thernstrom, *Poverty and Progress*.

31. "The Colorado Labor Convention," *Miners' Magazine*, 21 Jan. 1904, p. 3; "The Woman's Auxiliary," *Miners' Magazine*, 14 April 1904, pp. 12–13; "Dramatic Performance by Ladies of Victor Ladies' Auxiliary No. 2," *Miners' Magazine*, 14 April 1904, p. 11.

32. "The Situation in Colorado," *Miners' Magazine*, 16 June 1904, pp. 11–12; Ida Crouch-Hazlett, "A Colorado Heroine," *Miners' Magazine*, 30 March 1904, pp. 11–12.

33. See, for example, "The Situation in Colorado," *Miners' Magazine*, 3 Dec. 1903, p. 7; "The Situation in Colorado," *Miners' Magazine*, 28 Jan. 1904, pp. 8–12; "The Situation in Colorado," *Miners' Magazine*, 7 July 1904, pp. 8–11; "The Situation in Colorado," *Miners' Magazine*, 14 July 1904, pp. 8–11; Langdon, *The Cripple Creek Strike*, pp. 224–25; and Chapman interview. A contemporary document was recorded by a local photographer who clearly assumed that the militia would not shoot women. The sequence of photographs shows soldiers guarding union members brought to Victor on freight cars after the Battle of Dunnville. At first glance, the photographer appears to have been extremely brave, because the troops were stationed on top of the railroad cars, and they pointed their rifles at the crowd. On closer examination, however, it is clear that the photographer always kept a woman between himself and the militia.

Labor's belief that the militia would not jail or kill women and children lasted until the United Mine Workers' Ludlow strike, when the militia jailed Mary Harris ("Mother") Jones and burned the strikers' tent colony, killing two women and eleven children: Patricia Valdez and her four children, Elvira, Eulala, Mary, and Rudolph; Cedilano Costa, who was pregnant, and her children Onafrio and Lucy; and five other children, Gloria and Roderlo Podreon, Frank Lucy, and Joe Petrucci. Organized labor publicized the fact that the militia had killed women and children at Ludlow. It ignored ethnicity, although it is likely that the military felt less compunction in attacking "darker" Italians, Mexicans, and other immigrants than the "white" women and children of Cripple Creek.

34. WFM Executive Board Minutes, meeting of 22 Dec. 1904, p. 269, WFM Collection.

35. Langdon, *The Cripple Creek Strike*, p. 410; *Pueblo Labor Advocate*, 1 April 1904.

36. May Wing interview, 21 Oct. 1978. May Wing's cousin, Kathleen Welch Chapman, also knew these stories and added a story about her parents helping a militia member who was defecting. The man hid in the Welch woodpile. John Welch helped hide him, and Hannah supplied coffee and sandwiches for the man's escape. Chapman interview.

37. President's Report, 1904 WFM Convention, p. 204; *Pueblo Courier*, 13 March 1903.

38. "Argument of the Federation," *Miners' Magazine*, 1 Sept. 1904, p. 5.

39. Manuscript census, Teller County Colo., 1900, strike sample and lodge sample; *Press*, 17 Jan. 1903. Information on the Chamber of Commerce was not included with the lodges and fraternal organizations in chapter 4 but was gathered and processed in the same way.

40. Verdeckberg Papers, passim; *Press*, 24 July 1901; "The Situation in Colorado," *Miners' Magazine*, 3 Nov. 1904, p. 9; "The Situation in Colorado," *Miners' Magazine*, 8 Sept. 1904, p. 14. Leland was also a member of the Order of the Eastern Star, the Modern Woodmen of America, and the Woodmen of the World.

41. The pro-union activists included forty Democrats, six Republicans, one Silver Republican, three Populists, six Co-operatives, fifteen Socialists, five Social Democrats, and three members of the Bryan and Stevenson Club. The anti-union activists included eleven Democrats, fourteen Republicans, and one Co-operative. The most active—those arrested, deported, forced to resign offices, or organizers or relief distributors, included thirty-three Democrats, eight Republicans, a Silver Republican, a Populist, eight Co-operatives, sixteen Socialists, six Social Democrats, and two members of the Bryan and Stevenson Club. The

MOA, CA, and deportation committees included five Democrats and twelve Republicans. Although only a portion of strike activists are represented in these figures, it is clear that strike allegiances crossed party lines. Strike sample and political sample.

42. The *Press*, 28 Feb. 1902, reported Bell's election to the Mining Exchange. Some working-class Republicans felt particularly betrayed by Peabody and vowed to leave the party. See statements of Anna Ballard and Frank Waldron, both of whom served on a CSFL committee to meet with Peabody in January 1904. "The Colorado State Labor Convention," *Miners' Magazine*, 21 Jan. 1904, p. 5. The deposed officials who had belonged to organized labor included Teller County sheriff Henry Robertson, Deputy Sheriff James W. Gaughan, and Coroner M. J. Doran; Cripple Creek marshal W. J. Graham, Night Marshal Fred Harding, and justices of the peace J. P. Thomas and David Kelley; Victor aldermen J. W. Murphy and J. J. Tobin, Police Judge Michael Gibbons, City Marshal Michael O'Connell, Night Marshal Michael Lamb, and Jailer James Printy; Independence marshal Harvey Starbuck; Anaconda marshal E. E. Scott and several members of the city council; Goldfield marshal J. J. Brothers, Night Marshal Robert McCarthy, Aldermen J. F. Daugherty, Arthur Childers, Christopher Miller, M. D. Morrison, A. J. Burke, and the Goldfield city clerk, treasurer, street commissioner, and marshal. A number were also arrested, including Robertson, O'Connell, and Doran, all of whom witnessed key events on June 6, 1904, and five members of the Goldfield city council. *Labor Disturbances*, pp. 251–52.

43. William D. Haywood to President Theodore Roosevelt, 28 July 1904, quoted in *Miners' Magazine*, 28 July 1904, p. 5.

44. There were, however, exceptions who continued to support the Socialist Party. "Colorado Socialists," *Miners' Magazine*, 14 July 1904, p. 5; *Denver Clarion Advocate*, 30 Sept. 1904.

45. "The Situation in Colorado," *Miners' Magazine*, 8 Sept. 1904, p. 14.

46. *Denver Clarion Advocate*, 30 Sept. 1904, p. 4 (first quotation); *Miners' Magazine*, 20 Oct. 1904, p. 3 (second quotation); *Denver Times*, 25 Oct. 1904 (third quotation).

47. "The Situation in Colorado," *Miners' Magazine*, 17 Nov. 1904, pp. 10–11; *Denver Clarion Advocate*, 11 Nov. 1904, p. 1. Chris Miller was forced to resign his office on the Goldfield city council and at the time of his death was charged with precipitating the Victor riot.

48. *Denver Clarion Advocate*, 11 Nov. 1904.

49. "The Situation in Colorado," *Miners' Magazine*, 22 Dec. 1904, pp. 10–12; *Miners' Magazine*, 24 Nov. 1904, p. 3; "The Situation in Colorado," *Miners' Magazine*, 24 Nov. 1904, p. 12; "The Situation in Colorado," *Miners' Magazine*, 19 Jan. 1905, p. 10.

50. The statewide Socialist vote was 1,700, a considerable drop from 7,395 in 1902, *Miners' Magazine*, 8 Dec. 1904, p. 4; "The Situation in Colorado," *Miners' Magazine*, 5 Jan. 1905, p. 10.

51. Jenson, *Heritage of Conflict*, pp. 155–58; Suggs, *Colorado's War*, pp. 186–87; "The Situation in Colorado," *Miners' Magazine*, 14 Jan. 1905, p. 11; "The Situation in Colorado," *Miners' Magazine*, 26 Jan. 1905, pp. 10–11.

52. The remaining defendants accused of instigating the Victor riot included Peter Calderwood, William Boyle, Albert Bilat, L. R. Jenks, Frank Cochrane, Alf Miller, Arthur Parker, and Fred Minster. *Miners' Magazine*, 24 Nov. 1904, p. 4; *Miners' Magazine*, 29 Dec.

1904, p. 3; "The Situation in Colorado," *Miners' Magazine*, 5 Jan. 1905, p. 10; WFM Executive Board Minutes, meeting of 12 May 1905, p. 275; "The Situation in Colorado," *Miners' Magazine*, 24 Nov. 1904, p. 11; Frank Hangs, telegram to WFM Executive Board, 19 May 1905, WFM Executive Board Minutes, meeting of 19 May 1905, p. 285.

53. *Miners' Magazine*, 14 Jan. 1909, p. 3; Jim Warford, conversation with A. H. Rogers, Colorado State Prison, Canon City, 29 Jan. 1907, as reported by Rogers, Richardson Notes, p. 141. John Chipman corroborated the story that Edward Bell contracted for the murders. John Chipman, conversation with A. H. Rogers, 30 March 1907, as reported by Rogers, Richardson Notes, pp. 157–59.

54. WFM Executive Board Minutes, meeting of 16 Dec. 1904, p. 242, and meeting of 22 Dec. 1904, p. 268; "Strike Is Still On," *Miners' Magazine*, 20 April 1905, p. 5; *Official Proceedings of the Thirteenth Annual Convention, Western Federation of Miners* (Denver: Reed Publishing, 1905), p. 201. At the 1905 WFM Convention, Cripple Creek Engineers No. 82 reported twenty-five members, District Union No. 234 reported 134, and there was no information from any of the other District WFM locals. Ibid., pp. 204–8. WFM Executive Board Minutes, meeting of 9 Dec. 1907, pp. 9–11; *Miners' Magazine*, 11 Nov. 1909, p. 4.

55. CSFL—*Report of Proceedings of the Tenth Annual Convention, Salida, Colo., Sept. 11–13, 1905* (n.p.: Labor News Print, 1905), pp. 17, 160.

56. The opinion of Mayor Shockey of Cripple Creek, quoted in *Miners' Magazine*, 18 May 1905, p. 4.

57. *Miners' Magazine*, 11 April 1907, p. 4; Chapman interview; May Wing interview, 21 Oct. 1978; Leslie and Ruby Wilkinson interview; interview with May Wing and Beulah Pryor, Colorado Springs, Colo., 17 Feb. 1979; interview with Ralph and Mary Wing, Boulder, Colo., 26 Dec. 1978; Ileen Pryor interview.

58. "Doings in Boise, Idaho," *Miners' Magazine*, 27 June 1907, p. 9.

59. *Miners' Magazine*, 22 Nov. 1906, p. 15.

60. "A Scathing Reply," *Miners' Magazine*, 4 Oct. 1906, pp. 7–8; *Miners' Magazine*, 25 June 1914, p. 3.

61. *Official Proceedings of the Fourteenth Annual Convention Western Federation of Miners, May 28–June 3, 1906, Denver* (Denver: Reed Publishing, 1906), pp. 201–2; *Miners' Magazine*, 6 Dec. 1906, p. 3.

62. *Report of Proceedings of the Twelfth Annual Convention, CSFL, Pueblo, August 13–15, 1907* (Denver: Great Western Publishing, 1907), p. 7; "He Knows De Leon," *Miners' Magazine*, 8 Nov. 1906, pp. 13–14; "Meeting at Colorado City," *Miners' Magazine*, 7 March 1907, p. 13; "From Colorado City, Colorado," *Miners' Magazine*, 2 Feb. 1907, p. 13; "Colorado Socialists," *Miners' Magazine*, 14 July 1904, p. 5.

63. W. H. Leonard, for example, a former president of both Altman Stationary Engineers No. 75 and of Cripple Creek Engineers No. 82, held numerous District union offices and then moved to Denver after the strike, where he went in the coal, flour, and feed business and was a prominent Socialist Party leader for years. See *Official Proceedings of the Seventeenth Annual Convention, Western Federation of Miners, Denver, July 12–August 3, 1909* (Denver: W. H. Kistler Stationary Co., 1909), p. 3; *Official Proceedings of the Eighteenth*

Annual Convention, Western Federation of Miners, Denver, July 18–August 2, 1910 (Denver: Great Western Publishing, 1910), p. 3; 1912 WFM Convention, pp. 190–373. Despite the bravado of holding the 1912 convention in Victor, the small local No. 234 never gained members or bargaining power.

64. Chapman interview. Kathleen Chapman at various times said that her father was forty-eight when he died, that he was fifty-four, and that he died in 1914, when he would have been fifty. Her brother, who began work during the eighth grade and quit school as soon as he completed that year, was born in 1894, and it is likely that he took his father's place underground in 1909 or 1910, when Welch would have been forty-five or forty-six.

65. WFM Executive Board Minutes, meetings of 12 Dec. 1905, p. 328, and 17 Dec. 1906, p. 416; Western Federation of Miners Executive Board Minutes, July 1907–February 1909, WFM Collection, meetings of 11 Dec. 1907, p. 23, 18 Jan. 1909, p. 96, and 21 Jan. 1909, p. 102; Western Federation of Miners Executive Board Minutes, July 5, 1909–March 24, 1915, WFM Collection, meetings of 3 Jan. 1910, p. 21, and 11 July 1910, p. 41. Isaac Liebo's name is sometimes also spelled "Leabo" in these records.

APPENDIX A: METHODOLOGY

1. Taylor, *Cripple Creek*, pp. 203–5.
2. Ibid., p. 205; *Twelfth Census, Volume 1*, p. 88.
3. For more on my oral history methodology and my relationships with informants, see Elizabeth Jameson, "May and Me: Relationships with Informants and the Community," in *Insider/Outsider Relationships with Informants*, ed. Elizabeth Jameson, SIROW Working Paper no. 13 (Tucson: University of Arizona, 1982).

APPENDIX B: UNION MEMBERSHIP

1. Day Book and Ledger on Receipts, 1896 to 1898—CSFL; CSFL Day Book and Ledger on Receipts 1898 to 1900, Inc.; CSFL—Day Book and Ledger on Receipts 1900 to 1901; Ledger on Receipts and Day Book 1901 to 1904, CSFL (hereafter cited as CSFL Ledger, 1901–4, CSFL Collection); WFM Charter Book; "Local Unions Chartered in the State of Colorado."

2. In 1905, for example, Denver Carpenters' Local No. 55, UBCJA, had more than a thousand members. In July it voted to reaffiliate with the CSFL on the "basis of three hundred members," and in November it increased that figure to 450. Minutes of 10 July, 11 Nov. 1905, Local Union No. 55, United Brotherhood of Carpenters and Joiners of America, UCB.

3. CSFL Ledger, 1901–4, CSFL Collection; *Press*, 20 April 1902, 22 March 1901, 24 Jan. 1902; "Miners' Union New Hall," *Miners' Magazine*, May 1901, pp. 22–23.

4. WFM Charter Book; Rogers Memo; Minutes, Carpenters No. 547.

5. *Press*, 1 Jan. 1901, 4 Feb. 1902; "The Situation in Colorado," *Miners' Magazine*, 24 Dec. 1903, p. 8; Smith, *Eighth Biennial Report*, p. 86.

6. Computed from manuscript census, Teller County, Colo., 1900.

7. Taylor, *Cripple Creek*, p. 205.

8. Smith, *Eighth Biennial Report*, p. 86.

BIBLIOGRAPHY

ARCHIVAL MATERIAL

The Amon Carter Museum, Fort Worth, Tex.:
  Mazulla Collection
    Taped interview of Lillian Powers, 7 Nov. 1952, conducted by Caroline Bancroft and Fred and Jo Mazulla
Author's possession:
  "Local Unions Chartered in the State of Colorado." John S. Rogers, general secretary, United Brotherhood of Carpenters and Jointers of America, to Edward A. Rylands, executive secretary-treasurer, Colorado State Council of Carpenters, 13 Feb. 1981
Colorado State Historical Society, Denver:
  Albert Frost Collection
  Grand Army of the Republic Collection
  Edward Verdeckberg Papers
  Victor GAR Post No. 100, Correspondence and Minute Books
Colorado Springs Local No. 515, United Brotherhood of Carpenters and Joiners of America, Colorado Springs, Colo.:
  Minutes, 1895–1918, Colorado Springs Local No. 515
  Minutes, 1895–1909, Cripple Creek Local No. 547
Denver Public Library, Western History Department:
  Eben Smith (1831–1906) Collection
    Correspondence, Letterpress Books, and Papers
University of California, Berkeley, Graduate Social Science Library:
  Executive Committee Minutes, Western Federation of Miners, 1893–95 (microfilm)
  "Proceedings of the First Annual Convention of the Western Federation of Miners Held at Butte, Montana, May 15–19, 1893, Miners' Union Hall, Butte" (microfilm)
  "Proceedings of the Second Annual Convention of the Western Federation of Miners, Held at Salt Lake City, Utah, May 14, 1894" (microfilm)
  "Proceedings of the Third Annual Convention of the Western Federation of Miners, Denver, Colorado, May 12, 1895" (microfilm)
University of Colorado at Boulder Archives:
  Colorado State Federation of Labor
    Day Book and Ledger on Receipts 1898 to 1900, Inc.

Day Book and Ledger on Receipts 1901 to 1904, CSFL
Gross, John E., "Official History of the Colorado State Federation of Labor," prepared
    Dec. 1928
Minutes CSFL Executive Board, June 10, 1899–Nov.2, 1909
"Official Proceedings of the First Annual Convention of the Colorado State Federation
    of Labor Held in the City of Pueblo, Colo., May 1, 1896"
"Official Proceedings of the Second Annual Convention of the State Federation of La-
    bor, Held in City of Victor, Colo., April 30, 1897"
Mary McKinney Mining Company Collection
    Letter Book: General Correspondence, Aug. 10, 1901–Oct. 20, 1905
Pinkerton Detective Agency Reports
United Brotherhood of Carpenters and Joiners of America
    Minutes, 1897–1901, Denver Local No. 55
    Minutes, 1901–4, Denver Local No. 55
Western Federation of Miners/International Union of Mine, Mill and Smelter Workers
    Collection
    Official Charter Book, W.F.M. and I.U.M.M.&S.W.
    State of Idaho vs. Steve Adams (Defense Attorney Richardson's notes, affidavits and re-
        lated material 1906–9)
    Western Federation of Miners Executive Board Minutes, June 1902–July 1907
    Western Federation of Miners Executive Board Minutes, July 1907–Feb. 1909
    Western Federation of Miners Executive Board Minutes, July 5, 1909–March 24, 1915
Wisconsin State Historical Society, Madison:
    Adolph Germer Papers
    U.S. Mss. 14a., Victor Miners' Union, No. 32: Ledger, 1894–1903

PUBLISHED RECORDS OF LABOR ORGANIZATIONS

CSFL—*Report of Proceedings of the Tenth Annual Convention, Salida, Colo., Sept. 11–13,
    1905.* n.p.: Labor News Print, 1905.
Official Proceedings of the Ninth Annual Convention, Western Federation of Miners. Pueblo:
    Pueblo Courier Press, 1901.
Official Proceedings of the Tenth Annual Convention, Western Federation of Miners. Den-
    ver: Colorado Chronicle, 1902.
Official Proceedings of the Eleventh Annual Convention, Western Federation of Miners. Den-
    ver: Western Newspaper Union, 1903.
Official Proceedings of the Twelfth Annual Convention, Western Federation of Miners. Den-
    ver: Western Newspaper Union, 1904.
Official Proceedings of the Thirteenth Annual Convention, Western Federation of Miners.
    Denver: Reed Publishing, 1905.
Official Proceedings of the Fourteenth Annual Convention, Western Federation of Miners.
    Denver: Reed Publishing, 1906.
Official Proceedings of the Fifteenth Annual Convention, Western Federation of Miners.
    Denver: Allied Printing, 1907.

Official Proceedings of the Seventeenth Annual Convention, Western Federation of Miners, Denver, July 12–August 3, 1909. Denver: W. H. Kistler Stationary Co., 1909.

Official Proceedings of the Eighteenth Annual Convention, Western Federation of Miners, Denver, July 18–August 2, 1910. Denver: Great Western Publishing, 1910.

Official Proceedings of the Twentieth Annual Convention Western Federation of Miners, Victor, Colorado, July 15–July 26, 1912. Denver: Great Western Publishing, 1912.

Official Proceedings of the Twenty-Fourth Consecutive and Fourth Biennial Convention of the International Union of Mine, Mill and Smelter Workers, Held at Denver, Colorado, August 2d to 12th, Inclusive 1920. n.p.

Proceedings of Mass Convention of Organized Labor of Colorado Held under the Auspices of the Colorado State Federation of Labor, Held January 11–14, 1904. Denver: Great Western Publishing, 1904.

Proceedings of the Third Annual Convention, Colorado State Federation of Labor, Held at Colorado Springs, Colorado, May 2nd, 3rd, and 4th, 1898. Pueblo: Courier Printing, 1898.

Report of Proceedings of the Twelfth Annual Convention, Colorado State Federation of Labor, Held at Pueblo, Colorado, August 12, 13, 14, 15, 1907. Denver: Great Western Publishing, 1907.

NEWSPAPERS AND PERIODICALS

Colorado Springs Pink Iconoclast, Colorado Springs Weekly Gazette, The Coming Nation, Denver Clarion Advocate, Denver Colorado Chronicle, Denver Labor Enquirer, Denver Rocky Mountain Socialist, Miners' Magazine, Pueblo Courier, Pueblo Labor Advocate, Shullsburg Pick and Gad, and *Victor and Cripple Creek Daily Press*

DIRECTORIES

A Complete City Directory of Cripple Creek, Victor, and the Towns of the Cripple Creek Mining District. Colorado Springs: Gazette Publishing, 1897.

Cripple Creek District Directory 1900. Colorado Springs: Gazette Publishing, 1900.

Cripple Creek District Directory, 1902–3. n.p.: Gazetteer Publishing, 1902.

Cripple Creek District Directory 1912–13. Denver: Gazetteer Publishing, 1912.

Cripple Creek-Victor Mining District Directory. Cripple Creek: Directory Publishing, 1895.

GOVERNMENT DOCUMENTS
Colorado

Colorado Bureau of Labor Statistics. *Third Biennial Report of the Bureau of Labor Statistics of the State of Colorado, 1891–1892.* Colorado Springs: Gazette Printing, State Printers, 1892.

———. *Fourth Biennial Report of the Bureau of Labor Statistics of the State of Colorado, 1893–1894.* Denver: Smith-Brooks Printing, State Printers, 1894.

———. *Biennial Report of the Bureau of Labor Statistics, State of Colorado, 1895–1896.* Denver: Smith-Brooks Printing, State Printers, 1896.

Colorado State Bureau of Mines. *Report of the State Bureau of Mines, Colorado, for the Year 1897.* Denver: Smith-Brooks Printing, State Printers, 1898.

——. *Report of the State Bureau of Mines, Colorado, for the Years 1901–2*. Denver: Smith-Brooks Printing, State Printers, 1902.

——. *Report of the State Bureau of Mines, Colorado, for the Years 1903–4*. n.p.

Colorado State Inspector of Metalliferous Mines. *Biennial Report of State Inspector of Metalliferous Mines, December, 1894*. Denver: Smith-Brooks Printing, State Printers, 1894.

Henahan, T. R. *Twelfth Biennial Report of the Bureau of Mines of the State of Colorado*. Denver: Smith-Brooks Printing, 1912.

Lee, Henry A. *1896 Report of Bureau of Mines, Colorado*. Denver: Smith-Brooks Printing, State Printers, 1896.

Montgomery, W. H. *Ninth Biennial Report of the Bureau of Labor Statistics of the State of Colorado, 1903–1904*. Denver: Smith-Brooks Printing, State Printers, 1904.

Smith, James T. *Seventh Biennial Report of the Bureau of Labor Statistics of the State of Colorado, 1899–1900*. Denver: Smith-Brooks Printing, 1900.

——. *Eighth Biennial Report of the Bureau of Labor Statistics of the State of Colorado, 1901–1902*. Denver: Smith-Brooks Printing, State Printers, 1902.

United States

U.S. Department of Commerce. Bureau of the Census. *Abstract of the Twelfth Census of the United States, 1900*. Washington: Government Printing Office, 1902.

——. Manuscript Census, County of Denver, Colorado, 1920.

——. Manuscript Census, LaFayette County, Wisconsin, 1860, 1870, 1880.

——. Manuscript Census, Lake County, Colorado, 1900.

——. Manuscript Census, Teller County, Colorado, 1900.

——. *Twelfth Census of the United States Taken in the Year 1900, Volume 1*. Washington: United States Census Office, 1901.

——. *Twelfth Census of the United States, Taken in the Year 1900, Population, Volume 2, Part 2*. Washington: United States Census Office, 1901.

——. *Twelfth Census of the United States, Taken in the Year 1900, Manufactures, Volume 8, Part 2*. Washington: United States Census Office, 1902.

——. *U.S. Census, 1910, Population, Volume 3*. Washington: Government Printing Office, 1913.

——. *U.S. Census, 1930, Population, Volume 3, Parts 1 and 2*. Washington: Government Printing Office, 1932.

U.S. Congress. Senate. Commissioner of Labor. *A Report on Labor Disturbances in the State of Colorado, from 1880 to 1904, Inclusive*. S. Doc. 122, 58th Cong., 3d sess. Washington: Government Printing Office, 1905.

ORAL HISTORY INTERVIEWS

Chapman, Kathleen. Wheat Ridge, Colo., 27 April 1979.

Gatheridge, S. C. Denver, Colo., 21 Feb., 7 March 1979.

Pryor, Beulah. Colorado Springs, Colo., 6 May 1979.

Pryor, Beulah, and May Wing. Colorado Springs, Colo., 17 Feb. 1979.

Pryor, Ileen. Colorado Springs, Colo., 4 May 1979.

Stiverson, Clara. Golden, Colo., 29 July 1975.
Wilkinson, Leslie, and Ruby Wilkinson. Cripple Creek, Colo., 7 Sept. 1975.
Wing, Mary C., and Ralph O. Wing. Boulder, Colo., 26 Dec. 1978.
Wing, May. Boulder, Colo., 6 March 1976; Victor, Colo., 21 Oct. 1978; Colorado Springs, Colo., 16 Feb. 1979.
Wing, Ralph O. Boulder, Colo., 16 Feb. 1979.

THESES AND DISSERTATIONS

Brinley, John Ervin, Jr. "The Western Federation of Miners." Ph.D. dissertation, University of Utah, 1972.
Dumenil, Lynn. "Brotherhood and Respectability: Freemasonry and American Culture, 1880–1930." Ph.D. dissertation, University of California, Berkeley, 1981.
Huginnie, Andrea Yvette. "'Strikitos': Race, Class and Work in the Arizona Copper Industry, 1870–1920." Ph.D. dissertation, Yale University, 1991.
Jameson, Elizabeth. "The Creatures of Discontent: The Western Federation of Miners and the Radical Labor Movement, 1893–1916." B.A. thesis, Antioch College, 1970.
———. "High-Grade and Fissures: A Working-Class History of the Cripple Creek, Colorado, Gold Mining District, 1890–1905." Ph.D. dissertation, University of Michigan, 1987.
Jensen, Billie Barnes. "The Woman Suffrage Movement in Colorado." M.A. thesis, University of Colorado, 1959.
Johnson, Susan Lee. "Women's Households and Relationships in the Mining West: Central Arizona, 1863–1873." M.A. thesis, Arizona State University, 1984.
Murphy, Lucy. "Economy, Race, and Gender Along the Fox-Wisconsin and Rock Riverways, 1737–1832. " Ph.D. dissertation, Northern Illinois University, 1995.
Murphy, Mary. "Women on the Line: Prostitution in Butte, Montana, 1878–1917." M.A. thesis, University of North Carolina at Chapel Hill, 1983.
Petrik, Paula. "The Bonanza Town: Women and Family on the Rocky Mountain Mining Frontier, Helena, Montana, 1865–1900." Ph.D. dissertation, SUNY-Binghamton, 1982.
Rinker, Catherine. "The History of Cripple Creek, Colorado, 1891–1917." M.A. thesis, University of Colorado, 1934.
Shovers, Brian Lee. "Miners, Managers, and Machines: Industrial Accidents and Occupational Disease in the Butte Underground, 1880–1920." M.A. thesis, Montana State University, 1987.
Suggs, George Graham, Jr. "Colorado Conservatives Versus Organized Labor: A Study of the James Hamilton Peabody Administration, 1903–1905." Ph.D. dissertation, University of Colorado, 1964.

ARTICLES AND CHAPTERS IN BOOKS
Primary Sources

Baker, Ray Stannard. "The Reign of Lawlessness: Anarchy and Despotism in Colorado." McClure's Magazine, May 1904, pp. 43–57.
Keena, Leo J. "Cripple Creek in 1900." Colorado Magazine 30 (Oct. 1953): 269–75.

Secondary Sources

Barrett, James. "Americanization from the Bottom Up: Immigration and the Remaking of the Working Class in the United States, 1880–1930." *Journal of American History* 79 (Dec. 1992): 996–1020.

Bender, Thomas. "Wholes and Parts: The Need for Synthesis in American History." *Journal of American History* 73 (June 1986): 127–32.

Brundage, David. "Respectable Radicals: Denver's Irish Land League in the Early 1880s." *Journal of the West* 31 (April 1992): 52–58.

Dubofsky, Melvyn. "The Origins of Western Working Class Radicalism, 1890–1905." *Labor History* 7 (Spring 1966): 131–54.

Emmons, David. "Ethnic Cohesion and Advancement: Irish Worker Conservatism in Butte, 1876–1906." *Journal of the West* 31 (April 1992): 59–65.

———. "Immigrant Workers and Industrial Hazards: The Irish Miners of Butte, 1880–1919." *Journal of American Ethnic History* 5 (1985): 41–64.

Fink, Leon. "The New Labor History and the Powers of Historical Pessimism: Consensus, Hegemony, and the Case of the Knights of Labor." *Journal of American History* 75 (June 1988): 115–36.

Foster, James C. "Quantification and the Western Federation." *Historical Methods Newsletter* 10 (Fall 1977): 141–48.

Frank, Dana. "Housewives, Socialists, and the Politics of Food: The 1917 New York Cost-of-Living Protests." *Feminist Studies* 11 (Summer 1985): 255–85.

Garceau, Dee. "'I Got a Girl Here, Would You Like to Meet Her?': Courtship, Ethnicity, and Community in Sweetwater County, 1900–1925." In *Writing the Range: Race, Class, and Culture in the Women's West*, edited by Elizabeth Jameson and Susan Armitage, pp. 274–97. Norman: University of Oklahoma Press, 1997.

Glenn, Evelyn Nakano. "Racial Ethnic Women's Labor: The Intersection of Race, Gender and Class Oppression." *Review of Radical Political Economics* 17 (Fall 1985): 86–108.

Gonzalez, Rosalinda Mendez. "Distinctions in Western Women's Experience: Ethnicity, Class, and Social Change." In *The Women's West*, edited by Susan Armitage and Elizabeth Jameson, pp. 237–51. Norman: University of Oklahoma Press, 1987.

Griswold, Robert L. "Anglo Women and Domestic Ideology in the American West in the Nineteenth and Early Twentieth Centuries." In *Western Women: Their Land, Their Lives*, edited by Lillian Schlissel, Vicki L. Ruiz, and Janice Monk, pp. 13–33. Albuquerque: University of New Mexico Press, 1988.

Hirata, Lucie Cheng. "Chinese Immigrant Women in Nineteenth Century California." In *Women of America: A History*, edited by Carol Ruth Berkin and Mary Beth Norton, pp. 224–44. Boston: Houghton Mifflin, 1979.

Hulden, Patricia J. "The Rhetoric and Iconography of Reform: Women Coal Miners in Belgium, 1848–1914." *Historical Journal* 34 (June 1991): 411–36.

Hunt, Inez. "The Poverty Marchers of 1894." *Empire Magazine*, 16 Feb. 1969, pp. 14–18.

Ichioka, Yuji. "*Amerika Nadeshiko*: Japanese Immigrant Women in the United States, 1900–1924." *Pacific Historical Review* 49 (1980): 339–57.

"The I.W.W.: An Exchange of Views." *Labor History* 11 (Summer 1970): 355–72.

James, Ronald M. "Defining the Group: Nineteenth-Century Cornish on the North American Mining Frontier." In *Cornish Studies Two*, edited by Philip Payton, pp. 32–47. Exeter: University of Exeter Press, 1994.

Jameson, Elizabeth. "Imperfect Unions: Class and Gender in Cripple Creek, 1894–1904." In *Class, Sex, and the Woman Worker*, edited by Milton Cantor and Bruce Laurie, pp. 166–202. Westport: Greenwood Press, 1977.

———. "May and Me: Relationships with Informants and the Community." In *Insider/Outsider Relationships with Informants*, SIROW Working Paper no. 13. Edited by Elizabeth Jameson. Tucson: University of Arizona, 1982.

———. "Women as Workers, Women as Civilizers: True Womanhood in the American West." In *The Women's West*, edited by Susan Armitage and Elizabeth Jameson, 145–64. Norman: University of Oklahoma Press, 1987. .

Johnson, Susan L. "Sharing Bed and Board: Cohabitation and Cultural Difference in Central Arizona Mining Towns, 1863–1873." In *The Women's West*, edited by Susan Armitage and Elizabeth Jameson, pp. 77–92. Norman: University of Oklahoma Press, 1987.

Kaplan, Temma. "Female Consciousness and Collective Action: The Case of Barcelona, 1910–1918." *Signs* 7 (1982): 545–66.

Kerber, Linda K. "Separate Spheres, Female Worlds, Women's Place: The Rhetoric of Women's History." *Journal of American History* 75 (June 1988): 9–39.

Kerr, Clark, and Abraham Siegel. "The Interindustry Propensity to Strike." In *Industrial Conflict*, edited by Arthur Kornhauser, Robert Dubin, and Arthur M. Ross, pp. 89–212. New York: McGraw-Hill, 1954.

Kessler-Harris, Alice. "A New Agenda for American Labor History: A Gendered Analysis and the Question of Class." In *Perspectives on American Labor History*, edited by J. Caroll Moody and Alice Kessler-Harris, pp. 217–34. De Kalb: Northern Illinois University Press, 1989.

———. "Treating the Male as 'Other': Redefining the Parameters of Labor History," *Labor History* 34 (Spring-Summer, 1993): 190–204.

Kingsdale, Jon M. "The 'Poor Man's Club': Social Functions of the Urban Working-Class Saloon." In *The American Man*, edited by Elizabeth H. Pleck and Joseph H. Pleck, pp. 255–84. Englewood Cliffs: Prentice-Hall, 1980.

Leonard, Henry B. "American Immigration: An Historiographical Essay." *Ethnic Forum* (1987): 9–23.

Levine, Susan. "Workers' Wives: Gender, Class, and Consumerism in the 1920s United States." *Gender and History* 3 (Spring 1991): 44–64.

Murphy, Mary. "The Private Lives of Public Women." In *The Women's West*, edited by Susan Armitage and Elizabeth Jameson, pp. 193–206. Norman: University of Oklahoma Press, 1987.

Oestreicher, Richard. "Urban Working-Class Political Behavior and Theories of American Electoral Politics, 1870–1940." *Journal of American History* 74 (March 1988): 1257–86.

Pascoe, Peggy. "Race, Gender, and Intercultural Relations: The Case of Interracial Marriage." *Frontiers* 12 (1991): 5–18.

Peck, Gunther. "Charles Moyer and 'New' Immigrants: The Politics of Race and Ethnicity in the WFM, 1910–1912." Paper presented at the Western History Association, Austin, Tex., Oct. 1991.

——. "Padrones and Protest: 'Old' Radicals and 'New' Immigrants in Bingham, Utah, 1905–1912." *Western Historical Quarterly,* 24 (May 1993): 157–78.

Peterson, Richard H. "Conflict and Consensus: Labor Relations in Western Mining." *Journal of the West* 12 (Jan. 1973): 1–17.

Petrik, Paula. "'If She Be Content': The Development of Montana Divorce Law, 1865–1907." *Western Historical Quarterly* 18 (July 1987): 261–91.

Pomeroy, Earl. "Toward a Reorientation of Western History: Continuity and Environment." *Mississippi Valley Historical Review* 41 (March 1955): 579–600.

Preston, William. "Shall This Be All?: U.S. Historians versus William D. Haywood *Et Al.*" *Labor History* 12 (Summer 1971): 437–38.

Rosenzweig, Roy. "Boston Masons, 1900–1935: The Lower Middle Class in a Divided Society." *Journal of Voluntary Action Research* 6 (July–Oct. 1977): 199–26.

Schwantes, Carlos A. "The Concept of the Wageworkers' Frontier: A Framework for Future Research." *Western Historical Quarterly* 18 (Jan. 1987): 39–55.

Smith, Duane A. "The San Juaner: A Computerized Portrait." *Colorado Magazine* 52 (Spring 1975): 137–52.

Spivak, Gayatri Chakravorty. "Can the Subaltern Speak?" In *Marxism and the Interpretation of Culture,* edited by Gary Nelson and Lawrence Grossberg, pp. 271–313. Urbana: University of Illinois Press, 1988.

Spude, Robert L. "Cyanide and the Flood of Gold: Some Colorado Beginnings of the Cyanide Process of Gold Extraction." *Essays and Monographs in Colorado History,* no. 12 (1991): 1–35.

Stinneford, Earl. "Mines and Miners: The Eastern Europeans in Wyoming." In *Peopling the High Plains: Wyoming's European Heritage,* edited by Gordon Olaf Hendrickson, pp. 121–48. Cheyenne: Wyoming State Archives and Historical Department, 1977.

Suggs, George G., Jr. "Religion and Labor in the Rocky Mountain West: Bishop Nicholas C. Matz and the Western Federation of Miners." *Labor History* 11 (Spring 1970): 190–206.

Welter, Barbara. "The Cult of True Womanhood: 1820–1860." *American Quarterly* 18 (Summer 1966): 151–74.

West, Elliott. "Beyond Baby Doe: Child-Rearing on the Mining Frontier." In *The Women's West,* edited by Susan Armitage and Elizabeth Jameson, pp. 179–92. Norman: University of Oklahoma Press, 1987.

——. "Five Idaho Mining Towns: A Computer Profile." *Pacific Northwest Quarterly* 72 (July 1982): 108–20.

——. "Of Lager Beer and Sonorous Songs." *Colorado Magazine* 48 (Spring 1972): 108–28.

BOOKS

Primary Sources

Ellis, Anne. *The Life of an Ordinary Woman.* Boston: Houghton Mifflin, 1929. Reprint. Lincoln: University of Nebraska Press, 1980.

Hartzell, Charles. *The History of Colorado during the Turbulent Reign of "Davis the First."* Denver: C. J. Kelly, 1894.

Haywood, William Dudley. *Bill Haywood's Book: The Autobiography of Big Bill Haywood.* New York: International Publishers, 1929. Reprint. New York: International Publishers, 1974.

Howbert, Irving. *Memories of a Lifetime in the Pike's Peak Region.* New York: G. P. Putnam's Sons, 1925.

Langdon, Emma F. *The Cripple Creek Strike: A History of Industrial Wars in Colorado.* Denver: Great Western Publishing, 1904–5. Reprint. New York: Arno Press, 1969.

Lee, Mabel Barbee. *Back in Cripple Creek.* Garden City: Doubleday, 1968.

———. *Cripple Creek Days.* Garden City: Doubleday, 1958.

Mining Stock Association. *Official Summary of Certified Reports of Listed Companies.* Colorado Springs: Mining Stock Association, 1913.

Orchard, Harry . *The Confessions of Harry Orchard.* New York: McClure, 1907.

Spell, Leslie Doyle, and Hazel M. Spell. *Forgotten Men of Cripple Creek.* Denver: Big Mountain Press, 1959.

Sprague and Rohrbacker for the *Colorado Springs Evening Telegraph.* *The Fortunes of a Decade.* Colorado Springs: Colorado Springs Evening Telegraph, 1900.

Thomas, Lowell. *Good Evening Everybody.* New York: William Morrow, 1976.

Secondary Sources

Argersinger, Peter H. *The Limits of Agrarian Radicalism: Western Populism and American Politics.* Lawrence: University Press of Kansas, 1995.

Badger Historical Society of Shullsburg. *The Sesquicentennial History of Shullsburg, 1827–1977.* Shullsburg, Wisc.: Badger Historical Society of Shullsburg, 1977.

Barrios de Chungara, Domitila. *Let Me Speak: Testimony of Domitila, a Woman of the Bolivian Mines.* New York: Monthly Review Press, 1978.

Bodnar, John. *The Transplanted: A History of Immigrants in Urban America.* Bloomington: Indiana University Press, 1985.

Boyer, Richard O, and Herbert M. Morais. *Labor's Untold Story.* New York: Cameron Associates, 1955. Reprint. New York: United Electrical, Radio and Machine Workers of America, 1974.

Brown, Ronald C. *Hard-Rock Miners: The Intermountain West, 1860–1920.* College Station: Texas A&M University Press, 1979.

Brundage, David. *The Making of Western Labor Radicalism: Denver's Organized Workers, 1878–1905.* Urbana: University of Illinois Press, 1994.

Butler, Anne M., *Daughters of Joy, Sisters of Misery: Prostitutes in the American West, 1865–1890.* Urbana: University of Illinois Press, 1985.

Chan, Sucheng, ed. *Entry Denied.* Philadelphia: Temple University Press, 1991.

Clawson, Mary Ann. *Constructing Brotherhood: Class, Gender, and Fraternalism.* Princeton: Princeton University Press, 1989.

Clifford, James. *The Predicament of Culture: Twentieth-Century Ethnography, Literature, and Art.* Cambridge: Harvard University Press, 1988.

Conlin, Joseph R. *Big Bill Haywood and the Radical Union Movement*. Syracuse: Syracuse University Press. 1969.

Cumbler, John. *Working Class Community in Industrial America: Work, Leisure, and Struggle in Two Industrial Cities—1880–1930*. Westport: Greenwood Press, 1979.

Daniels, Roger, ed. *Anti-Chinese Violence in North America*. New York: Arno Press, 1978.

Dawley, Alan. *Class and Community: The Industrial Revolution in Lynn*. Cambridge: Harvard University Press, 1976.

Derickson, Alan. *Workers' Health, Workers' Democracy: The Western Miners' Struggle, 1891–1925*. Ithaca: Cornell University Press, 1988.

Deutsch, Sarah. *No Separate Refuge: Culture, Class, and Gender on an Anglo-Hispanic Frontier in the American Southwest, 1880–1940*. New York: Oxford University Press, 1987.

di Leonardo, Micaela. *The Varieties of Ethnic Experience: Kinship, Class, and Gender among California Italian-Americans*. Ithaca: Cornell University Press, 1984.

Dubofsky, Melvyn. *We Shall Be All*. New York: Quadrangle, 1969.

Emmons, David M. *The Butte Irish: Class and Ethnicity in an American Mining Town, 1875–1925*. Urbana: University of Illinois Press, 1989.

Feitz, Leland. *Myers Avenue: A Quick History of Cripple Creek's Red-Light District*. Pamphlet. Denver: Golden Bell Press, 1967.

Fell, James E. Jr. *Ores to Metals: The Rocky Mountain Smelting Industry*. Lincoln: University of Nebraska Press, 1979.

Ferguson, Charles W. *Fifty Million Brothers: A Panorama of American Lodges and Clubs*. New York: Farrar and Rinehart, 1937.

Filler, Louis. *Crusaders for American Liberalism*. New York: Harcourt, Brace, 1939. Reprint. Yellow Springs, Ohio: Antioch Press, 1964.

Fink, Leon. *Workingmen's Democracy: The Knights of Labor and American Politics*. Urbana: University of Illinois Press, 1983.

Foner, Philip S. *History of the Labor Movement in the United States*. Volume 2: *From the Founding of the American Federation of Labor to the Emergence of American Imperialism*. New York: International Publishers, 1955.

Foster, James C., editor. *American Labor in the Southwest: The First One Hundred Years*. Tucson: University of Arizona Press, 1982.

Foxhoven, Omer Vincent. *The City of God in the City of Gold*. n.p., n.p. June 1952.

Frank, Dana. *Purchasing Power: Consumer Organizing, Gender, and the Seattle Labor Movement, 1919–1929*. New York: Cambridge University Press, 1994.

Fuss, Diana. *Essentially Speaking: Feminism, Nature, and Difference*. New York: Routledge, 1989.

Gaboury, William Joseph. *Dissension in the Rockies: A History of Idaho Populism*. New York: Garland Publishing, 1988.

Geertz, Clifford. *The Interpretation of Cultures*. New York: Basic Books, 1973.

Gilkeson, John S. *Middle-Class Providence, 1820–1940*. Princeton: Princeton University Press, 1986.

Ginger, Ray. *The Bending Cross*. New Brunswick: Rutgers University Press, 1949.

Goldman, Marion S. *Gold Diggers and Silver Miners: Prostitution and Social Life on the Comstock Lode.* Ann Arbor: University of Michigan Press, 1981.

Graham, John, ed. *"Yours for the Revolution": The Appeal to Reason, 1845–1922.* Lincoln: University of Nebraska Press, 1990.

Greenberg, Brian. *Worker and Community: Response to Industrialization in a Nineteenth-Century American City, Albany, New York, 1850–1884.* Albany: State University of New York Press, 1985.

Griswold, Robert L. *Family and Divorce in California, 1850–1890.* Albany: State University of New York Press, 1983.

Gronlund, Laurence. *The Cooperative Commonwealth.* 1884. Reprint. Cambridge: Harvard University Press, 1965.

Gutman, Herbert G. *Work, Culture, and Society in Industrializing America: Essays in American Working-Class and Social History.* New York: Vintage Books, 1977.

Hampsten, Elizabeth. *Read This Only to Yourself: The Private Writing of Midwestern Women, 1890–1910.* Bloomington: Indiana University Press, 1982.

———. *To All Inquiring Friends: Letters, Diaries, and Essays in North Dakota 1880–1910.* Grand Forks: Department of English, University of North Dakota, 1979.

Hernández, Zoila. *El Coraje de las Mineras: Marginalidad Andino-Minera en Canaria.* Lima, Peru: La Asociación Aurora Vivar, 1986.

Hirsch, Susan E. *The Roots of the American Working Class.* Philadelphia: University of Pennsylvania Press, 1978.

Jameson, Elizabeth. *Building Colorado: The United Brotherhood of Carpenters and Joiners of America in the Centennial State.* Denver: Colorado State Council of Carpenters, 1984.

Jayne-Weaver, Ida M., and Emma D. Wood. *History of the Order of the Pythian Sisters.* Seattle: Peters Publishing, 1925.

Jenson, Vernon H. *Heritage of Conflict: Labor Relations in the Nonferrous Metals Industry Up to 1930.* Ithaca: Cornell University Press, 1950.

John, Angela V. *By the Sweat of Their Brow: Women Workers at Victorian Coal Mines.* London: Croom Helm, 1980.

Katz, Michael. *The People of Hamilton, Canada West: Family and Class in a Mid-Nineteenth-Century City.* Cambridge: Harvard University Press, 1979.

Larson, Robert W. *Populism in the Mountain West.* Albuquerque: University of New Mexico Press, 1986.

Laslett, John H. M. *Labor and the Left.* New York: Basic Books, 1970.

Laurie, Bruce. *The Working People of Philadelphia.* Philadelphia: Temple University Press, 1980.

Levine, Susan. *Labor's True Women: Carpet Weavers, Industrialism, and Labor Reform in the Gilded Age.* Philadelphia: Temple University Press, 1984.

Lingenfelter, Richard E. *The Hardrock Miners: A History of the Mining Labor Movement in the American West, 1863–1893.* Berkeley: University of California Press, 1974.

Lyman, Sanford M. *The Asian in the West.* Reno: University of Nevada Press, 1971.

Mann, Ralph Emerson. *After the Gold Rush: Society in Grass Valley and Nevada City, California, 1849–1870*. Stanford: Stanford University Press, 1982.

McNall, Scott G. *The Road to Rebellion: Class Formation and Kansas Populism, 1865–1900*. Chicago: University of Chicago Press, 1988.

Mellinger, Philip J. *Race and Labor in Western Copper: The Fight for Equality, 1896–1918*. Tucson: University of Arizona Press, 1995.

Mink, Gwendolyn. *Old Labor and New Immigrants in American Political Development*. Ithaca: Cornell University Press, 1986.

Mouat, Jeremy. *Roaring Days: Rossland's Mines and the History of British Columbia*. Vancouver: University of British Columbia Press, 1995.

Oestreicher, Richard. *Solidarity and Fragmentation: Working People and Class Consciousness in Detroit, 1873–1900*. Urbana: University of Illinois Press, 1986.

Ostler, Jeffrey. *Prairie Populism: The Fate of Agrarian Radicalism in Kansas, Nebraska, and Iowa, 1880–1892*. Lawrence: University Press of Kansas, 1993.

Palladino, Grace. *Another Civil War: Labor, Capital, and the State in the Anthracite Regions of Pennsylvania 1840–1868*. Urbana: University of Illinois Press, 1990.

Pascoe, Peggy. *Relations of Rescue: The Search for Female Moral Authority in the American West, 1874–1939*. New York: Oxford University Press, 1990.

Paul, Rodman. *California Gold: The Beginning of Mining in the Far West*. Cambridge: Harvard University Press, 1947.

Peavy, Linda, and Ursula Smith. *The Gold Rush Widows of Little Falls: A Story Drawn from the Letters of Pamelia and James Fergus*. St. Paul: Minnesota Historical Society Press, 1990.

———. *Women in Waiting in the Westward Journey: Life on the Home Frontier*. Norman: University of Oklahoma Press, 1994.

Perlman, Selig, and Philip Taft. *History of Labor in the United States, 1896–1932*. New York: MacMillan, 1935.

Peterson, Richard H. *The Bonanza Kings: The Social Origins and Business Behavior of Western Mining Entrepreneurs, 1870–1900*. Lincoln: University of Nebraska Press, 1977.

Petrik, Paula. *No Step Backward: Women and Family on the Rocky Mountain Mining Frontier, 1865–1900*. Helena: Montana Historical Society Press, 1987.

Rastall, Benjamin McKie. *The Labor History of the Cripple Creek District: A Study in Industrial Evolution*. Bulletin of the University of Wisconsin 198, Economic and Political Science Series. Volume 3, number 1. Madison: University of Wisconsin, 1908.

Riley, Glenda. *Divorce: An American Tradition*. New York: Oxford University Press, 1991.

Rosenzweig, Roy. *Eight Hours for What We Will: Workers and Leisure in an Industrial City, 1870–1920*. New York: Cambridge University Press, 1983.

Salvatore, Nick. *Eugene V. Debs: Citizen and Socialist*. Urbana: University of Illinois Press, 1982.

Saxton, Alexander. *The Indispensable Enemy—Labor and the Anti-Chinese Movement in California*. Berkeley: University of California Press, 1971.

Schwantes, Carlos A. *Coxey's Army: An American Odyssey*. Lincoln: University of Nebraska Press, 1985.

Shinn, Charles Howard. *Mining Camps: A Study in American Frontier Government*. New York: Charles Scribner's Sons, 1884. Reprint. New York: Harper and Row, 1965.

Smith, Duane A. *Rocky Mountain Mining Camps*. Lincoln: University of Nebraska Press, 1967.

Sprague, Marshall. *Money Mountain: The Story of Cripple Creek Gold*. Boston: Little, Brown, 1953. Reprint. New York: Ballantine Books, 1971, and Lincoln:University of Nebraska Press, 1979.

———. *Newport in the Rockies: The Life and Good Times of Colorado Springs*. Denver: Sage Books, 1961.

Stevens, Albert C., comp. and ed. *The Cyclopedia of Fraternities*. New York: E. B. Treat, 1907.

Suggs, George G., Jr. *Colorado's War on Militant Unionism: James H. Peabody and the Western Federation of Miners*. Detroit: Wayne State University Press, 1972.

Taylor, Robert Guilford. *Cripple Creek*. Indiana University Publications Geographic Monograph Series. Volume 1. Bloomington: Indiana University, 1966.

Thernstrom, Stephan. *Poverty and Progress: Social Mobility in a Nineteenth Century City*. Cambridge: Harvard University Press, 1964.

Thompson, E. P. *The Making of the English Working Class*. New York: Vintage Books, 1963.

Ubelhode, Carl; Benson, Maxine; and Smith, Duane, A. *A Colorado History*. 3d ed. Boulder: Pruett Publishing, 1972.

Walkowitz, Daniel J. *Worker City, Company Town: Iron and Cotton Worker Protest in Troy and Cohoes, New York, 1855–1884*. Urbana: University of Illinois Press, 1978.

Waters, Frank. *Midas of the Rockies: The Story of Stratton and Cripple Creek*. Chicago: Swallow Press, 1937.

West, Elliott. *The Saloon on the Rocky Mountain Mining Frontier*. Lincoln: University of Nebraska Press, 1979.

Whalen, William J. *Handbook of Secret Organizations*. Milwaukee: Bruce Publishing, 1966.

Wilentz, Sean. *Chants Democratic: New York City and the Rise of the American Working Class, 1788–1950*. New York: Oxford University Press, 1984.

Wright, James Edward. *The Politics of Populism: Dissent in Colorado*. New Haven: Yale University Press, 1974.

Wyman, Mark. *Hard Rock Epic: Western Miners and the Industrial Revolution, 1860–1910*. Berkeley: University of California Press, 1979.

INDEX

Adams, Alva, 243–45 election of 1896, 167

Adams, Stephen, 215; trial of, 228–29

African Americans: and exclusion, 150–54, 158; and prostitution, 128–29; racially segregated events, 101–2, 150–51; and womanhood, 142–43

Aiken, Frank, 229

Aikins, Frank, 223

Altman, Colo., 3, 5, 50, 54–55, 59, 63, 106, 112, 122, 140, 143, 169, 181, 184, 191–93, 205, 210; elections in, 165–67; and People's Party, 191; and Socialist Party, 192–93

Altman Engineers' Union No. 75, 69, 71, 101, 105, 172, 181; educational role of, 97; social role of, 94

Altman Free Coinage Miners' Union No. 19, 27, 31, 38, 54, 71, 90–91, 101, 152, 156, 174, 193, 208, 217, 236; benefits, 111–12; cross-class associations, 104; politics of, 168; and workplace dangers, 90

Altman Local Union No. 19: see Altman Free Coinage Miners' Union No. 19

Altman Miners' Union: see Altman Free Coinage Miners' Union No. 19

American Federation of Labor (AFL), 7, 12, 63–64, 160, 169, 246; anti-Asian sentiment, 155, 158; and challenge by Western Federation of Miners, 64, 77; see also Gompers, Samuel

American Labor Union (ALU), 63–64, 77, 91, 126, 160–61, 214, 220; anti-Asian sentiment, 158; politics of, 161, 178–79, 184; social role of, 95; see also Western Labor Union

American Labor Union Journal: see American Labor Union

American Order of Protection (AOOP), 111–12

American Protective Association (APA), 60, 148–49; and Gov. A. W. McIntire, 166; nativism of, 148

American Smelting and Refining Co. (ASARCO), 66, 68, 244

Anaconda, Colo., 206, 210, 222, 237

Anaconda Gold Mining Co., 52, 61

Anaconda Miners' Union No. 21, 31, 111, 224

Ancient Order of Hibernians, 89, 95, 106–7, 146; see also Degree of Honor; ethnic identity; ethnic politics

Ancient Order of United Workmen (AOUW), 87, 92–94, 104–6, 140, 241; benefits, 92, 106; connections to unions, 93–94; and working class, 108

Andrews, M. A., 64

Aspen, Colo., 21, 30–34, 36, 54, 56, 247; and Aspen Association, 33; unions founded in, 34

Australian ballot, 163–64, 167

Bailey, Morton, 167

Baker, James, 214

Barbee, Mabel: see Lee, Mabel Barbee

Barry, Leonora, 122

Battle Mountain, 3–4, 43, 53, 57, 61, 143, 209

Battle Mountain Gold Mining Co., 52

Baugh, G. W., 92; see also Victor Miners' Union No. 32

Bauman, Zygmunt, 10

Beacon Hill, 3

Beaver, Arthur, 92; see also Victor Miners' Union No. 32

Beck, Melvin, 211–12, 230

Beckman, Charles, 211

Worker City, Company Town: Iron and Cotton-Worker Protest in Troy and Cohoes, New York, 1855–84   *Daniel J. Walkowitz*

Life, Work, and Rebellion in the Coal Fields: The Southern West Virginia Miners, 1880–1922   *David Alan Corbin*

Women and American Socialism, 1870–1920   *Mari Jo Buhle*

Lives of Their Own: Blacks, Italians, and Poles in Pittsburgh, 1900–1960   *John Bodnar, Roger Simon, and Michael P. Weber*

Working-Class America: Essays on Labor, Community, and American Society   *Edited by Michael H. Frisch and Daniel J. Walkowitz*

Eugene V. Debs: Citizen and Socialist   *Nick Salvatore*

American Labor and Immigration History, 1877–1920s: Recent European Research   *Edited by Dirk Hoerder*

Workingmen's Democracy: The Knights of Labor and American Politics   *Leon Fink*

The Electrical Workers: A History of Labor at General Electric and Westinghouse, 1923–60   *Ronald W. Schatz*

The Mechanics of Baltimore: Workers and Politics in the Age of Revolution, 1763–1812   *Charles G. Steffen*

The Practice of Solidarity: American Hat Finishers in the Nineteenth Century   *David Bensman*

The Labor History Reader   *Edited by Daniel J. Leab*

Solidarity and Fragmentation: Working People and Class Consciousness in Detroit, 1875–1900   *Richard Oestreicher*

Counter Cultures: Saleswomen, Managers, and Customers in American Department Stores, 1890–1940   *Susan Porter Benson*

The New England Working Class and the New Labor History   *Edited by Herbert G. Gutman and Donald H. Bell*

Labor Leaders in America   *Edited by Melvyn Dubofsky and Warren Van Tine*

Barons of Labor: The San Francisco Building Trades and Union Power in the Progressive Era   *Michael Kazin*

Gender at Work: The Dynamics of Job Segregation by Sex during World War II   *Ruth Milkman*

Once a Cigar Maker: Men, Women, and Work Culture in American Cigar Factories, 1900–1919   *Patricia A. Cooper*

A Generation of Boomers: The Pattern of Railroad Labor Conflict in Nineteenth-Century America   *Shelton Stromquist*

DATE DUE

UNIVERSITY OF ILLINOIS PRESS
1325 SOUTH OAK STREET
CHAMPAIGN, ILLINOIS 61820-6903
WWW.PRESS.UILLINOIS.EDU